Anthropology

Second Canadian Edition

Anthropology

What Does it Mean to Be Human?

Robert H. Lavenda

Emily A. Schultz

Cynthia Zutter

OXFORD

UNIVERSITY PRESS

OXFORD

UNIVERSITY PRESS

Oxford University Press is a department of the University of Oxford.
It furthers the University's objective of excellence in research, scholarship,
and education by publishing worldwide. Oxford is a registered trade mark of
Oxford University Press in the UK and in certain other countries.

Published in Canada by
Oxford University Press
8 Sampson Mews, Suite 204,
Don Mills, Ontario M3C 0H5 Canada

www.oupcanada.com

First Canadian Edition published in 2016
Second Canadian Edition published in 2020

Anthropology: What Does It Mean to Be Human? was originally published in English in 2012.
This edition is published by arrangement with Oxford University Press. 198 Madison Avenue, New York, NY 10016-4314, USA.
Copyright © 2012, 2008 by Robert H. Lavenda and Emily A. Schultz

Library and Archives Canada Cataloguing in Publication
Title: Anthropology : what does it mean to be human? / Robert H. Lavenda, Emily A. Schultz, Cynthia
Zutter.
Names: Lavenda, Robert H., author. | Schultz, Emily A. (Emily Ann), 1949- author. | Zutter,
Cynthia, 1965- author.
Description: Second Canadian edition. | Includes bibliographical references and index.
Identifiers: Canadiana (print) 20190204419 | Canadiana (ebook) 20190204435 | ISBN 9780199032563
(softcover) | ISBN 9780199032600 (EPUB)
Subjects: LCSH: Anthropology—Textbooks. | LCGFT: Textbooks.
Classification: LCC GN25 .L38 2020 | DDC 301—dc23

Cover image: Feifei Cui-Paoluzzo/Moment Open/Getty Images
Cover and interior design: Laurie McGregor

Oxford University Press is committed to our environment.
Wherever possible, our books are printed on paper which comes from
responsible sources.

Printed and bound in the United States of America

1 2 3 4 — 23 22 21 20

Contents in Brief

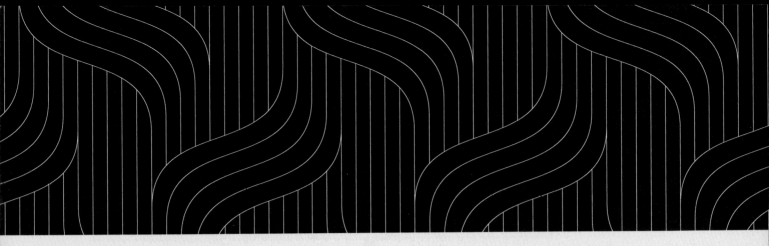

Contents

❶ What Is Anthropology?   1

❷ Why Is the Concept of Culture Important?   23

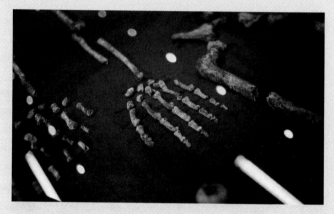

9 Why Did Humans Settle Down, Build Cities, and Establish States? 182

10 Why Do Anthropologists Study Economic Relations? 213

11 What Can Anthropology Teach Us about Sex, Gender, and Sexuality? 234

⓭ How Do Anthropologists Study Political Relations?   295

⓬ Where Do Our Relatives Come From and Why Do They Matter?   257

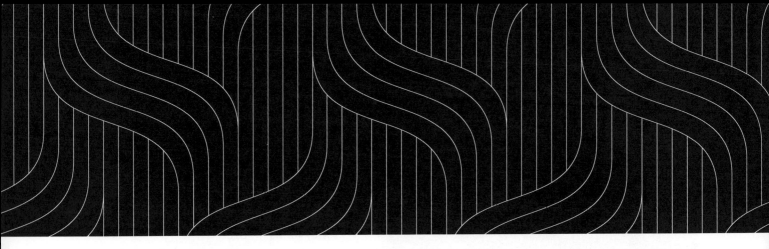

Preface

This original US version of this book emerged out of Robert Lavenda's and Emily Schultz's increasing dissatisfaction with all the available general anthropology texts. The authors found that these texts either overwhelmed beginning students with detail and the sheer volume of material or else provided overly brief introductions that failed to convey the richness of the field. They therefore set out to write a book that introduces this broad field concisely yet thoroughly, providing diverse perspectives and examples to foster not only an appreciation of anthropology but also a deeper engagement with it—one that helps students better understand themselves and the world around them. Anthropology professors (and their students) needed a general anthropology text that struck the right balance, fit into a 15-week semester, and came with a complete package of ancillary materials.

In preparing the Canadian edition, Cynthia Zutter has focused on two central themes, both of which Lavenda and Schultz strongly support. First, she has incorporated Canadian ideas and practices in as many ways as possible. Throughout the text, she has added discussions that focus on Canadian topics such as multiculturalism, bilingualism, same-sex marriage, and cultural resource management. She has also included many examples from across Canada, covering concerns such as how Canadian laws and policies affect people's everyday lives, how ethnicity and indigeneity are recognized, how Indigenous languages are being revitalized, and how French is being preserved in Acadia. In addition, Zutter has incorporated a wide variety of anthropological research carried out by Canadian anthropologists, both within Canada and in other regions—from Madagascar to Taiwan to Brazil. Second, like previous US editions of this text, this Canadian edition continues to address the central issues of the discipline, highlighting the controversies and commitments that shape contemporary anthropology in North America and around the world, and that make it interesting and exciting.

Approach

This book may be concise, but we cover the field effectively. We take a question-oriented approach that illuminates major concepts for students and shows them the relevance of anthropology in today's world. Structuring each chapter around an important question and its subquestions, we explore what it means to be human, incorporating answers from all four major subfields of anthropology—biological anthropology, archaeology, linguistic anthropology, and cultural anthropology—as well as from applied anthropology. We have made every effort to provide a balanced perspective, both in the level of detail we present and in our coverage of the major subfields.

The questioning approach not only sparks curiosity but orients students' reading and comprehension of each chapter, highlighting the concepts every student should take away from a general anthropology course. For example, students need to know about evolutionary theory, human variation, and the biological, social, and cultural critique of the concept of race, since knowledge in these areas is one of the great achievements of the discipline of anthropology. No other discipline (and possibly no other course) will teach about these matters the way anthropologists do, focusing on the idea of humans as biocultural organisms. Students need to know about the fossil evidence for the evolution of *Homo sapiens*, which they are not likely to learn about elsewhere. Students need to know what archaeology can tell us about the human past, as well as what ethnography can teach us about social complexity and inequality. They need to know that culture is more than just cultural festivals, regional foods, and interesting traditional costumes. They need to know about language and cognition and the central role of learning and play in human development. They need to understand the wellsprings of human creativity and imagination. It is valuable for them to see the many forms of human relatedness, and how people organize themselves. They need to know about globalization from the bottom up and not just the top down. They need to see how all the subfields of anthropology together can provide important, unique insights into all these topics, and how anthropology can provide a vital foundation for their university education.

The world we face as anthropologists has changed dramatically in the last quarter-century, and anthropology has changed, too. We have always felt it necessary to present students with a view of what contemporary anthropologists are doing; we therefore address the most current issues in the field and have thoroughly updated the text accordingly for this edition. Students will take away from the book an appreciation of how these areas of specialization have developed over time, and how they contribute to our understanding of the world in the twenty-first century.

Organization

Divided into 16 chapters with four "Focus" features online, this book is the ideal length for a one-semester course. Chapters 1 and 2 introduce the entire field and the concept of culture, which intersects all aspects of the discipline of anthropology. Following this comprehensive introduction, six chapters are devoted to biological anthropology and archaeology: evolution (Chapter 3); the primates (Chapter 4); the fossil record and human origins (Chapters 5 and 6); human variation (Chapter 7); the human past (Chapter 8); and the first farmers, cities, and states (Chapter 9). Topics in linguistic and cultural anthropology are covered in chapters on economics (Chapter 10); sex, gender, and sexuality (Chapter 11); kinship and marriage (Chapter 12); politics (Chapter 13); social inequality (Chapter 14, covering gender, class, caste, race, ethnicity, and nationalism); language and communication (Chapter 15); and symbolic practices (Chapter 16, covering play, art, myth, ritual, and religion). Throughout, the book incorporates discussions of indigeneity and gender, while paying special attention to issues of power and inequality in Canada and the contemporary world.

In the Canadian edition, Zutter placed the chapter on culture immediately after the introductory chapter to highlight the important role that culture plays in all aspects of anthropology, including biological anthropology and archaeology. She has also included additional emphasis on the biocultural nature of human organisms throughout, to facilitate the integration of biological and cultural approaches in anthropology.

In addition, the four brief "Focus" features (online) explore key concerns, methods, and approaches within each of the four major subfields of anthropology in greater depth, focusing on bioarchaeology and the stories that our skeletons hold (biological anthropology); methods for dating archaeological remains and hominin fossils (archaeology); the study of language use and the components of language (linguistic anthropology); and ethnographic methods commonly used in fieldwork (cultural anthropology).

—Robert H. Lavenda, Emily A. Schultz,
and Cynthia Zutter

Acknowledgements

My thanks goes out to all of the many people who helped me throughout the development of this Canadian edition of Robert Lavenda and Emily Schultz's *Anthropology: What Does It Mean to Be Human?* The editors at Oxford University Press have been a pleasure to work with, especially Tanuja Weerasooriya, Janice Evans, Leah-Ann Lymer, and Elizabeth Ferguson, who were patient and provided sage advice as they guided me through this project, and the entire production team. As well, I would like to extend a note of gratitude to Caroline Starr, who initiated and championed this project from its initial stages. Editorial assistance was provided by Rose Lorentzen, whose organizational skills were extremely helpful. My students at MacEwan University guided the project with their valuable comments and suggestions. In addition, I'd like to extend my gratitude to Robert

Lavenda and Emily Schultz for providing me with such a wonderful opportunity to combine their exceptional textbook with Canadian content.

Individual contributions from Canadian anthropologists form some of the key additions to this text, and I am grateful to those who provided personal explanations of their current research. My thanks goes out to Nicholas Bala, Michel Bouchard, Martin Cannon, Leslie Dawson, Carly Dokis, Parin Dossa, Linda Fedigan, Nicole Gombay, Sarah King, Jennifer Liu, Roderick McInnes, April Nowell, Kathryn Reese-Taylor, Tanya Romaniuk, Christine Schreyer, Sarah Shulist, Treena Swanston, Kisha Supernant, and Andrew Walsh. I appreciate their generosity in sharing their work for this project.

I would also like to extend my thanks to the following reviewers, as well as those who wish to remain anonymous:

Michel Bouchard, UNBC
Alexis Dolphin, Western University
Maciej Domanski, Dawson College
Nick Gabrilopoulos, Dawson College
Michael Gregg, Mount Allison University
Karoline Guelke, Camosun College
Helen R. Haines, Trent University
Brent Hammer, University of Alberta

Götz Hoeppe, University of Waterloo
David Hopwood, Vancouver Island University
Nicole Kilburn, Camosun College
Yin Lam, University of Victoria
Kathleen Lowrey, University of Alberta
Karen McGarry, McMaster University
Hugh McKenzie, MacEwan University
Lisa Mutch, MacEwan University
Brian Myhre, University of Winnipeg
Mark Prentice, Vanier College
Robbyn Seller, John Abbott College
Matthieu Sossoyan, Vanier College
Kisha Supernant, University of Alberta
Paul Thibaudeau, Carleton University
Tara Tudor, Camosun College
Jacky Vallée, Vanier College

Their insightful comments and suggestions contributed to the outcome of this Canadian edition.

This edition is dedicated to my family, including my siblings and my children, Kris, Troy, and Matthew. Their support and understanding throughout this process has been enduring. I am grateful to my husband, Mike, as well, for sharing in my journey as a Canadian anthropologist.

—Cynthia Zutter

Publisher's Preface

Oxford University Press is delighted to present the second Canadian edition of *Anthropology: What Does It Mean to Be Human?* This thought-provoking work offers an informative, practical, and comprehensive introduction to the discipline—one that not only reveals the richness of anthropological study but also fosters a deeper understanding of the many factors shaping human experience. Discussing issues and examples from across the globe, this comprehensive text shows Canadian students the relevance of anthropology in today's world—both at home and abroad.

Key Features

FIGURE 16.8 A crowd of hockey fans cheers on Team Canada during the 2010 Winter Olympic Games in Vancouver. These kinds of mass public events can create a feeling of communitas in today's nation-states.

relative ease into and out of play, but such is not the case with ritual.

Finally, play usually has little effect on the social order of ordinary life; as a result, play can safely create a wide range of commentary on the social order. Ritual is different: its role is explicitly to maintain the status quo, including the prescribed ritual transformations. Societies differ in the extent to which ritual behaviour alternates with everyday, non-ritual behaviour. When nearly every act of everyday life is ritualized and other forms of behaviour are strongly discouraged, we sometimes speak of *orthopraxy* ("correct practice"). Traditionally observant Jews and Muslims, for example, lead a highly ritualized daily life, attempting from the moment they awaken until the moment they fall asleep to carry out even the humblest of activities in a manner that is ritually correct. In their view, ritual correctness is the result of God's law, and it is their duty and joy to conform their every action to God's will.

Margaret Drewal (1992) argues that, at least among the Yoruba, play and ritual overlap (see EthnoProfile 16.3: Yoruba). Yoruba rituals combine spectacle, festival, play, sacrifice, and so on and integrate diverse media—music, dance, poetry, theatre, sculpture (Drewal 1992, 198). They are events that require improvisatory, spontaneous individual moves; as a result, the mundane order is not only inverted and reversed but may also be subverted through power play and gender play. For example, gender roles are rigidly structured in Yoruba society. Yoruba rituals, however, allow some cross-dressing by both men

How Are Play and Ritual Complementary?

How does the logic of ritual differ from the logic of play? Play and ritual are complementary forms of metacommunication, although play is not real and not serious while ritual is considered important and very real. The movement from non-play to play is based on the premise of metaphor ("Let's make believe"); the movement to ritual is based on the premise of literalness ("Let's believe"). From the perspective of the everyday social order, the result of these contrasting premises is the "inauthenticity" of play and the "truth" of ritual.

Because of the connection of ritual with self-evident truth, the metacommunication of the ritual frame ("This is ritual") is associated with an additional metacommunication: "All messages within this frame are true." It is ritual that asserts *what should be* to play's *what can be*. The ritual frame is more rigid than the play frame. Consequently, ritual is the most stable liminal domain, whereas play is the most flexible. Players can move with

orthopraxy "Correct practice"; the prohibition of deviation from approved forms of behaviour.

EthnoProfile 16.3

Yoruba

Region: Western Africa
Nation: Nigeria
Population: 40,000,000
Environment: Coastal and forest
Livelihood: Farming, commerce, modern professions
Political organization: Traditionally, kingdoms; today, part of a modern nation-state

For more information: Bascom, William. 1969. *The Yoruba of Southwestern Nigeria.* New York: Holt, Rinehart, and Winston.

ascribed statuses Social positions people are assigned at birth.

achieved statuses Social positions people may attain later in life, often as the result of their own (or other people's) effort.

achieved statuses, those social positions that people may attain later in life, often as the result of their own (or other people's) effort, such as becoming a spouse or college graduate. All societies have ways of incorporating outsiders into their kinship groups, however, which they achieve by converting supposedly ascribed kinship statuses into achieved ones, thus undermining the distinction between them. We will use the term *adoption* to refer to these practices that allow people to transform relationships based on nurturance into relations of kinship.

Adoption and Naming among the Inuit of Nunavut

In some societies, such as that of ancient Rome, people distinguish between Ego's biological father (or *genitor*) and Ego's social father (or *pater*); they may also distinguish between Ego's biological mother (or *genetrix*) and Ego's social mother (or *mater*). Social parents are those who nurture a child, and they are often the child's biological parents as well. Among the Inuit of Nunavut, these distinguishing factors are not strongly acknowledged (see EthnoProfile 12.4). Rather, the Inuit view of extended

family encompasses the concept of "custom adoption"—a traditional form of adoption in which the adoptee maintains flexible relationships with her or his birth and adoptive families. As Valerie Alia (2007, 35) has observed, in Nunavut communities, "children move daily among the homes of birth and adoptive parents ... receiving care, food, and companionship." Alia further notes that this form of adoption is generally considered to be "more welcoming and less stigmatized than adoption among *Qallunaat* [i.e., southerners]" (36). According to Alia's informants, "adoptions are a part of everyday life," and "giving a child for adoption is a way of making sure every *amauti* (or *amautik*) (the baby-carrying hood on a woman's parka, or *amautik*) carries a child" (36) (Figure 12.7). This practice of adoption encourages the formation of families, which contributes to a strong sense of community and provides families with many hands to help with hunting, fishing, preparing food, maintaining homes, and other sustenance tasks. Moreover, as Alia notes, "[w]hen communities are small and communication is open, adopted children grow up well nurtured and loved" (36).

To understand the cultural significance of custom adoption, it is important to understand the Inuit tradition of naming. According to the highly intricate *sauniq* naming system, Inuit parents and other relatives (usually women, sometimes men) assign the adoptee the name of a deceased relative. This act not only commemorates the deceased but also forms a vital, symbolic connection between the adoptee and her or his namesake, allowing the namesake to "live on" in the community. To the Inuit, the giving of a *sauniq* name is an act of extreme importance. As Alia (2007, 37) notes, "naming is a—perhaps *the*—central component of Inuit culture. It is

EthnoProfile 12.4

Inuit (Nunavut)

Region: North American Arctic
Nation: Canada
Population: 100,000
Environment: Arctic archipelago, tundra, shrub tundra
Livelihood: Hunting, fishing
Political organization: Traditionally, band societies; today, self-governing as part of a modern nation-state

For more information: McElroy, Ann. 2008. *Nunavut Generations: Change and Continuity in Canadian Inuit Communities.* Long Grove, IL: Waveland Press.

FIGURE 12.7 An Inuit mother carries her daughter in her *amauti* on Baffin Island, Nunavut.

Canadian focus. An array of Canadian examples makes the text highly relevant and accessible to students in Canada. Canadian scholarship and perspectives throughout also give readers insight into the many Canadian contributions to the field.

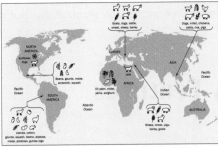

Global approach. Providing a broad context for analysis, the text features examples from around the world and highlights how globalization and the spread of capitalism has drastically shaped how people everywhere live their lives.

Coverage of gender and feminist anthropology. The authors tightly weave the topics of gender and sexuality into the fabric of the text. Discussion of issues such as gender identity, gender inequality, feminist archeology, and varieties of human sexual practice offers students insight into important areas of study within anthropology.

342   Anthropology: What Does It Mean to Be Human?

attentive to the spread of this discourse and the issues it raises, some of which we explore here.

Are Human Rights Universal?

Globalization has stimulated discussions about **human rights**: powers, privileges, or material resources to which people everywhere, by virtue of being human, are justly entitled. Rapidly circulating capital, images, people, things, and ideologies juxtapose different understandings about what it means to be human or what kinds of rights people may be entitled to. The context within which human rights discourse becomes relevant is often described as **multiculturalism**: living permanently in settings surrounded by people with cultural backgrounds different from your own and struggling to define with them the degree to which the wider society should accord respect and recognition to the cultural beliefs and practices of different groups. It is precisely in multicultural settings—found everywhere in today's globalized world—that questions of rights become salient and different cultural understandings of what it means to be human, and what rights humans are entitled to, become the focus of contention.

Human Rights Discourse as the Global Language of Social Justice

Discourses about human rights have proliferated in recent decades, stimulated by the original UN Universal Declaration on Human Rights in 1948 and followed by numerous subsequent declarations. For example, in 1992, the Committee for the Elimination of Discrimination against Women (CEDAW) declared that violence against women was a form of gender discrimination that violated the human rights of women. This declaration was adopted by the UN General Assembly in 1993 and became part of the rights platform at the Fourth World Conference on Women in Beijing, China, in 1995 (Figure 14.6). Anthropologist Sally Merry (2001) observes that this declaration "dramatically demonstrates the creation of new rights—rights which depend on the state's failure to protect women rather than its active violation of rights" and that "the emergence of violence against women as a distinct human rights violation depends on redefining the family so that it is no longer shielded from legal scrutiny" (36–7).

Although CEDAW has proven particularly contentious, other human rights documents have been signed without controversy by many national governments. Signing a human rights declaration supposedly binds governments to take official action to implement changes in local practices that might be seen to violate the rights asserted in the declaration. Human rights discourses are common currency in all societies, at all levels.

Because of the wide adoption of human rights discourses throughout the world, some people have come to speak of an emerging "culture of human rights," which has now become "the preeminent global language of social justice" (Merry 2001, 38). Important to this dialogue is the inclusion of Indigenous peoples' rights in the UN declaration of 1989. As Jane Cowan, Marie-Bénédicte Dembour, and Richard Wilson (2001) write, it is "no use imagining a 'primitive' tribe which has not yet heard of human rights . . . what it means to be 'indigenous' is itself transformed through interaction with human-rights discourses and institutions" (5). These developments mean that anthropologists must take note of the important influence of this human rights discourse as it shapes the community-focused research that they do.

What counts as "human rights" has changed over time, not only because of the action of international bodies like the UN but also because of the efforts of an increasing number of NGOs that have become involved in various countries of the world, many of them deeply committed to projects designed to improve people's lives and protect their rights (Figure 14.7). As Merry (2001) says, these developments "have created a new legal order" (35) that has given birth to new possibilities throughout the world for the elaboration and discussion of what human rights are all about.

In addition, because the "culture of human rights" is increasingly regarded, in one way or another, as the "culture of globalization," it would seem to be a topic well-suited to anthropological analysis in itself. This is because, as we shall see, human rights discourse is not as straightforward as it seems. On the face of things, defending human rights for all people would seem unproblematic. Few people who are aware of the devastation wrought by colonial exploitation, for example, would

> **human rights** Powers, privileges, or material resources to which people everywhere, by virtue of being human, are justly entitled.
>
> **multiculturalism** Living permanently in settings surrounded by people with cultural backgrounds different from one's own and struggling to define with them the degree to which the cultural beliefs and practices of different groups should or should not be accorded respect and recognition by the wider society.

What Can Anthropology Tell Us about Social Groups and Inequality?   327

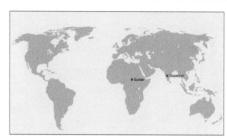

MAP 14.1 Location of societies whose EthnoProfiles appear in Chapter 14.

members of lower ranked classes have much more limited access to wealth (Figure 14.1).

The concept of class has a double heritage in modern anthropology, one stemming from Europe and the other from North America. European social scientists lived in states with a long history of social class divisions reaching back to the Middle Ages and, in some cases, to even earlier times. In their experience, social classes were well-entrenched and relatively closed classes. In the late 1700s, both the Industrial Revolution and the French Revolution promised to end the oppressive privileges of the ruling class and to equalize everyone's access to wealth. However, class divisions did not wither away in Europe during the nineteenth century; they just changed their contours. Followers of Karl Marx judged that, at best, an old ruling class had been displaced by a new one: feudal aristocrats had been replaced by bourgeois capitalists. The lowest level in European societies—rural peasants—were partially displaced as well, with the appearance of the urban working class. But the barriers separating those at the top of the class hierarchy from those at the bottom seemed just as rigid as ever.

As we described in Chapter 10, Marx defines classes in terms of their members' different relations to the means of production. This means that as long as a particular set of unequal productive relations flourishes in a society, the classes defined by these unequal roles in the division of labour will also persist. The French Revolution had triggered the displacement of aristocrats and peasants, who had played the key roles in European feudalism. They were replaced by new key classes—industrial entrepreneurs and the industrial working class—who were linked together within the capitalist mode of production. In time, Marx predicted, these industrial

FIGURE 14.1 Members of different social classes often live within easy sight of one another. Here, luxury apartments and squatter settlements rub shoulders in Rio de Janeiro, Brazil.

Current anthropological approaches to power and inequality. In-depth treatment of issues such as nationalism, racism, class, caste, and human rights helps students understand how power is manifested, deployed, resisted, and transformed.

A questions-oriented approach. Structuring each chapter around an important question and its sub-questions, the authors illuminate major concepts, incorporating answers from the main subfields of anthropology—biological anthropology, archaeology, linguistic anthropology, and cultural anthropology—as well as applied anthropology. This engaging approach sparks students' curiosity while focusing their learning around key topics in the field.

▲ The evolution of human ancestry, visible through changes in anatomy, is displayed at the National Museum of Natural Sciences in Kiev, Ukraine. Photo Andrii Zastrozhnov/Shutterstock

3 **Why Is Evolution Important to Anthropologists?**

Chapter Outline

- What Is Evolutionary Theory?
- What Material Evidence Is There for Evolution?
- Pre-Darwinian Views of the Natural World
- What Is Natural Selection?
- How Did Biologists Learn about Genes?
- Genotype, Phenotype, and the Norm of Reaction

- What Does Evolution Mean to Anthropologists?
- Chapter Summary
- For Review
- Key Terms
- References

FIGURE 6.16 Historical archaeologists, shown here excavating in the Roman Forum, supplement written documents with records of settlement patterns, structures, and artifacts, which reveal valuable information about the past that was never written down.

In 1980, Spector and her team began to dig at a site near Jordan, Minnesota, known by the Dakota as *Inyan Ceayak Atonwan*, or "Village at the Rapids." She examined historical documents that referred to the site for clues about what tasks were carried on by men and women at the site, as a guide to what kinds of material remains to look for. After several seasons, concerned that her work might be meaningless or offensive to the Dakota, Spector met a Dakota man who was a descendant of a man named Mazomani, one of the original inhabitants of the Village at the Rapids. Eventually, other descendants of Mazomani visited the site. By the 1985–1986 season, Dakota and non-Dakota were collaborating in teaching Dakota language, oral history, ethnobotany, ecology, and history at the site while digging continued. A Dakota elder conducted a pipe ceremony at the site shortly before the field season began, which symbolized for Spector the Dakota people's permission to work there.

Since the early 1980s, collaborative archaeological research of this kind has become increasingly common. Renfrew and Bahn (2008), for example, report on a multidisciplinary research project inside Kakadu National Park in the Northern Territory of Australia that began in 1981. Archaeologists wanted to learn more about the earliest occupation of tropical Australia, which began more than 23,000 years ago, and Kakadu National Park was an ideal place to look: the park contains a number of rockshelters filled with rich material traces of ancient human occupation, including rock paintings as old as those found in European caves such as Lascaux. Archaeologists wanted to build on previous work and to test the proposal made by an earlier researcher, George Chaloupka, who argued that the rock art in the region reflected changes in the environment triggered by rising sea levels (Renfrew and Bahn 2008, 521).

But Rhys Jones, the team leader from the Australian National University, knew that the site was legally owned by the local Aborigine community, whose permission would be needed before any excavation could begin. The Aborigine community was willing to give permission for the project, but they wanted to ensure that the dig was carried out in a way that was responsible and

respectful. They insisted that one member of the community supervise the project, primarily "to protect the diggers from doing something that could bring practical or ritual danger: the totemic geography of a region contains some 'dangerous places,' into which archaeologists might stray through ignorance" (Renfrew and Bahn 2008, 521). The archaeologists also had to agree to complete work at one site before moving on to another and to return all disturbed areas to the condition in which they had been prior to the excavation. But Aboriginal involvement in the project did not stop there. "Senior Aborigine men representing the relevant groups accompanied the team on field trips and carefully monitored the excavations, while trainee Aboriginal rangers helped in the laboratory, and were instructed in archaeological procedures" (Renfrew and Bahn 2008, 522). When the project was completed, the researchers did indeed find evidence that verified Chaloupka's hypothesis, but two other findings were perhaps even more exciting. The first was the discovery of plant remains as much as 6,000 years old, preserved thanks to the unusual microclimate present in one rockshelter. The second came from a second rockshelter and consisted of pieces of red ochre, a pigment used by ancient human populations in many parts of the world. These pieces were 53,000 years old, had been worked by hand, and might have been the sources of pigment for some of the rock art. Renfrew and Bahn (2008) judge this project "very successful" (528), and one measure of its success was the way it provided a model—as did Spector's work—of finding a way to do archaeology while working together with an indigenous community that had its own stake in the way the project was carried out, as well as in the outcome.

Cosmopolitan Archaeologies

A variety of far-reaching changes have swept the world since the end of the Cold War in 1989. As we will see in later chapters, these changes have affected the way all anthropologists do research, and archaeologists are no exception. Collaborative projects between local communities and archaeologists have become increasingly common in recent years, but these collaborations themselves have been affected by a number of broader changes. For example, global tourism has mushroomed, and huge numbers of tourists from all over the world now want to visit archaeological sites such as Machu Picchu or Kakaku National Park, both of which have been named UNESCO World Heritage Sites.

As we saw in the case of Machu Picchu, a lot of money can be made managing flows of wealthy tourists to well-known cultural heritage sites (see Figure 6.10). When tourist traffic threatens to destroy such sites, therefore, it is not merely the ruins themselves that are at stake; so are the livelihoods of local people and governments. Moreover, powerless minorities with traditional connections to these sites frequently find themselves shoved aside as national and international institutions step in and take over. In the past, most archaeologists tried to do their research while avoiding local legal and political involvements, hoping to achieve "a 'do no harm' model of coexistence" (Meskell 2009, 5). Today, many archaeologists have adopted the view that their first obligation should be to those local (and often marginalized) people with traditional connections to the archaeological sites where they work. But more and more archaeologists are finding that this kind of single-minded commitment is increasingly problematic because they and their local allies must find a way to deal with a range of other local and global stakeholders who have their own, often conflicting, ideas about how cultural heritage should be managed.

Like many contemporary cultural anthropologists (see Chapter 8), some archaeologists have been moved by these struggles to question a view of the world that divides it up into a patchwork quilt of distinct, neatly bounded "cultures," each of which embodies a unique heritage that must be protected from change at all costs. Again, like many of their cultural anthropologist colleagues, these archaeologists have concluded that the only way forward is to cultivate a "cosmopolitan" point of view. For many cultural anthropologists, **cosmopolitanism** means being able to move with ease from one cultural setting to another. Cultural anthropologists regularly develop cosmopolitan skills and awareness as they move in and out of fieldwork situations. Moreover, people everywhere—tourists, immigrants, or refugees, for example—have crafted a variety of different kinds of cosmopolitan skills to cope successfully with movement from one cultural setting to another. As you will see later, these movements have become the focus of new "multisited" forms of ethnographic research.

For archaeologists, adopting a cosmopolitan orientation means giving up universalistic assumptions about the meaning of the past. It means acknowledging, for example, that preservation of material artifacts may in fact sometimes go against the wishes of local groups with close connections to those artifacts. Dealing with

cosmopolitanism Being able to move with ease from one cultural setting to another.

Online "Focus on Four Fields" features. Engaging modules introduce students to the methods and approaches anthropologists use to conduct research within their various subfields.

Cross-chapter references. Marginal notes help readers make connections between topics, issues, and subfields of anthropology.

what makes them different from or similar to other animals. Early interest in these matters was a by-product of centuries of exploration and colonial expansion. Western Europeans found tremendous variation in the physical appearance of peoples around the world and tried to make sense of these differences. Some researchers developed a series of elaborate techniques to measure different observable features of human populations, including skin colour, hair type, and skull shape, hoping to find scientific evidence that would allow them to classify all the peoples of the world into a set of unambiguous categories based on distinct sets of biological attributes. Such categories were called **races**, and many scientists were convinced that clear-cut criteria for racial classification would be discovered if careful measurements were made on enough people from a range of different populations.

European scientists first applied racial categories to the peoples of Europe itself, but their classifications soon included non-European peoples, who were coming under increasing political and economic domination through colonial expansion by European and European American capitalist societies. These peoples differed from "white" Europeans not only because of their skin colour but also because of their unfamiliar languages and customs. In most cases, their technologies were also no match for the potent armaments of the West. In the early eighteenth century, using terms that are no longer in use today, the European biologist Carolus Linnaeus (Carl von Linné, 1707–1778) classified known human populations into four races (Amerindian, Caucasian, Asian, and Negro) based on skin colour (reddish, white, yellow, and black, respectively).

In the nineteenth century, influential natural scientists such as Louis Agassiz (1807–1873), Samuel George Morton (1799–1851), Francis Galton (1822–1911), and Paul Broca (1824–1880) built on this idea of race, ranking different populations of the world in terms of skull size; they found the brains of "white" Europeans and North Americans to be larger and saw the other "races" as representing varying grades of inferiority, with the two lowest grades being represented by Amerindians (i.e., Indigenous) and Africans (Gould 1996). These findings were used to validate the social practice of **racism**: the systematic oppression of members of one or more socially defined "race" by members of another socially defined "race" that is justified in terms of the supposed inherent biological superiority of the rulers and the supposed inherent biological inferiority of those they rule. For example, despite the fact that millions of Indigenous people were living and thriving in the Americas for thousands of years, racism and racist ideals supported the nineteenth-century colonial perspective that the land was nobody's (*terra nullius*) and open to be settled. Consequently, thousands of Indigenous people were enslaved, removed from their land, and died as their land was settled by European colonizers.

In the recent past, the treatment of Indigenous peoples in Canada exemplifies clear racist practices. By far one of the most devastating of these was the establishment of the residential school program in Canada. Indigenous children from across the country were taken from their families in an attempt to take the "Indian out of the Indian" and assimilate them into the Euro-Christian culture. As a result, these children were forced to live in boarding schools, subjected to horrendous living conditions, and not allowed to speak their Indigenous language; essentially, they had their Indigenous culture stripped away. These schools were in existence for over 100 years, impacting over 100,000 children, who essentially grew up without a connection to their culture. To redress the legacy of residential schools and this devastating loss of Indigenous culture, the Canadian government created a Truth and Reconciliation Commission (TRC). The TRC was created to hear the stories of the survivors of the residential school system and to lay the foundation for reconciliation. Ten principles of reconciliation and 94 Calls to Action were put forward to guide the process of repairing the broken relationship between Indigenous and non-Indigenous peoples in Canada. The Calls to Action are to be used to change all levels of government, including sectors that deal with child welfare, health, justice, and education (TRC 2015).

For further discussion of the Truth and Reconciliation Commission (TRC), see Chapter 13, p. 305, and Chapter 15, p. 366.

For expanded discussion of the methods anthropologists use to study human variation without using the term *race*, see Chapter 7, pp. 137–9. For a discussion of present-day racism and associated social issues in Canada, see Chapter 14, pp. 332–3.

races Social groupings that allegedly reflect biological differences.

racism The systematic oppression of members of one or more socially defined "race" by members of another socially defined "race" that is justified in terms of the supposed inherent biological superiority of the rulers and the supposed inherent biological inferiority of those they rule.

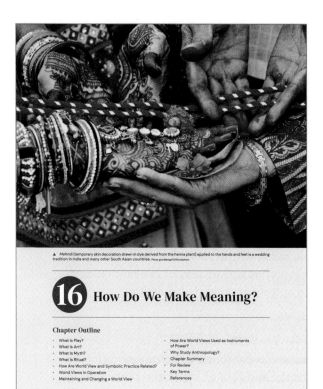

▲ Mehndi (temporary skin decoration drawn in dye derived from the henna plant) applied to the hands and feet is a wedding tradition in India and many other South Asian countries. Photo: goodlikeg20/iStockphoto.

16 How Do We Make Meaning?

Chapter Outline

- What Is Play?
- What Is Art?
- What Is Myth?
- What Is Ritual?
- How Are World Views and Symbolic Practice Related?
- World Views in Operation
- Maintaining and Changing a World View

- How Are World Views Used as Instruments of Power?
- Why Study Anthropology?
- Chapter Summary
- For Review
- Key Terms
- References

---

matrilineage belonging to either the Raven or the Eagle *k'waalaa* (clan). Strong feelings of reciprocity and social responsibility exist between the Ravens and the Eagles, and membership in a particular matrilineage and its *k'waalaa* shapes individuals' identities as well as social relationships (Krmpotich 2010). The Haida use matrilineal identity to navigate such matters as their participation in potlatches, their use of property, whom they should marry, their social status, and whom they can ask for economic support.

A Haida matrilineage can be thought of as a broad network of families linked through ancestry, property, and common social responsibilities. The most closely related members of a matrilineage tend to share the strongest bonds, which are based on love, friendship, history, obligations, shared work, and commitment. Indeed, matrilineal kin form the basis of each person's sense of family, and they play integral roles in major life events—for example, by leading rites of passage; by preparing feasts, potlatches, weddings, and other celebrations; and by mourning the deceased (Krmpotich 2010, 162). At the same time, individuals are generally encouraged to marry outside of their *k'waalaa*, a practice that facilitates non-matrilineal kinship bonds (e.g., between children and fathers).

Haida often wear crests to represent the matrilineage to which they belong. The designs of these crests are owned and inherited by members of the *k'waalaa* to which they correspond, and they can be painted or embroidered onto garments and even tattooed onto a person (Figure 12.5). These material expressions

perpetuate a sense of belonging and continuity of family and lineages. A significant factor in Haida kinship is the relationships between the living and the dead. Ancestors are often considered as guides for the living, providing opportunities and companionship. The recently deceased often accompany a relative for days or months after their death. Thus, kinship relationships are not only part of the living world; they transcend into the past, solidifying the matrilineal ties among the Haida (Krmpotich 2010, 163).

See Chapter 16, pp. 390–1, for a discussion of rites of passage.

Kinship Terminologies

People everywhere use special terms to refer to people they recognize as related to them. Despite the variety of kinship systems in the world, anthropologists have identified six major patterns of kinship terminology based on how people categorize their cousins. The six patterns reflect common solutions to structural problems faced by societies organized in terms of kinship. Kinship terminologies suggest both the external boundaries and the internal divisions of kinship groups, and they outline the structure of rights and obligations assigned to different members of the society. They also provide clues about how the vast and undifferentiated world of potential relations may be divided.

What Criteria Are Used for Making Kinship Distinctions?

Anthropologists have identified several criteria that people use to indicate how people are related to one another. See Table 12.1 for a list of the most common to the least common criteria.

By the early 1950s, kinship specialists in anthropology had identified six major patterns of kinship terminology, based on how cousins were classified. In recent years, however, anthropologists have become quite skeptical of the value of these idealized models, in large measure because they are highly formalized, neglect all kin categories except cousins, and fail to consider the full range of people's actual kinship practices. Perhaps the main value to come from formal kinship studies is the fact that they took seriously the ways other people classified their relatives and were able to display the logic that informed such classifications.

FIGURE 12.5 Haida use crests to physically represent the matrilineages to which they belong. Here, canoe paddles painted with family crests are stored in a longhouse on Graham Island, part of the Queen Charlotte Islands, in British Columbia.

Vibrant four-colour design. A wide array of photos, maps, tables, and illustrations helps bring anthropology to life!

---

care. According to anthropologist Merrill Singer (1998, 195), critical medical anthropology "is committed to the 'making social' and the 'making political' of health and medicine." Thus, critical medical anthropologists pay attention to the way social divisions based on class, "race," gender, and ethnicity can block access to medical attention or make people more vulnerable to disease and suffering. They draw attention to the way Western biomedicine "encourages people to fight disease rather than to make the changes necessary to prevent it," for example, by linking low birth weight in newborn babies to poor nutrition, but failing to note that poor nutrition "may be a major health factor among impoverished social classes and oppressed ethnic groups in developed countries despite an abundance of food in society generally" (Singer 1998, 106, 109).

The Uses of Anthropology

Why take a course in anthropology? An immediate answer might be that human fossils or broken bits of ancient pots or the customs of faraway peoples inspire a fascination that is its own reward. But the experience of being dazzled by seemingly exotic places and peoples carries with it a risk. As you become increasingly aware of the range of anthropological data, including the many options that exist for living a satisfying human life, you may find yourself wondering about the life you are living. Contact with the unfamiliar can be liberating, but it can

also be threatening if it undermines your confidence in the absolute truth and universal rightness of your previous understanding of the way the world works.

The contemporary world is increasingly interconnected. As people from different cultural backgrounds come into contact with one another, learning to cope with cultural differences becomes crucial. Anthropologists experience both the rewards and the risks of getting to know how other people live, and their work has helped to dispel many harmful stereotypes that sometimes make cross-cultural contact dangerous or impossible. Studying anthropology may help prepare you for some of the shocks you will encounter in dealing with people who look different from you, speak a different language, or do not agree that the world works exactly the way you think it does.

Anthropology involves learning about the kinds of living organisms we human beings are, the various ways we live our lives, and how we make sense of our experiences. Studying anthropology can equip you to deal with people with different cultural backgrounds in a less threatened, more tolerant manner. You may never be called on to eat termite paste. Still, you may one day encounter a situation in which none of the old rules seem to apply. As you struggle to make sense of what is happening, what you learned in anthropology class may help you relax and dare to try something totally new to you. If you do so, perhaps you too will discover the rewards of an encounter with the unfamiliar that is at the same time unaccountably familiar. We hope you will savour the experience.

Chapter Summary

1. Anthropology aims to describe in the broadest sense what it means to be human. The anthropological perspective is holistic, comparative, and evolutionary and has relied on the concept of culture to explain the diversity of human ways of life. Human beings depend on cultural learning for successful biological survival and reproduction, which is why anthropologists consider human beings to be biocultural organisms. Anthropology is also a field-based discipline. In North America today, anthropology is considered to have four major subfields: biological anthropology, archaeology, cultural anthropology, and linguistic anthropology;

many people also consider applied anthropology to be a fifth major subfield.

2. Biological anthropology began as an attempt to classify all the world's populations into different races. By the early twentieth century, however, most anthropologists had rejected racial classifications as scientifically unjustifiable and objected to the ways in which racial classifications were used to justify the social practice of racism. Contemporary anthropologists who are interested in human biology include biological anthropologists, primatologists, and paleoanthropologists.

---

5. Choose and defend one of the proposed explanations for the extinction of Neandertals. Explain why you chose this hypothesis. Refer to April Nowell's hypothesis regarding play in your answer.

6. How do archaeology and biological anthropology contribute to our understanding of the evolution of a modern human capacity for culture?

7. Describe the evidence that archaeologists, biological anthropologists, and others use to identify when the first people arrived in the Americas and who these people were. Are there any contradictions between different sets of data? Explain.

Key Terms

African hybridization and replacement model 115	blades 123	Mousterian tradition 119
anatomically modern human beings 115	composite tools 123	Neandertals 116
archaic *Homo sapiens* 113	Denisovans 122	regional continuity model 115
	Late Stone Age (LSA) 123	replacement model 115
	Middle Stone Age (MSA) 119	

References

Adovasio, J.M., J.D. Gunn, J.L. Donahue, and R. Stuckenrath. 1978. "Meadowcroft Rockshelter, 1977: An Overview." *American Antiquity* 43: 632–51.

Aiello, Leslie C. 1993. "The Fossil Evidence for Modern Human Origins in Africa: A Revised View." *American Anthropologist* 95: 73–96.

Arsuaga, Juan-Luis, Ignacio Martinez, Ana Gracia, José-Miguel Carretero, and Eudald Carbonell. 1993. "Three New Human Skulls from the Sima de los Huesos. Middle Pleistocene Site in Sierra de Atapuerca, Spain." *Nature* 362: 534–37.

Bar-Yosef, Ofer, and Steven L. Kuhn. 1999. "The Big Deal about Blades: Laminar Technologies and Human Evolution." *American Anthropologist* 101 (2): 322–38.

Bermúdez de Castro, José-María, J.L. Arsuaga, Eudald, Carbonell, A. Rosas, Ignacio Martínez, and Marina Mosquera. 1997. "A hominid from the lower Pleistocene of Atapuerca, Spain." *Science* 276 (5317): 1392–95.

Bräuer, Günter. 1989. "The Evolution of Modern Humans: A Comparison of the African and Non-African Evidence." In *The Human Revolution*, edited by Paul A. Mellars and Chris Stringer, 123–54. Princeton, NJ: Princeton University Press.

Cann, Rebecca L., Mark Stoneking, and Allen C. Wilson. 1987. "Mitochondrial DNA and Human Evolution." *Nature* 325: 31–6.

Chase, Philip G. 1989. "How Different was Middle Paleolithic Subsistence? A Zooarchaeological Perspective on the Middle to Upper Palaeolithic Transition." In *The Human Revolution*, edited by Paul A. Mellars and Chris Stringer, 123–54. Princeton, NJ: Princeton University Press.

Chatters, James C., Douglas J. Kennett, Yemane Asmerom, Brian M. Kemp, Victor Polyak, Alberta Nava Blank, Patricia A. Beddows, et al. 2014. "Late Pleistocene Human Skeleton and mtDNA Link Paleoamericans and Modern Native Americans." *Science* 344 (6185): 750–4.

Collard, Mark, and Mana Dembo. 2013. "Modern Human Origins." In *A Companion to Paleoanthropology*, edited by David Begun, 557–81. West Sussex, UK: John Wiley and Sons.

Defleur, Alban, Olivier Dutour, Helene Valladas, and Bernard Vandermeersch. 1993. "Cannibals among the Neanderthals?" *Nature* 362: 214.

Dillehay, Thomas D. 2000. *The Settlement of the Americas*. New York: Basic Books.

Fagan, Brian. 1990. *The Journey from Eden*. London: Thames and Hudson.

Foley, Robert. 1995. *Humans before Humanity*. Oxford: Blackwell.

Gamble, Clive. 1994. *Timewalkers*. Cambridge, MA: Harvard University Press.

Gould, Stephen J. 1996. *Full House: The Spread of Excellence from Plato to Darwin*. New York: Harmony Books.

Green, Richard F. Johannes Krause, Adrian W. Briggs, Tomislav Maricic, Udo Stenzel, Martin Kircher, Nick Patterson, et al. 2010. "A Draft Sequence of the Neandertal Genome." *Science* 328 (5979): 710–22.

Hoffmann, D.L., C.D. Standish, M. García-Diez, P.B. Pettitt, J.A. Milton, J. Zilhão, J.J. Alcolea-González, et al. 2018. "U-Th Dating of Carbonate Crusts Reveals Neandertal Origin of Iberian Cave Art." *Science* 359 (6378): 912–15. doi:10.1126/science.aap7778

Hublin, Jean-Jacques, Fred Spoor, Marc Braun, Frans Zonneveld, and Silvana Condemi. 1996. "A Late Neanderthal Associated with Upper Palaeolithic Artifacts." *Nature* 381: 224–6.

Hublin, Jean-Jacques, Abdelouahed Ben-Ncer, Shara E. Bailey, Sarah E. Freidline, Simon Neubauer, Matthew M. Skinner, et al. 2017. "New Fossils from Jebel Irhoud, Morocco and the Pan-African Origin of *Homo sapiens*." *Nature* 546: 289–92.

Klein, Richard G. 2009. *The Human Career: Human Biological and Cultural Origins*. 3rd ed. Chicago: University of Chicago Press.

Krings, Matthias, Anne Stone, Ralf W. Schmitz, Heike Krainitzki, and Mark Stoneking. 1997. "Neandertal DNA Sequences and the Origin of Modern Humans." *Cell* 90: 19–30.

Krings, Matthias, Helga Geisert, Ralf W. Schmitz, Heike Krainitzki, and Svante Pääbo. 1999. "DNA Sequence of the Mitochondrial Hypervariable Region II from the Neandertal Type Specimen." *Proceedings of the National Academy of Sciences* 96: 5581–5.

Engaging learning tools. Chapter outlines, marginal definitions of key terms, chapter summaries, questions for review, a glossary, and additional online content help students synthesize concepts and offer avenues for further exploration.

 Ancillary Resource Center

A Full Complement of Ancillaries

This text is supported by an array of supplementary resources, for both students and instructors, designed to enrich the learning experience. The companion websites for the second edition of *Anthropology* can be found at **www.oup.com/he/Lavenda2Ce**

For the Student

- **Student study guide.** An extensive package of review material—including chapter outlines, key points, and multiple choice, true/false, and essay questions, as well as lists of relevant readings, websites, films, and video links—is designed to reinforce and enhance student learning.

For the Instructor

- **Instructor's manual.** This comprehensive resource features chapter summaries, questions for discussion and debate, suggested activities and assignments, and lists of suggested readings, web links, and films.
- **PowerPoint slides.** Dynamic lecture slides summarize key points from each chapter and incorporate figures and tables from the text.
- **Image bank.** This expansive resource contains a wealth of full-colour figures, photographs, and tables that will make classroom lectures engaging and relevant for students.
- **Test generator.** A comprehensive bank of test questions provides hundreds of multiple-choice, true/false, and short-answer questions.

Boxes

"Anthropology in Everyday Life" Boxes

"Anthropology in Everyday Life" boxes. A range of fascinating examples and cases help students see the many ways in which anthropology is relevant today.

"In Their Own Words" Boxes

"In Their Own Words" boxes. Short commentaries capture diverse voices—including those of anthropologists, non-anthropologists, and Indigenous peoples—providing students with fresh perspectives on interesting topics related to chapter content.

EthnoProfile Boxes

EthnoProfiles. Brief overviews of geographic, linguistic, demographic, and organizational information offer students context regarding various societies discussed in the text.

▲ Anthropologists study artifacts to learn about the human past. This ceramic shard found at an early nineteenth-century site in Niagara-on-the-Lake, Ontario, Canada, can help paint a picture of the local economy in the region at that time.
Photo by Brittney Richardson

1 What Is Anthropology?

Chapter Outline

- What Is Anthropology?
- What Is the Concept of Culture?
- What Makes Anthropology a Cross-Disciplinary Discipline?
- Biological Anthropology
- Cultural Anthropology
- Linguistic Anthropology
- Archaeology

- Applied Anthropology
- Medical Anthropology
- The Uses of Anthropology
- Chapter Summary
- For Review
- Key Terms
- References

This chapter introduces the field of anthropology. We look at what anthropology is and explore its four main subfields: biological anthropology, cultural anthropology, linguistic anthropology, and archaeology. We touch on anthropology's key concept—culture—as well as its key research method—fieldwork. We conclude with a discussion of the ways anthropological insights are relevant in everyday life.

In early 1976, two of the authors of this book (Robert H. Lavenda and Emily A. Schultz) travelled to northern Cameroon, in western Africa, to study social relations in the town of Guider, where they rented a small house. In the first weeks they lived there, Lavenda and Schultz enjoyed spending the warm evenings of the dry season reading and writing in the glow of the house's brightest electric fixture, which illuminated a large, unscreened veranda. After a short time, however, the rains began, and with them appeared swarms of winged termites. These slow-moving insects with fat, two-inch abdomens were attracted to the light on the veranda, and the anthropologists soon found themselves spending more time swatting at the insects than reading or writing. One evening, in a fit of desperation, they rolled up old copies of the international edition of *Newsweek* and began an all-out assault, determined to rid the veranda of every single termite.

The rent Lavenda and Schultz paid for this house included the services of a night watchman. As they launched their attack on the termites, the night watchman suddenly appeared beside the veranda carrying an empty powdered milk tin. When he asked if he could have the insects they had been killing, Lavenda and Schultz were a bit taken aback but warmly invited him to help himself. He moved onto the veranda, quickly collected the corpses of fallen insects, and then joined the anthropologists in going after those termites that were still airborne. Although Lavenda and Schultz became skilled at thwacking the insects with their rolled-up magazines, their skills paled beside those of the night watchman, who simply snatched the termites out of the air with his hand, squeezed them gently, and dropped them into his rapidly filling tin can. The three individuals managed to clear the air of insects—and fill the night watchman's tin—in about 10 minutes. The night watchman thanked Lavenda and Schultz and returned to his post, and the anthropologists returned to their books.

The following evening, soon after Lavenda and Schultz took up their usual places on the veranda, the watchman appeared at the steps bearing a tray with two covered dishes. He explained that his wife had prepared the food for them in exchange for their help in collecting termites. The anthropologists accepted the food and carefully lifted the lids. One dish contained *nyiri*, a stiff paste made of red sorghum, a staple of the local diet. The other dish contained another pasty substance with a speckled, salt-and-pepper appearance, which Lavenda and Schultz realized was termite paste prepared from the insects they and the watchman had killed the previous night.

The night watchman waited at the foot of the veranda steps, an expectant smile on his face. Clearly, he did not intend to leave until the others tasted the food his wife had prepared. Lavenda and Schultz looked at each other. They had never eaten insects before, nor had they considered them edible in the North American, middle-class diet they were used to. To be sure, "delicacies" like chocolate-covered ants existed, but such items were considered by most North Americans to be food fit only for eccentrics. However, the anthropologists understood the importance of not insulting the night watchman and his wife, who were being so generous. They knew that insects were a favoured food in many human societies and that eating them brought no ill effects (Figure 1.1). So, they reached into the dish of *nyiri*, pulling off a small amount. They then used the ball of *nyiri* to scoop up a small portion of termite paste, brought the mixture to their mouths, ate, chewed, and swallowed. The watchman beamed, bid them good night, and returned to his post.

Lavenda and Schultz looked at each other in wonder. The sorghum paste had a grainy tang that was rather pleasant. The termite paste tasted mild, like chicken, not unpleasant at all. The anthropologists later wrote to their families about this experience. When their families wrote back, they described how they had told friends about Lavenda and Schultz's experience. Most of their friends had had strong negative reactions. But one friend, a home economist, had not been shocked at all. She had simply commented that termites are a good source of clean protein.

What Is Anthropology?

The above anecdote illustrates some of the central elements of the anthropological experience. Anthropologists want to learn about as many different human ways of life as they can. The people they come to know are members of their own society or live on a different continent, in cities or in rural areas. Their ways of life may involve patterns of regular movement across international borders, or they may make permanent homes in the borderlands themselves. Archaeologists reconstruct ancient ways of life from traces left behind in the earth that are hundreds or thousands of years old; anthropologists who strive to reconstruct the origin of the human species itself make use of fossil remains that reach back millions of years into the past. Whatever the case may be, anthropologists are sometimes exposed to practices that startle them. However, as they take the risk of getting to know such ways of life better, they are often treated to the sweet discovery of familiarity. This shock of the unfamiliar becoming familiar—as well as the familiar becoming unfamiliar—is something anthropologists come to expect and is one of the real pleasures of the field. In this book, we share aspects of the anthropological experience in the hope that you, too, will come to find pleasure, insight, and self-recognition from an involvement with the unfamiliar.

Anthropology can be defined as the study of human nature, human society, human language, and the human past (adapted from Greenwood and Stini 1977). It is a scholarly discipline that aims to describe in the broadest possible sense what it means to be human. Anthropologists are not alone in focusing their attention on human beings and their creations. Human biology, literature, art, history, linguistics, sociology, political science, economics—all these scholarly disciplines and many more—concentrate on one or another aspect of human life.

What is distinctive about the way anthropologists study human life? As we shall see, anthropology is *holistic, comparative, field-based,* and *evolutionary.* First, anthropology emphasizes that all the aspects of human life intersect with one another in complex ways and become integrated with one another over time. Anthropology is

FIGURE 1.1 Many people around the world eat insects. Here, a restaurant worker in Bangkok, Thailand, prepares grubs for cooking.

thus the **holistic** study of human nature, human society, human language, and the human past. This perspective draws together anthropologists whose specializations might otherwise divide them. At the most inclusive level, we may thus think of anthropology as the unified (or holistic) study of humans.

Second, in addition to being holistic, anthropology is a discipline interested in **comparison**. To generalize about human nature, human society, human language, and the human past requires evidence from the widest possible range of human societies. It is not enough, for example, to observe only our own social group, discover that we do not eat insects, and conclude that human beings as a species do not eat insects. When we compare human diets in different societies, we discover that insect eating is quite common and that our North American aversion to eating insects is nothing more than a dietary practice specific to our own society. Indeed, upon reflection we can identify some of our own dietary

anthropology The study of human nature, human society, human language, and the human past.

holistic A characteristic of the anthropological perspective that describes, at the highest and most inclusive level, how anthropology tries to integrate all that is known about human beings and their activities.

comparison A characteristic of the anthropological perspective that requires anthropologists to study similarities and differences across as many human societies as possible before generalizing about human beings and their activities.

practices that may seem strange to people in other societies. For example, Canadians have a strong affinity for a gooey liquid that flows from certain trees. Every year, thousands of trees in Quebec and Ontario are tapped to make some of the best maple syrup in the world, yet not all societies would recognize processed tree sap as a part of their regular diet.

Third, anthropology is also a field-based discipline. That is, for almost all anthropologists, the actual practice of anthropology—its data collection—takes place away from the office and in direct contact with the people, the sites, or the animals that are of interest. Whether they are biological anthropologists studying capuchins in Costa Rica, archaeologists excavating a site high in the Canadian Arctic, linguistic anthropologists learning an unwritten language in the rainforest of Colombia, or cultural anthropologists studying ethnic identity in small-town festivals in Quebec, anthropologists are in direct contact with the sources of their data. For most anthropologists, the richness and complexity of this immersion in other patterns of life is one of our discipline's most distinctive features. Field research connects anthropologists directly with the lived experiences of other people as the example from Cameroon suggests, or with other primates, or to the material evidence that humans have left behind. Academic anthropologists intersperse field research with the other tasks they perform as university professors. Other anthropologists—often referred to as applied anthropologists—regularly spend most or all of their time interacting with communities in the field. All anthropology begins with a specific group of people (or primates) and always returns to them as well.

Lastly, anthropologists look for characteristics that unite all of humanity and that are valid across space and time. Because anthropologists are interested in documenting and explaining change in the human past, **evolution** is at the core of the anthropological perspective. Anthropologists examine both biological and cultural evolution of the human species. *Biological evolution* looks at how the physical features and life processes of human beings have changed over time. It also

examines human origins and the genetic variation and inheritance in living human populations. *Cultural evolution* concerns change over time in beliefs, behaviours, and material objects that shape human development and social life.

Early anthropologists' discussions of cultural evolution emphasized a series of universal stages. However, this approach has been rejected by contemporary anthropologists who talk about cultural evolution, including William Durham (1991) and Robert Boyd (e.g., Richerson and Boyd 2005). Currently, there are lively theoretical debates in anthropology and other related fields, such as evolutionary biology and developmental psychology, concerning culture change and whether or not it should be referred to as "cultural evolution." In the midst of this debate, one of anthropology's most important contributions to the study of human evolution remains the demonstration that biological evolution is not the same as cultural evolution. Distinction between the two remains important as a way of demonstrating the fallacies and incoherence of arguments claiming that everything people do or think can be explained biologically, for example, in terms of "genes" or "race" or "sex."

What Is the Concept of Culture?

A consequence of human evolution that had the most profound impact on human nature and human society was the emergence of **culture**, which can be defined as sets of learned behaviour, ideas, and material goods that human beings share as members of society. Human beings use culture to adapt to and transform the world in which they live.

Human beings are more dependent than any other species on learning for survival because we have no instincts that automatically protect us and help us find food and shelter. Instead, we have come to use our large and complex brains to learn from other members of society what we need to know to survive. Learning is a primary focus of childhood, which is longer for humans than for any other species.

In order to understand the power of culture, anthropologists must also consider human biology. Anthropologists in North America traditionally have been trained in both areas so that they can understand

evolution A characteristic of the anthropological perspective that requires anthropologists to place their observations about human beings and their activities in a temporal framework that takes into consideration change over time.

culture Sets of learned behaviour, ideas, and material goods that human beings share as members of society.

how living organisms work and become acquainted with comparative information about a wide range of human societies. As a result, they can better evaluate how biology and culture contribute to different forms of human behaviour. Indeed, most anthropologists reject explanations of human behaviour that force them to choose either biology or culture as the cause. Instead, they emphasize that human beings are **biocultural organisms**. Our biological makeup—our brain, nervous system, and anatomy—is the outcome of developmental processes to which our genes and cellular chemistry contribute in fundamental ways. It also makes us organisms capable of creating and using culture. Without these biological endowments, human culture as we know it would not exist. At the same time, our survival as biological organisms depends on learned ways of thinking and acting that help us find food, shelter, and mates and that teach us how to rear our children. Our biological endowment, rich as it is, does not provide us with instincts that would automatically take care of these survival needs. Human biology makes culture possible; human culture makes human biological survival possible.

↻ For further discussion of how humans use culture to adapt to and transform the world in which they live, see Chapter 3, pp. 63–65.

What Makes Anthropology a Cross-Disciplinary Discipline?

Because of its diversity, anthropology does not easily fit into any of the standard academic classifications. The discipline is usually listed as a social science, but it spans the natural sciences and the humanities as well. What it is *not*, as we will see, is the study of the *exotic*, the *primitive*, or the *savage*, terms originally used in colonial times that anthropologists rejected long ago. Figure 1.2 illustrates the variety of interests that fall under the anthropological umbrella.

Traditionally, North American anthropology includes a holistic four-field approach: *biological anthropology, cultural anthropology, linguistic anthropology*, and *archaeology*. Many anthropology departments try to represent most or all of these subfields in their academic programs. However, universities in other parts of the world, such as Europe, usually do not bring all these specialties together. Many North American anthropologists, however, associate this holistic four-field North American anthropology with

biocultural organisms Organisms (in this case, human beings) whose defining features are co-determined by biological and cultural factors.

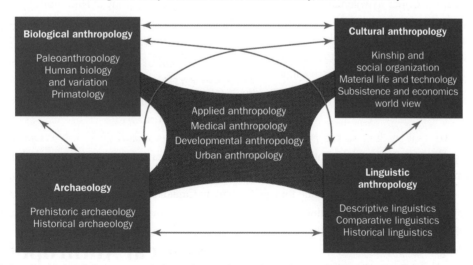

Anthropology
The integrated study of human nature, human society, and human history.

Biological anthropology

Paleoanthropology
Human biology
and variation
Primatology

Cultural anthropology

Kinship and
social organization
Material life and technology
Subsistence and economics
world view

Applied anthropology
Medical anthropology
Developmental anthropology
Urban anthropology

Archaeology

Prehistoric archaeology
Historical archaeology

Linguistic anthropology

Descriptive linguistics
Comparative linguistics
Historical linguistics

FIGURE 1.2 In the United States and Canada, anthropology is traditionally divided into four specialties: biological anthropology, cultural anthropology, linguistic anthropology, and archaeology. Applied anthropology draws on information provided by the other four specialties.

In Their Own Words

Anthropology as a Vocation

Michel Bouchard, an associate professor at the University of Northern British Columbia, describes his personal journey as an anthropologist. Moving throughout the circumpolar region and Canada, Bouchard's work is truly cross-disciplinary, investigating a variety of topics, ranging from individual and group identity formation to associations between language and status to interpretations of nationalism across different populations.

From a small town in northern Alberta to the distant tundra beyond the Arctic Circle of Russia, I have sought to understand identity, what makes us "Us," and how and why we distinguish between this "Us" and an "Other." This journey entailed trying to understand how language is used within communities, but also how the mundane rituals of daily life define us. Thus, I have analyzed Russian animated children's movies and visited graveyards in a largely Russian-speaking community on the margins of the Republic of Estonia to understand Russian nationalism, and I have sought to understand why in my home community of Falher, Alberta, it is "natural" to speak to babies and dogs in French, while English is used whenever there is a unilingual English speaker within earshot because it is "polite."

After completing my BA at the University of Toronto, I continued on to the Université Laval in Quebec to pursue my graduate research. Not having much funding, I chose to return home to live in my parents' basement while I conducted a study of my own community. I was a fourth-generation French speaker from Alberta who had grown up in a small region where the French language was still the dominant language throughout the community. Yet in other areas of Alberta, the province in which both my parents and I had been born, I was made to feel a stranger, as most Albertans believed that all French speakers lived in Quebec. As I conducted my research, I came to grips with issues of status and stigma, and how these issues influence the use of language and language maintenance. Even

before they start school, children know which language is dominant, which group has high status, and they act accordingly. Today I continue to investigate such themes as I conduct new research, in an attempt to understand how such feelings of stigma can be countered to ensure that minority languages are not lost.

From Falher I pushed into the Baltics and then Russia to better understand issues of nation and nationalism. There, I hit a roadblock, as the existing theory did not truly allow a nuanced explanation of how nation was understood and identity formulated. For over a decade, I have been working to develop a new, more relevant theoretical construct of nation—one that recognizes how nations are continually reconstituted in narrative in an act that I call *curating*—while acknowledging that nations are not modern inventions, but rather constructs that took root during the medieval period.

Recently, I have begun exploring a new topic, Métis ethnogenesis (i.e., the process by which Métis people have formed—and continue to form—a collective ethnic identity). This latest research seeks to understand how the emergence of a Métis identity is tied to the earlier *Canadien* identity that was adopted by the French speakers born in the colony of New France in the seventeenth century. I continue to use historical documents with an anthropological gaze to see how communities emerge and are shaped over time.

Source: Courtesy of Michel Bouchard, Professor at the University of Northern British Columbia.

the successful repudiation of nineteenth-century scientific racism by Franz Boas and other early twentieth-century anthropologists. They also recognize and value four-field anthropology as a cross-disciplinary discipline, where anthropologists are encouraged to bring together fresh concepts and knowledge from a variety of research traditions. Canadian anthropologist Regna Darnell, a distinguished professor at Western University, has intensively reviewed, documented, and analyzed the successful integration of the four fields of anthropology in academia throughout

North America (1992, 1998, 2000; see also Harrison and Darnell 2006 for an overview of the history of anthropology in Canada).

Biological Anthropology

Since the nineteenth century, when anthropology was developing as an academic field, anthropologists have studied human beings as living organisms in order to discover what makes them different from or similar to other animals. Early interest in these matters was a by-product of centuries of exploration and colonial expansion. Western Europeans found tremendous variation in the physical appearance of peoples around the world and tried to make sense of these differences. Some researchers developed a series of elaborate techniques to measure different observable features of human populations, including skin colour, hair type, and skull shape, hoping to find scientific evidence that would allow them to classify all the peoples of the world into a set of unambiguous categories based on distinct sets of biological attributes. Such categories were called **races**, and many scientists were convinced that clear-cut criteria for racial classification would be discovered if careful measurements were made on enough people from a range of different populations.

European scientists first applied racial categories to the peoples of Europe itself, but their classifications soon included non-European peoples, who were coming under increasing political and economic domination through colonial expansion by European and European American capitalist societies. These peoples differed from "white" Europeans not only because of their skin colour but also because of their unfamiliar languages and customs. In most cases, their technologies were also no match for the potent armaments of the West. In the early eighteenth century, using terms that are no longer in use today, the European biologist Carolus Linnaeus (Carl von Linné, 1707–1778) classified known human populations into four races (Amerindian, Caucasian, Asian, and Negro) based on skin colour (reddish, white, yellow, and black, respectively).

In the nineteenth century, influential natural scientists such as Louis Agassiz (1807–1873), Samuel George Morton (1799–1851), Francis Galton (1822–1911), and Paul Broca (1824–1880) built on this idea of race, ranking different populations of the world in terms of skull size; they found the brains of "white" Europeans and North Americans to be larger and saw the other "races" as representing varying grades of inferiority, with the two lowest grades being represented by Amerindians (i.e., Indigenous) and Africans (Gould 1996). These findings were used to validate the social practice of **racism**: the systematic oppression of members of one or more socially defined "race" by members of another socially defined "race" that is justified in terms of the supposed inherent biological superiority of the rulers and the supposed inherent biological inferiority of those they rule. For example, despite the fact that millions of Indigenous

people were living and thriving in the Americas for thousands of years, racism and racist ideals supported the nineteenth-century colonial perspective that the land was nobody's (*terra nullius*) and open to be settled. Consequently, thousands of Indigenous people were enslaved, removed from their land, and died as their land was settled by European colonizers.

In the recent past, the treatment of Indigenous peoples in Canada exemplifies clear racist practices. By far one of the most devastating of these was the establishment of the residential school program in Canada. Indigenous children from across the country were taken from their families in an attempt to take the "Indian out of the Indian" and assimilate them into the Euro-Christian culture. As a result, these children were forced to live in boarding schools, subjected to horrendous living conditions, and not allowed to speak their Indigenous language; essentially, they had their Indigenous culture stripped away. These schools were in existence for over 100 years, impacting over 100,000 children, who essentially grew up without a connection to their culture. To redress the legacy of residential schools and this devastating loss of Indigenous culture, the Canadian government created a Truth and Reconciliation Commission (TRC). The TRC was created to hear the stories of the survivors of the residential school system and to lay the foundation for reconciliation. Ten principles of reconciliation and 94 Calls to Action were put forward to guide the process of repairing the broken relationship between Indigenous and non-Indigenous peoples in Canada. The Calls to Action are to be used to change all levels of government, including sectors that deal with child welfare, health, justice, and education (TRC 2015).

↻ For further discussion of the Truth and Reconciliation Commission (TRC), see Chapter 13, p. 305, and Chapter 15, p. 366.

↻ For expanded discussion of the methods anthropologists use to study human variation without using the term *race*, see Chapter 7, pp. 137–9. For a discussion of present-day racism and associated social issues in Canada, see Chapter 14, pp. 332–3.

races Social groupings that allegedly reflect biological differences.

racism The systematic oppression of members of one or more socially defined "race" by members of another socially defined "race" that is justified in terms of the supposed inherent biological superiority of the rulers and the supposed inherent biological inferiority of those they rule.

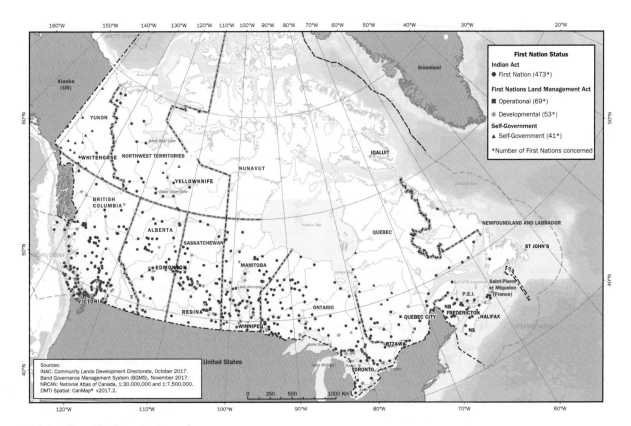

MAP 1.1 First Nations in Canada.
Sources: Geomatics Services, November 2017.

Biological or physical anthropology as a separate discipline had its origins in the work of scholars whose training was in some other discipline, often medicine. Johann Blumenbach (1752–1840), for example, whom some have called the "father of physical anthropology," was trained as a physician. Blumenbach identified five different races (Caucasoid, Mongoloid, American, Ethiopian, and Malayan), and his classification was influential in the later nineteenth and twentieth centuries (Molnar 2001, 6). He and his contemporaries assumed that the races of "mankind" (as they would have said) were fixed and unchanging subdivisions of humanity.

However, as scientists learned more about biological variation in human populations, some of them came to realize that traits traditionally used to identify races, such as skin colour, did not correlate well with other physical and biological traits, let alone mental and moral traits. Indeed, scientists could not even agree about how many human races there were or where the boundaries between them should be drawn.

By the early twentieth century, some anthropologists and biologists were arguing that "race" was a cultural label invented by human beings to sort people into groups and that races with distinct sets of biological attributes simply did not exist. Anthropologists including Franz Boas (1858–1942), for example, who in the early 1900s founded the first department of anthropology in North America, at Columbia University in New York, had long been uncomfortable with racial classifications in anthropology. Boas and his students devoted much energy to debunking racist stereotypes, using both their knowledge of biology and their understanding of culture. As the discipline of anthropology developed in the United States and later in Canada, students were trained in both human biology and human culture to provide them with the tools to fight racial stereotyping. After World War II, this position gained increasing strength in North American anthropology, under the forceful leadership of anthropologist Sherwood Washburn (1911–2000). The "new" physical anthropology that Washburn developed at the University of California, Berkeley, repudiated racial classification and shifted attention to patterns of variation and adaptation within the human species as a whole. This shift in emphasis led many of Washburn's followers to define their specialty as **biological anthropology**, a move that highlighted their differences with the older "physical anthropology" devoted to racial classification.

Some biological anthropologists work in the fields of **primatology** (the study of the closest living relatives of human beings, the non-human primates), **paleoanthropology** (the study of the fossilized bones and teeth of our earliest ancestors), and human skeletal biology (measuring and comparing the shapes and sizes—or morphology—of human bones and teeth using skeletal remains from different human populations) (Figure 1.3). Newer specialties focus on human adaptability in different ecological settings, on human growth and development, or on the connections between a population's evolutionary history and its susceptibility to disease (e.g., paleo-demography). Recent genetic studies in Quebec, for example, have investigated the link between certain medical issues occurring among current populations and similar issues among those who settled New France generations ago (Bhérer et al. 2011). In addition, forensic anthropologists use their knowledge of human skeletal anatomy to aid human rights investigations in places like Bosnia and Herzegovina

For further examples from primatology, see Chapter 4, p. 81.

(Skinner, York, and Connor 2002) or assist law enforcers with the identification of human remains (Mayne Correia and Beattie 2002). In both of these cases, biological anthropologists are participating in applied anthropology (see the discussion of applied anthropology later in this chapter).

Whether they study human biology, primates, or the fossils of our ancestors, biological anthropologists clearly share many methods and theories used in the natural sciences—primarily biology, ecology, chemistry, and geology. What tends to set biological anthropologists apart from their non-anthropological colleagues is the holistic, comparative, and evolutionary perspective that has been part of their anthropological training. That perspective reminds them always to consider their work as only part of the overall study of human nature, human society, and the human past.

> **biological anthropology (or physical anthropology)** The specialty of anthropology that looks at human beings as biological organisms and tries to discover what characteristics make them different from other organisms and what characteristics they share.
>
> **primatology** The study of non-human primates, the closest living relatives of human beings.
>
> **paleoanthropology** The study of human fossils and associated remains to understand our evolutionary history.

FIGURE 1.3 Some biological anthropologists are primatologists, such as Linda Fedigan, who studies capuchins, spider monkeys, and other primates in their natural habitats and is a professor emeritus at the University of Calgary (a). Other biological anthropologists are paleoanthropologists, such as Pamela Willoughby, who studies ancient human ancestors and teaches at the University of Alberta (b).

Cultural Anthropology

The second specialty within anthropology is **cultural anthropology**, which is sometimes called *sociocultural anthropology* or *social anthropology*. Sociology and anthropology developed alongside each other during the early twentieth century and share similar interests in the study of culture and social organization. What differentiated anthropology from sociology was the anthropological interest in comparing varieties of human social life around the globe. In the racist framework of nineteenth- and early-twentieth-century European and North American societies, some people viewed sociology as the study of "civilized" industrial societies and labelled anthropology as the study of all other societies, lumped together as "primitive." Today, by contrast, anthropologists are concerned with studying *all* human societies, and they reject the labels *civilized* and *primitive* for the same reason they reject the term *race*.

Because people everywhere use culture to adapt to and transform everything in the wider world in which they live, the field of cultural anthropology is vast. Cultural anthropologists tend to specialize in one or another domain of human cultural activity, such as gender or kinship but not limited to these. Others study the ways particular groups of human beings organize themselves to carry out collective tasks, whether economic, political, or spiritual. This focus within cultural anthropology bears the closest resemblance to the discipline of sociology, and from it has come the identification of anthropology as one of the social sciences.

Many anthropologists did significant research throughout the twentieth century to separate human biological variation from human cultural practices. By the latter part of the twentieth century, anthropologists also regularly distinguished between the biological sex of an individual and the culturally shaped **gender** roles considered appropriate for members of each sex in a given society. Many anthropological studies have highlighted how gender roles shape social changes in our global world; for example, Canadian anthropologist Marie-France Labrecque, at Université Laval, has spent many years researching the importance of women's roles in Latin America (see Labrecque 2012, 222). As we shall see throughout the text, attention to gender has become an integral part of all anthropological work.

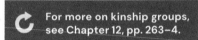

For a more in-depth discussion of sex, gender, and sexuality from an anthropological perspective, see Chapter 11.

Anthropologists discovered that people in many non-Western societies developed institutions of relatedness that enabled them to organize social groups through which they could live their lives. One form of relatedness, called *kinship*, links people to one another on the basis of birth, marriage, and nurturance. The study of kinship has become highly developed in anthropology and remains a focus of interest today. In addition, anthropologists have described a variety of forms of social

For more on kinship groups, see Chapter 12, pp. 263–4.

groups organized according to different principles, such as secret societies, age sets, and numerous forms of complex political organization, including states. In recent years, cultural anthropologists have studied contemporary issues of gender and sexuality, transnational labour migration, urbanization, globalization, the post–Cold War resurgence of ethnicity and nationalism around the globe, and debates about human rights.

Cultural anthropologists have investigated the patterns of material life found in different human groups. Among the most striking are worldwide variations in clothing, housing, tools, and techniques for getting food and making material goods. Some anthropologists specialize in the study of technologies in different societies or in the evolution of technology over time. Those interested in material life also describe the natural setting for which technologies have been developed and analyze the way technologies and environments shape each other. As well, other anthropologists have investigated the way non-Western people have responded to the political and economic challenges of colonialism and the capitalist industrial technology that accompanied it.

As cultural anthropologists have become increasingly aware of the sociocultural influences that stretch

cultural anthropology The specialty of anthropology that shows how variation in the beliefs and behaviours of members of different human groups is shaped by sets of learned behaviours and ideas that human beings acquire as members of society—that is, by culture.

sex The physical characteristics that traditionally distinguish two kinds of humans, females and males (for example, body shape, distribution of body hair, reproductive organs, sex chromosomes).

gender The culturally constructed roles assigned to males or females, which vary considerably from society to society.

across space to affect local communities, they have also become sensitive to those that stretch over time. As a result, many contemporary cultural anthropologists make serious efforts to place their cultural analyses in detailed historical context. Cultural anthropologists who do comparative studies of language, music, dance, art, poetry, philosophy, religion, or ritual often share many of the interests of specialists in the disciplines of fine arts and humanities.

Cultural anthropologists, no matter what their area of specialization, ordinarily collect their data during an extended period of close involvement with the people in whose way of life they are interested. This period of research, called **fieldwork**, has as its central feature the anthropologists' involvement in the everyday routine of those among whom they live (Figure 1.4). People who share information about their culture with anthropologists have traditionally been called **informants**; however, some anthropologists object to the use of this term because it suggests a role that is limited to supplying information for the benefit of the researcher. Therefore, some contemporary anthropologists prefer to describe these individuals as *respondents, collaborators, teachers, friends*, or simply *the people I work with* because these terms emphasize a relationship of equality and reciprocity. Fieldworkers gain insight into another culture by participating in social activities with members of that culture and by observing those activities as outsiders. This research method, known as *participant observation*, is central to cultural anthropology.

Cultural anthropologists write about what they have learned in scholarly articles or books and sometimes document the lives of the people they work with on film or video. An **ethnography** is a systematic study and description of a particular human culture; **ethnology** is the comparative study of two or more such groups (Radcliffe-Brown 1951). Thus, cultural anthropologists who write ethnographies are sometimes called *ethnographers*, and anthropologists who compare ethnographic information on many different cultural practices are sometimes called *ethnologists*. But not all anthropological writing is ethnographic. Some anthropologists specialize in reconstructing the history of our discipline, tracing, for example, how anthropologists' fieldwork practices have changed over time and how these changes may be related to wider political, economic, and social changes within the societies from which they came and within which they did their research (Harrison and Darnell 2006).

Courtesy Robert Lavenda

FIGURE 1.4 Cultural anthropologist Robert Laughlin with members of the Sna Jtz'ibajom puppet theatre troupe in San Cristóbal de las Casas, Mexico. Cultural anthropologists talk to many people, observe their actions, and participate as fully as possible in a group's way of life.

People everywhere are increasingly making use of material goods and technologies produced outside their own societies. Anthropologists have been able to show that contrary to many expectations, non-Western people do not slavishly imitate Western ways. Instead, they make use of Western technologies in ways that are creative and often unanticipated but that make sense in their own local cultural context. These forms of cultural exchange were powerfully accelerated after the end of the Cold War in 1989, when advances in the technologies of communication, manufacturing, and transportation seemed to dissolve, or at least seriously reduce, previous barriers of space and time. All parts of the world were drawn into these processes of **globalization**: the reshaping of local conditions by powerful global forces on an

fieldwork An extended period of close involvement with the people in whose way of life anthropologists are interested, during which anthropologists ordinarily collect most of their data.

informants People in a particular culture who work with anthropologists and provide them with insights about the local way of life. Also called *respondents, collaborators, teachers,* or *friends*.

ethnography A systematic study and description of a particular culture.

ethnology The comparative study of two or more cultures.

globalization Reshaping of local conditions by powerful global forces on an ever-intensifying scale.

every-intensifying scale. Globalization suggests a world full of movement and mixture, contacts and linkages, and persistent cultural interaction and exchange (Inda and Rosaldo 2002, 2). Some people have clearly benefited from globalization, whereas others have suffered, and people everywhere struggle to respond to effects of globalization that seem impossible to manage. In a globalized world, it is no longer possible to presume that peoples and cultures are firmly attached to specific geographical locations. As a result, many cultural anthropologists now pay increasing attention to the migrations undertaken by peoples all over the globe and have often focused on regions like the borderland between northern Mexico and the United States, where struggles with contradictory social practices and ambiguous identities have long been the rule, not the exception.

Research projects by contemporary cultural anthropologists occur in all areas of our interconnected world, including business and information technology (IT). A perfect example of this is the recent work of **design anthropologists**, who work with companies to design products that are culturally appealing to consumers (Wasson 2016). For example, design anthropologist Gray Graffam (2010) at the University of Toronto works on how anthropological research can contribute to marketing in business. Other interesting research includes the move of cultural anthropologists into fields including computer engineering or into ethnographic settings such as scientific laboratories or the Internet. This interest has also stimulated new approaches to material culture, especially the ways human beings and their computerized devices connect with each other.

Linguistic Anthropology

Perhaps the most striking cultural feature of our species is **language**: the system of arbitrary vocal symbols we use to encode our experience of the world and of one another. People use language to talk about all areas of their lives, from material to spiritual. **Linguistic anthropology**

design anthropology **The use of anthropological methods to develop new product ideas.**

language **The system of arbitrary vocal symbols used to encode one's experience of the world and of others.**

linguistic anthropology **The specialty of anthropology concerned with the study of human languages.**

therefore studies language, not only as a form of symbolic communication but also as a major carrier of important cultural information. In the early twentieth century, the focus of many anthropologists was to transcribe non-Western languages and to produce grammars and dictionaries of those languages as a means of preventing them from being lost. This sort of preservation remains important today as many languages are being lost around the world as modernization, colonization, and rapid globalization require the use of European languages in place of traditional languages.

In Canada, the residential school program of the early twentieth century had a devastating impact on Indigenous languages. Thousands of Indigenous children were forced to speak only English, and they experienced numerous other tragedies. In fact, today only 25 per cent of Indigenous people in Canada speak their traditional language, and only three Indigenous languages—Cree, Inuktitut, and Ojibwe—have enough people speaking and understanding them to ensure that future generations will be able to communicate using their traditional ways (Norris 2007). In response to this tragedy, the Truth and Reconciliation Commission of Canada enacted numerous Calls to Action that support Indigenous language revitalization. For example, Call to Action number 14 states the following:

> We call upon the Canadian government to enact an Aboriginal Languages Act that incorporates the following principles: i) Aboriginal languages are a fundamental and valued element of Canadian culture . . . ii) Aboriginal language rights are reinforced by the Treaties; iii) The . . . government has responsibility to provide sufficient funds for Aboriginal-language revitalization and preservation. (Truth and Reconciliation Commission of Canada 2015)

Today, many of these traditional languages are being taught in schools to the younger generations of Indigenous peoples to revitalize and maintain traditional knowledge and cultural practices.

Contemporary linguistic anthropologists and their counterparts in sociology (called *sociolinguists*) study the way language differences correlate with differences in gender, race, class, or ethnic identity. Some have specialized in studying what happens when speakers are fluent in more than one language and must choose which language to use under which circumstances. Others have written about what happens when speakers of unrelated languages are forced to communicate with one another, producing languages called *pidgins*. Some linguistic anthropologists study sign languages. Others look at the ways children learn language or the styles and strategies followed by fluent speakers engaged in conversation. More recently, linguistic anthropologists have paid attention to the way political ideas in a society contribute to people's ideas of what may or may not be said and the strategies speakers devise to escape these forms of censorship. Some take part in policy discussions about literacy and language standardization and address the challenges faced by speakers of languages that are being displaced by international languages of commerce and technology, such as English. Some linguistic anthropologists and others who study language even apply their knowledge to help create new languages for movies and TV shows, such as Klingon in *Star Trek* or Valyrian in *Game of Thrones* (Figure 1.5) (see the "Anthropology in Everyday Life" box).

UBC Okanagan/UBCO Media Services

FIGURE 1.5 Some linguistic anthropologists have helped to create new languages for movies and TV shows. Canadian linguistic anthropologist Christine Schreyer, shown here, developed a written form of Kryptonian for the 2013 movie *Man of Steel.*

In all these cases, linguistic anthropologists try to understand language in relation to the broader cultural and historical contexts that make it possible. For example,

Anthropology in Everyday Life

Language Revitalization: What Can We Learn from Conlang Communities?

It is not every day that an anthropologist finds herself on the set of a big-budget Hollywood movie production. Yet this is what happened to Canadian linguistic anthropologist Christine Schreyer, an assistant professor at the University of British Columbia's Okanagan campus. Schreyer was asked by the studio in charge of production to develop the written form of Superman's alien language, Kryptonian, for the 2013 movie *Man of Steel.*

Schreyer's training as an anthropologist equipped her with an intimate understanding of the interdependence that exists between language and culture, as each influences and shapes the other. Her work for *Man of Steel* was successful because she constructed the language in relation to the characteristics of Kryptonian culture that had been developed in past *Superman* comic books and movies. Yet the principles involved in creating and transmitting this fictional language have even greater significance for

language revitalization in the real world, a pressing issue among linguistic anthropologists today.

For years before she became involved with *Man of Steel*, Schreyer had been studying conlangs (constructed languages) in order to grasp how and why these linguistic creations have become established forms of communication among fandoms the world over. Indeed, many conlangs—such as those used in *Star Trek* and *The Lord of the Rings* trilogy—have grown substantial user communities since their creation. Schreyer decided to focus on speakers of the Na'vi language, which was created to be spoken by the aliens in the 2009 movie *Avatar*. In addition to learning about the Na'vi-speaking community itself, Schreyer was interested in discovering what threatened or endangered language communities might be able to learn from the successful spread of Na'vi.

Schreyer quickly discovered that conlang users have made expert use of social media and IT to build

Continued

up their communities. While these mediums have not always been useful to minority communities endeavouring to revitalize their traditional languages, Schreyer believes that there is potential for them to be more productive in the future. The key lies in analyzing why conlangs have been so successful and then applying the principles behind that success to endangered languages.

At least part of the answer seems to lie in the perceived prestige associated with each language. Conlangs draw their prestige from the lore surrounding the characters who use them in fictional realities. People generally wish to learn conlangs because of their attachment to a larger universe of wonder and fantasy. Similarly, a *lingua franca* such as English or Portuguese gains its prestige from dominating the economic marketplace—a realm that many people perceive as offering great economic and other benefits. Where do minority languages draw their prestige from? Predominately, this prestige originates in tradition and a sense of belonging to a culture—a sense of identity. Finding a way to increase the level of prestige attached to an endangered language, to increase its appeal to potential users, is vital to revitalization. How this can be achieved depends on the community in question.

Language revitalization is a very current, very critical issue in linguistic anthropology today. As different societies converge in the increasingly globalized marketplace, there seems to be little room for traditional languages. Yet these languages remain key to individual and group identities, and their preservation is important to the promotion of equal human rights across the globe. While not yet fully explored, the question of why some people are willing to spend so much time and energy learning conlangs may one day lead to new and creative solutions to this important issue.

Source: To read the original interview on which this piece is based, see http://blog.wennergren.org/2014/08. See also Schreyer 2011.

in Canada, the interplay between our two official languages is deeply affected by past and present tensions between French- and English-speaking Canadians. Contemporary linguistic anthropologists are trained in both linguistics and anthropology while many cultural anthropologists also receive linguistics training as part of their professional preparation.

Archaeology

Archaeology is another major specialty within anthropology. It is sometimes referred to as the cultural anthropology of the human past. Archaeologists are committed to the discovery and systematic study of the remnants of our past—everything from piles of bones and stones to the foundations of early great cities like Teotihuacan in Mexico. Through the analysis of **material culture**, archaeologists focus on reconstructing

---

archaeology The specialty of anthropology that studies the human past by analyzing material remains left behind by earlier societies.

material culture Objects created or shaped by humans and given meaning through cultural practices.

---

our human past. Archaeologists seek to understand past human cultural activity using a variety of methods: they conduct surveys of areas to understand where people lived; they try to reconstruct the types of houses in which people dwelled; they study garbage from past societies to understand what people ate; and they look closely at and even recreate tools people made in the past to survive. And, of course, archaeologists also excavate or dig archaeological *sites* (i.e., areas with high concentrations of human cultural remains) to recover *artifacts* (i.e., portable objects created or modified by humans).

Archaeologists rarely work alone. The complexity and vastness of the human past often requires a large team (or crew) of specialists working alongside archaeologists to assist in carrying out archaeological research. These teams may consist of geologists, botanists, wildlife biologists, metallurgists, pottery specialists, or others. Together, these experts work to better understand how humans lived in the past, what they ate to survive, how they manufactured their tools, and even what the environment was like when the site was occupied.

Archaeologists often work alongside paleoanthropologists as well, especially where human remains or burial sites are discovered, and their findings often complement each other. For example, archaeological information regarding successive stone-tool traditions in a particular region may correlate with human fossils that indicate ancient humans' prehistoric occupation of that region. In order to make these correlations, archaeologists must establish a clear sequence of events, or a timeline, for the artifacts and sites. To do this, they use a wide variety of dating techniques to establish the approximate ages of the artifacts.

Surveys of geographical areas are also important to create distribution maps of sites and artifacts across space. From this information, archaeologists can generate hypotheses about when certain societies existed, what their territorial ranges were, and what patterns of sociocultural change they experienced. For example, archaeologists often compare the appearance of certain cultural artifacts, such as pottery or stone tools, at one site to the appearance of those artifacts at another site, which allows them to hypothesize about the nature and degree of social contact between different peoples in the past. The sites and artifacts that archaeologists investigate sometimes relate to relatively recent events in the human past. For example, some archaeologists study what remains of seventeenth- and eighteenth-century fur-trade posts or explorers' ships (see Figure 1.6) or abandoned nineteenth-century industrial sites. As well, many archaeologists use oral histories of Indigenous peoples to help enhance our study of the

past (Martindale et al. 2017). Some contemporary archaeologists even dig through layers of garbage deposited by human beings within the last two or three decades, often uncovering surprising information about contemporary consumption patterns.

Unlike most fictional archaeologists like Indiana Jones and Lara Croft, anthropological archaeologists have ethical responsibilities to maintain and conserve the artifacts of humans. Looting of archaeological sites to remove artifacts to sell for profit along with the destruction of archaeological sites caused by industrial development are still very common, especially in countries with political unrest and widespread poverty. To combat such harmful actions, historic preservation laws exist throughout the world; these laws require archaeologists to seek government permission to excavate sites and to follow specific protocols for preserving and curating artifacts. Archaeologists are considered stewards of the past and accountable to the public for the interpretation, conservation, and preservation of the human past. Shared ethics and methods regarding the discovery of archaeological sites and artifacts are explicitly outlined on the websites of the Society for American Archaeology (SAA) and the Canadian Archaeological Association (CAA). A final note: the majority of professional archaeologists work in the field of cultural resource management (CRM), which is also known as salvage archaeology. These archaeologists work alongside environmental scientists to assess locations that are slated to be developed for industry and infrastructure projects. As a result, thousands of new sites are documented annually, and our knowledge of the human past is growing exponentially.

Applied Anthropology

Applied anthropology is the subfield of anthropology in which anthropologists use information gathered from the other anthropological specialties to propose solutions to practical cross-cultural problems (Figure 1.7). Some may use a particular group of people's ideas about illness and health to introduce new public

FIGURE 1.6 Canadian anthropologist Owen Beattie's work in the Canadian Arctic has led to a greater understanding of what became of the members of the "lost" Franklin expedition, which disappeared only months after beginning its search for the Northwest Passage in 1845.

applied anthropology The subfield of anthropology in which anthropologists use information gathered from the other anthropological specialties to solve practical cross-cultural problems.

REUTERS/Dado Ruvic

FIGURE 1.7 Some applied forensic anthropologists use their knowledge of skeletal anatomy to aid in human rights investigations. Here, a forensic expert working with the International Commission on Missing Persons (ICMP) checks human remains found in a mass grave near Tuzla, Bosnia and Herzegovina.

health practices in a way that makes sense to and will be accepted by members of the group. Others may use knowledge of traditional social organization to ease the problems of refugees trying to settle in a new land. Yet others may apply this knowledge to help communities adapt to changing local circumstances. A great example of this is the work being done by Mark Nuttall, from the University of Alberta, regarding the varied perceptions of northern Indigenous peoples to climate change and how policy-makers can work with these groups to facilitate their successful adaptation to their changing environments (2009; see also Crate and Nuttall 2009, 2016). Still other applied anthropologists may use their knowledge of traditional and Western methods of cultivation to help farmers increase their crop yields. Given the growing concern throughout the world with the effects of different technologies on the environment, this kind of applied anthropology holds promise as a way of bringing together Western and non-Western knowledge in order to create sustainable technologies that minimize pollution and environmental degradation. In addition, some applied anthropologists have become management consultants or carry out market research, and their findings may contribute to the design of new products.

> **medical anthropology** The specialty of anthropology that concerns itself with human health—the factors that contribute to disease or illness and the ways that human populations deal with disease or illness.

In recent decades, some anthropologists have become involved in policy issues, actively participating in social processes that attempt to shape the future of those people among whom they work (Moore 2005, 3). This development has involved a change in our understanding of what applied anthropology is. Anthropologists in Canada have a long history of working with Indigenous peoples to assist with government negotiations regarding land use and resource development as well as self-government. In fact, this focus on collaborating with Indigenous communities is what makes Canadian anthropology unique in North America (Waldram 2010). In his overview of the intersection between applied anthropology and Indigenous issues in Canada, Edward Hedican (2008) describes the many instances in which anthropologists have been employed by various bands to mediate development issues, such as the James Bay hydroelectric dam in Quebec (Salisbury et al. 1972) and the proposed Mackenzie Valley Pipeline through the Northwest Territories (Salisbury, Elberg, and Schneider 1974). Additionally, in Canada and elsewhere, applied anthropologists often work in the legal arena, providing their expertise to support tribal groups' efforts to claim official self-government status (e.g., Weaver 1997) or to defend Indigenous peoples' land rights and territorial land claims (e.g., Asch 1984, 2014).

Although many anthropologists believe that applied work can be done within any of the traditional four fields of anthropology, increasing numbers in recent years have come to view applied anthropology as a separate field of professional specialization (see Figure 1.2). More and more universities in Canada and the United States have begun to develop courses and programs in a variety of forms of applied anthropology. Anthropologists who work for government agencies or non-profit organizations or in other non-university settings often describe what they do as the *anthropology of practice*. In the twenty-first century, it has been predicted that more than half of all new PhDs in anthropology will become applied or practising anthropologists rather than take up positions as faculty in university departments of anthropology.

Medical Anthropology

Medical anthropology is one of the most rapidly growing branches of applied anthropology. Over the past half-century or so, it has developed into an important anthropological specialty that has offered new ways to link biological and cultural anthropology. Medical anthropology concerns itself with human health—the factors that contribute to disease or illness and the ways that human populations deal with disease or illness (Baer, Singer, and Susser 2003, 3). In many cases, medical anthropologists have cross-appointments with schools of medicine and may have been trained as either nurses or medical doctors. Some early work done in Canada in this field was led by Emőke Szathmáry (1986), who examined the high incidence of diabetes among the Dene in Northwest Canada, suggesting that there is a connection between the introduction of processed, Westernized foods and the rise of diabetes in this population. Medical anthropologists may consider the physiological and cultural variables that are involved with the perception of human health and disease, the environmental features that affect human well-being, and the way the human body adapts to various environments. Contemporary medical anthropologists engage in work that directly addresses the anthropological proposition that human beings must be understood as biocultural organisms (Figure 1.8). A great example of this is the work of Leslie Dawson of MacEwan University, who has tracked birth practices among the Tlicho in the

By permission of Mary Hayden

FIGURE 1.8 Medical anthropologist Mary Hayden works with traditional healers to track the spread of plague in Uganda. Working directly with informants in the field gives medical anthropologists the opportunity to study both the cultural and biological factors that impact human health.

Northwest Territories (NWT), Canada, noting how colonialism and Western medicine shaped perceptions of health and pregnancy (see "In Their Own Words" box).

In Their Own Words

Birth Places, Embodied Spaces: Tlicho Pregnancy Stories across Generations

Working with the Tlicho women of NWT, Canada, Leslie Dawson of MacEwan University explores the impact of colonization on maternal health through birthing stories.

Colonization of the Tlicho (formerly Dogrib) region in the Northwest Territories (NWT) is relatively recent, and the profound changes to the lives of the Tlicho can be heard in the stories across the generations. Grounded in women's narratives, particularly of Tlicho Elders and a traditional midwife, their stories reveal changes in the lived experiences of pregnancy and birth as reflecting different socio-historic locations within histories of colonization—from birth on the land with community and midwives, to the beginnings of settlement and birth in the mission hospital in Rae, and to lone evacuation to Yellowknife for medicalized birth in a biomedical hospital.

Birth, however, is not solely a physiological event but is shaped by cultural values and meanings; nor is a birth place simply a location in which a physiological event occurs. Birth places may be seen as social and cultural spaces endowed with cultural values and meanings fundamental to the rituals of birth. Similarly, the body may be seen as biological and social and cultural. Through the intersection of space, place, and the body, a space becomes embodied, or an *embodied space*, in which meaning is inscribed on the body. By considering Tlicho birth places as embodied spaces, I explored the social transformations in time and space brought about by the processes of missionization and medicalization to reveal how colonial histories of controlling birth experiences have become inscribed on Tlicho maternal bodies.

Continued

Birth on the Land: The Female Body as Powerful

In the traditional setting, birth on the land reflected the interconnected nature of humans, animals, and spirituality. The relationship to the land informed the rituals of birth and emplaced Tlicho birth experiences. Birth on the land was guided by midwives and saw women's knowledge around pregnancy and birth transmitted from mothers and grandmothers. Ritualized treatment of the umbilical cord and placenta reflected the interconnectedness of humans, animals, and spirituality, and the female body was seen as powerful. However, these rituals of birth were suppressed as Tlicho spirituality came under the missionaries' agenda of assimilation with aspects of Indigenous spiritualties. With suppression of Tlicho spirituality came a new interpretation of the female body.

Missionized Birth: The Female Body as Suffering

Missionization in the North, as with other areas of Canada, began with a desire to save Indigenous "souls" through conversion to Christianity. In response to the epidemics of infectious disease, the Faraud Mission Hospital was established in Fort Rae (Behchoko) in 1940. As part of the Roman Catholic Mission, the hospital setting revealed a shift in the transfer of women's knowledge of birth, as well as the imposition of Christian morality and the understanding of labour as the "curse of Eve," leading to views of the female body as suffering. As a mission hospital, Faraud was run by nuns who reinforced this view of suffering through prayers during labour as well as a moral interpretation of single mothers in labour: "No needle for you." Closure of the "Indian hospitals" began in the 1960s, and the full extent of the medicalization of birth began with the evacuation policy in the North. Spiritualties, both Tlicho and Christian, eventually gave way to dominant biomedical discourse with its emphasis on technology and risk, which led to new emplaced birth experiences and meanings inscribed on the female body.

Evacuated Birth: The Female Body as Risk

Beginning in the 1970s and still policy today, pregnant Tlicho women at 36 to 38 weeks gestational age—or sooner if a high-risk pregnancy—are evacuated to Yellowknife to wait to give birth. (This practice also occurs with other Indigenous women in rural and remote communities.) Contemporary childbirth for Tlicho women is medicalized and institutionalized predominately based on the idea that these babes and mothers are "at risk." With pregnancy no longer viewed as a natural process, the female body becomes inherently at risk, as well as "a site on which colonial goals of assimilation and civilization could be realized" (Lawford and Giles 2012, 332).

Revitalized Birth Places: The Female Body Decolonized

By considering birth places as embodied spaces, I revealed how colonial histories of missionization and medicalization created new birth experiences and inscribed Eurocentric meanings on Tlicho maternal bodies. Colonization became integrated into the lived experiences and rituals of birth and created birth places structured by the cultural values of the colonizer, whether saving souls or saving bodies. In order to decolonize this process and the female body, it is imperative to return birthing to the community. This would allow for traditional Tlicho customs of care by women during labour and childbirth to be revitalized and for perinatal care to be delivered in the women's language. Furthermore, attention to traditional practices would demonstrate respect, bolster Tlicho identity, and, in turn, improve overall health and wellness.

Source: Dawson, L. (2017). "Birth Places, Embodied Spaces: Tlicho Pregnancy Stories Across the Generations." In *Indigenous Experiences of Pregnancy and Birth*, edited by Jaime Cidro and Hannah Tait Neufeld, 144–62. Bradford, ON: Demeter Press.

Particularly significant has been the development of *critical medical anthropology*, which links questions of human health and illness in local settings to social, economic, and political processes operating on a regional, national, or global scale. A good example is the work of Dr Sandra Hyde (2007) from McGill University, who has studied the spread of HIV/AIDS in China, including how political forces in China have shaped public perception and response to the disease, and how the rise of HIV/AIDS has affected various groups throughout the country. Critical medical anthropologists have been among the most vocal in pointing out how various forms of suffering and disease cannot be explained only by the presence of microbes in a diseased body but may depend on—or be made worse by—the presence of social inequality and a lack of access to health care. According to anthropologist Merrill Singer (1998, 195), critical medical anthropology "is committed to the 'making social' and the 'making political' of health and medicine." Thus, critical medical anthropologists pay attention to the way social divisions based on class, "race," gender, and ethnicity can block access to medical attention or make people more vulnerable to disease and suffering. They draw attention to the way Western biomedicine "encourages people to fight disease rather than to make the changes necessary to prevent it," for example, by linking low birth weight in newborn babies to poor nutrition, but failing to note that poor nutrition "may be a major health factor among impoverished social classes and oppressed ethnic groups in developed countries despite an abundance of food in society generally" (Singer 1998, 106, 109).

The Uses of Anthropology

Why take a course in anthropology? An immediate answer might be that human fossils or broken bits of ancient pots or the customs of faraway peoples inspire a fascination that is its own reward. But the experience of being dazzled by seemingly exotic places and peoples carries with it a risk. As you become increasingly aware of the range of anthropological data, including the many options that exist for living a satisfying human life, you may find yourself wondering about the life you are living. Contact with the unfamiliar can be liberating, but it can also be threatening if it undermines your confidence in the absolute truth and universal rightness of your previous understanding of the way the world works.

The contemporary world is increasingly interconnected. As people from different cultural backgrounds come into contact with one another, learning to cope with cultural differences becomes crucial. Anthropologists experience both the rewards and the risks of getting to know how other people live, and their work has helped to dispel many harmful stereotypes that sometimes make cross-cultural contact dangerous or impossible. Studying anthropology may help prepare you for some of the shocks you will encounter in dealing with people who look different from you, speak a different language, or do not agree that the world works exactly the way you think it does.

Anthropology involves learning about the kinds of living organisms we human beings are, the various ways we live our lives, and how we make sense of our experiences. Studying anthropology can equip you to deal with people with different cultural backgrounds in a less threatened, more tolerant manner. You may never be called on to eat termite paste. Still, you may one day encounter a situation in which none of the old rules seem to apply. As you struggle to make sense of what is happening, what you learned in anthropology class may help you relax and dare to try something totally new to you. If you do so, perhaps you too will discover the rewards of an encounter with the unfamiliar that is at the same time unaccountably familiar. We hope you will savour the experience.

Chapter Summary

1. Anthropology aims to describe in the broadest sense what it means to be human. The anthropological perspective is holistic, comparative, and evolutionary and has relied on the concept of culture to explain the diversity of human ways of life. Human beings depend on cultural learning for successful biological survival and reproduction, which is why anthropologists consider human beings to be biocultural organisms. Anthropology is also a field-based discipline. In North America today, anthropology is considered to have four major subfields: biological anthropology, archaeology, cultural anthropology, and linguistic anthropology; many people also consider applied anthropology to be a fifth major subfield.

2. Biological anthropology began as an attempt to classify all the world's populations into different races. By the early twentieth century, however, most anthropologists had rejected racial classifications as scientifically unjustifiable and objected to the ways in which racial classifications were used to justify the social practice of racism. Contemporary anthropologists who are interested in human biology include biological anthropologists, primatologists, and paleoanthropologists.

3. Cultural anthropologists study cultural diversity in all living human societies, including their own. Linguistic anthropologists approach cultural diversity by relating varied forms of language to their cultural contexts. Both gather information through fieldwork, by participating with their informants in social activities, and by observing those activities as outsiders. They publish accounts of their research in ethnographies.

4. Over the past quarter-century, many anthropologists and other scholars have become involved in the interdisciplinary field of science studies, which subjects scientific laboratories and their activities to ethnographic investigation and has shown how successful science in action differs from traditional idealized accounts of scientific research. Science studies research highlighting the productive interconnections among human beings, non-human organisms, and technical apparatus has inspired anthropologists from many subfields to revise our understanding of relationships between nature and culture, people and artifacts, and people and other living species.

5. Archaeology is the cultural anthropology of the human past, with interests ranging from the earliest stone tools to twenty-first-century garbage dumps. Archaeologists focus on understanding how humans lived in the past, how past societies interacted with one another, and how cultures changed over time. Archaeologists are stewards of the human past, and they rely on historic preservation laws to protect archaeological remains from looting and destruction.

6. Applied anthropologists, who are frequently referred to as practising anthropologists, often use information from the other anthropological specialties to solve practical cross-cultural problems. Medical anthropology connects biological anthropology, cultural anthropology, and applied anthropology, focusing on cultural perceptions of health and illness, suffering, and well-being.

online

For more information about different ethnographic practices used to study and understand other cultures, see the Focus on Four Fields passage "Cultural Anthropology: Ethnographic Methods" on the companion website.

For Review

1. What is anthropology? What makes it different from the other social sciences? What do the qualities of being *holistic, comparative, field-based,* and *evolutionary* contribute to the discipline?

2. How do anthropologists define culture? In what ways is this definition different from other, less specialized definitions of culture? How would the anthropological definition of culture inform the way that anthropologists view data?

3. What makes anthropology a cross-disciplinary discipline? Why is a cross-disciplinary approach advantageous to anthropologists?

4. Describe the main subfields of modern anthropology. Include one area of study for each subfield. What sorts of research projects might require anthropologists from two or more of these subfields to work together?

5. Identify three aspects of biological anthropology that appeal to you, and describe why you think they are interesting.

6. What are some of the main topics of interest in cultural anthropology? Which of these topics appeal to you the most? Why?

7. Summarize the difference between ethnography and ethnology.

8. How do linguistic anthropologists learn about human languages? What types of research do these anthropologists conduct? What knowledge and skills would you need to develop in order to create a new language as Christine Schreyer did for *Man of Steel*?

9. What are some of the topics or things archaeologists study? Which of these topics or things do you find most interesting? Why?

10. What are the connections between applied anthropology and the other branches of anthropology? Outline the advantages of applied anthropology.

11. Why is critical medical anthropology an important area of focus within applied anthropology? What are some examples of this type of research?

Key Terms

anthropology 3

applied anthropology 15

archaeology 14

biocultural organisms 5

biological anthropology
   (or physical anthropology) 9

comparison 3

cultural anthropology 10

culture 4

design anthropology 12

ethnography 11

ethnology 11

evolution 4

fieldwork 11

gender 10

globalization 11

holistic 3

informants 11

language 12

linguistic anthropology 12

material culture 14

medical anthropology 16

paleoanthropology 9

primatology 9

races 7

racism 7

sex 10

References

Asch, Michael. 1984. *Home and Native Land: Aboriginal Rights and the Canadian Constitution*. Toronto: Methuen.

——. 2014. *On Being Here to Stay: Treaties and Aboriginal Rights in Canada*. Toronto: University of Toronto Press.

Baer, Hans, Merrill Singer, and Ida Susser. 2003. *Medical Anthropology and the World System*. 2nd ed. Westport, CT: Praeger.

Bhérer, Claude, Damian Labuda, Marie-Helene Roy-Gagnon, Lous Houde, Marc Tremblay, and Helene Vézina. 2011. "Admixed Ancestry and Stratification of Quebec Regional Populations." *American Journal of Physical Anthropology* 144: 432–441. doi:10.1002/ajpa.21424.

Crate, Susan A., and Mark Nuttall, eds. 2009. *Anthropology and Climate Change: From Encounters to Actions*. Walnut Creek, CA: Left Coast Press.

——. 2016. Anthropology and Climate Change: From Actions to Transformations. Walnut Creek, CA: Left Coast Press.

Darnell, Regna. 1992. "The Boasian Text Tradition and the History of Canadian Anthropology." *Culture* 17: 39–48.

——. 1998. "Toward a History of Canadian Departments of Anthropology: Retrospect, Prospect, and Common Cause." *Anthropologica* 40 (2): 153–69.

——. 2000. "Canadian Anthropologists, the First Nations, and Canada's Self-Image at the Millennium." *Anthropologica* 42 (2): 165–74.

Dawson, Leslie. 2017. "Birth Places, Embodied Spaces: Tlicho Pregnancy Stories across the Generations." In *Indigenous Experiences of Pregnancy and Birth*, edited by Jaime Cidro and Hannah Tait Neufeld, 144–162. Bradford, ON: Demeter Press.

Durham, William H. 1991. *Coevolution: Genes, Culture, and Human Diversity*. Stanford: Stanford University Press.

Gould, Stephen J. 1996. *Full House: The Spread of Excellence from Plato to Darwin*. New York: Harmony Books.

Graffam, Gray. 2010. "Anthropology Meets Marketing." *Anthropologica* 52 (1): 155.

Greenwood, David, and William Stini. 1977. *Nature, Culture, and Human History*. New York: Harper and Row.

Harrison, Julia, and Regna Darnell, eds. 2006. *Historicizing Canadian Anthropology*. Vancouver: UBC Press.

Hedican, Edward. 2008. *Applied Anthropology in Canada: Understanding Aboriginal Issues*. 2nd ed. Toronto: University of Toronto Press.

Hyde, Sandra. 2007. *Eating Spring Rice: The Cultural Politics of AIDS in Southwest China*. Berkeley: University of California Press.

Inda, Jonathan Xavier, and Renato Rosaldo. 2002. "Introduction: A World in Motion." In *The Anthropology of Globalization*, edited by Jonathan Xavier Inda and Renato Rosaldo. Malden, MA: Blackwell.

Labrecque, Marie-France. 2012. "Gender Mainstreaming and Market Fundamentalist in Rural Yucatan Mexico." In *Confronting Capital: Critique and Engagement in Anthropology*, edited by Pauline Gardiner Barber, Belinda Leach, and Winnie Lem, 222–38. New York: Routledge.

Lawford, Karen, & Giles, Audrey. (2012). "Marginalization and Coercion: Canada's Evacuation Policy for Pregnant First Nations Women Who Live on Reserves in Rural and Remote Regions. *Pimatisiwin* 10 (3): 327–40.

Martindale, Andrew, Susan Marsden, Katherine Patton, Angela Ruggles, Kisha Supernant, David Archer, Bryn Letham, Duncan McLaren, and Kenneth Ames. 2017. "The Role of Small Villages in Northern Tsimshian Territory from Oral and Archaeological Records." *Journal of Social Archaeology* 17 (3): 285–325.

Mayne Correia, Pamela, and Owen Beattie. 2002. "A Critical Look at Methods for Recovering, Evaluating, and Interpreting Cremated Human Remains." In *Advances in Forensic Taphonomy: Method, Theory, and Archaeological Perspectives*, edited by William D. Haglund and Marcella H. Sorg, 435–50. Baton Rouge: CRC Press.

Molnar, Stephen. 2001. *Human Variation*. New York: Prentice Hall.

Moore, Sally Falk. 2005. "Comparisons: Possible and Impossible." *Annual Review of Anthropology* 34: 1–11.

Norris, Mary Jane. 2007. "Aboriginal Languages in Canada: Emerging Trends and Perspectives on Second Language Acquisition." *Canadian Social Trends* 83 (Summer): 20.

Nuttall, Mark. 2009. "Living in a World of Movement: Human Resilience to Environmental Instability in Greenland." In *Anthropology and Climate Change: From Encounters to Actions*, edited by Susan A. Crate and Mark Nuttall, 292–310. Walnut Creek, CA: Left Coast Press.

Radcliffe-Brown, A.R. 1951. "The Comparative Method in Social Anthropology." *Journal of the Royal Anthropological Institute of Great Britain and Ireland* 81 (1/2): 15–22.

Richerson, Peter, and Robert Boyd. 2005. *Not by Genes Alone: How Culture Transformed Human Evolution*. Chicago: University of Chicago Press.

Salisbury, Richard F., N. Elberg, and R.H. Schneider. 1974. *Development? Attitudes to Development among the Native*

Peoples of the Mackenzie District. Montreal: McGill Programme in the Anthropology of Development.

Salisbury, Richard F., F. Filion, F. Rawji, and D.A. Stewart. 1972. *Development and James Bay: Social Implications of the Proposals for the Hydroelectric Scheme.* Montreal: McGill Programme in the Anthropology of Development.

Schreyer, Christine. 2011. "Media, Information, Technology, and Language Planning: What Can Endangered Language Communities Learn from Created Language Communities?" *Current Issues in Language Planning* 12 (3): 403–25.

Singer, Merrill. 1998. "The Development of Critical Medical Anthropology: Implications for Biological Anthropology." In *Building a New Biocultural Synthesis*, edited by Alan H. Goodman and Thomas L. Leatherman, 93–123. Ann Arbor: University of Michigan Press.

Skinner, Mark, Heather P. York, and Melissa A. Connor. 2002. "Postburial Disturbance of Graves in Bosnia-Herzegovina." In *Advances in Forensic Taphonomy: Method, Theory, and Archaeological Perspectives*, edited by William D. Haglund and Marcella H. Sorg, 293–308. Boca Raton, FL: CRC Press.

Szathmáry, Emőke. 1986. "Diabetes in Arctic and Subarctic Populations Undergoing Acculturation." *Collegium Antropologium* 10: 145–158.

Truth and Reconciliation Commission of Canada. 2015. *Honouring the Truth, Reconciling for the Future: Summary of the Final Report of the Truth and Reconciliation Commission of Canada.* http://www.trc.ca/assets/pdf/Honouring_the_Truth_Reconciling_for_the_Future_July_23_2015.pdf

Waldram, James B. 2010. "Engaging Engagement: Critical Reflections on a Canadian Tradition." *Anthropologica* 52 (2): 225–32.

Wasson, Christina. 2016. "Design Anthropology." *General Anthropology* 23 (2): 1–11.

Weaver, Sally M. 1997. "An Assessment of the Federal Self-Government Policy." In *Justice for Natives: Searching for Common Ground*, edited by Andrea P. Morrison. Montreal: McGill-Queen's University Press.

▲ Maasai women in Kenya wearing traditional Maasai clothing. Beadwork, body ornamentation, hair length, and clothing are symbolic of identity and cultural position within Maasai society. Photo: hadynyah/iStockphoto

2 Why Is the Concept of Culture Important?

Chapter Outline

In this chapter, we will examine in greater detail the concept of culture, one of the most influential ideas that anthropologists have studied and defined for many decades. While there are disagreements on how the concept is defined, all do agree that it consists of these five key elements: it is learned, it is shared, it has patterns, it is adaptive, and it is symbolic.

Human beings who develop and live together in groups are shaped by culture and are deeply affected by shared cultural experiences. They become different from what they would have been had they matured in isolation; they also become different from other people who have been shaped by different social and cultural patterns. Social scientists have long known that human beings who grow up isolated from meaningful social interactions with others do not behave in ways that appear recognizably human. Social living and cultural sharing are necessary for individual human beings to develop what we recognize as a human culture.

How Do Anthropologists Define Culture?

In Chapter 1, we defined *culture* as sets of learned behaviour and ideas that humans acquire as members of a society, together with the artifacts and structures we create and use. Culture is not reinvented by each generation; rather, we learn it from other members of the social groups we belong to, although we may later modify this heritage in some way. Children use their own bodies and brains to explore their world. At the same time, other people actively work to steer their activity and attention in particular directions. Consequently, children's exploration of the world is not merely trial and error. The path is cleared for them by others who shape their experiences. We use two terms in the social sciences to refer to this

socialization The process by which humans as material organisms, living together with other similar organisms, cope with the behavioural rules established by their respective societies.

enculturation The process by which humans living with one another must learn to come to terms with the ways of thinking and feeling that are considered appropriate in their respective cultures.

process of culturally and socially shaped learning. The first, **socialization**, is the process of learning to live as a member of a group. This involves mastering the skills of appropriate interaction with others and learning how to cope with the behavioural rules established by that group. The second term, **enculturation**, refers to the cognitive challenges facing humans who live together and must come to terms with the ways of thinking and feeling considered appropriate in their respective cultures.

Because children learn to act, think, feel, and speak at the same time, we will use the term *socialization/enculturation* to represent this holistic experience. Socialization/enculturation produces a socially and culturally constructed individual capable of functioning successfully in society. So, culture is *shared* as well as *learned*. But many things we learn, such as table manners and what is good to eat and where people are supposed to sleep, are never explicitly taught but rather are absorbed in the course of practical daily living. *Habitus*, according to French anthropologist Pierre Bourdieu, is the result of learning and is heavily influenced by our interactions with material culture. The cultural practices shared within social groups always encompass the varied knowledge and skills of many different individuals. For example, driving is part of North American culture, but no individuals could build a car in their backyard without the assistance of parts manufactured by others in our culture.

Human cultures also appear *patterned*; that is, related cultural beliefs and practices show up repeatedly in different areas of social life. Language is a good example of these patterns. Cultural patterns can also be traced through time: the fact that English and French are widely spoken in Canada, but not Fulfulde (a West African language), is connected to the colonial conquest and domination of Canada by speakers of English and French in past centuries. Cultural patterns also vary across space: for example, the English of Newfoundland and Labrador differs from the English of other provinces in style, rhythm, and vocabulary (Figure 2.1).

It is this patterned cultural variation that allows anthropologists (and others) to distinguish different "cultural traditions" from one another. But separate cultural traditions are often hard to delineate. That is because, in addition to any unique elements of their own, all contain contradictory elements, and all also share elements with other traditions. First, customs in one domain of culture may contradict customs in another domain, as when religion tells us to share with others and economics tells us to look out for ourselves alone. Second, people have always borrowed cultural elements from their neighbours, and many increasingly refuse to be limited in the present by cultural practices of the past. Thus, cultural patterns can be useful as a kind of shorthand, but it is important to remember that the boundaries between cultural traditions are always fuzzy. Ultimately, they rest on someone's judgment about how different one set of customs is from another set of customs.

So far we have seen that culture is learned, shared, and patterned. Cultural traditions are also reconstructed and enriched, generation after generation, primarily because human biological survival depends on culture. Thus, culture is also *adaptive*. Human newborns are not born with "instincts" that would enable them to survive on their own. On the contrary, they depend utterly on support and nurturance from adults and other members of the group in which they live. It is by learning the cultural practices of those around them that human beings come to master appropriate ways of thinking and acting that promote their own survival as biological organisms. Moreover, as Figure 2.2 illustrates, appropriate ways of thinking and acting are always scaffolded by artifacts and features of a particular local setting. In the 1970s, for example, young girls in Guider, Cameroon, promoted their own and their families' welfare by fetching water for their mothers, who were forbidden by propriety from leaving their household compounds alone during the day. The presence in town of public water spigots, only a few years old at the time, lightened the chore of bringing water back to homes that did not have plumbing. Imported metal basins and pails were more reliable than large calabashes for carrying water, especially for young water carriers who had mastered the impressive skill of balancing heavy loads on their heads (sometimes atop a flat fabric pad). Public spigots, together with recycled metal containers, a pole, and a rope, also afforded young men the opportunity to earn money by selling their services to residents who could not rely on young relatives

FIGURE 2.1 A street sign in St John's, Newfoundland, poses a friendly question to passersby. While the language on this sign would seem perfectly natural to most Newfoundlanders, it would seem strange to people living in other parts of Canada.

FIGURE 2.2 Of all living organisms, humans are the most dependent on learning for their survival. From a young age, girls in northern Cameroon learn to carry heavy loads on their heads and also learn to get water for their families.

to bring water to them. In such ways do tradition and innovation shape each other over time, mediated by material culture.

Finally, culture is *symbolic*. A **symbol** is something that stands for something else. Consider a red hexagon

symbol **Something that stands for something else.**

FIGURE 2.3 Stop sign in Morocco. The shape of the sign signals drivers to stop even if they are unable to read the language on the sign.

FIGURE 2.4 A chimpanzee uses a stick to get termites out of a hole in a large rock.

or a red triangle. For those who drive, these shapes are recognizable as meaning "stop" or "yield" at an intersection, even if they are written in a different language (Figure 2.3).

Everything we do in society has a symbolic dimension, from how we conduct ourselves at the dinner table to how we bury the dead. It is our heavy dependence on

For more on human biological and cultural evolution, see Chapters 5 and 6. For more on how researchers use archaeological techniques to learn about these past cultures, see Chapter 8, pp. 155–65.

hominins **All bipedal apes.**

symbolic learning that sets human culture apart from the apparently non-symbolic learning on which other species rely.

Human culture, then, is *learned*, *shared*, *patterned*, *adaptive*, and *symbolic*. And the contemporary human capacity for culture has also evolved over millions of years. Culture's beginnings can perhaps be glimpsed among Japanese macaque monkeys, who invented the custom of washing sweet potatoes; and among wild chimpanzees, who invented different grooming postures or techniques to crack open nuts or to gain access to termites or water (Leca, Huffman, and Vasey 2012; see Figure 2.4). Our ancestors likely shared similar aptitudes when they started walking on two legs some 6 million years ago. By 3.3 million years ago, their descendants were making stone tools. Thereafter, our **hominin** lineage gave birth to a number of additional species, all of whom depended on culture more than their ancestors had. Culture, then, is not something that appeared suddenly with the arrival of *Homo sapiens*. Rather, culture had long been an integral part of our evolutionary heritage by the time *Homo sapiens* appeared some 300,000 years ago. As such, paleoanthropological and archaeological work can offer startling insight into how past cultures functioned, survived, and changed.

As Rick Potts (1996, 197), a paleoanthropologist, suggests, human culture has its roots in primate culture. Monkeys and apes possess many basic abilities, such as learning how to wash sweet potatoes or bickering for status in troops, which is the reason they may be said to have simple cultural traditions. Certainly, our earliest hominin ancestors were no different.

Apes apparently also possess a rudimentary capacity for symbolic coding, or symbolic representation, something our ancestors undoubtedly possessed as well. But new species can evolve new capacities not found in their ancestors. This occurred in the human past when our ancestors first developed a capacity for complex symbolic representation, including the ability to communicate freely about the past, the future, and the invisible. Complex symbolic representation apparently was of great adaptive value for our ancestors. It created selective pressures that increased human symbolic capacities over time. Put another way, culture and the human brain coevolved, each adapting to key features of the environment (Deacon 1997, 44). We have used our complex symbolic abilities, moreover, to create institutions—complex, variable, and enduring forms of cultural practice that

The Nature/Culture of Genetic Facts

Anthropology can tell us a lot about human biology and heredity. However, as biological anthropologist Jonathan Marks testifies, it is important to realize that "natural facts" have cultural information (values, meanings) integrated into them.

Anthropology is positioned to try to explain why groups of scientists do and say the things they do, in parallel with why groups of Indigenous people do and say the things they do (Franklin 1995). The basic explanation lies in a significant contribution of twentieth-century anthropology, namely, the discovery that human facts are fundamentally biocultural.... Consequently, we are now understanding the facts of human biology not so much as facts of nature, but as facts of "nature/culture." ... After all, "innate" and "learned" are not antonyms, for the most fundamentally hard-wired human adaptations—walking and talking—are actively learned by every person, every generation.

The facts of human biology are, of necessity, facts of human culture in three ways. First, our evolutionary lineage has been coevolving with technology for millions of years, and consequently the environment into which our own species evolved and adapted was necessarily a cultural one.... Second, as individuals, we develop within environments that are profoundly cultural.... And third, these facts have always been produced in a context of conflicting interests of patronage, political ideologies of diverse kinds, professional aspirations, and cultural expectations.... [For example, a]rchaeological facts are often produced in the service of nationalism ... for they may authorize the historical identity of a nation.... The problem is not that culture corrupts our understanding of nature; it is that culture is integral to understanding nature (Franklin 1995, 2003). One literally cannot understand natural facts any way other than culturally.

Source: Marks 2013, 249. © 2013 by Annual Reviews, http://www.annualreviews.org

---

> ↻ For a more thorough description of human language and other communication systems, see Chapter 15.

organize social life, also unique to our species. As a result, for *Homo sapiens*, culture has become "the predominant manner in which human groups vary from one another . . . it swamps the biological differences among populations" (Marks 1995, 200). It is because of this coevolution of human biology (in particular, the human brain) and culture that anthropologists refer to humans as *biocultural organisms*.

Culture, History, and Human Agency

The human condition is rooted in time and shaped by history. As part of the human condition, culture is also historical, being worked out and reconstructed in every generation. Culture is also part of our biological heritage. Our biocultural heritage has produced a living species that uses culture to surmount biological and individual limitations and is even capable of studying itself and its own biocultural evolution.

This realization, however, raises another question: Just how free from limitations are humans? In Western societies, humans are recognized as agents who cannot escape the cultural and historical context within which they act but must frequently select a course of action when the "correct" choice is unclear and the outcome uncertain. Some anthropologists liken human existence to a minefield that we must painstakingly try to cross without blowing ourselves up. It is in such contexts that human beings exercise their **human agency** by making interpretations, formulating goals, and setting out in pursuit of those goals (Figure 2.5).

Many anthropologists insist that it is possible to develop a view of human beings that finds room for culture, history, and human agency. The anthropological point of

> **human agency** Human beings' ability to exercise at least some control over their lives.

FIGURE 2.5 People regularly struggle, often against great odds, to exercise some control over their lives. During the "Dirty War" in Argentina in the 1970s and early 1980s, women whose children had been "disappeared" by secret right-wing death squads began, at great personal risk, to stand every Thursday in the Plaza de Mayo, the central square of Buenos Aires, with photographs of their missing children. Called the Mothers of the Plaza de Mayo, they continue their weekly vigil today. They were a powerful rebuke to the dictatorship and to subsequent governments that were not forthcoming about providing information about the disappeared.

view called **holism** assumes that no sharp boundaries separate mind from body, body from environment, individual from society, my ideas from our ideas, or their traditions from our traditions. Rather, holism assumes that mind and body, body and environment, and so on, interpenetrate each other and even define each other. From a holistic perspective, attempts to divide reality into mind and matter are unsuccessful because of the complex nature of reality, which resists isolation and dissection. Anthropologists who have struggled to develop this holistic perspective on the human condition have made a contribution of unique and lasting value.

In anthropology, holism is traditionally understood as a perspective on the human condition in which the whole

holism A perspective on the human condition that assumes that mind and body, individuals and society, and individuals and the environment interpenetrate and even define one another.

coevolution The interconnected relationship between biological processes and symbolic cultural processes, in which each makes up an important part of the environment and to which the other must adapt.

(for example, a human being, a society, a cultural tradition) is understood to be greater than the sum of its parts. For example, from a holistic perspective, human beings are complex, dynamic living entities shaped by genes, culture, and experience into entities whose properties cannot be reduced to the materials out of which they were constructed. To be sure, human organisms are closed off from the wider world in some ways by how our cells, tissues, and organs are bound into a single body. At the same time, like all living organisms, human beings are open to the world in other ways: we breathe, eat, harbour colonies of intestinal bacteria to aid our digestion, excrete waste products, and learn from experience (see Deacon 2003, 296–7). Similarly, a society is not just the sum of its individual members; people in groups develop dynamic relationships that facilitate collective actions impossible for individuals to bring about on their own. And cultural traditions are not just a list of beliefs, values, and practices; rather, different dimensions of cultural activity, such as economics and politics and religion, are knotted together in complex ways. To understand any human community requires untangling those cultural threads in order to reveal the full range of factors that shape particular cultural practices in that community.

One useful way of thinking about the relationships among the parts that make up a whole is in terms of **coevolution**. A coevolutionary approach to the human condition emphasizes that human organisms, their physical environments, and their symbolic practices co-determine one another; with the passage of time, they can also coevolve with one another. A coevolutionary view of the human condition also sees human beings as organisms whose bodies, brains, actions, and thoughts are equally involved in shaping what they become. Coevolution produces a human nature connected to a wider world and profoundly shaped by culture. These connections make us vulnerable over the courses of our lives to influences that our ancestors never experienced. The open, symbolic, meaning-making properties of human culture make it possible for us to respond to those influences in ways that our ancestors could not have anticipated.

Why Do Cultural Differences Matter?

The same objects, actions, or events frequently mean different things to people with different cultures. In fact, what counts as an object or event in one tradition may not be recognized as such in another. This powerful lesson of anthropology was illustrated by the experience of some volunteers working with the United States' Peace Corps in southern Africa.

In the early 1970s, the Peace Corps office in Botswana was concerned by the number of volunteers who seemed to be "burned out," failing in their assignments, leaving the assigned villages, and increasingly hostile to their Tswana hosts. (See Map 2.1 and EthnoProfile 2.1: Tswana.) The Peace Corps asked American anthropologist Hoyt Alverson, who was familiar with Tswana culture and society, for advice. Alverson (1977) discovered that one major problem the Peace Corps volunteers were having involved exactly this issue of similar actions having very different meanings. The volunteers complained that the Tswana would never leave them alone. Whenever they tried to get away and sit by themselves for a few minutes to have some private time, one or more Tswana would quickly join them. This made the Americans angry. From their perspective, everyone is entitled to a certain amount of privacy and time alone. To the Tswana, however, human life is social life; the only people who want to be alone are witches and the insane. Because these young Americans did not seem to be either, the Tswana who saw them sitting alone naturally assumed that there had been a breakdown in hospitality and that the volunteers would welcome some company. Here, one behaviour—a person walking out into a field and sitting by himself or herself— had two very different meanings (Figure 2.6).

From this example, we can see that human experience is inherently ambiguous. Even within a single cultural tradition, the meaning of an object or an action may differ, depending on the context. To resolve the ambiguity, experience must be interpreted, and human beings regularly turn to their own cultural traditions in search of an interpretation that makes sense. They do this daily as they go about life among others with whom they share traditions. Serious misunderstandings may arise, however, when individuals confront the same ambiguous situation without realizing that their cultural ground rules differ.

Does Culture Explain Everything?

We believe that our view of the concept of culture as presented in this chapter is widely shared among contemporary cultural anthropologists. Nevertheless, in

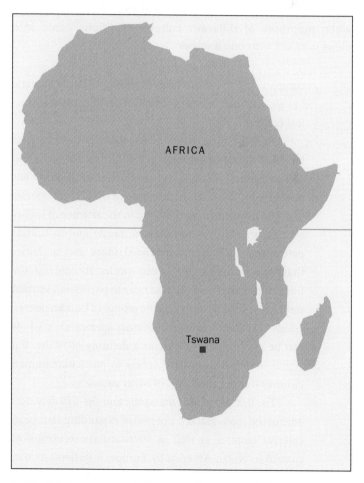

EthnoProfile 2.1

Tswana

Region: Southern Africa

Nation: Botswana

Population: 1,200,000 (also 1,500,000 in South Africa)

Environment: Savannah to desert

Livelihood: Cattle raising, farming

Political organization: Traditionally, chiefs and headmen; today, part of a modern nation–state

For more information: Comaroff, Jean. 1985. *Body of Power, Spirit of Resistance: The Culture and History of a South African People.* Chicago: University of Chicago Press.

MAP 2.1 Location of Tswana. For more information, see EthnoProfile 2.1.

recent years the concept of culture has been critically re-examined as patterns of human life have undergone major dislocations and reconfigurations. The issues are

FIGURE 2.6 For Tswana, human life is social life, and only witches or the mentally ill would choose to spend time isolated from others. For most Westerners, in contrast, alone or "private" time is a highly valued part of everyday life. These sorts of cultural differences can lead to misunderstandings when members of different cultural traditions come into close contact with one another.

complex and are more fully explored in later chapters, but we offer here a brief account to provide some historical context.

For at least the past 50 years, many anthropologists have distinguished between *Culture* (with a capital *C*) and *cultures* (plural with a lowercase *c*). The term *Culture* has been used to describe an attribute of the human species as a whole—its members' ability, in the absence of highly specific genetic programming, to create and to imitate patterned, symbolically mediated ideas and activities that promote the survival of our species. By contrast, the term *cultures* has been used to refer to particular, learned ways of life belonging to specific groups of human beings. Given this distinction, the human species as a whole can be said to have Culture as a defining attribute, but actual human beings have access to particular human cultures—either their own or other people's.

The last decades of the 1800s and the first few decades of the 1900s marked a period of expanding European colonial empires as well as westward consolidation of control in North America by European settlers. At that time, the social sciences were becoming established

in universities, and different fields were assigned different tasks. Anthropology was allocated the study of the so-called "primitive" world that was the target of **colonization**. Early Canadian anthropologists, such as Diamond Jenness (1922), were often charged with documenting and preserving the "disappearing savages," which included conducting intensive research of these supposedly "dying cultures." Moreover, since these early anthropologists were often employed by the National Museum of Canada, relics and artifacts of Indigenous peoples were often taken without permission, under the guise of "cultural preservation." In these and other cases, anthropologists became the official academic experts on societies whose members suffered racist denigration as "primitives" and whose ways of life were being undermined by contact with Western colonial "civilization."

Early twentieth-century anthropologists were determined to denounce these practices and to demonstrate that the "primitive" stereotype was false. Some found inspiration in the work of English anthropologist E.B. Tylor, who, in 1871, had defined "culture or civilization" as "that complex whole which includes knowledge, belief, art, morals, law, custom, and any other capabilities and habits acquired by man as a member of society" ([1871] 1958, 1). This definition had the virtue of blurring the difference between "civilization" and "culture," and it encouraged the view that even "primitives" possessed "capabilities and habits" that merited respect. Thus, in response to stereotypes of "primitives" as irrational, disorganized, insensitive, or promiscuous, anthropologists like Franz Boas were able to show that, on the contrary, so-called "primitives" possessed "cultures" that were reasonable, orderly, artistically developed, and morally disciplined (Figure 2.7). The plural use of *culture* allowed them to argue that, in their own ways, "primitives" were as fully human as "civilized" people were.

By the end of the twentieth century, however, some anthropologists became concerned about the way the plural concept of culture was being used. That is, the boundary that was once thought to protect vulnerability was starting to look more like a prison wall, condemning those within it to live according to "their" culture, just as their ancestors had done, like exhibits in a living museum, whether they wanted to or not. But if some group members criticize a practice, such as female genital cutting, that is part of their cultural tradition, does this mean that the critics are no longer "authentic" members of their own culture? To come to such a conclusion overlooks the

colonization The act of settling a region, establishing control over the Indigenous peoples who live there, and appropriating local lands and resources for one's own use.

FIGURE 2.7 Anthropologists like Franz Boas—seen here demonstrating a position in the Kwakiutl (Kwakwaka'wakw) Hamatsa dance ritual in 1894—showed that so-called "primitives" possessed reasonable and developed "cultures."

possibility that alternatives to a controversial practice might already exist within the cultural tradition and that followers of that tradition may themselves decide that some alternatives make more sense than others in today's world. The issue then becomes not just which traditions have been inherited from the past—as if "authentic" cultures were monolithic and unchanging—but, rather, which traditional practices ought to continue in a contemporary world, and who is entitled to make that decision.

What Is Ethnocentrism?

Ethnocentrism is the term anthropologists use to describe the opinion that one's own way of life is natural or correct or even superior, indeed the only way of being fully human. Ethnocentrism is one solution to the inevitable tension that arises when people with different cultural backgrounds come into contact. It reduces the other way of life to a version of one's own. Sometimes we correctly identify meaningful areas of cultural overlap. But other times, we are shocked by the differences we encounter. We may conclude that if our way is right, then their way can only be wrong. (Of course, from their perspective, our way of life may seem to be a distortion of theirs.)

The members of one society may go beyond merely interpreting another way of life in ethnocentric terms. They may decide to do something about the discrepancies they observe. They may conclude that the other way of life is wrong but not fundamentally evil and that the members of the other group need to be converted to their own way of doing things. If the others

are unwilling to change their ways, however, the failed attempt at conversion may enlarge into an active dualism: us versus them, civilization versus savagery, good versus evil. The ultimate result may be war and genocide—the deliberate attempt to exterminate an entire group based on race, religion, national origin, or other cultural features.

Is It Possible to Avoid Ethnocentric Bias?

One way to address the question of whether it is possible to avoid ethnocentric bias is to view relationships between individuals with different cultural backgrounds as not being fundamentally different from relationships between individuals with very similar cultural backgrounds. Even people with little in common can learn to get along, even if it is not always easy. Like all human relationships, relationships between individuals with different cultural backgrounds affect all parties involved, changing them as they learn about each other. People with a cultural background very different from your own may help you see possibilities for belief and action that are drastically at odds with everything your tradition considers possible. By becoming aware of these unsuspected possibilities, you become a different person. People from cultural backgrounds different from yours are likely to be affected in the same way.

For a more in-depth discussion of ethnocentrism in the context of social inequality, see Chapter 14, pp 336–7.

Learning about other cultures is at once enormously hopeful and immensely threatening; once it occurs, we can no longer claim that any single culture has a monopoly on truth. Although this does not mean that the traditions in question must therefore be based entirely on illusion or falsehood, it does mean that the truth embodied in any cultural tradition is bound to be partial, approximate, and open to further insight and growth.

What Is Cultural Relativism?

Anthropologists must come to terms with the tensions produced by cultural differences as they do their fieldwork. One result has been the formulation of the concept

ethnocentrism The opinion that one's own way of life is natural or correct and, indeed, the only true way of being fully human.

In Their Own Words

The Paradox of Ethnocentrism

Ethnocentrism is usually described in thoroughly negative terms. As anthropologist Ivan Karp points out, however, ethnocentrism is a more complex phenomenon than we might expect.

Anthropologists usually argue that ethnocentrism is both wrong and harmful, especially when it is tied to racial, cultural, and social prejudices. Ideas and feelings about the inferiority of blacks, the cupidity of Jews, or the lack of cultural sophistication of farmers are surely to be condemned. But can we do without ethnocentrism? If we stopped to examine every custom and practice in our cultural repertoire, how would we get on? For example, if we always regarded marriage as something that can vary from society to society, would we be concerned about filling out the proper marriage documents, or would we even get married at all? Most of the time we suspend a quizzical stance toward our own customs and simply live life.

Yet many of our own practices are peculiar when viewed through the lenses of other cultures. Periodically, for over fifteen years, I have worked with and lived among an African people. They are as amazed at our marriage customs as my students are at theirs. Both [North] American students and the Iteso of Kenya find it difficult to imagine how the other culture survives with the bizarre, exotic practices that are part of their respective marriage customs. Ethnocentrism works both ways. It can be practiced as much by other cultures as by our own.

Paradoxically, ethnographic literature combats ethnocentrism by showing that the practices of cultures (including our own) are "natural" in their own setting. What appears natural in one setting appears so because it was constructed in that setting—made and produced by human beings who could have done it some other way. Ethnography is a means of recording the range of human creativity and of demonstrating how universally shared capacities can produce cultural and social differences.

This anthropological way of looking at other cultures—and, by implication, at ourselves—constitutes a major reason for reading ethnography. The anthropological lens teaches us to question what we assume to be unquestionable. Ethnography teaches us that human potentiality provides alternative means of organizing our lives and alternative modes of experiencing the world.

Source: Karp, Ivan. 1990. Guest editorial in *Cultural Anthropology: A Perspective on the Human Condition*, by Emily Schultz and Robert Lavenda, 2nd ed. St Paul, MN: West. Excerpt from pp. 74–5.

of **cultural relativism**. Definitions of cultural relativism have varied as different anthropologists have tried to draw conclusions based on their own experience of other ways of life. For example, cultural relativism can be defined as "understanding another culture in its own terms sympathetically enough so that the culture appears to be a coherent and meaningful design for living" (Greenwood and Stini 1977, 182). According to this holistic definition, the goal of cultural relativism is to promote understanding of cultural practices, particularly those that an outsider finds puzzling, incoherent, or morally troubling. These practices range from trivial (such as eating insects) to questionable (such as female circumcision), but most are likely to be located somewhere between these extremes.

How Can Cultural Relativity Improve Our Understanding of Controversial Cultural Practices?

Rituals initiating girls and boys into adulthood are widely practised throughout the world. In some parts of Africa, this ritual includes genital cutting (Figure 2.8). For example, ritual experts may cut off the foreskins of the penises of adolescent boys, who are expected to endure

cultural relativism Understanding another culture in its own terms sympathetically enough that the culture appears to be a coherent and meaningful design for living.

Courtesy of Daniel Lavenda

FIGURE 2.8 Among many East African people, including the Maasai, female genital cutting is an important part of the transformation of girls into women. These young Maasai women are recovering from the operation. After undergoing the operation, Maasai women are proud of their new status as adults. Do you think this practice is a violation of human rights? Why or why not?

this operation without showing fear or pain. In the case of girls, ritual cutting may involve little more than nicking the clitoris with a knife blade to draw blood. In other cases, however, the surgery is more extreme. The clitoris itself may be cut off (or excised), a procedure called *clitoridectomy*. In some parts of eastern Africa, however, the surgery is even more extreme: the labia are excised along with the clitoris, and the remaining skin is fastened together, forming scar tissue that partially closes the vaginal opening. This version is often called *pharaonic circumcision* or *infibulation*. When young women who have undergone this operation marry, they may require further surgery to widen the vaginal opening. Surgery may be necessary again to widen the vaginal opening when a woman gives birth; and after she has delivered her child, she may expect to be closed up again. Many women who have undergone these procedures repeatedly can develop serious medical complications involving the bladder and the colon later in life.

The removal of the male foreskin—or circumcision—has long been a familiar practice in Western societies, not only among observant Jews, who perform it for religious reasons, but also among physicians, who have encouraged circumcision of male newborns as a hygienic measure. The ritual practice of female genital cutting (FGC), by contrast, has been unfamiliar to most people in Western societies until recently.

Genital Cutting, Gender, and Human Rights

In 1978, radical feminist Mary Daly grouped "African female genital mutilation" together with practices such as foot binding in China and witch burning in medieval Europe and labelled all these practices patriarchal "Sado-Rituals" that destroy "the Self-affirming being of women" (111). Feminists and other cultural critics in Western societies spoke out against such practices in the 1980s. In 1992, African American novelist Alice Walker published a bestselling novel, *Possessing the Secret of Joy*, in which the heroine is an African woman who undergoes the operation, suffers psychologically and physically, and eventually pursues the female elder who performed the ritual on her. Walker also made a film called *Warrior Marks* that condemned female genital cutting. Although many Western readers continue to regard the positions taken by Daly and Walker as formidable and necessary feminist assertions of women's resistance against patriarchal oppression, other readers—particularly women from societies in which female genital cutting is an ongoing practice—have responded with far less enthusiasm.

Does this mean that these women are in favour of female genital cutting? Not necessarily; in fact, many of them are actively working to discourage the practice in their own societies. But they find that when outsiders publicly condemn traditional African rituals including clitoridectomy and infibulation, their efforts may do more harm than good. Women anthropologists who come from African societies where female genital cutting is traditional point out that Western women who want to help are likely to be more effective if they pay closer attention to what the African women themselves have to say about the meaning of these customs: "Careful listening to women helps us to recognize them as political actors forging their own communities of resistance. It also helps us to learn how and when to provide strategic support that would be welcomed by women who are struggling to challenge such traditions within their own cultures" (Abusharaf 2000).

A better understanding of female genital cutting is badly needed in places like Canada, the United States, and the European Union, where some immigrants and refugees from Africa have brought traditions of female genital cutting with them. Since the mid-1990s, growing awareness and public condemnation of the practice has led to the passage of laws that criminalize female genital cutting in 18 African states and 12 industrialized nations, including Canada and the United States (Center for Reproductive Rights 2015). Non-profit advocacy organizations, such as the Center for Reproductive Rights, consider female genital cutting (which they call "female genital mutilation," or "FGM") a human rights violation.

Some women have been able successfully to claim asylum or have avoided deportation by claiming that they have fled their home countries to avoid the operation. However, efforts to protect women and girls may become increasingly complicated when immigrant or refugee mothers in Canada and the United States who seek to have their daughters ritually cut are stigmatized in the media as "mutilators" or "child abusers" and find that this practice is considered a felony punishable by up to five years in prison (Abusharaf 2000). A startling example of this is presented by cultural anthropologist Janice Boddy (2007) of the University of Toronto, who recalls that during her study of Sudanese immigrant women in Toronto, her university ethics board required her to report any young women with FGC to the police. Boddy suggests that this criminalization of FGC is part of the Western "climate of fear," where cultural practices from other nations are often misunderstood.

Genital Cutting as a Valued Ritual

Female genital cutting is clearly a controversial practice about which many people have already made up their minds. In such circumstances, is there any role to be played by anthropologists?

Yes, there is. In fact, Janice Boddy, a Canadian anthropologist, has written an ethnographic study that exemplifies the challenges of being culturally relative and sensitive to these "controversial" cultural practices. She has carried out field research since 1976 in a small Muslim village that she calls Hofriyat in rural Sudan, where female genital surgery is traditionally performed in childhood. She writes that it was difficult when she first observed the operation; nevertheless, "as time passed in the village and understanding deepened I came to regard this form of female circumcision in a very different light" (1997, 309). Circumcisions in Hofriyat were traditionally performed on both boys and girls, but the ritual had a different meaning for boys than it did for girls. Once circumcised, a boy takes a step toward manhood, but a girl will not become a woman until she marries. Female circumcision is required, however, to ensure that a girl is fertile and marriageable (310).

Boddy encountered a number of different explanations by scholars and other observers about the purpose of female genital cutting. In Hofriyat, female circumcision traditionally involved infibulation, to preserve chastity and curb female sexual desire. This made the most sense in rural Sudan, where women's sexual conduct is the symbol of family honour. Women who undergo the procedure do indeed suffer a lot, not only at the time of circumcision. They whenever they engage in sexual intercourse and give birth. They may also have difficulties with menstruation. What cultural explanation could make all this suffering meaningful to women?

The answer lies in the connection rural Sudanese villagers make between the infibulated female body and female fertility. Boddy believes that the women she knew equated the category of "virgin" more with fertility than with lack of sexual experience and believed that a woman's virginity and her fertility could be renewed and protected by the act of reinfibulation after giving birth. Women she knew described infibulated female bodies as clean and smooth and pure (1997, 313). Boddy concluded that the ritual was best understood as a way of socializing female fertility "by dramatically de-emphasizing [women's] inherent sexuality" and turning infibulated women into potential "mothers of men" (314). This means they are eligible, with their husbands, to found a new lineage section by giving birth to sons. Women who become "mothers of men" are more than mere sexual partners or servants of their husbands and may attain high status, with their name remembered in village genealogies.

Culture and Moral Reasoning

Boddy's relativistic understanding of female genital cutting, therefore, accomplishes several things. It makes the practice comprehensible and even coherent. It reveals how a physically dangerous procedure can appear perfectly acceptable—even indispensable—when placed in a particular context of meaning. It can help us see how some of the cultural practices that we take for granted, such as the promotion of weight loss and cosmetic surgery among women in our own society, are equally dangerous. Media and marketing pressure for cosmetic treatments that stop the visible signs of aging bombard middle-aged women, as Natasha Singer of *The New York Times* suggests (2007, E3). Singer quotes a 33-year-old real estate broker who has had Botox injections, chemical peels, and laser treatments, who said, "If you want to sell a million-dollar house, you have to look good . . . and you have to have confidence that you look good" (2007, E3). In Sudan, people say that virgins are "made, not born" (Boddy 1997, 313); perhaps in Canada, youth is also "made, not born." In Canada and in many other countries around the world today, the media message to women is that success in life requires not an infibulated body, but a face and a body that never age (Figure 2.9). In both cases, cultural practices recommend surgical intervention in the female life cycle to render permanent certain aspects of youthful female bodies that are otherwise transient (fertility and unlined faces, respectively).

Did Their Culture Make Them Do It?

Do these examples imply that women support harmful practices simply because "their culture makes them do it?" For some people, this kind of explanation is plausible, even preferable, to alternative explanations because it absolves individual people of blame. How can one justify accusing immigrant African women of being mutilators or abusers of children and throw them into prison if they had no choice in the matter, if their cultures conditioned them into believing that female circumcision was necessary and proper, and if they are powerless to resist?

As discussed earlier, women and men in Hofriyat are agents in their own culture and have the ability to change or at least reduce the harm of infibulation. Boddy (1997, 312) observed that a less radical form of the operation began to gain acceptance after 1969, and "men are now marrying—and what is more, saying that they prefer to marry—women who have been less severely mutilated," at least in part because they find sexual relations with these women to be more satisfying. This suggests that the women or men in Hofriyat are not passive beings, helpless to resist cultural indoctrination but rather are, according to Abusharaf (2000, 18), "political actors forging their own communities of resistance." Specifically, Boddy showed how increasing numbers of women (and men) continued to connect female genital cutting with properly socialized female fertility—but they no longer believed that infibulation was the only procedure capable of achieving that goal.

People everywhere may be repelled by unfamiliar cultural practices when they first encounter them. Sometimes when they understand these practices better, they change their minds and conclude that the practices

Photo by BSIP/UIG Via Getty Images

FIGURE 2.9 There is a great deal of pressure placed on women in North America, especially by the beauty and fashion industries, to maintain a youthful appearance for as long as possible. Here, a woman receives Botox injections to reduce fine lines and wrinkles by paralyzing the underlying muscles.

in question are more suitable for the people who employ them rather than their own practices would be. They might even recommend incorporating practices from other cultures into their own society. But the opposite may also be the case. It is possible to understand perfectly the cultural rationale behind such practices as slavery, infanticide, headhunting, and genocide—and still refuse to approve of these practices. Insiders and outsiders alike may not be persuaded by the reasons offered to justify these practices, or they may be aware of alternative arrangements that could achieve the desired outcome via less drastic methods. In fact, changing practices of female circumcision in Hofriyat seem to be based precisely on the realization that less extreme forms of surgery can achieve the same valued cultural goals. This should not surprise us: it is likely that any cultural practice with far-reaching consequences for human life will have critics as well as supporters within the society where it is practised. This is certainly the case in Canada, where abortion and euthanasia remain controversial issues. Indeed, the Supreme Court of Canada's 2015 ruling that allows doctor-assisted suicide in some cases demonstrates how cultural practices are open to change as well as how controversial such change can be.

As Boddy's ethnographic account of female circumcision suggests, cultural relativism makes moral reasoning more complex. It does not, however, require us to abandon every value our own society has taught us. Every cultural tradition offers more than one way of evaluating experience. Exposure to the interpretations of an unfamiliar culture forces us to reconsider the possibilities our own tradition recognizes in a new light and to search for areas of intersection as well as areas of disagreement. What cultural relativism does discourage is the easy solution of refusing to consider alternatives from the outset. It also does not free us from sometimes facing difficult choices between alternatives whose rightness or wrongness is less than clear-cut.

Culture Imperialism or Cultural Hybridity?

It is no secret that colonizing states have regularly attempted to determine the cultural priorities of those whom they conquered. Sending missionaries to convert colonized peoples to Christianity is one of the best-known practices of Western **cultural imperialism**. The concept of cultural imperialism is based on two notions. First, it claims some cultures dominate other cultures. In recent history the culture(s) of Europe or Canada or "the West" has (have) come to dominate all other cultures of the world, owing to the spread of colonialism and capitalism. Second, cultural domination by one culture is said to lead inevitably to the destruction of subordinated cultures and their replacement by the culture of those in power. Thus, Western cultural imperialism is seen as responsible for destroying, for example, local music, technology, dress and food traditions, replacing them with rock and roll, cell phones, t-shirts, blue jeans, and Coca-Cola. The inevitable outcome is seen as "the cultural homogenization of the world...dooming the world to uniformity" (Inda and Rosaldo 2002, 13, 14).

Anthropologists have long noted the spread of elements of Western culture among those they worked with. But cultural imperialism did not fully explain this spread, for at least three reasons (Inda and Rosaldo 2002, 22–4). First, cultural imperialism denies *agency* to non-Western peoples who make use of Western cultural forms, assuming that they are unable to resist anything of Western origin that is marketed to them. Second, cultural imperialism assumes that non-Western cultural forms never move "from the rest to the West." But this is clearly false; today, non-Western music and food

cultural imperialism The idea that some cultures dominate others and that domination by one culture leads inevitably to the destruction of subordinated cultures and their replacement by the culture of those in power.

and material culture have large and eager followings in western Europe and Canada. Finally, cultural imperialism ignores that cultural forms and practices sometimes move from one part of the non-Western world to other parts of the non-Western world, bypassing the West entirely. For instance, movies made in India have been popular for decades in northern Nigeria (Larkin 2002), Mexican soap operas have large followings in the Philippines, and karaoke is popular all over the world.

Cultural Hybridity

Dissatisfied with the discourse of cultural imperialism, anthropologists began to search for alternative ways of understanding global cultural flows. From the days of Franz Boas and his students, anthropologists had recognized the significance of cultural borrowing. But they always emphasized that borrowing cultural forms or practices from elsewhere must be understood as borrowing with modification. That is, people rarely accept ideas or practices or objects from elsewhere without finding a way of reconciling them with local practices in order to serve local purposes. For example, in the nineteenth and twentieth centuries, missionaries were sent to the far northeast of the Canadian Arctic to assist in "civilizing" the Inuit. Although these missionaries were initially resisted, eventually they made many converts. Indeed, the Inuit have incorporated many aspects of Christianity into their cultural traditions, and today most Inuit consider it to be part of their cultural heritage (Laugrand and Oosten 2010, 36). But how should this religious conversion be understood?

Doesn't the fact that most Inuit today are Christians demonstrate that federal officials and missionaries succeeded in their policies of Western Christian cultural imperialism? Maybe not. As Canadian anthropologists Frédéric Laugrand and Jarich Oosten (2010, 36) note, despite the fact that Christianity was widely adopted by many Inuit, their beliefs and practices continued through creatively integrating Inuit traditions and Christian beliefs. And despite the prevailing perceptions that these so-called primitive societies would die off with the expansion of the dominant Western civilization, the Inuit continued to thrive and adopted Western technologies and created new cultural practices that eased the challenges of living in one of the most isolated and inhospitable environments in the world.

The Inuit combined their traditional beliefs and practices with those of Christianity. Many prominent elders, including Inuit shamans (*angakkuit*), adopted

Christianity and were trained as missionaries and ministers, making Christianity highly attractive to others. Missionaries, in turn, actively sought to adapt Christian practices to traditional Inuit ways. For example, Anglican missionaries translated hymns and scriptures into the Inuktitut language of the Inuit using syllabics, and they distributed these translations in the form of "little red books" (Remie and Oosten 2002). These books were central to Christianizing the Inuit, and they became so popular that they often reached Inuit in isolated areas even before missionaries had established missions there. Another outcome of the creation of the "little red books" was that the Inuit rapidly learned to read and write using these texts, resulting in the literacy rate of Inuit matching that of many European countries by the end of the nineteenth century (Remie and Oosten 2002, 112).

It might be as accurate to say that the Inuit "Inuitized" Christianity, therefore, as it would be to say that missionaries "Christianized" the Inuit. For example, the shape of the cross can be recognized in the inukshuk represented on the Nunavut flag, and the traditional Inuit Sedna feast has become integrated with Christmas celebrations (Laugrand and Oosten 2010,

327). In addition, many of the shamans and elders who became lay preachers and ministers continued to practise traditional healing and divination in secret, combining integral Inuit traditions with Christian practice. Interestingly, the evangelical and Pentecostal movement known as Canada Awakening Ministries that has spread to Nunavut in recent years evokes many aspects of the elders' shamanism. For example, speaking in tongues, which is common to Pentecostalism, recalls shamanistic behaviour (Laugrand and Oosten 2010, 341).

By integrating Western traditions into their own culture, Inuit Christians have been able to convert what began as an exercise in cultural imperialism into a re-affirmation of traditional Inuit values. For example, by transforming the inukshuk into a symbol of the cross, they have effectively made the cross an Inuit symbol that encourages people to follow their ancestors in a modern context (Laugrand and Oosten 2010, 377). This challenges the presumption that "authentic cultures" never change. Such an inflexible concept of culture can accommodate neither the agency of Inuit Christians nor the validity of the ongoing and continually unfolding cultural traditions they produce.

Anthropology in Everyday Life

Anthropology and Indigenous Rights

Anthropologists are increasingly participating in organizations for the defence of human rights. In particular, they have contributed to the recognition by human rights legal advocates that the collective rights of groups (such as Indigenous groups) deserve as much attention as the rights of individuals do. In Canada, there have been numerous opportunities for anthropologists to work as advocates for First Nations groups to promote their rights as Indigenous peoples. One of the first arose during the 1970s in response to a proposal to construct an oil and gas pipeline that would run from Alaska through the Mackenzie Valley to the southern United States. The proposed project would have taken away and altered the traditional lands of the Dene and other First Nations groups living along its route. Concerned about the negative social and environmental consequences of the project, the Canadian government commissioned an inquiry and

charged Thomas Berger, a Supreme Court judge, with leading the investigation. Over the course of the investigation, which came to be known as the Berger Inquiry (Berger 1977), numerous anthropologists and First Nations peoples provided evidence to substantiate claims that the lands in question were essential to the well-being of the Dene and other Indigenous peoples and that these peoples' ways of life were not "becoming extinct." In the end, Berger recommended that the project be put on hold for 10 years in order for land claims and environmental concerns to be assessed.

Another early example arose in the 1970s when numerous anthropologists, mostly from McGill University, were asked to work with the James Bay Cree as they negotiated for rights to their traditional hunting lands, an area of about 380,000 square kilometres that the Quebec government planned to develop for

Continued

a hydroelectric plant. Harvey Feit (1995) and Richard Salisbury (1986) were among the first anthropologists invited to advocate for and assist the James Bay Cree. Feit was called upon by the Cree Grand Council to use his doctoral research on Cree ecological land use to defend their claims against the Quebec and federal governments. Between 1973 and 1978, multiple negotiations took place with numerous anthropologists advocating for the Cree's Indigenous rights. Their work led to the establishment of the James Bay and Northern Quebec Agreement, which was, at the time, the most comprehensive land claims settlement ever reached in Canada. The settlement included not only rights to land but also authority over education, health services, housing, and other social services as well as a role in future development plans in the area.

Since the late 1980s, anthropologist Ronald Niezen (2003) has spent much of his time involved in community-based research with the eastern James Bay Cree in northern Quebec as well as the Cross Lake Cree in Manitoba. As his involvement with these groups increased, Niezen found that the Cree valued his ability to provide a link between their own Indigenous government and the government of Canada. He was called on to perform many roles in addition to that of participant-observer, acting at various times "as an observer, witness, advocate, author—roles that were pretty much informally developed as needs became felt" (Niezen 2003, xiv).

As his work with the Cree evolved, and he moved back and forth from reservation to government meetings, Niezen came to realize that a global movement of Indigenous peoples had come into existence and was getting noticed at places such as the United Nations. His earlier research in Mali also became relevant in a new way when, during one of his trips to Geneva, he encountered delegates from West Africa who were coming to identify themselves as Indigenous peoples and who were working "to develop human-rights standards appropriate to their concerns" (Niezen 2003, xiv). So, in 1994, he travelled as an observer delegate with the Grand Council of the Cree to a meeting of the Working Group on Indigenous Populations at the United Nations in Geneva, Switzerland. People on Indigenous reservations were also learning via the Internet about the struggles of other Indigenous communities for rights, and some community leaders were starting to "see themselves as leading a cause for justice directly analogous to (and without distinguishing among) a variety of liberation movements, including the American

civil rights movement and resistance to South African apartheid" (Niezen 2003, xiii).

Indigeneity is supposed to refer to a primordial identity that preceded the establishment of colonial states. Yet the very possibility that groups from West Africa, Latin America, and North America might come together as Indigenous peoples "is predicated upon global sameness of experience, and is expressed through the mechanisms of law and bureaucracy" (Niezen 2003, 2–3). "Indigenous peoples" is not just a badge of identity, but also a legal term that has been included in international conventions issued by the International Labour Organization.

According to Niezen (2003), it is important to distinguish what he calls *ethnonationalism* from *indigenism*. Ethnonationalism, he believes, describes a movement of people who "have defined their collective identities with clear cultural and linguistic contours and who express their goals of autonomy from the state with the greatest conviction and zeal, sometimes with hatreds spilling over into violence" (8). For example, in Canada the advocates of sovereignty for Quebec have pushed for an independent French-speaking nation-state (8). Indigenism, by contrast, "is not a particularized identity but a global one, ... grounded in international networks" (9). What connects specific groups to this identity, whether they live in dictatorships or democratic states, "is a sense of illegitimate, meaningless, and dishonourable suffering" (13).

Unlike ethnonationalists, Indigenous-rights activists do not seek to form breakaway states of their own. Their approach is entirely different: Indigenous representatives lobby for their rights before international bodies such as the United Nations, attempting to hold states accountable for abusing their Indigenous citizens. In Niezen's (2003, 16) opinion, the strategy "shows some Indigenous leaders to be, despite their limited power and resources, some of the most effective political strategists on the contemporary national and international scenes." Their goal is to get nation-states to live up to their responsibilities and promises to Indigenous people, which are often explicitly stated in treaties. Thus, they seek affirmation of their rights to land and compensation for past losses and suffering; they seek cultural self-determination and political sovereignty. The goal of Indigenous liberation thus involves the recognition of *collective rights*.

While Niezen (2003, 23) urges us to acknowledge the daring and effectiveness of the Indigenous movement, he also warns against romanticizing it: "Significant obstacles remain to be overcome before a new order of relations between Indigenous peoples and the state can be said to have truly arrived." For example, the United Nations has been less responsive than many Indigenous delegates might have hoped because some of its member states continue to equate the movement for Indigenous sovereignty with ethnonationalism. Hence the UN Permanent Forum on Indigenous Issues is not called the UN Permanent Forum on Indigenous *Peoples* (160–4).

Some liberal human rights theorists are also concerned that the recognition of collective rights would serve as a green light to despotic governments, who could use the rights of distinct cultures as an excuse for repression. Niezen (2003, 219–21) concluded that

> if Indigenous claims to self-determination are to avoid playing into the hands of despotic governments, they must have individual rights built into them.... Human rights do not offer protection of cultural practices that themselves violate individual rights. The concept of "Indigenous peoples" developed principally within Western traditions of scholarship and legal reform ... has transcended its symbolic use by acquiring legal authority.... It has been taken control of by its living subjects—reverse-engineered, rearticulated, and put to use as a tool of liberation.

Today, a variety of groups, from Indigenous activists in Amazonia to immigrant activists in Europe, have incorporated the plural use of *culture* into their own self-definitions, and in some cases anthropologists defend this move as valuable and progressive. In addition, scholarly disciplines outside anthropology, from cultural studies to cognitive science, have incorporated *culture* into their own technical vocabularies. On the one hand, this can be seen (perhaps ironically) as a measure of the success of earlier generations of anthropologists in demonstrating the value of the culture concept. On the other hand, it means that today, *culture* is sometimes used in ways that anthropologists find objectionable but that they cannot control.

Can We Be at Home in a Global World?

When people from different cultural backgrounds are thrust by circumstance into one another's company and seek ways to get along with one another, links they attempt to make are likely to be clumsy and uncomfortable. This phenomenon is what anthropologist Anna Tsing has called **friction**: "the awkward, unequal, unstable aspects of interconnection across difference" (2005, 4). Friction in the struggle to bridge differences makes new things possible, and unequal encounters can lead to new arrangements of culture and power (Tsing 2005, 3–5). And these arrangements may also be seen as a source of hope.

Tsing's understanding of "friction" can be found when new and old cultural practices are at odds with each other, such as assisted suicide in Canada; or when individual rights are in conflict with shared views, such as the UN human rights versus the rights of individual cultures to practise infibulation or other forms of FGM.

> For more information on anthropological approaches to ethnicity, globalization, and identity, see Chapters 12, 13, and 14, respectively.

Many of the ethnographic cases in this book demonstrate the human ability to cope creatively with changed life circumstances. Nevertheless, successful outcomes are never ensured. As we approach the third decade of the twenty-first century, a critical awareness is needed, one that involves concerted practical attempts to wrestle with these stresses and contradictions.

The Promise of the Anthropological Perspective

The anthropological perspective on the human condition is not easy to maintain. It forces us to question the common-sense assumptions with which we are most comfortable. It compels us to consider the cultural contexts that influence how "scientific experts" conduct

> friction The awkward, unequal, unstable aspects of interconnection across difference.

their research. It only increases the difficulty we encounter when faced with moral and political decisions. It does not allow us an easy retreat, for once we are exposed to the kinds of experience that the anthropological undertaking makes possible, we are changed. We cannot easily pretend that these new experiences never happened to us.

Chapter Summary

1. Anthropologists have argued that culture distinguishes the human condition from the condition of other living species. Human culture is learned, shared, patterned, adaptive, and symbolic. It did not emerge all at once but evolved over time. Our biological evolution aligns with cultural influences, making our species essentially biocultural.

2. Many anthropologists have long thought holistically about human culture. Anthropological holism argues that objects and environments interpenetrate and even define each other. Thus, the whole is more than the sum of its parts. Human beings and human societies are open systems that cannot be reduced to the parts that make them up. The parts and the whole mutually define, or codetermine, each other and coevolve. This book adopts a coevolutionary approach to human nature, human society, and the human past. Human beings depend on symbolic cultural understandings to help them resolve the ambiguities inherent in everyday human experience.

3. Anthropologists believe that ethnocentrism can be countered by a commitment to cultural relativism, an attempt to understand the cultural underpinnings of behaviour. Cultural relativism does not require us to abandon every value our society has taught us; however, it does discourage the easy solution of refusing to consider alternatives from the outset. Cultural relativism makes moral decisions more difficult because it requires us to take many things into account before we make up our minds.

4. Human history is an essential aspect of the human story. Culture is worked out over time and passed on from one generation to the next. The cultural beliefs and practices we inherit from the past or borrow from other people in the present make some things easier for us and other things more difficult. At the same time, culture provides resources that human beings can make use of in the pursuit of their own goals. Thus, the anthropological understanding of human life recognizes the importance of human agency.

5. Many anthropologists have criticized the use of the term *cultures* to refer to particular, learned ways of life belonging to specific groups of human beings. Critics argue that this way of talking about culture seems to endorse a kind of oppressive cultural determinism. Supporters, however, argue that in some cases this version of the culture concept can be used to defend vulnerable social groups against exploitation and oppression by outsiders.

6. In recent years, cultural anthropologists who follow the vast contemporary population movements of migrants, refugees, and tourists have begun to study processes of cultural hybridity that cannot be reduced to forms of cultural imperialism. Rather, much of this cultural mixing appears to reflect new forms of multicultural, cosmopolitan consciousness.

For Review

1. Consider the five key attributes of human culture highlighted in this chapter. How do you experience these in your day-to-day life? Why is it important that culture is adaptive?

2. What are complex symbolic representation and institutions, and why are they especially important to human culture? Provide an example of one institution that you are involved in every

day. How you do think that institution shapes your life?

3. What is human agency? How does attention to human agency affect the way anthropologists interpret cultural phenomena?

4. What do anthropologists mean by *holism*? How do different factors combine to produce different human societies?

5. Describe the problems US Peace Corps volunteers were having in Botswana in the early 1970s and the explanation that was provided by anthropologist Hoyt Alverson. Have you ever experienced a misunderstanding with someone from a different culture? Analyze what happened. Do you think that there is a cultural explanation for your problem?

6. Explain the effects of ethnocentrism and cultural relativism on an individual's perception of another culture. Is there a cultural practice that you do not understand? Could cultural relativity help you understand this practice?

7. Some cultural practices, such as female genital cutting, are highly contentious. Discuss the issues at stake and think about how cultural relativism changes the discussion. Why is it important to remain culturally relative when discussing sensitive issues?

8. Distinguish between *Culture* (with a capital *C*) and *culture(s)* (with a lowercase *c*) by providing an example of each. What does this difference reflect for anthropologists?

9. Summarize the case study on Inuit Christianity with the five key attributes of culture in mind. Which attributes are discussed, and how does the case study highlight them?

Key Terms

coevolution 28	enculturation 24	hominins 26
colonization 30	ethnocentrism 31	human agency 27
cultural imperialism 36	friction 39	socialization 24
cultural relativism 32	holism 28	symbol 25

References

Abusharaf, Rogaia Mustafa. 2000. "Female Circumcision Goes beyond Feminism." *Anthropology News* 41 (March): 17–18.

Alverson, Hoyt. 1977. "Peace Corps Volunteers in Rural Botswana." *Human Organization* 36 (3): 274–81.

Berger, Thomas R. 1977. *Northern Frontier, Northern Homeland: Report of the Mackenzie Valley Pipeline Inquiry.* 2 vols. Ottawa: Supply and Services Canada.

Boddy, Janice. 1997. "Womb as Oasis: The Symbolic Context of Pharaonic Circumcision in Rural Northern Sudan." In *The Gender/ Sexuality Reader*, edited by Roger Lancaster and Micaela Do Leonardo, 309–24. New York: Routledge.

——. 2007. "Gender Crusades: The Female Circumcision Controversy in Cultural Perspective." In *Transcultural Bodies: Female Genital Cutting in Global Context*, edited by Ylva Hernlund and Bettina Shell-Duncan. New Brunswick, NJ: Rutgers University Press.

Center for Reproductive Rights. 2015. "Female Genital Mutilation (FGM): Legal Prohibitions Worldwide." http://www.reproductiverights .org/document/female-genital-mutilation-fgm-legal-prohibitions- worldwide

Comaroff, Jean. 1985. *Body of Power, Spirit of Resistance: The Culture and History of a South African People.* Chicago: University of Chicago Press.

Daly, Mary. 1978. *Gyn/Ecology: The Metaethics of Radical Feminism.* Boston: Beacon Press.

Deacon, Terrence. 1997. *The Symbolic Species: The Co-evolution of Language and the Brain.* New York: W.W. Norton.

——. 2003. "The Hierarchic Logic of Emergence: Untangling the Interdependence of Evolution and Self-Organization." In *Evolution and Learning: The Baldwin Effect Reconsidered*, edited by Bruce H. Weber and David J. Depew, 273–308. Cambridge, MA: MIT Press.

Feit, Harvey A. 1995. "Hunting and the Quest for Power: The James Bay Cree and Whitemen in the Twentieth Century." In *Native Peoples: The Canadian Experience*, 2nd ed., edited by R.B. Morrison and C.R. Wilson. Toronto: McClelland and Stewart.

Franklin, Sarah. 1995. "Science as Culture, Cultures of Science." *Annual Review of Anthropology* 24: 163–84.

——. 2003. "Re-thinking Nature–Culture: Anthropology and the New Genetics." *Anthropological Theory* 3: 65–85.

Greenwood, David, and William Stini. 1977. *Nature, Culture, and Human History.* New York: Harper and Row.

Inda, Jonathan Xavier, and Renato Rosaldo. 2002. "Introduction: A World in Motion." In *The Anthropology of Globalization*, edited by Jonathan Xavier Inda and Renato Rosaldo. Malden, MA: Blackwell.

Jenness, Diamond. 1922. *The Life of the Copper Eskimos*. Ottawa: FA Ackland.

Karp, Ivan. 1990. Guest editorial in *Cultural Anthropology: A Perspective on the Human Condition*, by Emily Schultz and Robert Lavenda, 74–5. 2nd ed. St Paul, MN: West.

Larkin, Brian. 2002. "Indian Films and Nigerian Lovers: Media and the Creation of Parallel Modernities." In *The Anthropology of Globalization*, edited by Jonathan Xavier Inda and Renato Rosaldo, 350–78. Malden, MA: Blackwell.

Laugrand, Frédéric B., and Jarich G. Oosten. 2010. *Inuit Shamanism and Christianity: Transitions and Transformations in the Twentieth Century*. Montreal: McGill-Queen's University Press.

Leca, Jean-Baptiste, Michael A. Huffman, and Paul L. Vasey, eds. 2012. *The Monkeys of Stormy Mountain: Sixty Years of Primatological Research on the Japanese Macaques of Arashiyama*. Cambridge Studies in Biological and Evolutionary Anthropology, no. 61. Cambridge: Cambridge University Press.

Marks, Jonathan. 1995. *Human Biodiversity*. New York: Aldine.

———. 2013. "The Nature/Culture of Genetic Facts." *Annual Review of Anthropology* 42: 247–67. doi:10.1146/annurev-anthro-092412-155558

Niezen, Ronald. 2003. *The Origins of Indigenism: Human Rights and the Politics of Identity*. Berkeley: University of California Press.

Potts, Richard. 1996. *Humanity's Descent*. New York: William Morrow.

Remie, Cornelius H.W., and Jarich Oosten. 2002. "The Birth of a Catholic Inuit Community: The Transition to Christianity in Pelly Bay, Nunavut, 1935–1950." *Inuit Studies* 26 (1): 109–41.

Salisbury, Richard F. 1986. *A Homeland for the Cree: Regional Development in James Bay 1971–1981*. Montreal: McGill-Queen's University Press.

Singer, Natasha. 2007. "Is Looking Your Age Now Taboo?" *New York Times*, March 1, E1, E3.

Tsing, Anna Lowenhaupt. 2005. *Friction: An Ethnography of Global Connection*. Princeton, NJ: Princeton University Press.

Tylor, E.B. (1871) 1958. *Primitive Culture*. New York: Harper and Row.

▲ The evolution of human ancestry, visible through changes in anatomy, is displayed at the National Museum of Natural Sciences in Kiev, Ukraine. Photo: Andrii Zastrozhnov/Shutterstock

3 Why Is Evolution Important to Anthropologists?

Chapter Outline

- What Is Evolutionary Theory?
- What Material Evidence Is There for Evolution?
- Pre-Darwinian Views of the Natural World
- What Is Natural Selection?
- How Did Biologists Learn about Genes?
- Genotype, Phenotype, and the Norm of Reaction

- What Does Evolution Mean to Anthropologists?
- Chapter Summary
- For Review
- Key Terms
- References

The question of why evolution is important to anthropologists is fundamental to contemporary anthropology and is a topic of great significance in wider scientific discussions. As introduced in Chapter 1, humans are considered biocultural organisms; as such, we are subject to the evolutionary processes that affect all life on earth. In this chapter, we will look at how the living world was understood before the nineteenth century, where Darwin's ideas came from, how they have been further elaborated since his time, and why evolutionary theory continues to be our most powerful tool for understanding biological processes today.

Philosopher of science Philip Kitcher (1982) has suggested that successful scientific theories are testable, unified, and fruitful. A theory is testable when its hypotheses can be independently matched up against nature. A theory is unified when it offers just one or a few basic problem-solving strategies that make sense of a wide range of material evidence. And a theory is fruitful when its central principles suggest new and promising possibilities for further research. The modern theory of biological evolution possesses all three characteristics. Evolutionary hypotheses are highly testable in a number of ways. As we shall see, material evidence from widely diverse sources has consistently fit evolutionary predictions. Because it is based on a few central concepts and assumptions, the evolutionary research program is also highly unified. Charles Darwin's *On the Origin of Species by Means of Natural Selection* appeared in 1859. As Kitcher (1982, 48) puts it, Darwin "gave structure to our ignorance." After that date, biologists could borrow Darwin's methods to guide them in new and promising directions. The study of life has not been the same since. As we begin our study of human evolution, you may be surprised at the number of terms and concepts that you are learning from biology, genetics, and ecology. The theory of evolution has engaged the efforts of many scientists for over 150 years. Their work has produced a still-developing, powerful, multi-stranded theory. To understand the arguments made by modern evolutionary biologists, we have to learn the language of evolution. The payoff will be a nuanced view of what the theory of evolution is really about and how powerful it really is.

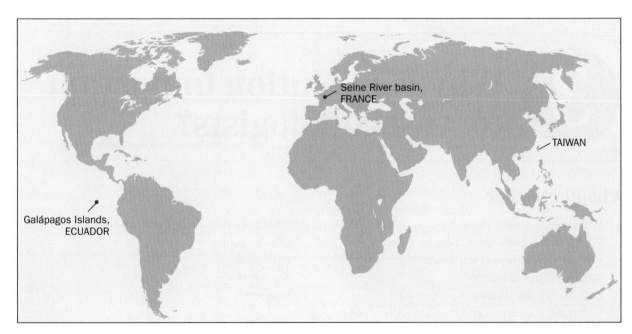

MAP 3.1 Major locations discussed in Chapter 3.

What Is Evolutionary Theory?

Evolutionary theory claims that living species can change over time and give rise to new kinds of species, with the result that all organisms ultimately share a common ancestry. Because of this common ancestry, information about biological variation in finches or genetic transmission in fruit flies can help us understand the roles of biological variation and genetics in human evolution.

What Material Evidence Is There for Evolution?

Two kinds of material evidence have been particularly important in the development of evolutionary theory: material evidence of change over time and material evidence of change across space. Geological research led to the discovery of the fossil record—the remains of life forms that had been preserved in the earth for a long time. When scientists compared these fossils with each other and with living organisms, they noted that the living organisms were quite different from the fossilized organisms. This was material evidence of change over time, or **evolution**, in the kinds of organisms that have lived on the earth. Any persuasive biological theory would have to find a way to explain this material evidence.

Equally important material evidence for the development of evolutionary theory came from the study of living organisms. Darwin himself was most interested in explaining the pattern of distribution of living species of organisms. In one of his best-known studies, Darwin noted that neighbouring geographic areas on the islands of the Galápagos archipelago were inhabited by species of finch different from the finch species found on the Ecuadorian mainland. At the same time, the various Galápagos species resembled one another closely and resembled mainland finch species (Figure 3.1). Species distribution patterns of this kind suggested change over space, which, again, any persuasive biological theory would have to explain.

In the centuries before Darwin, however, the fossil record was mostly unknown, and many of those concerned with biology did not see the pattern of distribution of living species as evidence for past change.

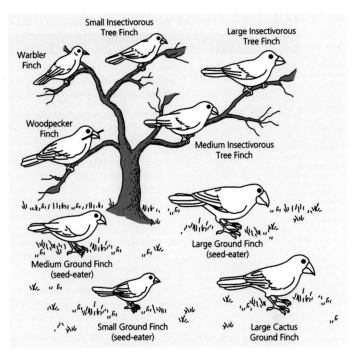

FIGURE 3.1 Charles Darwin and Alfred Russel Wallace explained the pattern of distribution of living species of organisms (such as the various species of finches living on the Galápagos Islands) by arguing that all the variants had evolved from a single ancestral species.

To understand why Darwin's ideas had such a powerful impact requires an understanding of pre-Darwinian views of the natural world (Table 3.1).

Pre-Darwinian Views of the Natural World

In the Western societies of antiquity, the Greeks thought the world had been, and would be, around forever; in the Judeo-Christian tradition, it was thought that the world was young and would end soon. Both traditions saw the world as fixed and unchanging.

Essentialism

If the world does not change, then the various forms of life that are part of it also do not change. We can trace

---

evolutionary theory The set of testable hypotheses that assert that living organisms can change over time and give rise to new kinds of organisms, with the result that all organisms ultimately share a common ancestry.

evolution The process of change over time.

TABLE 3.1 Pre-Darwinian Views of the Natural World

View	Key Features	Example
Essentialism	Each "natural kind" of living thing is characterized by an unchanging, perfect core of features that separates it from all other natural things. Based on ideas derived from Plato.	A panda has "pandaness" and is not a bear.
Great Chain of Being	A comprehensive framework used in the Middle Ages based on Aristotelian principles that linked all living things in an elaborate chain. It was based on three principles: 1. *Continuity:* Attributes of one kind of organism always overlap to some extent with the attributes of organisms closest to it in the classification. 2. *Plentitude:* A world of organisms created by a benevolent God can have no gaps but must include all logically conceivable organisms. 3. *Unilinear gradation:* All organisms can be arranged in a single hierarchy based on various degrees to which they depart from divine perfection.	A panda is like a bear living in a tree.
Catastrophism	The notion that natural disasters, such as floods, are responsible for the extinction of species, which are then replaced by new species. Introduced by French scientist Georges Cuvier.	Extinction of dinosaurs
Uniformitarianism	The belief that the natural processes (such as erosion or volcanism) that affect the earth's surface today were at work in the past. Thus, we can use our understanding of current processes to reconstruct the history of the earth. Popularized by British geologist Charles Lyell.	Volcanic eruptions in Iceland create new landscapes.
Transformational Evolution	Assuming essentialist species and a uniformly changing environment, proponents argued that all members of a species transform themselves in identical ways in order to adapt to commonly experienced changes in the environment. To explain why, they invoked (1) the law of use and disuse and (2) the inheritance of acquired characteristics. Introduced by French naturalist Jean-Baptiste de Monet de Lamarck.	Pandas have "thumbs" that they don't use.

this view back to the ancient Greek philosopher Plato (c. 429–c. 347 BCE). A central element of Plato's philosophy was a belief in an ideal world of perfect, eternal, unchanging forms that exist apart from the imperfect, changeable, physical world of living things. Plato believed that these two worlds—ideal and material—were linked and that every ideal form was represented in the physical, material world by a number of imperfect but recognizable forms—for example, the ideal form of "cowness" was represented by living cows of varying sizes, colours, temperaments, and so on. Plato also believed that when observers looked at living cows and saw their similarities despite all this variation, what they were really seeing was the ideal form, or essence, of "cowness" that each individual cow incarnated.

According to Plato, all living things that share the same essence belong to the same "natural kind," and there are many natural kinds in the world, each of which is the result of the imperfect incarnation in the physical world of one or another eternal form or ideal ("cowness," "humanness," "ratness," and the like). This view is called essentialism. For essentialists, as Ernst Mayr (1982, 256) explains, each species has a unique, unchanging essence that clearly separates it from all other species. That essence is what makes every individual cow a cow and not, say, a deer.

The Great Chain of Being

Greek ideas were adopted and adapted by thinkers in the Judeo-Christian religious tradition. By the Middle Ages, many scholars thought they could describe the organizing principles responsible for harmony in nature. According to Arthur Lovejoy ([1936] 1960), these scholars in the Middle Ages used the following idea that was developed by the ancient Greek philosopher Aristotle (384–322 BCE). Aristotle suggested that different kinds of organisms could be arranged in a single line from most primitive to most advanced, and he argued that the attributes of one kind of organism always overlap to some extent with the attributes of organisms closest to it in the classification so that the differences between adjacent organisms were very slight. Together, these ideas constituted a principle of continuity. Logically implied by the principle of continuity is the principle of plenitude, or fullness, which states that a world of organisms created by a benevolent God can have no gaps but must include all logically conceivable organisms. Finally, the assumption that God alone is self-sufficient and perfect, which was held by a variety of ancient and medieval philosophers, implied that each of God's creatures must lack, to a greater or lesser degree, some part of divine perfection. As a result, the various kinds of organisms can be arranged in a single hierarchy, or unilinear gradation, like a ladder or a chain, based on the degrees to which they depart from the divine idea.

When the notion of unilinear gradation was combined with the notions of continuity and plenitude, the result was called the Great Chain of Being, a comprehensive framework for interpreting the natural world. This framework suggested that the entire cosmos was composed "of an immense, or of an infinite, number of links . . . every one of them differing from that immediately above and that immediately below it by the 'least possible' degree of difference" (Lovejoy [1936] 1960, 59). Degrees of difference were understood in theological terms to be degrees of excellence. Creatures farthest away from divine perfection were lowest in the hierarchy whereas creatures most like God (such as the angels) ranked highest (Figure 3.2). Human beings occupied a unique position in the chain. Their material bodies linked them to other material beings; but, unlike other material creatures, they also possessed souls and were thereby linked to the spiritual realm by a God who had created them in his image.

For several hundred years—from the Middle Ages through to the eighteenth century—the Great Chain of Being was the framework in the Western world within which all discussions of living organisms were set. This framework of ideas continued as late as the mid-eighteenth century, influencing even Carolus Linnaeus (1707–1778), who is the father of modern biological **taxonomy** or classification (Figure 3.3). Linnaeus was committed to an essentialist definition of natural kinds. He focused on what modern taxonomists call the **genus** (plural *genera*) and used the form and structure of reproductive organs to define the "essence" of a genus (Mayr 1982, 178). (The term **species**, which modern biologists

FIGURE 3.2 In the Great Chain of Being, creatures were ranked according to their degree of divine perfection. Plants and fungi, which lack mobility and sensory organs, were ranked below animals, which were in turn ranked below human beings.

assign to subpopulations of the same genus that share certain specific attributes, was used more loosely in the past by essentialists and by non-essentialists.) Essentialists like Linnaeus knew that individuals sometimes differ markedly from what is considered "normal" for others of their kind. But these deviations were thought of as accidents, or "degradations," that could not affect the unity of the natural kind.

Catastrophism and Uniformitarianism

In the eighteenth century, unprecedented social and scientific discoveries gradually raised doubts about the

taxonomy In biology, a classification system used to organize various kinds of organisms.

genus The level of the Linnaean taxonomy in which different species are grouped together based on their similarities to one another. In modern taxonomies, genus is ranked between family (less specific) and species (more specific).

species For Linnaeus, a Platonic "natural kind" defined in terms of its essence. For modern biologists, a reproductive community of populations (reproductively isolated from others) that occupies a specific niche in nature.

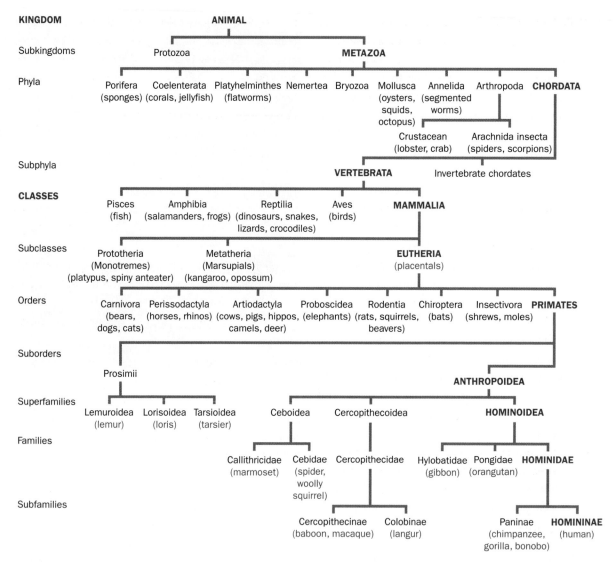

FIGURE 3.3 A modern biological taxonomy based on the Linnaean classification (popular names are in parentheses). Organisms sharing structural similarities are still grouped together, but their similarities are understood to be the result of common ancestry, indicated by the horizontal line connecting them.

Great Chain of Being. The principle of continuity was criticized by French scientist Georges Cuvier (1769–1832), a pioneer in modern anatomy who also carried out some of the first important excavations of fossils in the Seine River basin near Paris. He was a firm believer in the essentialist definition of natural kinds, but his anatomical studies convinced him that there were only four natural categories of living things: Vertebrates (humans), arthropods (spiders, insects, crabs), molluscs (shellfish), and Radiata (jellyfish, starfish). Each category was perfectly adapted to its way of life but had no connection to any of the others. Cuvier's studies of the fossil record convinced him that, over time, some species had been abruptly wiped out and replaced, equally abruptly, by new species from somewhere else. He called these abrupt transitions

"revolutions," although this term was translated into English as "catastrophe." Hence, the term *catastrophism* came to refer to the notion that natural disasters, such as floods, are responsible for the extinction of some natural kinds, which are later replaced by new natural kinds.

In some ways, Cuvier's ideas were perfectly traditional: he did not reject the essentialist understanding of species and never suggested that new species were simply old species that had changed. Yet his idea that some species might disappear in mass extinctions was quite radical because, according to Judeo-Christian theology, God had created all possible forms of life only once. In the same way, Cuvier's assertion in 1812 that there were no connections whatsoever among the four basic categories of living things seriously undermined the principle of unilinear gradation. That is, if the four categories had nothing in common with one another, then they could not be arranged in a simple chain of natural kinds, each precisely placed between the one slightly less advanced and the one slightly more advanced. Biologist Ernst Mayr (1982, 201) concluded that this argument dealt the Great Chain of Being its death blow.

But the Great Chain of Being did not die gently because its principles had become inextricably intertwined with Judeo-Christian beliefs about the natural world. By the late eighteenth and early nineteenth centuries, one result of this process of amalgamation was the development of an approach arguing that the perfection of each organism's adaptation could only be the result of intentional design by a benevolent creator. One group of thinkers, known as "catastrophists," modified Cuvier's theory and argued that the new species that replaced old ones had been specially created by God. Others subscribed to a position known as *uniformitarianism*, which stressed nature's overall harmonious integration as evidence for God's handiwork. These "uniformitarians" criticized the ideas of Cuvier and the catastrophists. God might allow the world to change, they admitted, but a benevolent God's blueprint for creation could not include sharp breaks between different forms of life and the abrupt disappearance of species through extinction. The uniformitarian position gained powerful support from the book *Principles of Geology* by Charles Lyell (1797–1875), a geologist, published between 1830 and 1833. Lyell argued that the same gradual processes of erosion and volcanism that change the earth's surface today had also been at work in the past. Assuming the uniformity of these processes, he contended that our understanding of current processes could be used to reconstruct the history of the earth.

The quarrel between catastrophists and uniformitarians has often been portrayed as a conflict between narrow-minded dogmatism (identified with the catastrophists) and open-minded, empirical science (identified with the uniformitarians). But, as paleontologist Stephen Jay Gould (1987) demonstrated, this portrayal misrepresents the nature of their disagreement. Both Cuvier and Lyell were empirical scientists: the former, a leading anatomist and excavator of fossils; the latter, a field-working geologist. Both confronted much of the same material evidence; however, as Gould points out, they interpreted that evidence in very different ways. Catastrophists were willing to accept a view of earth's history that permitted ruptures of harmony in order to preserve their belief that history, guided by divine

intervention, was going somewhere. By contrast, the harmonious, non-directional view of the uniformitarians was rooted in their belief that time was cyclic, like the changing seasons. Uniformitarians promoted the view that God's creation was the "incarnation of rationality"— that is, that God's creation unfolded in accordance with God's laws, without requiring subsequent divine intervention or a fixed historical trajectory.

Transformational Evolution

Thus, by the early years of the nineteenth century, traditional ideas about the natural world had been challenged by new material evidence and conflicting interpretations of that evidence. During this period, French naturalist Jean-Baptiste de Monet de Lamarck (1744–1829) grappled with the inconsistencies described above, dealing the first serious blow against essentialism (Figure 3.4). Lamarck

FIGURE 3.4 Jean-Baptiste de Monet de Lamarck. Lamarck wanted to preserve the traditional view of a harmonious living world, but his interpretation of the evidence of fossils eventually undermined exactly the view he was trying to defend.

wanted to preserve the traditional view of a harmonious living world. One of the most serious challenges to that view was the problem of extinction. How could perfectly adapted creatures suddenly be wiped out, and where did their replacements come from? Some suggested that the extinctions were the result of the biblical Noah's flood, but this could not explain how aquatic animals had become extinct. Others suggested that extinctions were the result of human hunting, possibly explaining why mastodons no longer roamed the earth. Some hoped that natural kinds believed to be extinct might yet be found inhabiting an unexplored area of the globe.

Lamarck suggested an original interpretation of the material evidence that had been used to argue in favour of extinction. In 1809, he noted that many fossil species bore a close resemblance to living species, and perhaps fossil forms were the ancestors of living forms. Fossil forms looked different from their descendants, he believed, because ancestral features had been modified over time to suit their descendants to changing climate and geography. Such a process would prove that nature was harmonious after all—that, although the world was a changing world, living organisms possessed the capacity to change along with it.

Many elements of the Great Chain of Being could be made to fit with Lamarck's scheme. Lamarck (1809) believed that once a natural kind had come into existence, it had the capacity to evolve over time into increasingly complex (or "perfect") forms. This could happen, Lamarck suggested, because all organisms have two attributes: (1) the ability to change physically in response to environmental demands and (2) the capacity to activate this ability whenever environmental change makes the organism's previous response obsolete. Otherwise, the resulting lack of fit between organisms and environment would create disharmony in nature. Lamarck never suggested that a species might adapt to change by splitting into two or more new species; rather, he suggested that every member of every species is engaged in its own individual adaptive transformation over time. Therefore, Lamarckian evolution has also been called *transformational evolution*.

Lamarck proposed two "laws" to explain how such transformation occurs. First, he said, an organ is strengthened by use and weakened by disuse (an early statement of "use it or lose it"). If environmental changes cause members of a species to rely more heavily on some organs than on others, the former will become enhanced and the latter reduced. This was known as the law of use and disuse. Lamarck further argued that this first law had

FIGURE 3.5 Lamarckian transformational evolution and Darwinian variational evolution offer two different explanations for how the panda got its "thumb." The "thumb" is actually an elongated wrist bone that aids pandas in stripping bamboo leaves, their favourite food, from bamboo stalks.

evolutionary consequences because the physical result of use or disuse could be passed from one generation to the next, which resulted in his second law: the inheritance of acquired characteristics.

Consider the following example: modern pandas possess an oversized, elongated wrist bone that aids them in stripping bamboo leaves, their favourite food, from bamboo stalks (Figure 3.5). This bone has been called the panda's "thumb," although pandas retain all five digits on each paw. Had Lamarck known about the panda's "thumb," he might have explained its origin as follows: suppose that pandas originally had wrist bones like those of other bears. Then the environment changed, obliging pandas to become dependent on bamboo for food. Pandas, unable to survive on bamboo unless they found an efficient way to strip the leaves off the stalk, were forced to use their forepaws more intensively (the law of use and disuse) in order to remove enough bamboo leaves to satisfy their appetite. Continual exercise of their wrists caused their wrist bones to enlarge and lengthen into a shape resembling a thumb. After acquiring "thumbs" through strenuous activity, pandas gave birth to offspring with elongated wrist bones (the law of inheritance of acquired characteristics). Thus, Lamarck's laws could explain how each species builds up new, more complex organs and attains, over many generations, higher levels of "perfection."

Because transformational evolution works through the efforts of individual members of a species, what would prevent different individuals from transforming themselves in different directions? Part of the answer is that Lamarck expected a changing environment to affect all individuals of the same species in the same way, leading to identical responses in terms of use and disuse. But the rest of the answer lies in the fact that Lamarck still accepted the essentialist belief that every individual member of a species was identical in essence to every other member. Only if this were so could all members of the same species respond in the same ways to the same environmental pressures and retain their species identity over time.

Lamarck's transformational theory of biological evolution was rejected by biologists in the early twentieth century when geneticists were able to demonstrate that neither the law of use and disuse nor the law of inheritance of acquired characteristics applied to genes. In the early nineteenth century, however, Lamarck's speculations opened the door for new ideas about how organisms develop and change through time.

What Is Natural Selection?

Lamarck had argued that a species could vary over time. Contemporaries of Lamarck, observing living organisms in the wild in Europe, the Americas, Africa, and Asia, had demonstrated that species could vary over space as well. Where did all this mutually coexisting but previously unknown living variation come from?

The mystery of geographical variation in living organisms was particularly vexing to Charles Darwin (1809–1882) (Figure 3.6) and Alfred Russel Wallace (1823–1913), whose field observations made it impossible to ignore. Wallace reasoned that the relationship between similar but distinct species in the wild could be explained if all the similar species were related to one another biologically—that is, if they

FIGURE 3.6 Charles Darwin (1809–1882).

were considered daughter (or sibling) species of some other parental species. Darwin, comparing the finches on the Galápagos Islands with finches on the Ecuadorian mainland, reasoned that the similarities linking the finches could be explained if all of them had descended from a single parental finch population. A recent study of these finches by Lamichhaney and colleagues (2015) corroborate and support Darwin's initial work and document how quickly new species developed on the Galápagos.

Independently of one another, Darwin and Wallace concluded that similar species must descend from a common ancestor, meaning that any species might split into a number of new species given enough time. But how much time? In the 1650s, James Ussher, the Anglican archbishop of Ireland, used information in the Bible to calculate that God had created the earth on 23 October 4004 BCE, a date that was still widely accepted. Charles Lyell and other geologists, however, claimed that the earth was much more than 6000 years old (indeed, it is about 4.5 billion years old). If the geologists were right, there had been ample time for what Darwin called "descent with modification" to have produced the species diversity we find in the world today.

Darwin had refrained from publishing his work on evolution for years but was moved to action when Lyell warned him that Wallace was ready to publish his ideas. As a result, Darwin and Wallace first published their views in a scientific paper carrying both their names. Darwin became better known than Wallace in later years, in part because of the mass of material evidence he collected in support of his theory together with his refined theoretical interpretations of that evidence.

The theory of **common ancestry**—"the first Darwinian revolution" (Mayr 1982, 116)—was in itself scandalous because it went far beyond Lamarck's modest suggestion that species can change without losing their essential integrity. Not only did Darwin propose that similar species can be traced to a common ancestor, but he also offered a straightforward, mechanistic explanation of how such descent with modification takes place. His explanation, the theory of **natural selection**, was "the second Darwinian revolution." That natural selection remains central to modern evolutionary theory is testimony to the power of Darwin's insight because it has been tested and reformulated for more than 150 years and remains the best explanation we have today for the diversity of life on earth.

Charles Darwin's theory of evolution was possible only because he was able to think about species in a new way. Although Lamarck had begun to do this when he suggested that species could change, Darwin completed the job. If organisms could change, then they did not have a fixed essence. This, in turn, meant that variation—or differences—among individual members of a species might be extremely important.

Thus, Darwin turned the essentialist definition of *species* on its head. He argued that the important thing about individual members of a species is not what they have in common but how they are different. The Darwinian theory of evolution by natural selection argued that variation, not a unitary essence, is the central condition of life. Therefore it is called **variational evolution**, in contrast to the transformational evolution of Lamarck (see, e.g., Lewontin 1982). The idea of variational evolution depends on what Ernst Mayr (1982) calls "population thinking"—that is, seeing the populations that make up a species as composed of biological individuals whose differences from one another are genuine and important.

Population Thinking

Darwin combined this new view of species with other observations about the natural world. Consider, for example, frogs in a pond. Nobody would deny that new frogs hatch from hundreds of eggs laid by mature females every breeding season, yet the size of the population of adult frogs in a given pond rarely changes much from one season to the next. Clearly, the great potential fertility represented by all those eggs is never realized or the pond would shortly be overrun by frogs. Something must keep all those eggs from maturing into adults. In order to explain this phenomenon, Darwin used the mainstream nineteenth-century capitalistic ideas of Thomas Malthus, who suggested that population numbers are limited by resource availability (Figure 3.7). Darwin noted that there was a limited food supply in the pond, which means that the hatchlings are forced to compete with one another for food. Darwin wondered what factors determined which hatchlings win and which lose. Pointing to the variation among all individuals of the species, he argued that those individuals whose traits better equip them to compete in the struggle for existence are more likely to survive and reproduce than those who lack such traits. Individuals who leave greater numbers of offspring are said to have superior fitness.

When Darwin interpreted his observations, he came up with the following three principles and one driving force to explain how biological evolution occurs:

1. *The principle of variation.* No two individuals in a species are identical in all respects; they vary in such features as size, colour, and so on.
2. *The principle of heredity.* Offspring tend to resemble their parents.
3. *The principle of natural selection.* Different variants leave different numbers of offspring.

The driving force, Darwin suggested, was the struggle for existence. In a later edition of *On the Origin of*

common ancestry Darwin's claim that similar living species must all have had a common ancestor.

natural selection A two-step, mechanistic explanation of how descent with modification takes place: (1) every generation, variant individuals are generated within a species because of genetic mutation, and (2) those variant individuals best suited to the current environment survive and produce more offspring than other variants do.

variational evolution The Darwinian theory of evolution, which assumes that variant members of a species respond differently to environmental challenges. Those variants that are more successful ("fitter") survive and reproduce more offspring, who inherit the traits that made their parents fit.

kjorgen/iStockphoto

FIGURE 3.7 Darwin used mainstream ideas about capitalism to explain the concept of fitness. Even though female turtles produce many offspring, such as those seen here, only those whose variant traits best equip them to compete for limited resources will survive to adulthood and reproduce.

Species, he borrowed a phrase coined by sociologist Herbert Spencer and described the outcome of the struggle for existence as "survival of the fittest."

Natural Selection in Action

To illustrate the operation of natural selection, let us return to the problem of how pandas got their "thumbs." Lamarck would explain this phenomenon by arguing that individual pandas all used their wrists intensively to obtain enough bamboo leaves to survive, causing their wrist bones to lengthen, a trait they passed on to their offspring. Darwin, by contrast, would explain this phenomenon by focusing attention not on individual pandas, but on a *population* of pandas and the ways in which members of that population differed from one another. He would argue that originally there must have

been a population of pandas with wrist bones of different lengths (the principle of variation). Because offspring tend to resemble their parents, pandas with long wrist bones gave birth to offspring with long wrist bones and pandas with short wrist bones gave birth to offspring with short wrist bones (the principle of heredity). When the climate changed such that pandas became dependent upon bamboo leaves for food, pandas with wrist bones of different lengths had to compete with one another to get enough leaves to survive (the struggle for existence).

Note that, in this example, "the struggle for existence" does not imply that the pandas were necessarily *fighting* with one another over access to bamboo. The pandas with long wrist bones functioning as "thumbs" for stripping bamboo stalks were simply more successful than pandas who lacked such a "thumb"; that is, in this new environment, their elongated wrist bones made them fitter than pandas with short wrist bones. Thus, pandas with "thumbs" survived and left more offspring than did those without "thumbs." As a result, the proportion of pandas in the population with elongated wrist bones in the next generation was larger than it had been in the previous generation and the proportion of pandas in the population with short wrist bones was smaller. If these selective pressures were severe enough, pandas with short wrist bones might not leave any offspring at all, resulting at some point in a population made up entirely of pandas with "thumbs."

In Darwinian terms, adaptation has been traditionally understood as the process by which an organism "is engineered to be in harmony with the natural environment" because of natural selection (Little 1995, 123). However, this concept contains ambiguities that can confuse the *process* of adaptation with its *outcomes* (also often called "adaptations"). In 1982, paleontologists Stephen Jay Gould and Elisabeth Vrba helped to resolve this confusion by distinguishing among **aptation**, **adaptation**, and **exaptation**. An *aptation* refers to any useful feature of an organism, regardless of its origin.

aptation The shaping of any useful feature of an organism, regardless of that feature's origin.

adaptation The shaping of a useful feature of an organism by natural selection for the function it now performs.

exaptation The shaping of a useful feature of an organism by natural selection to perform one function and the later reshaping of that feature by different selection pressures to perform a new function.

An *adaptation* refers to a useful feature of an organism that was shaped by natural selection for the function it now performs. An *exaptation*, by contrast, refers to a useful feature of an organism that was originally shaped by natural selection to perform one function but later re-shaped by different selection pressures to perform a new function.

The distinction between adaptation and exaptation is important because mistaking one for the other can lead to evolutionary misinterpretations. For example, it has been standard practice to explain an organism's current form (e.g., an insect's wing shape) as an adaptation for the function it currently carries out (i.e., flight). This kind of explanation, however, raises problems. If insect wings evolved gradually via natural selection, then the first modest appendages on which selection would operate could not have looked like—or worked like—the wings of living insects. As a result, those early appendages could not have been used for flying. But what adaptive advantage could something that was not yet a wing confer on insect ancestors? Gould and Vrba (1982) showed that appendages that were not yet wings could have been adaptive for reasons having nothing to do with flying. For example, the original adaptive function of insect appendages was body cooling, but these appendages were later exapted for the function of flying, once they had reached a certain size or shape (Figure 3.8). Specialists in human evolution, such as Pam Willoughby (2007), use the concepts of adaptation and exaptation to explain some of the twists and turns in human evolutionary history.

FIGURE 3.8 How did wings evolve for flight? Gould and Vrba (1982) suggest that wings on early insects were an adaptation for body cooling but later exapted for flying once those appendages had reached a certain size or shape.

Darwin's theory of evolution by natural selection is elegant and dramatic. As generations of biologists have tested its components in their own research, they have come to examine it critically. For example, much debate has been generated about the concept of fitness. Some people have assumed that the biggest, strongest, toughest individuals must be, by definition, fitter than the smaller, weaker, gentler members of their species. Strictly speaking, however, Darwinian, or biological, fitness is nothing more (and nothing less) than an individual's ability to survive and leave offspring. There is no such thing as "absolute" fitness. In a given environment, those who leave more offspring behind are fitter than those who leave fewer offspring behind. But any organism that manages to reproduce in that environment is fit. As geneticist Richard Lewontin (1982, 150) puts it, "In evolutionary terms, an Olympic athlete who never has any children has a fitness of zero, whereas J.S. Bach, who was sedentary and very much overweight, had an unusually high Darwinian fitness by virtue of his having been the father of twenty children."

Clearly, Darwinian theory has been challenged to show that biological heredity operates to produce ever-renewing variation and to explain how such variation is generated and passed on from parents to offspring. Darwin's original formulation of the theory of evolution by natural selection was virtually silent about these matters. Darwin was convinced on the basis of considerable evidence that heritable variation must exist, but he and his colleagues were completely ignorant about the sources of variation. Not until the beginning of the twentieth century did knowledge about these matters begin to accumulate, and not until the 1930s did a new evolutionary synthesis of Darwinian principles and genetics become established.

How Did Biologists Learn about Genes?

Offspring tend to look like their parents, which suggests that something unchanging is passed on from one generation to the next. At the same time, offspring are not identical to their parents, which raises the possibility that whatever the parents pass on may be modified by environmental forces. The question of whether biological inheritance was stable or modifiable, or both, challenged Darwin and his contemporaries.

In the absence of scientific knowledge about heredity, Darwin and many of his contemporaries adopted a theory of heredity that had roots in antiquity: the theory of pangenesis. **Pangenesis** was a theory of inheritance in which multiple particles from both parents blended in their offspring. That is, it claimed that an organism's physical traits are passed on from one generation to the next in the form of distinct particles. Supporters of pangenesis argued that all the organs of both mother and father gave off multiple particles that were somehow transmitted, in different proportions, to each of their offspring. For example, suppose that a child resembled her father more than her mother in a particular trait—say, hair colour. Pangenesis explained this by arguing that the child had received more "hair colour particles" from her father than from her mother. The particles inherited from both parents were believed to blend in their offspring. Thus, the child's hair colour would be closer to her father's shade than to her mother's.

As we know today, heredity is not the result of pangenesis. In the years since Darwin conducted his research, biologists have discovered that physical differences in offspring result from the way new sets of **chromosomes,** which contain an organism's genes, form during fertilization. To arrive at this discovery, they first had to realize that living cells reproduce by undergoing two kinds of division. The first kind, **mitosis,** is simply the way body cells split and make exact copies of themselves. The second kind, **meiosis,** is more central to the question of how offspring inherit traits from their parents. In meiosis, a cell divides its chromosome pairs in half, producing "sex cells" or "germ cells" (sperm and eggs) that contain only half of the genetic material contained in the original cell. When sperm and egg join, the individual chromosomes from both parents combine to create new paired chromosomes, resulting in a unique individual. A major contribution toward our modern understanding of genetic inheritance came from the experiments that Gregor Mendel conducted in the nineteenth century.

Mendel's Experiments

The notion of particulate inheritance was already common in the middle of the nineteenth century when the Austrian monk Gregor Mendel (1822–1884) began conducting plant-breeding experiments in the garden of his monastery. His great contribution was to provide evidence in favour of non-blending, single-particle inheritance, called **Mendelian inheritance**. When Mendel crossed peas with strikingly different traits, some of those traits did not appear in offspring of the first generation (F_1) (Figure 3.9). They did, however, reappear in their original form in the next generation (F_2). Had the particles blended, all the offspring of plants with red flowers and plants with white flowers should have been some shade of pink; but this did not happen, providing strong evidence that the particles responsible for the trait did not blend in offspring but remained discrete.

When Mendel carefully counted the number of offspring in the F_2 generation that showed each trait, he consistently came up with a 3:1 ratio of one form to the other, a factor nobody before him had noticed. This ratio recurred whenever Mendel repeated his experiments. If pangenesis were correct, no such ratios would have occurred because each individual would have inherited an unpredictable number of particles from each parent. However, the 3:1 ratio made excellent sense if, as Mendel assumed, each individual inherited only one particle from each parent (Mayr 1982, 721).

The results of his breeding experiments suggested to Mendel something else as well—that the particle responsible for one form of a particular trait (e.g., flower colour) could be present in an organism but go unexpressed. Those particles whose traits are expressed in an organism are said to be *dominant*; those whose traits are not expressed are said to be *recessive*. (We now know that sometimes both traits can be expressed, in which case they are said to be *codominant*.) Mendel thus concluded

---

pangenesis A theory of heredity suggesting that an organism's physical traits are passed on from one generation to the next in the form of multiple distinct particles given off by all parts of the organism, different proportions of which get passed on to offspring via sperm or egg.

chromosomes Sets of paired bodies in the nucleus of cells that are made of DNA and contain the hereditary genetic information that organisms pass on to their offspring.

mitosis The way body cells make copies of themselves. The pairs of chromosomes in the nucleus of the cell duplicate and line up along the centre of the cell. The cell then divides, each daughter cell taking one full set of paired chromosomes.

meiosis The way sex cells make copies of themselves, which begins like mitosis, with chromosome duplication and the formation of two daughter cells. However, each daughter cell then divides again without chromosome duplication and, as a result, contains only a single set of chromosomes rather than the paired set typical of body cells.

Mendelian inheritance The view that heredity is based on non-blending, single-particle genetic inheritance.

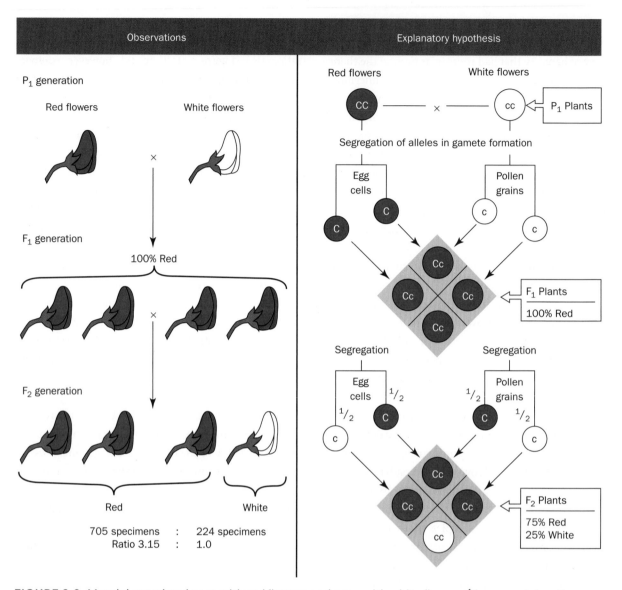

FIGURE 3.9 Mendel crossbred peas with red flowers and peas with white flowers (the parental, or P$_1$, generation). This produced a generation (F$_1$) of only red flowers. When Mendel crossed red-flowered peas from the F$_1$ generation, they produced the F$_2$ generation of peas, in which there were approximately three red-flowered plants for every one plant with white flowers. This 3:1 ratio of red to white flowers, together with the reappearance of white flowers, could be explained if each plant had two genetic factors and the factor for red flowers was dominant. Only a plant with two factors for white flowers would produce white flowers, whereas red flowers would appear in every plant that had at least one factor for red.

Source: From *New Evolutionary Timetable* by Steven M. Stanley, copyright © 1981. Reprinted by permission of Basic Books, an imprint of Hachette Book Group, Inc.

that the particles responsible for a particular trait, such as the pea's flower colour, occur in pairs. An individual

principle of segregation A principle of Mendelian inheritance in which an individual gets one particle (gene) for each trait (i.e., one-half of the required pair) from each parent.

principle of independent assortment A principle of Mendelian inheritance in which each pair of particles (genes) separates independently of every other pair when germ cells (egg and sperm) are formed.

gets one particle for each trait (i.e., one-half of the pair) from each parent. This is the **principle of segregation**. Mendel further argued that each pair of particles separates independently of every other pair when what he called "germ cells" (egg and sperm) are formed. This is the **principle of independent assortment**. As a result, each sperm and ovum is virtually guaranteed to be different from all others produced by an individual because the collection of particles that each contains will be distinct. Moreover, the pairs of particles that come together in any individual offspring are random, depending on which egg and which sperm happened to unite to form that individual.

The Emergence of Genetics

Mendel's insights were ignored for nearly 35 years until two biologists, William Bateson and W.L. Johannsen, rediscovered them at the beginning of the twentieth century, resulting in an explosion of research and vast growth of scientific knowledge about heredity. The British scientist William Bateson coined the term **genetics** in 1908 to describe the new science being built on Mendelian principles. He invented the term **homozygous** to describe a fertilized egg that receives the same particle from both parents for a particular trait and the term **heterozygous** to describe a fertilized egg that receives a different particle from each parent for the same trait.

In 1909, the Danish geneticist W.L. Johannsen suggested the term **gene** to refer to the particle itself. Although genes occur in pairs in any individual, geneticists discovered that there might be many more than two forms of a given gene. Bateson used the term **alleles** to refer to all the different forms that a particular gene might take.

At first, nobody knew what physical structures corresponded to the genes and alleles they had been describing. However, advances in cell biology led some scientists to suggest that the chromosomes in the cell nucleus might play an important role. These sets of paired bodies were easy to see under the microscope because they accepted a coloured stain very well (hence their name, from Greek, meaning "coloured bodies"). Animals of different species have different numbers of chromosomes (humans have 46), but all chromosomes are found in pairs (humans have 23 pairs).

Genes and Traits

Geneticists originally thought (and many non-scientists still believe) that one gene equals one trait. Sometimes a single allele does appear to govern a single physical trait. This may be true of many physical traits that show **discontinuous variation**—that is, sharp breaks from one individual to the next. Recall that the flowers on Mendel's pea plants were either red or white; they did not come in various shades of pink; thus, there is no blending of inheritance. This observation led Mendel to conclude that a single dominant particle (or two identical recessive particles) determines flower colour.

Early research, however, showed that one gene–one trait was too simplistic an explanation for many hereditary traits. Sometimes many genes are responsible for producing a single trait, such as skin colour; such traits are thus said to be the result of **polygeny**. Traits like skin colour in human beings are different from traits like flower colour in Mendel's peas because they show **continuous variation**. That is, the expression of the trait grades imperceptibly from one individual to another, without sharp breaks. The discovery of polygenic inheritance showed that Mendelian concepts could be used to explain discontinuous and continuous variation alike.

Perhaps even more surprising than polygenic activity was the discovery that a single gene may affect more than one trait, a phenomenon called **pleiotropy**. For example, the *S* allele that gives human red blood cells increased resistance to malarial parasites also reduces the amount of oxygen these cells can carry (Rothwell 1977, 18). Similarly, the allele that causes the feathers of chickens to be white also works to slow down their body growth (Lerner and Libby 1976). The discovery of pleiotropy showed that genes do not produce traits in isolation. Many geneticists came to focus attention on what the Russian geneticist Sergei Chetverikov called the "genetic milieu," investigating the effects that different genes could have on one another (Figure 3.10).

↻ For more on the connection between pleiotropy and human variation, see Chapter 7, p. 144.

---

genetics The scientific study of biological heredity.

homozygous Describes a fertilized egg that receives the same particle (or allele) from each parent for a particular trait.

heterozygous Describes a fertilized egg that receives a different particle (or allele) from each parent for the same trait.

gene The portion or portions of the DNA molecule that code for proteins that shape phenotypic traits.

alleles All the different forms that a particular gene might take.

discontinuous variation A pattern of phenotypic variation in which the phenotype (e.g., flower colour) exhibits sharp breaks from one member of the population to the next.

polygeny The phenomenon whereby many genes are responsible for producing a phenotypic trait, such as skin colour.

continuous variation A pattern of variation involving polygeny in which phenotypic traits grade imperceptibly from one member of the population to another without sharp breaks.

pleiotropy The phenomenon whereby a single gene may affect more than one phenotypic trait.

In Their Own Words

Culture: The Silent Language Geneticists Must Learn

The following is an excerpt from a speech that Roderick McInnes, professor of genetics and biochemistry at McGill University, gave at a meeting of the American Society of Human Genetics in 2010. In this speech, McInnes describes how important it is for human geneticists to consider the role of culture in their research and how it is essential to create ethical and respectful community-based research initiatives with Indigenous peoples.

The subject of my address, "Culture: The Silent Language Geneticists Must Learn," occurred to me when I recently discovered a reprint of a favourite book, *The Silent Language*, by Edward T. Hall, first published in 1959. The silent language referred to in the title is culture. He wrote that ". . . cultural patterns are literally unique, and therefore they are not universal. . . . Consequently, difficulties in intercultural communication are seldom seen for what they are." As geneticists and genomicists have reached out to study the world's populations, . . . the opportunities for cultural misunderstanding have grown. In some instances, remarkable progress has been made, both in doing research with Indigenous communities and [in] doing it in ways welcomed by them. In others, the cultural perspective of the researchers, and their more powerful cultural position in society, has prevented them from fully considering the priorities of the study population, . . . and the population under study has been left with a sense of mistrust, stigmatization, or weakened political authority (Manson 1989; Dukepoo 1999). . . .

A geneticist's first impression of an Indigenous culture is similar to viewing an iceberg: what you see isn't what you get. The obvious differences—the visible one-seventh of the iceberg above the water—are only a small fraction of all the distinct features of the Indigenous culture. These surface features poorly represent the larger substratum of profound differences hidden beneath the surface.

My first goal [in giving this speech] is to increase your awareness of the perspectives and concerns of Indigenous populations regarding genetic research. . . . Perhaps the predominant reality for Indigenous populations, with respect to research, is the fact that we, geneticists from Western-oriented cultures, are from the dominant [i.e., more powerful] culture. . . . This fact generally permeates almost all interactions between researchers and Indigenous populations. As exemplified by the experience of Mohatt and his colleagues in conducting research with Alaskan Natives, the researcher must . . . avoid unconsciously sending the "message that the researcher, as someone holding specialized knowledge and language, could tell the community what was right . . ." (Mohatt et al. 2004).

The power differential may be unwittingly and unfavourably tilted against the . . . Indigenous culture before even a word has been spoken.

My second goal is to present examples of both successful and unsuccessful research studies of Indigenous populations and to consider why some succeeded and others failed. Third, I will emphasize that the culture, priorities, values, and jurisdiction of the Indigenous community must be respected and that, in successful studies, they have been. The take-home message is that we must do "culturally competent" research; research that respects the Indigenous community's beliefs, their desire for self-determination, their desire to benefit from the research, and their wish to retain intellectual property rights and ownership of samples of DNA, tissues, and body fluids. One can visualize the ideal dynamic between researchers and Indigenous communities schematically: imagine that a large circle is us, the dominant culture, and that the Indigenous culture is a very much smaller circle within or partially within our culture (see below). The equality of the reach and influence of the Indigenous population over the whole research project can be represented by the arrows radiating out from the small central circle of the Indigenous community to the perimeter of the large circle . . .

One of the first unfortunate interactions between geneticists and an Indigenous population occurred in Canada and involved the Nuu-chah-nulth, a tribe whose people live on the west coast of Vancouver Island in British Columbia (Pullman and Arbour 2009). The Nuu-chah-nulth have a high frequency of rheumatoid arthritis. In the early 1980s, Dr R.H. Ward, at the time at the University of British Columbia, approached the tribal leaders about undertaking a search for HLA alleles that might be linked to the arthritis in this tribe. A study of 900 participants failed to demonstrate linkage. These studies were conducted according to ethical guidelines of the time. . . . The problems arose later. Between 1985 and up to 2000, the DNA was moved to other research centres without the knowledge or consent of the tribe and was used for research that hadn't been authorized. . . . Such misuse of DNA samples for studies outside the original research

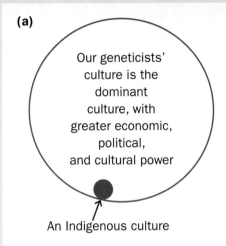

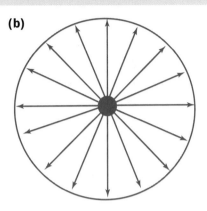

The relationship between the dominant Western culture and an Indigenous population. (a) The view of our culture from the perspective of an Indigenous culture. (b) The ideal equality of an Indigenous culture's influence over research is represented by the arrows reaching to the full perimeter of the dominant culture's circle of influence.

question has been a recurrent problem for Indigenous populations (Lee et al. 2009; Royal et al. 2010). . . .

The perception of researchers that DNA collected for research becomes their property is actually a common problem: once the DNA is taken, . . . it can be difficult for [the Indigenous community] to recover the samples. . . . Regrettably, the outcome for the Nuu-chah-nulth was a sense of betrayal and a loss of trust in researchers. But the tribe responded to this sense of mistrust with action. The elected chief formed a committee to establish conditions to be followed by researchers who wished to carry out research with their community. Subsequently, the Nuu-chah-nulth made important contributions to the development of the Canadian guidelines on research with Indigenous populations (CIHR 2010). . . .

One of the recurrent complaints of Indigenous people about research is that it benefits the researchers and not the population being studied. An Alaskan Native saying perfectly captures the resentment bred of experiences like those of the Nuu-chah-nulth: "Researchers are like mosquitoes; they suck your blood and leave" (Cochran et al. 2008). . . .

[In response to such negative outcomes in the field, m]any Canadian researchers realized that our "investigator-driven" paradigm had to be changed for studies with Indigenous populations. The outcome was the *Guidelines for Health Research Involving Aboriginal People* developed by the Canadian Institutes of Health Research [CIHR]. The community-based participatory approach outlined in these guidelines, and that all of us would be well advised to use, is exemplified

by a study undertaken by Laura Arbour and her colleagues in northern British Columbia with the Gitxsan people (Arbour et al. 2008). In the Gitxsan community, the long QT syndrome and sudden [infant] death are very prevalent. . . . Community members brought this problem to the attention of university researchers. To provide advice and govern the research, the Gitxsan Health Society formed a local research advisory committee consisting of lay community members and medical personnel. Laura's studies showed that up to approximately 1 out of 100 individuals carry [the mutation that is associated with the long QT syndrome]. This prevalence is about 50 fold greater than that found in the general population. . . .

The features of the Gitxsan long QT syndrome research that were characteristic of participatory research were that the Gitxsan initiated the research, participated in the development of the research protocol, and maintained an ongoing advisory and governance role. In addition, there were tribal research assistants, the community reviewed the results with the investigators, reviewed the paper before it was submitted for publication, and agreed with the decision to use their tribal name in the publication. . . .

With respect to genetic research with Indigenous populations, I suggest that we must now be invited into the metaphorical tent of the Indigenous communities. . . . If we succeed, both genetics and the populations of the world will be the richer.

Source: Reprinted from McInnes, Roderick, R. "Culture: The Silent Language Geneticists Must Learn." *American Journal of Human Genetics* 88 (3); 254–61, 2011, with permission from Elsevier.

Gene effects

An unusual case:
one gene = one trait

Polygeny trait:
many genes = a single trait

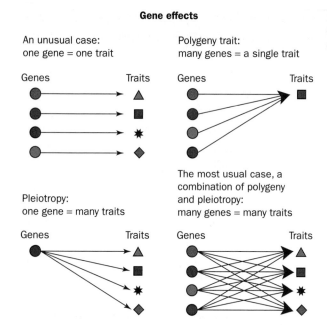

The most usual case, a
combination of polygeny
and pleiotropy:
many genes = many traits

Pleiotropy:
one gene = many traits

FIGURE 3.10 Only rarely is a single physical trait the result of the action of a single gene. Many traits are the result of gene interaction, involving polygeny, pleiotropy, or, as is usually the case, both.

Mutation

Early in the twentieth century, geneticists discovered that very occasionally a new allele can result when the old form of a gene suddenly changes (or undergoes a **mutation**) but that, otherwise, genes are stable. Mutation thus explains how genetic inheritance can be unchanging and still produce the variation that makes evolutionary change possible (Mayr 1982, 755). Being part of a process of stable inheritance means, however, that the occurrence of genetic mutations is random with respect to the adaptive challenges facing the organism in which it occurs: mutations do not occur because the organism "needs" them. Mutations can be harmful or helpful, but they may also have no effect at all (Figure 3.11). Mutations that neither help nor harm an organism are called "neutral" mutations.

Modern genetics, by contrast, assumes that, apart from mutation, genes are inherited unchanged from parent organisms and that it is impossible for an organism's experiences or "needs" to feed back and reshape the

mutation The creation of a new allele for a gene when the portion of the DNA molecule to which it corresponds is suddenly altered.

santiphotois/iStockphoto

FIGURE 3.11 The pale colouration of the white Bengal tiger is caused by a mutation in a protein called SLC45A2. How might this sort of visible mutation be either helpful or harmful?

genetic information in the sex cells. Natural selection can act only on randomly produced variation, which makes evolution by natural selection a two-step process. First, random genetic variation is produced. Second, those organisms whose variant traits better equip them to meet environmental challenges survive and produce more offspring than those whose traits equip them less well.

From a Darwinian point of view, *individual organisms* do not evolve genetically. Barring mutations (or the interventions of genetic engineering), individual organisms are stuck with the genes they are born with. However, the *populations* to which individuals belong *can evolve* as each generation contributes different numbers of offspring to the generation that comes after it. Put another way, from a Darwinian perspective, the only *biological* effect an individual can have on its population's evolution is in terms of the *number of offspring* that it bequeaths to the next generation. More (or fewer) offspring mean more (or fewer) copies of parental genes in the next generation. This is why Darwinian population biologists traditionally track evolutionary change by measuring changes in gene frequencies over time.

For more information on the connection between mutation and patterns of human variation, see Chapter 7, pp. 140–2.

DNA and the Genome

The discovery in the early 1950s of the structure of chromosomes greatly expanded our understanding of genetic mutation. We now know that chromosomes are made up largely of long molecules of **deoxyribonucleic acid**, or

DNA, parts of which are used by living cells as templates for the construction, or *synthesis*, of proteins that make up most of the tissues and organs of any living organism. The DNA molecule, assembled in the shape of a double helix, resembles a twisted ladder, the rungs of which are made up of chemical components called "bases." Although there are many bases, DNA ordinarily makes use of only four: guanine, cytosine, adenine, and thymine. Each rung of the DNA ladder is made up of two of these bases: guanine always links to cytosine, and adenine always links to thymine.

The sum of all the genetic material in the cell nucleus is called the **genome**. We know today that the human genome contains approximately 20,500 genes, but these account for less than 2 per cent of the entire genome. Geneticists know that some non-coding DNA in the genome is involved in regulatory functions, but we remain ignorant of the functions played by much of it. Recent work on DNA and stem cells has the potential to lead to a cure for many human diseases, but it is also ethically risky, as this form of research threatens to modify and even replicate the human genome. Anthropologist Jennifer Liu provides some insight into the practice and promise of stem-cell research and how it is being done in Taiwan (see the "In Their Own Words" box).

Discovery of the structure and operation of DNA solidified the rejection of Lamarckian views by geneticists. Simply put, no matter how useful or valuable a particular adaptation might be to an organism, genetic inheritance provides no mechanism whereby such information could be directly transmitted through that organism's tissues and cells in order to restructure the organism's DNA in a more "adaptive" form. At the same time, knowledge of DNA explained what mutations were: changes in the structure of the DNA molecule. Cosmic radiation, heat, and chemicals can all alter the structure of DNA; and when these alterations occur in the sex cells, they can be passed on to offspring.

Genotype, Phenotype, and the Norm of Reaction

Geneticists realized long ago that the molecular structure of genes (or **genotype**) had to be distinguished from the observable, measurable, overt characteristics of an organism that genes help to produce (its **phenotype**). For example, the sequences of bases on a stretch of DNA (genotypes) are used by living cells to assemble strings of amino acids that bond to form proteins (phenotypes), but bases are not the same thing as protein molecules. How does a genotype get realized in a phenotype? The question is not idle because fertilized eggs do not turn into organisms in a vacuum. Living organisms grow in a physical environment that provides them with nourishment, protection, and other vital resources to support their development over time until they are mature and able to reproduce their own offspring. Without the raw materials for protein synthesis supplied by the ovum, and later by food, genotypes can do nothing. At the same time, just as one gene does not equal one trait, different genotypes may be associated with the same phenotype. Mendel first showed this when he was able to demonstrate the existence of recessive genes. That is, red flowers could be produced by homozygous dominant parents (i.e., both red) as well as by heterozygous parents (i.e., one red and one white); but only one in every four offspring of heterozygous parents would have the chance of producing white flowers (i.e., if it received a recessive white gene from each parent). Nevertheless, individuals with the same genotype—identical twins, for example, or cuttings from a single plant or cloned animals—may also develop a range of different phenotypes (Figure 3.12).

To understand how we get from an organism's genotype to its phenotype, we must consider both genotype and phenotype in relation to the environment in which that organism developed. Biologists compare the phenotypic outcomes of organisms with the same genotype in different environments and with different genotypes in the same environment, and they plot these outcomes on what is called a **norm of reaction**. Levins and Lewontin (1985, 90–1) define the norm of reaction as

a table or graph of correspondence between the phenotypic outcome of development and the

---

DNA (deoxyribonucleic acid) The structure that carries the genetic heritage of an organism as a kind of blueprint for the organism's construction and development.

genome The sum total of all the genetic information about an organism, carried on the chromosomes in the cell nucleus.

genotype The genetic information about particular biological traits encoded in an organism's DNA.

phenotype The observable, measurable, overt characteristics of an organism.

norm of reaction A table or graph that displays the possible range of phenotypic outcomes for a given genotype in different environments.

In Their Own Words

Science, Democracy, and Taiwanese Stem Cells

Jennifer Liu, of the University of Waterloo, discusses her work on the processes and progress of stem-cell research in Taiwan, highlighting the importance of ethically led research and how science and genetic research is conducted in Taiwan.

In the early years of the new millennium, stem cells were being touted as the next big thing in medical science. These cells, it seemed, had the potential to regenerate all kinds of human cells and to treat a variety of seemingly intractable diseases. My own research started with a spark of anger at media stories in North America that seemed to suggest that East Asian countries would race ahead in stem-cell research because, as I heard phrased in various ways, "they don't care about the ethics." Informed by an anthropological sensibility that is suspect of essentializing discourses and that insists that cultural forms and norms must be examined in their specific contexts, I set about to study stem-cell research and its ethics in Taiwan.

Since I'm also interested in the relationship between science and democracy, Taiwan seemed an ideal site. Its complex modern political history includes 50 years as a colony of Japan (1895–1945), followed by 38 years of martial law (1949–1987). Full electoral democracy was established in 1996. Although Taiwan governs autonomously, it is claimed by the Chinese government as a province of China. While many on the island support closer relations with China, many also strenuously resist, and an independence movement flourishes.

Elsewhere, I write about the ways that stem-cell and related genetic research are used by some to articulate a uniquely Taiwanese identity in a biological register. I write about the morning I awoke in Taipei to headlines that Taiwanese researchers had created fluorescent pigs that glowed green "all the way through"; these became a kind of model animal for some kinds of stem-cell research there. I write about how policy was made in ways that conform to international standards of scientific research and democratic governance, and how Taiwanese scientists are, in many ways, transnational scientists, among other things. What I found in Taiwan did not at all support a claim that "they don't care about the ethics." The stem-cell scientific community cares deeply about ethics, but ethics are not necessarily configured in the same way as they are in North America.

Below, I introduce two Taiwanese human embryonic stem-cell scientists working in Taiwan and their respective ethics. They both operate in an ethical frame, but the right thing to do is configured differently and results in different practices for each. They each prioritize different values—on the one hand, of *biomedical* progress and Taiwanese inclusion, and on the other, of specific *bioethical* considerations.

Dr Lee had been recruited back to Taiwan specifically for his expertise in human embryonic stem-cell research. Before returning to Taiwan, he had used human embryos in his research almost without thinking, but after years back home he still has not used a single human embryo. Dr Pan, on the other hand, expands his quest to produce "Taiwanese" stem-cell lines. Both scientists are working on projects of ethical significance for both their science and their people, but they possess distinctly different views and approaches.

For Dr Pan, it involves pushing forward scientifically to develop "Taiwanese" stem-cell lines to include his people, with their unique genetics, in the promise of stem-cell therapeutics. This is made all the more urgent because several medical concerns in Taiwan are perceived as receiving inadequate attention in Western-dominated biomedical sciences.

For Dr Lee, this means delaying his research as he searches for bioethical clarity; this involves both personal reflection and active participation in the development of national policy. He was a member of several committees working on ethics and research protocols, regularly attended meetings, and helped to establish the regulatory structure for biomedical research. For Dr Lee, scientific progress means slowing his bench research in order to get the bioethical and institutional elements in order. His concern is with the inclusion of Taiwanese publics in an explicitly *bioethical* register. He wants to know, of a general public, of Buddhist groups, among others, "what do they *really* think?" and "do they *all* really think this?"

Source: Jennifer Liu, Associate Professor at the University of Waterloo. For more information, see Liu 2012a and 2012b.

FIGURE 3.12 Individuals with the same genotype may exhibit a range of different phenotypes. Identical twins, for example, develop unique fingerprints due to exposure to different environmental stressors in the womb.

environment in which the development took place. Each genotype has its own norm of reaction, specifying how the developing organism will respond to various environments. In general, a genotype cannot be characterized by a unique phenotype.

Different genotypes can produce the same phenotype in some environments, and the same genotype can produce different phenotypes in different environments. Despite very different genotypes, the eyes of newborn babies all tend to be the same colour, as does hair colour as we age. Indeed, the phenotype of a single individual can vary markedly from one environment to the next. As Lewontin (1982, 20) points out,

> People who "tend to be fat" on 5500 calories a day "tend to be thin" on 2000. Families with both "tendencies" will be found living in the same

towns in Northeastern Brazil, where two-thirds of the families live on less than what is considered a minimum subsistence diet by the World Health Organization.

Increasing numbers of biologists are addressing not only the ways in which the organism's phenotype is shaped by the environment in which it develops, but also how organisms shape the environments in which they develop. For example, in their book *Niche Construction*, F. John Odling-Smee, Kevin Laland, and Marcus Feldman (2003, 1) argue that organisms play two roles in evolution: carrying genes and interacting with environments.

> Specifically, organisms interact with environments, take energy and resources from environments, make micro- and macrohabitat choices with respect to environments, construct artifacts, emit detritus and die in environments, and by doing all these things, modify at least some of the natural selection pressures in their own and in each other's local environments. This second role for phenotypes in evolution is not well described or understood by evolutionary biologists and has not been subject to a great deal of investigation. We call it "niche construction."

Niche construction is understood to occur either when an organism actively perturbs the environment or when it actively moves into a different environment (Odling-Smee et al. 2003, 41). If the physical, environmental consequences of niche construction are erased between generations, this process can have no long-term effects on evolution. But if these consequences endure, they feed back into the evolutionary process, *modifying the selection pressures* experienced by subsequent generations of organisms (Figure 3.13). Odling-Smee et al. (2003, 50–115) provide numerous examples taken from all taxonomic groups of living organisms, including blue-green algae, earthworms, dam-building beavers, burrowing rodents, and nest-building birds. Their most controversial proposal is that niche construction be

niche construction When organisms actively perturb the environment in ways that modify the selection pressures experienced by subsequent generations of organisms.

WoodyUpstate/iStockphoto

FIGURE 3.13 Many species, including beavers, construct key features of their own ecological niches. Beaver dams can be extensive, up to 850 metres long, as in this photo of a dam in Wood Buffalo National Park, Alberta. These dams modify selection pressures experienced by beavers, but they also alter selection pressures experienced by neighbouring species whose own niches are altered by the presence of the beaver dam in their habitats.

incorporated into evolutionary theory as an additional adaptive process alongside natural selection and that non-genetic "legacies of modified natural selection pressures" be recognized in addition to the genetic legacies passed on in the egg and sperm. In their view, a suitably extended evolutionary theory would recognize both niche construction and natural selection as evolutionary processes contributing together to the dynamic adaptive match between organisms and environments (2–3).

Taking niche construction into account encourages biologists to look at organisms in a new way. Rather than picturing them as passively staying in place, subject to selection pressures they cannot affect, organisms are now seen as sometimes capable of actively intervening in their evolutionary fate by *modifying the environment*: Odling-Smee et al. (2003, 298) predict that "those members of the population that are least fit relative to the imposed selective regime will be the individuals that exhibit the strongest evidence for niche construction." Alternatively, organisms that *move into a new environment* with different selection pressures can no longer be automatically identified as the unquestionable losers in evolutionary competition in their former environment. Niche construction portrays all organisms (not just human organisms) as active agents living in environments that are vulnerable to the consequences of their

activities, contributing in potentially significant ways to the evolutionary histories of their own and other species.

According to Odling-Smee et al. (2003, 3), acknowledging niche construction as an adaptive process offers a way to link evolutionary theory and ecosystem ecology, and it also alters the relationship between evolutionary theory and the human sciences. They regard human beings as "virtuoso niche constructors" (367), and their arguments should be of great interest to anthropologists, especially cultural anthropologists who insist that any explanation of social and culture change must make room for human agency: the way people struggle, often against great odds, to exercise some control over their lives. The agency of organisms as niche constructors matters in evolution "because it introduces feedback into the evolutionary dynamic [which] significantly modifies the selection pressures [on organisms]" (Odling-Smee et al. 2003, 2; see also Deacon 2003). As we will see in later chapters, we as humans are never free to do exactly as we please but always have options

> ↻ For a thorough discussion of the connection between human niche construction and the cultural process of domestication, see Chapter 9, pp. 184–5.

for action. And the actions we choose to undertake can sometimes reshape the selective pressures we experience, exactly as niche construction theorists would predict.

What Does Evolution Mean to Anthropologists?

Ever since Darwin, evolutionary theory has been subjected to repeat testing. Although the results of those tests have led to modifications of the theory in certain respects, none of them has ever called the concept of evolution itself into question. Indeed, the power of evolutionary theory is illustrated by how the work of Linnaeus, Darwin, and Mendel meshes together so beautifully, even though each of them worked independently. Modern biologists agree that no process other than evolution can explain nearly as much about the history of life on earth.

The study of evolution in contemporary biology is very lively. New evidence and new ways of interpreting evidence have led many evolutionists to question the adequacy of their old ways of understanding and to develop different perspectives on the evolutionary process. They are keenly aware that a phenomenon as complex as evolution requires theoretical pluralism—that is, the recognition that a variety of processes operating at different levels work together to produce the similarities and differences that characterize the living world.

Life has a comprehensible history for modern evolutionists. How it is likely to change next, however, cannot be predicted with any certainty because random factors continue to play an important evolutionary role. Human biologists have been forced to rethink the place of their own species in the web of life. Unquestionably, the result has been to dislodge human beings from the centre. Most contemporary evolutionists would probably agree with Steven Stanley (1981, 151) that "not all paths lead toward *Homo sapiens*, and possibly no persistent path led directly toward him." Indeed, the very notion that organisms are "going somewhere" along a linear evolutionary "path" has been questioned. Stephen Jay Gould (1996, 162) has argued that apparent directional trends in evolution, such as increasing body size, are "really random evolution away from small size, not directed evolution toward large size." He suggests that a more appropriate way to think of the history of life is in terms of expansion or contraction over time in the total range of variation in living forms (i.e., life's "full house"). To do so is to recognize that bacteria have always been the most common form of life on this planet. Organisms of extreme complexity (such as human beings) were bound to appear as the range of variation expanded, but the kind of organisms they turned out to be "is utterly unpredictable, partly random, and entirely contingent—not at all foreordained by the mechanisms of evolution. . . . Humans are here by

the luck of the draw, not the inevitability of life's direction or evolution's mechanism" (Gould 1996, 174–5).

Moreover, once we consider our own species alongside other species whose comings and goings have been so well documented in the fossil record, we cannot avoid grappling with the following well-known facts:

> The only certainty about the future of our species is that it is limited. Of all the species that have ever existed 99.999 per cent are extinct. The average lifetime of a carnivore genus is only 10 million years, and the average lifetime of a species is much shorter. Indeed, life on earth is nearly half over: Fossil evidence shows that life began about 3 billion years ago, and the sun is due to become a red giant about 4 billion years from now, consuming life (and eventually the whole earth) in its fire. (Lewontin 1982, 169)

On the other hand, the story of our species has many unique twists and turns and is far from over. Compared to many living organisms on the earth, we are a relatively "recent" species; yet we have coevolved within changing environments for millions of years using our creative cultural tendencies to modify the world around us. And who knows? Perhaps we will find a way to spread beyond our solar system, and our descendants may escape the grim fate that awaits our planet in 4 billion years or so. In the meantime, we remain on earth, searching for answers about who we are and how we are to live our lives.

Chapter Summary

1. Evolutionary theory is a testable, unified, and fruitful scientific theory. Material evidence of evolutionary change over time can be found in the fossil record and in the pattern of distribution of living species of organisms.

2. Before Darwin, European thinkers divided living things into natural kinds, each of which was thought to have its own unchanging essence. The Great Chain of Being was understood as God's creation, naturally harmonious and without gaps, and it inspired Linnaeus's important eighteenth-century taxonomy of living organisms.

3. In the nineteenth century, catastrophism and uniformitarianism undermined the Great Chain of Being. Catastrophism was based on the ideas of Georges Cuvier, who argued that some species had become extinct in massive natural disasters, after which new species were introduced from elsewhere. Uniformitarianism was promoted by geologist Charles Lyell, who argued that the same processes of erosion and uplift that can be observed to change the earth's surface today had been at work in the past. Uniformitarianism implied that changes in life forms were as gradual and reversible as changes in the earth's surface.

4. Lamarck tried to preserve the view of a harmonious Great Chain of Being by claiming that fossil species had not become extinct. Lamarck argued that individual members of a species are all able to transform themselves in the same way when facing the same environmental pressures. Lamarckian transformational evolution has been rejected by contemporary evolutionary researchers. In contrast to Lamarck, Darwin and Wallace concluded that the similarities shared by distinct living species could be explained if all such species had descended from a single parental species that had lived in the past. In addition, Darwin proposed that such "descent with modification" could occur as a result of the straightforward, mechanistic process of natural selection.

5. Darwin's theory of evolution by natural selection (or variational evolution) was based on the principle of variation, the principle of heredity, and the principle of natural selection. Variational evolution was driven by what Darwin called the "struggle for existence" between individuals of the same species to survive and reproduce. In a given environment, those variant individuals who survive and leave greater numbers of offspring are said to have greater fitness than other members of their species who leave fewer offspring. There is no such thing as "absolute" fitness.

6. Evolutionary theorists use the concept of adaptation to refer both to a process of mutual adjustment between organisms and their environments and to the phenotypic features of organisms that are produced by this process. Reconstructing accurate evolutionary histories of organisms requires distinguishing adaptations from exaptations.

7. Darwin did not know why offspring tend to resemble their parents, nor did he understand how variation was introduced into populations. Answers to these questions were developed in the field of genetics. Genes are associated with particular portions of the DNA molecules located on the chromosomes in the cell nucleus. The machinery of the cell uses DNA to synthesize proteins necessary for life processes and makes it possible for chromosomes to be copied before cells divide. Gene interaction helps explain how continuous traits, such as skin colour or hair colour, are the result of unchanging inheritance. Different genotypes may produce the same phenotype, and the same genotype may produce different phenotypes, depending on the kinds of environments in which organisms possessing these genotypes live and grow. That is, each genotype has its own norm of reaction.

8. The study of evolution in contemporary biology is very lively. Modern biologists agree that life on earth has evolved, but they have different views about how evolutionary processes work. Many evolutionary thinkers are increasingly convinced that a phenomenon as complex as biological evolution requires theoretical pluralism.

For Review

1. How has the theory of evolution been important in shaping how anthropologists view human history?
2. Explain the kinds of material evidence that have been important in the development of evolutionary theory.
3. What are the beliefs that influenced essentialism and the Great Chain of Being? Provide an example from each theory that exhibits these beliefs.
4. Explain the difference between transformational (Lamarckian) evolution and variational (Darwinian) evolution.
5. Using the principles of natural selection, explain to a friend why pandas have thumbs. How does the role of populations factor into the Darwinian explanation of why pandas have thumbs?
6. Create a chart listing the terms associated with evolutionary theory. Provide examples of all terms.
7. Why is the principle of variation so important in evolutionary theory?
8. Explain non-blending, single-particle inheritance (Mendelian inheritance). Why are Mendel's experiments still important today?
9. What is the difference between discontinuous variation and continuous variation? What is meant by the "genetic milieu"?
10. What are the differences between genotype and phenotype? Why are these differences important?
11. What is a norm of reaction? Explain its significance for the evolution of human populations.

12. Clearly, an environment can have a profound effect on the evolution of a population, but what part, if any, does a population have in shaping its environment? Discuss Odling-Smee et al.'s "most controversial proposal." Make sure to discuss the main components of niche construction in your discussion.

Key Terms

adaptation 53
alleles 57
aptation 53
chromosomes 55
common ancestry 52
continuous variation 57
discontinuous variation 57
DNA (deoxyribonucleic acid) 61
evolution 45
evolutionary theory 45
exaptation 53
gene 57

genetics 57
genome 61
genotype 61
genus 47
heterozygous 57
homozygous 57
meiosis 55
Mendelian inheritance 55
mitosis 55
mutation 60
natural selection 52
niche construction 63

norm of reaction 61
pangenesis 55
phenotype 61
pleiotropy 57
polygeny 57
principle of independent
   assortment 56
principle of segregation 56
species 47
taxonomy 47
variational evolution 52

References

Arbour, Laura, Saman Rezazadeh, Jodene Eldstrom, Gwen Weget-Simms, Rosemarie Rupps, Zoe Dyer, Glen Tibbits, et al. 2008. "A KCNQ1 V205M Missense Mutation Causes a High Rate of Long QT Syndrome in a First Nations Community of Northern British Columbia: A Community-Based Approach to Understanding the Impact." *Genetics in Medicine* 10: 545–50.

CIHR (Canadian Institutes of Health Research). 2010. "CIHR Guidelines for Health Research Involving Aboriginal People." http://www.cihr-irsc.gc.ca/e/29134.html

Cochran Patricia A., Catherine A. Marshall, Carmen Garcia-Downing, Elizabeth Kendall, Doris Cook, Laurie McCubbin, and Reva Mariah Gover. 2008. "Indigenous Ways of Knowing: Implications for Participatory Research and Community." *American Journal of Public Health* 98: 22–7.

Deacon, Terrence. 2003. "The Hierarchic Logic of Emergence: Untangling the Interdependence of Evolution and Self-Organization." In *Evolution and Learning: The Baldwin Effect Reconsidered*, edited by Bruce H. Weber and David J. Depew, 273–308. Cambridge, MA: MIT Press.

Dukepoo, Frank C. 1999. "It's More than the Human Genome Diversity Project." *Politics and the Life Sciences* 18: 293–7.

Gould, Stephen J. 1987. *Time's Arrow, Time's Cycle*. Cambridge, MA: Harvard University Press.

———. 1996. *Full House: The Spread of Excellence from Plato to Darwin*. New York: Harmony Books.

Gould, Stephen J., and Elisabeth Vrba. 1982. "Exaptation—A Missing Term in the Science of Form." *Paleobiology* 8: 4–15.

Hall, Edward T. 1959. *The Silent Language*. Garden City, NY: Doubleday.

Kitcher, Philip. 1982. *Abusing Science*. Cambridge, MA: MIT Press.

Lamichhaney, Sangreet, Jonas Berglund, Markus Sällman Almén, Khurram Maqbool, Manfred Grabherr, Alvaro Martinez-Barrio, Marta Promerová, Carl-Johan Rubin, Chao Wang, Neda Zamani, B. Rosemary Grant, Peter R. Grant, Matthew T. Webster, and Leif Andersson. 2015. "Evolution of Darwin's Finches and Their Beaks Revealed by Genome Sequencing." *Nature* 518: 371–5. doi:10.1038/nature14181

Lee, Sandra Soo-Jin, Deborah A. Bolnick, Troy Duster, Pilar Ossorio, and Kimberly Tallbear. 2009. "The Illusive Gold Standard in Genetic Ancestry Testing." *Science* 325: 38–39.

Lerner, I. Michael, and William J. Libby. 1976. *Heredity, Evolution, and Society*. 2nd ed. San Francisco: W.H. Freeman.

Levins, Richard, and Richard Lewontin. 1985. *The Dialectical Biologist*. Cambridge, MA: Harvard University Press.

Lewontin, Richard. 1982. *Human Diversity*. New York: Scientific American Books.

Little, Michael. 1995. "Adaptation, Adaptability, and Multidisciplinary Research." In *Biological Anthropology: The State of the Science*, edited by Noel T. Boaz and Linda Wolfe, 121–47. Bend, OR: International Institute for Human Evolutionary Research.

Liu, Jennifer. 2012a. "Aboriginal Fractions: Enumerating Identity in Taiwan." *Medical Anthropology* 31 (4): 329–46.

———. 2012b. "Asian Regeneration? Technohybridity in Taiwan's biotech." *East Asian Science, Technology and Society* 6 (3): 401–14.

Lovejoy, Arthur O. (1936) 1960. *The Great Chain of Being*. New York: Harper Torchbooks.

McInnes, Roderick. 2011. "2010 Presidential Address: Culture: The Silent Language Geneticists Must Learn." *American Journal of Human Genetics* 88 (3): 254–61.

Manson, S.M. 1989. "Alcohol Study: Emphasis on Its Ethical and Procedural Aspects." *American Indian and Alaska Native Mental Health Research* 2: 5–6.

Mayr, Ernst. 1982. *The Growth of Biological Thought*. Cambridge, MA: Harvard University Press.

Mohatt, Gerald V., Kelly L. Hazel, James Allen, Mary Stachelrodt, Chase Hensel, and Robert Fath. 2004. "Unheard Alaska: Culturally Anchored Participatory Action Research on Sobriety with Alaska Natives." *American Journal of Community Psychology* 33: 263–73.

Odling-Smee, F. John, Kevin L. Laland, and Marcus W. Feldman. 2003. *Niche Construction: The Neglected Process in Evolution*. Princeton, NJ: Princeton University Press.

Pullman, Daryl, and Laura Arbour. 2009. "Genetic Research and Culture: Where Does the Offense Lie?" In *The Ethics of Cultural Appropriation*, edited by James O. Young and Conrad G. Brunk, 115–39. Hoboken, NJ: Wiley-Blackwell.

Rothwell, Norman V. 1977. *Human Genetics*. Englewood Cliffs, NJ: Prentice Hall.

Royal Charmaine D., John Novembre, Stephanie M. Fullerton, David B. Goldstein, Jeffrey C. Long, Micheal J. Bamshad, and Andrew G. Clark. 2010. "Inferring Genetic Ancestry: Opportunities, Challenges, and Implications." *American Journal of Human Genetics* 86: 661–73.

Stanley, Steven M. 1981. *The New Evolutionary Timetable*. New York: Basic Books.

Willoughby, Pamela. 2007. *The Evolution of Modern Humans in Africa: A Comprehensive Guide*. Lanham, MD: AltaMira Press.

▲ Japanese macaques (*Macaca fuscata*) relax in a hot spring pool in Hakodate, Japan. Photo: neptunestocks/iStockphoto

4 — What Can the Study of Primates Tell Us about Human Beings?

Chapter Outline

Our closest animal relatives are the primates. This chapter introduces you to the richness and variety of primate ways of life, and it provides an overview of primate evolution. Primates are fascinating in their own right, but they also can help us understand more about what it means to be human.

Human beings are primates, and the evolution of human beings constitutes one strand of the broader evolutionary history of the primate order. Because knowledge of living primate species offers important clues to their evolutionary past, this chapter begins with an overview of what we know about living primates. Because modern primates have their own evolutionary history but also share an evolutionary history with human beings, we now turn to a brief look at their evolution.

What Are Primates?

Western Europeans first learned about African apes in the seventeenth century. Ever since, these animals have been used as a mirror to reflect on and speculate about

anthropomorphism The attribution of human characteristics to non–human animals.

human nature. But the results of this exercise have been contradictory. The physical characteristics that humans share with primates have led many observers to assume that these primates also share our feelings and attitudes. This is called **anthropomorphism**, the attribution of human characteristics to non-human animals. In the twentieth century alone, Westerners vacillated between viewing primates as innocent and comical versions of human beings (e.g., Curious George) and as brutish and degraded versions of human beings (e.g., King Kong, Figure 4.1). When studying primates, we must remain aware of how our own human interests and habits can distort what we see (Haraway 1989). If you think humans are basically kind and generous, primates will look kind and generous; if you think humans are basically nasty and selfish, primates will look nasty and selfish. Pamela Asquith, a primatologist from the University of Victoria, has been studying the role of anthropomorphism in primatological studies for over 30 years, and she points out that awareness of anthropomorphism has enhanced our

FIGURE 4.1 In the West, primates are often portrayed in ways that embody human fears and anxieties. In the 1930s, the giant ape in the original *King Kong* (a) embodied a racial threat to the power of white males and the sexual virtue of white females. Since that time, our shifting interests and understandings seem to have influenced the 2005 remake of *King Kong* (b), in which the white human heroine and the giant ape become allies in an effort to evade greedy, abusive, and exploitative white males.

studies of primates, adding a more nuanced understanding of their lives (Asquith 2011, 243). She also insists on continued discussions of this topic in order to avoid either romanticizing or demonizing primates so that we might be able to understand these animals in their own right.

How Do Anthropologists Classify Primates?

The first step in understanding primates is to address the variety they exhibit. Primatologists, like other biologists, use biological **taxonomy** to group organisms together on the basis of morphological traits, behavioural traits, and geographical distribution (Mayr 1982, 192). The laboratory technique of DNA **hybridization** allows researchers to combine single strands of DNA from two species to see how closely they match. When human DNA is compared to primate DNA, these strands all match very closely. In fact, the similarity between human DNA and our closest primate relative, the chimpanzee, is as high as 99 per cent (Chimpanzee Sequencing and Analysis Consortium 2005). As we will see in Chapter 6, these kinds of comparisons are no longer limited to the DNA of living primates. New laboratory techniques that permit the recovery of ancient DNA from fossilized bones that are tens of thousands of years old are making it possible to reconstruct evolutionary continuity and divergence as measured in similarities and differences in the DNA of living species and their extinct relatives (Brown and Brown 2013).

Taxonomists classify organisms by assigning them to groups and arranging the groups in a hierarchy based on the seven levels originally recognized by Linnaeus: kingdom, phylum, class, order, family, genus, and species. Biologists continue to assign Latin names to species (e.g., *Homo sapiens*). The species name consists of (1) a generic name (always capitalized) that refers to the genus in which the species is classified and (2) a specific name that identifies particular species (any distinguishing name will do, including the Latinized name of the person who first identified the species). Genus and species names are always italicized. The taxonomy recognized by modern biologists is an inclusive hierarchy. That is, related lower groups are combined to make higher groups: related species make up a genus, related genera make up a family, and so on. Each species—and each set of related species grouped at any level of the hierarchy—is called a **taxon**

(plural, *taxa*). For example, *H. sapiens* is a taxon, as is Hominoidea (the superfamily to which humans and apes belong) and Mammalia (the class to which primates and all other mammals belong).

Contemporary taxonomies are designed to reflect the evolutionary relationships that modern biologists believe were responsible for similarities and differences among species, and taxonomists debate which kinds of similarities and differences they ought to emphasize. Traditional evolutionary taxonomies focused on the **morphology** of organisms—the shapes and sizes of their anatomical features—and related these to the adaptations the organisms had developed. Organisms that seemed to have developed similar adaptations at a similar level of complexity in similar environments were classified together in the same evolutionary division. In traditional systems, the primate order is classified into two main groups: **prosimians** (now referred to as **strepsirrhines**), which includes lemurs and lorises; and **anthropoids,** which includes tarsiers, monkeys, apes, and humans (now referred to as **haplorhines**).

This traditional approach to taxonomy has much to recommend it—especially to paleontologists—because what fossils there are, are often so incomplete that any classification more precise than "group" is likely to be misleading. Paleontologists realize that adaptive morphological similarity by itself is not a foolproof indicator of evolutionary relatedness. This is because similarity can arise in one of two ways: (1) members of different species inherit common features from a common

taxonomy A biological classification of various kinds of organisms.

hybridization When members of two or more different species mate and produce viable offspring.

taxon Each species as well as each group of species related at any level in a taxonomic hierarchy.

morphology The physical shape and size of an organism or its body parts.

prosimians The least complex evolutionary division of primates, which includes lemurs and lorises (now referred to as *strepsirrhines*).

strepsirrhines A suborder of primates that includes lemurs and lorises (formerly called *prosimians*).

anthropoid The primate evolutionary grade that includes tarsiers, monkeys, apes, and humans.

haplorhines The suborder of primates that includes tarsiers, monkeys, apes, and humans.

ancestor (**homology**), or (2) members of different species with very different evolutionary histories develop similar physical features as a result of adapting to similar environments (**homoplasy**, or convergent evolution). Examples of homoplastic traits include wings in birds and in bats; and long, hydrodynamic body shapes in fishes and in whales.

To avoid confusing homology with homoplasy, some twentieth-century taxonomists developed an alternative taxonomic method called *cladistics* that is based on homology alone (that is, on evolutionary relatedness alone). Cladistics attempts to reconstruct the degrees of similarity and difference that result from

> homology Genetic inheritance resulting from common ancestry.
>
> homoplasy Convergent, or parallel, evolution, as when two species with very different evolutionary histories develop similar physical features as a result of adapting to a similar environment.

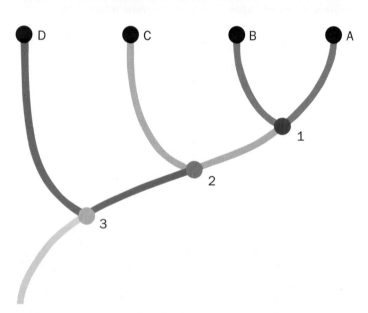

FIGURE 4.2 This cladogram shows the relationships among four hypothetical species: A, B, C, and D. Each is assigned separate species status on the basis of unique, derived traits. A and B together possess shared, derived traits not found among C or D, indicating that A and B share a recent common ancestor (1). A, B, and C together possess shared, derived traits that distinguish them from D, indicating that they, too, share a common—but more distant—ancestor (2). A, B, C, and D are grouped together for analysis on the basis of shared, primitive traits common to them all or shared, derived traits that distinguish their common ancestor (3) from an out-group not shown in the cladogram.

cladogenesis (the formation of one or more new species from an older species). First, cladists must distinguish between homologous and analogous physical traits, focusing on homologous traits only. Then, they must determine which of the homologous traits shared by a group of organisms belonged to the ancestral population out of which they all evolved. These traits are called "primitive traits."

To trace later evolutionary developments, cladists identify phenotypic features shared by some, but not all, of the descendant organisms. A group of organisms possessing such a set of shared, derived features constitutes a natural group called a *clade* that must be recognized in the taxonomy. Finally, if cladists find derived features that are unique to a given group, this too requires taxonomic recognition. A group of organisms sharing a set of unique, derived features that sets them apart from other such groups within the same genus would qualify as a species (Figure 4.2). This way of defining species exemplifies the *phylogenetic species concept*. In recent years, cladistic methods have been

For a discussion of the phylogenetic species concept and other species concepts that have been proposed, see Chapter 7, p. 135.

widely adopted by primatologists and human paleontologists, and the following discussion uses cladistic categories.

What Do We Know about the Kinds of Primates Living Today?

Primates are found today throughout the world, most often in the tropical regions. Some species, such as the Japanese macaque, have moved out of the tropics and into temperate climates. Primates are unusual, however, because, unlike most mammalian groups, their many and varied species are nearly all found in the tropics. Primates are studied in laboratories, in captive populations in zoos or research facilities, and in the wild. Primatologists must gather and compare information from all these settings to construct a picture of primate life that does justice to its richness and diversity.

And primate life is tremendously diverse. Different species live in different habitats, eat different kinds of food, organize themselves into different kinds of social configurations, and observe different patterns of mating and raising offspring. In light of all this diversity, most primatologists would probably caution against taking any single primate species as a model of early human social life (Cheney et al. 1987, 2). Alison Jolly (1985, 36) points out that any species' way of life—what it eats and how it finds mates, raises its young, relates to companions, and protects itself from predators—defines that species' **ecological niche**. And, she adds, "With primates, much of the interest lies in guessing how our ancestors evolved from narrow confinement in a particular niche into our present cosmopolitan state."

Strepsirrhines

Strepsirrhines include lemurs and lorises (see Figure 4.3), which are prosimians that have a rhinarium (a wet-looking, grooved nose) and a cleft upper lip that is attached to their gums by a web of skin (think of a dog's or a cat's nose and upper lip). Other shared, derived features that unite strepsirrhines include the tooth comb (forward-tilting lower incisors and canine teeth used for grooming), a grooming claw on the second digit of their feet, and an ankle bone (or talus) that flares to the side (Fleagle 2013). Strepsirrhine **dentition** (the sizes, shapes, and numbers of their teeth) displays the dental formula 2.1.3.3 (that is, each side of both upper and lower jaws has two incisors, one canine, three premolars, and three molars). Ancient and contemporary DNA comparisons indicate that all the Madagascar species (including the mouse lemur, the smallest living primate) form a clade separate from lorises and galagos,

although more detailed relations among many species remain unclear (Fleagle 2013).

Today, lemurs (Figure 4.4) are found only on the island of Madagascar, off the east coast of Africa, where they were isolated from competition from later-evolving primate species on the African mainland. Humans first arrived in Madagascar about 2000 years ago, and it appears that they were responsible for the extinction of a number of large-bodied lemur species, either by hunting or by destroying their habitats (Fleagle 2013).

Lorises are found in Africa and Asia and possess features in their cranium that differentiate them from lemurs. Both groups live in trees and are **nocturnal** (active at night) and are slow climbers (Fleagle 2013).

Haplorhines

Haplorhines include tarsiers, monkeys, apes, and humans. These are all primates with a dry-looking nose that is separate from their lips (rather than a rhinarium) and a continuous upper lip that is not attached directly to their gums (think of your own nose and upper lip). Some

> **ecological niche** A species' unique position within the ecosystem in which it exists, which is shaped by its way of life (e.g., what it eats and how it finds mates, raises its young, relates to companions, and protects itself from predators).
>
> **dentition** The sizes, shapes, and number of an animal's teeth.
>
> **nocturnal** Active during the night.

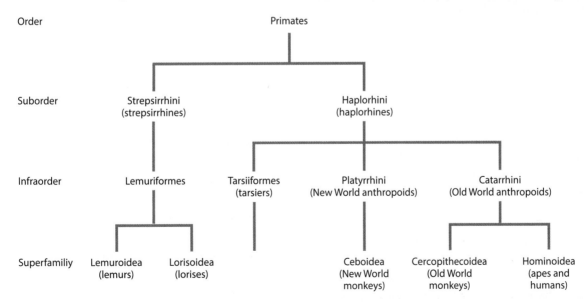

FIGURE 4.3 Cladistic taxonomy of the primates.

Source: Relethford, John. 1996. *The Human Species*, third edition, Mayfield Publishing Company, p. 175.

Edwin Butter/ Shutterstock

FIGURE 4.4 The striking black-and-white tail of the ring-tailed lemur lacks prehensile capabilities (i.e., the ability to grasp), but it serves another important function. During mating season, males compete for dominance via "stink wars," in which they cover their tails with an odorous secretion and wave them at their opponents.

taxonomists emphasize the features all Haplorhini share, and they recognize in their taxonomies three Haplorhini infraorders: Tarsiiformes (tarsiers), Platyrrhini (New World anthropoids), and Catarrhini (Old World anthropoids) (see Figure 4.3).

Tarsiers

Tarsiers (Figure 4.5) are small nocturnal primates that eat only animal food, such as insects, birds, bats, and snakes. Tarsiers used to be grouped with lemurs and lorises, but cladists have argued persuasively that they belong in the same clade as anthropoids. This is because they share a number of derived traits with the anthropoids, including dry noses, detached upper lips, a similarly structured placenta (and heavier infants), and a structure in their skulls called the "postorbital partition" (Bearder 1987).

Tarsier body morphology—a tiny body and enormous eyes and feet—is quite distinctive. Tarsier dentition is also unusual: tarsiers have no tooth comb but resemble lemurs and lorises in the upper jaw (2.1.3.3), although not the lower jaw (1.1.3.3). In other respects, tarsier tooth morphology resembles that of anthropoids (Fleagle 2013, 85).

> prehensile **The ability to grasp with fingers, toes, or tail.**

Noel Rowe/alltheworldsprimates.org

FIGURE 4.5 Although tarsiers used to be grouped together with lemurs and lorises because of similar observable traits, cladists point out that tarsiers share a number of derived traits with the anthropoids.

Platyrrhines and Catarrhines

These groups include New World monkeys, Old World monkeys, apes, and humans. New World monkeys are called *platyrrhines*, a term referring to their broad, flat noses; Old World monkeys, apes, and humans are called *catarrhines* in reference to their downward-pointing nostrils (Figure 4.6). Platyrrhines also differ from catarrhines in dentition: the platyrrhine dental formula is 2.1.3.3, whereas the catarrhine dental formula is 2.1.2.3. In other words, platyrrhines have three premolars, while catarrhines have two. Some platyrrhines have **prehensile**, or grasping, tails, whereas no catarrhines do. Finally, all platyrrhines are tree dwellers, whereas some catarrhine species live permanently on the ground. John Fleagle (2013) reminds us that all these features did not appear at once but, rather, evolved in a piecemeal fashion over millions of years.

New World monkeys are the only clade of primates that evolved in Central and South America. Titi monkeys are the least specialized of all New World monkeys and may bear the closest resemblance to the earliest

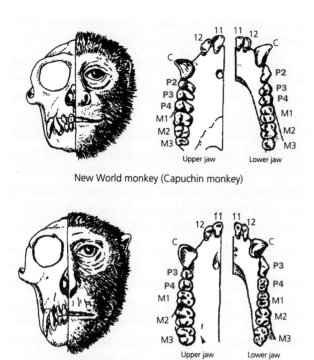

New World monkey (Capuchin monkey)

Old World monkey (Macaque monkey)

FIGURE 4.6 New World monkeys, such as the capuchin, have flat noses with nostrils pointing sideways and three premolars (P2, P3, and P4). By contrast, Old World anthropoids, including Old World monkeys such as the macaque (see Figure 4.9 also), have noses with downward-pointing nostrils and only two premolars (P3 and P4).

Source: Schultz, A.H. 1969. *The Life of Primates.* New York: Universe Books and from Rosenberger, A. L. 1986. "Platyrrhines, catarrhines and the anthropoid transition" in "Major topics in primate and human evolution," ed. B. A. Wood, L. Martin, and P. Andrews, 66–88. Cambridge: Cambridge University Press.

platyrrhines. Capuchins (or organ-grinder monkeys) are well known outside their habitats in the South American rainforest. Some populations in open habitats in Brazil have been observed walking on their hind legs, using tools to break open palm nuts, and making stone tools (Proffitt et al. 2018). The largest New World monkeys are the spider and howler monkey, which have prehensile tails (Figure 4.7). Their tails function much like a fifth limb, helping them to suspend themselves in trees. Overall, the adaptive diversity of New World monkeys is impressive. There is no evidence of hybridization among species of New World monkeys (Fleagle 2013).

Ground-dwelling species of baboons are perhaps the best known of all Old World monkeys. Hamadryas baboons (*Papio hamadryas*) and gelada baboons (*Theropithecus gelada*) are found in Africa. Although

© imageBROKER / Alamy Stock Photo

FIGURE 4.7 A well-known species of New World monkeys is the spider monkey. These monkeys' tails function much like a fifth limb, helping them to suspend themselves in trees.

they belong to different genera, they both live in social groups that possess a single breeding male. However, this superficial similarity turns out to be the result of very different social processes. Hamadryas males build up their one-male units by enticing females away from other units or by "adopting" immature females and caring for them until they are ready to breed (Figure 4.8). They carefully police the females in their units, punishing those that stray with a ritualized neck bite. In addition, hamadryas males thought to be kin form bonds to create a higher-level social unit known as a "clan." Several one-male units, several clans, and some individual males congregate in a band to forage together, and three or four bands may sleep together at night in a troop. By contrast, gelada baboons construct their one-male units on a core of strongly bonded female relatives that are closely influenced by the dominant female and that stay together even if the male of their group is removed (Stammbach 1987).

© Stephenmeese / Dreamstime.com

FIGURE 4.8 Hamadryas baboons live in highly complex, multi-levelled societies. At the lowest level are reproductive units, which consist of one male and several females, followed by clans, bands, troops, and communities.

© ZUMA Press, Inc. / Alamy Stock Photo

FIGURE 4.9 The Japanese macaques of Arashiyama, Japan, are one of the longest continuously studied primate populations in the world. Informal observations began as early as 1948, with formalized studies beginning around 1954; these studies have led to numerous longitudinal primate studies (Leca, Huffman, and Vasey 2012).

The most widely distributed primate genus in the world is *Macaca*—or the macaques—of which there are over 20 species (Figure 4.9). Their habitat ranges from Gibraltar and North Africa to Southeast Asia. All macaque species live in large multi-male groups with complex internal social structures. They do well in a wide variety of habitats and have been especially successful living in habitats disturbed by humans, with whom they

have a long history of interaction in many parts of the world (Fleagle 2013).

Hominoidea is the superfamily of catarrhines that includes apes and humans. Apes can be distinguished from Old World monkeys by morphological features, such as dentition (reduced canine size, changes in jaw shape and molar shape) and the absence of a tail. Traditional taxonomies divide living apes into three grades, or families: the lesser apes (gibbons), the great apes (orangutans, gorillas, and chimpanzees), and the hominins (humans). In recent years, however, many cladists have argued that classification within the great ape and human categories must be revised to reflect the results of biochemical and DNA testing, which show that humans and African apes (gorillas and chimpanzees) are far more closely related to one another than they are to orangutans. Moreover, because chimpanzees and humans share more than 98 per cent of their DNA, more and more taxonomists have concluded that these genetic similarities require placing chimpanzees and humans together in the same family, Hominidae; humans and their immediate ancestors are then grouped into a subfamily called Homininae and are called *hominins* (Goodman et al. 1990). This usage, now adopted by many leading authorities (e.g., Klein 2009, 74–5), will be followed in this book.

However, some biological anthropologists object that using genetics alone to determine taxonomy ignores important evolutionary information. For instance, emphasizing the genetic similarities between chimps and humans ignores wide adaptive differences between these taxa that illustrate Darwinian "descent with modification." These differences help explain why chimps and other apes are on the verge of extinction, largely as a consequence of human adaptive success. Biological anthropologist Jonathan Marks (2013, 251) asks this:

Who would say "nature" is reducible to "genetics" (aside from self-interested geneticists)? Certainly not the evolutionary "synthetic theorists" of the mid-twentieth century (Huxley 1947; Simpson 1949). If "evolution" refers to the naturalistic production of difference, then to say that we are apes is equivalent to denying that we have evolved. Or to put it another way, if evolution is descent with modification, then our ape identity implies descent without modification.

Both traditionalists and cladists agree that gibbons belong in their own family, Hylobatidae. Gibbons, the smallest of the apes, are found in the tropical rainforests of southeastern Asia. Most primate species show **sexual dimorphism** in size; that is, individuals of one sex (usually the males) are larger than individuals of the other sex. Gibbons, however, show no sexual dimorphism in size, although in some species males and females have different coat colours. Gibbons are monogamous, neither male nor female is consistently dominant, and males contribute a great deal of care to their offspring. Gibbon groups usually comprise the mated pair and one or two offspring, all of whom spend comparatively little time in social interactions with one another. Gibbon pairs defend their joint territory, usually by vocalizing together to warn off intruders but occasionally by engaging in physical encounters. Establishing a territory appears to be difficult for newly mated pairs, and there is some evidence that parents may assist offspring in this effort. Evidence also suggests that some young male gibbons inherit the territory of their parents by pairing with their widowed mothers, although these pairs do not seem to breed (Leighton 1987).

Orangutans are found today only in the rainforests of Sumatra and Borneo in southeastern Asia. Their dentition is different from that of chimpanzees and gorillas. Orangutans are an extremely solitary species whose way of life has made them difficult to study in the wild. Adult female orangutans and their offspring occupy overlapping ranges that also overlap the ranges of more than one male. Orangutan males come in two different adult forms, unflanged and flanged. Unflanged males are the size of females whereas flanged males grow protruding fleshy jowls, called flanges, and may be twice as large. Some orangutan populations have been documented demonstrating cultural differences in tool use and vocalization (Fleagle 2013). Biruté Galdikas, from Simon Fraser University, has spent most of her career studying these fascinating primates and has established a foundation (Orangutan Foundation International) to aid in the conservation of their ranges, which are becoming very limited as deforestation threatens to destroy their rainforest habitats (see the "Anthropology in Everyday Life" box about orangutan conservation in Borneo). Many primate species are threatened today, and most

> **sexual dimorphism** Observable phenotypic differences between males and females of the same species.

Anthropology in Everyday Life

Orangutan Conservation in Borneo

Globalization and economic growth have often come at a cost to various species, and in many cases primates in particular have suffered disastrous consequences. Primatologists such as Biruté Galdikas of Simon Fraser University have devoted their lives to the study and protection of endangered great apes, such as orangutans. Galdikas began working with the orangutans of Borneo in 1971, and in 1986 she founded the Orangutan Foundation International (OFI) to protect and revitalize dwindling orangutan populations. The OFI supports reforestation and rehabilitation programs and reintroduces back into their natural habitat orangutans that were captured and sold as pets. The foundation also provides information sessions to the inhabitants of Borneo to help curb poaching and

deforestation. These sessions are guided by decades of research that have been completed by Galdikas and her colleagues.

While mature orangutans are extremely solitary—particularly males, who can roam over a range of up to 40 kilometres—juvenile orangutans are highly dependent on their mothers. Orangutans depend on their mothers much longer than do any other primates, staying up to 10 years at their mothers' sides before becoming reclusive individuals at maturity. During these years, juvenile orangutans learn all they need to know to survive on their own. The rehabilitation program run by the OFI provides support for orangutans that have been taken and removed during this crucial time. Introduction back into the wild can be difficult for any animal that

Continued

has been removed from its habitat for a long period, but this process is particularly challenging for one that has been taken away before it has reached maturity.

In 1971, when Galdikas first arrived, poaching was widespread because various orangutan body parts were being used locally in medicinal products or sold as souvenirs to tourists. At the same time, kidnapping was common because orangutans, like many other primates, are desired as household pets and are often illegally exported to be sold as such. Poaching and kidnapping become easier as deforestation encroaches on orangutans' territory. As plant life is removed and the ecology of the tropical forests shifts, the fruits that orangutans depend upon grow less plentiful, causing individuals to forage farther in order to maintain a healthy diet. The removal of trees and forest cover also exposes orangutans to more predators and makes them vulnerable to human interference.

Since the early 1970s, Galdikas's extensive research has been instrumental in the development and success of the OFI. The reserve where Galdikas has maintained her long-term research project has been designated as a national park, known as the Tanjung Puting National Park. This development is a result of her intensive lobbying efforts in which she advocated for the preservation of the orangutans' natural habitat. From her first field season, Galdikas has done what was popularly believed to be impossible to do: she has cultivated a wealth of knowledge about orangutans, including their habits and their ecology, all the while preserving for future populations of orangutans the swampy lowlands in which they live.

Whether by design or by chance, Galdikas conducted much of her research through forming intimate relationships with orphaned orangutans that took her as a mother. These unlikely children went everywhere with Galdikas, as would infant orangutans with their biological mothers. From these interactions, Galdikas created long-term connections with creatures that are commonly very solitary and often difficult to spot in their forested homes. As the pressures of ever-intensifying globalization lead to deforestation, such efforts to understand species' needs and behaviours in the wild remain essential to finding ways of mitigating the harm too often brought on by human activity.

Biruté Galdikas with orangutans in Tanjung Puting National Park, located in Indonesian Borneo.

Source: Adapted from Yin 2011.

primatologists work to conserve the dwindling habitats of these important mammals.

There are five living subspecies of gorillas, all of which are found in Africa. The rarest subspecies, the mountain gorilla, is probably the best known, thanks to the work of American primatologist Dian Fossey, whose experiences have been popularized in books and film. Mountain gorillas eat mostly leaves. Like the New World howler monkeys, both male and female gorillas transfer out of the group in which they were born before they start breeding. The transfer, which does not appear forced, may occur more than once in a female's life. An adult female gorilla may produce three surviving offspring in her lifetime. Gorillas are highly sexually dimorphic in size, and the dominant

male often determines group activity and the direction of travel. Immature gorillas are attracted to dominant males, who ordinarily treat them with tolerance and protect them in dangerous situations (Stewart and Harcourt 1987).

Chimpanzees (*Pan troglodytes*) are probably the most studied of all the apes. British primatologist Jane Goodall and her associates in Gombe, Tanzania, have followed some chimpanzee groups for over 50 years. Other long-term field research on chimpanzees has been carried out elsewhere in eastern and western Africa as well (Boesch-Achermann and Boesch 1994). In recent years, a second species belonging to the genus Pan, *Pan paniscus*, known as the bonobo (Figure 4.10), has received increasing attention, both in the wild and in captivity. Bonobos are found only in central Africa south of the Zaire River and may number fewer than 100,000; forest destruction, human predation, and capture for illegal sale all threaten their survival (de Waal 1989). The two species differ morphologically: bonobos have less rugged builds, shorter upper limbs, and longer lower limbs than chimpanzees and sport a distinctive coiffure. Both species share a fluid social structure; that is, temporary smaller groups form within the framework of a larger community. Their patterns of social interactions differ, however. Bands of unrelated adult males are very common among chimpanzees but rare among bonobos. Bonds formed between unrelated females are relatively weak among chimpanzees but strong among bonobos. Bonds between the sexes are much stronger among bonobos as well. This means that female bonobos play a more central role in their society than female chimpanzees play in theirs.

Chimpanzees and bonobos eat both plant and animal foods. Indeed, one of Goodall's famous early discoveries was that chimpanzees deliberately make tools to help them find food. They have been observed preparing sticks to fish for insects in termite mounds or anthills, using leaf sponges to obtain water from tree hollows, and using rocks to smash open nuts. Indeed, patterns of tool use seem to vary regionally, suggesting the existence of separate cultural traditions in different chimpanzee groups. Male chimpanzees have been observed hunting for meat and sharing their kill with other members of the group; interestingly, forest-dwelling chimpanzees are more likely to hunt in groups, presumably because the foliage makes their prey harder to secure (Boesch-Achermann and Boesch 1994).

The sexual life of chimpanzees cannot compare with the highly eroticized social interactions typical of bonobos. Bonobo females are able and willing to mate during much of their monthly cycle, but researchers have also observed a high degree of mounting behaviour and sexual play between all members of bonobo groups, young and old, involving individuals of both the same sex and the opposite sex. Studying a captive colony of bonobos in the San Diego Zoo, Frans de Waal and his assistants observed 600 mounts, fewer than 200 of which involved sexually mature individuals, which suggests that this sexual behaviour is likely used to manipulate relationships rather than increase numbers of offspring. Also of note in a discussion of

FIGURE 4.10 Although they belong to the same genus, chimpanzees and bonobos differ markedly in social and behavioural characteristics. Unlike female chimpanzees, female bonobos have higher social status than males and develop strong social bonds with other females, even those who are unrelated.

same-sex sexual behaviour among primates is the research conducted by Paul Vasey, a primatologist from the University of Lethbridge, who has studied this sort of behaviour among Japanese female macaques over the past two decades. In his recent work, Vasey clearly outlines the differences between sexual behaviour in primates and sexual orientation in humans, cautioning against using these studies as any type of evolutionary model for human sexuality or sexual behaviour (Vasey and VanderLaan 2012).

When we try to summarize what makes primate life unique, we are struck by its flexibility, resilience, and creativity. Primates can get by under difficult circumstances, survive injuries, try out new foods or new social arrangements, and take advantage of the random processes of history and demography to do what none has done before (Jolly 1985). Simplistic models of primate behaviour assuming that all primates are fundamentally alike, with few behavioural options, are no longer plausible. As Mary Ellen Morbeck (1997, 14) observes, "Most current models are inadequate when applied to the complex lives of large-bodied, long-lived, group-living mammals, primates, and humans with big brains and good memories." Overall, it seems quite clear that flexibility is the hallmark of primate adaptations.

Anthropology in Everyday Life

Why Do Female Humans Experience Menopause?

Evolutionary theory posits that an individual's main driving force is to be reproductively successful. This is true across all species, yet female humans, unlike all other female primates, experience the end of menstrual cycles—and therefore cease being able to reproduce—decades before death. In contrast, other female primates continue producing viable offspring throughout their entire lives, even when they live to a relatively old age. What, then, might account for such early menopause in humans?

Primatologist Linda Fedigan, an Order of Canada recipient and professor emeritus from the University of Calgary, has investigated this question in some depth. While studying Japanese macaques, she became interested in the differences between the reproductive capabilities of female humans and those of female primates. She noted that female macaques reproduce throughout their entire lives, which is not the case for female humans, who enter menopause on average between 52 and 54 years of age and then continue to live for many more years. After discovering these differences, Fedigan combined her work with data from long-term studies on seven different primate species from around the world and compared it to ethnographic information on traditional societies, such as that of the Ju/'hoansi of the Kalahari Desert (EthnoProfile 10.1). Fedigan sought to establish whether the presence of modern medicine was affecting the time difference between reproductive cessation and death in female humans. However, her results showed that this was not the case. What, then, might account for these differences?

Fedigan notes that there are currently two proposed explanations that might provide the answer. Both have connections to evolutionary theory.

One explanation is known as the "grandmother hypothesis." This hypothesis notes that while it is true that reproductive success is the driving force of all species, the means to this end can differ greatly depending on the life cycle of the species in question. Human offspring are incredibly dependent for a significant portion of their early lives; therefore, they require a great amount of attention from their caregivers—first and foremost their mothers, followed by their fathers and other relatives. Cross-culturally, grandparents play a strong supportive role in caring for children. Thus, for humans, ceasing to reproduce around the age of 40 to 50 and instead focusing on existing children and grandchildren may be the best way to ensure the survival of future generations—to achieve reproductive success. In fact, some evidence gathered from hunter-gatherer populations suggests that young children have better survival rates when grandmothers are actively involved in their care. In evolutionary terms, the grandmother hypothesis suggests that as humans evolved, those who were invested in maintaining the longevity of a few offspring would have been more reproductively successful than those who were interested only in producing as many offspring as possible. This is a great example of "less is more."

The other explanation—and the one that Fedigan believes her research supports—is referred to as the "shelf-life of eggs hypothesis." The basis of this explanation is that because female primates are born with all of the eggs that they will ever have, and because those eggs deteriorate throughout a female's life, there are only a finite number of years that a female primate is capable of reproducing. Evidence to support this hypothesis comes from the fact that both female humans and female great apes—our closest primate relatives—cease to reproduce in their early fifties (on average, between 50 and 52 for great apes and between 52 and 54 for humans). In fact, no female mammal reproduces much beyond 54 years of age. The difference, however, is that while humans tend to live far beyond their early to mid-fifties, great apes do not. Thus, it seems that human females do not actually experience "early menopause" but, rather, "delayed death." From an evolutionary perspective, the shelf-life of eggs hypothesis proposes that while certain evolutionary pressures led to longer life spans in humans, there was no accompanying increase in the number or longevity of eggs in female humans.

Ultimately, both theories have their merits. Moreover, it may be that aspects of both are correct. While we cannot yet draw any conclusions about why there is such a long gap between the end of women's reproductive lives and the end of their biological lives, comparative studies such as Fedigan's have offered us new insights and new ways of thinking about human reproduction. This observation reflects the more general value of studying primates from an anthropological perspective—to help us understand not only where we have come from but where we are today and even where we are headed as a species.

Sources: Adapted from Montgomery 2014 and Rackow 2013.

What Is Ethnoprimatology?

Ethnoprimatology has been defined as the "theoretically and methodologically interdisciplinary study of the multifarious interactions and interfaces between humans and other primates" (Fuentes 2012, 102). As Agustín Fuentes explains, humans and other primates have long coexisted successfully in many global settings, but human activities now threaten the survival of many primate species in the wild. Indeed, ethnoprimatologists call into question the very notion of "the wild," given mounting knowledge that human niche construction is responsible for vast modifications of the living and nonliving world. Some scientists argue that this human-generated (or *anthropogenic*) environmental modification has been extensive enough to initiate a new geological epoch (the shortest geological time period), which is termed the *Anthropocene*: "the current geological epoch wherein anthropogenic agency is one of the prominent forces affecting global landscapes and climates" (Fuentes 2012, 102).

To study human–primate interactions in the Anthropocene requires reconfiguring the focus of primatological field research and broadening the kinds of questions researchers ask. For instance, if we all live in the Anthropocene, ethnoprimatologists must give up on the idea that there are any settings on the planet where primates are able to live beyond the influences of human activity. Acknowledging these multiple entanglements means that ethnoprimatologists must also explore a range of issues that go beyond their traditional focus on predator–prey relations. Overall, "Ethnoprimatology rejects the idea that humans are separate from natural ecosystems and mandates that anthropological and multiple stakeholder approaches be included in behavioral ecological and conservation research on other primates" (Fuentes 2012, 102). (See the "Anthropology in Everyday Life" box about orangutan conservation in Borneo on pp. 77–8).

How have different primate populations fared in their encounters with humans? The great apes seem to face the greatest threats: gorillas, chimpanzees, and orangutans reproduce at slow rates and all require large areas of forest to meet their dietary needs. They are threatened by forest destruction by human settlement and logging, as well as by hunters who capture infants for the exotic pet trade or prize the flesh of these animals as "bushmeat." In response to these conditions, Jane Goodall and her foundation have worked extensively with local communities throughout Africa to conserve habitats, especially for chimpanzees, and to restore previously forested lands (The Jane Goodall Institute of Canada 2014). As Carl Zimmer, science writer for *The New York Times* reported on 18 January 2017, nearly three-quarters of primate species are in decline, and about 60 per cent are now threatened with extinction. Some species, such as macaques and baboons, are better able to coexist with humans. These monkeys are generalist foragers who seem to thrive in areas disturbed by human settlement and are becoming important draws for tourists in Southeast Asia and South Africa.

In many situations, Fuentes (2012) argues, "ethnoprimatological projects provide a particularly robust arena for the (re)integration of sociocultural and biological perspectives in anthropology" (106). This reintegration of perspectives is clear in situations where ethnoprimatologists work with conservationists and local communities to find ways of managing human–non-human primate relations more successfully. Indeed, Fuentes reports, programs of this kind "that incorporate anthropological orientations and multistakeholder approaches show the most potential although in some cases it appears that the human social and economic crises will overwhelm attempts to find sustainable solutions that benefit alloprimates as well as humans" (109–10).

Are There Patterns in Primate Evolution?

How do we begin to trace evolutionary developments within the primate order? The first step is to create a framework for comparison. For example, to trace the evolution of the mammalian skeleton, paleontologists collect samples of fossil mammal bones that span a long stretch of geological time, and they distinguish the bones of the animal's head—the skull, or **cranium** (plural, *crania*), and lower jaw, or **mandible**—from the rest of the animal's bones, its **postcranial skeleton**. Homologous bones of different ages can then be compared for similarities

cranium The bones of the head, excluding the jaw.

mandible The lower jaw.

postcranial skeleton The bones of the body, excluding those of the head.

TABLE 4.1 Primates' Distinguishing Characteristics

Ancestral Characteristics	Evolutionary Trends	Unique Prehensile Features
• Five digits on hands and feet • Clavicle for flexible shoulders • Walking with the palms of the hands and the feet flat on the ground (plantigrade locomotion)	• Increased relative brain size • Reduced facial projection and reduced reliance on smell • Increased dependence on sight and development of stereoscopic vision • Reduced number of teeth • Increased infant dependency • Greater dependence on learned behaviour	• Opposable thumbs and toes • Nails instead of claws • Sensitive pads on tips of fingers and toes • Dermal ridges (fingerprints) on digits, soles, palms, and underside of prehensile tails

Source: Adapted from Le Gros Clark (1963) and others.

and differences. The fossilized and living species grouped together in the primate order share no single attribute that sets all of them apart from other living creatures. What does distinguish primates, living and extinct, are three different sets of features: (1) ancestral characteristics (often called "primitive characteristics"), (2) past evolutionary trends, and (3) unique prehensile features (Table 4.1). In addition, primates are unusual because they are "distinguished mainly by a tendency to retain specific parts that other animals have lost during their evolution" (Klein 2009, 68). This is why primates are often described as generalized organisms that can live in varied environments. So even though primates have adaptive features suited to arboreal ecosystems, they can survive in terrestrial ones as well (for example, baboons).

Ancestral characteristics that primates inherited from their earlier non-primate mammalian ancestors appear in their generalized postcranial skeletons. These characteristics include the following:

- The presence of five digits on the hands and the feet
- The presence of the clavicle, or collarbone, allowing for flexibility in the shoulder joint
- The use of the palms of the hands and the feet (rather than the toes) for walking, called plantigrade locomotion

W.E. Le Gros Clark (1963) identified four evolutionary trends that can be traced across the primate order since the first primates evolved away from their primitive mammalian ancestors:

1. An increase in brain size, relative to body size, and an increase in the complexity of the neocortex (or new brain)
2. A reduction of both the projection of the face and the reliance on the sense of smell
3. An increasing dependence on the sense of sight, resulting in the relocation of the eyes onto the same plane on the front of the face so that the visual field of each eye overlaps, producing depth perception (or **stereoscopic vision**) (Figure 4.11)
4. A reduction in the number of teeth

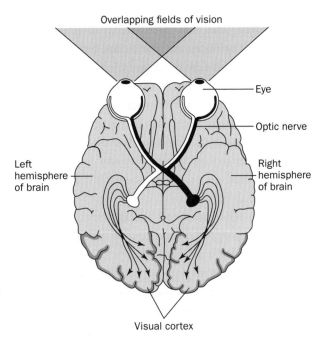

FIGURE 4.11 Primates have stereoscopic vision, which means that their fields of vision overlap, and the optic nerve from each eye travels to both hemispheres of the brain. The result is true depth perception.

stereoscopic vision A form of vision in which the visual field of each eye of a two-eyed (binocular) animal overlaps with the other, producing depth perception.

Some scholars have suggested two additional evolutionary trends: an increasing period of infant dependence and a greater dependence on learned behaviour.

Finally, primates' unique prehensile morphological features include the following:

- Opposable thumbs (i.e., the thumb is opposite the other fingers and can be "opposed to" the other fingers for grasping; most primates, aside from humans, also have opposable great toes)
- Nails rather than claws on at least some digits
- Pads at the tips of fingers and toes that are rich in nerve endings
- Dermal ridges, or friction skin, on the digits, soles, palms, and underside of prehensile tails

Le Gros Clark (1963) argued that primate evolutionary trends and unique features were the outcome of an arboreal adaptation—that is, adaptation to life in the trees. In his view, creatures with excellent grasping abilities, acute binocular vision, and a superior brain are well suited to an arboreal habitat. However, many other organisms (e.g., squirrels) have adapted to life in the trees without having evolved such traits. More recently, Robert Sussman (1991) and Katherine Milton (1993) have argued that switching from insect predation to consumption of edible plant parts and fruit set the stage for future primate evolution leading to grasping hands, visual acuity (including colour vision), larger brains, and increased behavioural flexibility. Combined, these evolutionary trends and unique features are all important when looking at primates.

How Do Paleoanthropologists Reconstruct Primate Evolutionary History?

The following survey of primate evolution begins approximately 65 million years ago (mya) with the onset of the Cenozoic geological era (a geological time period that can be divided into epochs) and continues throughout the subsequent six epochs until the current one, known as the Holocene. The Cenozoic era is divided into six geological epochs, known as the Paleocene, the Eocene, the Oligocene, the Miocene, the Pliocene, and the Pleistocene, listed from oldest to most recent

(Figure 4.12). During these millions of years, the earth's continents moved significantly to end up where they are today (Figure 4.13). Consequences of this continental drift include the creation of new land masses (e.g., islands like Madagascar and Iceland) along with new landforms (e.g., the Himalayan mountains and the Mediterranean Sea). In conjunction with these changes to the land, climate shifted from a warmer, more moderate, wet global climate to a cooler, more temperate climate with seasonal fluctuations. Combined, these modifications to the world and its climate had a direct impact on the evolution of primates, with those primates best suited to their environment continuing to create new generations. Although the first primate ancestors evolved in the Paleocene, around 65 mya (Figures 4.12 and 4.13), anthropoid evolution doesn't begin to flourish until the Miocene.

Primates of the Miocene

The Miocene lasted from about 23 to about 5 mya. Between 18 and 17 mya, the continents finally arrived at their present positions, when the African plate (which includes the Arabian Peninsula) contacted the Eurasian plate. This helps explain why fossil anthropoid from the early Miocene (about 23 to 16 mya) have been found only in Africa. More recent fossil anthropoids have been found from western Europe to China, presumably because their ancestors used the new land bridge to cross from Africa into Eurasia. During the middle Miocene (about 16 to 10 mya), anthropoid diversity declined. During the late Miocene (about 9 to 5 mya), cercopithecoid monkeys became very successful, many anthropoid species became extinct, and the first members of a new lineage, the hominins, appeared.

In the early Miocene, eastern Africa was covered with tropical forest and woodland. One well-known collection of early Miocene primate fossils has been assigned to the anthropoid genus of *Proconsul* (now referred to as genus *Ekembo*). The best evidence, including a nearly complete skeleton, exists for the species *Proconsul heseloni* (Figure 4.14), which was about the size of a modern gibbon (Klein 2009, 117). *Proconsul heseloni* is very ape-like in its cranium, teeth, and shoulder and elbow joints. However, its long trunk, arms, and hands resemble those of modern monkeys. It appears to have been a fruit-eating, tree-dwelling, four-footed (four-handed?) proto-ape that may have lacked a tail. Some argue that it is also generalized enough in its morphology to have been ancestral to later anthropoids,

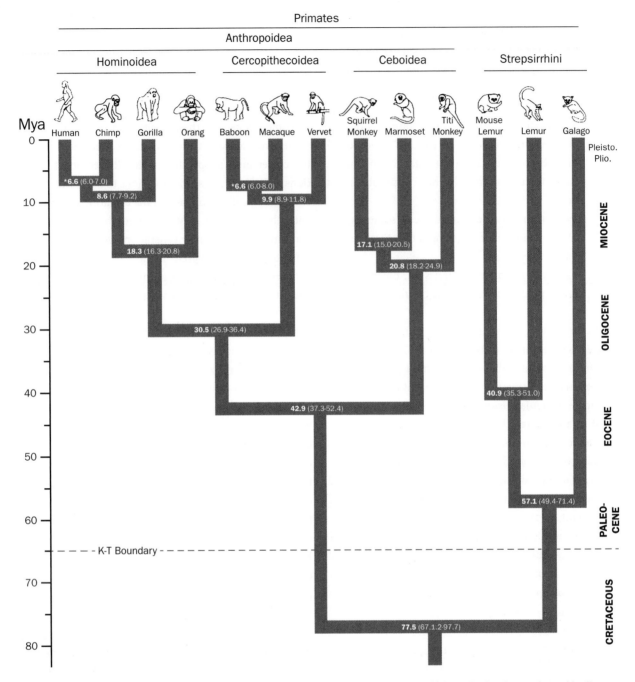

FIGURE 4.12 This timeline arranges the major fossil primate taxa by date and geological epoch and indicates estimated divergence dates in millions of years.

Source: Primate molecular divergence dates, Michael E. Steiper, Nathan M. Young, *Molecular Phylogenetics and Evolution* 41 (2006) 384–394.

including modern apes and human beings, although this is debated (Fleagle 1995). *Proconsul* and other early Miocene anthropoids were confined to Africa and the Arabian Peninsula.

Most taxonomists agree, however, that *P. heseloni* and other early-Miocene anthropoids were outside the modern anthropoid clade. These early anthropoids also retained many primitive catarrhine features lost by later cercopithecoid monkeys, showing that "Old World monkeys are a very specialized group of higher primates" (Fleagle 2013, 322).

The land bridge connecting Africa to Eurasia was formed during the middle Miocene (16 to 10 mya). The earliest fossils assigned to the modern anthropoid

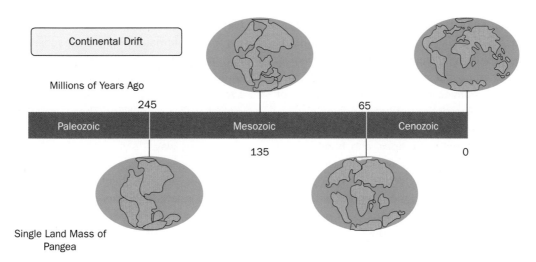

FIGURE 4.13 Across the history of the earth, the land masses that we recognize today as continents and islands have undergone a shift known as "continental drift." By the beginning of the Cenozoic era, the continents had completed much of their separation, but they had not yet arrived in their current positions.

clade date to the middle and late Miocene (10 to 5 mya) and come mostly from Africa, although one genus, *Kenyapithecus*, is also represented by a second species from Turkey (Fleagle 2013). Once anthropoids made it out of Africa, they experienced a rapid radiation throughout many parts of the Old World, and their fossils remain difficult to classify. Unfortunately, very few African anthropoid fossils of any kind date from the late Miocene (10 to 5 mya) or the early Pliocene (5 to 2.5 mya) (Benefit and McCrossin 1995, 251).

Recent finds of a 13-million-year-old complete skull of a Nyanzapithecus provides new data that may identify the common ancestor of African apes and human beings. The combined evidence from the skull suggests that Nyanzapithecines were early anthropoids, possibly the origin of extant apes (Nengo et al. 2017). With this, we know that it was during the late Miocene that the first ancestors in our own lineage appeared. Tracing their evolutionary history is the topic of the next chapter.

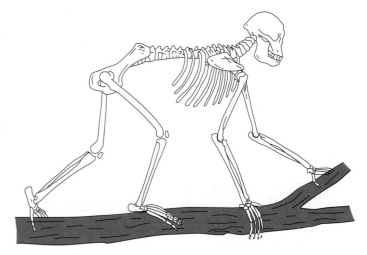

FIGURE 4.14 *Proconsul* is perhaps the best known of the earliest African anthropoids. Some argue that *Proconsul* is generalized enough in its morphology to have been ancestral to later anthropoids, including modern apes and human beings, although this is debated.

Chapter Summary

1. If we avoid anthropomorphism, careful comparison between human beings and primate species has the potential to offer enormous insight into our evolutionary past. Primatologists attempt to make sense of primate diversity by creating primate taxonomies. Traditional taxonomies of primates compared the phenotypes and adaptations of primates and recognized four primate grades. Cladistic

taxonomies ignore adaptation and the fossil record and classify organisms only on the basis of homologous evolutionary traits found in living species. Many primatologists combine features of both kinds of taxonomies to demonstrate relations of evolutionary relatedness between species.

2. Strepsirrhines include lemurs and lorises. Haplorhines include tarsiers, monkeys, apes, and humans and have forms that are distinctly identified as New World and Old World. New World monkeys evolved separately from Old World monkeys and differ from them in nose shape and the number of premolars; in addition, some New World monkeys evolved prehensile tails. All New World monkey species are tree dwellers.

3. Old World haplorhines include species of monkeys and apes, as well as human beings; all share the same nose shape and the same number of premolars. Apes are distinguished from Old World monkeys by dentition, skeletal shape and size, and the absence of a tail. The African apes are far more closely related to one another than to gibbons or orangutans, and human beings are more closely related to chimpanzees than to any other ape species. Chimpanzees deliberately make simple tools to help them find food. Bonobos are known for their highly eroticized social interactions and for the central role females play in their society.

4. Primates are distinguished from other species through a number of ancestral characteristics, evolutionary trends, and unique features associated with prehensility. These evolutionary developments have not affected all primate species in the same way.

5. Paleontologists assign primate fossils to various categories after examining and comparing cranial and postcranial skeletal material. They have concluded that the first undisputed primates appeared during the Eocene.

6. The first haplorhines that evolved in Africa during the early Miocene were very diverse. One of the best-known examples is *Proconsul heseloni*, which is generalized enough to have been ancestral to later apes and human beings. During the middle Miocene, haplorhines rapidly spread and diversified, and their fossils are found from Europe to eastern Asia. In the late Miocene, many haplorhines species became extinct. Paleoanthropologists agree that chimpanzees, gorillas, and human beings shared a common ancestor, possibly known as Nyanzapithecus, in the late Miocene.

For Review

1. As our closest evolutionary cousins, primates are often viewed by humans as living insights into our own evolutionary history. But what are some dangers of ascribing human traits to primates, and vice versa?

2. How do biologists classify primates? What are the advantages and disadvantages of the major approaches to taxonomy discussed at the beginning of this chapter?

3. Distinguish between homology and homoplasy. Comparing different species, what might be some examples of each?

4. What are clades? Illustrate with examples.

5. Summarize in a chart the names and features used to distinguish different kinds of primates from each other. What is distinctive about the platyrrhines and catarrhines?

6. Discuss the differences and similarities of chimpanzees and bonobos.

7. In what ways do ancestral characteristics, evolutionary trends, and unique morphological features distinguish primates from other species? What are some examples?

8. What adaptive explanations do paleoanthropologists give for the unique prehensile features of primates? Do you find these explanations convincing?

Key Terms

anthropoid 71
anthropomorphism 70
cranium 81
dentition 73
ecological niche 73
haplorhines 71
homology 72

homoplasy 72
hybridization 71
mandible 81
morphology 71
nocturnal 73
postcranial skeleton 81
prehensile 74

prosimian 71
sexual dimorphism 77
stereoscopic vision 82
strepsirrhines 71
taxon 71
taxonomy 71

References

Asquith, Pamela. 2011. "Of Bonds and Boundaries: What Is the Modern Role of Anthropomorphism in Primatological Studies?" *American Journal of Primatology* 73 (3): 238–44.

Bearder, Simon K. 1987. "Lorises, Bushbabies, and Tarsiers: Diverse Societies in Solitary Foragers." In *Primate Societies*, edited by Barbara Smuts, Dorothy Cheney, Robert Seyfarth, Richard Wrangham, and Thomas Struhsaker, 11–24. Chicago: University of Chicago Press.

Benefit, Brenda, and Monte L. McCrossin. 1995. "Miocene Hominoids and Hominid Origins." *Annual Review of Anthropology* 24: 237–56.

Boesch-Achermann, Hedwige, and Christophe Boesch. 1994. "Hominization in the Rainforest: The Chimpanzee's Piece of the Puzzle." *Evolutionary Anthropology* 3 (1): 9–16.

Brown, Keri A., and Terence A. Brown. 2013. "Biomolecular Archaeology." *Annual Review of Anthropology* 42: 159–74.

Cheney, Dorothy L., Robert M. Seyfarth, Barbara B. Smuts, and Richard W. Wrangham. 1987. "The Study of Primate Societies." In *Primate Societies*, edited by Barbara Smuts, Dorothy Cheney, Robert Seyfarth, Richard Wrangham, and Thomas Struhsaker, 1–10. Chicago: University of Chicago Press.

Chimpanzee Sequencing and Analysis Consortium. 2005. "Initial Sequence of the Chimpanzee Genome and Comparison with the Human Genome." *Nature* 437: 69–87. doi:10.1038/nature04072

de Waal, Frans. 1989. *Peacemaking among Primates*. Cambridge, MA: Harvard University Press.

Fleagle, John G. 1995. "Origin and Radiation of Anthropoid Primates." In *Biological Anthropology: The State of the Science*, edited by Noel T. Boaz and Linda Wolfe, 1–21. Bend, OR: International Institute for Human Evolutionary Research.

———. 2013. *Primate Adaptation and Evolution*. 3rd ed. Amsterdam: Elsevier/Academic Press.

Fuentes, Augustín. 2012. "Ethnoprimatology and the Anthropology of the Human-Primate Interface." *Annual Review of Anthropology* 41: 202–47.

Goodman, Morris, Danilo A. Tagle, David Fitch, Wendy Bailey, John Czelusniak, Ben Koop, Philip Benson, and Jerry L. Slightom. 1990. "Primate Evolution at the DNA Level and a Classification of the Hominoids." *Journal of Molecular Evolution* 30: 260–6.

Haraway, Donna. 1989. *Primate Visions*. New York: Routledge.

The Jane Goodall Institute of Canada. 2014. https://janegoodall.ca/

Jolly, Alison. 1985. *The Evolution of Primate Behaviour*. 2nd ed. New York: Macmillan.

Klein, Richard G. 2009. *The Human Career: Human Biological and Cultural Origins*. 3rd ed. Chicago: University of Chicago Press.

Leca, Jean-Baptiste, Michael A. Huffman, and Paul L. Vasey, eds. 2012. *The Monkeys of Stormy Mountain: Sixty Years of Primatological Research on the Japanese Macaques of Arashiyama*. Cambridge Studies in Biological and Evolutionary Anthropology, no. 61. Cambridge: Cambridge University Press.

Le Gros Clark, W.E. 1963. *The Antecedents*. 2nd ed. New York: Harper and Row.

Leighton, Donna Robbins. 1987. "Gibbons: Territoriality and Monogamy." In *Primate Societies*, edited by Barbara Smuts, Dorothy Cheney, Robert Seyfarth, Richard Wrangham, and Thomas Struhsaker, 135–45. Chicago: University of Chicago Press.

Marks, Jonathan. 2013. "The Nature/Culture of Genetic Facts." *Annual Review of Anthropology* 42: 247–67. doi:10.1146/annurev-anthro-092412-155558

Mayr, Ernst. 1982. *The Growth of Biological Thought*. Cambridge, MA: Harvard University Press.

Milton, Katherine. 1993. "Diet and Primate Evolution." *Scientific American* 269 (2): 86–93.

Montgomery, Marc. 2014. "Hot Flashes—Unique to Human Females." Radio Canada International. http://www.rcinet.ca/en/2014/01/08/hot-flashes-unique-to-human-females

Morbeck, Mary Ellen. 1997. "Life History, the Individual and Evolution." In *The Evolutionary Female: A Life-History Perspective*, edited by Mary Ellen Morbeck, Alison Galloway, and Adrienne Zihlman, 3–14. Princeton, NJ: Princeton University Press.

Nengo, Isaiah, et al. 2017. "New Infant Cranium from the African Miocene Sheds Light on Ape Evolution." *Nature* 548: 169–74.

Proffitt, Tomos, Michael Haslam, J.F. Mercader, Christophe Boesch, Lydia Luncz. 2018. "Revisiting Panda 100, the First Archaeological Chimpanzee Nut-Cracking Site." *Journal of Human Evolution* 124: 117–39.

Rackow, Frank. 2013. "The Upside to Menopause." *Homestretch*. CBC Radio One. http://www.cbc.ca/player/Radio/Local+Shows/Alberta/The+Homestretch/ID/2415513090/

Stammbach, Eduard. 1987. "Desert, Forest and Montane Baboons: Multilevel Societies." In *Primate Societies*, edited by Barbara Smuts, Dorothy Cheney, Robert Seyfarth, Richard Wrangham, and Thomas Struhsaker, 112–20. Chicago: University of Chicago Press.

Stewart, Kelly J, and Alexander H. Harcourt. 1987. "Gorillas: Variation in Female Relationships." In *Primate Societies*, edited by Barbara

Smuts, Dorothy Cheney, Robert Seyfarth, Richard Wrangham, and Thomas Struhsaker, 155–64. Chicago: University of Chicago Press.

Sussman, Robert. 1991. "Primate Origins and the Evolution of Angiosperms." *American Journal of Physical Anthropology* 23: 209–23.

Vasey, Paul, and Doug VanderLaan. 2012. "Is Female Homosexual Behavior in Japanese Macaques Truly Sexual?" In *The Monkeys of Stormy Mountain: Sixty Years of Primatological Research on the Japanese Macaques of Arashiyama,* edited by Jean-Baptiste Leca, Michael A. Huffman, and Paul L. Vasey, 153–72. Cambridge: Cambridge University Press.

Yin, Steph. 2011. "Scientist Sunday: Leakey's Angels Part III, Biruté Galdikas." *Ink-Chroma.* http://inkchromatography.wordpress.com /2011/12/20/scientist-sunday-leakeys-angels-part-iii-birute-galdikas/

Zimmer, Carl. 2017. "Most Primate Species Threatened with Extinction, Scientists Find." *The New York Times,* 18 January. https://www .nytimes.com/2017/01/18/science/almost-two-thirds-of-primate-species-near-extinction-scientists-find.html

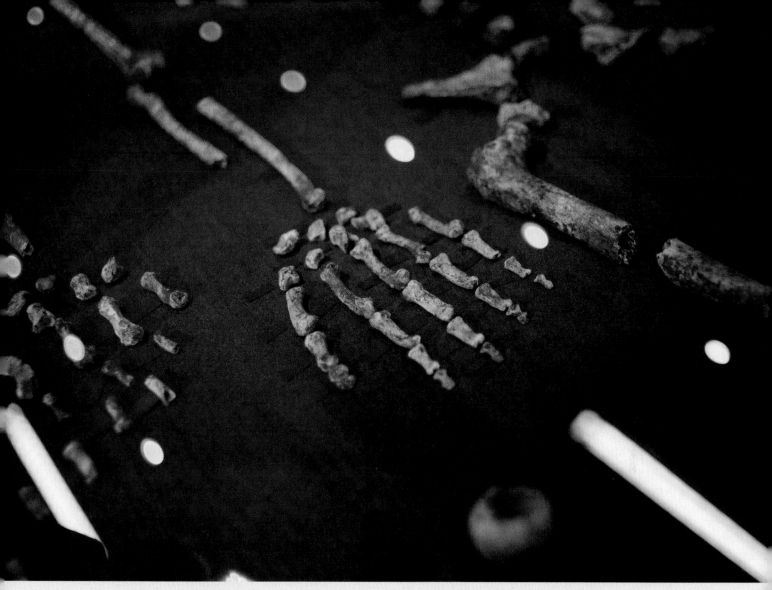

▲ Skeletons of *Homo naledi* were discovered at the Cradle of Humankind World Heritage Site outside Johannesburg, South Africa, in 2013. Standing at about 1.5 metres (5 feet) tall and weighing approximately 45 kilograms (100 pounds), *H. naledi* presents a striking combination of australopith-like and human-like features that help anthropologists understand hominin evolution. Photo: STEFAN HEUNIS/AFP/Getty Images

5 What Can the Fossil Record Tell Us about Human Origins?

Chapter Outline

Anthropology has made major contributions to our understanding of human biological and cultural evolution. This chapter tells the story of what we have learned from fossils, stone tools, and other cultural remains, from the appearance of our earliest known ancestors about 6 million years ago, including the appearance of *Homo erectus* and the migration of these hominins out of Africa and into new areas of the world.

Chapter 3 presented some of the central concepts of modern evolutionary theory, and Chapter 4 used some of these to locate human beings in the primate order. In this chapter, we look at the fossil record for evidence of the evolution of our species. As such, this chapter will adapt the perspective of macroevolution, which focuses on long-term evolutionary changes, including the origins of new species and their modifications across millions of years. **Macroevolution** is measured in geological time, spanning many generations and many ecological settings. **Microevolution**, by contrast, focuses on short-term evolutionary changes that generally occur within a given species over a few generations. It is measured in what is considered "ecological time" or the pace of time as experienced by organisms living and adapting to their ecological settings. The study of microevolution and how these processes are affecting the human species will be presented in Chapter 7.

What Is Macroevolution?

Macroevolution studies evolution at or above the species level over extremely long stretches of geological time and is concerned with tracing (and explaining) the extinction of old species and the origin of new species. Evidence for these processes comes from close study of fossils and of the comparative anatomy of living organisms. As we shall see, the way we understand macroevolution shapes our understanding of human evolution.

Until the 1970s, most evolutionary biologists were convinced that the problems of macroevolution had been solved in a satisfactory manner by Darwin himself. Darwin claimed, and neo-Darwinians agreed, that macroevolution—the origin of new species—is simply what happens when microevolution continues over a long enough period of time. Such a view seemed plausible because, as we have seen, all these evolutionary thinkers assumed that, over time, genetic and environmental changes are inevitable. Mutation (if unchecked by natural selection) inevitably changes a species' physical attributes over time in the same way that the natural environment, perpetually subject to uniformitarian processes of erosion and uplift, never remains constant. Evolution was thought to occur when independent processes of genetic change and environmental change intersect in the phenotypes of organisms living in a particular habitat.

In his final formulation of the theory of natural selection, Darwin argued that there is no such thing as a fixed species, precisely because evolution is gradual. And evolution is gradual because environments change slowly. Lamarck's concept of long-term evolutionary change was also gradualistic, except that he pictured *individual members* of a long-lived natural kind (and their offspring) tracking the changing environment over a long period of time. For Darwin, however, one species gradually transforms itself over time into a new species, a process called **anagenesis**, although the actual boundary between species can never be detected but only drawn arbitrarily. Darwin's theory of the origin of new species is called **phyletic gradualism** (Figure 5.1 and Table 5.1).

Arguing for phyletic gradualism made a lot of sense in Darwin's day, given the kind of opposition he faced; and it has many defenders today. But some biologists

macroevolution A subfield of evolutionary studies that focuses on long-term evolutionary changes, especially the origins of new species and their diversification across space and over millions of years of geological time.

microevolution A subfield of evolutionary studies that devotes attention to short-term evolutionary changes that occur within a given species over relatively few generations of ecological time.

anagenesis The slow, gradual transformation of a single species over time.

phyletic gradualism A theory arguing that one species gradually transforms itself into a new species over time, yet the actual boundary between species can never be detected but only drawn arbitrarily.

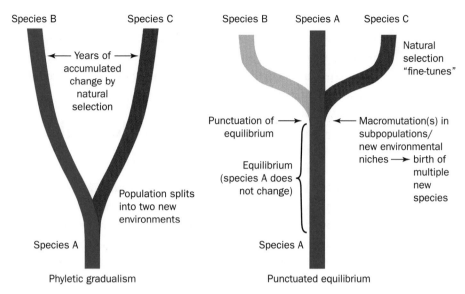

FIGURE 5.1 Two models of macroevolution: phyletic gradualism (left) and punctuated equilibrium (right). Research and theories about punctuated equilibrium have challenged the common neo–Darwinian understanding of speciation by means of phyletic gradualism.

have argued that phyletic gradualism does not explain a number of things that evolutionary theory must explain. In particular, it cannot explain the fact that a single fossil species often seems to have given birth to a number of descendant species, a process called **cladogenesis**. What about those breaks in the fossil record that led Georges Cuvier to argue that old species disappeared, and new species appeared with what, from the point of view of geological time, was extreme rapidity? Is this just the result of poor preservation of intermediate forms, or do new species arise suddenly without having to go through any drawn-out intermediate stages? Or do the

fossils that we thought represented intermediate stages in the anagenesis of a single species actually belong to several different species that resulted from the process of cladogenesis?

In the early 1970s, these problems led evolutionists Stephen Jay Gould and Niles Eldredge to propose that the rate and manner of evolutionary change may differ at the level of genes, of organisms, and of species. They argued

cladogenesis The birth of a variety of descendant species from a single ancestral species.

TABLE 5.1 Models of Macroevolution

	Phyletic Gradualism	Punctuated Equilibrium
Originator(s)	Charles Darwin (in the late 1800s)	Stephen Jay Gould and Niles Eldredge (in the 1970s)
Macroevolution	A uniform process, the eventual outcome of microevolution, given enough time	*Different* from microevolution, not a uniform process
Motor of Speciation	The result of *anagenesis*, the gradual transformation of one species into another species	The result of *cladogenesis*, the rapid production of multiple new species alongside parent species
Species Boundary	Species boundaries are arbitrary	Species boundaries are real
Consequences	No sharp breaks in fossil record between old and new species	Speciation achieves the shifting of "genetic and morphological centres of gravity of parent and daughter species" such that "each species is now free to accumulate more variation and hence more potential species differences" (Tattersall 1998, 163)

↺ The similarities between living primates and humans are outlined in Chapter 4, on pp. 82–3.

that patterns in the fossil record (including the patterns Cuvier had recognized) suggest that phyletic gradualism might not explain all cases of evolutionary change. Between the breaks in the fossil record, many fossil species show little—if any—change for millions of years. Moreover, it is often the case that new species appear in the fossil record alongside their unchanged ancestors (Eldredge and Tattersall 1982). We find evidence of this phenomenon when we compare ourselves to the other living primates. Gould and Eldredge (1977) contended that evolutionary change is not a uniform process but, rather, that most of evolutionary history has been characterized by relatively stable species coexisting in equilibrium (plural, *equilibria*). Occasionally, however, that equilibrium is punctuated by sudden bursts of speciation, when extinctions are widespread and many new species appear. This view is called the theory of **punctuated equilibrium** (see Figure 5.1 and Table 5.1).

But if phyletic gradualism is not the rule, where do new species come from? Gould and Eldredge (1977) argue that drastic changes in the natural environment trigger extinction and speciation by destroying habitats and breaking reproductive communities apart. When this happens, the populations that remain have both a radically modified gene pool and the opportunity to construct a new niche in a radically modified environment. When adaptive equilibria are punctuated this way, speciation is still thought to require thousands or hundreds of thousands of years to be completed. From the perspective of ecological time, the process still appears "gradual," but from the perspective of geological time, speciation appears "rapid" when compared to the long periods of stasis that precede and follow it.

punctuated equilibrium **A theory claiming that most of evolutionary history has been characterized by relatively stable species coexisting in an equilibrium that is occasionally punctuated by sudden bursts of speciation, when extinctions are widespread and many new species appear.**

bipedalism **Walking on two feet.**

australopiths **An informal term used to refer to all hominins that were the earliest bipedal hominins.**

mosaic evolution **A process of change over time in which different phenotypic traits, responding to different selection pressures, may evolve at different rates.**

These suggestions regarding punctuated equilibria remain highly controversial. Many modern evolutionary biologists remain convinced that phyletic gradualism is well supported by the fossil records of many species.

What Is Hominin Evolution?

About 10 million years ago (mya), when the Miocene epoch was ending, grasslands increased at the expense of forests, and many species of haplorhines became extinct throughout Europe, Asia, and Africa. Some African haplorhines seem to have adapted to the changed conditions by spending more time on the ground, a move that apparently exposed them to new selective pressures favouring **bipedalism**—walking on two feet rather than four. *Hominins* (bipedal hominoids) first appeared in Africa at the end of the Miocene or beginning of the Pliocene, between 10 and 5 mya.

As we saw in Chapter 4, contemporary taxonomists classify the African great apes and humans together as *hominoids*; and within the hominoid category, they separate out humans and other bipedal species, who are classified together as *hominins*. Within the hominin category, a further distinction is also commonly made between recent hominin species assigned to the genus *Homo* and earlier hominin species assigned to such genera as *Ardipithecus*, *Australopithecus*, or *Paranthropus*. Several authorities informally refer to all these earlier hominins as **australopiths**, and that is what we will do here.

Fossil hominins are grouped together with living human beings because of a set of skeletal features that indicate habitual bipedalism, a feature that seems to be the first of our distinctive anatomical traits to have appeared (Figure 5.2). Hominin evolution has also been marked by additional evolutionary changes in dentition. Finally, some hominins developed an expanded brain and ultimately came to depend on tools and language—that is, on culture—for their survival (Table 5.2). These developments did not occur all at once but were the result of **mosaic evolution** (different traits evolving at different rates). For this reason, anthropologists speak of the evolution of our species as a process, not an event, using the term *human origins* (Silcox 2013).

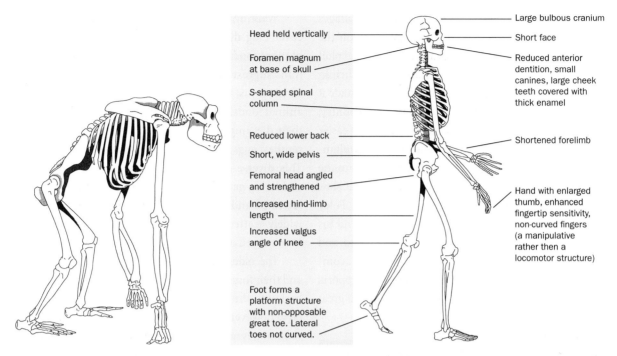

Head held vertically

Foramen magnum at base of skull

S-shaped spinal column

Reduced lower back

Short, wide pelvis

Femoral head angled and strengthened

Increased hind-limb length

Increased valgus angle of knee

Foot forms a platform structure with non-opposable great toe. Lateral toes not curved.

Large bulbous cranium

Short face

Reduced anterior dentition, small canines, large cheek teeth covered with thick enamel

Shortened forelimb

Hand with enlarged thumb, enhanced fingertip sensitivity, non-curved fingers (a manipulative rather then a locomotor structure)

FIGURE 5.2 Apes (*left*) are adapted anatomically for a form of quadrupedal locomotion called knuckle walking, although they often stand upright and occasionally may even walk on their hind limbs for short distances. A human skeleton (*right*) shows the kinds of reshaping that natural selection performed to produce the hominin anatomy, which is adapted to habitual bipedalism.

Who Were the First Hominins (6–3 mya)?

The Origin of Bipedalism

The skeletons of all primates allow upright posture when sitting or swinging from the branches of trees. Many primates often stand upright and occasionally walk on their hind limbs for short distances. Because bipedalism requires upright posture, primates have already, so to speak, taken a step in the right direction. Put another way, we could say that hominoid morphology for upright posture that evolved in an arboreal context led to hominin bipedalism in a terrestrial context.

What sort of selective pressures might have favoured bipedal locomotion in hominoids? To answer this

TABLE 5.2 Four Major Trends in Hominin Evolution

Trend	Development	Dates and Species
Bipedalism	Evidence of bipedalism marks the appearance of the hominin line.	• Between 10 and 5 mya • *Ardipithecus ramidus* ("Ardi")
Distinctive Dentition	The development of huge cheek teeth (molars) and much smaller front teeth was characteristic of the australopiths.	• Between 4 to 2 mya • *Australopithecus afarensis* ("Lucy")
Expanded Brain	Brain expansion beyond the 350 to 550 cm³ of the australopiths was characteristic of the genus *Homo*.	• Beginning 2.4 mya • *Homo habilis* ("handy man")
Culture	Greater reliance on learned and shared patterns of behaviour and thought. Use of stone tools. Later, communication through spoken language. Combined, these are key building blocks for human culture.	• Beginning 2.5 mya • *Homo habilis* ("handy man") and a variety of other hominins

question, paleoanthropologists examine the advantages bipedalism would have conferred. Moving easily on the ground might have improved hominoids' ability to exploit food resources outside the protective cover of the shrinking Miocene forests. Upright posture would have made it easier for them to spot potential predators in open country, and skilful bipedal locomotion would have made it easier for them to escape. Finally, walking upright simultaneously reduces the amount of skin surface exposed to the sun, allows greater distances to be covered (albeit at slow speeds), and is more energy-efficient (Day 1986, 189; Foley 1995, 143). Research by archaeologist Alan Cross and his colleagues at Simon Fraser University (Cross, Collard, and Nelson 2008, 2011) that relies on three-dimensional computer-generated models of bipedal movement supports this idea that walking on two feet is efficient and a great way to regulate heat from the sun.

omnivorous **Eating a wide range of plant and animal foods.**

Walking would have enabled the first hominins to cover long distances between widely scattered sources of plant food or water. Indeed, the teeth of these hominins suggest that they were probably **omnivorous**, not carnivorous; that is, they ate a wide range of plant and animal foods. Equipped with just a simple digging stick, their diet might have included a variety of fruits, roots, reptiles, eggs, birds, fish, and possibly small mammals. This diverse diet is very close to that of chimpanzees and living gatherer/hunters (Mann 1981). As the forests retreated and stands of trees became smaller and more widely scattered, groups of bipedal hominins appear to have ranged over a variety of environments.

The oldest known hominins are the australopiths, and their fossils come from Africa (Map 5.1), some dating back into the Miocene. The oldest remains are fragmentary, however, and their significance for later hominin evolution is not clearly understood. The most noteworthy of recent australopith finds are *Sahelanthropus tchadensis* (6 to 7 million years old), from Chad (Brunet et al.

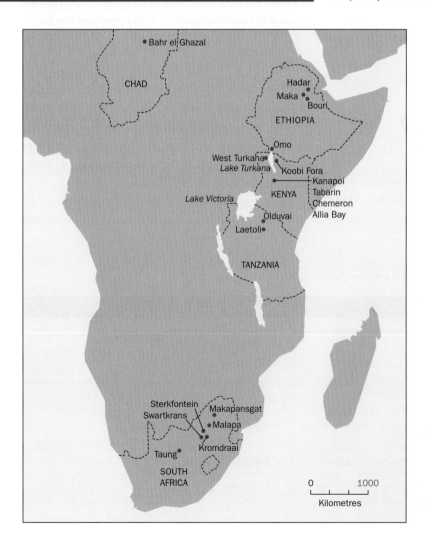

MAP 5.1 Major sites in Africa (for the most part, eastern and southern Africa) from which fossils of australopiths and early *Homo* have been recovered.

FIGURE 5.3 The fossils of *Ardipithecus ramidus*, pictured above, have been interpreted as belonging to a bipedal hominoid living in a forested environment, which challenges the traditional notion that bipedalism evolved in an open, savannah environment.

FIGURE 5.4 The earliest evidence of hominin bipedalism comes from the 3.6-million-year-old fossil footprints preserved in hardened volcanic ash at Laetoli, Tanzania.

2002, 6); *Orrorin tugenensis* (6 million years old), from Kenya (Senut et al. 2001); and *Ardipithecus kadabba* (5.2 to 5.5 million years old) and *Ardipithecus ramidus* (4.4 to 5.8 million years old), from Ethiopia (White et al. 2009). The discovery of "Ardi," a relatively complete skeleton of *Ar. ramidus*, was announced in 2009, representing a hominin that apparently could walk bipedally on the ground, although in a manner different from later australopiths and members of the genus *Homo* (see Figure 5.3). Most paleoanthropologists have traditionally viewed bipedal locomotion as an adaptation to life in open African grasslands called *savannah*. However, *Ar. ramidus* apparently lived in a more wooded environment, suggesting that "Ardi" spent more time in trees than later australopiths and that its gait was likely more similar to bipedalism in chimpanzees than in humans.

Most early hominin fossils showing skeletal evidence of bipedalism have been placed in the genus *Australopithecus*. The oldest of these is *Australopithecus anamensis*, whose fossils come from Kanapoi and Allia Bay in Kenya. *Au. anamensis* dates from 4.2 to 3.9 mya. *Au. anamensis* shows that bipedalism had evolved at least a few hundred thousand years before the date of 3.6 mya provided by the Laetoli footprints (Leakey et al. 1995). The Laetoli footprints, discovered by paleoanthropologist Mary Leakey, are a trail of footprints preserved in a layer of hardened volcanic ash laid down in the middle Pliocene at the site of Laetoli, Tanzania. These footprints are the earliest direct evidence of hominin bipedalism.

Most of the remaining early hominin fossils have been assigned to the species *Australopithecus afarensis*. Fossils assigned to this taxon have also been found at Laetoli and in a region of Ethiopia known as the Afar Depression—hence the species name "afarensis" (see the location of Hadar on Map 5.1). These fossils, which are quite numerous, range between 3.9 and 3.0 million years of age (Johanson and Edey 1981). The famous *Au. afarensis* fossil "Lucy" (named after the Beatles's song "Lucy in the Sky with Diamonds") (Figure 5.5) was found 40 per cent intact and undisturbed where she had died, which allowed paleoanthropologist Donald Johanson and his colleagues to reconstruct her postcranial skeleton in great detail (see the "In Their Own Words" box on finding fossils). The first fairly complete adult skull of *Au. afarensis*, found in the early 1990s, confirmed its small-brained, ape-like features. The 0.9-million-year age range of these Hadar fossils suggests a period of prolonged evolutionary stasis within *Au. afarensis*.

Some features of the skeleton of *Au. afarensis* reveal its adaptation to habitual bipedalism, which are key differences between apes and humans. First of all, the spinal column of an ape joins its head at the back of the skull, as is normally the case in quadrupedal animals. This is revealed by the position of a large hole, the *foramen magnum*, through which the spinal cord passes on its way to the brain. Second, the ape pelvis is long and broad, and the knee is almost directly in line with the femur (or thigh bone) and therefore ill-adapted to support the ape's centre of gravity when it tries to move on its hind legs. As a result, when apes walk bipedally, they appear to waddle in an awkward attempt to stay upright. Lastly, the great toe of the ape foot diverges like a thumb from the rest of the digits, a feature that allows apes to use their feet for grasping but inhibits their ability to use this toe for the "push-off" so important for effective bipedalism.

By contrast, the modern human head balances on the top of the spinal column. The foramen magnum in humans is located directly beneath the skull rather than at its back. The basin-shaped human pelvis is the body's centre of gravity, supporting and balancing the torso above it. Finally, the bones of human legs have a knock-kneed appearance, with the femur pointing inward toward the knee joint at the *valgus angle*. As a result, humans can easily transfer their centre of gravity directly over the stepping foot during bipedal walking.

The skeleton of *Au. afarensis* more closely resembles that of modern human beings than that of apes. For example, as paleoanthropologist Michelle Drapeau (2012) of the University of Montreal has observed, *Au. afarensis*'s great toes were generally in line with its other toes. In addition, its femur bent inward toward the knee joint at the valgus angle, and its pelvis was short

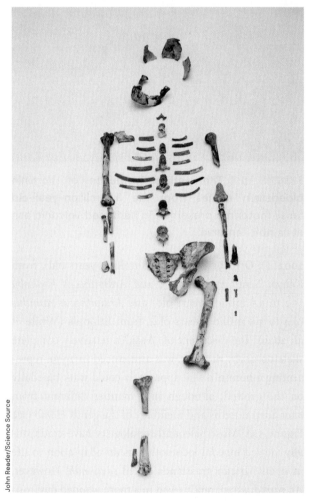

John Reader/Science Source

FIGURE 5.5 Forty per cent of Lucy's bones were found undisturbed, and her remains included much of her postcranial skeleton.

and basin-like (Figure 5.6). In addition, the skull of *Au. afarensis* balanced on the top of the spinal column, as shown by the position of its foramen magnum. Nevertheless, elements of the postcranial skeleton of *Au. afarensis* still identify its recent ape ancestry (Figure 5.7). It has longer arms, in proportion to its legs, than any other hominin. Also, the bones of its fingers and toes are slightly curved, and the toes are much longer, resembling the finger and toe bones of apes. Because these features

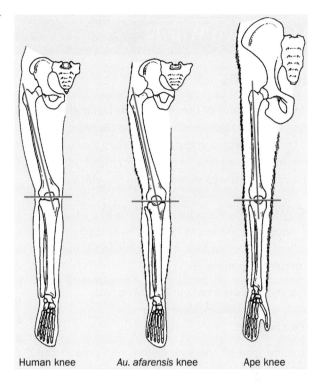

Human knee   *Au. afarensis* knee   Ape knee

FIGURE 5.6 The bones of human legs have a somewhat knock-kneed appearance, with the femur pointing inward toward the knee joint at the valgus angle. This allows human beings to easily transfer the centre of gravity directly over the foot in the course of bipedal walking. Ape femurs do not angle inward in this manner, so apes waddle when they try to walk bipedally. Because *Au. afarensis* is human-like in its valgus angle and in the shape of its pelvis, we conclude that, like us, it walked bipedally.

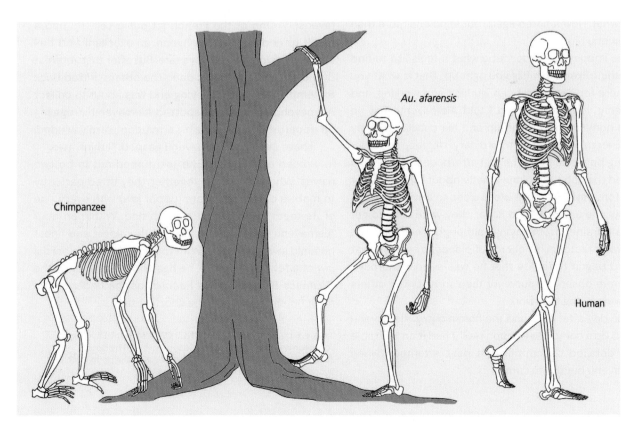

Chimpanzee

Au. afarensis

Human

FIGURE 5.7 Although *Au. afarensis* was human-like in some respects, in other respects its skeleton retained adaptations to life in the trees.

In Their Own Words

Finding Fossils

Searching for remains of the human past is not glamorous work. As he relates the experiences of Alemayehu, one of the most successful fossil hunters on his team, Donald Johanson reveals both the extraordinary discipline required for the search and the near delirium that ensues when the search is successful. (Note that Johanson uses the term hominid *in place of* hominin *to mean "humans and their immediate ancestors"; this usage is consistent with the common usage of the word in the 1980s.)*

One day Alemayehu found a small piece of a lower jaw with a couple of molars in it. They were bigger than human molars, and he told me that he had a baboon jaw with funny big teeth.

"You think this is a baboon?" I asked him.
"Well, with unusually large molars."
"It's a hominid."

The knee joint of the year before had proved the existence of hominids at Hadar. Everyone had been sanguine about finding more of them in 1974. In fact, the French had been so eager that they had gone rushing out to survey on the very first day, leaving it to the Americans to put up the tents. But after weeks of searching without results, that ardour had dimmed somewhat. Now it flared again, but in no one more than Alemayehu himself.

It is impossible to describe what it feels like to find something like that. It fills you right up. That is what you are there for. You have been working and working, and suddenly you score. When I told Alemayehu that he had a hominid, his face lit up and his chest went way out. Energized to an extraordinary degree, and with nothing better to do in the late afternoons, Alemayehu formed the habit of poking quietly about for an hour or so before dark. He chose areas close to camp because, without the use of a Land Rover, they were easy to get to. He refrained from saying—although I feel sure that this was a factor in his choice of places to survey—that he had begun to realize that he was a more thorough and more observant surveyor than some of the others who were doing that work.

The day after he found the hominid jaw, Alemayehu turned up a complete baboon skull. I had it on the table for a detailed description the next afternoon when Alemayehu burst into camp.

His eyes were popping. He said he had found another of those things. After having seen one, he was sure this was another human jaw. I dropped the baboon skull and ran after Alemayehu, forgetting that I was barefoot. I began to cut my feet so badly on the gravel that I was forced to limp back to my tent to put on shoes. Guillemot and Petter, who were with me, kept going. When I rejoined them, it was in a little depression just a few hundred yards beyond the Afar settlement. Guillemot and Petter were crouching down to look at a beautiful fossil jaw sticking out of the ground. Guillemot ruefully pointed out his own footprints, not ten feet away, where he had gone out surveying that first morning in camp and seen nothing.

A crowd of others arrived and began to hunt around feverishly. One of the French let out a yell—he had a jaw. It turned out to be a hyena, an excellent find because carnivores are always rare. But after that, interest dwindled. It began to get dark. The others drifted back to camp. I stopped surveying and was about to collect Alemayehu's jaw when I spotted Alemayehu struggling up a nearby slope, waving his arms, completely winded.

"I have another," Alemayehu gasped. "I think, two."

I raced over to him. The two turned out to be two halves. When I put them together, they fitted perfectly to make a complete palate (upper jaw) with every one of its teeth in position: a superb find. Within an hour Alemayehu had turned up two of the oldest and finest hominid jaws ever seen. With the addition of the partial jaw of a few days before, he has earned a listing in the *Guinness Book of World Records* as the finder of the most hominid fossils in the shortest time.

are related to the typical tree-climbing adaptation of most hominoids, some paleoanthropologists have concluded that *Au. afarensis* must have had significant tree-climbing ability along with bipedalism (Klein 2009, 213).

A final early hominin species of note is *Australopithecus bahrelghazali*, which was contemporaneous with *Au. afarensis*. In 1995, the discovery of 3.5-million-year-old fossil remains from this australopith in Chad extended the known range of australopiths far beyond southern and eastern Africa (Brunet et al. 1995) (Map 6.1).

Changes in Hominin Dentition

Once the first australopiths regularly ventured down from the trees and into a variety of new habitats, they presumably began to rely on new food sources, which would create changes that are evident in the teeth of *Au. afarensis*. To assess the importance of these changes, it helps to compare the teeth of *Au. afarensis* with those of modern apes and humans.

A striking feature of ape dentition is a *U*-shaped dental arch that is longer front to back than it is side to side. By contrast, the human dental arch is parabolic, or gently rounded in shape and narrower in front than in back. Apes have large, sexually dimorphic canine teeth that project beyond the tooth row. In addition, they possess a *diastema* (plural, *diastemata*), or space in the tooth row for each canine of the opposite jaw to fit into when the jaws are closed. Human canine teeth do not project beyond the tooth row and show little sexual dimorphism, and humans have no diastemata. Ape teeth show functional specialization, with biting incisors, shearing canines, and grinding molars. In addition, the incisors are about the same size as the molars, and the canines are the largest teeth of all. Functional specialization in human teeth is very different. Humans have canines and incisors that are similar in shape and much smaller than their molars.

How does *Au. afarensis* compare? As Figure 5.8 shows, the *Au. afarensis* dental arcade is *U*-shaped, like that of the apes. Its canines, though relatively smaller than those of apes, still project somewhat; and 45 per cent of the *Au. afarensis* specimens examined have diastemata (Lewin 1989, 70). As *Au. afarensis* canines were getting smaller, their molars were getting larger, marking the beginning of an evolutionary trend toward smaller front teeth and enormous cheek teeth that occurs among australopiths that flourished a million years after *Au. afarensis*. The increase in the size of later australopith molars is greater than would be expected if it were merely the result of a larger-bodied hominin having

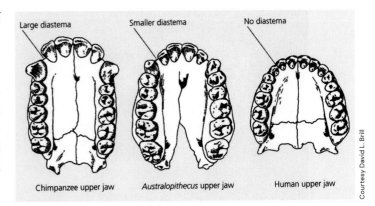

Large diastema   Smaller diastema   No diastema

Chimpanzee upper jaw   *Australopithecus* upper jaw   Human upper jaw

Courtesy David L. Brill

FIGURE 5.8 The upper jaw of *Au. afarensis* shows some ape-like features, but its dentition shows signs of change in the direction of smaller front teeth and large cheek teeth that would appear fully developed in later australopith species.

proportionately larger teeth. Thus, paleoanthropologists deduce that the enlarged molars were produced as an effective adaptation to grassland diets consisting of coarse vegetable foods. Because projecting canine teeth prevent the side-to-side jaw movement that grinding tough foods requires, natural selection may have favoured australopiths whose canines did not project beyond the tooth row.

Who Were the Later Australopiths (3–1.5 mya)?

Fossils of 3-million-year-old australopiths with small front teeth and large cheek teeth were found first in southern Africa and later in eastern Africa. Some of them possessed the typical late-australopith enlargement of the cheek teeth, but their faces were small and lightly built; they were classified together as *Australopithecus africanus* and came to be known as the "gracile australopiths" (Figure 5.9a). *Au. africanus* lived between 3 and 2 mya. Other australopith fossils with more rugged jaws, flatter faces, and enormous molars have been assigned to the species *Paranthropus robustus*, and they are called the "robust australopiths" (Figure 5.9b). *P. robustus* is generally estimated to have lived between 2.5 and 0.7 mya. Research using micro-computed tomography (micro-CT) has revealed the patterns of surface wear on teeth, giving us clues that suggest their diet consisted mainly of plants (Skinner et al. 2008).

It turns out that the striking morphological differences between gracile and robust australopiths have to do almost exclusively with their chewing anatomy. To begin

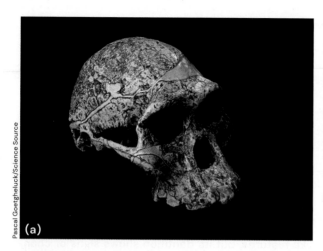
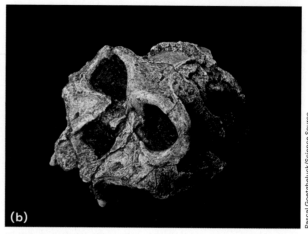

FIGURE 5.9 Two-million-year-old bipedal hominins with small front teeth and large cheek teeth fall into two major categories: (a) gracile australopiths (such as this specimen of *Au. africanus* from Sterkfontein, South Africa) have smaller, more lightly built faces; (b) robust australopiths (such as this specimen from Swartkrans, South Africa) have more rugged jaws, flatter faces, truly enormous molars, and sagittal crests.

with, selection seems to have favoured large molars to grind tough plant foods. But large molars are ineffective without jaws massive enough to absorb the shock of grinding and muscles large enough to move the jaws. The robust australopiths had the flattest faces because their cheekbones had expanded the most, to accommodate huge jaw muscles that attached to bony crests along the midlines of their skulls.

Both gracile and robust australopith fossils show the same adaptation to bipedalism found in *Au. afarensis*. The foramen magnum of both forms is found directly underneath the skull. Also, the size of the braincase (or **cranial capacity**) in both forms increased in size by approximately 25 to 35 per cent, to between 400 and 550 cm³. There are some possible behavioural changes among the australopiths as well. Current research by Michelle Drapeau (2012) supports the hypothesis that these and other australopiths had highly dexterous hands that they could have used to shape and manipulate tools. Her work suggests that despite having slightly longer and rounded fingers, *Au. afarensis* had very "human-like" hands that would have allowed for the use and creation of tools, possibly giving this species an adaptive advantage (242).

All australopith fossils from southern Africa have been recovered from limestone quarries or limestone caves. Unfortunately, none of the deposits from which these fossils came can be dated by traditional numerical methods, although newer uranium-series and paleomagnetic

techniques are more promising. Dating is much easier at eastern African sites, such as Olduvai Gorge, Tanzania, where volcanic rock layers can be dated using isotopic methods (Figure 5.10). Since 1959, eastern Africa has become the most important source of hominin fossils in the world.

How Many Species of Australopith Were There?

Fleagle (2013, 365) counts six species of *Australopithecus* that are generally recognized, but he also observes that

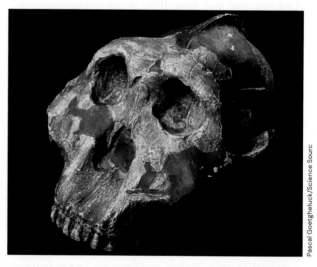

FIGURE 5.10 The "Zinjanthropus" skull, classified as *Paranthropus boisei*. When the potassium–argon method was used in 1959 to date the volcanic rock lying above the sediment in which this fossil was found, the date of 1.75 million years stunned the scientific community.

cranial capacity The size of the braincase.

TABLE 5.3 Increase in Cranial Capacity in Hominins*

Hominin	Date Range (years ago)	Cranial Capacity (cm³)
Sahelanthropus tchadensis	7–6 million	350
Orrorin tugenensis	6 million	a
Ardipithecus kadabba	5.5–5.2 million	a
Ardipithecus ramidus	5.8–4.4 million	a
Australopithecus anamensis	4.2–3.9 million	a
Australopithecus afarensis	3.9–3.0 million	375–550
Australopithecus africanus	3–2 million	420–500
Australopithecus bahrelgazali	3.5–3 million	a
Australopithecus sediba	1.95–1.78 million	420
Australopithecus garhi	2.5 million	a
Paranthropus aethiopicus	2.6–2.3 million	410
Paranthropus robustus	2.0–1.5 million	530
Paranthropus boisei	2.1–1.1 million	530
Homo habilis	2.4–1.5 million	500–800
Homo georgicus	1.8 million	600–680
Homo erectus	1.8 million–700,000	750–1225
Homo ergaster	1.8–1.3 million	910
Homo antecessor	780,000	a
Homo heidelbergensis	600,000–200,000	1200
Homo neanderthalensis	230,000–27,000	1520
Denisovans	400,000–30,000	a
Homo naledi	300,000	500
Homo floresiensis	100,000	380
Homo sapiens	200,000–present	1400

* There are many species that are currently being studied, and this table will continue to change as these discoveries are reported.
a Unknown at present.

"more are probably waiting to be uncovered" (see Table 5.3). Gracile australopiths apparently flourished between 3 and 2 mya, in both southern and eastern Africa, suggesting an early divergence between the robust and gracile australopith lineages. It now appears that robust australopiths go back some 1.75 million years in southern Africa and perhaps 2.5 million years in eastern Africa, becoming extinct between 1.2 and 0.7 mya.

How Can Anthropologists Explain the Human Transition?

By 2 mya, bipedal hominins with specialized teeth and expanded brains were walking the open environment of the east African savannah. At least some of them made artifacts out of wood, stone, and bone and may have used fire. Some observers have concluded that meat eating led to a need for stone tools to kill and butcher animals and that stone-tool manufacture led natural selection to favour hominins with expanded brains. This is the "man the hunter" story about human origins, which purports to explain nearly every physical and behavioural trait that makes humans human as the outcome of our ancestors' devotion to hunting. In 1968, for example, anthropologists Sherwood Washburn and C.S. Lancaster (1968, 299–300) concluded that "the biological bases for killing have been incorporated into human psychology." This story seemed to be supported by early primatological work reporting that savannah baboons lived by a rigid hierarchy in a closed society: large males with huge canines dominated much smaller females and juveniles. As Canadian primatologist Linda Fedigan (1986, 36) remarked, this model of human origins "can be said to have been traditional and consistent with contemporary role expectations for Western men and women." As a result, the baboon model was quickly accepted by those who considered Western gender-role expectations as natural rather than culturally imposed.

However, the baboon model was quickly debunked, both because anthropologists could not agree about how to define *hunting* and because ethnographic fieldwork showed that plant food gathered by women was more important to the survival of foraging peoples than was meat hunted by men (Fedigan 1986, 33–4). For many anthropologists, the Ju/'hoansi people of southern Africa provide helpful insights concerning the social and economic life of the first hominins (see EthnoProfile 10.1: Ju/'hoansi). Richard Lee, a Canadian ethnographer from the University of Toronto, who has worked among the Ju/'hoansi since the 1960s, suggested that several "core features" of Ju/'hoansi society may have characterized the first hominin societies: a flexible form of kinship organization that recognized both the male and the female lines, group mobility and a lack of permanent attachment to territory, small group size (25 to 50 members) with fluctuating group membership, equitable food distribution that leads to highly egalitarian social relations, and a division of labour that leads to sharing (Lee 1974). In addition, women in foraging societies appear to arrange their reproductive lives around their productive activities, giving birth on average to one child every three to four years (Fedigan 1986, 49).

> For further discussion of Fedigan's comparative studies of female primates and humans, see Chapter 4, p. 80.

In sum, ethnographic evidence suggested that females played active roles in the adaptations of our early hominin ancestors. Some feminist anthropologists used this evidence to construct stories of human evolution that stressed the importance of "woman the gatherer," in which the key tools for human adaptation were digging sticks, slings to carry infants, and containers for gathered foods, all of which, they suggest, were probably invented by women. Rather than using an Old World monkey (i.e., the baboon) as a primate model, they used the chimpanzee. Jane Goodall's early reports from Gombe, in Tanzania, suggested that chimpanzee females were not constrained within a rigid hierarchy or dominated by aggressive males; they were active and mobile, feeding themselves and their young and spending most of their lives apart from their mates. Their closest bonds were with their offspring, and the mother–infant group was the most stable feature of chimpanzee society. Perhaps the first human food sharing was between women and their children; perhaps even hunters would have most likely shared food with their

mothers and siblings rather than with their mates. This "woman the gatherer" account—no less extremist than the "man the hunter" scenario—tested earlier assumptions about the foundations of human society and found them wanting.

All reconstructions of the lives of ancestral hominins, however, are tempered by the realization that the key features of human behaviour did not all appear at the same time. As such, identifying how and when hominins developed "culture" is not an easy thing to do, especially when we have limited material evidence. Many theories are being developed regarding this idea, and each of these must be considered and tested on its own merits and evidence. As in the case of our skeletal morphology, human behaviour also appears to be the product of mosaic evolution.

What Do We Know about Early *Homo* (2.4–1.5 mya)?

About 2.5 to 2 mya, the drying trend that had begun in Africa in the late Miocene became more pronounced, possibly causing a wave of extinction as well as the appearance of new species. During this period, the gracile australopiths disappeared, either by evolving into or being replaced by a new kind of hominin.

Expansion of the Australopith Brain

Whereas the brains of all australopith species varied within the range of 350 to 550 cm³, the new hominins had larger relative brain sizes. Were these merely advanced gracile australopiths, or did they belong to a new species or even a new genus? For paleoanthropologist Louis Leakey, who discovered at Olduvai in 1963 a skull with a cranial capacity of 680 cm³, the answer was clear. He asserted that the skull belonged to the genus *Homo* and named it *Homo habilis*—"handy man." Eventually, Leakey and his allies discovered more fossils that were assigned to *H. habilis*. But some paleoanthropologists believed that these fossils showed too much internal variation for a single species, and they proceeded to sort the fossils into new categories.

How Many Species of Early *Homo* Were There?

How do paleoanthropologists decide if a gracile fossil younger than 2 million years should be placed in the

> ***Homo*** The genus to which taxonomists assign large-brained hominins approximately 2 million years old and younger.

genus *Homo*? The key criterion they use is cranial capacity. In general, the cranial capacities of these early *Homo* fossils range from 510 to 750 cm³. Larger brains resided in larger, differently shaped skulls. Compared to the more elongated australopith cranium, the cranium of early *Homo* has thinner bone and is more rounded; the face is flatter and smaller in relation to the size of the cranium; and the teeth and jaws are less rugged, with a more parabolic arch. Most significantly, early *Homo*'s expansion in brain size was not accompanied by a marked increase in body size, meaning that the enlarged brain was a product of natural selection (Figure 5.11). But what advantages did having a bigger brain offer to early *Homo* species? Many researchers have sought to answer this question. For example, paleoanthropologist Carol MacLeod, from Langara College in Vancouver, has analyzed the differences between ape and human brains, and she has concluded that the most significant changes occurred in our lateral cerebellum (located below the larger cerebral cortex), which allowed us to improve our memory and learning abilities (MacLeod et al. 2003).

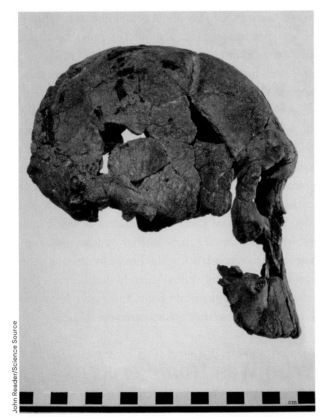

FIGURE 5.11 Perhaps the best-known fossil of an early *Homo* is KNM–ER 1470, found by Richard Leakey and his team near Lake Turkana in northern Kenya.

However, we know little about the actual postcranial morphology of any early *Homo* species.

Our understanding of the early *Homo* fossil record was enriched by two new finds in 2015, one from Ethiopia and one from South Africa. The fossils that received the most publicity came from Rising Star Cave in South Africa, where paleoanthropologists announced the discovery of a rich trove of hominin fossils that they argued were distinct from other early species of *Homo* previously identified (Dirks et al. 2015). Called *Homo naledi*, these fossils had small cranial capacities comparable to those of the early *Homo* line (between 465 and 560 cc). Other features of their anatomy, however, more closely resembled fossils assigned to australopithecines. The sediments that yielded these fossils have recently been dated to between 300,000 and 200,000 BP, suggesting that species evolved alongside early members of our species, *Homo sapiens* (Dirks et al. 2017).

The second early *Homo* find of 2015 came from the Ledi-Geraru in the Afar region of Ethiopia (Villmoare et al. 2015). This find consisted of a single lower jawbone with teeth, but Villmoare and his colleagues argue that it displays morphological features associated with *Homo*. Most exciting was the age of this fossil, which dates to between 2.8 and 2.75 mya—some 400,000 years earlier than previously known fossils of early *Homo*.

Today, it is widely believed that several species belonging to the genus *Homo* coexisted in eastern Africa in the early Pleistocene (Fleagle 2013, 376) at the same time as the robust australopiths of eastern Africa (which became extinct only around 1 mya), so it appears that more than one hominin genus coexisted. This situation challenges the evolutionary theory of phyletic gradualism but is understandable from the point of view of punctuated equilibria.

Earliest Evidence of Culture: Stone Tools of the Oldowan Tradition

Stone tools are the most enduring evidence we have of human-created artifacts. Paleoanthropologist Ian Tattersall (1998) emphasizes that the earliest hominins who made identifiable stone tools "*invented* efficient tool-making from materials they consciously chose" (57). The oldest undisputed stone tools are at least 3.3 million years old, found at Lomekwi in Kenya (Harmand et al. 2015). Other similar tools, dating from 2.5 to 2 mya, have been found elsewhere in eastern and southern Africa. For the most part, these tools consist of *cores* (tennis ball–sized rocks with a few flakes knocked off to produce cutting edges) and **flakes** (chipped-off pieces of rocks that may or may not have been used as small cutting tools). In general, these early styles of stone-toolmaking are referred to as the **Oldowan tradition** (Figure 5.12).

Oldowan tools are extremely simple and it is challenging for paleoanthropologists to conclude that they are dealing with deliberately fashioned artifacts rather than objects modified by natural processes. Paleoanthropologists who specialize in stone-tool analysis often use manufacturing techniques and **taphonomy** to examine stones and bones for evidence of human activity. Stones used as tools, for example, have characteristic manufacturing scars and wear patterns along their flaked edges. Flaked rocks that lack these identifiers are not usually considered to be tools unless they are unmistakably associated with other evidence of human activity.

An example of these taphonomic analyses was completed by paleoanthropologists Pat Shipman, Rick Potts, and Henry Bunn, who examined bones for marks of butchery by early hominins. Shipman learned how modern hunters butcher animals and discovered that carnivore tooth marks and stone cut marks on fresh bone look very different under the scanning electron microscope (Figure 5.13). Shipman, Potts, and Bunn examined over 2500 fossil bones that had been found at Olduvai and dated at 2 million years old and they found the following: (1) fewer than half the cut marks seemed to be associated with meat removal; (2) the stone-tool cut marks and carnivore tooth marks showed basically the same pattern of distribution; (3) nearly three-quarters of the cut marks occurred on bones with little meat, suggesting they resulted from skinning; and (4) in 8 out of 13 cases where cut marks and tooth marks overlapped, the cut marks were on top of the tooth marks. Taken together, these patterns suggested to her and her colleagues that, rather than hunting for meat, the Olduvai hominins regularly scavenged carcasses killed by carnivores, taking what they could get (Shipman 1984). It is now widely accepted that scavenging for meat was more likely than hunting among early hominins.

How had all of these stones and bones accumulated at Olduvai 2 mya? Rick Potts (1993) used a computer simulation to identify that the most efficient way for early hominins to get stones and animal carcasses together would be to cache (or hide) stones at various spots in areas where they hunted and bring carcasses to the nearest cache for processing. He called this the "stone cache hypothesis," where early hominins might have created the first stone caches accidentally but would have returned to them regularly whenever stone tools were needed, thus reconstructing their niche by creating a collection of stones and animal parts. In Potts's view, stone cache sites could turn into home bases once hominins could defend these sites against carnivores.

> **flakes** Chipped-off pieces of stone that may or may not have been used as small cutting tools.
>
> **Oldowan tradition** A stone-tool tradition named after the Olduvai Gorge (in Tanzania).
>
> **taphonomy** The study of the various processes that objects undergo in the course of becoming part of the fossil and archaeological records.

Kristie Cannon-Bonventre/AnthroPhoto

FIGURE 5.12 An Oldowan chopper with flakes removed from one side (or face).

Who Was *Homo erectus* (1.8–0.3 mya)?

Fossils of early *Homo* species disappear during the Pleistocene, about 1.8 mya. It is assumed that these species either evolved into the large-brained, robust

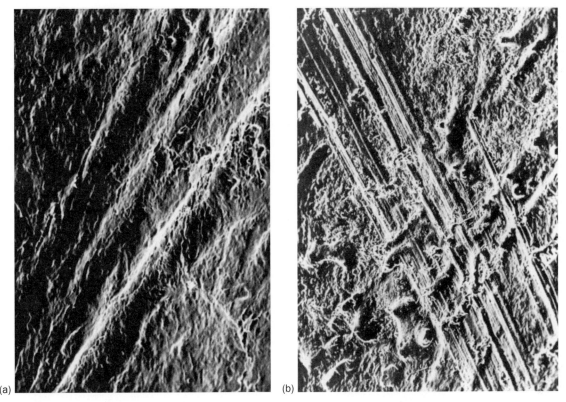

FIGURE 5.13 The scanning electron microscope allows taphonomists to distinguish between different kinds of marks on bones. (a) Hyena tooth marks on modern bones. (b) *V*-shaped stone-tool cut marks on modern bones.

hominins called ***Homo erectus*** or were replaced by them (Map 5.2). *H. erectus* seems to have coexisted in eastern Africa with the robust australopithecines until between 1.8 and 0.7 mya, and was the first hominin species to migrate out of Africa, apparently shortly after it first appeared. A collection of cranial and postcranial hominin fossils found in the Republic of Georgia (located northeast of Turkey) date to 1.8 mya and seem to represent an early *Homo erectus* population of this kind. Five adult crania from this population showed a range of phenotypic variation that may have characterized early populations of *Homo erectus* in general (Lordkipanidze et al. 2013). One of these crania belonged to an individual who had lost all his teeth long before he died, which suggests that this individual's survival is evidence of support from other members of his social group. Rocks yielding *H. erectus* fossils from Java have been dated to 1.8 and 1.7 mya; and Chinese fossils, including the famous specimens from Zhoukoudian, near Beijing, are 900,000 years old. No agreed-upon *H. erectus* fossils have been found in western Europe, though artifacts have been found at European sites that date from the time when *H. erectus* was living in Africa and Asia (Klein 2009, 367).

The earliest known African *H. erectus* fossil (sometimes called *H. ergaster*) is of a boy found on the west side of Lake Turkana, Kenya (Figure 5.14). Dated to 1.7 mya, the Turkana (or Nariokotome) boy is the most complete early hominin skeleton ever found and differs from other *H. erectus* specimens in several ways. First, the boy was taller than other specimens and had a slim build, which may be an adaptation to heat (Klein 2009, 326). Second, the size and shape of the Turkana boy's thoracic canal is less developed than our own, casting doubt on his ability to communicate using a spoken language (Walker 1993). Third, the Turkana boy looks very different from *H. erectus* living in Java at the same time, and paleoanthropologists have created new evolutionary trees where there may be more than one species of *H. erectus*.

> ***Homo erectus*** **The species of large-brained, robust hominins that lived between 1.8 and 0.3 mya.**

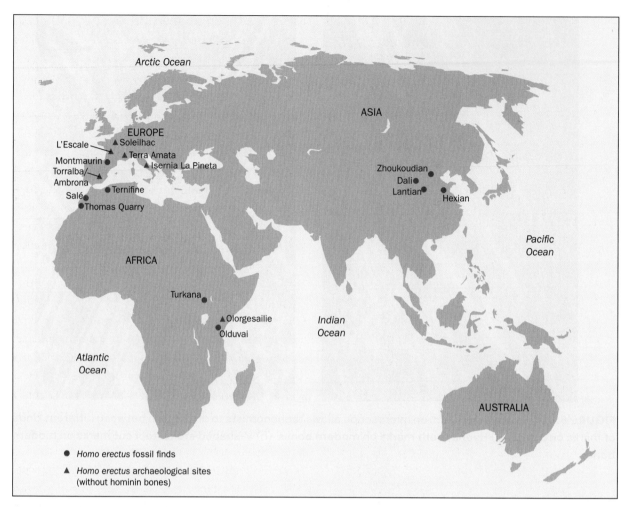

MAP 5.2 The major sites where *H. erectus* fossils or evidence of *H. erectus* settlement (without *H. erectus* fossils) have been found.

Morphological Traits of *H. erectus*

Morphological traits traditionally used to assign fossils to *H. erectus* involve its cranium, its dentition, and its postcranial skeleton. The cranial capacity of *H. erectus* averages around 1000 cm³, a significant increase over early *Homo*, for whom cranial capacity ranged from approximately 500 to 700 cm³. In addition, the skull of *H. erectus* possesses a number of distinctive morphological features, including heavy brow ridges, a five-sided cranial profile (when viewed from the rear), and a bony protuberance at the rear of the skull called a "nuchal crest." The molars of *H. erectus* are reduced in

size and the jawbones are less robust than those of early *Homo*. In addition, the wear patterns on teeth are different from those found on the molars of early *Homo*. The enamel of *H. erectus* is heavily pitted and scratched, suggesting that its diet was different from that of previous hominins. The postcranial skeleton of *H. erectus* is somewhat more robust than modern human skeletons but is otherwise like our own (see Figure 5.14).

The Culture and Stone Tools of *H. erectus*

Traditionally, the appearance of *H. erectus* in the fossil record has been linked to the appearance of a new stone-tool tradition in the archaeological record: the **Acheulean tradition**. Acheulean stone tools come in a variety of forms, but the Acheulean biface, or "hand ax," is the most characteristic (Figure 5.15). Acheulean bifaces are manufactured from stone cores using technical skills that are more

Acheulean tradition A Lower Paleolithic stone-tool tradition associated with *Homo erectus* and characterized by stone bifaces, or "hand axes."

quite unique in eastern Asia (Klein 2009, 256). The best-known stone-tool **assemblages** associated with *H. erectus* in China lack large bifaces and consist mostly of flakes. Archaeologist Brian Fagan (1990, 119) explains this phenomenon by suggesting that bamboo and other forest materials in Asia would have made excellent tools capable of doing the work performed elsewhere by stone bifaces.

H. erectus also used and controlled fire, a very important and useful tool that likely influenced diet, lifestyle, and living conditions. Not only would fire have allowed *H. erectus* to cook food, making its food easier to digest, but it also would have provided a source of heat and a gathering focal point for these hominins. In essence, fire creates a hearth, a central space for socialization and interaction. Fire was likely also a contributing factor that allowed *H. erectus* to disperse into Europe and other temperate zones. The best evidence of fire use by *H. erectus* is found at the site of Gesher Benot Ya'akov in Israel (780,000 years ago); and in Zhoukoudian, China, and Europe (between 670,000 and 400,000 years ago) (Klein 2009, 412–13). As well, burned cobbles and bones from a southern African site suggest that African *H. erectus* (*H. ergaster*) may have had intermittent control of fire a million years earlier than this (Tattersall 2012, 111–12).

Biological anthropologist Richard Wrangham (2009, 194) suggests that the transition to *H. erectus* aligns with the control of fire, and led to an increasing reliance on cooked food. In his view, cooking was of major importance in human evolution, allowing for humans' bodies to easily digest and more readily acquire nutrients from their diet. Cooked food led to smaller teeth, smaller guts, bigger brains, and reduced body hair.

H. erectus the Hunter?

Earlier in the chapter, we discussed the hypothesis that bipedal locomotion enabled endurance walking and daylight hunting among the australopiths. Recent research has suggested that *endurance running* may also have played a crucial role in the evolution of later hominins, linking the emergence of new forms of hunting with the appearance of *H. erectus*. Biological anthropologist Daniel Lieberman and human biologist Dennis Bramble point

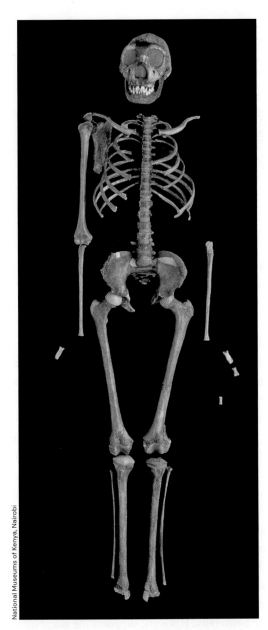

National Museums of Kenya, Nairobi

FIGURE 5.14 The most complete *H. erectus* skeleton ever discovered is KNM–WT 15000 from Kenya. Believed to have been a 12-year-old boy, this fossil includes a nearly complete postcranial skeleton.

refined those used to make Oldowan tools. Acheulean tools appear in the archaeological record shortly after the appearance of *H. erectus*. Together the Acheulean and the Oldowan stone-tool traditions are assigned by archaeologists to a single period known as the Lower Paleolithic in Europe and the **Early Stone Age (ESA)** in Africa.

The Acheulean stone-tool tradition changed little over a period of 1 million years, suggesting it was a very well-adapted tool for life in the Pleistocene environments of Europe and Africa; however, these stone tools were

Early Stone Age (ESA) The name given to the period of Oldowan and Acheulean stone-tool traditions in Africa.

assemblages Artifacts and structures from a particular time and place in an archaeological site.

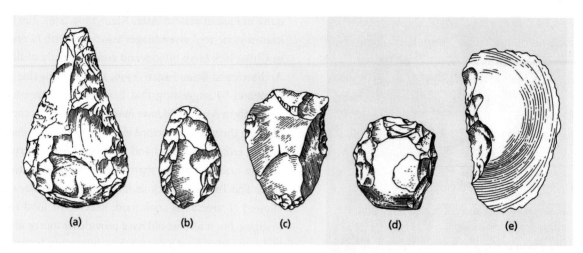

FIGURE 5.15 Although the biface, or "hand ax" (a), is the best-known tool from the Acheulean tradition, other core tools, such as scrapers (b), choppers (c and d), and cleavers (e), have also been found.

Source: From F. Bordes, *The Old Stone Age*, Weidenfeld Publishers Ltd., 1968.

out that endurance running is not found among primates other than humans and that the distinctive characteristics of human endurance running are unusual among mammals in general. For example, many people are aware that most mammals can out-sprint human beings, but they may not realize that humans can outrun almost all other mammals (sometimes even horses) for marathon-length distances (Lieberman and Bramble 2007, 289). Lieberman and Bramble argue that endurance running could have been a very powerful adaptation to the environments in which later hominins such as *H. erectus* were living.

Three sets of adaptations make human endurance running possible: *energetics* (the flow and transformation of energy), *stabilization* (how the body keeps from falling), and *temperature regulation* (maintaining body temperature within limits). Human energetic adaptations include tendons and ligaments in the legs and feet that are absent or very much smaller in other primates. These anatomical structures store energy and then push the body forward in a gait that is fundamentally different from the mechanics of walking. Human stabilization adaptations affect the centre of mass and balance during running. These adaptations include a ligament that helps keep the head stable during running and an enlarged *gluteus maximus* (the muscle that makes up the distinctively large human buttocks). The *gluteus maximus*, which hardly contracts during level walking, contracts strongly during running, stiffening the torso and providing a counterbalance to the forward tilt of the trunk.

Human temperature regulation adaptations address what Lieberman and Bramble (2007, 289) consider to be the biggest physiological challenge that runners face: muscle activity generated by running generates as much as 10 times more heat than does walking. Most mammals stop galloping after short distances because they cannot cool their body temperature fast enough to prevent *hyperthermia*, or overheating. "Humans, uniquely, can run long distances in hot, arid conditions that cause hyperthermia in other mammals, largely because we have become specialized sweaters" (Lieberman and Bramble 2007, 289). Humans have less body hair and many more sweat glands than do other mammals, which allows for effective body cooling through evapotranspiration.

Exactly how these hominins regulated (and how present-day humans regulate) their body temperatures during exercise was analyzed by Alan Cross at Simon Fraser University. His work supports the suggestion that *H. erectus* was able to run long distances effectively. It also reveals how different lengths of limbs, both arms and legs, can influence thermoregulation of the body in both hot and cold temperatures (Cross et al. 2008; Cross and Collard 2011). Specifically, longer limbs tend to be better at releasing excess heat and are thus advantageous in warmer climates, while shorter limbs tend to be better at retaining heat and are thus advantageous in cooler climates. Thus, it is not surprising that we find evidence of relatively long limbs in *H. erectus* living in warmer regions.

When and why did hominins become good at running long distances? Lieberman and Bramble (2007) argue that running emerged about 2 million years ago, at the time of the transition to *H. erectus* and long after bipedal walking evolved. They argue that endurance running made scavenging meat and especially hunting of medium- to large-sized mammals increasingly successful. They also argue that it made persistence hunting possible: long-distance hominin runners forced prey animals to run at speeds that these animals could not endure for long, driving them to hyperthermia. The animals could then be killed by the only weapons available to hominins such as *H. erectus*—simple stone tools and sharpened, untipped, thrusting spears.

This chapter has reviewed the current data assembled by paleoanthropologists, geneticists, and archaeologists to help reconstruct the evolutionary history of our species. But as with most historic sciences, many questions remain and daily new discoveries are made, as we have only begun to discover the past and there are new ways to interpret our data; moreover, the future of genetic studies holds many new promises. Generally, all agree that bipedalism was a marked change in primate evolution, leading to an ability for some of our ancestors to use their hands and to begin to create material items, such as tools. As well, the overall trend of larger brain capacity aligns with changes to teeth and diet, contributing to the migration out of Africa of *Homo erectus* and the controlled use of fire. In the next chapter, we move further along the evolutionary tree, providing evidence for the beginnings and creative pursuits of our species, *Homo sapiens*.

Chapter Summary

1. Bipedal hominoids that appeared in Africa at the end of the Miocene are known as hominins and are placed in the same lineage as living human beings. Bipedalism may have been favoured by natural selection in hominoids exploiting food resources on the ground, outside the protection of forests. Their diet was probably omnivorous, and they could carry infants, food, and tools in their newly freed hands. The earliest hominin skeletal fossils are 6 to 7 million years old. The best-known early hominin fossils are 2 to 3 million years younger and have been placed in the genus *Australopithecus*. The earliest direct evidence of hominin bipedalism is a 3.6-million-year-old trail of fossilized footprints found in Laetoli, Tanzania.

2. Hominin adaptations apparently led to changes in dentition. The teeth of australopiths show an evolutionary trend toward smaller front teeth and enormous cheek teeth. This dental pattern is interpreted as an adaptation to diets of coarse vegetable foods that required grinding. Fossils of hominins between 3 and 2 million years old with this dental pattern have been found at southern and eastern African sites and have been classified into two groups: the gracile australopiths and the robust australopiths. Robust australopiths had more rugged jaws, flatter faces, and larger molars than did the gracile australopiths. Apart from these differences, the gracile and robust australopiths had similar postcranial skeletons and chimpanzee-sized cranial capacities.

3. The first members of the genus *Homo* appeared about 2.4 mya. Many paleontologists believe that more than one species belonging to *Homo* may have coexisted in eastern Africa in the early Pleistocene alongside the eastern African robust australopiths.

4. Fossils of early *Homo* disappear about 1.8 mya, either by evolving into or being replaced by *Homo ergaster or Homo erectus*, the first *Homo* species to spread out of Africa. The cranium of *H. erectus* averages around 1000 cm³, within the lower range of modern human beings. *H. erectus* may have been, to some extent, capable of speech. Wear patterns on teeth suggest that *H. erectus* had a diet different from that of previous hominins. The postcranial skeleton of *H. erectus* is more robust than that of modern humans and shows a marked reduction in sexual dimorphism compared to earlier hominins. *H. erectus* probably did not hunt big-game animals as a major source of food.

5. The oldest undisputed stone tools, classified in the Oldowan tradition, were found in Ethiopia, date to at least 3.3 mya, and may have been made by early *Homo*. Acheulean bifaces are associated with *H. erectus*. In recent years, however, archaeologists have concluded that it is misleading to associate individual stone-tool traditions with only one hominin species. Some archaeologists have suggested that bamboo was available for toolmaking in those areas in Asia where Acheulean bifaces are lacking.

Oldowan and Acheulean traditions are usually grouped together in a single period known as the Lower Paleolithic in Europe and the Early Stone Age in Africa.

online For a thorough discussion of the anthropological subfield of bioarchaeology, see the Focus on Four Fields passage "Biological Anthropology: Bioarchaeology and the Analysis of Human Remains" on the companion website.

For Review

1. What is the evolutionary importance of bipedalism and its effects on human mobility?
2. Outline the distinctive characteristics of hominin dentition. What can our teeth tell us about our diet?
3. Explain the differences between robust and gracile australopiths.
4. There is more than one explanation for the evolutionary transition from early hominins to the genus *Homo*. Choose one and write a paragraph defending it by using what you have learned about hominin evolution.
5. Describe how time, soil, and weather conditions might affect the evidence that paleoanthropologists (and archaeologists) study. What methods and tools might researchers use to understand these natural processes?
6. Summarize what is known about *Homo erectus*, morphologically and culturally.

Key Terms

Acheulean tradition 106
anagenesis 90
assemblages 107
australopiths 92
bipedalism 92
cladogenesis 91
cranial capacity 100

Early Stone Age (ESA) 107
flakes 104
Homo 102
Homo erectus 105
macroevolution 90
microevolution 90
mosaic evolution 92

Oldowan tradition 104
omnivorous 94
phyletic gradualism 90
punctuated equilibrium 92
taphonomy 104

References

Brunet, Michel, Alain Beauvilain, Yves Coppens, Emile Heintz, Aladji H.E. Moutaye, and David Pilbeam. 1995. "The First Australopithecine 2500 Kilometers West of the Rift Valley (Chad)." *Nature* 378: 273–5.

Brunet, Michel, Franck Guy, David Pilbeam, Hassane Taisso Mackaye, Andossa Likius, Djimdoumalbaye Ahounta, Alain Beauvilain, et al. 2002. "A New Hominid from the Upper Miocene of Chad, Central Africa." *Nature* 418: 145–51.

Cross, Alan, and Mark Collard. 2011. "Estimating Surface Area in Early Hominins." *PLOS One* 6 (1): e16107.

Cross, Alan, Mark Collard, and Andrew Nelson. 2008. "Body Segment Differences in Surface Area, Skin Temperatures and 3-D Displacement and the Estimation of Heat Balance During Locomotion in Hominins." *PLOS One* 3 (6): e2464.

Day, Michael H. 1986. "Bipedalism: Pressures, Origins, and Modes." In *Major Topics in Primate and Human Evolution*, edited by Bernard A. Wood, Lawrence B. Martin, and Peter Andrews, 188–202. Cambridge: Cambridge University Press.

Dirks Paul, Lee R. Berger, Eric M. Roberts, Jan D. Kramers, John Hawks, Patrick S. Randolph-Quinney, Marina Elliott, et al. 2015. "Geological and Taphonomic Evidence for Deliberate Body Disposal by the Primitive Hominin Species *Homo naledi* from the Dinaledi Chamber, South Africa." *eLife* 4: e09561. doi:10.7554/eLife.09561

Dirks, Paul, Eric M. Roberts, Hannah Hilbert-Wolf, Jan D. Kramers, John Hawks, Anthony Dosseto, Mathieu Duval, et al. 2017. "The Age of *Homo naledia* and Associated Sediments in the Rising Star Cave, South Africa." *eLife*. doi:10.7554/elife.24231

Drapeau, Michelle S.M. 2012. "Forelimb Adaptations in Australopithecus Afarensis." In *African Genesis: Perspectives on Hominin Evolution*, edited by Sally C. Reynolds and Andrew Gallagher. Cambridge: Cambridge University Press.

Eldredge, Niles, and Ian Tattersall. 1982. *The Myths of Human Evolution*. New York: Columbia University Press.

Fagan, Brian. 1990. *The Journey from Eden*. London: Thames and Hudson.

Fedigan, Linda M. 1986. "The Changing Role of Women in Models of Human Evolution." *Annual Review of Anthropology* 15: 25–66.

Fleagle, John G. 2013. *Primate Adaptation and Evolution*. 3rd ed. Amsterdam: Elsevier/Academic Press.

Foley, Robert. 1995. *Humans before Humanity*. Oxford: Blackwell.

Gould, Stephen J., and Niles Eldredge. 1977. "Punctuated Equilibria: The Tempo and Mode of Evolution Reconsidered." *Paleobiology* 3: 115–51.

Harmand, Sonia, Jason Lewis, Craig Feibel, Christopher Lepre, Sandrine Prat, Lenoble Arnaud, Xavier Boës, et al. 2015. "3.3-million-year-old Stone Tools from Lomekwi 3, West Turkana, Kenya." *Nature* 521: 310–15.

Johanson, Donald, and Maitland A. Edey. 1981. *Lucy: The Beginnings of Humankind*. New York: Simon and Schuster.

Klein, Richard G. 2009. *The Human Career: Human Biological and Cultural Origins*. 3rd ed. Chicago: University of Chicago Press.

Leakey, Meave G., Craig S. Feibel, Ian McDougall, and Alan C. Walker. 1995. "New Four-Million-Year-Old Hominid Species from Kanapoi and Allia Bay, Kenya." *Nature* 376: 565–71.

Lee, Richard B. 1974. "Male–Female Residence Arrangements and Political Power in Human Hunter-Gatherers." *Archaeology of Sexual Behavior* 3: 167–73.

Lewin, Roger. 1989. *Human Evolution*. 2nd ed. Boston: Blackwell Scientific Publications.

Lieberman, Daniel E., and Dennis M. Bramble. 2007. "The Evolution of Marathon Running." *Sports Medicine* 37 (4/5): 288–90.

Lordkipanidze, David, Marcia S. Ponce de Leon, Ann Margvelashvili, Yoel Rak, G. Philip Rightmire, Abesalom Vekua, and Christopher P.E. Zollikofer. 2013. "A Complete Skull from Dmanisi, Georgia, and the Evolutionary Biology of Early *Homo*." *Science* 342: 326–31.

MacLeod, Carol E., Karl Zilles, Axel Schleicher, James K. Rilling, and Kathleen R. Gibson. 2003. "Expansion of the Neocerebellum in Hominoidea." *Journal of Human Evolution* 44 (4): 401–29.

Mann, Alan E. 1981. "Diet and Human Evolution." In *Omnivorous Primates*, edited by Robert S.O. Harding and Geza Teleki, 10–36. New York: Columbia University Press.

Potts, Richard. 1993. "Archaeological Interpretations of Early Hominid Behavior and Ecology." In *The Origin and Evolution of Humans and Humanness*, edited by D. Tab Rasmussen, 49–74. Boston: Jones and Bartlett.

Senut, Brigitte, Martin Pickford, Dominique Gommery, Pierre Mein, Kiptalam Cheboi, and Yves Coppens. 2001. "First Hominid from the Miocene (Lukeino Formation, Kenya)." *Comptes Rendus Des Seances de l'Academie Des Sciences* 332: 137–44.

Shipman, Pat. 1984. "Scavenger Hunt." *Natural History* (April): 22–7.

Silcox, Mary T. 2013. "Primate Origins." In *A Companion to Paleoanthropology*, edited by D.R. Begun, 339–57. Oxford: Blackwell.

Skinner, Matthew M., Bernard A. Wood, Christophe Boesch, Anthony J. Olejnczak, Antonio Rosas, Tanya M. Smith, and Jean-Jacques Hublin. 2008. "Dental Trait Expression at the Enamel-Dentine Junction of Lower Molars in Extant and Fossil Hominoids." *Journal of Human Evolution* 54: 173–86.

Tattersall, Ian. 1998. *Becoming Human: Evolution and Human Uniqueness*. San Diego: Harcourt Brace.

———. 2012. *Masters of the Planet: The Search for Our Human Origins*. New York: Palgrave-Macmillan.

Villmoare, Brian, William H. Kimbel, Chalachew Seyoum, Christopher J. Campisano, Erin N. DiMaggio, John Rowan, David R. Braun, et al. 2015. "Early *Homo* at 2.8 Ma from Ledi-Geraru, Afar, Ethiopia." *Science* 347 (6228): 1352–5. doi:10.1126/science.aaa1343

Walker, Alan. 1993. "The Origin of the Genus *Homo*." In *The Origin and Evolution of Humans and Humanness*, edited by D. Tab Rasmussen. Boston: Jones and Bartlett.

Washburn, Sherwood, and C.S. Lancaster. 1968. "The Evolution of Hunting." In *Man the Hunter*, edited by R. Lee and I. DeVore, 293–303. Chicago: Aldine.

White, Tim D., Berhane Asfaw, Yonas Beyene, Yohannes Haile-Selassie, C. Owen Lovejoy, Gen Suwa, and Giday Wolde-Gabriel. 2009. "*Ardipithecus ramidus* and the Paleobiology of Early Hominids." *Science* 326: 64, 75–86.

Wrangham, Richard. 2009. *Catching Fire: How Cooking Made Us Human*. New York: Basic Books.

▲ A Neanderthal flint point was discovered next to the skeleton of a mammoth outside Paris, France. Artifacts such as these give anthropologists clues about the daily lives of Neanderthals and early anatomically modern humans, and how early cultures evolved. Photo: LOIC VENANCE/AFP/Getty Images

6 How Did *Homo sapiens* Evolve?

Chapter Outline

We present the earliest evidence for the appearance of our species, modern *Homo sapiens,* in this chapter. Beginning around 300,000 years ago, unique biological traits and cultural innovations were introduced that define the evolution of our species. We also look at the relationships between *H. sapiens* and other hominins, including Neanderthals, and how *H. sapiens* were the first to occupy all the corners of the world, including Australia and the Americas.

In this chapter, we present the biological and cultural records that mark the evolution of our species, *Homo sapiens*. Physical changes were less pronounced than in the earlier hominins while cultural innovations, tools, technologies, and artistic expression changed rapidly, allowing our ancestors to live throughout the world, from the ice-covered north to the extreme heat of the south. And we were not alone. In fact, other hominins, including the Neanderthals, lived in the same places and spaces as *H. sapiens*. We examine how we interacted with other hominins and what genetic evidence suggests our relationship with these other species. No agreed-upon *H. erectus* fossils have been found in western Europe, though artifacts have been found at European sites that date from the time when *H. erectus* was living in Africa and Asia (Klein 2009, 367).

How Did *Homo sapiens* Evolve?

What Is the Fossil Evidence for the Transition to Modern *H. sapiens*?

The relatively rich and reasonably uniform fossil record associated with *H. erectus* disappeared after about 700,000 years ago, to be replaced by a far patchier and more varied fossil record. Some 30 sites in Africa, Europe, and Asia have yielded a collection of fossils sometimes called early or **archaic *Homo sapiens*** (Map 6.1 and Figure 6.1). Most of these fossils consist of fragmented crania, jaws, and teeth. Postcranial bones thought to belong to archaic *H. sapiens* are robust, like those of *H. erectus*, but they are difficult to interpret because they are few in number and poorly dated and show considerable variation. However, these are important finds that help us to understand not just the fate of *H. erectus* but also the birth of our own species.

Paleoanthropologist Günter Bräuer used cladistic methods to compare all the skulls from Africa that had been assigned to archaic *H. sapiens*. Bräuer (1989, 132) argued that his morphological analysis showed that modern *H. sapiens* evolved from *H. erectus* only once, in Africa, and that the period of transition from archaic *H. sapiens* to modern *H. sapiens* was slow, taking some tens of thousands of years. Such a conclusion might be interpreted as an argument for the evolution of modern *H. sapiens* as a result of phyletic gradualism. But is a period of tens of thousands of years relatively long or relatively short, geologically speaking? G. Philip Rightmire (1995), another paleoanthropologist, favours a punctuationist analysis of the evolution of modern *H. sapiens*. That is, he regards *H. erectus* "as a real species, stable during a long time period" (1995, 487; see also Rightmire 1990). The appearance of modern *H. sapiens* would have followed the punctuation of this equilibrium some 200,000 years ago. If Rightmire's analysis is correct, then the period of evolutionary stability he claims for *H. erectus* would continue up to the appearance of the first anatomically modern populations of *H. sapiens*.

Paleoanthropologist Ian Tattersall also favours a punctuationist explanation for the origins of *H. sapiens*, but he does not agree that all regional populations assigned to *H. erectus* belonged to a single species. Tattersall includes all archaic *H. sapiens* fossils between 600,000 and 200,000 years of age, from Europe, Africa, and China, in the fossil species *Homo heidelbergensis*; he describes *H. heidelbergensis* as the first "cosmopolitan" hominin species, and he locates its origin somewhere within early African *Homo* (Tattersall 2012, 135–6). Tattersall also believes that *H. heidelbergensis* was responsible for a number of cultural innovations dated to this time period: shelter construction, domestication of fire, fabrication of spears, and the prepared-core technique of

---

archaic *Homo sapiens* Hominins dating from 500,000 to 200,000 years ago that possessed morphological features found in both *Homo erectus* and *Homo sapiens*.

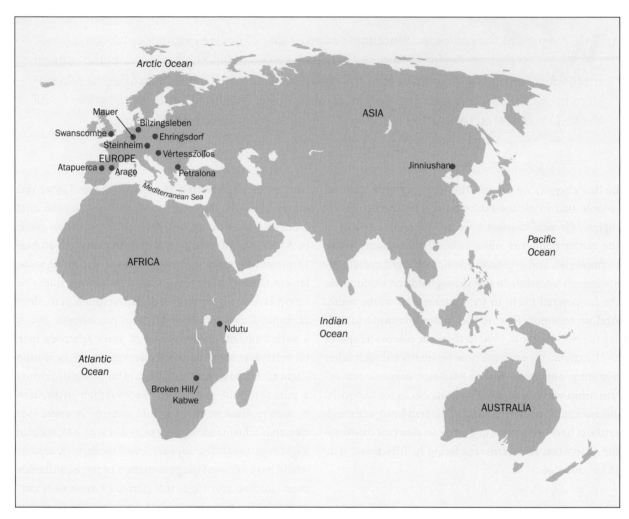

MAP 6.1 The major sites providing fossils assigned to archaic *H. sapiens*.

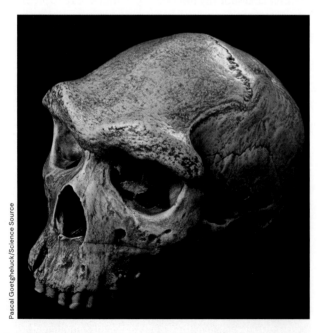

Pascal Goetgheluck/Science Source

FIGURE 6.1 Fossils assigned to archaic *H. sapiens* include the Broken Hill skull, from Kabwe, Zambia.

stone-tool manufacture (Tattersall 2012, 138–41). In the mid-1990s, moreover, paleoanthropologists working in limestone caves in the Sierra de Atapuerca, Spain, discovered fragments of hominin bones and teeth that are nearly 800,000 years old (Bermúdez de Castro et al. 1997). They argue that these are the remains of an offshoot of *H. ergaster* (African *H. erectus*) and may be ancestral to both *H. heidelbergensis* and *H. sapiens*. Not only are these the earliest well-dated hominin fossils ever found in Europe, but they also display a mix of modern and *erectus*-like features that do not match those of *H. heidelbergensis*. As a result, the Spanish scholars assigned these fossils to a new species, *Homo antecessor* (*antecessor* is Latin for "explorer, pioneer, early settler," an appropriate name for the earliest known hominin population in Europe). Other paleoanthropologists seem willing to accept *H. antecessor* as a valid species but believe that not enough evidence yet exists to link it firmly to other species that came before or after it.

The same team of Spanish paleontologists also discovered hominin fossils at Atapuerca that appear to represent a very early stage in Neanderthal evolution (Arsuaga et al. 1993). In 2007, improved uranium-series dating methods showed that these fossils were at least 53,000 years old (Tattersall 2012, 156).

Today, most experts place the African and European fossils once classified as "archaic *H. sapiens*" into the species *H. heidelbergensis*, which Tattersall (2009, 281) describes as a "truly cosmopolitan" hominin species, originating in Africa some 600,000 years ago. *H. heidelbergensis* may be the origin of the European and African lineages that led to the Neanderthals and modern humans, respectively. This conclusion is based on the fact that these fossils all show morphological features not present in *H. erectus*, but none show any of the features that are distinctive of either Neanderthals or modern humans.

Where Did Modern *H. sapiens* Come From?

There are three competing theories that are used to explain the origin of *H. sapiens*: the *replacement model*, the *regional continuity model*, and the *African hybridization and replacement model*, which is a combination of the first two.

Punctuationists, as we saw, view *H. erectus* as a single, long-lived, geographically dispersed species. They hypothesize that only one subpopulation of this species, probably located in Africa, underwent a rapid spurt of evolution to produce *H. sapiens* 300,000 to 100,000 years ago. After that, *H. sapiens* itself multiplied and moved out of Africa, gradually populating the globe and eventually replacing any remaining populations of *H. erectus* or their descendants. This scenario is usually called the "out of Africa" or **replacement model**.

The factor triggering this evolutionary spurt is usually thought to be the pattern of fluctuating climate and environmental change caused by the repeated advance and retreat of ice sheets during the late Pleistocene. In Europe, warming and cooling periods have fluctuated since 128,000 years ago until about 12,000 years ago when the large continental glaciers in northern Europe and North America retreated. In Africa, by contrast, hominin populations experienced strong arid–moist fluctuations called "megadroughts" between about 135,000 and 75,000 years ago; by 12,000 years ago, the climatic pattern we know today had been established.

However, some gradualists reject this scenario of *H. sapien* evolution, arguing that evolution from

H. erectus to *H. sapiens* occurred gradually throughout the traditional range of *H. erectus*. According to paleoanthropologist Milford H. Wolpoff (1985), as each regional population evolved from *H. erectus* to *H. sapiens*, it retained its distinct physical appearance, which was the result of adaptation to regional selection pressures. He finds morphological similarities between European *H. erectus* and later European Neanderthals, between *H. erectus* from Java and later Australian *H. sapiens*, and between Chinese *H. erectus* and later Chinese *H. sapiens*. This model assumes a complex pattern of gene flow that would have spread any new genetic mutations arising in one regional population to all the others while at the same time preventing those populations from evolving into separate species. This view is called the **regional continuity model**.

A debate has persisted between proponents of these two models, but as paleoanthropologist Leslie Aiello (1993, 73) points out, "neither of these hypotheses, in their extreme forms, are fully consistent with the known fossil record for human evolution in the Middle and Late Pleistocene." As a result, biological anthropologist John Relethford (2001) proposed what has been called the "mostly out of Africa" model. He agrees with advocates of the replacement model that the fossil evidence suggests an African origin for modern human *anatomy* but that this did not necessarily mean that the entire contents of the modern human *gene pool* were exclusively from Africa. Current genetic evidence suggests that there was some, albeit limited, gene flow between modern humans and other hominins (Collard and Dembo 2013). This evidence tends to support a third model of modern human evolution, known as the **African hybridization and replacement model**. This third model is essentially a combination of the replacement and regional continuity models in

---

replacement model The hypothesis that only one subpopulation of *Homo erectus*, probably located in Africa, underwent a rapid spurt of evolution to produce *Homo sapiens* 300,000 to 100,000 years ago. After that time, *H. sapiens* would itself have multiplied and dispersed, gradually populating the globe and eventually replacing any remaining populations of *H. erectus* or their descendants.

regional continuity model The hypothesis that evolution from *Homo erectus* to *Homo sapiens* occurred gradually throughout the traditional range of *H. erectus*.

African hybridization and replacement model The hypothesis that anatomically modern humans evolved in Africa between 300,000 and 100,000 years ago and then moved out into Europe, Asia, and Australasia, interbreeding to some extent with the hominin populations in those areas.

which anatomically modern humans evolved in Africa between 300,000 and 100,000 years ago and then moved out into Europe, Asia, and Australasia, interbreeding to some extent with the hominin populations in those areas.

Who Were the Neanderthals (230,000– 27,000 Years Ago)?

Neanderthals get their name from the Neander Tal ("Neander Valley") in Germany, where a fossil skull-cap and some postcranial bones were discovered in 1856. Thereafter, paleoanthropologists used the name Neanderthal to refer to other fossils from Europe and

Neanderthals An archaic species of *Homo* that lived in Europe and western Asia 230,000 to 27,000 years ago.

western Asia that appeared to belong to populations of the same kind (Map 6.2). The first Neanderthals appeared about 230,000 years ago, during a period of global cooling. The most recently dated Neanderthal fossil, from France, is about 35,000 years old; and another, from Spain, may be even younger, at 27,000 years of age (Hublin et al. 1996). After this date, Neanderthals disappear from the fossil record.

Because numerous cranial and postcranial bones have been recovered, paleoanthropologists have been able to reconstruct Neanderthal morphology with some confidence. Neanderthals were shorter and more robust than modern *H. sapiens*, with massive skulls; continuous brow ridges; and protruding, chinless faces. Neanderthal teeth are larger than those of modern humans and have enlarged pulp cavities and fused roots, a condition known as *taurodontism*. Unlike the jaws of modern human beings, Neanderthal lower jaws possess a gap behind the third molar called a *retromolar space*, which results from

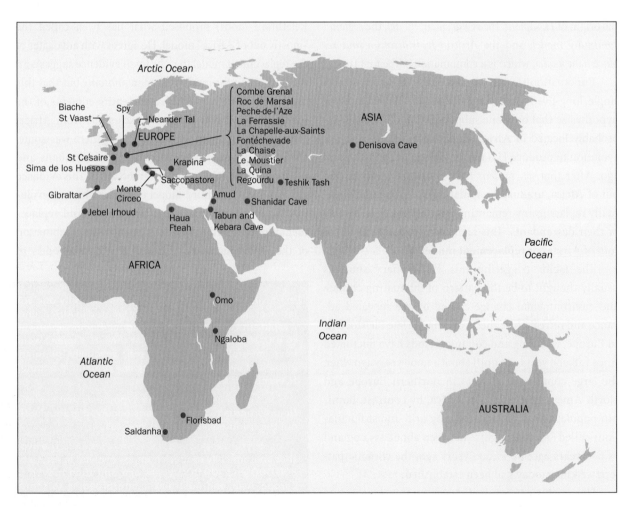

MAP 6.2 Major Neanderthal sites, indicating the concentration of these hominins in Europe and south-western Asia.

the extreme forward placement of teeth in the jaw. This forward placement and the characteristic wear patterns on Neanderthal incisors suggest that Neanderthals regularly used their front teeth as a tool.

The average Neanderthal cranial capacity (1520 cm³) is actually larger than that of modern human populations (1400 cm³), and the braincase is elongated, with a receding forehead, unlike the rounded crania and domed foreheads of modern humans. Fossilized impressions of Neanderthal brains appear to show the same pattern of difference between the left and right halves (*brain asymmetry*) that is found in modern human brains. Among other things, this suggests that Neanderthals were usually right-handed, and since Neanderthal and anatomically modern human populations descended from the same ancestral group (i.e., some form of archaic *H. sapiens*), then it is likely that both groups inherited similarly functioning brains.

Neanderthal postcranial skeletons are not significantly different from those of modern human beings, except for shape of the pelvis and the femur. Neanderthals were extremely muscular, as indicated by the markings for muscle attachment on the bones of their limbs, and Neanderthal hands suggest to paleoanthropologists that Neanderthals had an unusually powerful grip. The Neanderthal pubic bone is longer and thinner than that of modern human beings, which may be the result of posture and locomotion.

The morphological differences that distinguish modern human beings from the Neanderthals are not considered greater than the differences that distinguish two subspecies within some species of mammals. Moreover, genetic information from ancient DNA suggests that Neanderthals may have been genetically similar enough to our direct human ancestors to have interbred with them. Paleoanthropologists these days are recognizing that mobility and interaction among ancient hominin populations were much greater than suspected, and they are reconsidering how boundaries between fossil species ought to be understood.

In Their Own Words

Growing Up Fast: Young Neanderthals Had No Time for Imaginary "What If?" Games

April Nowell, of the University of Victoria, describes her recent work on Neanderthals, culture, and the importance of childhood games for creative activity.

As a Paleolithic archaeologist, I study the archaeological record of our earliest human ancestors, from 2.5 million years ago when we have the first stone tools to 10,000 years ago when the last Ice Age ended. My research focuses on the evolution of language, art, and symbol use and the emergence of modern cognition. In particular, I specialize in Neanderthals and what we can learn about their lifeways from studying the remains they left behind and how they used the landscape around them. Because of these research interests, I currently direct an international team of scientists in the excavation and analysis of Lower and Middle Paleolithic sites in Jordan. We have found many stone tools, including some that have blood residue on them from animals that went extinct thousands of years ago.

Over the past few years, I have become interested in the archaeology of children. In prehistoric societies, children likely made up 40 to 60 per cent of the population, but archaeologists have largely been silent about the lives they led and the contributions they made; however, through the work of many dedicated people, this is beginning to change. My own research in this area focuses on how Neanderthal children grew and developed and what this can tell us about the adults they became. The following is an excerpt from an article I wrote for *New Scientist* in 2013:

Humans today live in what we call a symbolic culture. All the objects around us have a symbolic dimension. The clothes we wear, for instance, send out signals about us that are unrelated to their practical function. We form symbolic relationships where no biological relationship exists, with a husband, sister-in-law, godchild, blood-brother, for example. Language, of course, is another key example; the relationship between the words and the objects and concepts to which they refer is completely arbitrary and that is the essence of a symbol.

Continued

Neanderthals created few symbolic artifacts. Before about 50,000 years ago there is very little evidence of any that stand up to scientific scrutiny. A few Neanderthal sites dating from 50,000 to 30,000 years ago contain some beads, pigments, raptor talons, and indirect evidence for feathers—all presumably for some kind of body decoration. . . .

The ability to reproduce a three-dimensional form on a two-dimensional surface, or to "see" a figure in ivory, requires a completely different way of imagining the world. Neanderthals created nothing like these artefacts, and I believe this can be explained by the games they played, or more correctly did not play, as children.

Neanderthals matured more slowly than earlier hominins such as *Homo erectus*, but more quickly than modern humans. As a result, they had a shorter childhood than us. We know this because Neanderthals occasionally buried their dead, so we have a relatively large collection of Neanderthal infants and children from which to measure their development. One study in particular was a game changer. In 2010, Tanya Smith from Harvard University and colleagues studied Neanderthal and early human teeth, counting daily growth lines to calculate the exact age. By comparing this to the individual's patterns of growth, Smith concluded that Neanderthals grew relatively rapidly and spent less time dependent on their parents.

Why should this make a difference to the minds of Neanderthals compared to modern humans? To understand this, we need to take a closer look at childhood. In general, species like us, with longer dependency periods, tend to play more and engage in many more types of play. This influences our minds, because play is an important part of the healthy cognitive development of many animals, not just humans, and being deprived of opportunities to play can be detrimental. For example, a study on rats demonstrated that those raised normally but without access to playmates suffered from

Courtesy of April Nowell

Canadian archaeologist April Nowell excavating Neanderthal sites in Jordan.

the same kinds of problems as rats with damage to their prefrontal cortex, a region of the brain involved in social behaviour, abstract thinking, and reasoning. In other words, play shapes the brain. But the kind of brain we have also shapes the type of play we engage in.

Humans are unique in that we engage in fantasy play, part of a package of symbol-based cognitive abilities that includes self-awareness, language, and theory of mind. Its benefits include creativity, behavioural plasticity, imagination, and the ability to plan. Being able to imagine novel solutions to problems and to work out their consequences before implementing them would have been an enormous advantage for our early human ancestors—this is exactly what we are practising when we play "what if" games. From what we can tell, it is unlikely that Neanderthals were able to engage in fantasy play, and it is this level of imagination that underlies the differences in material culture between Neanderthals and early humans.

What Do We Know about the Culture of the Middle Paleolithic/Middle Stone Age?

Late archaic human populations in Europe, Africa, and southwestern Asia are associated with a new stone-tool tradition, the **Mousterian tradition**, named after the cave in Le Moustier, France, where the first samples of these tools were discovered. Mousterian tools are assigned to the Middle Paleolithic, whereas similar tools from Africa are assigned to the **Middle Stone Age (MSA)**. They differ from the Lower Paleolithic/ESA tools in that they consist primarily of flakes, not cores. Many Mousterian flakes, moreover, were produced by a new method of tool production known as the Levallois technique of core preparation, a highly precise manufacturing process. The earliest MSA tool industries in Africa are probably about 200,000 years old. The earliest Mousterian industries of

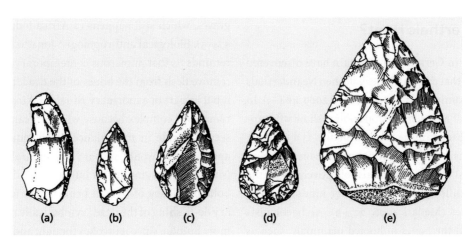

FIGURE 6.2 Mousterian tools were primarily flake tools, commonly produced by the Levallois technique of core preparation.

Source: From F. Bordes, *The Old Stone Age*, Weidenfeld Publishers Ltd., 1968.

Europe may be equally old, but dating is far less certain because radiometric techniques cannot provide reliable dates for this period.

Despite differing names and a distribution that covers more than one continent, most Mousterian/MSA stone-tool assemblages are surprisingly similar, consisting of flake tools that were retouched to make scrapers and points (Figure 6.2). Flint was the stone of choice in Europe and southwestern Asia, but quartzite and some volcanic rock types were widely used in Africa, where flint is absent. Most Mousterian/MSA sites are rock shelters located near what were once sources of fresh water. The rock shelters were probably living sites because many contained hearths as well as stone tools. Interestingly, Mousterian sites found in the European part of the former Soviet Union appear to be the earliest hominin sites that exist in these areas. This might mean that Neanderthals were the first hominins capable of settling areas with such a cold, harsh climate.

What other cultural remains are there from the Middle Paleolithic? In western Europe, Neanderthals left traces of hearths, although their sites were not centred on hearths, as is typical of the Upper Paleolithic. The evidence for stone walls is ambiguous, but there is good evidence for pits and even a post hole, especially at Combe-Grenal in France, where archaeologist François Bordes excavated (Mellars 1996, 295). Moreover, we know that Neanderthals deliberately buried their dead, often with arms and legs folded against their upper bodies. A number of the most famous Neanderthal finds, such as La Ferrassie in France and Shanidar Cave in Iraq, are grave sites. Many paleoanthropologists interpret deliberate burials as evidence for the beginnings of human belief systems. Accumulations of bear skulls found at some European sites have been interpreted as collections Neanderthals made for use in a "cave bear cult." Flower pollen scattered over the Shanidar burial was interpreted as the remains of flowers mourners had placed on the grave. Fragments of natural red or black pigments were interpreted as possible ritual cosmetics. Recent evidence suggests that Neanderthals created elaborate cave art in La Pasiega, Spain, and in other caves in the Iberian peninsula (Hoffmann et al. 2018).

Combined, these burials and cave art are evidence that illustrate the culture of the Neanderthals while the biological/fossil data indicate that Neanderthals lived hard lives in a difficult habitat, with many bones showing evidence of injuries, disease, and premature aging. To survive as long as they did, the individuals to whom these bones belonged would have needed to rely on others to care for them (Chase 1989, 330). As Klein (2009, 585) observes, "This group concern for the old and sick may have permitted Neanderthals to live longer than any of their predecessors, and it is the most recognizably human, non-material aspect of their behaviour that can be directly inferred from the archaeological record."

Mousterian tradition A Middle Paleolithic stone-tool tradition associated with Neanderthals in Europe and southwestern Asia and with anatomically modern human beings in Africa.

Middle Stone Age (MSA) The name given to the period of Mousterian stone-tool tradition in Africa, 200,000 to 40,000 years ago.

Did Neanderthals Hunt?

Archaeologists in Germany and Britain have discovered wooden spears that date to the period when Neanderthals were the only hominins in Europe (Klein 2009, 404–5). In addition, several Mousterian stone points show what appears to be impact damage, suggesting use as a weapon. Animal remains at some sites in France and on the island of Jersey suggest that Neanderthals collectively drove the animals over cliffs or engaged in other kinds of mass-killing strategies (Mellars 1996, 227–9). Archaeologists have also found the bones of hoofed mammals, such as deer, bison, and wild species of oxen, sheep, goats, and horses, at Eurasian Mousterian sites.

Archaeologist P.G. Chase has argued that Neanderthals were skilled hunters of large game and that their diet does not seem to have differed much from that of the modern people who eventually replaced them. Recent research done by archaeologist Eugene Morin of Trent University concurs with Chase regarding Neanderthals' capacity to hunt. Morin (2008) analyzed the mammal remains from various Neanderthal sites, identifying a high percentage of reindeer. Reindeer are migratory mammals, and their herd numbers are not stable. Thus, as Morin has noted, the Neanderthals put themselves at risk as their reliance on reindeer intensified, and they likely experienced years of feast and famine as a result.

What about the flesh of other Neanderthals? Persuasive evidence of cannibalism in association with Neanderthals has been reported from the 100,000-year-old site of Moula-Guercy, in France (Defleur et al. 1993) and from the 49,000-year-old site of El Sidron, in Spain (Lalueza-Fox et al. 2010). In both sites, the bones of a number of Neanderthal individuals show unmistakable signs of cut marks that indicate some or all of the following: the deliberate cutting apart of bodies, the cutting away of muscles, or the splitting of bones to extract marrow. The question is how to interpret these findings. Middle Paleolithic archaeologist Richard Klein suggests that the damage to these bones may have been the work of carnivores that feasted on bodies they had dug out of

graves, which still happens in Africa today (Klein 2009, 574–5). Biological anthropologist Jonathan Marks (2009) reminds us that numerous contemporary human groups remove flesh from the bones of the dead, not to consume it but as part of a mortuary ritual. Making sense of these remains is complex because what it means to be human seems to ride in the balance: if Neanderthals ate one another, they would appear "behaviourally non-human (since the consumption of human flesh lies on the symbolic boundary of human behaviour)," whereas mortuary de-fleshing of the dead "symbolically renders them as more human, since it invokes thought and ritual" (Marks 2009, 225).

What Do We Know about Anatomically Modern Humans (300,000 Years Ago to Present)?

During the period when classic Neanderthal populations appeared in Europe and western Asia, a different kind of hominin appeared to the south—one that possessed an anatomy like that of modern human beings. These hominins had an average cranial capacity of more than 1350 cm³, domed foreheads, and round braincases. These early modern people also had flatter faces than Neanderthals, usually with distinct chins. Their teeth were not crowded into the front of their jaws, and they lacked retromolar spaces. The postcranial skeleton of these **anatomically modern human beings** was much more lightly built than that of the Neanderthals, and over time it gradually became smaller and less robust; this trend is most evident in the fossil record of Europe. Many paleoanthropologists believe that these changes were a by-product of niche construction as anatomically modern human beings became increasingly dependent on culture and buffered themselves from selection pressures that favoured physical strength.

Experts long thought that anatomically modern human beings first appeared about 40,000 years ago in Europe. However, discoveries in recent years have profoundly altered our understanding of modern human origins. It is now accepted that the earliest evidence for anatomically modern humans comes from Jebel Irhoud in Morocco, with these fossils and associated culture items dating to approximately 300,000 years ago

anatomically modern human beings Hominins assigned to the species *H. sapiens*, with anatomical features similar to those of living human populations: short and round skulls, small brow ridges and faces, prominent chins, and gracile skeletal build.

(Hublin et al. 2017). Other fossils attributed to early anatomically modern *Homo sapiens* have been found elsewhere in Africa and the world (see Map 6.3).

Until recently, dating fossils as old as those found in Jebel Irhoud had been problematic, as traditional radiocarbon methods tend to be ineffective for dating fossils that are more than 60,000 or so years old. As a result, scientists have had to develop new methods that can more accurately date older fossils. Some examples include uranium-series dating, thermoluminescence dating, and methods that measure electron spin resonance. As these methods are being refined, they are providing firmer and firmer dates for the earliest fossils of anatomically modern humans.

As well, between 127,000 and 71,000 years ago, a total of at least 45,000 years, Neanderthals and modern humans apparently lived side by side or took turns occupying southwestern Asia. These sites are important discoveries in our evolutionary past as they indicate that Neanderthals and anatomically modern human beings were living at the same time, thereby disputing theories that claim that modern humans descended from Neanderthals.

What Can Genetics Tell Us about Modern Human Origins?

Based on the assumption that genetic mutations accumulate in DNA at a constant rate, geneticists have been able to construct a "molecular clock" that reveals approximate timespans between crucial genetic developments in our evolutionary past. These timespans are most accurately measured using mitochondrial DNA (mtDNA), which is found in the mitochondria of cells, outside the nucleus, and is transmitted only along the female line (unlike eggs, sperm carry only nuclear DNA). The results of such analyses suggest that the ancestors of modern humans originated in Africa some 100,000 to 200,000 years ago (Cann, Stoneking, and Wilson 1987; Wilson and Cann 1992). Other analyses of variation in the Y (i.e., the male) chromosome of different regional human populations have also suggested an African origin for modern *H. sapiens* (e.g., Rouhani 1989). Over the past few decades, information about the DNA of many living species, not just our own, has grown at an impressive rate (see Chapter 3).

But most exciting of all has been the invention of techniques that can successfully extract ancient DNA from bones that are tens of thousands of years old. These operations have been performed on the bones of many extinct species, but the successes achieved using bone from Neanderthals and their contemporaries has been dazzling. In 1997, molecular geneticists working in the laboratory directed by Svante Pääbo at the Max Planck Institute for Evolutionary Anthropology in Leipzig, Germany, extracted a sequence of mtDNA with 378 base pairs from the original 1856 Neanderthal-type specimen and compared the Neanderthal sequence with 994 human mtDNA lineages taken from a worldwide sample

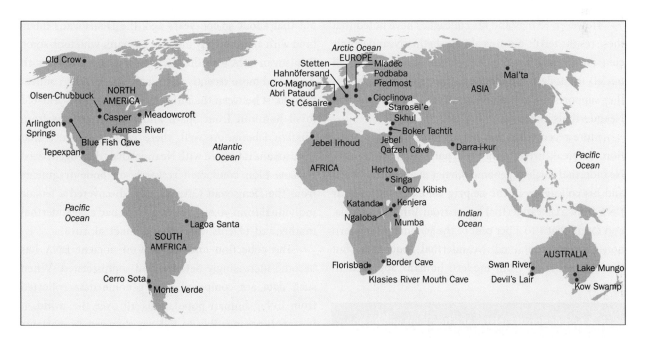

MAP 6.3 Fossils of anatomically modern human beings and/or their archaeological remains have been recovered from these Old World and New World sites.

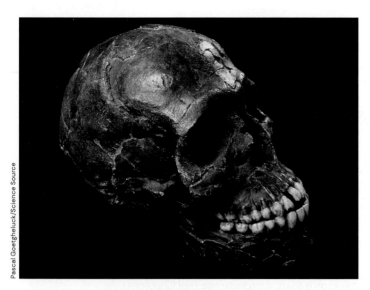

Pascal Goetgheluck/Science Source

FIGURE 6.3 Using thermoluminescence, uranium-series dating, and electron spin resonance, researchers have been able to date the remains of an anatomically modern human, found in Qafzeh Cave, Israel, to between 130,000–92,000 years ago.

of living human populations. They concluded that Neanderthal females contributed no mtDNA to modern human populations and reaffirmed that the ancestor of the mtDNA pool of contemporary humans lived in Africa (Krings et al. 1997). Shortly thereafter, they concluded that the last common mtDNA ancestor of Neanderthals and modern humans lived approximately half a million years ago (Krings et al. 1999).

However, Krings and his colleagues have noted that these results tell us nothing about whether Neanderthals contributed *nuclear* genes (i.e., genes located in our cell nuclei) to modern populations. Thus, this research neither supports nor refutes whether modern humans and Neanderthals interbred.

More recent work has begun to answer this question. A breakthrough was the publication of a draft Neanderthal nuclear genome (Green et al. 2010). Green and his colleagues in the Leipzig lab extracted nuclear DNA from 21 Neanderthal bones from Vindija, Croatia, and found that 1 to 4 per cent of the genomes of modern non-Africans contained Neanderthal sequences, but that no sequences from modern humans appeared in

the Neanderthal genome. They concluded, therefore, that most genetic variation in modern humans outside Africa originated with our anatomically modern ancestors. Finally, because they thought the Neanderthal genome was equally distant from the genomes of modern individuals from around the world, they concluded that the interbreeding between modern humans and Neanderthals probably took place in southwestern Asia, before modern humans spread out and diversified throughout the Old World. These results do not support the regional continuity model but would be consistent with the African hybridization and replacement model.

At the same time, new evidence of our modern human ancestors having interbred with another extinct hominin species, the **Denisovans**, has come to light from northeast Asia. In 2010, Svante Pääbo and his colleagues extracted both mtDNA and nuclear DNA from two tiny fossils found at Denisova Cave in Siberia. When the Denisova sequences were compared with those of Neanderthals and modern human populations, three key findings emerged: (1) although they lived between 400,000 and 30,000 years ago, the Denisovans were genetically distinct from Neanderthals; (2) the Denisovans and Neanderthals shared a common ancestor who had left Africa nearly 500,000 years ago; and (3) the Denisovan genome was very similar to the genome of modern humans from New Guinea. Pääbo and his colleagues concluded that the Denisovan and Neanderthal populations must have split apart after leaving Africa, but that about 50,000 years ago, the Denisovans interbred with anatomically modern humans, who took some Denisovan DNA with them when they moved into South Asia. And more recently still, as we saw earlier, connections exist between the mtDNA from a 300,000-year-old fossil hominin from Spain and the Denisovans from Russian Siberia. As well, there is now evidence that Denisovans interbred with Neanderthals. Paleogeneticist Viviane Slon conducted research on bone fragments from the Denisovan Cave and she discovered a female individual from 90,000 years ago that had a Neanderthal mother and a Denisovan father (Slon et. al. 2018).

The collection and analysis of ancient DNA has become increasingly detailed and sophisticated. When such data are compared with genome data collected from living human populations all over the world, it is sometimes possible to tell whether genetic variants found in living human populations were part of the gene pool of these ancient populations. For example, a variant

Denisovans A population of Pleistocene hominins known only from ancient DNA recovered from two tiny, 41,000-year-old fossils deposited in Denisova Cave in Siberia.

of the *MC1R* gene, which affects skin pigmentation in modern human populations, has been recovered from Neanderthal bones in Spain and Italy; tests on its functioning suggest that Neanderthals had light skin and red hair (Lalueza-Fox et al. 2007).

Although there is lingering concern that modern DNA might have contaminated some ancient fossil samples, this new genetic evidence is exciting and accumulating at an impressive rate. Still, some perspective is called for. Jonathan Marks (2011, 139) reminds us that "while our DNA matches that of a chimpanzee at over the 98 per cent level, it matches the DNA of the banana the chimpanzee is eating at over the 25 per cent level. Yet there is hardly any way we can imagine ourselves to be over one-quarter banana—except in our DNA." So do we really share 1 to 4 per cent of our genome with Neanderthals? Many paleontologists and archaeologists are likely to be cautious about endorsing the DNA evidence until it is backed up by additional fossil evidence.

What Do We Know about the Upper Paleolithic/Late Stone Age (40,000–10,000 Years Ago)?

Middle Paleolithic/MSA tools disappear in Africa and southwestern Asia by approximately 40,000 years ago and in Europe after about 35,000 years ago. What replaces them are far more elaborate artifacts that signal the beginning of the Upper Paleolithic in Europe and southwestern Asia and the **Late Stone Age** (LSA) in Africa.

The stone-tool industries of the Upper Paleolithic/LSA are traditionally identified by the high proportion of blades they contain when compared with the Middle Paleolithic/MSA assemblages that preceded them. A **blade** is defined as any flake that is at least twice as long as it is wide. Despite that fact that blades have traditionally been associated with the anatomically modern humans, there is a multitude of evidence that blades were manufactured in over a dozen sites in western Eurasia and Africa that also contain Middle Paleolithic or MSA stone-tool assemblages rich in blades (Figure 6.4). Further, new evidence from Tanzania uncovered by paleoanthropologist Pam Willoughby, of the University of Alberta, suggests that there is a gradual transition to more blade manufacturing in Africa beginning approximately 500,000 years ago and leading up to the LSA

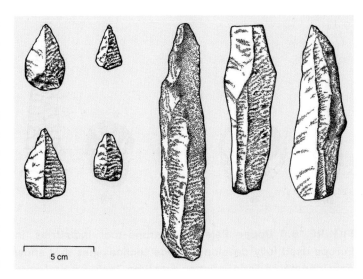

FIGURE 6.4 Blade tools dating as far back as 90,000 years (during the Middle Stone Age) have been found in the Klasies River Mouth Cave in South Africa.

Source: From F. Bordes, *The Old Stone Age*, Weidenfeld Publishers Ltd., 1968.

(Willoughby and Collins 2010). There is no reason to suppose that Neanderthals or Denisovans or *H. heidelbergensis* were incapable of making blades; therefore, one cannot assume that the presence of blades indicates the presence of anatomically modern humans. Rather, it is more important to recognize the high proportion and rapid spread of blades, along with many other artifacts, found at archaeological sites as an indication of the LSA.

During the Upper Paleolithic, tools made from blades or blade segments were regularly attached to wood, bone, antler, or ivory in order to form **composite tools,** such as bows and arrows. Archaeologists Bar-Yosef and Kuhn (1999) note that composite tools require interchangeable parts, so the efficient production of standardized blades would have been advantageous and would have encouraged the spread of blade production techniques that allowed toolmakers better control over the sizes and shapes of the blades they produced; such production also reflects the emergence of significant patterns of economic and social interactions.

Late Stone Age (LSA) The name given to the period of highly elaborate stone-tool traditions in Africa, 40,000 to 10,000 years ago, in which blades were important.

blades Sharp-edged stone tools that are at least twice as long as they are wide.

composite tools Tools such as bows and arrows in which several different materials are combined (e.g., stone, wood, bone, ivory, antler) to produce the final working implement.

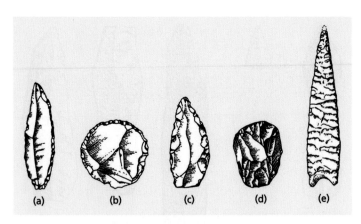

(a)   (b)   (c)   (d)   (e)

FIGURE 6.5 Upper Paleolithic stone-tool industries in Europe used fully developed blade technologies that show considerable stylistic variation over time. Tools *a*, *b*, and *c* are from the Perigordian culture, a variety of the Gravettian; tool *d* is from the Aurignacian; and tool *e* is from the Solutrean.
Source: From F. Bordes, *The Old Stone Age*, Weidenfeld Publishers Ltd., 1968.

Indeed, Upper Paleolithic/LSA people clearly had a new capacity for cultural innovation. Although Mousterian/MSA tool types persist with little change for over 100,000 years, several different Upper Paleolithic/LSA tool traditions replace one another over the 30,000 years or so of the Upper Paleolithic/LSA. Each industry is stylistically distinct and possesses artifact types not found in the others (Figure 6.5). For the earliest anatomically modern people to abandon the Mousterian/MSA culture that had served them well for so long, something important must have happened. Many experts believe this something was a reorganization of the brain, producing the modern capacity for culture. This anatomical change, if it occurred, has left no fossil evidence. However, as knowledge about the genomes of living humans, other primates, and fossil hominins accumulates, it may become increasingly possible to find and date key mutations associated with brain expansion or language ability (Klein 2009, 638ff). For the present, such a change must be inferred from the cultural evidence produced by anatomically modern humans after about 40,000 years ago.

What Happened to the Neanderthals?

The first appearance of the Upper Paleolithic tool tradition in Europe is important because of what it can tell us about the fate of the Neanderthals. If Neanderthals gradually evolved into modern human beings, it is argued, then this gradual evolution should be documented in archaeological assemblages. In the search for evidence to support this position, the Châtelperronian and Aurignacian stone-tool industries have attracted the most attention.

Châtelperronian assemblages from France are 35,000 to 30,000 years old and contain a mixture of typical Mousterian backed knives and more advanced pointed cutting tools called "burins." They also contain bone tools and pierced animal teeth. Other mixed assemblages similar to the Châtelperronian have been found in Italy, central and northern Europe, and southern Russia (Mellars 1996, 417–18). Aurignacian assemblages, which are roughly 34,000 to 30,000 years old, are Upper Paleolithic blade assemblages. We know that Neanderthals were capable of making Châtelperronian tools because two Neanderthal skeletons were found in 32,000-year-old Châtelperronian deposits at Saint-Césaire, France. If Neanderthals invented Aurignacian technology as they evolved into anatomically modern human beings, then the Châtelperronian and other mixed assemblages might be transitional between the Mousterian and the Aurignacian.

Some archaeologists argue, however, that Neanderthals may have borrowed elements of Upper Paleolithic technology from a culturally more advanced population of outsiders. For example, deposits found in some cave sites in southwestern France and northern Spain show Châtelperronian layers on top of some Aurignacian layers, suggesting that two different cultural groups coexisted and occupied the same caves at different times (Mellars 1996, 414). These archaeologists believe that anatomically modern people invented the Aurignacian industry in southwestern Asia and brought it with them when they migrated into central and western Europe 40,000 to 35,000 years ago. The skeletons of anatomically modern human beings begin to appear at European sites around this time, when the ice sheets had begun to melt and the climate was improving. For many archaeologists, the arrival in Europe of both modern human beings and Aurignacian culture during the same time period seems too well correlated to be an accident. No Aurignacian assemblages have been found in eastern Europe, which suggests that the Upper Paleolithic developed differently there (Klein 2009, 586–8, 605).

Even if European Neanderthals borrowed Upper Paleolithic technology from southwestern Asian immigrants, they were gone a few thousand years later. What happened to them? There is no evidence that the replacement of Neanderthals by modern people involved conquest and extermination, although this has been proposed from time to time. European Neanderthals may have disappeared because they evolved into anatomically modern people, developing Aurignacian tools as they did so, in line with the regional continuity model. This hypothesis, however, runs afoul of the fact that Neanderthals and moderns apparently originated on different continents and coexisted in southwestern Asia for 45,000 years, both of them making and using Mousterian tools. European Neanderthals may have disappeared as they interbred with the in-migrating modern people and as their descendants adopted Aurignacian tools. If this happened, then contemporary European populations might be expected to share morphological traits with their alleged Neanderthal ancestors. As we saw earlier, morphological evidence for such interbreeding during the Pleistocene is stronger for populations in eastern Europe and western Asia than for the classic Neanderthals of western Europe, and Neanderthal genes make up 1 to 4 per cent of our modern nuclear genome. Neanderthals may have retreated as modern people spread throughout Europe, decreasing in number until, around 27,000 years ago, they simply died out. In sum, at this time, the archaeological evidence is no more able than the fossil or genetic evidence to resolve disputes about the fate of the Neanderthals.

How Many Kinds of Upper Paleolithic/Late Stone Age Cultures Were There?

Although blades and composite tools are the classic tools of Upper Paleolithic/LSA industry, other tool types appear that are not found in Mousterian/MSA assemblages, such as endscrapers, burins, and numerous artifacts of bone, ivory, and antler (Figure 6.6). Brian Fagan (1990, 157) calls this technological explosion the "Swiss army knife effect": "like its modern multipurpose counterpart, the core and blade technique was a flexible artifact system, allowing Upper Paleolithic stoneworkers to develop a variety of subsidiary crafts, notably bone and antler working, which likewise gave rise to new weapons systems and tailored clothing."

FIGURE 6.6 Upper Paleolithic stoneworkers developed bone-, antler-, and ivory-working techniques to a high degree, as is shown by these objects from Europe.

As we saw earlier, the most distinctive Upper Paleolithic artifacts are composite tools, such as spears and arrows, made of several different materials. The oldest undisputed evidence of wooden bows and arrows in Europe dates from 12,000 to 11,000 years ago; however, bows and arrows may have been used as long as 20,000 years ago in Africa and Eurasia, where researchers have found indirect evidence in the form of stone points, backed bladelets, and bone rods resembling arrow shafts (Klein 2009, 679–80). Archaeologists have also found the skeletons of fur-bearing animals whose remains suggest they were captured for their skins, not for food; pointed bone tools that were probably used to sew skins together (the oldest eyed needles appeared between 35,000 and 28,000 years ago); and the remains of tailored clothing in Upper Paleolithic burials dating from between 26,000 and 19,000 (Klein 2009, 673).

Evidence for regular hunting of large game is better at Upper Paleolithic sites than at sites from earlier periods, especially in Europe and Asia. Researchers have found hunting tools as well as the bones of mammoths, reindeer, bison, horses, and antelope, animals that provided not only meat but also ivory, antler, and bone. The mammoth, for instance, supplied bones used for building shelters. Fresh bones and animal droppings were also probably burned as fuel. The Upper Paleolithic way of life may have resembled that of contemporary foragers. Consequently, plant foods probably formed a larger part of the diet than did meat. Reliance on plant foods was likely greater among those living in warmer areas of Africa and southwestern Asia, whereas those living in the cooler climates of eastern Europe and northern Asia may have relied more on animals for food.

The richness and sophistication of Upper Paleolithic culture is documented in many other ways. Upper Paleolithic burials are more elaborate than Mousterian/ MSA burials, and some burial sites contain several bodies (Klein 2009, 690–1). Some Upper Paleolithic sites have yielded human bones that have been shaped, perforated, or burned or that show cut marks suggesting de-fleshing. Some paleoanthropologists conclude that Upper Paleolithic peoples may have been cannibals. However, the shaped or perforated bones may have been trophies or mementos of individuals who had died for other reasons; the burned bones may be the remains of deliberate cremation or accidental charring under a hearth; and the flesh may have been removed from human bones after death for ritual purposes, a practice documented in modern ethnographic literature.

The most striking evidence of modern human culture and creativity is represented in the multitude of unique art forms from the Upper Paleolithic/LSA. In Africa, ostrich-eggshell beads were made at least 50,000 years ago, identifying an early form of personal adornment. As Jennifer Miller and Pam Willoughby (2014) from the University of Alberta suggest, these beads represent important innovations that align with new social interactions. Animal paintings on rocks date to at least 19,000 and possibly 27,500 years ago. Fire-hardened clay objects shaped like animals or human beings, dating to about 28,000 to 27,000 years ago, have been recovered at a Gravettian site in the former Czechoslovakia. This and other Gravettian sites in western and central Europe have yielded human figurines, some of which depict females with exaggerated breasts and bellies, thought to have been made between 27,000 and 20,000 years ago. Over 200 caves in southern France and northern Spain, including Lascaux and Altamira, contain spectacular

FIGURE 6.7 Upper Paleolithic cave paintings, like this one from Lascaux, France, have been dated to between 15,000 and 11,000 years ago.

wall paintings or engravings (Figure 6.7). Other painted caves exist in Italy, Portugal, and the former Yugoslavia, and spectacular wall art from rock shelters in northern Australia may be especially old (Renfrew and Bahn 2004, 523). The European paintings portray several animal species now extinct and were probably painted between 15,000 and 11,000 years ago, during Magdalenian times. Recently, new techniques have permitted archaeologists to analyze the recipes of pigments used to make these wall images, while accelerator mass spectrometry can be used to date the charcoal used to make other drawings. As a result, archaeologists are increasingly able to determine when images were painted and whether all the images in a particular cave were painted at the same time.

Where Did Modern *Homo sapiens* Migrate in Late Pleistocene Times?

Upper Paleolithic peoples were more numerous and more widespread than previous hominins. In Europe, there are more Upper Paleolithic sites than Mousterian sites, and they also have a more varied assortment of material remains. As well, skeletons dating from this period show few injuries and little evidence of disease or violence, and they possess relatively healthy teeth. The presence of skeletons belonging to older or incapacitated individuals at Upper Paleolithic sites suggests that these people, like the Neanderthals, cared for the old and the sick. Analysis indicates that the life expectancy of Upper Paleolithic people was greater than that of the Neanderthals and not very different from that of modern-day foragers (Klein 2009).

Archaeologists have found amber, seashells, and even flint in Upper Paleolithic/LSA sites located tens to hundreds of kilometres away from the regions where these items occur naturally. They must have been deliberately transported to these sites, suggesting that Upper Paleolithic peoples, like contemporary foragers, participated in trading networks or that they migrated over long distances. However, no evidence of trade-based social contacts exists for earlier times. Perhaps the linguistic and cultural capacities of fully modern humans were necessary before such contacts could develop.

Eastern Asia and Siberia

Physically and culturally modern human beings were the first hominins to occupy the coldest, harshest climates in Asia. Upper Paleolithic blade industries developed in central Asia about 40,000 to 30,000 years ago with the oldest reliable dates for human occupation in Siberia between 35,000 and 20,000 years ago (Klein 2009, 673). During this glacial time, a land bridge known as the Bering land bridge connected eastern Siberia to Alaska. Ice Age animals and Upper Paleolithic peoples ranged

across this area, referred to as Beringia, establishing sites in Alaska and Canada; these sites have been found to contain artifacts similar to those of northeast Siberia that date to between 15,000 and 12,000 years ago. Artifacts from one of these sites, Bluefish Caves in the Yukon, may even be more than 20,000 years old. Migration over land to areas below the glaciers was blocked by continuous ice between 25,000 and 14,000 years ago. Alternatively, recent archaeological finds and DNA analysis support a migration route southward along the northwestern coast of North America by approximately 16,000 years ago (Llamas et al. 2016). Soon after this, continental glaciers melted, facilitating both land and water migration into uninhabited regions to the south.

The Americas

Genetic studies strongly support an Asian origin for Indigenous populations in America (Klein 2009, 707). The earliest known skeletal remains found in the Americas have recently been dated between 13,000 and 11,000 years old, and their morphological variation suggests that the Americas were colonized more than once (Map 6.4)

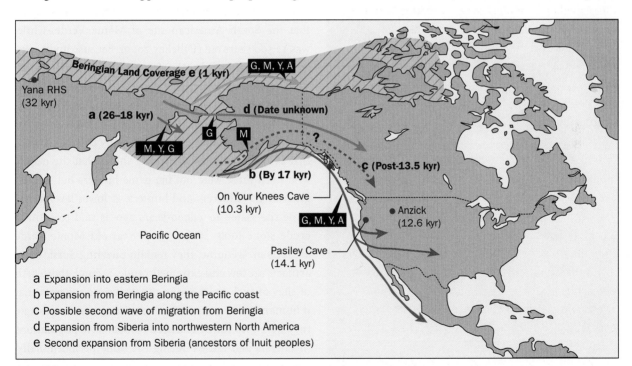

MAP 6.4 Map of hypothesized migration routes of humans from Asia into North America, with several significant archaeological sites (indicated by black dots). The orange arrows represent possible routes of people from Beringia, while the blue arrows represent possible routes of people from Siberia. The letters *G* (for genomic), *Y* (for Y-chromosome), *M* (for mitochondrial), and *A* (for archaeological) indicate the type of evidence that supports each hypothesized route. The shading around Asia and northwestern North America represents the estimated extent of Beringia during the last glacial maximum. Note that *kyr* stands for "thousand years ago" (Raff and Bolnick 2014).

(Raff and Bolnick 2014). New evidence that provides both morphological and genetic information about the earliest inhabitants of the Americas is being recovered in unusual places (Chatters et al. 2014). In underground caves along Mexico's Yucatan peninsula, researchers have found the skeleton of a juvenile female, whom they have named "Naia," estimated to be more than 12,000 years old. Geoarchaeologist Eduard Reinhardt of McMaster University is part of the international team working to recover Naia's remains from their watery grave as well as reconstruct the environmental conditions that existed in Central America when humans were first settling in it. Naia's skeleton represents the earliest human remains recovered in the Americas so far. The youth's morphology supports an early migration out of Beringia, likely along the west coast, and her genetic signature identifies a population continuity model that began in eastern Asia and moved into the Americas.

AP Photo/The Daily Oklahoman, Chad Love

FIGURE 6.8 Stone tools made by Paleoindian peoples have been found at sites that provide some of the oldest reliable dates for human occupation in North America. The Clovis point pictured here was probably attached to a shaft to make a spear.

Research in other regions of the Americas has suggested that the first anatomically modern human beings to inhabit these continents, called "Paleoindians" or "Paleoamericans," were successful hunting peoples. Reliable evidence of their presence comes from sites dated between 11,500 and 11,000 years ago, which contain stone tools called Clovis points (Figure 6.8). Meadowcroft Rockshelter in Pennsylvania may represent an early Clovis site (Adovasio et al. 1978). Clovis points were finely made and probably attached to shafts to make spears. Rapidly following the Clovis culture were a series of different stone-tool cultures, all of which were confined to North America. Some experts believe that Paleoindian hunting coupled with postglacial climatic changes may have brought about the extinction of mammoth, camel, horse, and other big-game species in North America, but evidence is inconclusive.

For many years, researchers believed that the people who made these exquisite Clovis points represented the earliest human culture to have existed in the Americas. In 1997, however, the "Clovis barrier" of approximately 11,500 years ago was finally broken when a group of archaeologists and other scientists formally announced that the South American site of Monte Verde, Chile, was 12,500 years old (Dillehay 2000). Because it was covered by a peat bog shortly after it was inhabited, Monte Verde contained many well-preserved organic remains, including stakes lashed with knotted twine, dwellings with wooden frames, and hundreds of tools made of wood and bone. Archaeologist Thomas Dillehay argues that evidence from Monte Verde shows that the people who lived there were not big-game hunters but, rather, generalized gatherers and hunters. A lower level at the same site, dated to 33,000 years ago, is said to contain crude stone tools. If the 33,000-year-old Monte Verde artifacts are genuine, they remain puzzling. First, these artifacts are few and extremely crude. Second, the dearth of sites of such great age in the Americas suggests that if human beings were in the Americas 30,000 years ago, they were very thinly scattered compared to populations in Eurasia and Africa during the same period. Finally, blood-group and tooth-shape evidence supports the idea that the ancestors of Indigenous peoples of the Americas migrated into North America from Asia. If the makers of 33,000-year-old Monte Verde artifacts also came from Asia, archaeologists must explain how these people could have reached South America from Siberia by that date. Possibly, they travelled over water and ice, but how they got to South America remains a mystery.

In 2011, evidence for pre-Clovis occupations in North America was found at the Debra L. Friedkin site near Austin, Texas: more than 15,000 artifacts assigned to the Buttermilk Creek Complex, dating between 13,200 and 15,000 years ago, were discovered in soil beneath a Clovis assemblage (Waters et al. 2011). The archaeologists who discovered the tools view them as potentially representing the technology from which Clovis was developed; other archaeologists remain unconvinced.

Today ancient DNA analysis is helping resolve some of these questions, even as it opens up entirely new sets of questions. Ancient mitochondrial DNA and Y-chromosome DNA were extracted from the skeleton of a male infant found in western Montana (see the "Anzick" location on Map 6.4); the remains were discovered in association with Clovis artifacts and buried around 12,600 years ago, leading to the conclusion that the population to which this individual belonged is more closely related to populations from Central and South America than to populations from anywhere else (Rasmussen et al. 2014). This connection suggests that the child belonged to a population "from which many contemporary Native Americans are descended and is closely related to all indigenous American populations" (Rasmussen 2014, 227–8). These ancient DNA studies are forming an important component of scientific efforts to answer questions about ancient human migrations all over the world.

Two Million Years of Human Evolution

By 12,000 years ago, modern human beings had spread to every continent except Antarctica, a fact that we take for granted today but that could not have been predicted 2 mya in Africa, when the first members of the genus *Homo* walked the earth. In fact, the more we learn about hominins and their primate ancestors, the more zigs and zags we perceive in our own past. Our species' origin must be regarded as "an unrepeatable particular, not an expected consequence" (Gould 1996, 4). Some paleoecologists have concluded that "human features may not be adaptations to some past environment, but exaptations . . . accidental by-products of history, functionally disconnected from their origins" (Foley 1995, 47).

For example, paleoanthropologist Rick Potts argues that, rather than "survival of the fittest" (i.e., survival of a species narrowly adapted to a specific environment), modern *H. sapiens* better illustrates "survival of the generalist" (i.e., survival of a species that had the plasticity, the "weed-like resilience," to survive the extremes of the rapidly fluctuating climate of the Ice Ages). In other words, our ancestors' biological capacity to cope with small environmental fluctuations was exapted to cope with larger and larger fluctuations. In Potts's view, selection for genes favouring open programs of behaviour "improve an organism's versatility and response to novel conditions" (1996, 239).

Archaeologist Clive Gamble (1994, 182) believes that the social and cognitive skills that allowed our ancestors to survive in novel habitats were used by *H. sapiens* to colonize the world: "We were not adapted for filling up the world. It was instead a consequence of changes in behaviour, and exaptive radiation produced by the cooption of existing elements in a new framework of action." Gamble is sensitive to the ways human-constructed niches modified the selection pressures our ancestors faced: he argues that all the environments of Australia could never have been colonized so rapidly without far-flung social networks that enabled colonizers to depend on one another in times of need. He sees the colonization of the Pacific as a deliberate undertaking, showing planning and care (1994, 241; see also Dillehay 2000).

The role of niche construction is also implicated in the approach of Richard Klein (2009, 72), who lists a series of "related outcomes of the innovative burst behind the out of Africa expansion" that are detectable in the archaeological record after 50,000 years ago, ranging from standardization and elaboration of artifacts to evidence for increasing elaboration of a built environment (with campsites, hearths, dwellings, and graves) to evidence of elaborate trading networks, ritual activity, and successful colonization of challenging cold climates.

Paleoanthropologists, geneticists, and archaeologists have assembled many of the pieces of the human evolutionary puzzle, but many questions remain. Experts differ, for example, on how to reconstruct the human family tree. Figure 6.9 shows one recent attempt to summarize what is known (and what remains to be established) about the evolution of human beings. Because new data and interpretations appear in the news almost daily, you may want to find out how much

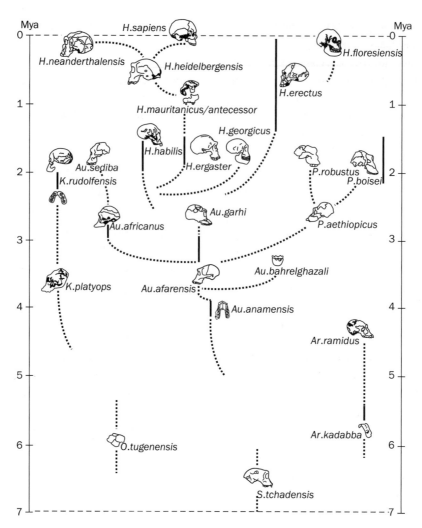

FIGURE 6.9 This summary of what is currently known about hominin evolution is open to modification by new data and new interpretation.

Source: Klein, Richard G. 2009. p. 244.

this summary has been modified by the time you read this book! Another knotty problem concerns how we interpret mounting evidence that human biology and human culture evolved at different rates. Finally, within a few thousand years after the glaciers retreated, human groups in Asia and the Americas were settling in villages and domesticating plants and animals. Why they should have done so at this time is addressed in Chapter 9.

Chapter Summary

1. Around 500,000 years ago, *H. erectus* fossils disappear from the fossil record, to be replaced by fossils that show a mosaic of features found in *H. erectus* and *H. sapiens*. Many paleoanthropologists classify these fossils as *Homo heidelbergensis*. A lively debate continues between punctuationists and gradualists about the fate of *H. erectus* and the origin of *H. sapiens*. Punctuationists and cladists favour the replacement model; gradualists favour the regional continuity model. The African hybridization and replacement model is a combination of the replacement and regional continuity models and is the most readily accepted model used by paleoanthropologists.

2. Neanderthals flourished between 230,000 and 27,000 years ago. They were shorter and more robust than anatomically modern *H. sapiens*. Their molars showed taurodontism, their jaws possessed retromolar spaces, and they may have habitually used their incisors as a clamp. Their average cranial capacity was larger than that of modern human populations, although their skull was shaped differently. Neanderthal fossils found in Europe are typically associated with the Mousterian stone-tool tradition. Similar tools found in southwestern Asia and Africa have been assigned to the Middle Paleolithic/Middle Stone Age, which probably began at least 200,000 years ago.

3. Anatomically modern human beings began to appear around 300,000 years ago. Fossil evidence suggests that Neanderthals and moderns likely lived side by side or took turns occupying the same areas in southwestern Asia for at least 45,000 years, and both populations used the same kinds of Mousterian tools. Studies of ancient DNA have shown that modern humans share 1 to 4 per cent of their nuclear genome with Neanderthals; what this means is still under discussion.

4. By 40,000 years ago in southwestern Asia and 35,000 years ago in Europe, Mousterian/Middle Stone Age tools are replaced by far more elaborate artifacts that signal the beginning of the Upper Paleolithic/Late Stone Age. Upper Paleolithic people made many different stone tools as well as tools and ornaments out of bone, ivory, and antler; composite tools, such as spears and arrows; and clothing from animal fur. They regularly hunted large game and used bones from animals such as mammoths to construct dwellings and to burn as fuel. Upper Paleolithic burials were far more elaborate than Middle Paleolithic burials. Cave paintings and personal ornaments offer the most striking evidence in the Upper Paleolithic for the modern human capacity for culture.

5. Some Upper Paleolithic assemblages, like the Châtelperronian industry from France, contain a mixture of typical Mousterian tools and more elaborate cutting tools, bone tools, and pierced animal teeth. Paleoanthropologists disagree about what these mixed assemblages represent. Some interpret the Châtelperronian industry as evidence that Neanderthals gradually invented Upper Paleolithic tools on their own, which would support the regional continuity model. Others argue that Châtelperronian Neanderthals borrowed Upper Paleolithic techniques from in-migrating modern people who already possessed such techniques under their Aurignacian tradition. This view is compatible with the replacement model. If Aurignacian moderns did replace Neanderthals in Europe, there is no evidence that this was the result of conquest or extermination.

6. Upper Paleolithic peoples showed few signs of injury or disease, and their life expectancy was longer than that of Neanderthals. Upper Paleolithic peoples apparently constructed niches that allowed them to participate in widespread trading networks. Anatomically modern people with Upper Paleolithic cultures were the first humans to migrate into the northernmost regions of Asia and into the New World, arriving at least 12,000 years ago, probably earlier. Further, DNA research provides evidence that the New World was populated by more than one wave of immigrants from Siberia.

For Review

1. Clearly describe the fossil evidence for the evolutionary transition to modern *Homo sapiens*. In what ways does this species differ from Neanderthals?

2. Outline the hypothesis for the African hybridization and replacement model of the origin of modern *Homo sapiens*. What evidence do biological anthropologists use to defend this model? How does this model contrast with the earlier replacement model and the regional continuity model?

3. Biological anthropologists have been studying Neanderthals for hundreds of years. What do we know about them, and how does this knowledge influence how we think about human society and culture?

4. Summarize the features anthropologists emphasize in distinguishing anatomically modern humans from other archaic populations of *Homo*. Why are these features important?

5. Choose and defend one of the proposed explanations for the extinction of Neanderthals. Explain why you chose this hypothesis. Refer to April Nowell's hypothesis regarding play in your answer.

6. How do archaeology and biological anthropology contribute to our understanding of the evolution of a modern human capacity for culture?

7. Describe the evidence that archaeologists, biological anthropologists, and others use to identify when the first people arrived in the Americas and who these people were. Are there any contradictions between different sets of data? Explain.

Key Terms

African hybridization and replacement model 115

anatomically modern human beings 120

archaic *Homo sapiens* 113

blades 123

composite tools 123

Denisovans 122

Late Stone Age (LSA) 123

Middle Stone Age (MSA) 119

Mousterian tradition 119

Neanderthals 116

regional continuity model 115

replacement model 115

References

Adovasio, J.M., J.D. Gunn, J.L. Donahue, and R. Stuckenrath. 1978. "Meadowcroft Rockshelter, 1977: An Overview." *American Antiquity* 43: 632–51.

Aiello, Leslie C. 1993. "The Fossil Evidence for Modern Human Origins in Africa: A Revised View." *American Anthropologist* 95: 73–96.

Arsuaga, Juan-Luis, Ignacio Martinez, Ana Gracia, José-Miguel Carretero, and Eudald Carbonell. 1993. "Three New Human Skulls from the Sima de los Huesos, Middle Pleistocene Site in Sierra de Atapuerca, Spain." *Nature* 362: 534–37.

Bar-Yosef, Ofer, and Steven L. Kuhn. 1999. "The Big Deal about Blades: Laminar Technologies and Human Evolution." *American Anthropologist* 101 (2): 322–28.

Bermúdez de Castro, José-María, J.L. Arsuaga, Eudald. Carbonell, A. Rosas, Ignacio Martinez, and Marina Mosquera. 1997. "A Hominid from the Lower Pleistocene of Atapuerca, Spain." *Science* 276 (5317): 1392–95.

Bräuer, Günter. 1989. "The Evolution of Modern Humans: A Comparison of the African and Non-African Evidence." In *The Human Revolution*, edited by Paul A. Mellars and Chris Stringer, 123–54. Princeton, NJ: Princeton University Press.

Cann, Rebecca L., Mark Stoneking, and Allan C. Wilson. 1987. "Mitchondrial DNA and Human Evolution." *Nature* 325: 31–6.

Chase, Philip G. 1989. "How Different was Middle Palaeolithic Subsistence? A Zooarchaeological Perspective on the Middle to Upper Palaeolithic Transition." In *The Human Revolution*, edited by Paul A. Mellars and Chris Stringer, 321–7. Princeton, NJ: Princeton University Press.

Chatters, James C., Douglas J. Kennett, Yemane Asmerom, Brian M. Kemp, Victor Polyak, Alberta Nava Blank, Patricia A. Beddows, et al. 2014. "Late Pleistocene Human Skeleton and mtDNA Link Paleoamericans and Modern Native Americans." *Science* 344 (6185): 750–4.

Collard, Mark, and Mana Dembo. 2013. "Modern Human Origins." In *A Companion to Paleoanthropology*, edited by David Begun, 557–81. West Sussex, UK: John Wiley and Sons.

Defleur, Alban, Olivier Dutour, Helene Valladas, and Bernard Vandermeersch. 1993. "Cannibals among the Neanderthals?" *Nature* 362: 214.

Dillehay, Thomas D. 2000. *The Settlement of the Americas*. New York: Basic Books.

Fagan, Brian. 1990. *The Journey from Eden*. London: Thames and Hudson.

Foley, Robert. 1995. *Humans before Humanity*. Oxford: Blackwell.

Gamble, Clive. 1994. *Timewalkers*. Cambridge, MA: Harvard University Press.

Gould, Stephen J. 1996. *Full House: The Spread of Excellence from Plato to Darwin*. New York: Harmony Books.

Green, Richard E., Johannes Krause, Adrian W. Briggs, Tomislav Malicic, Udo Stenzel, Martin Kircher, Nick Patterson, et al. 2010. "A Draft Sequence of the Neandertal Genome." *Science* 328 (5979): 710–22.

Hoffmann, D.L., C.D. Standish, M. García-Diez, P.B. Pettitt, J.A. Milton, J. Zilhão, J.J. Alcolea-González, et al. 2018. "U-Th Dating of Carbonate Crusts Reveals Neandertal Origin of Iberian Cave Art." *Science* 359 (6378): 912–15. doi:10.1126/science.aap7778

Hublin, Jean-Jacques, Fred Spoor, Marc Braun, Frans Zonneveld, and Silvana Condemi. 1996. "A Late Neanderthal Associated with Upper Palaeolithic Artifacts." *Nature* 381: 224–6.

Hublin, Jean-Jacques, Abdelouahed Ben-Ncer, Shara E. Bailey, Sarah E. Freidline, Simon Neubauer, Matthew M. Skinner, et al. 2017. "New Fossils from Jebel Irhoud, Morocco and the Pan-African Origin of *Homo sapiens*." *Nature* 546: 289–92. |

Klein, Richard G. 2009. *The Human Career: Human Biological and Cultural Origins*. 3rd ed. Chicago: University of Chicago Press.

Krings, Matthias, Anne Stone, Ralf W. Schmitz, Heike Krainitzki, and Mark Stoneking. 1997. "Neandertal DNA Sequences and the Origin of Modern Humans." *Cell* 90: 19–30.

Krings, Matthias, Helga Geisart, Ralf W. Schmitz, Heike Krainitzki, and Svante Pääbo. 1999. "DNA Sequence of the Mitochondrial Hypervariable Region II from the Neandertal Type Specimen." *Proceedings of the National Academy of Sciences* 95: 5581–5.

Lalueza-Fox, Carles, Holger Rompeler, David Caramelli, Claudia Staubert, Giulio Catalano, David Hughes, Nadin Rohland, et al. 2007. "A Melanocortin 1 Receptor Allele Suggests Varying Pigmentation among Neanderthals." *Science* 318: 1453–5.

Lalueza-Fox, Carles, Antonio Rosas, Almudena Estalrrich, Elena Gigli, Paula F. Campos, Antonio Garcia-Tabernero, Samuel Garcia-Vargas, et al. 2010. "Genetic Evidence for Patrilocal Mating Behavior among Neandertal Groups." *PNAS* 108 (1): 250–3. doi:10.1073/pnas.1011553108

Llamas, Bastien, Lars Fehren-Schmitz, Guido Valverde, Julien Soubrier, Swapan Mallick, Nadin Rohland, Susanne Nordenfelt, et al. 2016. "Ancient Mitochondrial DNA Provides High-Resolution Time Scale of the Peopling of the Americas." *Science Advances* 2 (4): e1501385. doi:10.1126/sciadv.1501385

Marks, Jonathan. 2009. *Why I Am Not a Scientist: Anthropology and Modern Knowledge.* Berkeley: University of California Press.

———. 2011. *The Alternative Introduction to Biological Anthropology.* New York: Oxford University Press.

Mellars, Paul. 1996. *The Neandertal Legacy.* Princeton, NJ: Princeton University Press.

Miller, Jennifer M., and Pamela R. Willoughby. 2014. "Radiometrically Dated Ostrich Eggshell Beads from the Middle and Later Stone Age of Magubike Rockshelter, Southern Tanzania." *Journal of Human Evolution* 74 (1): 118–22.

Morin, Eugene. 2008. "Evidence for Declines in Human Population Densities during the Early Upper Paleolithic in Western Europe." *Proceedings of the National Academy of Sciences* 105 (1): 48–53.

Nowell, April. 2013. "All Work and No Play Left Little Time for Art." *New Scientist* 217 (2905): 28–9.

Potts, Richard. 1996. *Humanity's Descent.* New York: William Morrow.

Raff, Jennifer A., and Deborah A. Bolnick. 2014. "Palaeogenomics: Genetic Roots of the First Americans." *Nature* 506: 162–3. doi:10.1038/506162a

Rasmussen, Morten, Sarah L. Anzick, Michael R. Waters, Pontus Skoglund, Michael DeGiorgio, Thomas W. Stafford Jr, Simon Rasmussen, et al. 2014. "The Genome of a Late Pleistocene Human from a Clovis Burial Site in Western Montana." *Nature* 506: 225–9.

Relethford, John. 2001. *Genetics and the Search for Modern Human Origins.* New York: Wiley.

Renfrew, Colin, and Paul Bahn. 2004. *Archaeology: Theories, Methods and Practice.* 4th ed. London: Thames and Hudson.

Rightmire, G. Philip. 1990. *The Evolution of* Homo erectus. Cambridge: Cambridge University Press.

———. 1995. "Diversity within the Genus *Homo.*" In *Paleoclimate and Evolution, with Emphasis on Human Origins*, edited by Elisabeth Vrba, George Denton, Timothy Partridge, and Lloyd Burckle, 483–92. New Haven, CT: Yale University Press.

Rouhani, Shahin. 1989. "Molecular Genetics and the Pattern of Human Evolution: Plausible and Implausible Models." In *The Human Revolution*, edited by Paul A. Mellars and Chris Stringer, 47–61. Princeton, NJ: Princeton University Press.

Slon, Viviane, Fabrizio Mafessoni, Benjamin Vernot, Cesare de Filippo, Steffi Grote, Bence Viola, Mateja Hajdinjak, et al. 2018. "The Genome of the Offspring of a Neanderthal Mother and a Denisovan Father." *Nature* 561: 113–16.

Tattersall, Ian. 2009. *The Fossil Trail.* 2nd ed. New York: Oxford University Press.

———. 2012. *Masters of the Planet: The Search for Our Human Origins.* New York: Palgrave-Macmillan.

Waters, Michael R., Steven L. Forman, Thomas A. Jennings, Lee C. Nordt, Steven G. Driese, Joshua M. Feinberg, Joshua L. Keene, et al. 2011. "The Buttermilk Creek Complex and the Origins of Clovis at the Debra L. Friedkin Site, Texas." *Science* 331: 1599–1603.

Willoughby, Pamela, and Benjamin Collins. 2010. "The Faunal Analysis of Magubike and Mlambalasi, Two MSA-LSA Archaeological Sites from Iringa District, Tanzania." *Journal of Taphonomy* 8 (1): 33–68.

Wilson, Allan C., and Rebecca L. Cann. 1992. "The Recent African Genesis of Humans." *Scientific American* (April): 68–73.

Wolpoff, Milford H. 1985. "Human Evolution at the Peripheries: The Pattern at the Eastern Edge." In *Hominid Evolution: Past, Present and Future*, edited by Phillip V. Tobias, 355–65. New York: Alan R. Liss.

▲ Due to extended isolation after its occupancy by Irish, Scottish, and Scandinavian settlers over 1200 years ago, the population of Iceland possesses relatively low genetic diversity. Photo: ARCTIC IMAGES / Alamy Stock Photo

7 · What Can Evolutionary Theory Tell Us about Human Variation?

Chapter Outline

N ot everyone looks the same. Why is that? Does it make a difference? Do the differences cluster together? In this chapter, we will look at the way evolutionary theory explains patterns of human biological variation. In particular, we will show why anthropologists have concluded that these patterns cannot be explained by the cultural concept of "race."

Chapter 5 presented some of the central concepts of modern evolutionary theory, specifically macroevolution and how it is applied to the history of humans and their closest relatives. Continuing on the theme of evolution, this chapter investigates how biologists and anthropologists have used evolutionary theory in their research. This chapter will focus on **microevolution**, which attends to short-term evolutionary changes that occur within a few generations of a given species, which can range from a few years to hundreds of years (i.e., insects versus turtles). Microevolution involves what is sometimes called "ecological time," or the pace of time as experienced by organisms living in and adapting to their ecological settings.

What Is Microevolution?

The Modern Evolutionary Synthesis and Its Legacy

In the 1930s and 1940s, biologists and geneticists worked to formulate a new way of thinking about evolution that combined Darwinian natural selection and Mendelian ideas about heredity. Until recently, this approach (called the "modern evolutionary synthesis" or "neo-Darwinism") dominated research and thinking in biology. As we saw in the last chapter, contemporary evolutionary theorists have challenged, expanded, and enriched this neo-Darwinian research program, much the way the formulators of the modern synthesis had earlier challenged, expanded, and enriched the contributions made by Darwin, Mendel, and other early evolutionary thinkers. But some achievements of the modern synthesis remain fundamental to our understandings of living organisms. In anthropology, perhaps the most significant contribution of neo-Darwinism was the way it undermined the nineteenth-century anthropological misconception of "biological race," refocusing attention on a new understanding of biological species. After World War II, many anthropologists rejected the biased, race-based physical anthropology of

the nineteenth and early twentieth centuries and replaced it with a "new physical anthropology" or "biological anthropology." Research in biological anthropology took for granted the common membership of all human beings in a single species, considered humans as biocultural organisms, and addressed human variation using concepts and methods drawn from neo-Darwinism (Strum, Lindburg, and Hamburg 1999).

Biologists have proposed alternative definitions of *species* that attempt to respect the purpose of Darwinian taxonomy, which is to represent scientists' best current understanding of the relationships between and among organisms. Field biologists use the following definition of *species*: a reproductive community of a population, isolated from others, that occupies a specific niche in nature. This definition, commonly referred to as the *biological species concept*, has been useful to field biologists studying populations of living organisms. However, this definition has been less useful for scientists studying fossils.

As we noted in Chapter 4, many taxonomists working with living primates prefer to use the *phylogenetic species concept*, which identifies species based on a set of unique features (morphological or genetic) that distinguish their members from other related species. Contemporary paleoanthropologists also often rely on this concept of species by calculating the measurable morphological differences between living species. They then assume that similar degrees of morphological difference may also be used to distinguish species in the

> ↻ For further discussion of the links between race, biological anthropology, and culture, see Chapter 1; for in-depth treatment of race and social stratification, see Chapter 14, pp. 332–6.

> **microevolution** A subfield of evolutionary studies that devotes attention to short-term evolutionary changes that occur within a given species over relatively few generations of ecological time.

fossil record. Fleagle (2013, 2) observes that this concept can be a useful way to sort fossils in a continuously changing lineage "in which the endpoints may be very different but individual samples overlap."

Species normally are subdivided into *populations* that are more or less scattered, although the separation is not complete. That is, populations of the same species (or individual members of those populations) may be separated at one time but may merge together again, and successfully reproduce, at a later time. Evolutionary theorists Ian Tattersall and Rob DeSalle (2011, 50) describe this process of species differentiation and reintegration as "reticulation." They emphasize that reticulation takes place *within* a species and that the "resulting web-like pattern of relationships is very different from the dichotomous pattern *among* species" on which the phylogenetic species concept is based. For example, prior to the rise of the great ancient civilizations, the human species was made up of widely scattered populations. Those populations living in North America had been separated from populations in Europe for thousands of years, until the European explorations of the Americas began in the fifteenth century. However, when Europeans and the Indigenous peoples of North America did come into contact, they were able to interbreed and produce viable, fertile offspring. From the perspective of the biological species concept, this ability to interbreed and produce fertile offspring indicates that members of these different populations belong to the same reproductive community and hence the same species. Proponents of the phylogenetic species concept can specify the set of unique features that distinguish all successfully interbreeding populations of the human species from populations of other related species.

Finally Darwinian population thinking requires biologists to recognize the distinctiveness of each individual *organism* that belongs to a particular population of a given species. It is variation among individual organisms in particular populations in particular environmental circumstances that engenders the Darwinian struggle for existence. To follow arguments made by evolutionary biologists, therefore, these three nesting concepts—*species* made up of *populations* made up of *organisms*—must be kept distinct from one another. Keep in mind that even if individual organisms from populations of different species occasionally mate with one another, such matings do not necessarily dissolve the species boundary. For instance, horses and donkeys can interbreed to produce mules, but mules are infertile, so the species boundary between horses and donkeys is unaffected by these matings.

Neo-Darwinians were also concerned about the genetic makeup of species. They introduced the concept of the **gene pool**, which includes all of the genes in the bodies of all members of a given species (or a population of a species). Using mathematical models, evolutionary theorists can estimate the **gene frequency** of particular genes—that is, the frequency of occurrence of gene variants or alleles within a particular gene pool. Measuring the stability or change of gene frequencies in populations over time allowed geneticists to trace short-term evolutionary change, in a new field called **population genetics**. Once population geneticists had identified a target population, they analyzed its gene pool by calculating the frequencies of various alleles within that gene pool and trying to figure out what would happen to those frequencies if the carriers of the various alleles were subjected to particular selection pressures (Table 7.1). Some evolutionary geneticists tested these predictions on such organisms as fruit flies, but others concentrated on human beings.

The ability of human beings from anywhere in the world to interbreed successfully is the most important measure of membership in our species. However, comparing our genotypes provides additional evidence of our biological closeness. As we discussed in Chapter 3, most alleles come in a range of different forms (i.e., are **polymorphous**), and known polymorphous variants fall into one of two groups. The first group, polymorphic alleles, accounts for most genetic variation across populations. Populations differ not because they have mutually exclusive sets of alleles but because they possess different *proportions* of the same set of alleles. An example is the ABO blood groups: the polymorphic alleles *A*, *B*, and *O* are found in all human populations, but the frequency of each allele differs from population to population.

For a related discussion of evidence of cross-species hybridization in the human fossil record, see Chapter 6, p. 115.

gene pool All the genes in the bodies of all members of a given species (or a population of a species).

gene frequency The frequency of occurrence of the variants of particular genes (i.e., of alleles) within the gene pool.

population genetics A field that uses statistical analysis to study short-term evolutionary change in large populations.

polymorphous Describes alleles that come in a range of different forms.

TABLE 7.1 Example of Allele Frequency Computation

Imagine you have just collected information on *MN* blood group genotypes for 250 humans in a given population. Your data are the following:
Number of *MM* genotype = 40
Number of *MN* genotype = 120
Number of *NN* genotype = 90
The allele frequencies are computed as follows:

Genotype	Number of People	Total Number of Alleles	Number of *M* Alleles	Number of *N* Alleles
MM	40	80	80	0
MN	120	240	120	120
NN	90	180	0	180
Total	**250**	**500**	**200**	**300**

The relative frequency of the *M* allele is computed as the number of *M* alleles divided by the total number of alleles: 200/500 = 0.4.
The relative frequency of the *N* allele is computed as the number of *N* alleles divided by the total number of alleles: 300/500 = 0.6.
As a check, note that the relative frequencies of the alleles must add up to 1.0 (0.4 + 0.6 = 1.0).
Source: Relethford, John. 1996. *The Human Species*, third edition, Mayfield Publishing Company, p. 66.

The second group, private polymorphisms, includes alleles that are found in the genotypes of some, but usually not all, members of a particular population. One example is a genetically determined blood cell antigen known as the "Diego antigen." The Diego antigen occurs only in Asian and African populations, although 60 to 90 per cent of the members of these populations do not have it (Marks 1995, 165).

Such results support the inescapable conclusion that the traditional Western concept of "race" is biologically and genetically meaningless. There is not a simple line that can be drawn to distinguish groups of humans based on their genetic makeup. In fact, evolutionary geneticist Richard Lewontin (1972) demonstrated more than four decades ago that more genetic variation could be found within conventionally identified racial groups than could be found between them. These results, based on population thinking, make it clear that "humankind . . . is not divided into a series of genetically distinct units" (Jones 1986, 324). Ian Tattersall and Rob DeSalle (2011, 141) point out that Lewontin's claims have successfully withstood attempts to reject them experimentally for more than 40 years. Initially, Lewontin's interpretations were questioned (Edwards 2003), but with new methods and approaches, his underlying outcomes are generally accepted. This means that the boundaries said to define human "races" have been culturally imposed on shifting and unstable clusters of allele (Marks 1995, 117).

It turns out that genetic variation in human populations is mostly a matter of differences in the relative proportions of the same sets of alleles. In fact, the distribution of particular phenotypes shifts gradually from place to place across populations as the frequencies of some alleles increase while those of others decrease or stay the same. Moreover, the distributions of some traits (like skin colour) do not match the distributions of other traits (like hair type). This sort of gradual intergradation of genetic variation from population to population is called a **cline**. Clines can be represented on maps, as in Map 7.1, which shows the gradually shifting distribution of differences in human skin colours from the equator to the poles.

If you were to walk from Stockholm, Sweden, to Kampala, Uganda, you would perceive gradual changes in average skin colour as you moved from north to south (or vice versa). Evolutionary biologists argue that skin pigmentation is distributed in this way as a consequence of natural selection: in regions close to the equator, individuals with darker skin pigmentation had a selective advantage over individuals with lighter pigmentation. By contrast, populations farther away from the equator faced less intense selection pressure for darkly pigmented skin and perhaps even selective pressures in favour of lighter skins. But *different* selection pressures would have been at work on other traits, such as stature or hair type, within the same population, which is why the geographical distributions of these traits do *not*

cline The gradual intergradation of genetic variation from population to population.

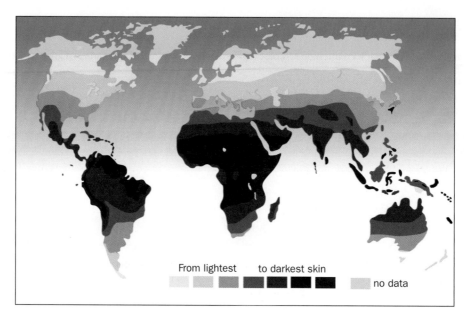

From lightest   to darkest skin

no data

MAP 7.1 This map illustrates the continuum, or cline, of skin colours exhibited among Indigenous peoples around the world. What evolutionary, environmental, and/or cultural forces might have contributed to the development of this cline?

Source: Chaplin, G. 2004. "Geographic Distribution of Environmental Factors Influencing Human Skin Coloration." *American Journal of Physical Anthropology* 125: 292–302; map updated in 2007. With permission from John Wiley and Sons.

match up neatly with the distribution of skin pigmentation. To make things even more complex, different genes may be involved in the production of similar phenotypic traits in different populations: for example, although different ancestral populations of humans living near the equator have dark skin, the identity and the number of alleles involved in the production of this phenotypic trait may be different in different populations.

These sorts of observations about global variations in human phenotypes led biological anthropologist Frank Livingstone (1964, 279) to declare over 50 years ago that "There are no races, there are only clines." Clinal variation explains why people searching for "races" have never been able to agree on how many there are or how they can be identified. *Clines are not groups.* The only group involved in clinal mapping is the entire human species. Each cline is a map of the distribution of a *single* trait. Biologists might compare the clinal maps of trait A and trait B to see if they overlap and, if so, by how much. But the more clines they superimpose, the more obvious it becomes that the trait distributions they map *do not coincide* in ways that neatly subdivide into distinct human subpopulations. Since the biological concept of "race" predicts exactly such overlap, it cannot be correct. In other words, *clinal analysis tests the biological concept of "race" and finds nothing in nature to match it.* And if

biological races cannot be found, then the so-called races identified over the years can only be symbolic constructs, based on cultural elaboration of a few superficial phenotypic differences—skin colour, hair type and quantity, skin folds, lip shape, and the like. In short, early race theorists "weren't extracting races from their set of data, they were imposing races upon it" (Marks 1995, 132).

The Molecularization of Race?

During the 1960s and 1970s, anthropologists and others explained that there was no biological basis for race; in other words, all humans are part of a single species. Although there is internal variation within the species, it does not easily fall into the cultural categories of "race" as they had been defined. In the past 30 years, however, there has been a resurgence of attempts to explain distinct genetic groupings in terms of "race." For example, controversial books such as *The Bell Curve: Intelligence and Class Structure in American Life* (Herrnstein and Murray 1994) or *A Troublesome Inheritance: Genes, Race, and Human History* (Wade 2014) attempt to align genetic traits with behaviours "innate" to specific biological "races."

Perhaps a no more complicated set of questions has been raised

Further descriptions of the history of race and racism can be found in Chapter 1, p. 7, and in Chapter 14, pp. 332–6.

about race in the twenty-first century than those that have emerged following the completion of the Human Genome Project (HGP) in 2003. The goals of the project were as follows:

- To identify all the approximately 20,500 genes in human DNA
- To determine the sequences of the 3 billion chemical base pairs that make up human DNA
- To store this information in databases
- To improve tools for data analysis
- To transfer related technologies to the private sector
- To address the ethical, legal, and social issues that may arise from the project (US Department of Energy 2014)

As anthropologist Nadia Abu El-Haj (2007) has suggested, some molecular biologists quickly mobilized the information produced by the HGP to attempt to develop forms of medical treatment based on the identification of genes associated with particular diseases. Some formed private biomedical research companies that promised to help create a future of *personalized medicine*: therapies based on knowledge of individuals' genomes that were precisely tailored to a particular individual's degree of genetic risk for a particular disease.

In recent years, the cost of sequencing individual genomes has been dropping; Tattersall and DeSalle (2011, 184) predict that "with the $1000 genome on the horizon, we will soon have the ultimate tool for individualized medicine." However, the cost has been high enough that many researchers have used genetic data from other members of populations to which individuals belong to stand in for certain parts of an individual's particular genome. For example, if your mother's brother suffers from a particular disease with a genetic component, researchers may conclude that you and other biological relatives have an increased risk for that disease. In this case, information about your biological family stands in for information about you. As Abu El-Haj (2007) explains, some biomedical researchers also use information about "racial" groups' genetics to stand in for genetic information particular to individuals who consider themselves to be members of such groups. The thinking is that if a disease marker shows up in the genomes of some people said to be members of a particular "race," then this may be an indication that other people

classified in the same "race" might also be at risk for the disease.

Does this pragmatic use of race in medical research mean that researchers are committed to the doctrines associated with scientific racism? Abu El-Haj (2007, 284) says no, for two reasons. First, the old race concept focused on the classification of *phenotypes*, whereas the new race concept classifies *genotypes*. The transition from a phenotypic to a genotypic view of race came about, she says, as a consequence of changing historical understandings of sickle-cell anemia in North America. In the first part of the twentieth century, sickle-cell anemia was identified as a disease of "black" people—of people with African ancestors. But later, its cause was traced to molecular genes: the presence of an abnormal "sickling" hemoglobin allele at a particular locus on a chromosome. "At the meeting point between these two definitions of the disease . . . the commitment to race as a molecular attribute took form," leading over time to "the correlation of disease risk and racial difference" (Abu El-Haj 2007, 287).

Second, nineteenth-century race science aimed to discover how many races existed and to assign all individuals to their "true race." The commercial technologies used by biomedical researchers do distinguish human populations in terms of the continents from which their ancestors presumably came. But all these technologies assume that everyone has a mixed ancestry of some kind; the goal is to measure how much of which ancestry markers are present in each population, thereby determining the degree of risk that members of that population face for genetic diseases associated with particular ancestries. As Abu El-Haj says, ancestry markers "are not used to discover one's 'true' race. . . . Instead, ancestry markers are used, for example, to understand the Puerto Rican population's risk for asthma" (Abu El-Haj 2007, 288). That is, if genome analysis determined that some ancestral population contributed genes to contemporary Puerto Rican populations that enhanced their risk for developing asthma, this information would be crucial in devising personalized drugs precisely keyed to individuals with different risks for asthma.

However, unless studies and trials of drugs are well planned, these biomedical treatments aimed at members of a particular "race" can be problematic as is the case with the development and distribution of the drug BiDil in the United States. On its BiDil website, Arbor Pharmaceuticals (2015), the current manufacturer of BiDil, describes this drug as "a fixed-dose combination medicine consisting of isosorbide dinitrate and hydralazine hydrochloride. It is approved by the FDA for the treatment of heart failure in self-identified African American patients when added to standard heart failure medicines." Approval from the US Food and Drug Administration (FDA), the site reports, was based on results of the African-American Heart Failure Trial (or A-HeFT), which "studied 1050 self-identified African American patients with heart failure: It is the largest number of African American patients ever studied in a major heart failure trial.... A-HeFT was started on May 29, 2001, and the study was halted early in July 2004 due to a significant survival benefit seen with BiDil as compared to standard therapy alone."

Even though neither the researchers who developed the drug nor the FDA endorses nineteenth-century racial categories, there were clear problems with the original A-HeFT study. Most notably, the drug trial involved only "self-identified" African American subjects, which the FDA agrees is a "highly imperfect" but "useful proxy" for whatever factors are responsible for the observed "racial differences." The FDA admits that other individuals besides self-identified African Americans might well benefit from BiDil, but this was not demonstrated by the A-HeFT drug trial because all of its participants were African American. In other words, the drug was proven only to work on African Americans because it was tested only on African Americans. This is a circular argument that has led to much controversy surrounding the drug as well as the financial collapse of the drug's original developer, NitroMed.

Abu El-Haj (2007, 293) notes that the successful production and marketing of drugs such as BiDil have transformed race into "a potentially profitable commodity." Moreover, "giving federal recognition to a drug like BiDil implies recognizing the biological reality of race." The current situation is perplexing, to say the least: such notions as "race" and "biology" are still with us, but their meanings appear to have changed, producing consequences that seem to be both positive and negative. She concludes that "Nature, too ... has a history," and that history "may well differ not just across time but between the various disciplines.... The same of course is true of race" (294).

Biological evidence has not in the past and will not in the future dismantle oppressive sociopolitical structures created as a result of racist ideologies, but it can provide an important component in the struggle to eliminate these practices from our societies. Anthropologists need to be vigilant, emphasizing in no uncertain terms the lack of biological justification for the racial categories promoted by scientific racists. As Jonathan Marks (1995, 117) reminds us, it was the recognition that human variation did not come in neat divisions called "races" that "began to convert racial studies into studies of human microevolution."

Human Variation and the Four Evolutionary Processes

What controls the patterns of gene frequencies that characterize a given population? Modern evolutionists recognize four evolutionary processes that can alter the frequencies at which genes occur in a given population: *natural selection, mutation, gene flow,* and *genetic drift.* To understand how these processes work, let's begin by considering an example that involves the first two, natural selection and mutation, which were introduced in Chapter 3.

Mutation is responsible for variant alleles that may be present at a single locus on a chromosome. Some of these mutations are mobilized during development to help produce specific physical traits. When a trait proves helpful, evolutionary theory predicts that the frequency of the alleles involved in its production will be increased by natural selection. Perhaps the best-known instance of microevolution of such a trait by means of natural selection concerns a variant of hemoglobin, one of the proteins in red blood cells.

In many human populations, only one allele—hemoglobin A (*HbA*)—is present. In other populations, however, mutant forms of hemoglobin A may also be present. One such mutant allele, known as *HbS*, alters the structure of red blood cells, distorting them into a characteristic sickle shape and reducing their ability to carry oxygen (Figure 7.1). When individuals inherit the *HbS* allele from both parents, they develop sickle-cell anemia. About 85 per cent of those with the *HbS/HbS* genotype do not survive to adulthood and, hence, do not reproduce. Although many people in the United States think that sickle-cell anemia affects only people with ancestors who came from Africa, in fact many people in India, Saudi Arabia, and Mediterranean countries such as Turkey, Greece, and Italy also suffer from the disease.

↻ For more background on the processes of natural selection and mutation, see Chapter 3, pp. 51–61.

Because the *HbS* allele seems to be harmful, we would expect it to be eliminated through natural selection. But in some populations of the world, it has a frequency of up to 20 per cent in the gene pool. Why should that be? It turns out that the *HbS* allele also conveys an evolutionary advantage—higher resistance to malaria. Research has shown that people exposed to malaria have a better chance of resisting the parasite if their hemoglobin genotype is *HbA/HbS* rather than the normal *HbA/HbA*. Thus, in regions of the world where malaria is common, having the *HbS* allele is advantageous to survival; not surprisingly, it is in these same regions that the *HbS* allele appears in its highest frequencies.

The *HbA/HbS* genotype is an example of what geneticists call a "balanced polymorphism," in which the heterozygous genotype is fitter than either of the homozygous genotypes. In Mendelian terms, we would say that the *HbA* and *HbS* alleles are codominant, with the result that a single *HbS* allele changes the structure of red blood cells enough to inhibit malarial parasites but not enough to cause sickle-cell anemia.

The rise of malarial infection in human beings appears to have begun only a few thousand years ago (Livingstone 1958). Before that time, the people who lived where malaria is now found gathered and hunted wild foods for a living. This way of life kept forests intact, leaving few open areas where water could collect and malaria-carrying mosquitoes could breed in large numbers. As these inhabitants began to cultivate plants for food, however, they needed to clear large tracts of forest for their fields, creating large open spaces where rainwater could collect in stagnant pools, providing ideal breeding conditions for mosquitoes. And as the population of cultivators grew, so grew the number of hosts for the malaria parasite.

If the *HbS* allele first appeared in the populations of gatherers and hunters, it probably had a low frequency. But once cultivation began, selection pressures changed. At that point, individuals with the *HbA/HbS* genotype were fitter because they had a greater probability of surviving and reproducing than individuals with *HbA/HbA* or *HbS/HbS*. As a result, the frequency of *HbS* increased in the population, despite the fact that in a double dose it was generally lethal. This example also illustrates the way niche construction—the enduring consequences of efforts organisms make to modify the environments in which they live—can reshape the selection pressures that a population experiences. In this case, a switch from one pattern of food acquisition to another created new niches

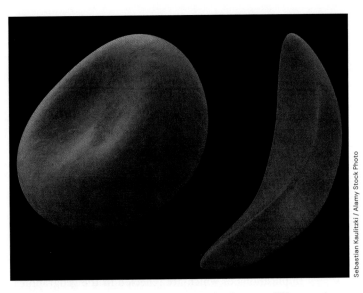

Sebastian Kaulitzki / Alamy Stock Photo

FIGURE 7.1 Normal red blood cells look very different from the distorted, "sickled" red blood cells. Sickled red blood cells carry less oxygen than do normal red blood cells; however, they also offer an evolutionary advantage to populations living in some regions of the world.

for humans, mosquitoes, and malaria parasites, simultaneously reshaping the selection pressures experienced by all three populations (Odling-Smee et al. 2003).

The above example illustrates how gene frequencies are most commonly altered within a relatively closed, relatively stable population. However, gene frequencies can also be altered—often quite drastically—if a given population experiences a sudden expansion due to the in-migration of outsiders from another population of the species, which is called **gene flow**. **Genetic drift**, on the other hand, occurs when there are random changes in gene frequencies from one generation to the next. Genetic drift can be the result of two differing processes: the *bottleneck effect,* where disease or disasters reduce the number of individuals in a population; or the *founder effect,* where small subgroups establish themselves apart from a larger population (i.e., migrate to a new area). Both of these effects accidentally eliminate large numbers of alleles.

gene flow The exchange of genes that occurs when a given population experiences a sudden expansion due to in-migration of outsiders from another population of the species.

genetic drift Random changes in gene frequencies from one generation to the next due to a sudden reduction in population size as a result of disaster, disease, or the out-migration of a small subgroup from a larger population.

The effects of genetic drift have been studied in relation to the French Canadian population of Quebec. Today, this population consists of approximately 6 million people, most of whom are descendants of the approximately 8500 French settlers who arrived in New France in the period from the early seventeenth century to the late eighteenth century (Laberge et al. 2005). The availability of both genomic and genealogical data for this population has allowed researchers to distinguish several founder events and establish related indices (see Moreau et al. 2011; Roy-Gagnon et al. 2011). For example, Laberge et al. (2005) have found evidence that the various migrations of these settlers and their early descendants led to a series of regional founder effects, the genetic implications of which are reflected in the geographical distribution of certain genetic diseases among French Canadians in Quebec today. In their study, Laberge et al. identified conditions that had never before been uncovered in any other population as well as conditions that were far more common among French Canadians than among members of the wider Canadian population. Other studies have identified certain groups within past French Canadian populations whose relatively high fertility rates have had a disproportionately high impact on the genetic makeup of the current population. In review, modern evolutionists recognize four evolutionary processes: mutation, natural selection, gene flow, and genetic drift. Table 7.2 summarizes the effects of the four standard evolutionary processes on gene frequencies within and between populations.

Chance plays a role in each of these evolutionary processes. The occurrence of a mutation is random, and there is no guarantee that a useful mutation will occur when it is needed; many mutations are neutral, neither helping nor harming the organisms in which they occur. Nor is there any way to predict the factors that make population migrations possible or to foresee the natural accidents that diminish populations. Unpredictable changes in the environment can modify the selection pressures on a given population, affecting its genetic makeup. Moreover, as we discussed in Chapter 3, *niche construction* can sometimes alter the selection pressures that individuals, their descendants, and other neighbouring organisms experience in those environments. For example, control of fire and the invention of clothing made it possible for early humans to colonize cold environments that were inaccessible to earlier ancestors, who lacked these cultural skills. Niche construction of this kind buffers us from experiencing some selection pressures, but it simultaneously exposes us to others (see Creanza, Fogarty, and Feldman 2013).

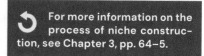
For more information on the process of niche construction, see Chapter 3, pp. 64–5.

Today, many biologists and anthropologists agree that the most intense selection pressures our species faces come from disease organisms that target our immune systems and from human-made environmental threats, such as pollution and the ozone hole (Leslie and Little 2003; Farmer 2003; Figure 7.2). Evidence that microorganisms are a major predatory danger to humans comes from research on the connection between infectious diseases and polymorphic blood groups (i.e., blood groups that have two or more genetic variants within a population). Biological anthropologists James Mielke, Lyle Konigsberg, and John Relethford (2011) point out, for example, that the diseases human beings have suffered from have not always been the same. When our ancestors were living in small foraging bands, they were susceptible to chronic parasitic infections, such as pinworms, and diseases transmitted from animals. After the domestication of plants and animals, however, human diets changed, settled life in towns and cities increased, and sanitation worsened. Populations expanded, individuals had more frequent contact with one

TABLE 7.2 Effects of the Four Evolutionary Processes on Variation within and between Populations

Evolutionary Process	Variation within Populations	Variation between Populations
Mutation	Increases	Increases
Gene Flow	Increases	Decreases
Genetic Drift	Decreases	Increases
Natural Selection	Increases or decreases	Increases or decreases

another, and the stage was set for the rise and spread of *endemic* diseases (i.e., diseases particular to a population) that could persist in a population without repeated introduction from elsewhere. It was these endemic diseases that had devastating impacts on the populations of Indigenous peoples in North America during colonization, creating the current limited genetic variety among their population.

This was especially true during the colonization of the Americas, when these European diseases killed thousands of North and South American Indigenous people, drastically reducing their populations and their genetic diversity, which has been identified in recent studies of ancient mitochondrial DNA (Llamas et al. 2016).

Several evolutionary processes may affect a population at the same time. For example, a rare, helpful allele might appear in a population through mutation. However, if a natural disaster such as an earthquake struck the population while the new allele was still rare, it might be completely lost if its few carriers were among those who perished (genetic drift). Alternatively, the frequency of a harmful new allele might increase in subsequent generations if its carriers survived such a disaster and if they introduced the new allele into a larger population through interbreeding (gene flow). Niche construction could also be implicated if, for example, gene flow were enabled or intensified as a result of persisting, environment-modifying activities of the populations exchanging genes.

Measuring the interaction among these evolutionary processes allows population geneticists to predict the probable effects of inbreeding and outbreeding on a population's gene pool. Inbreeding tends to increase the proportion of homozygous combinations of alleles already present in a population. If some of these alleles are harmful in a double dose, inbreeding increases the probability that a double dose will occur in future generations and thus decrease fitness. If helpful combinations of alleles occur in an inbreeding population, their proportions can increase in a similar way.

At the same time, inbreeding over several generations tends to reduce genetic variation. Natural selection on genes has a better chance of shaping organisms to changed environments if it has a wider range of genetic variation to act on. Perhaps for this reason, mating with individuals from out-groups is widely observed in the animal kingdom. Monkeys and apes, for example, regularly transfer into a new social group before they

FIGURE 7.2 Some of the most intense selection pressures faced by humans today are human-made. In countries such as China, air pollution is believed to be the cause behind the unusually high rates of asthma and other respiratory problems among children.

begin to reproduce (Figure 7.3). Human beings ordinarily do the same thing, with our reproductive practices shaped by culture; people in different societies draw the boundaries around in-groups and out-groups differently. In one society, the children of brothers and sisters (what we consider first cousins) may be considered members of the same "family" and, thus, off limits for marriage; in another, they may be considered members of different "families" and, thus, ideal marriage partners. However,

FIGURE 7.3 Among rhesus monkeys, young adult males will typically leave the group in which they were born to enter another social group before mating.

cultural rules forbidding *incest*, or sexual relations with close kin, do not always succeed in preventing such relations from occurring.

Adaptation and Human Variation

One of the breakthroughs of modern genetics was the discovery of *gene interaction*. That is, a single gene may contribute to the production of more than one phenotypic feature (*pleiotropy*), and many genes may combine forces to produce a single phenotypic feature (*polygeny*). Pleiotropy and polygeny help explain how it is that genes, which are discrete, could influence phenotypic traits such as body size or skin colour, which show continuous gradations. Traits that are the product of multiple genes offer multiple and varied opportunities for natural selection to shape phenotypic traits in ways that are adaptive for the organisms in which they are found.

In discussions of gene action, biologists commonly distinguish between genes of major effect and polygenes of intermediate or minor effect. A gene of major effect is a gene at one locus whose expression has a critical effect on the phenotype. The *HbS* allele that produces the sickling trait in red blood cells is an example of a gene of major effect. But phenotypic traits that depend on one or a few genes of major effect are rare. The evolution of a phenotypic trait may begin with selection on genes of major effect, but the products of such genes may be pleiotropic, producing adaptive as well as harmful consequences for the organism. Further selection on multiple polygenes of intermediate or minor effect that also affect the trait, however, may modify or eliminate those harmful consequences (West-Eberhard 2003, 101–4). Finally, because gene expression does not take place in an environmental vacuum, many phenotypic traits in organisms are even more finely tuned for their adaptive functions by inputs from environmental factors such as nutrients, temperature, humidity, altitude, or day length. Human phenotypic traits such as body size or skin colour, for example, are the outcome of complex interactions among multiple gene products and environmental influences throughout the life cycle.

phenotypic plasticity Physiological flexibility that allows organisms to respond to environmental stresses, such as temperature changes.

adaptation The mutual shaping of organisms and their environments.

Many students of human genetics have devoted attention to the way natural selection may mould complex human phenotypic traits, better adapting human populations to their specific environments. More recently, developmental biologists have been able to show how the responsiveness of organisms to their environments also contributes to the abilities of those organisms to adapt to their environments. A fertilized human egg (or zygote) has its own phenotype, and the zygote's phenotype can respond to environmental influences—such as those encountered in a woman's uterus—*even before its own genes are active*. This responsiveness is called **phenotypic plasticity**: "the ability of an organism to react to an environmental input with a change in form, state, movement, or rate of activity" (West-Eberhard 2003, 35). For example, the leaves of dandelion plants will grow differently in sunny versus shaded locations; the resulting difference in size between plants is due to environmental variability rather than actual genetic differences. Because all living organisms exhibit phenotypic plasticity, it is *incorrect* to assume that genes "direct" the development of organisms or "determine" the production of phenotypic traits. Indeed, much of the "action" that goes into producing adult organisms with distinctive phenotypes goes on during development.

Note that acknowledging the phenotypic plasticity of organisms has nothing to do with Lamarckian ideas of use and disuse and the inheritance of acquired characteristics, neither of which is accepted by modern evolutionary biologists.

Some of the most exciting work in evolutionary biology today involves linking new understandings about developmental influences on phenotypes with understandings of traditional evolutionary processes such as mutation, gene flow, genetic drift, and natural selection (West-Eberhard 2003).

Adaptation as a process refers to the mutual shaping of organisms and their environments. However, the term *adaptation* can also be used to refer to the phenotypic traits that are the outcome of adaptive processes (see Chapter 3). Biological anthropologists traditionally distinguish between three levels of phenotypic adaptation: genetic adaptations, short-term adaptations, and developmental adaptations. Each of these shows differing degrees of phenotypic plasticity. The sickling trait in hemoglobin described in the previous section is a classic example of a genetic adaptation because the form of the hemoglobin molecule is the phenotypic product of a single-locus gene of major effect. Most human phenotypic traits, however, are the product of pleiotropy, polygeny, and inputs from the environment.

Often the environmental input operates as a triggering mechanism for an adaptive response. This is the case for the shivering response, an adaptive physiological response in human beings sometimes called "short-term **acclimatization**." Human beings are warm-blooded organisms who need to maintain a constant internal body temperature to function properly. When the surrounding temperature drops, however, and threatens to cool our internal organs below this threshold temperature (roughly 37°C, or 98.6°F), this temperature drop triggers a twitching response in the muscles that surround our vital organs, as a way of generating heat. If we are able to increase our body temperature above the threshold—by going indoors, putting on clothes, or moving closer to the fire—the shivering stops.

Other forms of acclimatization are longer lasting than the shivering response and take shape over the course of many months or years as human beings are born, grow up, or come to spend much of their lives in particular environments. The physiological or morphological changes these individuals undergo are consequences of human phenotypic plasticity, not genetic variation. For example, among northern peoples, there are a number of physiological changes that have allowed them to be exposed to cold temperatures for long periods of time without sustaining major cold-related injuries. One such change is the development of a higher-than-average basal metabolic rate (BMR), which contributes to a higher body temperature. Another is the development of a superior "hunters' response"—the process by which blood vessels alternately constrict and then dilate, in a cyclical pattern, in response to exposure to the cold (see Figure 7.4). This response protects core body temperature as well as maintains blood flow to the extremities, thus protecting against frostbite (see So 1980, 69; Steegmann 1977).

Another form of acclimatization is found among peoples who live in mountain environments, such as

acclimatization A change in the way the body functions in response to physical stress.

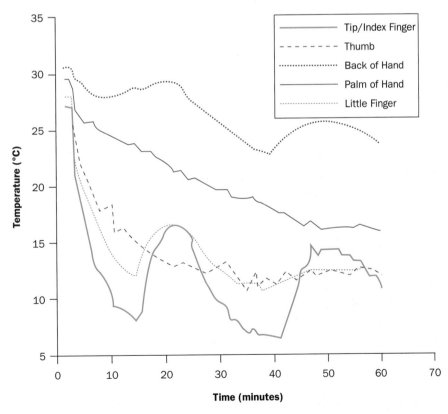

FIGURE 7.4 Over time, extremities exposed to very cold temperatures experience alternating vasoconstriction and vasodilation, which results in a cyclical rise and fall in tissue temperature. The lines in this graph represent the change in temperature in the various parts of a hand exposed to extreme cold.

the highlands of the Andes in South America. Human populations who live at these high altitudes are subject to hypoxia, a deficiency in the amount of oxygen in the blood, because less oxygen is available to breathe than at lower altitudes. Studies have shown that people who grow up in high altitudes adapt to lower oxygen levels by developing greater chest dimensions and lung capacities than do people living at low attitudes. Studies have also shown that individuals who were not born in such an environment increased in chest dimensions and lung capacity the longer they lived in such an environment and the younger they were when they moved there (Greska 1990). These sorts of changes, sometimes called "developmental acclimatization," are consequences of human phenotypic plasticity that occur when the human body is challenged—in this case, by a low level of oxygen in the environment.

Skin Colour

Skin colour is a highly visible, complex, continuous phenotypic trait in human populations (Figure 7.5). Variation in skin colour seems to be the product of a few genes of major effect, additional polygenes of intermediate or minor effect, and input from the environment. As Nina Jablonski (2004, 613) suggests, "determination of the relative roles of variant genes and varying environments has proven extremely challenging"; in addition, it is not clear how many alleles are involved or whether identical genes are responsible for the dark skin of apparently unrelated human populations (Marks 1995,

FIGURE 7.5 Skin colour in human populations is a complex phenotypic trait that shows continuous variation—different skin shades grade imperceptibly into one another without sharp breaks. This variation results from the interaction of a few genes of major effect, various polygenes of intermediate or minor effect, and input from the environment.

167–8). Biological anthropologists agree that skin colour is adaptive and related to the degree of ultraviolet radiation (UVR) that human populations have experienced in particular regions of the globe.

Note that "similar skin colours have evolved independently in human populations inhabiting similar environments," making skin colour "useless as a marker for membership in a unique group or 'race'" (Jablonski 2004, 615). Indeed, some of the most striking features of human skin are clearly consequences of developmental and phenotypic plasticity: variations in skin thickness are a function of age and history of sun exposure; the outer layers of the skin in darkly pigmented or heavily tanned people have more, and more compact, cell layers, making the skin more effective as a barrier to sun damage. The overall intensity of skin colour is thus determined by a combination of morphological, physiological, environmental, and developmental factors. When the intricate articulation of these factors is destabilized, the outcome can be anomalous skin conditions such as *albinism* (an absence of pigmentation), abnormally intense pigmentation, or a patchy spotting of light and dark skin.

As mentioned earlier, human skin colour exhibits clinal variation, with average pigmentation growing gradually lighter in populations that live closer to the poles (Map 7.1). The pigments in human skin (melanin) protect the skin against sunburn by absorbing and scattering UVR and by protecting DNA from damage that can lead to cancer (Jablonski 2004, 590). Of course, as humans we are at risk of sun damage to the skin because we do not grow fur coats, as our closest primate relatives do. Dark fur coats can actually protect primates from tropical heat by absorbing short-wave radiation (UVB) near the surface of the coat and reflecting much longwave radiation (UVA) away before it reaches the skin.

These advantages of fur, however, are reduced if the fur is wet with sweat, which can happen if the temperature rises or the organism's activity level increases. Under these conditions, "thermal sweating as a method of cooling becomes more important," and it is "greatly facilitated by the loss of body hair" (Jablonski 2004, 599). It is now hypothesized that the last common ancestor of humans and chimpanzees probably had light skin covered with dark hair, like other Old World primates. However, the loss of hair created new selection pressures in favour of increasingly darker skin, such that by 1.2 million years ago, early members of the genus *Homo* would have had darkly pigmented skin (Rogers, Iltis, and Wooding 2004).

Exposure of human skin to solar radiation has complex and contradictory consequences. Too much sunlight produces sunburn and destroys folic acid, which is a crucial factor in the prevention of spina bifida and neural tube defects. At the same time, solar radiation also has positive consequences: it stimulates the synthesis of vitamin D in human skin. Vitamin D is crucial for healthy bone development and other cellular processes. According to Jablonski and Chaplin (2000), these selective pressures have produced two opposing clines of skin pigmentation. The first cline grades from dark skin at the equator to light skin at the poles and is an adaptive protection against sun damage. The second cline grades from light pigmentation at the poles to dark pigmentation at the equator and is an adaptive response favouring vitamin D production. In the middle of these two clines, they argue, natural selection favoured populations with enhanced phenotypic plasticity who could tan more easily during hot, sunny seasons but easily lose their tans in seasons when temperature and sunlight levels decreased.

Jablonski (2004, 604) concludes that "the longer wavelengths of UVR, which are capable of penetrating deep into the dermis of the skin, have been the most important agents of natural selection in connection with the evolution of skin pigmentation." At the same time, because people have always migrated, different populations vary in the numbers of generations exposed to the selective pressures of any single regime of solar radiation. Human cultural practices (urbanization, wearing clothes, using sun block, staying indoors) have shaped the levels of pigmentation and levels of vitamin D production in particular individuals or populations. Megan Brickley et al. (2014) from McMaster University studied the long-term effects of vitamin D deficiency and found interesting correlations between the movement of people into cities. Her group found that the skeletons of ancient Greeks as well as people from the Middle Ages who lived in urban centres exhibited much higher frequencies of rickets and other indications of vitamin D deficiencies than skeletons from those living on farms.

Many of these factors may explain why the skin colours of the Indigenous peoples of South America are lighter than those of Indigenous populations in Asia or Europe who live at similar latitudes. Most anthropologists estimate that these populations migrated from the Old World perhaps 10,000 to 15,000 years ago, which means they have had far less time to experience the selective pressures associated with local solar radiation levels anywhere on the continent. In addition, these migrants were modern humans with many cultural adaptations to help them modify the negative effects of solar radiation, including both protective clothing and a vitamin D–rich diet. Obtaining vitamin D from food rather than sunlight has thus altered selection pressures that otherwise would have favoured lighter skin. Thus, the darker skin pigmentation of circumpolar peoples may be the consequence of selection pressures for darker skin as a protection against solar radiation reflected from snow and ice (Jablonski 2004, 612).

Intelligence

Intelligence may be the most striking attribute of human beings. However, attempts to define and measure "intelligence" have a long history of controversy. Is intelligence a single, general, unitary "thing" that people have more or less of? If not, what attributes and skills ought to count? Psychologist Howard Gardner (2000, 1) points out that "Every society features its ideal human being." In his view, "the intelligent person" in modern Western societies has been exemplified by individuals who could do well at formal schooling and succeed in commerce. It is perhaps not surprising, then, that tests developed in Western societies purporting to measure individuals' intelligence quotient (IQ) traditionally have equated high scores on verbal and mathematical reasoning with high intelligence.

But these are not the only areas in which humans display differing levels of ability or skill. Gardner, for example, has long argued that in addition to linguistic and logico-mathematical intelligence, human beings possess different types of intelligence, including bodily–kinesthetic intelligence (displayed by exceptional athletes and dancers), interpersonal or intrapersonal intelligence (displayed by individuals with exceptional understanding of social relations or their own psyches), musical intelligence, spatial intelligence, and naturalist intelligence (which attunes us to plants and animals in the world around us). In Gardner's view, these types of intelligence can probably be enhanced in all individuals, given the right kind of environmental support (Figure 7.6). Indeed, even linguistic intelligence and logico-mathematical intelligence require the proper environmental support—long-term training and practice in rich cultural settings—to produce the highest levels of achievement.

FIGURE 7.6 According to Howard Gardner, there are multiple types of intelligence that human beings can display, and each of these types can be enhanced with the right environmental support. Here, children in Brazil learn to play the recorder, helping to enhance their musical skill.

Because the definition of intelligence is so controversial, and because not all forms of intelligence are equally rewarded in Canada and the United States, great controversy results when attempts to measure intelligence are applied not only to individuals but also to entire social groups, defined on the basis of gender, class, or "race." The former president of Harvard University was subjected to strong criticism when he acknowledged that fewer women than men become scientists and suggested, in the face of massive evidence to the contrary, that perhaps this meant that women simply had less "intrinsic aptitude" for science and engineering than men did (Summers 2005). Controversies have been as great or greater when ideas about intelligence have been linked to ideas about race. In Canada, for example, people tend to assign each other to "races" on the basis of phenotypic criteria such as skin colour. As we have seen, such "races" are then often regarded as different natural kinds, each sharing its own biological essence. From this assumption, it is a short step to conclude that differences between races must include differences in intelligence. Some scientists have devised IQ tests that they claim can measure intelligence, the results of such testing repeatedly showing, for example, that the average IQ score for African North Americans and Indigenous peoples of North America is below that of European North Americans, which is below that of Asian North Americans, a false premise that only perpetuates inequality and racist attitudes.

Do IQ scores show that racial differences in intelligence are clear-cut and genetically determined? They do not. First, the idea that races are natural kinds assumes that racial boundaries are clear and that traits essential to racial identity (e.g., skin colour) are discrete and non-overlapping. However, as we noted above, skin colour is a continuously varying phenotypic trait, both among members of the so-called racial groups as well as across the boundaries of those groups. Particular shades of skin colour cannot be assigned exclusively to particular socially defined races, nor can they be used to infer any other so-called racial attribute, such as intelligence or athletic ability.

Second, it is far from clear that there is a single, accurately measurable substance called "intelligence" that some people have more of than others. Performing well on paper-and-pencil tests tells us very little about practical problem-solving skills and creativity, which might equally deserve to be called "intelligence." Third, even if intelligence is such a measurable substance, we do not know that IQ tests actually measure it. People can score badly on an IQ test for many reasons that have nothing to do with intelligence: they may be hungry or ill or anxious, for example. When different social groups within a society consistently score differently as groups, however, we may suspect that the test itself is to blame. Arguing that IQ tests measure cultural knowledge far more than they measure intelligence, many critics contend that the vocabulary items used on most IQ tests reflect experiences typical of European North American middle-class culture. People from different cultural backgrounds do poorly on the test because their experiences have not provided them with the knowledge being tested. In Canada, for example, research has shown that Indigenous Canadian students' poor performance on standardized intelligence tests reflects differences in cultural understanding and language barriers, not intelligence (Common and Frost 1988). When researchers have looked at more culturally sensitive mechanisms of measuring intelligence and learning, Indigenous Canadian children match closely with other Canadian children (Wilgosh, Mulcahy, and Watters 1986).

Many studies have shown that how an individual will do on an IQ test is more accurately predicted by social class and educational background than by "race." When students of different "racial" backgrounds are compared in this way, "race"-based differences in IQ scores are not apparent. In the United States, for example, when African American and European American students are matched by class and educational background, the differences in average IQ scores disappear (Molnar 1992). Similarly, African American children adopted by middle-class European American parents tend to score significantly higher on IQ tests compared to African American children living in lower-income communities (Woodward 1992). Studies like these demonstrate repeatedly that IQ scores are not phenotypic traits uniquely determined by genes; rather, they are individual traits that are powerfully affected by a range of environmental factors over the course of the human life cycle.

Phenotype, Environment, and Culture

In recent years, many evolutionary biologists and biological anthropologists have recognized that trying to attribute every phenotypic trait of an organism to adaptation is problematic. Sometimes an adaptive explanation seems transparently obvious, as with body shape in fish and whales or wing shape in bats and birds, which equips these animals for efficient movement through water and air. Other times, adaptive explanations seem less obvious, or even contrived. As we saw in Chapter 3, the wings of contemporary insects are better understood as an exaptation, when appendages that evolved as an adaptation to one set of selective pressures began at some point to serve an entirely different function.

> For more information on exaptation, aptation, and adaptation, see Chapter 3, p. 53.

In other words, the trait an organism possesses today may not be the direct result of adaptation but, instead, may be the by-product of some other feature that was being shaped by natural selection. It may also be the consequence of random effects. Jonathan Marks (1995) has observed, for example, that anthropologists have tried, without notable success, to offer adaptive explanations for the large, protruding brow ridges found in populations of human ancestors. He suggests that brow ridges might well have appeared "for no reason at all—simply as a passive consequence of growing a fairly large face attached to a skull of a small frontal region" (190).

We must also remember that phenotypes are shaped by environment as well as by genes. For example, some have argued that slow growth in height, weight, and body composition and delayed onset of adolescence among Guatemalan Mayan children constitute a genetic adaptation to a harsh natural environment. However, by comparing measurements of these traits in populations of Mayans who migrated to the United States with similar measurements to those in Guatemala, Barry Bogin (1995, 65) was able to disprove these claims, for "the United States–living Maya are significantly taller, heavier, and carry more fat and muscle mass than Mayan children in Guatemala." Similarly, other biological anthropologists working in the Andean highlands have refuted the hypothesis that hypoxia is responsible for poor growth among some Indigenous populations (de Meer, Bergman, and Kusner 1993; Leonard et al. 1990). They point out that the genetic explanation fails to consider the effects that poverty and political marginalization can have on human health and maturation rates.

At the beginning of the twenty-first century, it has become fashionable for many writers, particularly in the popular media, to treat genes as the ultimate explanation for all features of the human phenotype. Given the great achievements by molecular biology that followed the discovery of the structure of the DNA molecule, this enthusiasm is perhaps understandable. But discussions of human adaptive patterns that invoke natural selection on genetic variation alone are extremely unsatisfactory. For one thing, they mischaracterize the role genes play in living organisms. Speaking as though there were a separate gene for each identifiable phenotypic trait ignores pleiotropy and polygeny, as well as phenotypic plasticity. It also ignores the contribution of the other classic evolutionary processes of genetic drift and gene flow, as well as the influences of historical and cultural factors on human development (as in the case of the Mayan migrants). Researchers in the Human Genome Project originally expected that, given our phenotypic complexity, the human genome would contain at least 100,000 genes; today, we know that the actual number is closer to 20,500, which is remarkably close to the number of genes in the genome of the roundworm *Caenorhabditis elegans*, one of the simplest organisms that exists. Clearly, the number of genes possessed by an organism is not coupled in any straightforward way with its phenotypic complexity.

The gene-centred approach gained considerable influence in anthropology after 1975 because of the widespread theoretical impact of a school of evolutionary thought called "sociobiology." Sociobiology attracted some anthropologists who proposed explanations of human adaptations based on sociobiological principles. Other anthropologists have been highly critical of sociobiology. However, after 40 or so years, some proposals emerging from this debate have come a long way toward meeting the objections of sociobiology's original critics.

Anthropology in Everyday Life

Examining the Remains of Richard III

One way to learn about our present and our future is by exploring our past. Nowhere is this approach more prevalent than in the anthropological study of genetics. The sequencing of ancient genomes allows researchers to explore not only the lives of persons in the past but also the lives that we are living today. Below is one example of a DNA-sequencing project that promises to change the way we think about life, both past and present.

In 2012, archaeologists found skeletal remains while excavating a parking lot in Leicester, England. While they were hoping to find the remains of a monastery that was said to be buried beneath hundreds of years of infrastructure, they found much more than they were expecting: skeletal remains that were later identified as those of Richard III, England's last king to die in battle. His remains have since been reinterred, but not before his entire genome was sequenced by Canadian geneticist Turi King and her colleagues at the University of Leicester. In King's own words, this project is important because it "will help to teach us not only about him, but ferment discussion about how our DNA informs our sense of identity, our past and our future" (quoted in Wellcome Trust 2014). Because of King's work, Richard III's DNA will be accessible to future researchers in all disciplines.

The positive identification of Richard III's skeletal remains was an exceptional find for geneticists, as researchers are rarely given the chance to examine DNA from an ancient person whose identity is known to them. Moreover, Richard is one of only a limited group of ancient humans whose DNA has been sequenced. Others include Neanderthal specimens, hunter-gatherers from Spain, an Inuit ancestor from Greenland, and Ötzi the Iceman.

The identification of Richard III's remains would not have been possible without modern gene-sequencing technologies and access to Richard III's distant living relatives. King was able to retrieve mitochondrial DNA (mtDNA) from two known descendants of Richard's sister, Canadian-born Michael Ibsen and Australian Wendy Duldig, who were tracked down using a variety of historical documents. King found that the mtDNA of both Ibsen and Duldig matched that of the skeleton excavated from the Leicester parking lot. Thus,

according to King, "there is, at its most conservative, a 99.999 per cent probability that these are indeed the remains of Richard III" (quoted in Treble 2015).

Sequencing ancient mtDNA is no small feat, as an individual's biological material becomes degraded as the body decomposes. Only after numerous hours of painstakingly intricate work was King able to compare the mtDNA from Ibsen and Duldig to that from the skeleton found under the parking lot. Her results were then independently scrutinized by two other laboratories that specialize in working with ancient DNA. In both cases, King's results were verified. Richard III had been discovered more than 500 years after his death.

The data King and her colleagues have uncovered provides biological anthropologists, archaeologists, and historians with concrete facts that can be used to verify or refute written accounts and other historic documents from the period in which Richard III lived. For example, Richard III had been described by some, including his rival and successor, Henry Tudor, as a "poisonous hunch-back'd toad"; other contemporaries described him as having a bodily shape of low stature. These descriptions fit with the story told by the skeletal remains recovered from the parking lot, as the remains show clear signs of scoliosis, which deforms the spine into an *S* shape. Thus, while King's findings cannot offer insight into Richard's historical reputation of being a vile, untrustworthy murderer, they do provide physical evidence of what his body was like in life and in death and, by extension, how he lived and died.

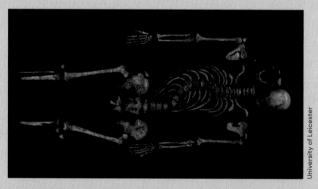

The skeletal remains of Richard III shows a curvature of the spine due to scoliosis.

Source: Adapted from Wellcome Trust 2014 and Treble 2015. For more information on the results of King's research, see King et al. 2014.

Can We Predict the Future of Human Evolution?

Current arguments among evolutionary biologists illustrate these researchers' varied attempts to grasp the meaning of evolution. How we classify the natural world matters not only to scientists, who want to be sure their classifications match what they find when they go to nature, but also to non-scientists. How we make sense of evolution is important because people of all societies see a connection between the way they make sense of the natural world and the way they make sense of their own lives. Many people believe that human morality is, or ought to be, based on what is natural. For such people, evolutionary interpretations of nature can be threatening even if they portray a natural world that is orderly. If nature's order is dog-eat-dog and if human morality must be based on nature's order, then survival at any cost must be morally correct because it is "natural." This is clearly why many people find the more extreme claims of human sociobiology so repugnant. For those who want to root compassion and generosity in human nature, sociobiology offers a portrait of human nature in which such behaviour has little or no value.

But perhaps the uncontrolled and uncontrollable pursuit of food and sex is no more natural in our species than sharing, compassion, and non-violent resolution of differences. As we noted in Chapter 4, many primatologists have evidence to show that, most of the time, most apes and monkeys do not live by the "law of the jungle." Possibly, the law of the jungle is not a law after all.

Human beings, like all living organisms, are subject to evolutionary processes. Like other organisms, our species shares a gene pool whose various combinations, together with environmental input, create different phenotypes that are able, within certain limits, to allow a certain range of adaptive responses. But we are not like other organisms in all respects, and this is what makes the study of human nature, human society, and the human past necessary. In order to adapt to our environments—to make a living and replace ourselves—we have options that do not exist for other organisms: cultural adaptations that are passed on by learning, even when there is no biological reproduction (see Figure 7.7).

The rich heritage of human culture is the source of much wisdom to guide us in our moral dealings with one another. The more we learn about biology, however, the more we realize that neither genotypes nor phenotypes nor environmental pressures provide obvious answers to our questions about how to live. If anything, "nature" offers us mixed messages about what is, or is not, likely to promote survival and reproduction. And in any case, with the development of culture, human beings have long been concerned not only with survival and reproduction but also with what it takes to lead a meaningful life. This search for a meaningful life has been part of the human condition for millennia and is likely to remain with us long after our contemporary scientific debates have become history.

Photo by Maher Attar/Sygma via Getty Images

FIGURE 7.7 An individual may have high cultural fitness and no genetic fitness at all. Here, a religious teacher who is celibate (thereby reducing her genetic fitness to zero) passes cultural knowledge to a new generation of other people's offspring.

Chapter Summary

1. The neo-Darwinian evolutionary synthesis of the 1930s and 1940s combined Darwinian natural selection with Mendelian ideas about heredity. Neo-Darwinians studied populations of reproductively isolated species, concentrating on the population's gene pool, estimating the frequency

of occurrence of different alleles of a particular gene, and predicting how those gene frequencies might be affected by different selection pressures.

2. Human population genetics has shown that different human populations from all over the world share basically the same range of genotypic variation, no matter how different they may appear phenotypically, reinforcing the position that the concept of "race" is biologically meaningless.

3. Natural selection, mutation, gene flow, and genetic drift are four evolutionary processes that can affect change in gene frequencies in a population over time. Sometimes one evolutionary process may work to increase the frequency of a particular allele while a different process is working to decrease its frequency. Inbreeding over several generations can be harmful because it decreases genetic variation and increases the probability that any alleles for deleterious traits will be inherited in a double dose, one from each parent.

4. Natural selection seems to have moulded many complex human phenotypic traits, better adapting human populations to their environments. Anthropologists have studied how variations in traits such as skin colour appear to have been shaped by natural selection. Anthropologists have also shown how variations in IQ test scores reflect variations in cultural background, social class, and educational background rather than "race."

5. Many evolutionary biologists and biological anthropologists recognize that trying to attribute every phenotypic trait of an organism to adaptation is problematic. Some traits may not be the result of adaptation but the by-product of some other feature that was shaped by natural selection—or even the consequence of random effects.

6. Gene-centred explanations of human evolution gained considerable influence in anthropology after 1975 because of the widespread theoretical impact of a school of evolutionary thought called "sociobiology."

For Review

1. Distinguish between microevolution and macroevolution. Explain why this distinction is important to anthropologists.

2. How did neo-Darwinians define a species? What is the significance of a "reproductive community" in regard to different human populations?

3. Explain what a cline is and why it is important. Consider the example of a cline discussed in this chapter and explain it to one of your friends.

4. Explain what is meant by the "molecularization of race." How has the Human Genome Project changed the scientific discussion of "race"?

5. What are the four evolutionary processes outlined in this chapter? In what ways can they overlap to affect one another? Provide examples.

6. Describe how natural selection explains why a high proportion of the sickling allele is maintained in certain human populations but not others.

7. What is phenotypic plasticity, and why is it important?

8. Explain the difference between short-term acclimatization and developmental acclimatization.

9. What factors influence IQ? Why do anthropologists and many other scholars insist that IQ is not determined by genes alone?

10. Explain why natural selection on genetic variation alone is not sufficient to explain the range of human adaptive patterns revealed by archaeology, ethnography, and history.

Key Terms

acclimatization 145
adaptation 144
cline 137
gene flow 141

gene frequency 136
gene pool 136
genetic drift 141
microevolution 135

phenotypic plasticity 144
polymorphous 136
population genetics 136

References

Abu El-Haj, Nadia. 2007. "The Genetic Reinscription of Race." *Annual Review of Anthropology* 36: 283–300.

Arbor Pharmaceuticals. 2015. *BiDil*. https://arborpharma.com/

Bogin, Barry. 1995. "Growth and Development: Recent Evolutionary and Biocultural Research." In *Biological Anthropology: The State of the Science*, edited by Noel T. Boaz and Linda Wolfe, 49–70. Bend, OR: International Institute for Human Evolutionary Research.

Brickley, Megan, Lori D'Ortenzio, Bonnie Kahlon, Menno L.P. Hoogland, Barbara Veselka, and Andrea L. Waters-Rist. 2014. "Biocultural Perspectives of Vitamin D Deficiency in the Past." *Journal of Anthropological Archaeology* 36: 48–59. doi:10.1016/j.jaa.2014.08.002

Common, R.W., and L.G. Frost. 1988. "The Implications of the Mismeasurement of Native Students' Intelligence through the Use of Standardized Intelligence Tests." *Canadian Journal of Native Education* 15 (1): 18–30.

Creanza, Nicole, Lauren Fogarty, and Marcus Feldman. 2013. "Exploring Cultural Niche Construction from the Paleolithic to Modern Hunter-Gatherers." In *Dynamics of Learning in Neanderthals and Modern Humans*. Volume 1. 211–28. Springer Japan.

de Meer, K., R. Bergman, and J.S. Kusner. 1993. "Differences in Physical Growth of Aymara and Quechua Children Living at High Altitude in Peru." *American Journal of Physical Anthropology* 90: 59–75.

Edwards, Paul A.W. 2003. "Human Genetic Diversity: Lewontin's Fallacy." *Bioessays* 25 (8): 798–801.

Farmer, Paul. 2003. *Pathologies of Power: Health, Human Rights, and the New War on the Poor*. Berkeley: University of California Press.

Fleagle, John G. 2013. *Primate Adaptation and Evolution*. 3rd ed. Amsterdam: Elsevier/Academic Press.

Gardner, Howard. 2000. *Intelligence Reframed: Multiple Intelligences for the Twenty-First Century*. New York: Basic Books.

Greska, Lawrence P. 1990. "Developmental Responses to High-Altitude Hypoxia in Bolivian Children of European Ancestry: A Test of the Developmental Adaptation Hypothesis." *American Journal of Human Biology* 2: 603–12.

Herrnstein, Richard, and Charles Murray. 1994. *The Bell Curve*. New York: Free Press.

Jablonski, Nina G. 2004. "The Evolution of Human Skin and Skin Color." *Annual Review of Anthropology* 33: 585–623.

——, and George Chaplin. 2000. "The Evolution of Skin Coloration." *Journal of Human Evolution* 39: 57–106.

Jones, J.S. 1986. "The Origin of *Homo sapiens*: The Genetic Evidence." In *Major Topics in Primate and Human Evolution*, edited by B. Wood, L. Martin, and P. Andrews, 317–30. Cambridge: Cambridge University Press.

King, Turi, Gloria Gonzalez Fortes, Patricia Balaresque, Mark G. Thomas, David Balding, Pierpaolo Maisano Delser, Rita Neumann, et al. 2014. "Identification of the Remains of King Richard III." *Nature Communications* 5. http://www.nature.com/ncomms/2014/141202/ncomms6631/full/ncomms6631.html

Laberge, A.M., J. Michaud, A. Richter, E. Lemyre, M. Lambert, B. Brais, and G.A. Mitchell. 2005. "Population History and Its Impact on Medical Genetics in Quebec." *Clinical Genetics* 68 (4): 287–301.

Leonard, W.R., R.L. Leatherman, J.W. Carey, and R.B. Thomas. 1990. "Contributions of Nutrition versus Hypoxia to Growth in Rural Andean Populations." *American Journal of Human Biology* 2: 612–26.

Leslie, Paul W., and Michael Little. 2003. "Human Biology and Ecology: Variation in Nature and the Nature of Variation." *American Anthropologist* 105 (1): 28–37.

Lewontin, Richard. 1972. "The Apportionment of Human Diversity." *Evolutionary Biology* 6: 381–98.

Livingstone, Frank B. 1958. "Anthropological Implications of Sickle Cell Gene Distribution in West Africa." *American Anthropologist* 60: 533–62.

——. 1964. "On the Nonexistence of Human Races." In *The Concept of Race*, edited by M.F. Ashley-Montagu, 46–60. New York: Collier.

Llamas, Bastien, Lars Fehren-Schmitz, Guido Valverde, Julien Soubrier, Swapan Mallick, Nadin Rohland, Susanne Nordenfelt, et al. 2016. "Ancient Mitochondrial DNA Provides High-Resolution Time Scale of the Peopling of the Americas." *Science Advances* 2 (4): e1501385 doi:10.1126/sciadv.1501385

Marks, Jonathan. 1995. *Human Biodiversity*. New York: Aldine.

Mielke, James H., Lyle W. Konigsberg, and John H. Relethford. 2011. *Human Biological Variation*. New York: Oxford University Press.

Molnar, Stephen. 1992. *Human Variation: Races, Types, and Ethnic Groups*. 3rd ed. Englewood Cliffs, NJ: Prentice Hall.

Moreau, Claudia, Claude Bhérer, Hélène Vézina, Michèle Jomphe, Damian Labuda, and Laurent Excoffier. 2011. "Deep Human Genealogies Reveal a Selective Advantage to Be on an Expanding Wave Front." *Science* 334: 1148–50.

Odling-Smee, F. John, Kevin L. Laland, and Marcus W. Feldman. 2003. *Niche Construction: The Neglected Process in Evolution*. Princeton, NJ: Princeton University Press.

Relethford, John. 2008. *The Human Species: An Introduction to Biological Anthropology*. 7th ed. New York: McGraw-Hill.

Rogers, Alan R., David Iltis, and Stephen Wooding. 2004. "Genetic Variation at the MC1R Locus and the Time since Loss of Human Body Hair." *Current Anthropology* 45: 105–7.

Roy-Gagnon, Marie-Hélène, Claudia Moreau, Claude Beherer, Pascal St-Onge, Daniel Sinnett, Catherine Laprise, Hélène Vézina, and Damian Labuda. 2011. "Genomic and Genealogical Investigation of the French Canadian Founder Population Structure." *Human Genetics* 129 (5): 521–31.

So, Joseph K. 1980. "Human Biological Adaptation to Arctic and Subarctic Zones." *Annual Review of Anthropology* 9: 63–82.

Steegmann, A.T Heodore. 1977. "Finger Temperatures during Work in Natural Cold: The Northern Ojibwa." *Human Biology* 49 (3): 349–62.

Strum, Shirley, Donald G. Lindburg, and David Hamburg, eds. 1999. *The New Physical Anthropology: Science, Humanism, and Critical Reflection*. Upper Saddle River, NJ: Prentice Hall.

Summers, Lawrence H. 2005. "Remarks at NBER Conference on Diversifying the Science and Engineering Workforce." Cambridge, MA: President and Fellows of Harvard College. http://www.harvard.edu/president/speech/2005/remarks-nber-conference-on-diversifying-science-engineering-workforce

Tattersall, Ian, and Rob DeSalle. 2011. *Race? Debunking a Scientific Myth*. College Station: Texas A&M University Press.

Treble, Patricia. 2015. "Canada's Connection to King Richard III: The Inside Story." *Maclean's*, 22 March, http://www.macleans.ca/society/canadas-connection-to-king-richard-iii-the-inside-story

US Department of Energy. 2014. "Human Genome Project Information Archive 1990–2003." http://web.ornl.gov/sci/techresources/Human_Genome/index.shtml

Wade, Nicholas. 2014. *A Troublesome Inheritance: Genes, Race and Human History*. New York: Penguin Press.

Wellcome Trust. 2014. "Genomes of Richard III and His Living Descendants to Be Sequenced." http://www.wellcome.ac.uk/News/Media-office/Press-releases/2014/WTP055654.htm

West-Eberhard, Mary Jane. 2003. *Developmental Plasticity and Evolution*. Oxford: Oxford University Press.

Wilgosh, L., R. Mulcahy, and B. Watters. 1986. "Assessing Intellectual Performance of Culturally Different, Inuit Children with the WISC-R." *Canadian Journal of Behavioural Science* 18 (3): 270–7.

Woodward, Val 1992. *Human Heredity and Society*. St Paul, MN: West.

▲ The rock carvings at Petroglyph Provincial Park in Nanaimo, British Columbia, Canada, were done over 1000 years ago by the First Nations people of the area. Photo: Chase Clausen/Shutterstock

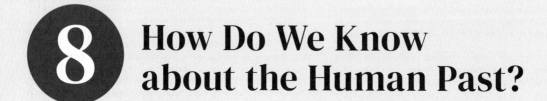

How Do We Know about the Human Past?

Chapter Outline

In this chapter, you will learn about what archaeologists do: how they excavate the remains of past human societies and then interpret what they find. We will discuss important issues about the past, including laws that protect historic sites and how in some cases these laws are being disregarded through the illegal destruction of precious sites and illegal sales of artifacts by looters. We will also explore new approaches to archaeological research, and we will consider questions such as "Who owns the past?" and "Why is understanding the past important to understanding humanity in its entirety?"

There are essentially two types of anthropologists who study the human past: paleoanthropologists and archaeologists. Paleoanthropologists focus on hominin skeletal fossils and genetic remains from the distant past, analyzing our biological evolution from our earliest ancestors through to the appearance of our own species. Archaeologists, on the other hand, focus primarily on reconstructing changes in past human societies using the **archaeological record**—material evidence of human modification of the physical environment. Beginning with humble stone tools, the archaeological record encompasses many types of artifacts (pottery, metalwork, textiles, and other technological developments) as well as large-scale cultural remnants (architecture, irrigation canals, and ancient farm fields). Archaeology, however, is more than digging up things and looking at old buildings. It provides a long-term perspective on humanity and reveals evidence about how human cultures have changed and adapted to their environments in the past.

What Is Archaeology?

Archaeologists study human prehistory by analyzing the material remains created by our ancestors. These remains include everything from the simplest stone tools to the impressive Mayan cities of Central America. The main goals of archaeology are to reconstruct how humans lived in the past, to identify how cultures have changed through time, and to understand what influenced these changes. But how do archaeologists do this? What kinds of analytical tools do they use? Essentially, archaeologists use a combination of scientific methods similar to those used by environmental biologists and geologists (e.g., analysis of soils and plants) as well as interpretative frameworks that rely on social science perspectives (see Figure 8.1 for an outline of the

archaeological process). The former are central to surveying and excavating archaeological **sites** as well as analyzing material remains found at those sites (see Map 8.1 for the major locations discussed in this chapter). Surveying involves carefully examining geographical regions to identify potential sites of interest and collecting preliminary data about those sites. Excavations require taking precise measurements, from which three-dimensional reconstructions of houses and other structures can be made. Lab analysis involves using a variety of methods, including palynology (the study of plant pollen) and trace element analysis to understand past physical environments. Throughout the process, archaeologists apply well-thought-out research questions and hypotheses about human behaviour to frame interpretations of the material remains. In this way, archaeologists combine systematic techniques from both the physical and the social sciences to provide the fullest possible understanding of the human past.

The Archaeological Process

The first step in archaeological research involves identifying the precise geographical locations of the remains of past human activity. Once archaeologists have found such a location, they may do small-scale excavations, using a shovel to dig small pits over a large area, or large-scale excavations of entire sites or large portions of sites. In some cases, anthropologists focus on a single site; more commonly, they work to compare several sites in a given region, noting similarities and differences. Archaeologists pay attention not only to portable

archaeological record All material objects and structures created by humans and our hominin ancestors.

site A precise geographical location of the remains of past human activity.

The Archaeological Process

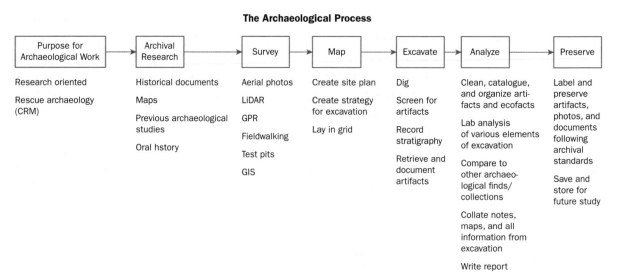

Purpose for Archaeological Work	Archival Research	Survey	Map	Excavate	Analyze	Preserve
Research oriented Rescue archaeology (CRM)	Historical documents Maps Previous archaeological studies Oral hstory	Aerial photos LiDAR GPR Fieldwalking Test pits GIS	Create site plan Create strategy for excavation Lay in grid	Dig Screen for artifacts Record stratigraphy Retrieve and document artifacts	Clean, catalogue, and organize artifacts and ecofacts Lab analysis of various elements of excavation Compare to other archaeological finds/collections Collate notes, maps, and all information from excavation Write report	Label and preserve artifacts, photos, and documents following archival standards Save and store for future study

FIGURE 8.1 A flow chart of the general pattern for archaeological research. Note that this is a general pattern and may change depending on the site and research project.

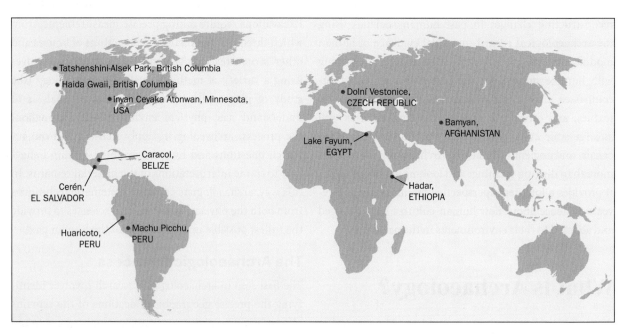

MAP 8.1 Major locations discussed in Chapter 8.

artifacts of human manufacture but also to non-portable remnants of material culture, such as house walls or ditches, which are called **features**. They also note the presence of **ecofacts**—remains that are not themselves artifacts but that are likely the by-products of human activity (e.g., plant seeds or animal bones connected with food consumption).

When archaeologists study sites through survey or excavation, they carefully record the immediate *matrix* (e.g., soil, gravel, sand, or clay) in which an object is found and its **provenance**, which is the precise three-dimensional position of the find within the matrix. For each object, they also record any other remains that they

> **artifacts** Objects that have been deliberately and intelligently shaped by humans or our hominin ancestors.
>
> **features** Non-portable items created by humans, such as house walls or ditches.
>
> **ecofacts** Biological remains that are likely associated with food consumption or other human activities.
>
> **provenance** The three-dimensional position of an artifact within the matrix of an archaeological site.

find near it, in order to identify associations and relationships between objects (known as their *context* within an archaeological site), which can lead to greater understanding of how the objects may have been used in the past. For example, finding a bowl and a spoon together may suggest that these artifacts were used for food preparation or consumption. Archaeologists also note disturbances to the site made by other humans or small animals, as these sorts of disturbances can cause artifacts to move from where they were originally deposited. This strong emphasis on the *context* in which artifacts are found makes archaeology a holistic undertaking. Undisturbed archaeological sites are important because they contain evidence that may answer key questions about human lifestyles or settlement in certain places at particular times.

Archaeologists must know what to look for to identify sites and the remains that can serve as evidence. They have to think about the kinds of human behaviour past populations are likely to have engaged in and what telltale evidence for that behaviour might have been left behind. Sometimes the artifacts themselves tell the story: a collection of blank flint pieces, partly worked flint tools, and a heap of *flakes* suggest that a site was used for flint-tool manufacture. Other times, when archaeologists are unclear about the significance of remains, they use a method called **ethnoarchaeology**, which is the study of the way present-day societies use artifacts and structures and how these objects become part of the archaeological record. Archaeologists studying how contemporary foraging people build traditional shelters—what kinds of materials are employed and how they are used in construction—can predict which materials would be most likely to survive in a buried site and the patterns they would reveal if they were excavated. If such patterns turn up in sites used by prehistoric foragers, archaeologists will already have important clues to assist in their interpretation. Archaeologists are very aware, however, that these contemporary foragers are not "living fossil cultures" that are replicates of those in the past. Instead, these contemporary cultures provide clues and possible explanations to assist in understanding the past.

However, archaeologists must not overlook the possibility that a variety of natural and human forces may have interfered with remains once they are left behind at a site. An important source of information about past human diets may be obtained from animal bones found in association with other human artifacts; but just because hyena bones, stone tools, and human bones are found together does not in itself mean that the humans ate hyenas. Careful study of the site may show that all these remains came together accidentally after having been washed out of their original resting places by flash flooding. This is known as *taphonomy*, or the study of the various processes that may have affected the formation of a particular site. Human activity can have particularly damaging effects on anthropological sites. Modern industrial agricultural practices are one of the most widespread and destructive taphonomic processes; thousands of sites and artifacts across North America have been accidentally destroyed

For more on the effect of natural taphonomic processes on hominin sites, see Chapter 5, p. 104.

through the mechanized plowing of millions of acres of land. Another highly destructive human activity is the pillaging and looting of archaeological sites, which will be discussed more thoroughly later in this chapter.

Even in ideal situations, where a site has lain relatively undisturbed for hundreds, thousands, or millions of years, some kinds of important human activity may not be represented by preserved remains. Wood and plant fibres decay rapidly, and their absence at a site does not mean that its human occupants did not use wooden tools. The earliest classification of ancient human cultural traditions in Europe was based on stone, bronze, and iron tools, all of which can survive for long periods. Baked clay—whether in the form of human-made pottery and figurines or naturally occurring deposits that were accidentally burned in a fire—is also quite durable. Fire can also create charred plant seeds that are virtually indestructible, allowing important dietary clues to survive.

Extreme climates can enhance artifact preservation. Hot, dry climates, such as those in Egypt or northern Chile, hinder decay. Sites in these regions contain not only preserved human bodies but also other organic remains, such as plant seeds, baskets, cordage, textiles, and artifacts made of wood, leather, and feathers. Cold climates provide natural refrigeration, which also slows decay. Burial sites in northern or high-mountain regions with extremely low winter temperatures may never thaw

ethnoarchaeology The study of the way present-day societies use artifacts and structures and how these objects become part of the archaeological record.

FIGURE 8.2 Some archaeological sites are well preserved as a result of natural disasters. This adobe house in Cerén, El Salvador (a), was buried under several layers of lava following a series of volcanic eruptions. Sometimes, organic remains leave impressions in the soil where they decayed. These remains of a corn crib and ears of corn from Cerén (b) are actually casts made by pouring dental plaster into a soil cavity.

out once they have been sealed, preserving even better than dry climates the flesh of humans and animals, plant remains, and artifacts made of leather and wood. This spectacular form of preservation is illustrated by the *Kwäd̯ąy Dän Ts'ìnchi̯* ("long ago person found") discovery, in which well-preserved human remains were recovered from a retreating glacier in the Tatshenshini-Alsek Park, British Columbia, in August 1999 (Hebda, Greer, and Mackie 2017). A range of artifacts were discovered in association with this roughly 500-year-old frozen body, including a robe-style fur garment, a plant-fibre hat, and various wooden artifacts (Beattie et al. 2000).

Occasionally, archaeological sites are well preserved as a result of natural disasters, such as volcanic eruptions (Figure 8.2). Similarly, mudslides may cover sites and protect their contents from erosion, while water-logged sites free of oxygen can preserve a range of organic materials that would otherwise decay. Peat bogs, for example, are exemplary airless, waterlogged sites that have yielded many plant and animal remains, including artifacts made of wood, leather, and basketry, as well as the occasional human body. Log pilings recovered from Swiss lakes have been useful both for reconstructing ancient sunken dwellings and for establishing tree-ring sequences in European dendrochronology.

survey The physical examination of a geographical region in which promising sites are most likely to be found.

Surveys

Often, a research problem requires a trip to the field. Traditionally, this meant surveying the region in which promising sites were likely to be found and then excavating the most promising of them. As archaeologists have increasingly come to recognize, however, excavations cost a lot of money and are inevitably destructive. Fortunately, non-destructive remote-sensing technologies have improved significantly in recent years. **Survey** archaeology can now provide highly sophisticated information about site types, their distribution, and their layouts, all without any earth being turned. Surveys have other advantages as well, as archaeologists Colin Renfrew and Paul Bahn (2008, 79) remind us: "Excavation tells us a lot about a little of a site, and can only be done once, whereas survey tells us a little about a lot of sites, and can be repeated." As the kinds of questions archaeologists ask have changed, larger regions—entire landscapes, contrasting ecological zones, trading zones, and the like—are increasingly of interest. And for this kind of research, surveys are crucial.

Surveys can be as simple as walking slowly over a field with eyes trained on the ground. They are as important to paleontologists as to archaeologists. For example, paleontologist Donald Johanson and his colleagues discovered the bones of "Lucy" when they resurveyed a locality in the Hadar region of Ethiopia that had yielded nothing on previous visits (see Chapter 5). Between their previous visits and the one during which they found Lucy's bones, the rainy season had come and gone, washing away soil and exposing the bones. Had Johanson or his colleagues not noticed those bones at that time, another rainy season probably would have washed away Lucy's remains (Johanson and Edey 1981).

Of course, Johanson and his team were not in Hadar accidentally; they had decided to look for sites in areas that seemed promising for good scientific reasons. Archaeologists ordinarily decide where to do their field surveys based on previous work, which can give them clues about where they will most likely find suitable sites. Local citizens who may know of possible sites are also important sources of information. For instance, the *Kwäday Dän Ts'ìnchi* discovery mentioned above was made by a group of First Nations hunters who stumbled upon a body that was melting out of the retreating glaciers (Hebda, Greer, and Mackie 2017). Government archaeologists and members of the nearby Champagne and Aishihik First Nations (CAFN) (see EthnoProfile 8.1) collaborated closely to excavate and examine the body. When DNA analysis of the body was conducted, 17 living members of the CAFN discovered that they were related to the "long ago person found" directly through their mother's lineage (Pringle 2008). As well, diseases that are common among the northern peoples today, including tuberculosis, were identified by Dr Treena Swanston, MacEwan University, within the gut of this ancient individual (see "In Their Own Words" box). After scientific analysis had been completed, the body was respectfully laid to rest in a traditional CAFN ceremony.

Aerial surveys can be used for mapping purposes or to photograph large areas with attributes that may suggest the presence of otherwise invisible sites. For example, when contemporary crops are planted in fields that were once used for other purposes, seeds sown over features such as buried walls or embankments will show growth patterns different from those of the plants around them, casting a shadow that is easily seen in aerial photographs. Black-and-white aerial photography is the oldest form of aerial reconnaissance and can provide fairly good image resolution. However, infrared and digital photography, as well as remote-sensing techniques using false-colour, heat-sensitive, or radar imaging, generally produce better results. Recent advances in remote-sensing techniques that are being used to detect archaeological sites include unmanned aerial vehicles (UAVs, or drones) and LiDAR systems. UAVs are a low-cost option whereby small remote-controlled planes are fitted with imaging

---

EthnoProfile 8.1

Champagne and Aishihik First Nations (CAFN)

Region: Northwestern North America

Nation: Canada

Population: 34,000

Environment: Boreal forest, subarctic

Livelihood: Hunting, fishing, gathering

Political organization: Part of a modern nation–state but also organized according to their own First Nations government

For more information: Champagne and Aishihik First Nations website: www.cafn.ca

---

equipment that can take aerial photos from hundreds to thousands of metres in the air. LiDAR uses laser technology that can penetrate dense forest cover to detect archaeological features and sites on the ground. The lasers are attached to low-flying planes and generally used in places covered by rainforests—for example, in Central America and Asia. An impressive example of the benefits of LiDAR is provided by a study of the Mayan Caracol site in Belize, where not only the topography of the site but also causeways and agricultural terraces from 2000 years ago were detected (Chase and Chase 2017) (Figure 8.3). More recent studies in Guatemala using this same technology reveal an intricate network of roads that connect more than 60,000 homes, temples, and fortresses (Ferrira 2018).

Thanks to modern technology, archaeologists can learn a lot about a site without actually digging. This is sometimes referred to as "archaeology of the invisible." Some machines can detect buried features and gravitational anomalies using echo sounding or by measuring the electrical resistivity of the soil. Magnetic methods can detect objects made of iron or baked clay, and metal detectors can locate buried metal artifacts. In recent years, ground penetrating radar (GPR) has become more readily available for archaeological use. GPR reflects pulsed radar waves off features below the surface. Because the radar waves pass through different kinds of materials at different rates, the echoes that are picked up reflect back

In Their Own Words

Kwädąy Dän Ts'ìnchį ("Long Ago Person Found"): Disease and Lineage

Treena Swanston, Assistant Professor, MacEwan University, was part of a research team that identified disease-causing pathogens in Kwädąy Dän Ts'ìnchį.

In the summer of 1999, the frozen remains of a man and a number of artifacts were discovered melting out of a glacier in northern British Columbia on the traditional territory of the Champagne and Aishihik First Nations (CAFN). The site was given the name *Kwädąy Dän Ts'ìnchį* ("Long Ago Person Found"). Based on radiocarbon dating of a plant fibre hat, an Arctic ground squirrel robe, and a sample from the individual, it is thought that the man lived between 1720 and 1850 AD. A management committee was formed that included CAFN members, the BC Archaeology Branch, and the Royal BC Museum. The committee decided to collaborate with the scientific community to learn more about the individual and the artifacts.

My initial analysis of microbial DNA associated with normal flora or pathogens (disease-causing microorganisms) in the tissues was unsuccessful because I could not determine if the amplified DNA was originally associated with the individual or if it was a modern contaminant. I then decided to look specifically for two different types of bacteria, *Helicobacter pylori* and *Mycobacterium tuberculosis*.

H. pylori, a bacterium in stomach tissue, can be found in half of the world's population, but only 15 per cent of infected individuals will have clinical symptoms. Studies have shown that variations in the virulence-associated genes correspond to different populations because transmission occurs vertically (within families) and corresponds with ancient population movement. *H. pylori* DNA was identified in the stomach tissue of the Long Ago Person Found and interestingly, the strain was 98 per cent similar to two modern strains isolated from individuals in Alaska. This finding supports the knowledge that the ancient individual relates to the modern local community.

Mycobacterium tuberculosis (MTB) is a bacterium that infects one in three globally. Only one in ten of those infected will develop active tuberculosis, but this disease is still a serious problem despite advances in treatments. The ancient individual did not have evidence of the disease tuberculosis. The analysis of his lung tissue revealed MTB DNA and the presence of a latent infection, but he would not have been infectious to others.

Source: Courtesy of Dr. Treena Swanston, Assistant Professor, MacEwan University, 2018.

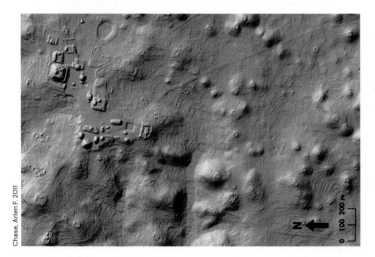

Chase, Arlen F. 2011

FIGURE 8.3 In this LiDAR image of the Caracol site in Belize, the jungle cover has been removed, revealing the linear patterns on the hillsides that represent the agricultural terraces ancient Mayans used to grow food.

changes in the soil and sediment encountered as well as the depth at which those changes are found. Advances in data processing and computer power make it possible to produce large three-dimensional sets of GPR data that can be used effectively to produce three-dimensional maps of buried archaeological remains. GPR is very useful when the site to be studied is associated with people who forbid the excavation of human remains.

Geographic information systems (GIS) are also becoming increasingly important in archaeological research. A GIS is a "computer-aided system for the collection, storage, retrieval, analysis, and presentation of spatial data of all kinds" (Fagan and DeCorse 2005, 188). In essence, a GIS is a database with a map-based interface. Anything that can be given a location in space—information about topography, soil, elevation, geology, climate, vegetation, water resources, site location, and

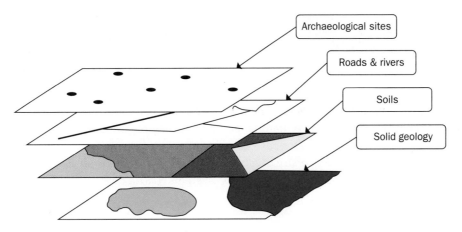

FIGURE 8.4 The layers of landscape information produced by a geographic information system.

field boundaries, as well as aerial photos and satellite images—may be entered into the database, and then maps can be generated with the selected information that the researcher requires. At the same time, statistical analysis can be done on the database, allowing archaeologists to generate new information and to study complex problems of site distribution and settlement patterns over a landscape. GIS is being used to construct predictive models, as well. That is, if certain kinds of settlement sites are found in similar places (close to water, sheltered, near specific food sources), then a GIS model for an area can be used to predict the likelihood of finding a site at a particular location (see Figure 8.4). For archaeologists, the drawback to this kind of predictive modelling is a tendency to overemphasize environmental features as the determining factors in past human settlement patterns. It is easy to measure, map, and digitize features of the natural environment. Social and cultural modifications of the environment, however, are equally important but more difficult to measure using GIS methods.

Archaeological Excavation

Excavation is necessary when archaeologists need to know "a lot about a little of a site" (Renfrew and Bahn 2008). In other words, if an archaeologist is focusing on a specific culture at a specific time, then excavation becomes a necessary component of archaeological research. Excavation is the systematic uncovering of archaeological remains through removal of the deposits of soil and other material covering and accompanying them (Renfrew and Bahn 2008, 580). Note that excavation is a form of destruction; a site, once excavated, is gone forever. Archaeologists today will excavate only a small part of a site on the assumption that future archaeologists will

have better techniques and different questions if they return to the same site. Some sites are shallow, with only one or a few occupation events, while other sites, such as caves that were used for centuries by successive human groups or urban sites that were used for hundreds or thousands of years, are far more complex. In either case, however, excavators keep track of what they find by establishing a rigorous three-dimensional grid system that allows them to record accurate positions of all aspects of the site.

As Renfrew and Bahn (2008, 107) point out, a multi-layered site contains two kinds of information about human activities: (1) contemporary activities that take place horizontally in space, and (2) changes in those activities that take place vertically over time. Artifacts and features associated with one another in an undisturbed context provide evidence for contemporary activities. As excavators uncover one stratum after another in sequence, they gradually reveal evidence for changes in human activities over time. The more levels of occupation at a site, the more likely it is that some of the levels will have been disturbed by subsequent humans, other animals, or natural forces. It then becomes the excavator's job to determine the degree of disturbance that has occurred and its effect on the site.

Only in shallow sites, like those of the Canadian Arctic, are archaeologists likely to expose an entire occupation level. However, this procedure is prohibitively expensive and destructive on large, multi-levelled

excavation The systematic uncovering of archaeological remains through removal of the deposits of soil and other material covering them and accompanying them.

In Their Own Words

GIS and Métis Settlement

One of the central issues in anthropology is determining how new identities, new peoples, and new cultures emerge and take hold. Archaeologists often use material culture and use of space to understand how people change, but what happens when you have a historical example where you know a new culture emerged? Kisha Supernant, a Métis archaeologist from the University of Alberta, asks that question by studying the emergence of the Métis Nation using archaeology and geographic information systems (GIS) in collaboration with contemporary Métis people.

The Métis of Canada are a post-contact Indigenous people who arose as a new Nation out of the history of the fur trade and contact between Indigenous and European peoples in Canada. Archaeology has the potential to explore the daily lives and identities of Métis people during a time where they were not writing their own history. Much of the written history of the Métis focuses on political and social activities at and around Red River, located in what is today Winnipeg, Manitoba. However, the Métis were a highly mobile people who moved extensively throughout the prairie, parkland, and boreal forest of western Canada. During the mid-1800s, Métis families began building cabins and spending the winter out on the prairie and parkland. This practice, known as an overwintering or *hivernant* way of life, left archaeological traces at locations where Métis people would live for six to seven months of the year.

Kisha Supernant explores Métis overwintering sites by combining archaeological analysis of past material culture and extensive site mapping using GIS. Archaeological excavations reveal patterns of Métis daily life, including diet, social activities, technologies, and the importance of social practices, such as Métis beading. Using high-precision mapping techniques, Dr Supernant places the tiny traces of human activity into a spatial context, drawing conclusions about how Métis people used space at different scales, from the insides of cabins to site layouts to comparison between different sites.

One of the key wintering sites she works on is the Buffalo Lake Métis Wintering site, located on the northeast corner of Buffalo Lake, Alberta. This site was occupied from 1872 to 1878 and may have had 400 cabins of Métis families during the winter of 1875 (Doll, Kidd, and Day 1988). If 400 cabins were present in 1875, the Buffalo Lake site would have been the largest concentration of people between Red River, Manitoba, and the Pacific Ocean, with potentially 1000 to 2000 people overwintering there. Many of the cabin locations have been subject to disturbance, but Dr Supernant and her team used GIS mapping, remote sensing, and targeted excavation to explore the full extent of the site. She has also been excavating a wintering site at Chimney Coulee, Saskatchewan, where cabin excavations have revealed thousands of artifacts that tell the story of Métis daily life during the late 1800s.

The archaeological record of overwintering sites can be used to explore how Métis patterns might be distinguished from settler or First Nations material culture and use of space, highlighting the importance of geographic mobility during the fur trade as a defining characteristic of a Métis cultural landscape. Working in collaboration with contemporary Métis communities allows modern people to connect to a history of Métis daily life that is often untold or forgotten in the story of Canada. In an era of reconciliation, objects from the past can be powerful ways for contemporary people to learn about the vibrant lives of Indigenous ancestors in Canada and for Indigenous people to reconnect with their identity. Traces of the Métis past also tell us whether or not we can see the emergence of new cultures and new identities in the archaeological record, contributing to the central anthropological question: How do we belong?

Source: Courtesy of Dr Kisha Supernant, Associate Professor, University of Alberta, 2018.

sites, especially those found in caves and rock shelters. Archaeologists often use statistical sampling techniques to choose which portions of large, complex sites to excavate, aiming for a balance between major features and outlying areas.

As the excavation proceeds, researchers document the artifacts and site details by taking photographs, writing descriptive field notes, and drawing profiles of the stratigraphic layers exposed during digging. Such record keeping is especially important for structures that will be destroyed as digging continues. Excavated soil is sifted through screens to recover tiny artifacts such as stone flakes or remains of plants or animals. Flotation methods allow archaeologists to separate light plant matter that floats (e.g., bits of wood, leaves, fibres, some seeds, stems, and charcoal) from heavier items that sink (e.g., rocks, sand, bones, pottery, and chipped stone). Everything is labelled and bagged for more detailed analysis in the laboratory.

Work on an archaeological excavation ranges from the backbreaking shifting of dirt to the delicate brushing away of soil from a key fossil or artifact. Each dig brings special challenges. Archaeologist Robert Wenke (1999, 84) describes his team's daily routine during the first three months of a six-month field season as they searched for evidence of the emergence of agriculture after 7000 BCE at a site on the southern shore of Lake Fayum in Egypt:

> We began by making a topological map of the area we intended to work in. We then devised a sampling program and collected every artifact in the sampling units defined, that is, in the hundreds of 5 × 5 meter squares in our study area. The average temperature during much of this work was over 40°C (104°F), and by mid-day the stone tools were often so hot we would have to juggle them as we bagged them. Afternoons were spent sorting, drawing, and photographing artifacts, drinking warm water, and drawing each other's attention to the heat.

Most of the labour of cleaning, classifying, and analyzing artifacts and ecofacts usually takes place in laboratories after the dig is over and frequently requires several years to complete. Researchers clean the artifacts well enough for close examination—but not so well that possible organic residues (grain kernels inside pots, traces of blood on cutting edges) are lost. They then classify the artifacts according to the materials out of which they are made, their shapes, and their surface decoration, if any, and arrange them in typologies, using ordering principles similar to those used for fossil taxonomies. Once the artifacts are classified, researchers analyze records from the dig for the context or patterns of distribution in space or time. Note that all sources of information collected during the excavation—notebooks, drawings, plots of artifact distributions, photographs, and computer data— are as much a part of the results of the excavation as the materials excavated are.

As you will recall from Chapter 5, the artifacts and structures from a particular time and place in a site are called an *assemblage*. Cultural change at a particular site may be traced by comparing assemblages from lower levels with those found in more recent levels. When surveys or excavations at several sites turn up the same assemblages, archaeologists refer to them as an "archaeological culture." Such groupings can be very helpful in mapping cultural similarities and differences over wide areas during past ages.

One pitfall, however, which earlier generations of archaeologists did not always avoid, is assuming that archaeological cultures necessarily represent real social groups as they actually existed. As archaeologist Ian Hodder (1982) has reminded us, archaeological cultures are the product of scientific analysis and may not represent all aspects of past human behaviour. Hodder's ethnoarchaeological research among several contemporary ethnic groups in eastern Africa showed that artifact distributions do sometimes coincide with ethnic boundaries when the items in question are used as symbols of group identity. He found, for example, that the ear ornaments worn by women of the Tugen, Njemps, and Pokot groups were distinct from one another and that women from one group would never wear ear ornaments typical of another. However, other items of material culture, such as pots or tools, which were not used as symbols of group identity, were distributed in patterns very different from those typical of ear ornaments. Such artifact distribution patterns could be misinterpreted by future researchers and result in a misleading archaeological culture.

Correlations between archaeological cultures and present-day cultures are important because they can help archaeologists explain cultural variation and reconstruct cultural change through time. Anthropologists seek to answer a variety of questions regarding

For more on the process of plant and animal domestication, see Chapter 9, pp. 185–192.

how humans lived in the past and the reasons new technologies and ways of life developed. One of the major cultural changes in the human past involves small bands of foragers who decided to settle down and farm for a living. When, where, and why did this happen? Further, why did some of these settlements then grow into large and complex urban centres? Patterned distributions of artifacts offer clues about groups of people who might have been responsible for these developments; however, we need to remember the risks of associating these distributions too rigidly with real past societies.

Digital Heritage and Archaeology

We described earlier new approaches in contemporary archaeology that include new types of computerized data obtained through a variety of new technologies, including GIS, ground penetrating radar, and LiDAR. In recent decades, the digital revolution of a myriad of technologies offers "the potential of connecting data to spatial coordinates, fleshing out site and landscape, and rendering simulated pasts in photographic detail, . . . [and create] as complete a model of the past as possible; a digital

> **digital heritage** Digital information about the past available on the Internet. It can include a range of materials, from digitized documents and photographs, to images of artifacts, to video and sound recordings.
>
> **archaeogaming** The utilization and treatment of immaterial space to study created culture, specifically through video games.

heritage" (Olsen et al. 2012, 88). However, the creation and successful management of **digital heritage** relies on clear partnerships among archaeologists, digital experts, and the Indigenous (or other) communities for whom digital heritage has meaning. This includes maintenance and sustainability of the digital records, as well as the updating of hardware and software along with ensuring online access to these resources.

One of the positive outcomes of digital media is the extensive documentation of various forms of archaeological data. For example, Chris Haukass and Lisa Hodgetts from Western University have used photogrammetry extensively to document archaeological resources in the Western Arctic (2016). Her current work (2019) with the Inuvialuit, to co-create a digital archaeology and heritage resource, responds to the Calls to Action of the Truth and Reconciliation Commission. Specifically, her project will address article 11: "Indigenous peoples have the right to practice and revitalize their cultural traditions

Anthropology in Everyday Life

Archaeogaming: Video Games and Archaeology

There is a long history of using games in education, in museum outreach, and in public archaeology. Yet rarely, as Shawn Graham (2016) from Carleton University suggests, are games used to make scholarly arguments about how to better understand the past. Graham, a self-proclaimed gamer, views "historical" video games as a means for students and the general public to question ideas about the past in the same way that archaeologists do. He states that these video games have a larger historical narrative within which the game's narrative must take place (2016, 17). In other words, to design the game and to play the game involves a kind of historical thinking that characterizes professional thinking about the past. Game players think about the past in the same way that we teach our students to think about the past, asking questions like "Why did that happen?"

Furthermore, training archaeologists has always emphasized how to do archaeology by performing archaeology. Hands-on experiences in the lab and field influence how we think and understand the past. Playing video games involves this same aspect of performance, where it is important to understand "Who made the game"? and "How did they imagine the world?" These systems of game rules are similar to the rules we use to construct our ideas about the past (Graham 2016, 17). Moreover, gamers internalize these systems of the rules and relationships, and often the learning that happens through video games is deep and tied to what psychologists call "flow." The best games adjust their level of difficulty to challenge the player, and the best learning is tied to this same sense of mastery.

Games about the past will be played, experienced, and internalized by many more people than who will ever read a formal paper on archaeology. And their experience with the past will resonate far more deeply than any visit to a site or to museums. Graham (2016) suggests that **archaeogaming** should become a sub-discipline of archaeology that requires the same standard of practice as the physical collection of excavated data, only with a different toolset (18). He also warns, that if "We ignore games as a venue for our scholarship [it is] at our peril" (18).

and customs. This includes the right to maintain, protect and develop the past, present and future manifestations of their cultures, such as archaeological and historical sites, artefacts, designs, ceremonies . . ." (TRC 2015). Hodgett's project exemplifies the importance of creating a digital heritage with the Inuvialuit and working with them to assist with meeting the Calls to Action by Canadian archaeologists.

How Do Archaeologists Interpret the Past?

Archaeological Objectives and Approaches

Renfrew and Bahn (2008, 17) outline four objectives or approaches that have guided archaeological interpretation since it developed as a discipline in the early to mid-1900s. Initially, archaeologists used traditional approaches that focused only on *reconstructing the material remains* of the past by putting together pots, reassembling statues, and restoring houses, known as the *culture history* approach. This was followed by a focus on *reconstructing the lifeways*—the culture—of the people who left those material remains, referred to as the *cultural ecology* approach. Since the 1960s, however, a third objective has been *explaining the cultural processes* that led to ways of life and material cultures of particular kinds. This has been the focus of what came to be known as *processual archaeology*, or *new archaeology*.

Processual archaeologists "sought to make archaeology an objective, empirical science in which hypotheses about all forms of cultural variation could be tested" (Wenke 1999, 33). They integrated mathematics into their work, using statistics to analyze the distribution of artifacts at a site, the transformations of artifact usage over time, or the dimensions of trade networks. Their interest in human adaptations to various environments in the course of cultural evolution led to an interest in the field of cultural ecology, in which cultural processes must be understood in the context of climate change, the variability of economic productivity in different environments, demographic factors, and technological change. As a general rule, processual archaeologists downplayed explanations in which people play an active role as agents who are conscious, to a greater or lesser degree, of what is happening around them and whose activities contribute to cultural maintenance or change.

In recent years, however, archaeologists have begun to ask new questions—leading to a fourth objective. Many have concluded that processual archaeology neglected human agency and the power of ideas and values in the construction of ancient cultures. A variety of new approaches, which are sometimes called *post-processual* or *interpretive archaeology*, stress the *symbolic and cognitive aspects of social structures and social relations*. Some post-processual archaeologists focus on power and domination in their explanations of certain aspects of the archaeological record; they draw attention to the ways that archaeological evidence may reflect individual human agency and internal contradictions within a society. Other post-processual archaeologists point out that similar-looking features can mean different things to different people at different sites, which is why it can be seriously misleading to assume that all cultural variation can be explained in terms of universal processes, such as population growth or ecological adaptation. (We will look at varieties of post-processual archaeology in the archaeology and gender section at the end of this chapter.)

However, while objectives such as these can lead to better understandings of past societies, we must always remember that increasingly precise archaeological methods and subtle archaeological theorizing are worthless if there is nothing left to study. By the twenty-first century, the looting and destruction of archaeological sites had reached crisis proportions. Michael Bisson provides a salient example of this when he describes finding a prehistoric artifact for sale in a Canadian pawn shop (Bisson and Bolduc 1994). Thus, archaeologists have come to recognize that stewardship of the remains of the human past may be their most pressing responsibility (Fagan and DeCorse 2005, 25).

Subsistence Strategies

One of the most important aspects that anthropologists seek to understand about the human past is how we lived and survived. All organisms, including human beings, construct their own ecological niches by inventing ways of using their relationships with one another and with the physical environment to make a living.

> ↻ Connections between subsistence strategies and economic practices are fully outlined in Chapter 10.

Subsistence is the term often used to refer to the satisfaction of the most basic material survival needs: food, clothing, and shelter. The different ways that people in different societies go about meeting subsistence needs are called **subsistence strategies**.

Anthropologists have devised a typology of subsistence strategies that has gained wide acceptance (Figure 8.5). The basic division is between food collectors, or *foragers* (those who gather, fish, or hunt), and food producers (those who depend on domesticated plants or animals or both). The strategies followed by food collectors depend on the richness of the environments in which they live. Small-scale food collectors live in harsher environments and are likely to change residence often in search of resources, as the Ju/'hoansi traditionally did. By contrast, complex food collectors live in environments richly endowed with dependable food sources and may even, like the Indigenous peoples of the northwest coast of North America, build settlements with permanent architecture. As we shall see, archaeological evidence shows that some of the first food producers in the world continued food collection for many generations, raising a

For more on the Ju/'hoansi, see EthnoProfile 10.1, on p. 215.

subsistence strategies **The ways that people in a particular society go about meeting their basic material survival needs.**

few crops on the side and occasionally abandoning food production to return to full-time foraging.

Food producers may farm exclusively, or herd exclusively, or do a little of both. Those who depend on herds are called *pastoralists*. Among those who farm, there are further distinctions. Some farmers depend primarily on human muscle power plus a few simple tools, such as digging sticks, or hoes, or machetes. They clear plots of uncultivated land, burn the brush, and plant their crops in the ash-enriched soil that remains. Because this technique exhausts the soil after two or three seasons, the plot must then lie fallow for several years as a new plot is cleared and the process is repeated. This form of cultivation is called *extensive agriculture*, emphasizing the extensive use of land as farm plots are moved every few years (see Figure 8.6). Other farmers use plows, draft animals, irrigation, fertilizer, and the like. Their method of farming—known as *intensive agriculture*—brings much more land under cultivation at any one time and produces significant crop surpluses. Finally, *mechanized industrial agriculture* is found in societies in which farming or animal husbandry has become organized along industrial lines. Agribusiness "factories in the field" or animal feedlots transform food production into a large-scale, technology-dependent industry of its own.

At the same time, archaeologists are interested in why certain kinds of subsistence types came about in

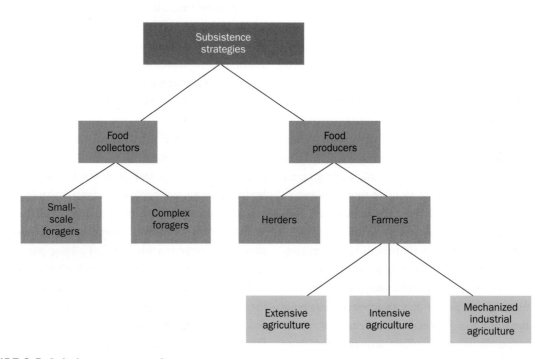

FIGURE 8.5 Subsistence strategies.

one place and time rather than another. Prehistorians note that there were numerous settled villages in southwest Asia 10,000 years ago, but only a few of them became cities or city-states. Some foragers settled down to become farmers or animal herders in some times and places while some of their neighbours managed to find a way to continue to survive by gathering and hunting right up until the end of the twentieth century. Indeed, in parts of the world, such as Afghanistan, herders continue to thrive and attempts to establish centralized states regularly fail. Archaeology, history, and ethnography can help explain why these developments have (or have not) occurred by seeking to identify social structural elements and cultural practices that may enhance, or impede, the transformation of one kind of social form into another. However, classification is not an end in itself.

Intensified processes of globalization in the late twentieth and early twenty-first centuries have revitalized the interest of many anthropologists in cultural borrowing, vindicating the Boasians' claims about the porous nature of social boundaries and the cultural adaptability of which all human societies are capable. At the same time, it has become clear that not all kinds of movements across social and cultural boundaries are equally easy or equally welcome everywhere. Anthropologists continue to pay attention to those structural features of contemporary societies—such as political boundaries between nation-states and international economic structures—that continue to modulate the tempo and mode of cultural, political, and economic change.

Whose Past Is It?

As a social science discipline, archaeology has its own theoretical questions, methodological approaches, and history. In recent years, archaeologists have explicitly had to come to terms with the fact that they are not the only people interested in what is buried in the ground, how it got there, how it should be interpreted, and to whom it belongs. In some cases, archaeological sites have come to play an important role in identity formation for people who see themselves as the descendants of the builders of the site. Machu Picchu in Andean Peru, the pyramids in Egypt, the Acropolis of Athens in Greece, Great Zimbabwe in Zimbabwe, and Masada in Israel are just a few examples of ancient monuments that have great significance for people living in modern states today. The meanings people take from them do not

Morley Read/Alamy Stock Photo

FIGURE 8.6 Extensive agriculture, sometimes known as *swidden* or *slash-and-burn horticulture*, requires a substantial amount of land since soils are exhausted within a couple of years and may require as many as 20 years to lie fallow before they can be used again.

always coincide with the findings of current archaeological research. At the same time, these sites, and a great many others, have become major tourist destinations. Geographically remote Machu Picchu, for example, now receives about 300,000 tourists per year, a number that is both impressive and worrisome since the constant movement of tourists may be doing permanent damage to the site (Figure 8.7). Nations, regions, and local communities have discovered that the past attracts tourists and their money, which can provide significant income in some parts of the world. The past may even be mobilized by the entertainment industry: for example, increasingly popular "time capsule" sites invite tourists to visit places where local people wear costumes and carry out the occupations associated with a "re-created" past way of life.

Nevertheless, not all peoples welcome either archaeologists or tourists. For example, as former colonies became independent states, their citizens became interested in uncovering their own past and gaining control over their heritage. This has often meant that the artifacts discovered during archaeological research must stay in the country in which they were found. Ownership of a peoples' heritage and antiquities is an important form of control over that peoples' history, and citizens of places like Greece and Egypt are now asking museums in Western countries to return cultural property—substantial quantities of material artifacts—that were removed long ago by colonizers. Still, many of the artifacts and relics acquired by European colonial powers during the eighteenth and

Leandro Mise/Alamy Stock Photo

FIGURE 8.7 Although Machu Picchu is a spectacular example of human ingenuity and achievement, it has had to endure increasing pressure from visitors who come to admire it. The Peruvian government has proposed closing the Inca trail during the rainy season to protect the sites.

nineteenth centuries, often illegally or by force, have yet to be returned to their rightful owners. These items include Nefertiti's bust, which was crafted in Egypt in the fourteenth century BCE and is currently held in a German museum; the Rosetta stone, which was inscribed in Egypt in the second century BCE and is currently held in the British Museum; and the Parthenon Marbles, which were sculpted in Greece in the fifth century BCE and are also currently held in the British Museum. These and other objects, some of which are considered sacred by their makers and were not intended for public view, have been openly displayed in Western museums for many years. Is displaying sacred objects in public, even among people who

do not believe in their sacredness, disrespectful to their makers? Is it just another way of representing the political power of the current owners? Renfrew and Bahn (2004, 552) suggest that the matter may be more complex:

> [One can] ask whether the interest of the great products of human endeavor does not in fact transcend the geographical boundaries of modern-day nationalism. Does it make sense that all the Paleolithic hand axes and other artifacts from Olduvai Gorge or Olorgesaillie in East Africa should remain confined within the bounds of the modern nations where they have been found? Should we not all be able to benefit from the insights they offer? And is it not a profound and important experience to be able, in the course of one day in one of the world's great museums, to be able to walk from room to room, from civilization to civilization, and see unfolded a sample of the whole variety of human experience?

But artifacts are not all that have come out of the ground over the course of a century-and-a-half of archaeological research. Human skeletal material has also been found and excavated, often from intentional burial sites. For archaeologists and biological anthropologists, this skeletal material offers important data on past patterns of migration, disease, violence, family connections, social organization and complexity, technology, cultural beliefs, and many other phenomena. Constantly improving analytical techniques are increasing the quality of data that can be extracted from skeletal remains, making this material even more valuable to understand the human past. Yet these may be the remains of ancestors of peoples now living in the area from which the bones were removed, and many of these peoples believe that the dead should not be disturbed and that it is disrespectful to have their ancestors' bones analyzed.

This has been a particularly important issue for archaeology in the United States and Canada because most of the collections of skeletal materials (and sacred objects) came from Indigenous populations. Most Indigenous and Inuit groups are deeply upset by the excavation of Indigenous burials and by the subsequent scientific analysis and public display of the bones of their ancestors (Figure 8.8). For these groups, excavation, analysis, and display of their ancestors exemplifies the disrespect and colonial domination of Indigenous peoples in North America that has existed since

Europeans first arrived. Thus, their objections have both spiritual and political dimensions. In the United States, these objections were recognized in the Native American Graves Protection and Repatriation Act, passed by the US Congress in 1990. In Canada, the heritage protection laws are quite different.

There is no federally mandated legal framework that protects all archaeological sites on lands and waters controlled by the federal and provincial governments in Canada. Rather, individual provinces and territories enact their own heritage protection and repatriation legislation, which they enforce on all sites within their boundaries except for national historic sites that are protected and controlled by Parks Canada. Generally, the regulations regarding site protection and **cultural resource management** (CRM) are similar across Canada, but the implementation and enforcement of these regulations may differ. For example, in Ontario engagement and partnering with local Indigenous peoples is a mandatory step implemented as part of all archaeology conducted in that province. In addition, archaeologists working in Canada are encouraged to follow the Principles of Ethical Conduct created by the Canadian Archaeological Association (CAA), which requires them to "exercise respect for archaeological remains and for those who share an interest in these irreplaceable and non-renewable resources" and to work respectfully with Indigenous peoples of Canada (CAA 2015).

Because of their training and expertise, archaeologists are frequently involved in protecting and managing cultural resources in Canada. In fact, CRM constitutes approximately 90 per cent of all archaeological investigations in this country. In northern Alberta, for example, rapid development of the oil and gas industry has called for an exponential number of CRM regional surveys and site discoveries. In addition, in regions such as northern Quebec and Labrador, Indigenous and Inuit peoples play a large role in managing archaeological sites and cultural heritage. In all cases, however, CRM archaeological investigations require that only qualified individuals (i.e., those with a Master's degree in archaeology and field experience) are issued permits to work in the area (Thomas, Kelly, and Dawson 2009, 479–84).

With respect to human remains and burial goods, questions of repatriation are often negotiated between the province or territory and local Indigenous or Inuit groups on a case-by-case basis. In British Columbia, human remains are considered "archaeological objects"

FIGURE 8.8 Deeply concerned that the remains of Haida ancestors had been stored in museums and moved to distant locations, the Haida Repatriation Committee (HRC) has undertaken extensive work on behalf of the Haida Nation to bring ancestral remains housed in museums home to Haida Gwaii (an archipelago off the northern coast of British Columbia). Once returned, the remains are respectfully buried according to traditional Haida ceremonies. Here, one of the founding members of the HRC, Andy Wilson, stands in front of the Royal British Columbia Museum holding a hand-crafted burial box designed to hold the remains of an ancestor.

and, as such, are subject to the province's heritage conservation legislation, while in Saskatchewan, burials not found in a cemetery are considered property of the federal government. In some cases, human remains may be studied for scientific analysis if permission to do so is granted by the local Indigenous community. In Alberta, the First Nations Sacred Ceremonial Objects Repatriation Act gives Indigenous peoples the right to apply for the return of sacred ceremonial objects that are currently in the possession of government entities. Recently in Ontario, the University of Toronto returned over 1700 *Huron-Wendat* skeletons to their local

cultural resource management (CRM) Archaeological projects that are focused on mitigating the effects of development through identifying and interpreting significant cultural and heritage sites; sometimes referred to as "salvage archaeology."

Indigenous groups in Ontario and Quebec. This unique and successful repatriation event led to the establishment of alliances between the university and local Indigenous communities (Pfeiffer and Lesage 2014).

In all cases, Canadian institutions are working proactively with Indigenous communities to develop repatriation policies and procedures, especially to work toward reconciliation with Indigenous peoples as part of the Calls to Action of the Truth and Reconciliation Commission. The Canadian Museum of Civilization (2011), for example, has developed detailed policies on repatriation. Thomas, Kelly, and Dawson (2009, 484) describe an example of a working relationship between Manitoba's provincial museum and the Nisichawayasihk Cree First Nation:

> A partnership between Nisichawayasihk (Nelson House) Cree First Nation and the Manitoba Museum was formed as part of the 1977 Northern Flood Agreement with the Province of Manitoba. The partnership was defined to work out the recovery, analysis, and display of artifacts found within the Churchill diversion basin in northern Manitoba. Under this agreement, burials are excavated in cooperation with Elders from Nelson House and the Manitoba Museum. Elders view the excavations as ethical because they believe that the ancestors are allowing themselves to be discovered, so that adults and children in their community can learn about the past. Scientific analysis has been allowed by the Cree First Nation, with the understanding that the burials and grave goods will be eventually returned to Nelson House for re-internment.

The *Kwäday Dän Ts'ìnchį* ("long ago person found") discovery in 1999, discussed earlier in this chapter, provides another example of a successful partnership between researchers and Indigenous peoples. Following the initial discovery of the human remains, a collaborative research committee was formed that included representatives from the Champagne and Aishihik First Nations, on whose land the body was found, as well as biological anthropologists and archaeologists (Hebda, Greer, and Mackie 2017). This group worked together to oversee the sampling procedures and the analysis of results, which was followed by the cremation of the body and the ceremonial distribution of the ashes. As the above examples suggest, the negotiation-based repatriation process in

Canada can be highly productive and has great potential to be able to meet the diverse needs of Indigenous peoples across the country (see Koehler 2007).

Indigenous peoples in Canada and the United States are not the only ones concerned with the treatment of human remains unearthed by archaeologists and others. In Australia, Aboriginal people have successfully pressed for the return of the remains of their ancestors, remains that were often collected unethically, sometimes through grave robbing and even murder. In recent years, the Australian government has established programs for the repatriation of cultural material and human remains that are held in Australian museums or other institutions, and it has worked to secure the repatriation of Aboriginal remains from outside Australia:

> The aim of the program is to repatriate all ancestral remains and secret sacred objects from the eligible museums to their communities of origin. The four specific objectives are to: identify the origins of all ancestral remains and secret sacred objects held in the museums where possible; notify all communities who have ancestral remains and secret sacred objects held in the museums; arrange for repatriation where and when it is requested; appropriately store ancestral remains and secret sacred objects held in the museums at the request of the relevant community. (Department of Communications, Information Technology, and the Arts 2005)

The Australian Archaeological Association has supported these initiatives.

Plundering the Past

Many people in the world were shocked and appalled in March 2001 when the extremist Taliban government of Afghanistan decided to destroy the Bamiyan Buddhas, two giant sculptures carved into the face of a cliff about 1500 years ago (Figure 8.9). Even though almost no Buddhists live in Afghanistan today, these sculptures had long been part of the cultural heritage of the Afghan people. Despite world condemnation of this decision—including fierce objection from representatives of the Islamic Conference, which represented 55 Muslim nations—the Taliban insisted that these human images were impious

REUTERS/Muzammil Pasha

(a)

REUTERS/Sayed Salahuddin

(b)

FIGURE 8.9 Many people in the world were shocked when the Taliban leaders of Afghanistan blew up two 1500-year-old statues of the Buddha, which were located in the province of Bamyan, Afghanistan. The photos above show (a) one of the statues before its destruction and (b) the empty cutout left behind following the destruction of the statues.

and destroyed them along with even older objects in the national museum. This act distressed many people, perhaps not only because it seemed so narrow-minded and thoughtless but also because the statues were irreplaceable examples of human creative power.

Nevertheless, destruction of the human past on a much greater scale goes on every day as a consequence of land development, agriculture, and looting for sale to collectors. The construction of roads, dams, office buildings, housing developments, libraries, subways, and so on has enormous potential to damage or destroy evidence of the past. As mechanized agriculture has spread across the world, tractors and deep plows tear across settlement sites and field monuments. While construction, development, and agriculture cannot be stopped, they can be made more sensitive to the potential damage they can do.

Unfortunately, such cannot be said for looting and the market in stolen antiquities. There is nothing really new about looting—the tombs of the pharaohs of Egypt

were looted in their own day—but the scale today surpasses anything that has come before. Indeed, any region of the world with archaeological sites also has organized looting, and the devastation looters leave behind makes any scientific analysis of a site impossible. We have seen how important it is for archaeologists to record the precise placement (i.e., provenance) of every object they excavate. When that context is destroyed, so too is the archaeological value of a site:

In the American Southwest, 90 per cent of the Classic Mimbres sites (c. 1000 CE) have now been looted or destroyed. In southwestern Colorado, 60 per cent of prehistoric Anasazi sites have been vandalized. Pothunters work at night, equipped with two-way radios, scanners, and lookouts. They can be prosecuted under the present legislation only if caught red-handed, which is almost impossible. (Renfrew and Bahn 2008, 563)

Looters steal to make money. Buyers, including museums and private collectors, have been willing to overlook the details of the process by which ancient objects come into their hands. While museum owners have taken some steps to make sure that they purchase (or accept as gifts) only objects that have been exported legally from their countries of origin, private collectors remain free to feed on the illegal destruction of the heritage of the world's people.

A shocking example of the illegal artifact trade came to light in 1993 when Michael Bisson, of McGill University, walked into an antiquities store in Montreal and was handed a small sculpture of an unclothed pregnant woman, carved in ivory and obviously extremely old. The piece was similar to European Upper Paleolithic figurines generally considered to be around 20,000 years old. In total, the antiquities dealer had seven of these figurines, which had been stolen from the Grimaldi Caves site in Italy during a dig in the late nineteenth century. The significance of the statues Bisson happened upon is huge, as they displayed previously unknown variations in the style of the representations and in the details they depicted (e.g., some of the figurines depicted women in the process of giving birth). The fact that these figurines had been stolen and hidden away in private collections before they could be scientifically examined within the context in which they were originally discovered demonstrates the irreparable harm that can be caused by the commercial artifact trade (Bisson and Bolduc 1994, 459–62).

To combat these sorts of destructive actions, historic protection laws were developed in the 1960s and 1970s in Canada. To meet the requirements of these laws, the archaeological specialty of cultural resource management (CRM) was developed. (See definition in earlier discussion.) CRM is an attempt to ensure that cultural resources threatened by development projects are properly managed—"recorded, evaluated, protected, or, if necessary, salvaged" (Fagan and DeCorse 2005, 483). CRM is a multi-million-dollar undertaking and the major source of employment for archaeologists in Canada; it is practised by private companies, federal agencies, universities,

> **feminist archaeology** A research approach that explores why women's contributions have been systematically written out of the archaeological record and suggests new approaches to the human past that include such contributions.

and individuals. There are strict guidelines for CRM archaeologists that underline the qualifications of those who can then undertake these projects. CRM surveys must often be conducted prior to the start of large-scale development projects involving pipelines, bridges, roadways, and other structures that reshape the natural landscape. This type of work typically requires archaeologists to collaborate with provincial (or in some cases federal) administrative offices that issue permits and require comprehensive reporting of archaeological finds (Lea and Frost 2012). If these procedures are not clearly followed, there can be dire consequences. For example, in Ontario there is a $1 million fine and a 12-month jail term for knowingly damaging archaeological materials. In addition, CRM projects always require establishing partnerships with First Nations communities when development occurs on reserve land. Originally, the legal grounds for CRM developed out of a concern for conservation rather than research. Over time, however, it has become clear that CRM archaeology contributes in a significant way not just to the preservation of the past but also to basic archaeological research and theory. In this way, we see again how archaeologists have become the stewards of the past, a role that requires great energy and skill.

Contemporary Trends in Archaeology

As we have seen, contemporary social issues lead archaeologists to rethink how they study the human past. We now consider three examples of contemporary archaeology that illustrate these developments.

Archaeology and Gender

By the 1980s, awareness of the unequal treatment of women in modern European and American societies had led archaeologists (both women and men) to examine why women's contributions had been systematically written out of the archaeological record. Building on anthropological studies of living people, **feminist archaeology** rejected biological determinism of sex roles, arguing that cultural and historical factors were responsible for how a society allocated tasks and that this allocation could change over time. The goal was to develop a view of the past that "replaces focus on remains with a focus on people as active social agents" (Conkey and Gero 1991, 15).

Feminist archaeology did not depend on new technological breakthroughs in excavation methods to pursue this goal. Rather, by using what they already knew about living human societies, together with available historical documents, feminist archaeologists asked new kinds of questions. For example, Joan Gero (1991) drew attention to male bias in discussions of the oldest, best-known collections of human artifacts: stone tools. Gero showed how traditional archaeological discussion of stone-tool technologies focused on highly formalized, elaborately retouched, standardized core tools. This focus, together with the assumption that such tools were made by men to hunt with, turns men and their activities into the driving force of cultural evolution. It simultaneously downplays or ignores the far more numerous flake tools that were probably made and used by women in such tasks as processing food or working wood and leather. Gero cited ethnographic and historical reports that describe women as active makers of stone tools, including more elaborate core tools, exposing as false the supposition that women were neither strong nor smart enough to produce these tools.

Gero then applied her findings to her analysis of a multi-layered site at Huaricoto in highland Peru. The lowest occupation level at Huaricoto dates from a period in which the site was a ceremonial centre visited by foragers who apparently made elaborate biface (two-sided) core tools out of imported stone in a workshop on the site. The most recent occupation level dates from a later period, when the site was no longer a ritual centre but had become a residential settlement whose inhabitants used many flake tools made of local stone for a variety of subsistence tasks. Gero (1991, 184) pointed out that "the flake tool performs many of the same actions unceremoniously that bifaces perform in a ritualistic setting." She suggests that the change from ceremonial centre to village settlement probably involved a shift not in the use of stone tools but rather in their social significance: male status may have been connected with stone-tool production during the early period but had probably become connected with some other kind of prestige goods instead (perhaps ceramics or textiles) by the later period. Stone tools continued to be made and used, but they were utilitarian flake tools, and their makers and users were most likely women.

Insights from feminist archaeology inform more recent work in **gender archaeology**, which "addresses the needs of contemporary gender studies for an understanding of how people come to understand themselves as different from others; how people represent these differences; and how others react to such claims" (Joyce 2008, 17). Contemporary gender studies asks, for example, why archaeologists often assume that the meanings of artifacts from all societies across space and over time should be interpreted in terms of a universal male–female division. As Rosemary Joyce observes, "The experiences of people in the contemporary world are actually a good deal more varied than those expected under the normative two-sex/two-gender model" (18). Gender archaeologists have found that new questions can be asked about variation in sex, gender, and other kinds of human difference in past societies if attention shifts away from the universals and focuses instead on detailed contextual features of specific archaeological sites.

Focusing on site-specific details affects the kinds of interpretations that archaeologists make. First, the meaning of a common artifact, whether found in a household rubbish dump or in a burial site, cannot be assumed to remain unchanged over time. This insight was central to Gero's reinterpretation of stone tools and their use at Huaricoto. Gero's approach also illustrates a second point: archaeological analyses that focus on the highly elaborated artifact can downplay or ignore patterns that would be visible if all relevant artifacts, ordinary and extraordinary, are considered. Joyce argues that Paleolithic figurines depicting females with exaggerated breasts and bellies have been misunderstood. Because of a widely shared assumption that *all* figurines depicting human females had to be "fertility symbols," archaeologists have tended to ignore other contemporary figurines that did not easily fit such an interpretation. For example, the 30,000-year-old central European Paleolithic site of Dolní Vestonice yielded figurines representing animals and human males as well as human females; moreover, the only figurines that depicted the wearing of woven clothing were some of the female figurines (Figure 8.10). Since most female and all male figurines lacked any representation of clothing, archaeologists now suggest that the female figurines with clothing represent a few women at this time and place who "gained individual status from their skill at producing textiles" (Joyce 2008, 15). This interpretation is

gender archaeology Archaeological research that draws on insights from contemporary gender studies to investigate how people come to recognize themselves as different from others, how people represent those differences, and how others react to such claims.

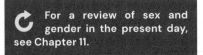

For a review of sex and gender in the present day, see Chapter 11.

strengthened by evidence from contemporary burials that clothing of men and women was not differentiated by gender and did not resemble the images of clothing portrayed on figurines (2008, 15).

For her third point about how focusing on site-specific details affects the kinds of interpretations that archaeologists make, Joyce stresses the need for archaeologists to think of material artifacts "as having had lives of their own . . . made, used, and discarded, and during which people's experiences and associations with them would have varied" (2008, 28). Focusing on the social lives of individual artifacts shifts attention away from artifacts to the individuals who made those artifacts and highlights the variety of motivations they may have had for making those artifacts the way they did. It also draws attention to the likelihood that all images were not accepted at face value but instead offered "a means for the circulation of propositions that might be contested" (2008, 16). As a result, the same

FIGURE 8.10 Sculpture head of a woman, Dolní Vestonice. The Dolní Vestonice site in the Czech Republic has yielded an extensive number of figures, some of which seem to represent women of status.

images might well have meant different things to different members of the social group that produced or used them. This approach provides "a critical basis for challenges to orthodox interpretations that might otherwise ignore complexities in human societies now as much as in the past" (2008, 16, 17).

The value of such an approach is displayed in the work of bioarchaeologist Sandra Hollimon, who was faced with interpreting remains of Chumash burials in California. As Joyce (2008) explains, contemporary Chumash culture traditionally recognized a third gender: "two-spirited" men whose status is neither male nor female. Moreover, as is the case in a number of Indigenous North American societies, such two-spirited individuals were often skilled craftspeople, who were given baskets in exchange for their work. Hollimon first expected that the graves of two-spirited individuals would stand out from the graves of women or other men because they would contain male skeletons accompanied by baskets. It turned out, however, that baskets were found together with the skeletal remains of both women and men. This prompted Hollimon to wonder if gender distinctions were not important in Chumash mortuary practices. She looked for other patterns of difference in the remains and discovered a typically female form of spinal arthritis in the skeletons of two young males. This form of arthritis was associated with regular use of digging sticks, typically women's work but also the work of two-spirited men.

These two particular male skeletons had been buried both with digging stick weights and with baskets, which strengthened the conclusion that they belonged to two-spirited males. However, digging sticks and baskets were tools traditionally associated with Chumash *undertakers*, who could be either two-spirited men or postmenopausal women. Hollimon concluded that the *status* of undertaker apparently was more significant in Chumash burial practices than was the *gender* of the individual being buried: "In Chumash society, these people helped the spirits of the dead make the transition to their next stage of life. To be able to do this, they needed a special spiritual status. This special status was limited to those whose sexual activity could not lead to childbirth" (Joyce 2008, 60). The lesson is clear: "Not finding three burial patterns led to a realization that sex may not have been the most significant basis for the identity of these people. . . . Genders were not permanent categorical identities, but rather distinctive performances related to sexuality that could change over a person's life" (2008, 61).

The Natural History Museum/Alamy Stock Photo

Indigenous Partnerships in Studying the Past

Janet Spector was one of the first archaeologists in North America to initiate an Indigenous partnership research program with the descendants of the people who had once occupied the sites she excavated. Her work in Minnesota is an example of **historical archaeology** (Figure 8.11)—the study (in this case) of post-European contact sites in North America. Like other feminist archaeologists, Spector wanted to shift attention from the artifacts to the people who made them, from a preoccupation with active men and passive women to a more realistic assessment of active women and men, and from a focus on the remains as evidence of European contact to what these remains suggested about "Indian responses or resistance to European expansion and domination" (Spector 1993, 6).

In 1980, Spector and her team began to dig at a site near Jordan, Minnesota, known by the Dakota as *Inyan Ceyaka Atonwan*, or "Village at the Rapids." She examined historical documents that referred to the site for clues about what tasks were carried out by men and women at the site, as a guide to what kinds of material remains to look for. After several seasons, concerned that her work might be meaningless or offensive to the Dakota, Spector met a Dakota man who was a descendant of a man named Mazomani, one of the original inhabitants of the Village at the Rapids. Eventually, other descendants of Mazomani visited the site. By the 1985–6 season, Dakota and non-Dakota were collaborating in teaching Dakota language, oral history, ethnobotany, ecology, and history at the site while digging continued. A Dakota elder conducted a pipe ceremony at the site

> **historical archaeology** The study of archaeological sites associated with written records; frequently, the study of post-European contact sites.

FIGURE 8.11 Historical archaeologists, shown working on an archaeological dig at the Colony of Avalon in Newfoundland, supplement written documents with records of settlement patterns, structures, and artifacts, which reveal valuable information about the past that was never written down.

© Robert Bird/Alamy Stock Photo

shortly before the field season began, which symbolized for Spector the Dakota people's permission to work there.

Since the early 1980s, collaborative archaeological research of this kind has become increasingly common. In Canada, there are a number of projects in which archaeologists work with Indigenous peoples to include their world views and traditional perspectives. In these projects, researchers interpret artifacts and sites using combined ideas about history, which they form by taking into account oral stories, songs, place names, and landscape use. A great example of this is the work done by Gerry Oetelaar, from the University of Calgary, in association with Blackfoot (Niitsitapi) elders in the Northern Plains region. In this project, the elders assist Oetelaar in the interpretation of patterns of stone circles (i.e., teepee rings) to reconstruct patterns of how people arranged space and socialized within past settlements. Other projects that involve collaboration with Indigenous peoples include the stewardship program led by Dana Lepofsky of Simon Fraser University (see the "Anthropology in Everyday Life" box) and the Aboriginal internship program established at the Manitoba Museum by E. Leigh Syms. Through his program, Syms created positive relationships with First Nations groups in Manitoba, initiating and guiding the process of co-operative education regarding First Nations heritage. Training Indigenous

peoples to become professional archaeologists is an outcome of Syms's program. One of the most accomplished graduates of this program is Kevin Brownlee, who is currently the curator of archaeology at the Manitoba Museum.

Cosmopolitan Archaeologies

A variety of far-reaching changes associated with globalization have swept the world in recent decades. These changes have affected the way all anthropologists do research, and archaeologists are no exception. A major change that has impacted archaeological work in the field is the rapid expansion of global tourism. Today, huge numbers of tourists from all over the world want to visit archaeological sites, such as Machu Picchu or Kakadu National Park in Australia, both of which have been named UNESCO World Heritage Sites.

As we discussed earlier in this chapter, nations, regions, and local communities can make a lot of money managing flows of wealthy tourists to well-known cultural heritage sites. When tourist traffic threatens to destroy such sites, therefore, it is not merely the ruins themselves that are at stake; the livelihoods of local people and governments are also threatened. Moreover, powerless minorities with traditional connections to these sites frequently find themselves shoved aside as national and international institutions step in and take over. In the past, most archaeologists tried to do their research while avoiding local legal and political involvements, hoping to achieve "a 'do no harm' model of co-existence" (Meskell 2009, 5). Today, many archaeologists have adopted the view that their first obligation should be to those local (and often marginalized) people with traditional connections to the archaeological sites where they work. This is the view taken, for example, by many archaeologists who advocate for the protection of sites located in Canada's fragile North, such as the Dorset site on Qikertaaluk Island, Nunavut (Figure 8.12). But more and more archaeologists are finding that this kind of single-minded commitment is increasingly problematic as they and their local allies must find a way to deal with a range of other local and global stakeholders who have their own, often conflicting, ideas about how cultural heritage should be managed.

Like many contemporary cultural anthropologists, some archaeologists have been moved by these struggles to question a view of the world that divides it up into a patchwork quilt of distinct, neatly bounded "cultures,"

FIGURE 8.12 Fragile sites, such as this Dorset petroglyph site at Qajartalik, on Qikertaaluk Island (Nunavut), which roughly dates to between 500 to 1000 CE, require careful monitoring to ensure they are not damaged by careless visitors and other threats, such as acid rain, climate change, etc. For decades, archaeologists of the Avataq Cultural Institute have taken into account the perspectives of local inhabitants as they work to record, monitor, and protect this site.

Daniel Arsenault; copyright: Avataq Cultural Institute

Anthropology in Everyday Life

Archaeology as a Tool of Civic Engagement

Barbara J. Little and Paul A. Shackel (2007) use the term *civic engagement* to refer to an important direction in contemporary archaeology. Civic engagement in archaeology refers to involvement and participation in public life, especially in directing people's attention to "the historical roots and present-day manifestations of contemporary social justice issues" (Little and Shackel 2007, 2). Civic engagement also refers to connecting archaeologists and the work they do to the communities that are connected in one way or another to archaeological sites and the history they embody.

An excellent example of civic engagement comes from a community-based stewardship program being run out of Simon Fraser University. Led by Dana Lepofsky, the Tla'amin–Simon Fraser University Archaeology and Stewardship Program is a combined field school and research project as well as a useful venue for spreading knowledge about a community's cultural heritage. Its guiding principles and goals include collaboration with the Tla'amin First Nation and training of Tla'amin youth and university students. The research crews work together with Tla'amin elders to facilitate exchanges of knowledge and history between the Indigenous peoples and the researchers. Through its work, the field school has formed bridges between groups that in other instances may be at odds. As Lepofsky (2011, 17) states, "Discussions of land claims are put aside to hold a projectile point and marvel at the fact that someone held this same point several millennia before. The artifact in these instances becomes more than just a stone tool; it is the medium by which intercommunity communication begins."

Involving local Tla'amin youth is an important part of this community-based project. Digging at the site, touching artifacts, and listening to the elders' accounts of their peoples' history encourages the youth of today to actively form connections between the past and the present. The outcome is a richer experience for all; the young people acquire a more in-depth understanding of the cultural heritage of the Tla'amin while older members of the Tla'amin First Nation are able to use information garnered from this work to advance their goals of self-governance and self-representation.

The following are but a few of the ways that Lepofsky (2011, 19) recommends engaging the community in local archaeological research projects and to communicate to community members the importance of the past:

1. Host a community potluck at which issues related to the research project can be discussed.
2. Create an artifact kit and make it available to the public so people can touch the artifacts that have been found.
3. Make an engaging pamphlet about the research project and pass it out at public events.
4. Go to local schools or community centres and educate students about the heritage of the sites.
5. Create an engaging website that discusses the project's progress and disseminates its findings.

For more on the goals and achievements of the Tla'amin–Simon Fraser University Archaeology and Stewardship Program, see the project's website: www.sliammonfirstnation.com/archaeology.

each of which embodies a unique heritage that must be protected from change at all costs. Again, like many of their cultural anthropologist colleagues, these archaeologists have concluded that the only way forward is to cultivate a "cosmopolitan" point of view. For many cultural anthropologists, *cosmopolitanism* means being able to move with ease from one cultural setting to another. Cultural anthropologists regularly develop cosmopolitan

skills and awareness as they move in and out of fieldwork situations. Moreover, people everywhere—tourists, immigrants, and refugees, for example—have crafted a variety of different kinds of cosmopolitan skills in order to cope successfully with movement from one cultural setting to another.

For archaeologists, adopting a cosmopolitan orientation means giving up Western/colonial assumptions about the meaning of the past. It means acknowledging, for example, that preservation of material artifacts may in fact sometimes go against the wishes of local groups with close connections to those artifacts. Dealing with such challenges means that cosmopolitan archaeologists will no longer be able to avoid involvement in legal and political debates about the future of cultural heritage, even as they come to recognize that their views may carry less weight than the views of other stakeholders: "Cosmopolitans suppose . . . that all cultures have enough overlap in their vocabulary of values to begin a conversation. Yet, counter to some universalists, they do not presume they can craft a consensus" (Meskell 2009, 7).

Archaeologist Chip Colwell-Chanthaphonh (2009, 143), for example, asks, "Can the destruction of heritage ever be ethically justified? If so, by what principle, why, and under what conditions?" He speaks of "the preservation paradox"—that is, the idea that "the concept of preservation is itself culturally conceived," with the result that "one group's notion of cultural preservation can be another group's notion of cultural destruction." Colwell-Chanthaphonh describes disagreements about the ethics of preservation of artifacts valued in different ways by different groups in the American southwest. Commitment to a "salvage ethic" led nineteenth-century collectors to "rescue" sculptures that the Zuni purposefully left to deteriorate in sacred shrines. "This is the core of the salvage ethic, the urge to 'preserve' objects by physically protecting them. But for the Zunis, such acts that aspired to cultural preservation were in fact acts of cultural destruction" (Colwell-Chanthaphonh 2009, 146).

Conflict over whether to preserve or to destroy ancient rock carvings is an issue that divides the Navajo people and the Hopi people, both of whom have lived in the American southwest for a very long time. Hopi people wish to preserve these rock carvings, which they regard as "monuments to Hopi history, proof of ancestral homelands and clan migrations" (Colwell-Chanthaphonh 2009, 149). Navajo people, however, regard all ruins from the past, including these rock carvings, as products of human evil or the activity of witches. Contact with the rock carvings is believed to cause sickness or other misfortunes, and curing ceremonies involve the destruction of the carvings. These

days, moreover, the Hopi and Navajo peoples are far from being the only groups who assign meaning to carvings and ancient ruins in the American southwest. As Colwell-Chanthaphonh points out,

> the ancient ruins of Chaco Canyon in New Mexico are at once a Hopi ancestral site, a locus of Navajo spiritual power, a ritual space for New Agers, an archaeological and scientific resource, a National Historical Park of the United States, and a UNESCO World Heritage Site. . . . Clearly, in anthropological as much as ethical terms, such a complex convergence of people, communities, and institutions cannot be reduced to just intra-nationalist, nationalist, or internationalist claims. The key ethical problem . . . is not so much categorizing rights but trying to illuminate the relationships. (151)

This is the reason a cosmopolitan approach appeals to him: "We must develop a sophisticated understanding of how heritage works from the individual level, to the community, to the nation and beyond it. . . . A just solution cannot simply pick out the rights of one group but must instead interweave these multiple values" (152). Colwell-Chanthaphonh recommends what he calls "the principle of complex stewardship": that is, "we should maximize the integrity of heritage objects for the good of the greatest number of people, but not absolutely" (160). To maximize the integrity of heritage objects would support those who want objects preserved. Concern for the good of the greatest number, however, would mean that the positions of other stakeholders with different views would also be included and might carry great weight, especially if they outnumbered the preservationists. Even then, however, the majority position might not necessarily carry the day because special consideration would need to be given to those whose ancestors made the objects or who are closely connected to them in other ways. The principle of complex stewardship is not a ready-made solution to disputes about the management of cultural heritage; rather, it is "a frame archaeologists can use to begin deliberations on ethical predicaments" (161). Finding solutions, for cosmopolitans, involves negotiations whose outcome cannot be predicted in advance.

Chapter Summary

1. Around 10,000 years ago, cultural variation, not biological species differences, distinguished human populations from one another. Archaeologists interpret cultural variation and cultural change in the human past.

2. Archaeologists trace patterns in past human cultures by identifying sites and regions of human occupation and by recovering artifacts, features, and other remains of human activity from these sites. In all cases, they are concerned with recording information about the context in which these remains are found.

3. The survival of archaeological remains depends on what they are made of and the conditions they experienced over time. Very dry and very cold climates and oxygen-free, waterlogged settings preserve many organic remains that would decay under other circumstances. Natural catastrophes, such as mudslides and lava flows, sometimes bury sites and preserve their contents remarkably well. Ethnoarchaeology and taphonomy are two methods archaeologists use to help them interpret the meaning of the remains they find.

4. Before archaeologists begin their work, they survey the region they are interested in. Surveys, whether on the ground or from the air, can yield important information that cannot be gained from excavations. Excavations are done when archaeologists want to know a lot about a small portion of a site. The style of excavation depends on the kind of site being excavated. As the excavation proceeds, archaeologists keep careful records to preserve contextual information. Much of the final analysis of the remains is carried out in laboratories.

5. Artifacts and structures from a particular time and place in a site are grouped together in assemblages; similar assemblages from many sites are grouped together in archaeological cultures. Archaeological cultures are constructed by archaeologists to reflect patterns in their data, so these cultures cannot be assumed to represent specific ethnic groups that existed in the past.

6. Archaeology has changed focus over time, from reconstructing material remains or lifeways of past human groups to explaining the cultural processes that led to particular kinds of material culture to emphasizing the role of human agency and the power of ideas and values in the construction of past cultures. Contemporary archaeologists also recognize that stewardship of the remains of the human past is one of their most important responsibilities.

7. Material remains indicating a past culture's subsistence strategy can tell archaeologists a lot about how members of that culture lived and survived. Traditionally, archaeologists distinguish between food collectors and food producers, although they also recognize that many societies across history have depended on features of both of these strategies to meet their basic material survival needs.

8. In recent years, many archaeologists have rethought their traditional methods. Feminist archaeologists have explored why women's contributions have been systematically written out of the archaeological record. Gender archaeologists have questioned the assumption that a male–female gender division is universal and have asked instead how variation in sex, gender, and other kinds of difference can be inferred from archaeological remains of past societies. Collaborative forms of archaeological research have increasingly involved co-operation between scientists and members of groups with past or current connections to the sites under investigation. In recent years, however, archaeological sites and artifacts have become the target of claims by a number of additional groups, including local and national governments, international institutions such as UNESCO, and tourists. These groups do not always agree about the value of cultural heritage preservation or about who has the right to decide the fate of remains from the past. Many archaeologists have concluded that it is vital to develop a cosmopolitan understanding of the claims of these varied stakeholders and to promote conversations among them, even if achieving consensus may not be possible.

For Review

1. What do archaeologists do? Consider popular cultural representations of archaeologists (e.g., Indiana Jones). Do these representations align with what you have learned in this chapter?
2. Create a flow chart that represents all of the steps involved in archaeology research projects (i.e., initial analysis [discovery, background data], surveys, etc.).
3. What kinds of questions do archaeologists ask about the human past? What kinds of evidence do they look for in order to answer these questions?
4. List the different human subsistence strategies presented in this chapter. How have cultural anthropologists and archaeologists contributed to the identification of these strategies?
5. Do you play any video games that depict ancient societies or even archaeology? Do you think the game developers have done a good job depicting the reality of archaeological research?
6. Who owns the past? In your answer, draw on examples presented in this chapter.
7. Research some of the provincial repatriation laws that are used in Canada. What are some similarities and differences between the different laws? How do these laws compare with repatriation laws used in other countries?
8. Explain why the looting of archaeological sites is so problematic for archaeological attempts to reconstruct the human past.
9. Using case studies in which gender considerations inform archaeological work, describe feminist archaeology.
10. What sorts of collaborative approaches do archaeologists take in studying the past? Describe some of the methods that Dana Lepofsky has used to engage local communities with her field school.
11. In what ways can archaeologists strike a balance between ensuring the protection of archaeological sites and promoting cultural knowledge through tourism?
12. What does it mean to speak of a "cosmopolitan" orientation in archaeology? Refer in your answer to the examples given in this chapter.

online

For more information about different archaeological techniques used to establish the approximate ages of artifacts, see the Focus on Four Fields passage "Archaeology: Dating Methods in Archaeological and Paleoanthropology" on the companion website.

Key Terms

archaeogaming 164
archaeological record 155
artifacts 156
cultural resource
   management 169
digital heritage 164

ecofacts 156
ethnoarchaeology 157
excavation 161
features 156
feminist archaeology 172
gender archaeology 173

historical archaeology 175
provenance 156
site 155
subsistence strategies 166
survey 158

References

Beattie, Owen, Brian Aplaud, Erik Blake, James A. Cosgrove, Sarah Gaunt, Sheila Greer, Alexander Mackie, et al. 2000. "The *Kwäday Dän Ts'ìnchj* Discovery from a Glacier in British Columbia." *Canadian Journal of Archaeology* 24: 129–47.

Bisson, Michael S., and P. Bolduc. 1994. "Previously Undescribed Figurines from the Grimaldi Caves." *Current Anthropology*: 458–68.

CAA (Canadian Archaeological Association). 2015. "Principles of Ethical Conduct." https://canadianarchaeology.com/caa/about/ethics/principles-ethical-conduct

Canadian Museum of Civilization. 2011. "Repatriation Policy." http://www.historymuseum.ca/wp-content/uploads/ 2011/09/ REPATRIATION-POLICY.pdf

Chase, Arlen F., Diane Z. Chase, John F. Weishampel, Jason B. Drake, Ramesh L. Shrestha, K. Clint Slatton, Jaime J. Awe, and William E. Carter. 2011. "Airborne LiDAR, Archaeology, and the Ancient Maya Landscape at Caracol, Belize." *Journal of Archaeological Science* 38: 387–398.

Chase, Diane, and Arlen Chase. 2017. "Caracol, Belize, and Changing Perceptions of Ancient Maya Society." *Journal of Archaeological Research* 25 (3): 185–249.

Colwell-Chanthaphonh, Chip. 2009. "The Archaeologist as World Citizen: On the Morals of Heritage Preservation and Destruction." In *Cosmopolitan Archaeologies*, edited by Lynn Meskell, 140–65. Durham, NC: Duke University Press.

Conkey, Margaret W., and Joan M. Gero. 1991. "Tensions, Pluralities, and Engendering Archaeology: An Introduction to Women and Prehistory." In *Engendering Archaeology*, edited by Joan M. Gero and Margaret W. Conkey, 3–30. Oxford: Blackwell.

Department of Communications, Information Technology, and the Arts. 2005. *Return of Indigenous Cultural Property Program*. Canberra: Government of Australia. http://www.dcita.gov.au/arts/councils/return_of_indigenous_cultural_property_(ricp)_program

Doll, Maurice F.V., Robert S. Kidd, and John P. Day. 1988. *The Buffalo Lake Metis Site: A Late Nineteenth Century Settlement in the Parkland of Central Alberta*. Human History Occasional Paper No. 4. Edmonton: Provincial Museum of Alberta.

Fagan, Brian, and Christopher DeCorse. 2005. *In the Beginning: An Introduction to Archaeology*. 11th ed. New York: HarperCollins.

Ferrira, V. 2018. "Laser Survey of Guatemalan Jungle Reveals Thousands of Complex Structures, Roads Built by Ancient Maya." *National Post*, 5 February.

Gero, Joan M. 1991. "Genderlithics: Women's Roles in Stone Tool Production." In *Engendering Archaeology*, edited by Margaret Conkey and Joan Gero, 163–93. Oxford: Blackwell.

Graham, Shawn. 2016. "The Archaeologist Who Studies Video Games and the Things He Learned There." *SAA Archaeological Record* 16 (5): 12–15.

Hebda, Richard, Sheila Greer, and Alexander Mackie. 2017. *Kwädąy Dän Ts'ìnchj: Teachings from Long Ago Person Found*. Victoria, BC: Royal BC Museum Press.

Hodder, Ian. 1982. *Symbols in Action*. Cambridge: Cambridge University Press.

Haukass, Chris, and Lisa Hodgetts. 2016. "The Untapped Potential of Low-Cost Photogrammetry in Community-Based Archaeology: A Case Study from Banks Island, Arctic Canada." *Journal of Community Archaeology and Heritage* 3 (1): 40–56.

Hodgetts, Lisa M., and Laura Kelvin. *Forthcoming [2019]*. "At the Heart of the Ikaahuk Archaeology Project." In *Archaeology of the Heart and Emotion*, edited by Kisha Supernant, Jane Toswell, Sonya Atalay, and Natasha Lyons. New York: Springer Press.

Johanson, Donald, and Maitland A. Edey. 1981. *Lucy: The Beginnings of Humankind*. New York: Simon and Schuster.

Joyce, Rosemary A. 2008. *Ancient Bodies, Ancient Lives: Sex, Gender, and Archaeology*. New York: Thames and Hudson.

Koehler, Elizabeth M. 2007. "Repatriation of Cultural Objects to Indigenous Peoples: A Comparative Analysis of US and Canadian Law." *International Lawyer* 41 (1): 103–26.

Lea, Joanne, and Karolyn Smardz Frost. 2012. "Public Archaeology in Canada." In *New Perspectives in Global Public Archaeology*, edited by Katsuyuki Okamura and Akira Matsuda, 57–76. Springer: New York.

Lepofsky, Dana. 2011. "Everyone Loves Archaeology: Bridging Communities through Archaeological Research." *The SAA Archaeological Record* 11 (5): 17–19.

Little, Barbara J., and Paul A. Shackel, eds. 2007. *Archaeology as a Tool of Civic Engagement*. Walnut Creek, CA: AltaMira.

Meskell, Lynn, ed. 2009. *Cosmopolitan Archaeologies*. Durham, NC: Duke University Press.

Olsen, Bjørnar, Michael Shanks, et al. 2012. *Archaeology: The Discipline of Things*. Berkeley: University of California Press.

Pfeiffer, Susan, and Louis Lesage. 2014. "The Repatriation of Wendat Ancestors, 2013." *Canadian Journal of Archaeology* 38: 5–12.

Pringle, Heather. 2008. "The Messenger." *Canadian Geographic* (December): 73.

Renfrew, Colin, and Paul Bahn. 2004. *Archaeology: Theories, Methods and Practice*. 4th ed. London: Thames and Hudson.

———. 2008. *Archaeology: Theories, Methods and Practice*. 5th ed. London: Thames and Hudson.

Spector, Janet D. 1993. *What This Awl Means*. St Paul: Minnesota Historical Society Press.

Thomas, David Hurst, Robert L. Kelly, and Peter C. Dawson. 2009. *Archaeology*. 1st Canadian ed. Toronto: Nelson Education.

Truth and Reconciliation Commission of Canada. 2015. "Honouring the Truth, Reconciling for the Future: Summary of the Final Report of the Truth and Reconciliation Commission of Canada." http://www.trc.ca/assets/pdf/Honouring_the_Truth_Reconciling_for_the_Future_July_23_2015.pdf

Wenke, Robert J. 1999. *Patterns in Prehistory: Humankind's First Three Million Years*. 4th ed. Oxford: Oxford University Press.

▲ The terraced city of Medina Azahara (Madinat al-Zahra) outside Córdoba, Spain, was built in the mid-tenth century as the seat of the Caliphate of Córdoba. Featuring infrastructure such as roads, bridges, water systems, buildings, and decorative objects, Medina Azahara provides anthropologists with in-depth knowledge of the Islamic civilization of al-Andalus.
Photo: By permission of Lauren Duenas

Why Did Humans Settle Down, Build Cities, and Establish States?

Chapter Outline

Modern human beings took what appear in retrospect to have been three major steps that profoundly transformed the lives of their descendants: (1) some of them settled in one place for extended periods of time; (2) some of them later began to intervene in the reproductive cycle of plants and animals; and (3) about 7500 years ago, a number of cultures independently developed social systems characterized by structural complexity and status inequality. In this chapter, we survey what anthropological research can tell us about the causes and consequences of these developments.

Today, many of us take settled life and dependence on agriculture for granted, but anthropologists argue that this was neither an easy nor an inevitable outcome of human history. In this chapter, we provide an overview of what anthropologists are able to say about the changes in human subsistence patterns, especially the factors responsible for the domestication of plants and animals. We then consider the impact of human dependence on culturally constructed agricultural niches for subsequent developments in human cultural evolution.

How Is the Human Imagination Entangled with the Material World?

Human dependence on culture is as much a requirement for survival as it is a source of freedom. Human imagination and cultural experimentation can suggest which aspects of the material world to pay attention to, and these suggestions can become part of a cultural tradition. At the same time, once a group commits itself to paying attention to some parts of the material world rather than others, it entangles itself in a set of relationships that it may not be able to abandon freely. These relationships become entrenched: they exert a determinant pressure on future choices. As we shall see, when people began to rely on cultivated plants and domesticated animals, not only did their use of the same landscape change, but also they found that they could not easily go back to their previous ways of using the environment to gather wild plants and hunt animals.

A good place to begin to study the relationship between human imagination and the material world is to consider how the need to make a living has led human beings to develop different ways of making a living in different natural environments. It turns out, however, that people can make a living in much the same way in different environments or in different ways in the same environment. For example, people work in factories in the tropical coastlands of Nigeria and in the bitter cold of Siberia in Russia; in Papua New Guinea, in similar environments some people garden whereas others have established huge plantations. Our study therefore requires us to pay attention to factors that do not depend on the natural environment alone: features of a group's cultural tradition, for example, or external influences due to unpredictable historical encounters with other human groups. In sum, documenting and accounting for major transformations in human material adaptations requires attention to ecological, economic, and sociocultural factors.

As we have seen, paleoanthropologists and archaeologists combine their knowledge with that of other scientific specialists to reconstruct earlier modes of human life. Based on these reconstructions, we know that our ancestors lived by foraging for foods and hunting for animals for most of the human past. But about 10,000 years ago, at the beginning of the Holocene, the ice sheets melted, sea levels rose, and environments changed. In some places around the globe, human beings responded to these changes by systematically interfering with the reproduction of other species, to modify those species to better suit human purposes. This process is called **domestication**, and it occurred independently in seven

↻ For more discussion on the analysis of subsistence practices in archaeology, see Chapter 8, pp. 165–6.

domestication Variety of ways that humans affected the reproduction of another species, with the result that specific plants and animals become more useful to and dependent on people.

© Igorj/ Dreamstime.com

FIGURE 9.1 A population is said to have adapted to a particular habitat when it has found its ecological niche within the larger community of organisms living in that habitat.

different areas of the world between 10,000 and 4000 years ago (Smith 1995, 12–13).

To appreciate the ways human beings responded to these environmental and ecological changes, anthropologists have used, and needed to draw on, concepts taken from the discipline of ecology. To begin with, ecologists are not content to speak vaguely of "the environment" when they discuss the relationships that species develop with each other and with the material world in which they live. Rather, they look for patterns in these relations in specific geographic settings. Traditionally, a population of a species is said to have adapted to a particular local physical environment, or *habitat*, when it has found a place, or *ecological niche*, for itself in the local community of organisms within that habitat (Figure 9.1). An *ecological niche* includes the space the population occupies and what it eats. Broader definitions also include how different populations relate to one another and the impact of their activities on the community. Many contemporary ecologists would argue that ecological niches are best defined in terms of the activities of a particular species, including the space, time, and resources that a population utilizes on a daily or seasonal basis (Odling-Smee, Laland, and Feldman 2003, 39).

Traditional ecological studies of animal populations in particular habitats have explained the social organization of that population's members—a troop of baboons,

evolutionary niche **Sum of all the natural selection pressures to which a population is exposed.**

for example—by conceiving of space, time, and resources as limiting factors to which that population must adapt if it is to survive and reproduce successfully. Biologists studying changing adaptations over time convert this ecological niche concept into an **evolutionary niche** concept by treating

> the niche of any population as the sum of all the natural selection pressures to which the population is exposed . . . that part of its niche from which it is actually earning its living, from which it is not excluded by other organisms, and in which it is either able to exclude other organisms or to compete with coexisting organisms. (Odling-Smee, Laland, and Feldman 2003, 40)

Two further ecological concepts are used to describe the dynamics relating organisms to their niches: *morphological features*, a term ecologists apply to the phenotypic traits or characteristics of organisms; and *environmental factors*, a term that refers to subsystems of the organism's environment: "Thus, natural selection can be described as promoting a matching of features and factors" (Odling-Smee, Laland, and Feldman 2003, 41).

Ordinarily, ecologists and evolutionary biologists assume that environmental factors are more powerful than morphological features of organisms: that is, natural selection involves an organism's adaptation *to* the environment. Ever since Darwin, it has been clear that this process of adaptation has played a powerful role in the evolution of life on earth. However, as we noted in earlier chapters and as the notion of ecological niche implies, organisms are not passive occupants of rigid environmental slots. Their activities regularly modify the factors in their habitats, as when birds build nests, gophers dig burrows, or beavers build dams. Organisms can pass these sorts of modification processes, known as *niche construction*, on to their descendants (or to other organisms living in their local communities). To qualify as niche construction, the modifications made by organisms to their environments must persist and/or accumulate over time. The legacy of altered environments with modified selection

↻ For additional discussion of niche construction and selection pressures in an evolutionary context, see Chapter 3, pp. 63–4.

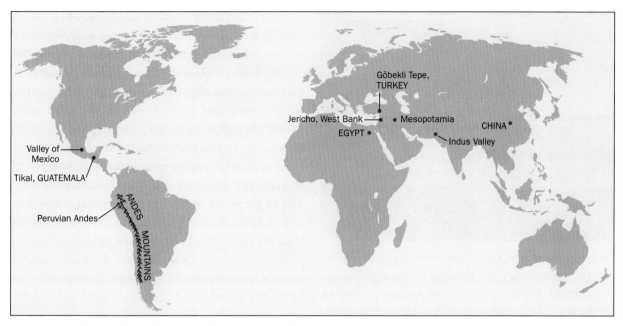

MAP 9.1 Major locations discussed in Chapter 9. (See Map 9.2 later in the chapter for the locations of major Natufian sites discussed in this chapter.)

pressures is what Odling-Smee, Laland, and Feldman (2003) call an "ecological inheritance."

How widely the process of niche construction can be successfully applied throughout the living world is not easily seen, but it clearly explains the history of human adaptations. For example, Odling-Smee, Laland, and Feldman (2003, 348–50) argue that the effects of niche construction (or its absence) should be visible when we consider the morphologies of organisms living in particular habitats. If niche construction is absent, we should expect to find that successful organisms have adapted to their environments through modifications of their phenotypes. However, if niche construction has been present in evolution, organisms should show less phenotypic change in response to environmental changes. That is, the organisms modify their environments to buffer them against having to undergo morphological changes, which is exactly what we seem to find in human evolution. People who live in extremely cold climates do not adapt by growing fur—they modify their environment by making clothing, building shelters, and heating those shelters.

As we saw in the previous chapter, the archaeological record documents a changing legacy of human modifications to environments that, at certain points, also allowed our ancestors to make a successful living in geographical regions of the world that previously had been impenetrable to them. Particularly in the past 200,000

years, we see minor physical changes in humans alongside dramatic expressions of human cultural changes and environmental modification. It is within this context that questions about transitions in human adaptive patterns are most fruitfully addressed.

Is Plant Cultivation a Form of Niche Construction?

For many years, scholars have argued about the extent to which plant domestication was accidental or intentional. Biologist David Rindos (1984), for example, suggests that domestication could have occurred without people's full awareness of what they were doing. Some archaeologists were wary of this way of approaching plant domestication. First, to argue that domestication was an unconscious process overlooks the fact that human beings of the late Pleistocene were fully modern and highly aware of their environment. Thus, they likely deliberately selected those plants that were easier to harvest, more nourishing, and tastier. In this view, humans actively intervened in the gene pool of the wild plants; domestication was a conscious decision. Second, women in contemporary foraging societies are primarily responsible for gathering wild plants, which makes women likely candidates as the first humans to have experimented with plant domestication. To assume,

FIGURE 9.2 Industrial agriculture converts acres of habitat into a uniform agroecology for growing commercial crops. These constructed niches offer protection from disease, drought, and insect infestations that the plants would be highly susceptible to in other environments. Canola, one of Canada's most economically valuable crops, is planted and harvested on more than 5 million hectares of land across the country.

FIGURE 9.3 In Australia, hunter–gatherers burn vegetation to encourage the growth of certain types of plants.

therefore, that plant domestication was a passive, unconscious process may be interpreted as a sexist stereotype, suggesting that women were not able to develop domestication. Third, paying attention only to the plants and the people involved in domestication ignores the kinds of *environmental modifications* needed

agriculture The systematic modification of the environments of plants and animals to increase their productivity and usefulness.

agroecology The systematically modified environment (or constructed niche) that becomes the only environment within which domesticated plants can flourish.

to make plant domestication successful, which clearly depended on conscious, active human intervention.

But what is the difference between domestication and cultivation? *Domestication* is human influence on the reproduction of another species, with the result that specific plants and animals become both more useful to and dependent on people. Domestication modifies the genotypes and phenotypes of plants and animals making them dependent upon humans. *Cultivation*, by contrast, is a concentrated process involving the activities of preparing fields, sowing, weeding, harvesting, and storing products, which requires a new way of thinking about subsistence and new technology to bring it about (Price and Gebauer 1995, 6). That is, habitats suitable for domesticated species to be cultivated must be carefully constructed and maintained for the domesticated species to mature and be harvested successfully. Indeed, the same process is required for successful animal domestication.

From this perspective, **agriculture** is best understood as the systematic modification of "the environments of plants and animals to increase their productivity and usefulness" (Wenke 1999, 270). Price and Gebauer call this systematically modified environment (or constructed niche) the **agroecology**, which becomes the only environment within which the plants (or animals) can flourish (Figure 9.2). Bruce Smith (1995) emphasizes that activities that led to domestication were conscious, deliberate, active attempts by foraging peoples to "increase both the economic contribution and the reliability of one or more of the wild species they depended on for survival, and thus reduce risk and uncertainty" (16). Such activities include burning off vegetation to encourage the growth of preferred plants that thrive in burned-over landscapes or to attract wild animals that feed on such plants (Figure 9.3). Burning land is a clear example of niche construction by humans that led to the domestication of grass plants, such as wheat and barley, which thrive in areas that were burned and disturbed.

More recently, some anthropologists have argued that niche construction theory can clarify relationships among people, plants, and animals that emerge in processes of domestication. Melinda Zeder, for example, suggests that such relationships are best understood as *coevolutionary* and that "niche-construction plays a role in each of three distinctive pathways that humans, plants, and animals follow into domestication" (2016, 326). First, humans engage in ecosystem modification to enhance the conditions of growth for plants and animals (e.g., burning). Second, plants and animals enter into relations with humans in order to take advantage of opportunities created by human-modified environments. Third, humans may begin interfering with the reproduction of plants and animals to suit them better to human purposes. This third step is what has traditionally been understood by "domestication," but the degree of control humans exercise in this coevolutionary network of relations can vary.

What obstacles faced those who first interfered in the life cycles of wild plants? If the plant was a grass, such as wheat, they had to cope with that plant's reproductive pattern. The wheat kernel, both domesticated and wild, is encased in a spikelet and attached to the cereal shaft by a structure called the "rachis" (Figure 9.4). In wild wheat, the rachis becomes extremely brittle as the kernel ripens, and the kernels on any stem ripen from bottom to top over a week or two. As each kernel ripens, the rachis can be broken by an animal walking through the stand of wheat or even by a gust of wind, dispersing the kernel into the air and eventually onto the ground. Wild wheat has two rows of kernels on each stalk. Because the kernels ripen at different times, the seeds have a greater chance of scattering in different directions and not all landing at the foot of the parent plant in a clump. The kernel of wild wheat is enclosed in a tough outer husk called a "glume," which protects the kernel from frost and dehydration and allows it to remain viable for as long as 20 years in the ground.

To be used successfully by humans, wheat would require a much less brittle rachis, seed heads that mature at the same time, and a softer glume. It would also require a larger, more easily visible seed head (in terms of both kernel size and number of kernel rows on a stalk). Plants with these variations would have had a selective advantage once human beings began to eat them. As the genes responsible for these increased in the wheat plant population, the plants would have contributed more and more to the human diet. The earliest domesticated wheat shows precisely these evolutionary trends, including six rows of kernels on a stalk rather than two.

The constructed niches favourable for cultivation have also varied over time and space in several important ways, and they did not appear overnight. David Harris (1989, 17) provides a useful overview of these patterns and classifies the relationships between plants and people into four major food-yielding systems: (1) wild plant–food procurement, (2) wild plant–food production, (3) cultivation, and (4) agriculture (Figure 9.5). Harris notes that

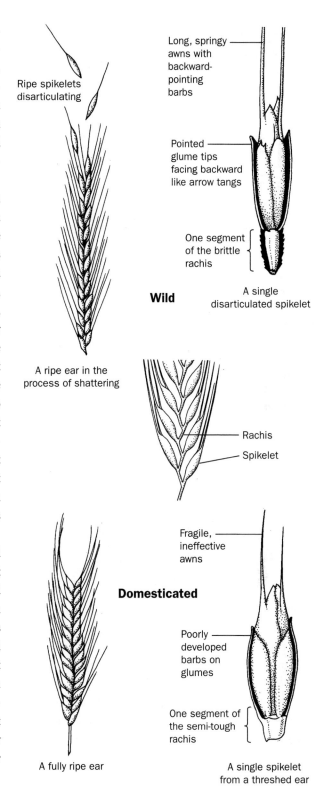

FIGURE 9.4 Wheat kernels form within spikelets that attach to the plant by a structure called the "rachis." The rachis of wild wheat is brittle, which aids in the dispersal of seeds. The rachis of domesticated wheat is not brittle, and spikelets remain attached to the ear during harvest.

Source: *The Emergence of Agriculture*, Bruce D. Smith, 1994. W.H. Freeman and Co. New York NY.

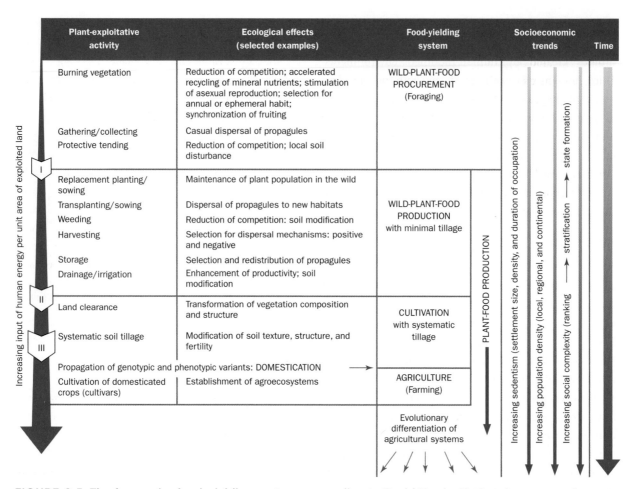

FIGURE 9.5 The four major food-yielding systems according to David Harris. Notice that energy-input to energy-output ratios jump sharply where wild plant–food production begins, where cultivation begins, and where agriculture begins. (The *propagules* referred to in the second column are the forms by which plants are reproduced: seeds, shoots, and so on).

Source: From David Harris and Gordon Hillman, *Foraging and Farming: The Evolution of Plant Exploitation, One World Archaeology*, Vol. 13, 1989, Unwin Hyman. Reprinted with permission from Routledge.

there are three points at which the amount of energy people put into plant-food activities increases sharply: (1) when wild plant–food production begins, (2) when cultivation begins, and (3) when agriculture begins.

When considering the development of domestication, note that it differs from **sedentism**, which is the process of humans staying and living in one place. People do not have to become farmers to become sedentary. The Indigenous peoples of the northwest coast of Canada (e.g., the Haida; *XaaydaGa Waadluxan Naay*) are considered sedentary foragers as they depended on seasonally re-occurring salmon runs that occurred in the same place in the same river. These reliable sources of fish were "harvested" as regularly as domesticated crops but involved minimal ecological interference and no processes of domestication.

Sedentism directly modifies the environment of those who come to depend on subsistence resources in a fixed location, be it a riverbank or a cultivated field or a pasture. Human beings who farm for a living must stay in one place to plant, water, maintain, and harvest their crops. These farmers are often able to support larger populations as they buffer themselves against food shortages that foraging peoples may be subject to during various seasons. At the same time, farmers are vulnerable to a variety of new issues brought about by sedentary life:

> For a discussion of how sedentism and agricultural practices contributed to the spread of malaria-carrying mosquitoes in tropical regions, see Chapter 7, p. 141.

sedentism The process of increasingly permanent human habitation in one place.

exposure to threats from agricultural pests and thieves as well as disease organisms that breed and spread more successfully among settled people than among foragers. As we saw, the clearing of forest by the first farmers in West Africa apparently created ecological conditions favouring larger pools of standing water, which were the ideal breeding grounds for malaria-carrying mosquitoes. This, in turn, created a new selection pressure in favour of the sickle-cell allele, which offers heterozygous carriers some protection against malaria (Odling-Smee, Laland, and Feldman 2003, 251).

How Do Anthropologists Explain the Origins of Animal Domestication?

Animal domestication can be defined as "the capture and taming by human beings of animals of a species with particular behavioural characteristics, their removal from their natural living area and breeding community, and their maintenance under controlled breeding conditions for mutual benefits" (Bökönyi 1989, 22). This definition views animal domestication as a consequence of people's attempts to control the animals they were hunting, which assumes active human intervention in selecting which animals to domesticate and how to domesticate them. Animals are more mobile than plants, and although culling wild herds can induce some changes in the gene pool, it is only by confining animals or maintaining them in captivity that human beings can intervene in their breeding patterns. As we discussed earlier, however, Zeder (2016) and others have begun to draw attention to the forms of mutualism between humans and animals that lay at the heart of domestication, contributing to an emerging field of *social zooarchaeology* that draws attention to the animal side of human–animal mutualism (Honeychurch and Makarewicz 2016). A great example of this is captured in the work of archaeologist Kristin Armstrong Oma (2010), where she suggests that people and animals were able to live together in Scandinavian Bronze Age longhouses because the animals considered humans as extended members of their herd. Despite this closeness, the relationship between humans and animals was not one of equals since humans will choose to act in ways that favour their interests over those of their animals.

Similar to the domestication of plants, humans have modified a range of different environments to domesticate animals of different species, with differing degrees of success. These environmental modifications range from protecting selected animals from other predators; to supplying them with food and water; to monitoring of their life cycles, from birth to slaughter. And, again, human commitment to the construction of niches that favour domesticated animals will in many ways modify human cultural behaviours as well. For example, in order to obtain a reliable supply of meat and skins, humans must follow a herd or seasonally move herds to reliable supplies of water and forage. Moving around would make humans vulnerable to encountering other humans, as well, and they would have to establish ways to coexist with these groups in order for their way of life to succeed. Not all people are pleased when herders pasture their animals in areas where cultivated plants are growing. And there are differing levels of animal–human–environment relationships that exist.

As mentioned, wild-hunted and domesticated-herded are but extreme ends of a continuum of animal–human–environment relationships. M.R. Jarman, G.N. Bailey, and H.N. Jarman (1982, 51–4) outline six stages on a continuum of relationships between domesticated animals, humans, and the environment. The first is *random hunting*, in which hunters make no attempt to control herds but hunt animals as they find them. The second stage, *controlled hunting*, involves the selective hunting of herds—killing young males, for example. This is the beginning of regular human intervention in the herd species' gene pool. In the third stage, *herd following*, specific herds and specific groups of people begin to interact regularly; as the herd moves from place to place, the people also move. The fourth stage, *loose herding*, is when people begin to control the movements of the herd. They move the herd at various times of the year, ensuring that all of the animals move safely at the same time. They also actively intervene in the herd's gene pool through selective breeding and culling. The fifth stage, *close herding*, is the most familiar practice in much of Canada, the United States, and western Europe. The animals' mobility is limited, and their gene pool is actively managed. In the sixth stage, *factory farming*, there is very intensive human intervention in all aspects of the animals' lives, and in most cases, animals never leave the building or feedlot in which they are raised.

Not all animals that were hunted, even in a controlled way, were domesticated. The bison/buffalo is a good example: there is evidence of controlled hunting using buffalo jumps and paddocks in the Canadian Prairies and elsewhere in North America as early as 4000 years ago, and selective hunting may have led to significant changes in the bison/buffalo gene pool, but there is no evidence of domestication. Clearly, culling herds of certain kinds of animals—male rather than female, less woolly rather than more woolly, thinner rather than fatter—affects the gene pool in ways that demonstrate that people have an influence on animals even if the animals are not fully domesticated. Thus, *herd following* blends almost imperceptibly into *loose herding*.

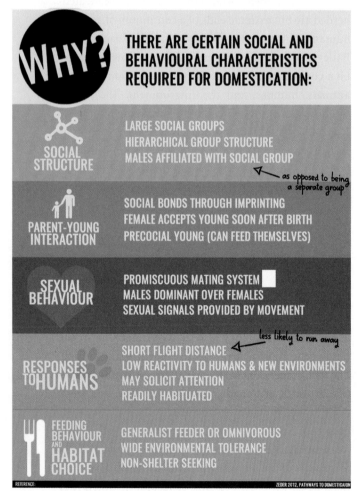

FIGURE 9.6 Animal domestication.

Source: https://www.witheringworld.com/animal-domestication-infographic/

When and Why Did Animal Domestication Begin?

The beginning of animal domestication is difficult to identify with precision in the archaeological record. However, Wenke (1999) provides four main types of evidence that may be used by archaeologists to assess this process.

First, the presence of an animal species outside its natural range may indicate herding. For example, because the southern Levant (the coastal area at the eastern end of the Mediterranean Sea; see Map 9.2 later in the chapter) is outside the area in which wild sheep evolved, scholars say that sheep remains found there constitute evidence of herding: the sheep must have been brought into the area by people. But for this argument to be effective, we must be sure we know precisely what the natural range of the wild species was.

Second, morphological changes occur in most animals as domestication progresses (Figure 9.6). Wenke and Olszewski (2007) point out that the shape and size of sheep horns reflect the process of domestication. Wild sheep have larger, stronger horns than do domesticated sheep since large horns are connected with the breeding hierarchies that males establish through fighting. The selective pressure for these horns was reduced as sheep were domesticated, so horn size and shape changed.

Third, an abrupt population increase of some species relative to others at a site is often taken as evidence of domestication. About 9000 years ago in southwestern Asia, archaeological sites were dominated by large numbers of gazelle bones that decreased rapidly, to be replaced by high percentages of bones from sheep and goats.

The fourth main type of evidence that archaeologists may use to infer the existence of domesticated animals is the age and sex of animals from archaeological sites. Abundant remains of immature or juvenile herd animals, especially males, represent human involvement with the herd. Why? In the wild, animals that were killed for meat come from a much wider age range; there is no emphasis on younger, especially younger male, animals. Also, human beings who manage herds kill immature males more readily than females because only a small number of males are required for reproduction, while larger numbers of females provide more offspring; more milk; and other products, such as dung, wool, and hair. Therefore, differences in age and sex indicated by animal remains can help to identify the presence of a domesticated herd and establish its function: for example, a meat herd contains a lot of adolescent and young adult animals while a dairy herd consists mostly of adult females.

The earliest known domesticated animal was the dog, likely because there were significant mutual advantages for both dogs and humans to team up in the hunt. The earliest undisputed evidence of dog domestication was found at a 14,700-year-old site in Germany, in a grave containing two human skeletons and the jawbone of a dog. Mitochondrial DNA analysis identified the dog remains as belonging to an ancestor of contemporary dogs (Giemsch and Feine 2015) (see Figure 9.7)

It seems that other animals were domesticated to provide food rather than to help get food. Frank Hole (2007) argues that people in different areas experimented with animals found around them to determine which

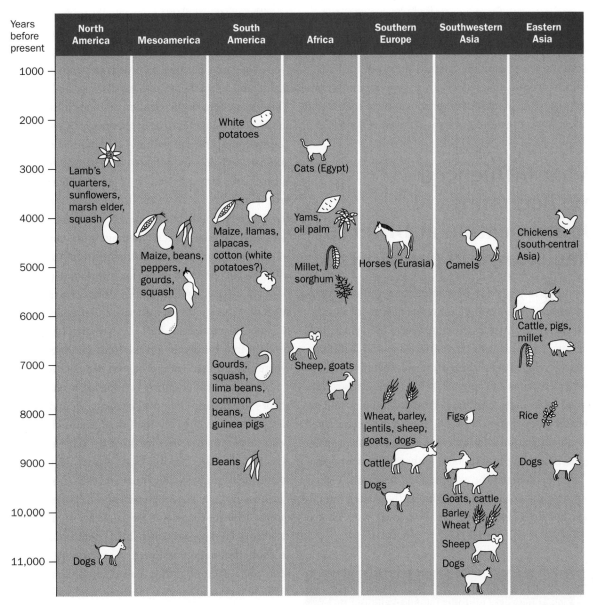

FIGURE 9.7 A chronology of probable dates when various plants and animals were domesticated in different regions.

ones were both desirable as food and amenable to human control. Both sheep and goats were relatively harmless, gregarious herd animals that had multiple uses for human beings and were found seasonally alongside the plants that people wanted to harvest.

However, the evidence, as summarized by Hole (2007), puts sheep and goats in different ecological zones of northern Mesopotamia, and it is likely that their distribution did not overlap much, if at all (see Map 9.4 later in the chapter and Figure 9.7). So it is likely that sheep and goats were domesticated in different places and at different times. The earliest evidence for goat herding is about 11,000 to 10,000 years ago, in a narrow zone along the Zagros Mountains (in modern-day southern Iran). The earliest sites for domesticated sheep were in central Anatolia (the Asian part of modern Turkey) while the evidence for cattle and pigs is much more difficult to assess. There are multiple domestication sites for cattle spanning from China to western Europe around 11,000 years ago while domesticated pig bones have been found throughout southwestern Asia as far back as 8000 years.

What Influenced the Beginnings of Domestication at Different Places around the World?

About 10,000 years ago, after more than 4 million years of hominin evolution and thousands of years of successful foraging by *H. sapiens*, human beings living in distant and unconnected parts of the world nearly simultaneously developed subsistence strategies that involved domesticated plants and animals. Why? Some scholars have argued for a single, universal explanation that would explain all cases of domestication. Thus, it has been argued that domestication is the outcome of population pressure as the increasing hunting-and-gathering human population overwhelmed the existing food resources. Others point to climate change or famine as the postglacial climate got drier. Increasing archaeological research has

broad-spectrum foraging A subsistence strategy based on collecting a wide range of plants and animals by hunting, fishing, and gathering.

made it clear, however, that the evidence in favour of any single-cause, universally applicable explanation is weak.

Some scholars have proposed universally applicable explanations that take several different phenomena into account. One such multifaceted explanation is called **broad-spectrum foraging**. This explanation is based on the reconstruction of the environmental conditions around 12,000 years ago, when the land glaciers in Europe, Asia, and North America melted and the very large Ice Age animals (e.g., mammoths, giant sloths) began to die out and were replaced by increased numbers of smaller animals (e.g., deer). As sea levels rose to cover continental shelves, and lakes became abundant, fish and shellfish became more plentiful in the warmer, shallower waters.

The effects on plants were equally dramatic as forests and woodlands expanded into new areas. Consequently, these scholars argue, people had to change their diets from big-game hunting to broad-spectrum foraging of plants and animals by hunting, fishing, and gathering. This broadening of the economy is said to have led to a more secure subsistence base, the emergence of sedentary communities, and a growth in population. In turn, population growth pressured the resource base of the area, and people were forced to eat "third-choice" foods, particularly wild grain, which was difficult to harvest and process but which responded to human efforts to increase yields. Although the broad-spectrum foraging argument appears to account for plant domestication in the Americas, the most recent evidence from ancient southwestern Asia does not support it. There is also evidence for the development of broad-spectrum gathering in Europe, but domestication did not follow. Rather, domesticated crops were brought into Europe by people from southwestern Asia, where a broad-spectrum revolution had not occurred.

Barbara Bender (1977) introduced a very different theory to explain the development of domestication that is based on the idea that local groups competed to achieve dominance over each other through feasting. According to this theory, there was an increasing expenditure of resources on ritual and exchange, engaging neighbours in a kind of prehistoric feasting extravaganza. To meet increasing demands for food and other resources, land use was intensified, and the development of food production followed. This argument emphasizes social factors, rather than environmental or technical factors, and takes a localized, regional approach. It is supported by ethnographic accounts concerning competitive exchange activities, such as the traditional *potlatch* ceremonies of the Indigenous peoples from the northwest coast of Canada. These peoples were foragers in a rich environment that enabled them to settle in relatively permanent villages without farming or herding. Competition among neighbouring groups led to ever more elaborate forms of competitive exchange, with increasingly large amounts of food and other goods being given away at each subsequent potlatch. Recently, archaeologists have found increasing evidence of feasting among early farmers. Brian Hayden, Neil Canuel, and Jennifer Shanse (2013), of Simon Fraser University, and others have suggested that plant domestication in both the Americas and in southwestern Asia was linked to brewing alcoholic drinks (from various plants including maize, grains, and cocoa) for feasts. Analysis of pottery and other vessels from these times reveals plant residues that include chemical signatures indicating alcoholic content. Although this evidence is not definitive, it does support Bender's argument.

Recently, archaeologists tend to avoid grand theories claiming that a single, universal process was responsible for domestication wherever it occurred. Many prefer to take a regional approach, searching for causes particular to one area that may or may not apply to other areas. Currently, the most powerful explanations seem to be *multiple-strand theories* that consider the combined local effect of climate, environment, population, technology, social organization, and diet on the emergence of domestication. The multiple-strand approach is well illustrated in an article by McCorriston and Hole (1991), and their work forms the basis for the following case study of domestication in ancient southwestern Asia.

How Did Domestication, Cultivation, and Sedentism Begin in Southwestern Asia?

Southwestern Asian domestication is thought to have begun about 12,500 years ago with the Natufian foragers, who relied on the intensive exploitation of wild cereals (notably wild wheat and barley), nuts (e.g., acorns, pistachios, and almonds), and wild game (e.g., gazelle and red deer) (Belfer-Cohen 1991, 167). Because of the climatic and ecological changes in the world that followed the retreat of the glaciers, the Natufians were able to exploit what

were, at first, increasingly rich supplies of wild cereals and large herds of gazelle, which made sedentism possible. Although many Natufian sites are small hunting camps, researchers have discovered at least two dozen Natufian villages, or base camps, that reached a size of 1000 square metres (about a quarter of an acre) and beyond (Belfer-Cohen 1991, 176–7). Henry (1989, 218) estimates that the Natufian hamlets ranged from 40 to 150 people; they were five to ten times larger than the mobile foraging camps of the people who preceded them (Map 9.2).

Evidence that these early Natufian villages were more than just campsites is revealed in the structure of their houses. Natufian houses were dug partially into the ground and had walls of stone and mud with timber posts and probably roof beams. At the Mallaha site, archaeologists have found houses with plaster-lined storage pits and burials beneath the floors. Archaeologists infer that such buildings, which required a considerable amount of labour and materials to build, were not constructed for brief residence only. Archaeologists have also found massive stone mortars used to grind seeds, which people would not have transported nor invested the time and effort to make if they were going to abandon them after

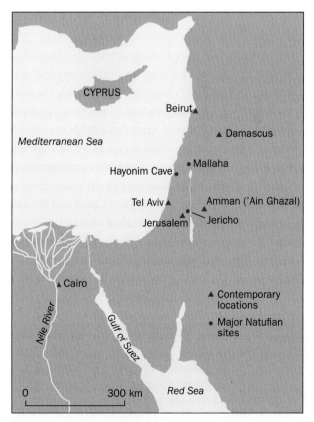

MAP 9.2 Major Natufian sites in the southern Levant in relation to other contemporary features.

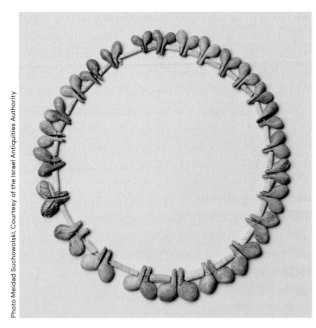

Photo Meidad Suchowolski; Courtesy of the Israel Antiquities Authority

FIGURE 9.8 A Natufian collar with 25 fragments of dentalia (a type of shell) separating bone beads. This collar was found in a male burial site.

one season's use. In addition, the remains of migratory birds and a great number of young gazelle bones indicate year-round hunting from the hamlets because migratory birds fly over the area during different seasons and young gazelles are born at one time only during the year.

Finally, artistic production among the Natufians was high. Anna Belfer-Cohen and others suggest that artistic activity may be closely associated with a sedentary way of life. In these situations, the production of artistic objects as personal ornaments helps to create a sense of identity among smaller groups while allowing members of those groups to participate in a larger society (Belfer-Cohen 1988). Elaborate ritual and ceremonial activities, with the consumption of food and brewed beverages, would also have soothed interactions and reduced tensions in increasingly large communities where co-operation was essential (Hayden, Canuel, and Shanse 2013).

grave goods **Objects buried with a corpse.**

social stratification **A form of social organization in which people have unequal access to wealth, power, and prestige.**

chiefdom **A form of social organization in which a leader (the chief) and close relatives are set apart from the rest of the society and allowed privileged access to wealth, power, and prestige.**

Natufian Social Organization

Information about social organization from the archaeological record is indirect, often interpreted from burials and **grave goods**. However, Donald Henry (1989) believes that over time Natufian society developed social divisions with unequal access to wealth, power, and prestige. That is, Natufian society showed **social stratification**, an important sign of social complexity. His evidence comes from Natufian burials.

In early Natufian times, the dead were buried together in small groups, which Henry believes corresponded to subgroups of a larger community (e.g., extended family burials). At the Hayonim Cave site in Israel, almost half the skeletons showed evidence of the genetically recessive trait *third-molar agenesis* (failure of the third molars, or wisdom teeth, to develop), a trait that occurs in the general human population between 0 and 20 per cent of the time. This skeletal evidence suggests that the group that lived at Hayonim Cave mated with other members of their own group rather than with outsiders for about 1000 years (Henry 1989, 208). As well, these group burials sometimes included decorative shell headdresses and collars (Figure 9.8) or elaborate grave goods or dogs that were buried with children. Overall, these burial practices indicate a differentiation of subgroups and infer inherited status differences.

In later times, there were still differences in grave goods from one burial to the next, but the dead were buried individually in cemeteries. This new pattern suggests that the old boundaries around descent groups had been destroyed and replaced by a new pattern in which resources were controlled by an entire community and stratification was community wide. Some people now coordinated activities

For a discussion of chiefdoms in relation to other forms of social organization, see Chapter 13, pp. 296–8.

for the group as a whole and had come to occupy high-status positions that cross-cut subgroup boundaries. For these reasons, Henry (1989) suggests that Natufian social organization had come to resemble what is called a "chiefdom" in anthropological literature. **Chiefdoms** are societies in which a leader (the chief) and close relatives are set apart from the rest of the society and allowed privileged access to wealth, power, and prestige.

Natufian Subsistence

The Natufians obtained 98 per cent of their meat protein mostly from gazelles, whose bones make up 40 to 80 per cent of all the animal bones recovered from Natufian sites. There is also evidence that meat was provided by red deer, wild sheep, and wild goats. Henry (1989) believes entire herds of gazelle were hunted communally in game drives. Woodlands were burned to promote the growth of young plants, which are particularly attractive to gazelle and deer. Henry points out that the increased attention to gazelles, wild grains, and nuts also represented specialization of subsistence activities by Natufian foragers (91). They were what we refer to as *complex foragers*, who live in areas of abundant resources that may appear to be inexhaustible (Price and Gebauer 1995), making them different from *generalized foragers*, who live in less generous environments and cope with shortages by diversifying their subsistence activities.

Unfortunately for the Natufians, the choices they made were destabilizing in the long run. They fed an increasingly large population by intensively exploiting small areas, and they gave up mobility by settling down. The short-term stability of sedentism and intensive collection increased the rigidity of their society, making it vulnerable to disruptive environment changes that occurred about 10,500 years ago. These included the drying up of the shallow interior lakes of the southern Levant and the loss of up to one-half of the local Mediterranean woodlands. Natufians in the southern part of the region abandoned their settlements and returned to simple foraging, developing what archaeologists refer to as the "Harifian culture." However, in the central core of the Natufian region the people tried to grow cereal plants, beginning the process of domestication.

The first evidence for domesticated cereals—specifically, wheat and barley—in this core Natufian area dates to about 10,300 years ago. Both wheat and barley were found at Jericho; and barley alone, at other sites. For archaeologists, the appearance of domesticated plants signals the end of the Paleolithic and the beginning of the **Neolithic**. This transition from the Natufian culture is marked in the southern Levant by the appearance of a new culture called the Pre-Pottery Neolithic A (PPNA), in which cultivation was practised but pottery had not yet been invented.

Jericho, a PPNA site, was located on the edge of an *alluvial fan* (a fan-shaped accumulation of sediment from flowing water at the mouth of a ravine) on a permanent stream, near hills rich in gazelle, wild grains, and nuts. The stream provided clear drinking water while the alluvial fan provided mud for bricks, and its regular floods

Israel Ancient Art and Architecture Collection Ltd./Bridgeman Images

FIGURE 9.9 By about 9300 years ago, the inhabitants of Jericho had built a stone wall, probably to protect the settlement from yearly flooding.

provided rich soil for plants. Jericho was much larger than the preceding Natufian settlements, with a surface area of about 2.5 hectares (about 6 acres) and perhaps 300 or more inhabitants (Smith 1995, 3). Henry (1989) suggests that this was due to the concentration of populations from smaller, more numerous hamlets in a setting where "large tracts of arable land, suitable for hoe cultivation, adjoined year-round water sources" (53–4).

By about 9300 years ago, the inhabitants of Jericho had built a stone wall 3 metres thick, 4 metres high, and perhaps 700 metres in circumference (Figure 9.9). The wall, it is now thought, was likely erected as protection from the floods since similar protections from flooding are found at other PPNA sites, although none is as elaborate as the wall of Jericho (Bar-Yosef and Kislev 1989, 635).

Trade was also significant in PPNA Jericho. Obsidian is an extremely sharp and highly prized volcanic glass that is found in relatively few places worldwide (Map 9.3). Anatolia, in modern Turkey, contained the major sites for obsidian in Neolithic southwestern Asia. Archaeologists have found Anatolian obsidian in Jericho, some 700 kilometres from Anatolia; it is unlikely that residents travelled that distance to get it themselves. Jericho also

Neolithic The "New Stone Age," which began with the domestication of plants 10,300 years ago.

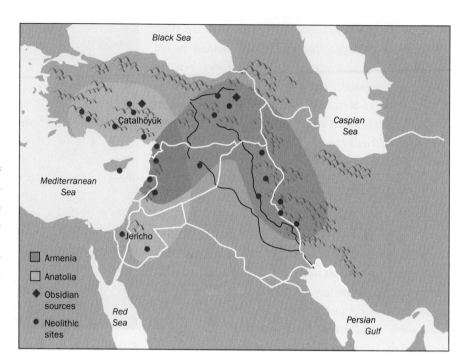

MAP 9.3 The distribution of obsidian in Neolithic south-western Asia from sources in Anatolia (west) and Armenia (east). Obsidian is an extremely sharp and highly prized volcanic glass. It was traded widely in Neolithic times and has been found as far as 800 kilometres away from its source.

contained marine shells from the Mediterranean Sea and the Black Sea as well as *amulets* (charms against evil or injury) and greenstone beads. These objects suggest not just trade from village to village but also trade between the settled farmers and the foraging peoples living in the semi-arid regions or higher areas.

Beginning about 9100 years ago, the PPNA culture was replaced by the Pre-Pottery Neolithic B (PPNB) culture, which represents the rapid expansion of agriculture. Although there are but a handful of PPNA sites, all in a small area around Jericho, there are more than 140 PPNB sites, many of which are very large and some of which are found in Anatolia and the Zagros Mountains. As the new farming technology moved north and east, it was adapted to fit local circumstances. At some point, farmers met herders from the Zagros Mountains and north **Mesopotamia** who had domesticated sheep and goats, animals that were well known in their wild state throughout the area. The agriculturalists adopted these herding techniques, which spread quickly, resulting in the creation of family farming systems throughout the entire region. By 8000 years ago, farmers in southwestern

Asia practised a mixed agricultural strategy, incorporating grains and livestock.

Architecture became more sophisticated during the PPNB times, with the construction of buildings that may have been used as temples. At Göbekli Tepe, a site located in modern-day Turkey, structures with impressive carved stone pillars suggest that specialized ritual spaces were becoming part of PPNB people's social practices. Edward Banning (2011), from the University of Toronto, has closely analyzed these structures to determine if they were in fact specialized temples or elaborate houses. His results suggest that they were in fact both—domestic houses with richly symbolic contents and uses.

Domestication Elsewhere in the World

The conditions under which domestication began, and the times at which it began, varied around the world (Map 9.4). In highland Mexico, for example, the pre-domestication population was relatively stable and sedentism had not yet occurred. There are no indications of the kinds of long-term shifts in resource density in Mexico that were characteristic of the eastern Mediterranean. As noted earlier, many scholars agree that broad-spectrum foraging was practised prior to the transition to domestication in the Americas, including Mexico. The mix of crops characteristic of domestication in the Americas also differs from that of the eastern Mediterranean. In Mesoamerica, maize (corn) and squash appeared

Mesopotamia The area made up of the Tigris–Euphrates river system, corresponding to modern-day Iraq, Kuwait, the northeastern section of Syria, and parts of Turkey and Iran. Often referred to as the "cradle of civilization" where early complex societies developed.

between 9000 and 4000 years ago, with beans about 2000 years ago (Smith 1995). In eastern Canada, maize appeared around 1500 years ago, while it appeared around 1000 years ago at Head-Smashed-In Buffalo Jump in Alberta. Maize (corn) forms the cornerstone of plant domesticates in the Americas and has been the focus of Dr Michael Blake's (University of British Columbia) research for many years. With colleagues across Canada and the world, Blake has created an interactive website, "Ancient Maize Map," documenting the recent discoveries of maize throughout North, Central, and South America (http://en.ancientmaize.com). As well, Blake's recent book (2015) *Maize for the Gods* outlines the intersections of maize as a food for survival and one for spiritual beings. Other plants, including goosefoot, marsh elder, sunflowers, and squash, were also domesticated in eastern North America (Smith 1995, 189–90). In South America, maize appears between 4000 and 3000 years ago but was only one of several domesticates. In other areas of South America, soil conditions, altitude, and climate favoured root crops—manioc or potatoes—as well as beans and quinoa (a high-altitude grain), which were of greater importance. Cocoa and chili, which were domesticated around 4000 years ago, were also important

in this region (Powis et al. 2008). Animal domestication was far less important in the Americas than it was in Mesopotamia as the ideal wild herd animals, such as goats and sheep, were not common in the Americas. The Andean llama is the largest animal domesticated in the Americas while the turkey was also domesticated and became a valuable food source.

Other notable plants were domesticated in Africa, such as coffee, millet, okra, and sorghum, while a large number of domesticates came from eastern Asia, including rice, yam, tea, sugarcane, garlic, onion, apple, and carrot (Map 9.4 and Figure 9.7).

Archaeologists are coming to agree that complex foragers living in areas of relatively abundant resources were probably responsible for domestication wherever it developed (Price and Gebauer 1995; Smith 1995). Rich and complex archaeological and genetic evidence from specific areas of the world downplays single-cause explanations of domestication and stresses the need to consider each domestication event on its own terms. Melinda A. Zeder and Bruce D. Smith (2009) are impressed by abundant and varied data from southwestern Asia showing that during several thousand years prior to the appearance of agriculture, "people appear to have

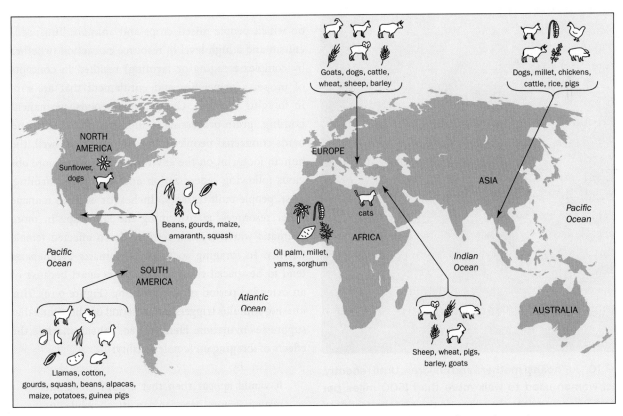

MAP 9.4 A map of probable locations where various plants and animals were domesticated.

been auditioning a wide variety of region-specific plants and animals for leading roles as domesticated resources in the absence of population increase or resource imbalance" (683). In eastern North America, the evidence is similar: climate change at the end of the Pleistocene around 10,000 years ago, with early plant domestication around 8000 years ago, the development of a complex of domesticated crops by 4000 years ago, and the key shift to maize agriculture by 2000 years ago. Thus, climate change appears to be a necessary precondition for the beginning of agriculture rather than other explanations, such as population growth.

In the face of such evidence, Zeder and Smith (2009) conclude that the process of niche construction is an important concept when considering the initiation of agriculture. Humans were actively shaping niches that would improve the productivity and density of targeted plant and animal populations. Bruno (2009) also emphasizes the importance for archaeologists of *historical ecology*, which "focuses on how long-term, accumulative human activities cause observable changes in the natural environment thus creating a 'landscape'" (704). The incorporation of niche construction and historical ecology concepts into anthropological theories of cultural transitions, such as the origins of agriculture or social complexity, promises to shed important new light on these developments.

What Were the Consequences of Domestication and Sedentism?

Constructed agricultural niches, within which domesticated plants and animals could thrive, promoted sedentism and transformed human life in ways that still have repercussions today. First, land was no longer free, available to anyone; instead, it was transformed into particular territories, collectively or individually owned, on which people raised crops and animals. Thus, sedentism and a high level of resource extraction (whether by complex foraging or farming) resulted in concepts of property ownership and entitlement that are rare in foraging societies. Graves, grave goods, permanent housing, grain-processing equipment, and fields and herds connected people to specific places. As well, the human footprint on the environment became more obvious following sedentization and the rise of farming. First, people built terraces, ditches, or walls to manage water resources, transforming the landscape in more dramatic ways. Second, settling down affected female fertility. In foraging societies, a woman's pregnancies tend to be spaced three to four years apart because of an extended period of breastfeeding (Figure 9.10). This nursing stimulus triggers the secretion of a hormone that suppresses ovulation. Henry (1989, 43) summarizes the effects of foraging on female fertility:

It would appear then that a number of interrelated factors associated with a mobile foraging strategy are likely to have provided natural

Hoberman/UIG/Maxx Images

FIGURE 9.10 Ju/'hoansi mothers and children. Until recently, Ju/'hoansi women used to walk more than 1500 miles per year with children and other burdens on their backs. Children nursed for several years.

controls on fertility and perhaps explain the low population densities of the Paleolithic. In mobile foraging societies, women are likely to have experienced both long intervals of breastfeeding by carried children as well as the high energy drain associated with subsistence activities and periodic camp moves. Additionally, their diets, being relatively rich in proteins, would have contributed to maintaining low fat levels, thus further dampening fecundity.

With complex foraging and increasing sedentism, female fertility would have increased—so much so that the population of humans may have increased 12-fold during the Holocene as a result of changing from a nomadic foraging way of life to one of sedentary agriculture (Bocquet-Appel 2011). A diet increasingly rich in cereals would have significantly changed the ratio of protein to carbohydrate in the diet. This would have changed the levels of prolactin, increased the positive energy balance, and reduced birth spacing as well as increased the rate of growth in the young and caused an earlier age for first menstruation. The ready availability of ground cereals would have enabled mothers to feed their infants soft, high-carbohydrate porridges and gruels.

The influence of cereals on fertility has been observed by Richard Lee (1992) among the Ju/'hoansi, who recently settled and began to eat cereals and experienced a marked rise in fertility. Renee Pennington (1992) notes that the increase in Ju/'hoansi reproductive success also seems to be related to a reduction in infant and child mortality rates (Figure 9.10). Although diets based on high-carbohydrate grains enabled an increase in female fertility, there is skeletal evidence that these diets are in fact less nutritious than the diets of foragers. Skeletons from Greece and Turkey in late Paleolithic times indicate an average height of 5 feet 9 inches (1.75 metres) for men and 5 feet 5 inches (1.65 metres) for women. With the adoption of agriculture, the average height declined sharply: by about 5000 years ago, the average man was about 5 feet 3 inches (1.60 metres) tall, and the average woman was about 5 feet (1.52 metres) tall. Even modern Greeks and Turks are still not, on average, as tall as the late Paleolithic people of the same region.

For more on the Ju/'hoansi, see EthnoProfile 10.1, on p. 216.

In the short term, agriculture was probably developed in ancient southwestern Asia, and perhaps elsewhere, to increase food supplies to support an increasing population at a time of serious resource stress. Because the agroecology created an environment favourable to domesticated plants, farmers were able to cultivate previously unusable land. The process of diverting water to the land between the Tigris and Euphrates rivers in Mesopotamia, for example, allowed the land on which wheat and barley were not native to actually support dense stands of these domesticated grains. The greater yield of domesticated plants per unit of ground also led to a greater proportion of cultivated plants in the diet, even when wild plants were still being eaten and were as plentiful as before. But as cultivated plants took on an increasingly large role in prehistoric diets, people became dependent on plants, and the plants in turn became completely dependent on the agroecology created by the people. According to Richard Lee (1992, 48), the Ju/'hoansi, who live in the Kalahari Desert, use more than 100 plants (14 fruits and nuts; 15 berries; 18 species of edible gum; 41 edible roots and bulbs; and 17 leafy greens, beans, melons, and other foods). By contrast, modern farmers rely on less than 20 plants; of those, only three—wheat, maize, and rice—feed most of the world's people. Historically, only one or two grain crops were staples for a specific group of people. If hail, floods, droughts, infestations, frost, heat, weeds, erosion, or other factors destroyed the crop or reduced the harvest, the risk of starvation increased. Deforestation, soil loss, silted streams, and the loss of many native species followed domestication. In the lower Tigris–Euphrates Valley, irrigation water used by early farmers carried high levels of soluble salts, poisoning the soil and making it unusable to this day (Figure 9.11).

New features of the agroecology also created new opportunities for the spread of diseases, such as malaria and tuberculosis. As we discussed earlier, in sub-Saharan Africa, the clearing of land for farming created standing water, which provided an excellent environment for malaria-carrying mosquitoes. As increasing numbers of people began to live near each other in relatively permanent settlements, the disposal of human (and eventually animal) waste also became increasingly problematic as vectors for many different diseases. Food storage was a key element in agroecological niches, but stored grains attracted pests, including rats

FIGURE 9.11 The lower Tigris–Euphrates Valley. Irrigation water used by early farmers carried high levels of soluble salts, poisoning the soil and making it unusable to this day.

FIGURE 9.12 A major challenge for societies that rely on food storage is preventing the stored food from attracting pests, such as rats and mice. A common solution to this problem—illustrated by the design of this *stabbur*, or food-storage cabin, in Norway—has been to raise food-storage facilities high off the ground, where rodents cannot easily access them.

and mice (Figure 9.12). Some of these pests also spread disease-causing microorganisms that thrived in human, animal, and plant wastes. The larger the number of people living very near each other, the greater the likelihood of communicable disease transmission: by the time one person recovers from the disease, someone else reaches the infectious stage and can re-infect the first; as a result, the disease never leaves the population. As well, the nutritional deficiencies of an agricultural diet may have reduced people's resistance to disease. Foragers could just walk away from disease, reducing the likelihood that it would spread; but this option is closed for settled people. Thus, increased exposure to epidemic disease was a major consequence of the modified selection pressures to which human populations became vulnerable as a consequence of their ancestors' construction of agroecological niches.

Maintaining an agroecology that supported domesticated plants and animals required much more labour than did foraging. People had to clear the land, plant the seeds, tend the young plants, protect them from predators, harvest them, process the seeds, store them, and select the seeds for planting the next year; similarly, people had to tend and protect domesticated animals, cull the herds, shear the sheep, milk the goats, and so on. This heavy workload was not divided up equally among members of the population. Increasing dependence on agriculture produced an increasingly complex division of labour, which set the stage for the emergence of complex hierarchical societies with different forms of social inequality.

Once societies develop ways to preserve and store food and other material goods, however, new possibilities open up. Archaeological evidence indicates that the more food there is to store, the more people invest in storage facilities (e.g., pits, pottery vessels) and the more quickly they become sedentary. Large-scale food-storage techniques buffer a population from ecological fluctuations for long periods of time. But techniques of food storage alone predict nothing about the "changes of hands" that food will undergo once it has been stored. Food-storage techniques have been associated with all subsistence strategies, including that of complex food collectors. This suggests that economic relations of consumption, involving the transfer of rights in stored food, have long been open to considerable cultural elaboration and manipulation (Halperin 1994, 178).

When people initially cultivated plants, they could not have anticipated all of the challenges that this process would create. Initially, agriculture had several apparent advantages, the foremost of which was that farmers could extract far more food from the same amount of land than could foragers. Put another way, a dry farmer needs 20 times less land than a forager, and an irrigation farmer needs 100 times less land, to feed the same number of people (Figure 9.13). Foragers know that they will find enough food to eat, but they never know how much of any given food resource they will find or exactly when or where they will find it. By contrast, farmers can predict, with a given amount of seed—and favourable conditions—the approximate size of a harvest. Herders can predict how many lambs they will have in the spring based on the number of rams and ewes in their herds, but hunters will not know how many animals will be available to kill. Sedentism and a fairly reliable and predictable domesticated food supply provided new opportunities for social complexity.

How Do Anthropologists Define Social Complexity?

Early Neolithic farming and herding societies differed little from the foraging societies they replaced. For the Natufians, foraging continued to be important alongside cultivation for many generations. In the same way, the social organization of these societies differed little from that of foraging societies; although people began to settle in permanent villages, archaeological evidence suggests that no great differences in wealth, power, or prestige divided villagers initially. Put another way, these early farming villages continued to practise **egalitarian social relations**. Things began to change, however, beginning about 5000 years ago in southwestern Asia and shortly thereafter in Egypt, the Indus Valley (India), China, Mesoamerica (the Valley of Mexico), and the Andes (Peru) (see Map 9.1). These six regions of the globe were the first to independently develop a new way of organizing society called social stratification, based on the assumption that different groups in society were entitled to different amounts of wealth, power, and prestige (mentioned earlier).

A move from egalitarian forms of social organization to social stratification involves the development of social complexity. Social stratification was made possible when societies produced amounts of food

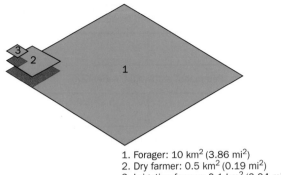

1. Forager: 10 km² (3.86 mi²)
2. Dry farmer: 0.5 km² (0.19 mi²)
3. Irrigation farmer: 0.1 km² (0.04 mi²)

FIGURE 9.13 Each square shows the proportionate amount of land needed to feed a single individual using three different food-getting strategies: foraging, dry farming, and irrigation farming.

that exceeded the basic subsistence needs of the population. Storage of excess food resulting from **surplus production** and control over its distribution made it possible for some members of a society to stop producing food altogether and to specialize in various occupations (e.g., weaving, pot making) or in new social roles (e.g., warrior, priest). In some cases, **occupational specialization** also created a wide gulf between most members of a society and members of a more prestigious social **class** of rulers who successfully claimed the bulk of this new surplus as their own. Societies organized in this way could support many more people than could the egalitarian societies that preceded them, not only because they successfully produced, stored, and distributed more food but also because they invented new ways of compelling people to carry out many new tasks (see Figure 9.14). As a result, anthropologists refer to these as the first **complex societies** to appear in the archaeological record.

egalitarian social relations Social relations in which no great differences in wealth, power, or prestige divide members from one another.

surplus production The production of amounts of food that exceed the basic subsistence needs of the population.

occupational specialization Specialization in various occupations (e.g., weaving or pot making) or in new social roles (e.g., king or priest) that is found in socially complex societies.

class A ranked group within a hierarchically stratified society whose membership is defined primarily in terms of wealth, occupation, or other economic criteria.

complex societies Societies with large populations, an extensive division of labour, and occupational specialization.

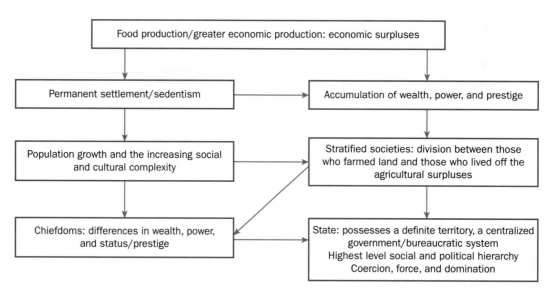

FIGURE 9.14 Changes involved in the evolution of complex societies.

Source: H. M. Ashraf Ali, MacEwan University.

In Their Own Words

The Food Revolution

Although dietary quality declined for the earliest full-time farmers, later contact and trade among different farming societies enriched diets everywhere. Over the past 500 years, as Jack Weatherford emphasizes, foods domesticated in the New World have played a particularly important role in the "food revolution."

On Thanksgiving Day North Americans sometimes remember the Indians who gave them their cuisine by dining upon turkey with cornbread stuffing, cranberry sauce, succotash, corn on the cob, sweet potato casserole, stewed squash and tomatoes, baked beans with maple syrup, and pecan pie. Few cooks or gourmets, however, recognize the much broader extent to which American Indian cuisine radically changed cooking and dining in every part of the globe from Timbuktu to Tibet. Sichuan beef with chilies, German chocolate cake, curried potatoes, vanilla ice cream, Hungarian goulash, peanut brittle, and pizza all owe their primary flavourings to the American Indians.

The discovery of America sparked a revolution in food and cuisine that has not yet shown any signs of abating. Tomatoes, chilies, and green peppers formed the first wave of American flavourings to circle the globe, but the American Indian garden still grows a host of plants that the world may yet learn to use and enjoy. These plants may have practical uses, such as providing food in otherwise unusable land or producing more food in underused land. They also vary the daily diets of people throughout the world and thereby increase nutrition. Even in this high-tech age, the low-tech plant continues to be the key to nutrition and health. Despite all the plant improvements brought about by modern science, the American Indians remain the developers of the world's largest array of nutritious foods and the primary contributors to the world's varied cuisines.

Source: Weatherford 1988, 115.

Why Is It Incorrect to Describe Foraging Societies as "Simple"?

Although the concept of a complex society seems straightforward enough, anthropologists must define this expression carefully to avoid misunderstanding. It is common to assume that the opposite of *complex* is *simple*, yet foraging and farming societies are not "simple" societies. As we saw, not even all foragers were alike; and in any case, foragers had to file away in their minds an enormously complex amount of information about different varieties of plants, seasonal habits of animals, details of kinship, and nuances of their religion and art. It was the comparatively simple technology of foragers—based on wood, stone, and bone tools that could be easily made by everyone—that was very different from the more complex technology that had to be developed and mastered in order to build massive pyramids, weave cloth, or smelt and mould metals such as copper, tin, and iron. These activities not only required highly specialized knowledge of architecture, textiles, and metallurgy but also presupposed a form of social organization that permitted some members of society to become highly specialized in certain activities while other members carried out different tasks.

Differences in technology and social organization say nothing about the complexity of the minds of the people involved. However, such differences strongly shaped the scale and texture of life in the two kinds of society. Setting up camp in a foraging society involved fewer decisions, in terms of technology and social organization, than did the construction of a pyramid. Pyramid building required more than architectural skill; suitable materials had to be found, quarried, or produced and transported to the site. Additionally, suitable workers had to be found, trained, supervised, fed, and lodged for the duration of construction, which may have taken decades. Finally, all these specialized activities had to occur in the right order for the project to be successfully completed. Not only would a foraging band—some 50 individuals of all ages—have been too small to carry out such a project, but their traditional egalitarian social relations also would have made the giving and taking of orders impossible. Indeed, the whole idea of building massive pyramids would have probably seemed pointless to them.

A society that not only wants to build pyramids but also has the material, political, and social means to do so is clearly different from a foraging band or a Neolithic farming village. For archaeologist T. Douglas Price (1995, 140), a complex society has "more parts and more connections between parts." Anthropologist Leslie White (1949) spoke in terms of a major change in the amount of energy a society can capture from nature and use to remodel the natural world to suit its own purposes. The members of foraging bands also depended on energy captured from the natural world but on a scale vastly smaller than that required to build pyramids. Archaeologist Robert Wenke (1999, 348) emphasizes that, in complex societies, "the important thing is that the ability and incentive to make these investments are

radically different from the capacities of Pleistocene bands, in that they imply the ability of some members of society to control and organize others."

What Is the Archaeological Evidence for Social Complexity?

How do archaeologists recognize social and cultural complexity when they see it? Important clues are certain kinds of remains that begin to appear in the archaeological record after about 5000 years ago. Among the most widespread indicators of social complexity are the remains of **monumental architecture**. Contemporary monumental architecture includes such structures as the Eiffel Tower in Paris, France; the National Library in Ottawa; and the Petronas Towers in Kuala Lumpur, Malaysia (Figure 9.15). Ancient monumental architecture

FIGURE 9.15 Monumental modern architecture: the Petronas Towers dwarf the surrounding city of Kuala Lumpur, Malaysia.

monumental architecture Architectural constructions of a greater-than-human scale, such as pyramids, temples, and tombs.

included public buildings, private residences, tombs, settlement walls, irrigation canals, and so on. Together with monumental architecture, however, archaeologists usually find evidence of technologically simpler constructions. Assemblages that demonstrate such architectural variability contrast with those from earlier periods, when dwellings were simpler and more uniform and monumental structures were absent.

Everywhere it is found, the earliest monumental architecture consisted of raised platforms, temples, pyramids, or pyramid-like structures (Figure 9.16). Different building techniques were used to construct these monuments in different areas, and the structures did not all serve the same purposes. Therefore, archaeologists have long rejected the notion that all pyramid-building societies derived from ancient Egypt. Rather, the cross-cultural similarities of these structures appear to have a more practical explanation. None of the architects in the earliest complex societies knew how to build arches and barrel vaults. In all cases, builders were limited by the types of materials and technologies to which they had access. Moreover, in the lowlands of modern Central America, builders had to work without metal, winches, hoists, or wheeled carts. Under these circumstances,

© SimonDennhauer/ Dreamstime.com

FIGURE 9.16 Among the most widespread indicators of early social complexity are the remains of monumental architecture, such as the Temple of the Great Jaguar at the Mayan site of Tikal, Guatemala.

concentrations of particular artifacts Sets of artifacts indicating that particular social activities took place at a particular area in an archaeological site when that site was inhabited in the past.

the only tall structures they could have built were such basic geometric forms as squares, rectangles, and pyramids (Wenke 1999, 577). The size and scope of civilizations such as the Maya have been difficult to ascertain because of the dense jungles that currently cover the areas they are located in. Recent research conducted by the Pacunam foundation, a cultural heritage preservation nonprofit group in Guatemala, has given us a better idea of what the Mayans were able to accomplish using only human strength. Images produced by light detection and ranging technology (LiDAR) show a vast area in the Maya Biosphere Reserve covered by settlements and quarries that were connected by highways. Mayan civilization reached its peak 1200 years ago and is estimated to have hosted a population of 10 to 15 million people at that time rather than the mere 5 million previously calculated. The infrastructure revealed by LiDAR suggests that Mayan culture was at the same level of cultural complexity as Ancient Greece or China (Clynes 2018).

Among the monumental structures built in the earliest complex societies were tombs. Differences in the size and construction of burials closely align with differences in the size and construction of residences, and both suggest the emergence of a stratified society. Graves that are larger and built of more costly materials often contain a variety of grave goods that were buried with the corpse. The occurrence of smaller, more modest graves, often with few or no grave goods, in the same place and time provides evidence for social stratification. The number and quality of grave goods found with a corpse give clues regarding the wealth and status of the buried individual. Many of the grave goods recovered from rich tombs are masterpieces of ceramics, metallurgy, weaving, and other crafts, indicating that the society had achieved a high degree of technological skill and, thus, a complex division of labour. In some cases, ritual burials of animals, either alongside people or on their own, offer evidence of the highly stratified nature of a society. For example, Haskel Greenfield, of the University of Manitoba, and his colleagues (Greenfield, Shai, and Maeir 2012) have found evidence connecting the ritual burial of a domesticated ass—an animal that likely played an important role in manual labour and trade—to the existence of a "commoner neighbourhood" on the outskirts of a city in the Levant.

Archaeologists often recover evidence of complex occupational specializations by noting high **concentrations of particular artifacts** in specific areas of a site. For example, broken pots or kilns found evenly distributed throughout a settlement might suggest that pottery was made by individual families. However, evidence of pottery manufacture concentrated within a particular area strongly suggests the existence of a potter's workshop and, thus, occupational specialization. Remains of the tools and materials used to make artifacts—potter's wheels, spindle whorls, or iron slag, for example—often provide important information about the degree to which craft technology developed at a particular time and place.

The emergence of complex societies seems connected with a phenomenal explosion of architectural and artistic creativity. Although anthropologists admire the material achievements of these ancient societies, many are struck by the "wasteful" expenditure of resources by a tiny ruling elite. Why, for example, did virtually every original complex society build monumental architecture? Why did they not invest their increasing technological and organizational power in less elaborate projects that might have benefited the ordinary members of society? Why were masterpieces of pottery, metallurgy, and weaving often hoarded and buried in the tombs of dead rulers instead of being more widely available? These excesses apparently did not develop in the early Harappan civilization of the Indus Valley, but they are so widespread elsewhere that the questions remain important. Archaeologist Michael Hoffman, an expert on prehistoric Egypt, proposed that the key to understanding the first complex societies lies in their social organization. For the first time in human history, tremendous power was concentrated in the hands of a tiny elite—who undoubtedly found their privileges challenged by their new subjects. Under such circumstances, the production of monumental architecture and quantities of luxury goods served as evidence of the elite's fitness to rule. Hoffman (1991, 294) prefers to call these objects "powerfacts" rather than "artifacts" because their role was to demonstrate the superior power of the rulers (see also Hayden 1995, 67) (Figure 9.17).

So far, we have described the kinds of archaeological remains that suggest that a site was once part of a complex society. But complex societies ordinarily consisted of a number of settlements organized in a hierarchy, usually based on the size of the settlement and/or the presence of monumental architecture. For example, today this hierarchy would be represented in ascending order by hamlets, villages, towns, and cities. To establish the presence of different types of sites, archaeologists must survey the region to determine how any given site

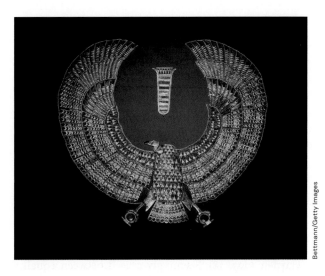

FIGURE 9.17 A "powerfact" from the tomb of Tutankhamun, a fourteenth-century BCE Egyptian pharaoh. This collar, found around the neck of Tutankhamun's mummy, is composed of gold, coloured glass, and obsidian. There are 250 inlaid segments, and each claw is grasping a *shen*, a symbol of totality.

compares to other settlements occupied at the same time in the same area. The most common and helpful surface artifacts recovered during such surveys are often pieces of broken pots called pottery sherds. When the survey is completed, archaeologists tabulate and create maps showing the different kinds of pottery that were used in an area to help determine changes in settlement size and population in the region. Systematic survey and mapping work in southern Iraq permitted Robert Adams and Hans Nissen to show how the small, scattered settlements that prevailed in the countryside of ancient Mesopotamia around 8000 years ago were gradually abandoned over the centuries, such that by about 5200 years ago virtually everyone was living in a handful of large settlements, which Adams and Nissen (1972) call "cities."

Why Did Stratification Begin?

Archaeologists typically organize their findings using a set of four categories that serve as benchmarks in the history of human social organization. These categories— *bands, tribes, chiefdoms, states*—were developed together with cultural anthropologists and rest on insights derived from the study of living and historically documented societies of different kinds as well as of the material remains they all tend to leave behind (Wenke 1999, 340–4). Up to 10,000 years ago, our ancestors lived in foraging *bands*, after which they began to experiment with new subsistence strategies and forms of social organization. Following this, those who came to farm or herd for a living could support larger populations and are classified as *tribes* (Hayden 1995, 18). Morton Fried (1967) preferred to call a society of this kind a "rank" society. Elman Service (1962), who was attempting to identify key turning points in the course of the human past, viewed tribes as a transitional form rather than a well-defined societal type. The ambiguity of terms such as *rank society* or *tribe* has led some archaeologists to substitute the term *transegalitarian society* to describe all societies that are neither egalitarian nor socially stratified (Hayden 1995, 18). Seemingly poised between equality and hierarchy, transegalitarian societies have flourished at various times and places up to the present day.

Unlike a transegalitarian society, a *chiefdom* is an example—indeed, the earliest clear example—of a socially stratified society, as we saw among the southern Natufians. Ordinarily in a chiefdom, only the chief and close relatives are set apart and allowed privileged access to wealth, power, and prestige; other members of the society continue to share roughly similar social status. Chiefdoms are generally larger than tribes and show a greater degree of craft production, although such production is not yet in the hands of full-time specialists. Chiefdoms also exhibit a greater degree of hierarchical political control, centred on the chief, relatives of the chief, and their great deeds. Archaeologically, chiefdoms are interesting because some, such as the southern Natufians, apparently remained as they were and then disappeared, whereas others went on to develop into states.

> ↻ Descriptions of the categories anthropologists use to classify forms of human societies can be found in Chapter 13, p. 297.

The *state* is a stratified society that possesses a territory that is defended from outside enemies with an army and from internal disorder with police. States, which have separate governmental institutions to enforce laws and to collect taxes and tribute, are run by an elite that possesses a monopoly on the use of force. In early states, government and religion were mutually reinforcing: rulers were often priests or were thought to be gods. State societies are supported by sophisticated food-production and food-storage techniques. Craft production is normally specialized and yields a dazzling variety of goods, many of which are refined specialty items destined for the ruling elite. Art and architecture also flourish, and writing frequently has developed in state societies. Shortly after the appearance of the first state in an area, other states usually develop nearby. From time to time, one might conquer its neighbours, organizing them into a vaster political network called an *empire*.

Monumental public buildings of a religious or governmental nature, highly developed crafts (e.g., pottery, weaving, and metallurgy), and regional settlement patterns that show at least three levels in a hierarchy of social complexity are all archaeological evidence of a state. Interstate conflict is suspected when towns and cities are surrounded by high walls and confirmed by artifacts that served as weapons, by art depicting battle, and by written documents that record military triumphs. Because writing developed in most of the early states, various inscriptions often provide valuable information on social organization that supplements the archaeologist's reconstructions.

Archaeologists assume regional integration when they find unique styles in architecture, pottery, textiles, and other artifacts distributed uniformly over a wide area; such evidence is called a *cultural horizon*. For archaeologists, the term *civilization* usually refers to the flowering of cultural creativity that accompanies the rise of state societies and persists for a long time. Widespread uniformity in material culture, however, need not imply a single set of political institutions. Archaeologists who wish to speak of a state or an empire, therefore, require additional evidence, such as a hierarchy of settlement patterns or written records that spell out centralized governmental policies. Cultural change in all early complex societies tended to alternate between periods of relative cultural uniformity and political unity and periods of regional differentiation and lack of political integration.

We should note that the preceding categories and the framework for cross-cultural comparison that they provide have been critiqued in recent decades. Post-processual archaeologists including Shanks and Tilley (1987), for example, argue that traditional comparisons of ancient "state" societies pay too much attention to environmental and technological similarities while ignoring or dismissing the significance of the distinct cultural patterns of meanings and values that made each of these ancient civilizations unique. Other archaeologists, however, maintain that the similarities among ancient civilizations are just as striking as the cultural differences among those civilizations and require explanation (Trigger 1993). While this debate continues, many archaeologists have tried to strike a balance, acknowledging the overall descriptive value of a formal category such as "state" but carrying out research projects that highlight the cultural variation to be found among societies grouped together as "states" (Wenke 1999, 346).

How Can Anthropologists Explain the Rise of Complex Societies?

Given that humans lived in foraging bands for most of their history and that, in some parts of the world, village farming remained a stable, viable way of life for hundreds or thousands of years, it is not obvious why complex societies should ever have developed at all. Over the years, anthropologists have proposed a number of explanations. Some of their hypotheses (such as those designed to explain our ancestors' turn to domestication or sedentism) argue for a single, uniform cause, or prime mover, that triggered the evolution of complex society worldwide. Indeed, as we will see, many of these prime movers are the same factors suggested to explain the development of domestication and sedentism.

For a long time, scholars thought that the domestication of plants and sedentary life in farming villages offered people the leisure time to invent social and technological complexity. This explanation is questionable, however, because many farming societies never developed beyond the village level of organization. In addition, social complexity apparently can develop without the support of a fully agricultural economy, as among the Natufians. Finally, ethnographic research has shown that foraging people actually have more leisure time than most village farmers do.

Other scholars suggest that social complexity depended on arid or semi-arid environments (Figure 9.18). The first complex societies in Egypt, Mesopotamia, and the Indus Valley were located in dry regions crossed by a major river, which provided water for intensified agricultural production following the construction of irrigation canals. The apparent connection between farming in an arid environment, the need for irrigation water, and the rise of complex societies led Karl Wittfogel (1957) to hypothesize that complex societies first developed in order to construct and maintain large irrigation systems.

Wittfogel argued that these irrigation systems could not have functioned without a ruling elite to direct operations. Thus, he sees the development of what he calls *hydraulic agriculture* as the key to the evolution of complex society. This hypothesis, although suggestive, has also been called into question. First, societies such as the Hohokam of the American southwest apparently operated an extensive irrigation system without developing social stratification or cultural complexity (Wenke 1999, 356). Second, the sorts of complex irrigation systems Wittfogel had in mind—those requiring a bureaucracy—appear late in the archaeological record of several early civilizations, long after the first appearance of monumental architecture, cities, and other signs of social complexity (see, e.g., Adams 1981, 53). Irrigation may have played a role in the development of complex societies, but it was apparently not the single prime mover that brought them into existence.

Because many early groups of village farmers never developed a high degree of social complexity, archaeologists see its appearance more as the exception, not the rule. Some suggest that population pressure was the decisive force: if the food supply could not keep up with a growing population, social chaos would have resulted unless someone were able to exercise power to allocate resources and keep the peace. This scenario is rejected,

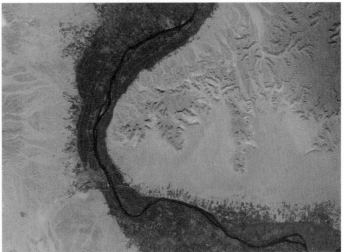

FIGURE 9.18 The civilization of ancient Egypt was supported by agricultural practices that relied on the regular flooding pattern of the Nile River. In this photograph taken from a space shuttle, the wide, dark band crossing the light desert region is the cultivated floodplain of the Nile. The river itself is the very dark, narrow line snaking its way through this cultivated area.

however, by those who argue that social inequality developed in societies where resources were abundant and opportunistic individuals could gain power by using surpluses to indebt others to them through competitive feasting or control of labour (Arnold 1995; Hayden, Canuel, and Shanse 2013). Also, archaeological evidence from more than one part of the world shows that population pressure was not a problem when social complexity first appeared. Some archaeologists now suggest that human societies were able to limit population growth if they chose to do so, whether by migration, infanticide, abortion, contraception, or late marriage. Finally, the greatest decline in fertility in the modern Western world did not occur among the hungry, nor was it triggered by the invention of new birth-control technology: it was the well-fed, middle-class families, not the poverty-stricken workers, who began to have fewer children in capitalist societies. The forces that change reproductive rates are far more complex than a simple population-pressure model would allow.

If population pressure did not undermine the egalitarian social relations of village farmers, perhaps conflict with other villagers was to blame. If all available farmland were settled, for example, making it impossible for people to move away at times of conflict, the only solution, apart from chaos, would have been to establish rules to resolve conflicts, thus leading to the development of more complex political structures (Nissen 1988, 60–1). Sooner or later, however, if chaos could not be contained, warfare might have broken out between neighbouring villages. Indeed, Brian Hayden (1995) suggests that power-seeking individuals might well have manipulated such tensions, using economic surpluses to settle conflicts and amassing personal wealth and power in the process. This could not occur, in his view, until people were willing to accept **bloodwealth**, a crucial innovation not found in egalitarian societies (Hayden 1995, 32). Bloodwealth is a payment by perpetrators to compensate their victims for their loss, and if bloodwealth created a surplus in some individuals or groups over others, social relations among these people would no longer be egalitarian.

Warfare, population pressure, and arid environments all play roles in Robert Carneiro's (1970) theory of the rise of the first states in Peru, Mesopotamia,

bloodwealth　**Material goods paid by perpetrators to compensate their victims for their loss.**

and Egypt; and of later, secondary states elsewhere. In Carneiro's scheme, population pressure would have led to increasing conflict between neighbouring villages once it was no longer possible for villagers to cultivate new lands. This situation, which he calls *environmental circumscription*, might have been especially likely in early farming societies that grew up along river valleys running through deserts, such as those in Mesopotamia, Egypt, and coastal Peru. When the desert barrier halted village expansion, new farmlands could be obtained only by taking them away from other villages by force. Carneiro's theory has stimulated much discussion. However, the role he assigns to population pressure is open to the criticism raised earlier, and many archaeologists still have not found evidence that would confirm or refute Carneiro's hypotheses.

All the prime movers discussed so far involve technological, economic, environmental, or biological factors that would have forced societies into complexity no matter what their previous cultural traditions might have been. Realizing that these external factors were less powerful than once believed, many anthropologists turned their attention to internal, sociocultural factors that might have led to the rise of social complexity. For example, external trade in luxury items by the leaders of early chiefdoms may have generated conflict between the chief's family (whose interests were served by trade) and the common people (whose interests were undermined by it) (Kipp and Schortman 1989). Such a conflict of interests might eventually have thrown a chiefdom completely out of equilibrium, leading to warfare and people desperate for social order. In this case, people may accept a more socially stratified society if it restored stability within the group.

Written documents, when available, can sometimes provide enough detailed insight into social organization to identify social hierarchies and trace their development over time. But for ancient complex societies that lacked writing—and this includes all six of the first such societies—the Marxian approach is exceedingly difficult to apply to archaeological materials. Many of the remains of the earliest complex societies are incomplete and could be compatible with more than one form of social organization. Indeed, any theory, Marxian or not, that seeks to explain the rise of a complex society in terms of social relations, political culture, or religious beliefs faces the same problem: however important they may have been, such phenomena do not fossilize and cannot be reliably inferred on the basis of archaeological data alone, an uncomfortable fact that continues to frustrate archaeologists trying to reconstruct the human past.

Anthropologists cannot offer a single, sweeping explanation of cultural evolution. But their attempts to test various hypotheses that promise such explanations have led to a far richer appreciation of the complexities of social and cultural change. Archaeologist Robert Wenke observes that "cultural evolution is not a continuous, cumulative, gradual change in most places. 'Fits and starts' better describes it" (1999, 336). He further emphasizes the remarkable adaptability of cultural systems, noting in a discussion of Mesoamerica that environmental and ecological analyses can only explain so much: "once we get beyond this simple ecological level of analysis, we encounter a welter of variability in sociopolitical forms, economic histories, settlement patterns, and the other elaborations of these complex societies" (609).

Chapter Summary

1. About 10,000 years ago, the retreat of the last glaciers marked the end of the Pleistocene. The earth's climate changed significantly, affecting the distribution of plants and animals and transforming the ecological settings in which human beings made their livings. Soon thereafter, human beings began to develop new ways of adapting by intervening in these changed environmental settings in order to create new niches for themselves.

2. Plant and animal domestication are usefully understood as forms of niche construction. Not only did human beings interfere with the reproduction of local species, to make them more useful for human purposes, but they also remodelled the environmental settings in which plants were grown and animals were fed and watered. When the invention of agriculture is viewed as niche construction, there is no question that it involved conscious human choice. Intelligent human beings consciously chose to domesticate wild plants that were easy to harvest, nourishing, and tasty; but they also had to consciously create the tools and plan the activities that would make cultivation of a domestic crop possible and successful.

3. The niches human beings construct to exploit plants are not all the same. Anthropologists have identified four major ways in which humans relate to plant species: wild plant–food procurement, wild plant–food production, cultivation, and agriculture. In each successive form, the amount of energy people apply to get food from plants increases, but the energy they get back from plants increases even more.

4. Animal domestication apparently developed as people consciously attempted to control the animals that they were hunting in order to intervene in their breeding patterns. Archaeological evidence for animal domestication may be indicated in one of four ways: when an animal species is found outside its natural range, when animal remains show morphological changes that distinguish them from wild populations, when the numbers of some species at a site increase abruptly relative to other species, and when remains show certain age and gender characteristics. The earliest animal domesticated, some 16,000 years ago, was the dog. Although archaeologists can pinpoint the regions where goats were domesticated, the earliest sites for domesticated sheep are not clear. It seems that cattle and pigs were domesticated at different sites in the Old World. Domestication of animals seems to have been slower and less important in the New World than it was in the Old World.

5. The niches humans have constructed to make use of animals vary. They include random hunting, controlled hunting, herd following, loose herding, close herding, and factory farming. Not all animals people hunted were domesticated. Once humans domesticated animals, their focus shifted from hunting wild animals to raising and slaughtering domesticated animals, which may have triggered concern for private property.

6. Scholars have suggested different factors responsible for plant and animal domestication; none alone is entirely satisfactory. Today, most archaeologists prefer multiple-strand theories that focus on the particular sets of factors that were responsible for domestication in different places. One good example of a multiple-strand approach to domestication is shown by recent studies of the

Natufian cultural tradition in southwestern Asia, which developed about 12,500 years ago. Post-Pleistocene human niches involving sedentism and domestication had both positive and negative consequences for human beings who came to depend on them. By the time farmers became fully aware of agriculture's drawbacks, their societies had probably become so dependent on agriculture that abandoning it for some other subsistence strategy would have been impossible.

7. Neolithic farming villages were basically egalitarian societies, like the foraging societies that had preceded them. However, beginning about 5000 years ago in southwestern Asia and shortly thereafter in Egypt, the Indus Valley (India), China, Mesoamerica (the Valley of Mexico), and the Andes (Peru), humans independently developed social stratification. Social stratification occurred when surplus food production made it possible for some members of society to stop producing food altogether and to specialize in various occupations. A wide gulf developed between most members of a society and members of a new social class of rulers who controlled most of the wealth. The earliest socially stratified societies were chiefdoms in which the chief and close relatives had privileged access to wealth, power, and prestige while other members of the society continued to share roughly similar social status.

8. Archaeological evidence of social complexity includes the remains of monumental architecture, elaborate burials alongside much simpler burials, and concentrations of particular artifacts in specific areas of an archaeological site that might indicate occupational specialization. Complex societies are normally made up of a number of settlements organized in a hierarchy: state organization is suspected when regional settlement patterns show at least three levels in the settlement hierarchy. Art and written inscriptions may provide further information about ancient social organization. Cultural change in all early complex societies tended to alternate between periods of relative cultural uniformity and political unity and periods of regional differentiation and lack of political integration.

9. Anthropologists have devised a number of different hypotheses to explain why complex societies developed. Frequently, the hypothesis places emphasis on a single cause, or prime mover. Although some of the causes that have been proposed as this prime mover were important in some places, they were not all important everywhere. Nevertheless, attempts to test these hypotheses about prime movers have led to a far richer appreciation of the complexities of social and cultural change in the human past.

For Review

1. Why do archaeologists use concepts borrowed from ecology to understand how humans have responded to their environments? What are these concepts, and how can they help us understand the human past?

2. What differentiates domestication from agriculture? Illustrate your answer with examples from this chapter.

3. Describe the different explanations offered by archaeologists for the domestication of plants and animals by humans. Select the one that you agree with most, and write a paragraph outlining your argument.

4. Summarize the discussion of the beginnings of domestication in southwestern Asia.

5. Who were the Natufians? What does archaeological research tell us about the processes of plant and animal domestication in Natufian society?

6. Summarize the key consequences of domestication and sedentism for human ways of life. In what ways have these consequences shaped modern ways of life in Canada?

7. What is social complexity? What is the archaeological evidence for social complexity?

8. Explain what Michael Hoffman means by the term *powerfacts*. In modern North American societies, what objects might serve a purpose similar to that of powerfacts in early complex civilizations?

9. What were the world's first complex societies, and where were they located? What was unique about these locations?

10. Outline the different hypotheses that archaeologists put forward to explain the beginning of complex societies. How did sedentism affect social complexity?

Key Terms

agriculture 186
agroecology 186
bloodwealth 208
broad-spectrum foraging 192
chiefdom 194
class 201
complex societies 201

concentrations of particular
  artifacts 204
domestication 183
egalitarian social relations 201
evolutionary niche 184
grave goods 194
Mesopotamia 196

monumental architecture 203
Neolithic 195
occupational specialization 201
sedentism 188
social stratification 194
surplus production 201

References

Adams, Robert. 1981. *Heartland of Cities*. Chicago: University of Chicago Press.

——, and Hans Nissen. 1972. *The Uruk Countryside*. Chicago: University of Chicago Press.

Armstrong Oma, Kristin. 2010. "Between Trust and Domination: Social Contracts between Humans and Animals." *World Archaeology* 42: 175–8.

Arnold, Jeanne E. 1995. "Social Inequality, Marginalization, and Economic Process." In *Foundations of Social Inequality*, edited by T. Douglas Price and Gary M. Feinman, 87–103. New York: Plenum.

Banning, Edward B. 2011. "So Fair a House." *Current Anthropology* 52 (5): 619–60.

Bar-Yosef, Ofer, and Mordechai Kislev. 1989. "Early Farming Communities in the Jordan Valley." In *Foraging and Farming: The Evolution of Plant Exploitation*, edited by David Harris and Gordon Hillman, 632–42. Vol. 13 of *One World Archaeology*. London: Unwin Hyman.

Belfer-Cohen, Anna. 1988. *The Natufian Settlement at Hayonim Cave*. PhD. diss. Jerusalem: Hebrew University.

——. 1991. "The Natufian in the Levant." *Annual Review of Anthropology* 20: 167–86.

Bender, Barbara. 1977. "Gatherer–Hunter to Farmer: A Social Perspective." *World Archaeology* 10: 204–22.

Blake, Michael. 2015. *Maize for the Gods: Unearthing the 9,000-Year History of Corn*. Berkeley: University of California Press.

Bocquet-Appel, Jean-Pierre. 2011. "When the World's Population Took Off: The Springboard of the Neolithic Demographic Transition." *Science* 333 (6042): 560–1. doi:10.1126/science.1208880

Bökönyi, Sandor. 1989. "Definitions of Animal Domestication." In *The Walking Larder: Patterns of Domestication, Pastoralism, and Predation*, edited by Juliet Clutton-Brock, 22–27. Vol. 14 of *One World Archaeology*. London: Unwin Hyman.

Bruno, Maria C. 2009. "Practice and History in the Transition to Food Production." *Current Anthropology* 50 (5): 703–6.

Carneiro, Robert. 1970. "A Theory of the Origin of the State." *Science* 169: 733–8.

Fried, Morton H. 1967. *The Evolution of Political Society*. New York: Random House.

Giemsch, Lianne, and Susanne Feine. 2015. Interdisciplinary Investigations of the Late Glacial Double Burial from Bonn-Oberkassel. *Hugo Obermaier Society for Quaternary Research and Archaeology of the Stone Age: 57th Annual Meeting in Hiedenheim*, April 7–11, 36–37.

Greenfield, Haskel J., Itzhaq Shai, and Aren Maeir. 2012. "Being an 'Ass': An Early Bronze Age Burial of a Donkey from Tell Es-Safi/Gath, Israel." *Bioarchaeology of the Near East* 6: 21–52.

Halperin, Rhoda H. 1994. *Cultural Economies: Past and Present*. Austin: University of Texas Press.

Harris, David. 1989. "An Evolutionary Continuum of People–Plant Interaction." In *Foraging and Farming: The Evolution of Plant Exploitation*, edited by David Harris and Gordon Hillman, 1–30. Vol. 13 of *One World Archaeology*. London: Unwin Hyman.

Hayden, Brian. 1995. "Pathways to Power." In *Foundations of Social Inequality*, edited by T. Douglas Price and Gary Feinman, 15–86. New York, Springer.

——, Neil Canuel, and Jennifer Shanse. 2013. "What Was Brewing in the Natufian? An Archaeological Assessment of Brewing Technology in the Epipaleolithic." *Journal of Archaeological Method and Theory* 20 (1): 102–50.

Henry, Donald. 1989. *From Foraging to Agriculture: The Levant and the End of the Ice Age*. Philadelphia: University of Pennsylvania Press.

Hoffman, Michael A. 1991. *Egypt before the Pharaohs: The Prehistoric Foundations of Egyptian Civilization*. Rev. ed. Austin: University of Texas Press.

Hole, Frank. 2007. "Agricultural Sustainability in the Semi-Arid Near East." *Climate of the Past* 3: 193–203.

Honeychurch, William, and Cheryl Makarewicz. 2016. "The Archaeology of Pastoral Nomadism." *Annual Review of Anthropology* 45: 341–59. doi.org/10.1146/annurev-anthro-102215-095827

Jarman, M.R., G.N. Bailey, and H.N. Jarman, eds. 1982. *Early European Agriculture: Its Foundations and Development*. Cambridge: Cambridge University Press.

Kipp, Rita Smith, and Edward M. Schortman. 1989. "The Political Impact of Trade in Chiefdoms." *American Anthropologist* 91: 370–85.

Lee, Richard B. 1992. *The Dobe Ju/'hoansi*. 2nd ed. New York: Holt, Rinehart, and Winston.

McCorriston, Joy, and Frank Hole. 1991. "The Ecology of Seasonal Stress and the Origins of Agriculture in the Near East." *American Anthropologist* 93: 46–69.

Nissen, Hans J. 1988. *The Early History of the Ancient Near East, 9000–2000 BC*. Chicago: University of Chicago Press.

Odling-Smee, F. John, Kevin L. Laland, and Marcus W. Feldman. 2003. *Niche Construction: The Neglected Process in Evolution*. Princeton, NJ: Princeton University Press.

Pennington, Renee. 1992. "Did Food Increase Fertility? Evaluation of !Kung and Herero History." *Human Biology* 64: 497–501.

Powis, Terry G., W. Jeffrey Hurst, María del Carmen Rodríguez, Ortíz C. Ponciano, Michael Blake, David Cheetham, Michael D. Coe, and John G. Hodgson. 2008. "The Origins of Cacao Use in Mesoamerica." *Mexicon 30*: 35–8.

Price, T. Douglas. 1995. "Social Inequality at the Origins of Agriculture." In *Foundations of Social Inequality*, edited by T. Douglas Price and Gary M. Feinman. New York: Plenum Press.

——, and Anne Birgitte Gebauer, eds. 1995. *Last Hunters, First Farmers*. Santa Fe, NM: SAR Press.

Rindos, David. 1984. *The Origins of Agriculture: An Evolutionary Perspective*. New York: Academic Press.

Service, Elman. 1962. *Primitive Social Organization*. New York: Random House.

Shanks, Michael, and Christopher Tilley. 1987. *Social Theory and Archaeology*. Oxford: Polity Press.

Smith, Bruce. 1995. *The Emergence of Agriculture*. New York: Scientific American Library.

Trigger, Bruce. 1993. *Early Civilizations: Ancient Egypt in Context*. Cairo: American University in Cairo Press.

Weatherford, Jack. 1988. *Indian Givers: How the Indians of the Americas Transformed the World*. New York: Fawcett.

Wenke, Robert J. 1999. *Patterns in Prehistory: Humankind's First Three Million Years*. 4th ed. Oxford: Oxford University Press.

——, and Deborah I. Olszewski. 2007. *Patterns in Prehistory: Humankind's First Three Million Years*. 5th ed. New York: Oxford University Press.

White, Leslie. 1949. *The Science of Culture*. New York: Grove Press.

Wittfogel, Karl. 1957. *Oriental Despotism: A Comparative Study of Total Power*. New Haven, CT: Yale University Press.

Zeder, Melinda A. 2016. "Domestication as a Model System for Niche Construction Theory." *Evolutionary Ecology* 30: 325–48.

——, and Bruce D. Smith. 2009. "A Conversation on Agricultural Origins." *Current Anthropology* 50 (5): 681–91.

▲ A vendor sells spices at a local market in Baheri, India. Photo: SoumenNath/iStockphoto

10 Why Do Anthropologists Study Economic Relations?

Chapter Outline

All human groups must organize themselves to make available to their members the material things they need for survival, such as food, shelter, and clothing. This chapter explores the variety of economic patterns human societies have developed over the millennia. It also draws attention to the way large-scale connections forged by trade or conquests continue to shape—and be reshaped by—the local economic practices of societies throughout the world.

Human beings are material organisms, and the seemingly endless meaningful ways we can imagine to live must always come to terms with the material realities of day-to-day existence. Culture contributes to the way human beings organize their social lives to meet such challenges. **Social organization** can be defined as the patterning of human interdependence in a given society through the actions and decisions of its members.

How Do Anthropologists Study Economic Relations?

Although our physical survival depends on our making adequate use of the resources around us, our culture tells us which resources to use and how to use them. Economic anthropologists study the many variations in human livelihood that anthropologists have found in different societies (see Map 10.1 for locations of societies discussed in this chapter). Richard Wilk (1996, xv) has defined **economic anthropology** as "the part of the discipline that debates issues of *human nature* that relate directly to the decisions of daily life and making a living."

In ordinary conversation, when we speak of making a living, we usually mean doing what is necessary to obtain the material things—food, clothing, shelter—that sustain human life. In earlier chapters, we discussed "making a living" interchangeably with the concept of subsistence strategies, or the ways that people go about

getting food resources. As a review, anthropologists use a generalized typology of subsistence strategies to understand the basic division between **food collectors**, or *foragers* (those who gather, fish, or hunt), and **food producers** (those who depend on domesticated plants or animals or both). The strategies followed by food collectors depend on the richness of the environments in which they live. Small-scale food collectors live in harsher environments and are likely to change residence often in search of resources, as the Ju/'hoansi (see EthnoProfile 10.1) traditionally did. By contrast, complex food collectors live in environments richly endowed with dependable food sources and may even, like the Indigenous peoples of the northwest coast of North America, build settlements with permanent architecture.

> For more discussion on subsistence strategies, see Chapters 8 and 9.

Food producers may farm exclusively or herd exclusively or do a little of both. Those who depend on herds are called *pastoralists*. Among those who farm, there are further distinctions. Some farmers, who are referred to as *extensive agriculturalists* or *horticulturalists*, depend primarily on human power and simple tools, such as digging sticks, to cultivate their fields. *Horticulturalists* often burn brush in order to clear plots of uncultivated land and plant their crops in the ash-enriched soil that remains. Because this technique exhausts the soil after two or three seasons, the plot must then lie fallow for several years as a new plot is cleared and the process is repeated. Other farmers use plows, draft animals, irrigation, fertilizer, and the like. Their method of farming—known as *intensive agriculture*—brings much more land under cultivation at any one time and produces significant crop surpluses. Lastly, *mechanized industrial agriculture* is found in societies in which farming, or animal husbandry, has become organized along industrial lines and is often associated with capitalism. Agribusiness "factories in the field" or animal feedlots transform food production into a large-scale, technology-dependent industry of its own.

social organization **The patterning of human interdependence in a given society through the actions and decisions of its members.**

economic anthropology **"The part of the discipline [of anthropology] that debates issues of *human nature* that relate directly to the decisions of daily life and making a living" (Wilk 1996, xv).**

food collectors **Societies that gather, fish, and hunt to subsist.**

food producers **Societies that depend on domesticated plants or animals or both to subsist.**

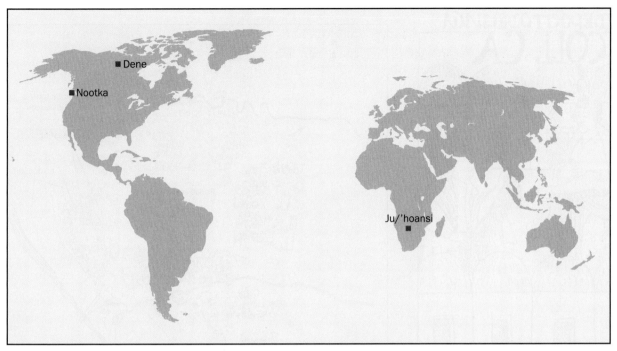

MAP 10.1 Locations of societies whose EthnoProfiles appear in Chapter 10.

How Do Anthropologists Study Production, Distribution, and Consumption?

Anthropologists generally agree that economic activity is usefully subdivided into three distinct phases: *production*, *distribution*, and *consumption*. Production involves transforming nature's raw materials into products useful to human beings, such as food collection or food production. Distribution involves getting those products to people. Consumption involves using up the products—for example, by eating food or wearing clothing. When analyzing economic activity in a particular society, however, anthropologists differ in the importance they attach to each phase. For example, the distributive process known as *exchange* is central to the functioning of capitalist free enterprise. Some anthropologists have assumed that exchange is equally central to the functioning of all economies and have tried to explain the economic life of non-Western societies in terms of exchange. Anthropologists influenced by the work of Karl Marx, however, have argued that exchange cannot be understood properly without first studying the nature of *production*. They point out that production shapes the context in which exchange can occur, determining which parties have how much of what kind of goods to exchange. Other anthropologists have suggested

EthnoProfile 10.1

Ju/'hoansi (!Kung)

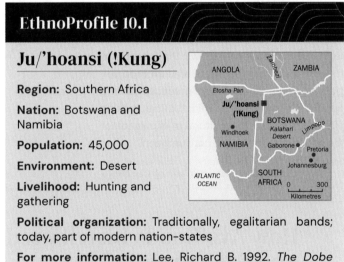

Region: Southern Africa

Nation: Botswana and Namibia

Population: 45,000

Environment: Desert

Livelihood: Hunting and gathering

Political organization: Traditionally, egalitarian bands; today, part of modern nation-states

For more information: Lee, Richard B. 1992. *The Dobe Ju/'hoansi.* 2nd ed. New York: Holt, Rinehart, and Winston.

that neither production nor exchange patterns make any sense without first specifying the *consumption* priorities of the people who are producing and exchanging. Consumption priorities, they argue, are certainly designed to satisfy material needs. But the recognition of needs and of appropriate ways to satisfy them is shaped by historically contingent cultural patterns. Finally, many would agree that patterns of production, exchange, and consumption are seriously affected by the kind of *storage* in use in a particular society (Figure 10.1).

> ↻ For a discussion of the links between storage and sedentism, see Chapter 9, pp. 199–200.

FIGURE 10.1 (Above) A seventeenth-century drawing of storage warehouses built at the height of the Inka Empire. (Right) The plan of Huánuco Pampa, Peru, shows the location of these storage warehouses. Some anthropologists argue that food-storage practices buffer a population from ecological fluctuations, making possible considerable cultural manipulation of the economic relations of consumption.

Source: *After Peruvian Prehistory: An Overview of Pre-Inca and Inca Society*, ed. Richard W. Keating, Cambridge: Cambridge University Press, 1988, p. 240.

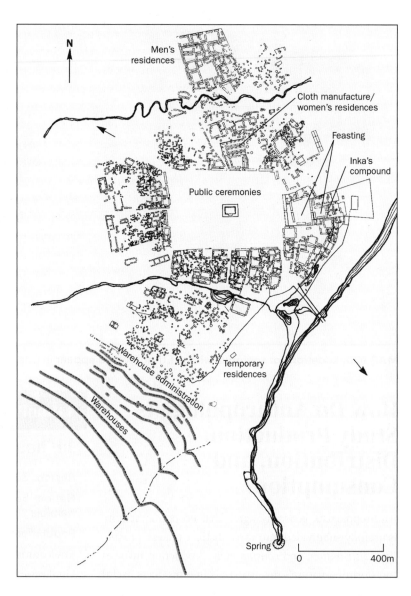

How Are Goods Distributed and Exchanged?

Capitalism and Neoclassical Economics

The discipline of economics was born in the late 1700s, during the early years of the Industrial Revolution in western Europe. At that time, such thinkers as Adam Smith and his disciples struggled to devise theories to explain the profound changes in economic and social life that European societies had recently begun to experience.

Capitalism differed in many ways from the feudal economic system that had preceded it, but perhaps the most striking difference was how it handled distribution. Feudal economic relations had allotted goods and services to different social groups and individuals on the basis of status, or position in society. Because lords had high status and many obligations, they had a right to more goods and services. Peasants, with low status and few rights, were allowed far less. This distribution of goods was a time-honoured tradition not open to modification. The customs derived from capitalist economic relations, by contrast, were considered "free" precisely because they swept away all such traditional restrictions. As we shall see in Chapter 13 in our discussion of "Sedaka"

> **capitalism** An economic system dominated by the supply–demand–price mechanism called the "market"; an entire way of life that grew in response to and in service of that market.

For our discussion of "Sedaka" Village, see Chapter 13, pp. 300–2.

Village, Malaysia, capitalism also swept away traditional protections. In any case, distribution under capitalism was negotiated between buyers and sellers in the market.

Capitalist market exchange of goods for other goods, for labour, or (increasingly) for cash was an important development in Western economic history. It is not surprising, therefore, that Western economic theory was preoccupied with explaining how the capitalist market worked. Markets clearly had a new, decisive importance in capitalist society, which they had not possessed in feudal times. Toward the end of the nineteenth century, the views of early economic thinkers such as Adam Smith were transformed into **neoclassical economics,** which remains the foundation of formal economics today. As Hann and Hart (2011) explain, neoclassical economics "still celebrated the market as the main source of increased economic welfare; but it replaced the classical view of economic value as an objective property of produced commodities, to be struggled over by the different classes, with a focus on the subjective calculations of individuals seeking to maximize their own utility" (37). This was a key turning point in the history of economics; it produced the divergent theoretical positions, identified by Wilk and Cliggett (2007), about which economists and economic anthropologists continue to disagree today.

Self-Interest, Institutions, and Morals

Wilk and Cliggett (2007) argue that it is possible to identify three theoretical camps in economic anthropology, each of which depends on a different set of assumptions about human nature.

The first model Wilk and Cliggett identify is the *self-interested model.* This model of human nature originated during the Enlightenment and is based on the assumption that individuals are first and foremost interested in their own well-being, that selfishness is natural. Economists since Adam Smith have argued that people's resources—for example, money—are not, and never will be, great enough for them to obtain all the goods they want. This view of economy also assumes that economic analysis should focus on *individuals,* who must maximize their utility (or satisfaction) under conditions of scarcity. An economizing individual is supposed to set priorities and to allocate resources according to those priorities.

Economic anthropologists who accept the self-interest model of human behaviour should therefore investigate the different priorities set by different societies and study how these priorities affect the maximizing decisions of individuals.

Other economic anthropologists, however, are committed to the *social model of human nature.* This means that they pay attention to "the way people form groups and exercise power" (Wilk and Cliggett 2007, 42). This view of human nature assumes that people ordinarily identify with the groups to which they belong and, in many cases, cannot even conceive of having a self with interests that diverge from the interest of the group. This view of human nature suggests that economics ought to focus on **institutions**—stable and enduring cultural practices that organize social life—not on individuals. From an institutional point of view, a society's economy consists of the culturally specific processes its members use to provide themselves with material resources.

Wilk and Cliggett (2007) introduce a third model used in economic anthropology, which is referred to as the *moral model,* where people's motivations are shaped by culturally specific belief systems and values guided by a culturally patterned view of the universe. People are socialized and enculturated into these values and practices over a lifetime, such that they will experience distress and conflict if tempted to make decisions—including economic decisions— that are contrary to their internalized morality. Wilk and Cliggett do not consider any one model as a fact and are more interested in paying close ethnographic attention to the particularities of real human beings in real sociocultural settings.

For a description of the concept of holism and its importance to the anthropological study of culture, see Chapter 2, p. 28.

Modes of Exchange

Some anthropologists argued that taking self-interested, materialistic decision making in the capitalist market as the prototype of human rationality was ethnocentric. They pointed out that the capitalist market is a relatively

neoclassical economics A formal attempt to explain the workings of capitalist enterprise, with particular attention to distribution.

institutions Complex, variable, and enduring forms of cultural practices that organize social life.

recent cultural invention in human history. Western capitalist societies distribute material goods in a manner that is consistent with their basic values, institutions, and assumptions about human nature. So non-Western, non-capitalist societies might be expected to have devised alternative modes of exchange that distribute material goods in ways that are in accord with their basic values and institutions. In the early twentieth century, for example, French anthropologist Marcel Mauss ([1950] 2000) contrasted non-capitalist **gift exchanges** (which are deeply embedded in social relations and always require a return **gift**) with impersonal **commodity exchanges** typical of the capitalist market (in which **commodities**, or goods, are exchanged for cash, and exchange partners need have nothing further to do with one another, for example, buying something from a grocery store). For other anthropologists, however, Mauss's binary division seemed to exclude too much variation. For example, Marshall Sahlins (1972) drew on the work of economic historian Karl Polanyi (e.g., 1977) to propose that three **modes of exchange** could be identified historically and cross-culturally: *reciprocity, redistribution,* and *market exchange.*

The most ancient mode of exchange was **reciprocity**. Reciprocity is characteristic of an egalitarian society, which the Ju/'hoansi once was (see EthnoProfile 10.1: Ju/'hoansi). Sahlins identified three kinds of reciprocity. (1) *Generalized reciprocity* is found when those who exchange do so without expecting an immediate return and without specifying the value of the return. Everyone assumes that the exchanges will eventually balance out. Generalized reciprocity usually characterizes the exchanges that occur between parents and their children. In Canada, for example, parents ordinarily do not keep a running tab on what it costs them to raise their children; nor do they then present their children with repayment schedules when they reach the age of 18. The expectation is that children will eventually reciprocate by meeting the needs of their aged parents as best they can, whatever those needs turn out to be. (2) *Balanced reciprocity* is found when those who exchange expect a return of equal value within a specified time limit (e.g., when cousins exchange gifts of equal value with one another at Christmas). Lee (1992, 103) notes that the Ju/'hoansi distinguish between barter, which requires an immediate return of an equivalent, and *hxaro*, which is a kind of generalized reciprocity that encourages social obligations to be extended into the future. (3) Finally, *negative reciprocity* is an exchange of goods and services in which at least one party attempts to get something for nothing without suffering any penalties. Such attempts can range from haggling over prices to outright theft and even slavery.

Redistribution, the second mode of exchange, requires some form of centralized social organization. Those who control the central position receive economic contributions from all members of the group. It is then their responsibility to redistribute the goods they receive in a way that provides for every member of the group. In Canada, the income taxes that we pay to the government are probably the most recognizable form of redistribution. Everyone pays the government, which in turn redistributes the money for roads, schools, and various other social services. A classic anthropological example of redistribution is the *potlatch* of the Indigenous peoples of the northwest coast of Canada. In the highly stratified fishing and gathering society of the Nootka (Nuu-chah-nulth), for example, nobles sought to outdo one another in generosity by giving away vast quantities of goods during the potlatch ceremony (see EthnoProfile 10.2: Nootka [Nuu-chah-nulth]). The noble who was giving the potlatch accumulated goods produced in one village and redistributed them to other nobles attending the ceremony. When the guests returned to their own villages, they in turn redistributed the goods among their followers. In the late nineteenth century, the Canadian government outlawed this form of redistribution as

gift exchanges Non-capitalist forms of economic exchange that are deeply embedded in social relations and always require a return gift.

gift A good or service exchanged as part of social relations.

commodity exchanges Impersonal economic exchanges typical of the capitalist market in which goods are exchanged for cash and exchange partners need have nothing further to do with one another.

commodities Goods exchanged for cash.

modes of exchange Patterns according to which distribution takes place: *reciprocity, redistribution,* and *market exchange.*

reciprocity The exchange of goods and services of equal value. Anthropologists distinguish three forms of reciprocity: *generalized,* in which neither the time nor the value of the return is specified; *balanced,* in which a return of equal value is expected within a specified time limit; and *negative,* in which parties to the exchange hope to get something for nothing.

redistribution A mode of exchange that requires some form of centralized social organization to receive economic contributions from all members of the group and to redistribute them in such a way as to provide for every group member.

a means of establishing control over the Indigenous peoples of Canada's northwest coast. The potlatch ban lasted until 1951, and it wasn't until 1952 that the first legal potlatch was celebrated on Vancouver Island.

Market exchange, invented in capitalist society, is the most recent mode of exchange, according to Polanyi (1977) (Figure 10.2). Polanyi was well aware that trade, money, and market institutions had developed independently of one another historically. He also knew that they could be found in societies outside the West. The uniqueness of capitalism was how all three institutions were linked to one another in the societies of early modern Europe.

According to Polanyi (1977), different modes of exchange often coexist within a single society although only one structures the society's principal economy. Canada's economy, for example, is structured by the market mode of exchange, yet redistribution and reciprocity have not disappeared. Within the family, parents who obtain income from the market redistribute that income, or goods obtained with that income, to their children. Generalized reciprocity also characterizes much exchange within the family, where parents regularly provide their children with affection, food, and clothing without expecting any immediate return, and children regularly feel obligated to do what they can to meet the needs of their parents as they age.

FIGURE 10.2 Items for sale at a market in Byblos, Lebanon. Markets can be found in many societies, but capitalism links markets to trade and money in a unique way.

The Maisin and Reciprocity

John Barker (2016), from the University of Toronto, has studied the Maisin of Collingwood Bay, Papua New Guinea, for many years. Part of his research has looked at the way in which reciprocity forms the social structure of the Maisin and how the cash economy and the reciprocity economy have affected each other.

Barker notes that Maisin society is based on reciprocity. A steady give-and-take of gifts, labour, and advice should characterize the relationship of close relatives. The Maisin do not keep track of what each person gives, gets, or is owed. Rather, people demonstrate their mutual trust and support by allowing things to balance out over time. This is what we have just referred to as *generalized* reciprocity. This kind of sharing is what the Maisin refer to as *marawawawe*, which translates as "love, peace, or social amity," and is a Maisin central value (50). It represents the way family and close friends should treat each other: "Indeed, it is what makes family and close friends." It is at this level that the obligation to reciprocate is most strongly felt.

Barker distinguishes three different types of generalized reciprocity at this level: complementary, asymmetrical, and symmetrical. Sisters and brothers and wives and husbands employ *complementary reciprocity*,

© Edwardkaraa/ Dreamstime.com

EthnoProfile 10.2

Nootka (Nuu-chah-nulth)

Region: Northwestern North America

Nation: Canada (Vancouver Island)

Population: 6000 (1970s)

Environment: Rainy, relatively warm coastal strip

Livelihood: Fishing, hunting, gathering

Political organization: Traditionally, ranked individuals, chiefs; today, part of a modern nation-state

For more information: Rosman, Abraham, and Paula G. Rubel. 1971. *Feasting with Mine Enemy: Rank and Exchange among Northwest Coast Societies.* New York: Columbia University Press.

---

market exchange The exchange of goods (trade) calculated in terms of a multipurpose medium of exchange and standard of value (money) and carried out by means of a supply-demand-price mechanism (the market).

with each making distinct contributions to the household. Their exchanges denote separate if not equal status. Parents and children and older and younger siblings engage in *asymmetrical reciprocity*—the elder should take care of the child or younger sibling by providing general food and good advice, and the child or younger sibling should listen respectfully and obey the parents' or older siblings' wishes. Over the course of a lifetime, children should return the original gifts of food or support to bring the relationship into balance. Exchange among members of different households, clan mates, and friends is *symmetrical*, such that the exchange is more or less in balance. This marks their equivalence.

At another level, the circle of neighbours and relatives in which the steady give-and-take is found tends not to extend much beyond nearby households that usually belong to close relatives. While these circles overlap, forming what Barker calls a dense interwoven exchange network, they do not form a unitary system. Rather, the more distant people are in terms of relatedness and residence, the harder it is to create the easy give-and-take of the inner circle. Exchanges are far less frequent, more carefully organized, and are recognized as balanced. This is *balanced reciprocity*.

Finally, as one moves from trusted family and close friends to increasingly distant exchange partners, one reaches the edges of social relationships, whereby *negative reciprocity* can occur. Negative reciprocity in the Maisin world happens between parties that have little or no social connection and so have no moral obligation to each other. They are strangers or nearly so. As Barker puts it,

> Reciprocity lies at the heart of the Maisin subsistence economy, but it should be clear by now that it is neither simple nor limited to the business of moving items between producers and consumers. Reciprocity provides the key means by which the Maisin create and sustain social relationships. The constant give-and-take of daily exchanges embodies an essential assumption that social relationships cannot be taken for granted. They must be created, affirmed, reproduced, and modified through giving and receiving. (54)

But there is more to the story. As well as growing their own food and building their own houses out of material from the forest, since the 1890s, the Maisin have simultaneously lived in a world of cash and commodities,

a world with different rules and a different moral logic. Over the years, Barker tells us, villagers have become increasingly dependent on purchased commodities, ranging from clothing or fish hooks to soccer balls and cigarettes, to the cost of travel to visit relatives in town, to school fees for their children (56–7). Although villagers complain about the problems money brings, no one wants to return to a time when people relied on local resources alone.

Opportunities for the Maisin to earn money locally are limited; the best and most reliable source of money now is remittances from relatives who are working elsewhere, either in Papua New Guinea or in another country. Villagers expect that their relatives who find work outside the village will "not forget" the people at home: "While life in the towns is expensive, most employed Maisin routinely put aside part of their salaries to assist their rural relatives in medical emergencies, bride wealth exchanges, funerals, and local business start-ups. They accommodate relatives visiting from the village and send them home with parcels of clothing and other goods" (58). They do this because they have been brought up in a world based on reciprocal exchange and because their rural relatives regularly remind them of the debt owed to those who brought them up. They also do it in order to leave open the possibility of being able to retire in their native village. By helping their rural relatives, they are assisting the people who care for the land and protect their property rights. As of 2016, almost all adult Maisin have lived for a time—and in many cases, a long time—in their towns, either working or visiting employed relatives.

There appears to be a conflict between a "traditional" economic system built on reciprocal exchange and a "modern" one based on money and commodities. The conflict can be seen as between an egalitarian system, in which there are no permanent ranked socioeconomic classes, and a money-based economy based on unequal access to wealth and prestige. Money can disrupt the obligation to return a gift, in part because it can be hidden:

> At a deeper level, money and markets imply a different type of morality, one focused on the individual who through hard work, good luck, or a combination of both succeeds on his or her own merits, with no help from others. Thus the introduction of money can be understood as the main engine of a series of transformations—for

reciprocity between people to transactions mediated by abstract markets in which value is set; from self-reliance to dependence upon wages paid by employers; from a relatively egalitarian to an economically stratified society; from a moral emphasis upon one's kin and community to the celebration of the self-reliant individual. (60–1)

Although there are indications of a market-oriented change in Maisin society, Barker observed that at every stage, Maisin have used their assumptions about reciprocity and morality to shape their understanding and use of money. The requirement to reciprocate remains strong and public. Indeed, employed Maisin often complained privately to Barker about the pressure they receive from villagers to share their cash. Yet most people share what they have because it is the normal thing to do. Those who have more take pleasure and pride in demonstrating their generosity. The subsistence, reciprocity-based economy is actually being subsidized by the cash economy.

Barker (2016) concludes his discussion of the interacting economic systems by noting that in recent years, the Maisin have become more tolerant of the inequalities money creates. Some households are better off than others. Villagers have become accustomed to using money in the village. Even so, reciprocity remains central to both the Maisin economy and moral system:

> There is no hunger in Maisin communities; the requirement to share, to support others, is too compelling. Maisin are keenly aware of the dangers money can bring or the threat it represents to their ancestral way of life. They need money; there is no turning back. Yet, at least for the time being, the Maisin appear to have been more or less successful in balancing the opposed logic of gift and commodity systems of value. (63–4)

Does Production Drive Economic Activities?

Some economic anthropologists have argued that production is the driving force behind economic activity, creating supplies of goods that must accommodate people's demand, thereby determining levels of consumption. Anthropologists who take this view borrow their perspective, as well as many key concepts, from the works of Karl Marx. They argue that studying production explains important economic processes ignored by views that emphasize market exchange as the driving force of economic activity.

Labour

Labour is perhaps the most central Marxian concept these anthropologists have emphasized. It is the activity linking human social groups to the material world around them: human beings must actively struggle together to transform natural substances into forms they can use. Human labour is therefore always *social* labour. Marx emphasized the importance of human physical labour in the material world, especially in the production of food, clothing, shelter, and tools. But Marx also recognized the importance of mental or cognitive labour: human intelligence allows us to reflect on and organize productive activities in different ways.

Modes of Production

Marx attempted to classify the ways different human groups carry out production. Each way is called a **mode of production**. Anthropologist Eric Wolf (1982) defined a mode of production as the way labour is organized within a society using specific tools, skills, organization, and knowledge. Tools, skills, organization, and knowledge constitute what Marx called the **means of production**. The social relations linking human beings who use a given means of production within a particular mode of production are called the **relations of production**. That is, different productive tasks (clearing the bush, planting, harvesting, and so on) are assigned to different social groups, which Marx called *classes*, all of whom must work together for production to be successful. Wolf notes that Marx speaks of at least eight different modes of production in his own writings, although he focused mainly on the capitalist mode.

---

labour The activity linking human social groups to the material world around them; from the point of view of Karl Marx, labour is, therefore, always social labour.

mode of production The way that labour is organized within a society using specific tools, skills, organization, and knowledge.

means of production The tools, skills, organization, and knowledge used to make a living.

relations of production The social relations linking the people who use a given means of production within a particular mode of production.

FIGURE 10.3 This drawing from 1562 shows Indigenous American men breaking the soil and Indigenous American women planting, a gender-based division of labour.

Source: Theodor de Bry after 1564 watercolor by Jacques Le Moyne/Library of Congress Rare Book and Special Collections Division Washington, D.C. 20540 USA.

Wolf (1982) finds the concept of "mode of production" useful and suggests that three modes of production have been particularly important in human history:

1. A *kin-ordered mode* (Figure 10.3), in which social labour is deployed on the basis of kinship relations (e.g., a family farm where husbands/fathers clear the fields, the whole family plants, mothers/wives weed, children keep animals out of the field)

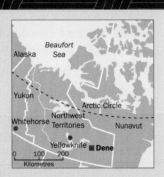

EthnoProfile 10.3

Dene

Region: Northern North America

Nation: Canada (Northwest Territories)

Population: 2000

Environment: Subarctic tundra and boreal forest

Livelihood: Fishing, hunting, and gathering

Political organization: Traditionally, ranked individuals, chiefs; today, part of a modern nation-state

For more information: Dokis, Carly. 2015. *Where the Rivers Meet: Pipelines, Participatory Resource Management, and Aboriginal–State Relations in the Northwest Territories.* Vancouver: UBC Press.

2. A *tributary mode*, "in which the primary producer, whether cultivator or herdsman, is allowed access to the means of production while tribute [a payment of goods or labour] is exacted from him by political or military means" (79)

3. A *capitalist mode*, which has three main features: the means of production are private property owned by members of the capitalist class, workers must sell their labour power to the capitalists in order to survive, and surpluses of wealth are produced that capitalists may retain as profit or reinvest in production to increase output and generate further surpluses and higher profits, such as agribusiness

The kin-ordered mode of production is found among foragers and those farmers and herders whose political organization does not involve domination by one group. An example of this mode of production is found among the Dene in the Sahtu Region of the Northwest Territories (Dokis 2015) (see EthnoProfile 10.3). The tributary mode is found among farmers or herders living in a social system that is divided into classes of rulers and subjects. Subjects produce both for themselves and for their rulers, who take a certain proportion of their subjects' produce or labour as tribute. The capitalist mode, the most recent to develop, can be found in the industrial societies of North America and western Europe beginning in the seventeenth and eighteenth centuries. The concept of mode of production thus draws attention to many of the same features of economic life highlighted in traditional anthropological discussions of subsistence strategies. Yet the concept emphasizes forms of social and political organization as well as material productive activities and shows how they are interconnected. That is, the kin-ordered mode of production is distinctive as much for its use of the kinship system to allocate labour to production as for the kind of production undertaken, such as farming. In a kin-ordered mode of production, the *relations of kinship* serve as the *relations of production* that enable a particular *mode of production* to be carried out. Farm labour organized according to kin-ordered relations of production, where labourers are relatives to whom no cash payment is due, is very different from farm labour organized according to capitalist relations of production, where labourers are often non-relatives who are paid a wage.

In Their Own Words

Treating Your Food Good: Changing Natures and Economies in the Northwest Territories

Carly Dokis from Nipissing University describes how the Dene people living in the Sahtu Region of the Northwest Territories form connections with their landscape and the food they rely on for sustenance.

Dene people in the Sahtu Region of the Northwest Territories have drawn sustenance from their lands since time immemorial. While a vast majority of people in the Sahtu continue to hunt, fish, and gather plants and berries for most of their food, the sustenance that people obtain from their lands extends beyond material needs to include personal, subjective, emotive, and spiritual connections to the places and other-than-human beings who inhabit the landscape. Spending time "in the bush" allows for the development of skills and knowledge that people associate with being Dene; it connects people to the places and stories that explain how the world was created and how it will come to be in the future; it fosters community cohesion through the sharing of knowledge, food, and senses of common identity; and it is in the bush [that] Dene people are free of imposed systems of state control.

For the majority of Sahtu Dene people, the landscape is composed of powerful animate beings. The land is seen as a leader (*k'aowe*), rather than a passive receptor of human management. In order to maintain proper relationships with the land and the other-than-human beings that dwell there, Dene people often talk about maintaining a Universal Law, or *Dene ʔeʔah*, which is a set of moral codes that one ought to live by in order to be a good human being. Part of the Universal Law includes engaging in respectful and reciprocal relationships with other-than-human beings, including making offerings before travelling, hunting, fishing, or gathering; respecting the bodies of animals killed in the hunt or fish caught during fishing; a consideration not to take too much or to interfere in the lives of other-than-human beings; and . . . sharing—with other-than-human beings and with one another. As one Dene elder put it, "if you treat your food good, it will treat you good too."

While there is a continued emphasis on the importance of spending time in the bush, and [on] maintaining the Universal Law, Dene people in the Sahtu face increased challenges to spending time on the land. Over the last half-century, Dene people have witnessed a change from life lived primarily on the land to living primarily in permanent settlements. Young people now spend a majority of their time in town, where they attend school, and adults must obtain cash in order to pay for the high cost of housing, fuel, and other necessities. Somewhat ironically, the high price of gas, ammunition, and equipment such as snowmobiles and traps necessitates that people who continue to spend time on the land, or their families, must also participate in a cash economy. This, of course, means that some people cannot travel great distances or for long periods of time because they have to come back to town to work.

The Sahtu Region has also experienced a significant increase in oil and gas exploration over the past 20 years. Some local people see the development of a hydrocarbon-based economy as an opportunity to provide jobs, business contracts, and increased revenue through access and benefits agreements, some of which could be used to support land-based activities. Others, however, express concerns about the impacts of oil and gas activities, including environmental contamination, changes in local lifeways such as decreased Slavey language use and greater influence of popular culture, and of course interferences with the ability to spend time in the bush. Importantly, increased extractive industries are also seen to seriously interfere in human–other-than-human relationships in ways that are moral in nature. That is, the impacts of oil and gas activities on moose or birds or fish are not just viewed as ecological, but may also come to bear on the responsibility that people have to maintain the Universal Law and proper relationships with the landscape.

When state agencies and regulators consider the potential impacts of extractive industries, even under systems of resource co-management, the impacts and risks associated with resource extraction are often evaluated in technocratic terms that serve to measure and quantify what for Sahtu Dene cannot be represented in graphs and tables—those subjective attachments that people have to their land and components

Continued

of life that are associated with being Dene. Additionally, mitigation measures adopted to avoid the risks of extractive projects are often technical in nature, for example moving a pipeline right-of-way, rather than seriously questioning the desirability of the proposed project itself or the effects of the project on local subjectivities or relational and emotive connections to land. When mitigation cannot be accomplished, the proposed solution is often economic compensation, implying that trapping, hunting, and gathering plants and medicines are solely economic activities that have little or no connection to other realms of peoples' lives.

The state-driven assessment of extractive projects in the Sahtu and elsewhere raise[s] a series of important questions: How can environmental assessments account for the impacts of extractive industries in ways that reflect the moral relationships that Sahtu Dene people have with their land? In what ways does the assessment of extractive projects require a reconfiguration of how people talk about and define their relationships to the land? If regulators find no quantifiable evidence of risk, as most environmental assessments do, does this mean that there are "no significant impacts" on affected communities? And, if such impacts do exist, how do we place a value on the way of life of a people?

Source: Carly Dokis, Nipissing University, 2015. For more on this topic, see Dokis 2015.

The Role of Conflict in Material Life

Anthropologists traditionally have emphasized the important links between a society's organization (kinship groups, chiefdom, state) and the way that society meets its subsistence needs, either to demonstrate the stages of cultural evolution or to display the functional interrelationships between its parts. In both cases, however, the emphasis of the analysis has been on the harmonious fashion in which societies operate. For some observers, this carried the additional message that social stability was "natural" and should not be tampered with. Social change was possible, but it would take place in an orderly fashion, in the fullness of time, according to laws of development beyond the control of individual members of society.

Many anthropologists, however, have not been persuaded that social organization is naturally harmonious or that social change is naturally orderly. Instead, they tend to use Marxian approaches because these sorts of approaches recognize that conflict and disorder are a natural part of the human condition. The concept of mode of production makes a major contribution to economic anthropology precisely because it acknowledges that the potential for conflict is built into the mode of production itself. And the more complex and

↻ For more on the link between economic and political relations, see Chapter 13, p. 297.

consumption The using up of material goods necessary for human survival.

unequal the involvement of different classes in a mode of production, the more intense is the struggle between them likely to be. The links between economic and political relations become particularly obvious and must be addressed.

Why Do People Consume What They Do?

Consumption usually refers to the use of material goods necessary for human survival. These goods include—at a minimum—food, drink, clothing, and shelter; they can and often do include much more. Until quite recently, the study of consumption by economists and others has been much neglected, especially when compared to the study of distribution or production. It seemed clear either that people consume goods for obvious reasons (i.e., because they need to eat and drink to survive) or that they consume goods as a result of idiosyncratic personal preferences (e.g., "I like the flavour of licorice and so I eat a lot of it, but my neighbour hates the flavour and would never put it into his mouth"). In either case, studying consumption seemed unlikely to reveal any interesting cultural patterns. As we will see below, however, anthropologists have always noticed striking differences in consumption patterns in different societies that seemed hard to reconcile with accepted economic explanations. Historically, anthropologists have taken three basic approaches to account for these patterns: (1) the internal explanation, (2) the external explanation, and (3) the cultural explanation.

The Internal Explanation: Malinowski and Basic Human Needs

The internal explanation for human consumption patterns comes from the work of Bronislaw Malinowski. Malinowski's version of functionalist anthropology explains social practices by relating them to the basic human needs that each practice supposedly fulfills. Basic human needs can be biological or psychological. Whatever their origin, if these needs go unmet, Malinowski argued, a society might not survive. Malinowski (1944) proposed a list of basic human needs, which includes nourishment, reproduction, bodily comforts, safety, movement, growth, and health. Every culture responds in its own way to these needs with some form of the corresponding institutions: food-getting techniques, kinship, shelter, protection, activities, training, and hygiene (91).

Malinowski's approach had the virtue of emphasizing the dependence of human beings on the physical world in order to survive. In addition, Malinowski was able to show that many customs that appear bizarre to uninitiated Western observers make sense once it is seen how they help people satisfy their basic human needs. However, Malinowski's approach fell short of explaining why all societies do not share the same consumption patterns. After all, some people eat wild fruit and nuts and wear clothing made of animal skins, others eat bread made from domesticated wheat and wear garments woven from the hair of domesticated sheep, and still others eat millet paste and meat from domesticated cattle and go naked. Why should these differences exist?

The External Explanation: Cultural Ecology

A later generation of anthropologists was influenced by evolutionary and ecological studies. They tried to answer this question with an external explanation for the diversity of human consumption patterns. As we saw in earlier chapters, ecology has to do with how living species interact with one another and how they interact with their physical environment. To explain patterns of human consumption (as well as production and distribution), cultural ecologists tend to focus on the available resources in particular habitats that are exploited by particular human groups. Hence, the particular consumption patterns found in a particular society cannot depend just on the obvious, internal hunger drive, which is the same for all people everywhere; instead, people depend on the particular external resources present in the local habitat to which their members must adapt. Nicole Gombay's (2010) work with Inuit peoples in northern Quebec provides an excellent example of how a society has adapted to and thrived in a generally hostile environment (see the "In Their Own Words" box on making a living).

For a discussion on how archaeologists have used cultural ecology, see Chapter 8, p. 165.

In Their Own Words

Making a Living: Place, Food, and Economy in an Inuit Community

In her study among the Inuit of Puvirnituq in northern Quebec, Nicole Gombay considers the meaning of food in the context of the changing local economy.

The Inuit economy, until relatively recently, has operated according to altogether other means than the Western market economy. . . . In most instances, Inuit are well aware of the means by which their food was produced. Because of people's participation not only in the eating of food, but also in the getting and distributing of it, they are generally aware both of its importance to them and of their wish to preserve their capacities to continue participating in these processes. For many Inuit, these processes are tied to their way of life. The production, distribution, exchange, and consumption of food is closely linked to how they conceive of and construct the world around them. These conceptions reflect not simply the mechanical processes involved in procuring food, but are linked to larger cosmological notions about the nature of existence and the place of humans in the world. These, in turn, are linked to a host of other processes: ideas about the role of the

Continued

individual in relation to society, the experience of being in the elements rather than removed from them, notions of temporality and understandings of history grounded in place. An important component of these elements is that they developed and operated outside the market economy. Since time immemorial, without markets and without money, Inuit have managed to make a living and supply themselves with the necessities of life.

Try to imagine how you would have to live were you to be involved in producing everything you ate. Try to imagine how that would affect how you interacted with the world around you and how you spent your time. How would you relate to others and to the environment that provided you with food? How would you make your living? What would your day be filled with from morning to night, from season to season, from year to year? Then think about what happens when the market economy comes into the equation. How would all these things be affected when you no longer had to produce everything you ate but could buy your food? Where would you get the money? How would you spend your time? How would this change in your circumstances affect your concerns about the world around you? These questions are inherently economic, and are intimately tied to the quality of our lives.... They are the questions Inuit society is confronting, at a fundamental level.

For Inuit, the economy operates in two fundamental realms, neither of which is isolated from the other. First there is the local economic system that is a reflection of Inuit beliefs and ways of working. Such an economy has been called variously an "indigenous" economy or a "community" economy. Either term is used to describe economies that are related to systems that are linked to a specific place and its people. Such economies are often linked to the idea that people are barely surviving and has the effect of freezing the Inuit in time, preventing them from commercial development. For these reasons, I have chosen to use the term "vernacular" economy to identify the economy associated with the ideas, processes, social relations, values, and institutions that Inuit link to the products of hunting, fishing, and gathering. The term [acknowledges that the Inuit] are constantly changing, while at the same time implying that such change has a local flavour . . . and that important links exist between economy and place.

The second economic realm in which Inuit now function is the market system that came with the arrival of non-Inuit to their region. It is an economy in which transactions rely on money as a medium of exchange. Under a market economy, prices are self-regulating, which means that markets must be allowed to function

without interference. In the process, nature becomes interwoven with processes of commoditization as its products become fodder for the market. Each market exchange is discrete; there is no expectation that it will entail an ongoing social relationship. As a result, social relations become embedded in the economy rather than the economy being embedded in social relations.

These two economies, the market and the vernacular, have been operating in tandem—sometimes in apparent isolation, but in fact increasingly overlapping and mixing together, with the distinction between them becoming blurred. Inuit are not living in isolation from the market, but must come to terms with the fact that their economy exists within the market. The term that is commonly used to denote this is a "mixed economy," where each is connected to the other. At issue for the Inuit, though, is to understand what this means for them and how to make sense of the mixing. What I argue is that, to comprehend how the market economy interacts with the Inuit economy we must take into consideration how the Inuit recognize the importance of and how their values are linked to community and the social institutions that sustain it.

On the one hand, Inuit have expressed a desire to hold on to their traditions of hunting, fishing, and trapping. This has been at the root of all Inuit land claims negotiated in Canada. On the other hand, they are aware that their economies cannot rely solely on traditions of the past. They know they need money even to pursue the traditional elements of their economy. Bullets, rifles, gas, Ski-Doos, and canvas for tents, among other things, all cost money, and as far as money is concerned, one thing is clear: for many Inuit it is in short supply.

By southern standards, northern economies are based on a limited set of activities, so the options for gaining access to cash are few. Since the period of contact with Europeans, Inuit have earned cash through . . . the fur trade, whaling, the sale of arts and crafts, social transfer payments, and [limited] employment in and assortment of public and private ventures [e.g., public services, development activities]. These forms of income have generally proved either unsustainable or of limited impact, and are open only to a few....

One potential way to expand the sources of cash income has been to sell the produce from people's hunting, fishing, and gathering commonly referred to as "country foods." This has led to a meeting of the two economic systems, the market and the vernacular. In the past, these economies generally operated separately, and under quite different rules. The vernacular economy of Inuit is predicated on sharing, . . . [while the] market economy . . . is predicated on monetary exchange. . . . How does a local economic system adjust itself to a global economic system when each is predicated on different concepts of value . . . and different concepts of access to and control over resources? In selling country foods, Inuit are obliged to confront these questions and learn how to accommodate the influx of new ideas and ways of living with [traditional] concepts about how the world operates. They are not alone: in their encounters with the forces of globalization, vernacular economies the world over have had to make similar adjustments.

The Cultural Explanation of Consumption

Why do people *X* raise peanuts and sorghum? The internal, Malinowskian explanation would be to meet their basic human need for food. The external, cultural ecological explanation would be because peanuts and sorghum are the only food crops available in their habitat that, when cultivated, will meet their subsistence needs. Both these answers sound reasonable, but they are also incomplete. To be sure, people must consume something to survive, and they will usually meet this need by exploiting plant and animal species locally available. However, Malinowski and many cultural ecologists assume that patterns of consumption are dictated by the environment that a group lives in and that human beings are by and large powerless to modify what the environment offers (at least, it is sometimes implied, until the invention of modern technology).

But we have seen that human beings (along with many other organisms) are able to actively construct their own niches, buffering themselves from some kinds of selection pressures while exposing themselves to other kinds. This means that human populations, even those with foraging technologies, are not passive in the face of environmental demands. On the contrary, people have the agency to produce a range of cultural inventions—tools, social relations, domesticated crops, agroecologies, and so on.

The Original Affluent Society

Based on the perceptions of early colonial settlers, it was long believed by many Westerners that foraging peoples led the most miserable of existences, spending all their waking hours in a food quest that yielded barely enough to keep them alive. To test this assumption in the field, Canadian anthropologist Richard Lee, from the University of Toronto, went to live among the Dobe Ju/'hoansi, a foraging people of southern Africa (see EthnoProfile 10.1:

Ju/'hoansi). Living in the central Kalahari Desert of southern Africa in the early 1960s, the Ju/'hoansi of Dobe were among the few remaining groups of the San peoples who returned to full-time foraging when economic ties with neighbouring herders became too onerous. Although full-time foraging has been impossible in the Dobe area since the 1980s and the Ju/'hoansi have had to make some difficult adjustments, Lee documented a way of life that contrasts vividly with their current settled existence.

Lee accompanied the Ju/'hoansi as they gathered and hunted in 1963, and he recorded the amounts and kinds of food they consumed. The results of his research were surprising. It turned out that the Ju/'hoansi provided themselves with a varied and well-balanced diet based on a selection from among the food sources available in their environment. At the time of Lee's fieldwork, the Ju/'hoansi classified more than 100 species of plants as edible, but only 14 were primary components of their diet (Lee 1992, 45ff.). Some 70 per cent of this diet consisted of vegetable foods; 30 per cent was meat. Mongongo nuts, a protein-rich food widely available throughout the Kalahari, alone made up more than one-quarter of the diet. Women provided about 55 per cent of the diet, and men provided 45 per cent, including the meat. The Ju/'hoansi spent an average of 2.4 working days—or about 20 hours—per person per week in food-collecting activities. Ju/'hoansi bands periodically suffered from shortages of their preferred foods and were forced to consume less desired items. Most of the time, however, their diet was balanced and adequate and consisted of foods of preference (Lee 1992, 56ff.) (Figure 10.4).

Marshall Sahlins coined the expression "the original affluent society" to refer to the Ju/'hoansi and other foragers like them. In an essay published in 1972,

affluence The condition of having more than enough of whatever is required to satisfy consumption needs.

FIGURE 10.4 Ju/'hoansi women returning from foraging with large quantities of mongongo nuts.

Sahlins challenged the traditional Western assumption that the life of foragers is characterized by scarcity and near-starvation (see Sahlins 1972). **Affluence**, he argued, is having more than enough of whatever is required to satisfy consumption needs. There are two ways to create affluence. The first, to *produce much*, is the path taken by Western capitalist societies; the second, to *desire little*, is the option, Sahlins argues, that foragers have taken. Put another way, the Ju/'hoansi foragers used culture to construct a niche within which their wants were few but abundantly fulfilled by their local environment. Moreover, it is not that foragers experience no greedy impulses; rather, according to Sahlins, affluent foragers live in societies whose institutions do not reward greed. Sahlins concluded that, for these reasons, foragers should not be considered poor, although their material standard of living is low by Western measures.

Original affluent foraging societies emphasize the long-standing anthropological observation that the concept of economic "needs" is vague (Douglas and Isherwood 1979). Hunger can be satisfied by beans and rice or steak and lobster. Thirst can be quenched by water or beer or soda pop. In effect, human beings in differently constructed niches define needs and provide for their satisfaction according to their own *cultural* logic, which is reducible to neither biology nor psychology nor ecological pressure. In every case, the human need for food is met selectively, and the selection that humans make carries a social message. But what about cases of consumption that do not involve food and drink (e.g., consumption of wood to make ceremonial masks or paper to make money)?

Banana Leaves in the Trobriand Islands

Anthropologist Annette Weiner (1980) travelled to the Trobriand Islands in the 1970s, more than half a century after Malinowski carried out his classic research there. To her surprise, she discovered a venerable local tradition involving the accumulation and exchange of banana leaves, which were known locally as "women's wealth" (Figure 10.5). Malinowski had never described this tradition, even though there is evidence from photographs and writing that it was in force at the time of his fieldwork. Possibly, Malinowski overlooked these transactions because they are carried out by women, and Malinowski did not view women as important actors in the economy. However, Malinowski might also have

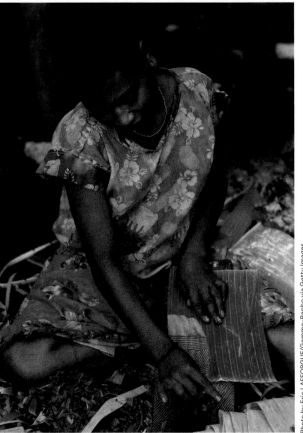

FIGURE 10.5 In the Trobriand Islands, women's wealth, made from banana leaves, is displayed during a funeral ritual called the *sagali*, which serves to reaffirm the status of the women's kinship group.

In Their Own Words

Fake Masks and Faux Modernity

Christopher Steiner addresses the perplexing situation all of us face in the contemporary multicultural world: given mass reproduction of commodities made possible by industrial capitalism, how can anybody distinguish "authentic" material culture from "fake" copies? The encounter he describes took place in Ivory Coast, western Africa.

In the Plateau market place, I once witnessed the following exchange between an African art trader and a young European tourist. The tourist wanted to buy a Dan face mask which he had selected from the trader's wooden trunk in the back of the market place. He had little money, he said, and was trying to barter for the mask by exchanging his Seiko wrist watch. In his dialogue with the trader, he often expressed his concern about whether or not the mask was "real." Several times during the bargaining, for example, the buyer asked the seller, "Is it really old?" and "Has it been worn?" While the tourist questioned the trader about the authenticity of the mask, the trader, in turn, questioned the tourist about the authenticity of his watch. "Is this the real kind of Seiko," he asked, "or is it a copy?" As the tourist examined the mask—turning it over and over again looking for the worn and weathered effects of time—the trader scrutinized the watch, passing it to other traders to get their opinion on its authenticity.

Although, on one level, the dialogue between tourist and trader may seem a bit absurd, it points to a deeper problem in modern transnational commerce: an anxiety over authenticity and a crisis of misrepresentation. While the shelves in one section of the Plateau market place are lined with replicas of so-called "traditional" artistic forms, the shelves in another part of the market place—just on the other side of the street—are stocked with imperfect imitations of modernity: counterfeit Levi jeans, fake Christian Dior belts, and pirated recordings of Michael Jackson and Madonna. Just as the Western buyer looks to Africa for authentic symbols of a "primitive" lifestyle, the African buyer looks to the West for authentic symbols of a modern lifestyle. In both of their searches for the "genuine" in each other's culture, the African trader and the Western tourist often find only mere approximations of "the real thing"—tropes of authenticity which stand for the riches of an imagined reality.

Source: Steiner 1994, 128–9.

For more on the Trobriand Islanders, see EthnoProfile 16.2 on p. 388.

The different forms of descent, including patrilineal, matrilineal, and bilateral, are described in detail in Chapter pp. 263–70.

considered banana leaves to be an unlikely item of consumption because he recognized as "economic" only those activities that satisfied biological survival needs, and banana leaves are inedible. Transactions involving women's wealth, however, turn out to be crucial for the stability of Trobrianders' relationships to their relatives.

Banana leaves might be said to have a "practical" use because women make skirts out of them but these skirts are also highly valued. Why bother to exchange great amounts of money or other goods to obtain bundles of banana leaves? This would seem to be a classic example of irrational consumption. However, the value of these "bunches of leaves" is linked to the most fundamental relationships in their social system: their kinship system (Weiner 1980).

Trobrianders are *matrilineal* (i.e., they trace descent through women; see Chapter 12), and men traditionally prepare yam gardens for their sisters. After the harvest, yams from these gardens are distributed by a woman's brother to her husband. Weiner's research suggests that what Malinowski took to be the *redistribution* of yams, from a wife's kin to her husband, could be better understood as a *reciprocal exchange* of yams for women's wealth. The parties central to this exchange are a woman, her brother, and her husband. The woman is the person through whom yams are passed from her own kin to her husband and through whom women's wealth is passed from her husband to her own kin.

Transactions involving women's wealth occur when someone in a woman's kinship group dies. Surviving relatives must "buy back," metaphorically speaking, all the yams or other goods that the deceased person gave to others during his or her lifetime. Each payment marks a social link between the deceased and the recipient, and the size of the payment marks the importance of their relationship. All the payments must be made in women's wealth.

The dead person's status, as well as the status of her or his family, depends on the size and number of the payments made; and the people who must be paid can number into the hundreds. Women make women's wealth themselves and exchange store goods to obtain wealth from other women, but when someone in their matrilineage dies, they collect it from their husbands. Indeed, a woman's value is measured by the amount of women's wealth her husband provides. Furthermore,

> if a man does not work hard enough for his wife in accumulating wealth for her, then her brother will not increase his labour in the yam garden. . . . The production in yams and women's wealth is always being evaluated and calculated in terms of effort and energy expended on both sides of production. The value of a husband is read by a woman's kin as the value of his productive support in securing women's wealth for his wife. (Weiner 1980, 282)

Weiner argues that women's wealth upholds the kinship arrangements of Trobriand society. It balances out exchange relationships between lineages linked by marriage, reinforces the pivotal role of women and matriliny, and publicly proclaims, during every funeral, the social relationships that make up the fabric of Trobriand society. The system has been stable for generations, but Weiner suggests that it could collapse if cash ever became widely substitutable for yams. Under such conditions, men might buy food and other items on the market. If they no longer depended on yams from their wives' kin, they might refuse to supply their wives' kin with women's wealth. This had not yet happened at the time of Weiner's research, but she saw it as a possible future development.

How Consumption Is Being Studied Today

The foregoing examples focus attention on distinctive consumption practices in different societies and demonstrate that the Western market is not the only way to measure the value of goods. These studies represent alternative consumption practices that, in different times and places, have worked as well as or better than capitalist markets to define needs and provide goods to satisfy those needs. But many anthropologists also recognize how Western colonialism has regularly undermined such alternatives, attempting to replace them with new needs and goods defined by the capitalist market. At the beginning of the twenty-first century, however, the consumption of market commodities occurs everywhere in the world. Moreover, not only are Western commodities sometimes embraced by those we might have expected to reject them (e.g., video technology by Indigenous peoples of the Amazon), but this embrace frequently involves making use of these commodities for local purposes, to defend or to enrich local culture, rather than to replace it.

Daniel Miller (1995) has therefore urged anthropologists to recognize that these new circumstances require that they move beyond a narrow focus on the destructive potential of mass-produced commodities to a broader recognition of the role commodities play in a globalizing world. But this shift does not mean that concern about the negative consequences of capitalist practices disappears. In a global world in which everyone everywhere increasingly relies on commodities provided by a capitalist market, one must consider how unsustainable this system is as the population of the world continues to grow. (For a contemporary example that relates to many of these themes, see the "In Their Own Words" box in this chapter on changing natures and economies among the Dene people of the Northwest Territories.)

The Anthropology of Food

The anthropology of food is a recent field of study undertaken by economic anthropologists and tends to focus on the way the global capitalist food market works and the influence of political forces on how food is produced, distributed, and accessed around the world. For example, Alan and Josephine Smart (2011) of the University of Calgary have investigated how quarantines, health inspections, and import bans have been used as political tools to control the transport of beef across international borders, especially in North America. At the same time, exploring links between food and culture in a globally complex world reveals the many ways different kinds of food and cooking can be embraced by different groups in society to bolster their gender, sexual, racial, ethnic, class, or national identities.

FIGURE 10.6 Tuscan women making pasta in a farm kitchen.

Carole Counihan is a pioneering anthropologist of food. Beginning in 1970, she lived and worked in Italy for 14 years. During this time she developed a "long-term relationship with a Florentine I call Leonardo" and most of the data for her book *Around the Tuscan Table* (Counihan 2004) comes "from 56 hours of food-centered life histories tape-recorded in Italian with Leonardo's 23 living relatives in 1982–84" (2).

Counihan began collecting food-centred life histories from women but eventually collected them from men as well. Because these life histories came from individuals from different generations, they reflected historical changes in the political economy of food that had shaped the lives of her interview subjects over time. For example, situating the food memories of the oldest members of her sample required reconstructing the traditional *mezzadria* sharecropping system in Tuscany. This system was based on large landholdings worked by peasant labourers whose households were characterized by a strict division of labour by gender: the patriarch (male head of the family) managed food production in the fields, and his wife supervised food preparation for the large extended family. The *mezzadria* system would disappear in the early twentieth century, but it constituted the foundation of Tuscan food practices that would follow. Counihan's interviewees ate a so-called "Mediterranean" diet consisting of "pasta, fresh vegetables, legumes, olive oil, bread, and a little meat or

fish" (2004, 7) (Figure 10.6). Food was scarce in the first part of the twentieth century but more abundant after World War II.

Food-centred life histories from Counihan's oldest interviewees traced nearly a century of changing Tuscan food practices and revealed, surprisingly, older people's nostalgia for the more constrained patterns of food consumption in their youth:

> When my older subjects were young before and during the Second World War, consumption was highly valued because it was scarce and precarious. Yet their children, born after the war in the context of the Italian economic miracle, grew up in a world where consumption was obligatory, taken for granted, and essential to full personhood—a transformation lamented by older people. (Counihan 2004, 5)

Even as Counihan's research documents continuities in Tuscan diet and cuisine, it also demonstrates the way deeply rooted consumption practices were upended by the Italian state under Mussolini in the 1920s and 1930s and by the international cataclysm of World War II. As this example demonstrates, economic life cannot be considered apart from political relations in any society, which will be further discussed in Chapter 13.

Chapter Summary

1. Contemporary cultural and economic anthropologists are interested in how cultures change, but they are suspicious of evolutionary schemes that give the impression that social arrangements could not have been—or could not be—other than the way they are. They also point out that no society anywhere is static. The power that human beings have to reproduce or to change their social organization is an important focus of anthropological study. Anthropological approaches can provide insights often overlooked by other disciplines.

2. Human economic activity is usefully divided into three phases—production, distribution, and consumption—and is often shaped in important ways by storage practices. Formal neoclassical economic theory developed in Europe to explain how capitalism works, and it emphasizes the importance of market exchange. Economic anthropologists have shown that non-capitalist societies regularly relied on non-market modes of exchange, such as reciprocity and redistribution, which still play restricted roles in societies dominated by the capitalist market.

3. Marxian economic anthropologists view production as more important than exchange in determining the patterns of economic life in a society. They classify societies in terms of their modes of production. Each mode of production contains within it the potential for conflict between classes of people who receive differential benefits and losses from the productive process.

4. In the past, some anthropologists tried to explain consumption patterns in different societies either by arguing that people produce material goods to satisfy basic human needs or by connecting consumption patterns to specific material resources available to people in the material settings where they lived. Ethnographic evidence demonstrates that both these explanations are inadequate because they ignore how culture defines our needs and provides for their satisfaction according to its own logic.

5. Particular consumption preferences that may seem irrational from the viewpoint of neoclassical economic theory may make sense when the wider cultural practices of consumers are taken into consideration. In the twenty-first century, those whom Western observers might have expected to reject Western market commodities often embrace them, frequently making use of them to defend or enrich their local culture rather than to replace it. In a global world in which everyone everywhere increasingly relies on commodities—including food—provided by a capitalist market, some anthropologists focus on inequalities of access and the negative impact of contemporary economic institutions on most of the world's population.

For Review

1. Explain the connection between culture and livelihood. Create a table with the differing forms of subsistence strategies, and outline their different modes of production.

2. Visit "The Story of Stuff Project" (http://storyof-stuff.org/movies/story-of-stuff). Then, create a flow chart that shows the steps of production, distribution, and consumption for an article of clothing you own. Note any international connections in your flow chart. What do these connections suggest about the modes of production operating in today's world?

3. Explain the significance of food storage and food sharing in economic activity.

4. Discuss the role of distribution in capitalism as explained by neoclassical economics.

5. According to Eric Wolf's definition of *mode of production* (see p. 221), what mode of production is in use in Canada today? Compare and contrast the Canadian mode of production with the other modes listed by Wolf in this chapter.

6. Consider Marxian approaches to economic theory and explain why these are favoured in anthropology.

7. Explain the complex interchange that occurs in Northern Quebec between the Inuit economy and the Western one, according to Nicole Gombay. Discuss which of the modes of exchange are at work in each economy.

8. Which of the three explanations of consumption do you agree with? Why?

9. Outline the key elements in Marshall Sahlins's argument about "the original affluent society." Do you agree with Sahlins? Why or why not?

10. This chapter offers two case studies on how consumption is culturally patterned: one about the Dobe Ju/'hoansi as the original affluent society, and one about the significance of banana leaves to the Trobriand Islanders. Explain how each of these case studies illuminates the cultural construction of human needs.

11. Discuss the connections between culture and food in Italy, as presented by Carole Counihan.

Key Terms

affluence   227
capitalism   216
commodities   218
commodity exchanges   218
consumption   224
economic anthropology   214
food collectors   214

food producers   214
gift   218
gift exchanges   218
institutions   217
labour   221
market exchange   219
means of production   221

mode of production   221
modes of exchange   218
neoclassical economics   217
reciprocity   218
redistribution   218
relations of production   221
social organization   214

References

Barker, John. 2016. *Ancestral Lines: The Maisin of Papua New Guinea and the Fate of the Rainforest.* Toronto: University of Toronto Press.

Counihan, Carole M. 2004. *Around the Tuscan Table: Food, Family, and Gender in Twentieth-Century Florence.* New York: Routledge.

Dokis, Carly. 2015. *Where the Rivers Meet: Pipelines, Participatory Resource Management, and Aboriginal–State Relations in the Northwest Territories.* Vancouver: UBC Press.

Douglas, Mary, and Baron Isherwood. 1979. *The World of Goods: Towards an Anthropology of Consumption.* New York: W.W. Norton.

Gombay, Nicole. 2010. *Making a Living: Place, Food, and Economy in an Inuit Community.* Saskatoon, SK: Purich Publishing.

Hann, Chris, and Keith Hart. 2011. *Economic Anthropology: History, Ethnography, Critique.* Malden, MA: Polity Press.

Lee, Richard B. 1992. *The Dobe Ju/'hoansi.* 2nd ed. New York: Holt, Rinehart, and Winston.

Malinowski, Bronislaw. 1944. *A Scientific Theory of Culture and Other Essays.* Oxford: Oxford University Press.

Mauss, Marcel. [1950] 2000. *The Gift: The Form and Reason for Exchange in Archaic Societies.* New York: W.W. Norton.

Miller, Daniel. 1995. "Consumption and Commodities." *Annual Review of Anthropology* 24: 141–61.

Polanyi, Karl. 1977. *The Livelihood of Man.* New York: Academic Press.

Rosman, Abraham, and Paula G. Rubel. 1971. *Feasting with Mine Enemy: Rank and Exchange among Northwest Coast Societies.* New York: Columbia University Press.

Sahlins, Marshall. 1972. *Stone Age Economics.* Chicago: Aldine.

Smart, Alan, and Josephine Smart. 2011. "(Im)mobilizing Technology: Slow Science, Food Safety, and Borders," *Identities: Global Studies in Culture and Power* 18 (6): 529–50.

Steiner, Christopher. 1994. *African Art in Transit.* Cambridge: Cambridge University Press.

Weiner, Annette. 1980. "Stability in Banana Leaves: Colonization and Women in Kiriwina, Trobriand Islands." In *Women and Colonization: Anthropological Perspectives,* edited by Mona Etienne and Eleanor Leacock, 270–93. New York: Praeger.

Wilk, Richard. 1996. *Economies and Cultures: Foundations of Economic Anthropology.* Boulder, CO: Westview Press.

——, and Lisa Cliggett. 2007. *Economies and Cultures: Foundations of Economic Anthropology.* Boulder, CO: Westview Press.

Wolf, Eric. 1982. *Europe and the People without History.* Berkeley: University of California Press.

▲ *Muxes* (considered a third gender in Indigenous Zapotec culture) take part in the traditional procession during the Muxes Festival in Juchitán, Mexico. *Muxes* represents those who identify differently from the gender they were assigned at birth.
Photo: Jan Sochor/Getty Images

11 What Can Anthropology Teach Us about Sex, Gender, and Sexuality?

Chapter Outline

Cultural anthropologists have been interested in sex, gender, and sexuality since the beginnings of anthropology as a discipline, but their preferred approaches to these topics have changed over time, along with broader theoretical developments in the discipline and wider historical shifts in the world. This chapter focuses primarily on perspectives and concepts that have developed since the 1960s and 1970s in Euro-American sociocultural anthropology. However, scholarship and activism on issues surrounding sex, gender, and sexuality extend far beyond the discipline of anthropology. As a result, anthropologists and other social scientists have shared perspectives and borrowed concepts from one another. The result, for sociocultural anthropologists, has been the production of a vast and expanding body of ethnographic research exploring sex, gender, and sexuality both in Euro-American societies and in societies outside the Western world. (See Map 11.1 for a map of societies mentioned in this chapter.)

How Did Twentieth-Century Feminism Shape the Anthropological Study of Sex, Gender, and Sexuality?

Twentieth-century feminism has been responsible for a series of pivotal transformations in social science scholarship. **Feminism** argues that women and men are equally human and therefore that women are entitled to enjoy the same rights and privileges as men. As a social movement in North America, the first wave of feminism emerged in the nineteenth century, but after women in Canada obtained the right to vote in the early twentieth century, the struggle for women's rights lost momentum. However, by the 1960s and 1970s, in the wake of the Civil Rights Movement, a second-wave feminist movement rose up, challenging many remaining forms of inequality between men and women. Second-wave feminists pointed out that even though Western societies were supposed to be democratic, and women now had the right to vote, many domains of social life continued to be organized in terms of **patriarchy**—that is, by the domination of men over women and children.

Feminists coined the term **sexism** (based on an analogy with racism) to describe the systematic sociocultural structures and practices of inequality, derived from patriarchal institutions, that continue to shape relations between women and men. As with racism, sexism was seen to involve more than prejudiced individual

beliefs alone; as a result, achieving full equality between women and men was understood to require not only changing beliefs but also dismantling patriarchal institutions and practices.

A rallying cry for many second-wave feminists was that "the personal is political." These feminists confronted the **public/private divide**, a barrier that law and custom had erected between "private" domestic life in the family, conceived as "women's place," and public life, outside the family, conceived as the domain of men.

Feminists pointed out that women were oppressed by domestic forms of patriarchy that were considered "private" and, thus, understood to be matters beyond the "public" reach of the law. Ostensibly, women's husbands and fathers both looked after women's interests within private, male-headed households and protected women from the harsh effects of the public, male domain. However, women who sought education or employment outside the home, or who lacked husbands or private homes altogether, found themselves at the mercy of

feminism The theory that women and men are equally human and therefore that women are entitled to enjoy the same rights and privileges as men.

patriarchy The domination of men over women and children.

sexism The systematic sociocultural structures and practices of inequality, derived from patriarchal institutions, that continue to shape relations between women and men (based on an analogy with racism).

public/private divide A barrier that laws and customs erected between "private" domestic life in the family, conceived as "women's place," and public life, outside the family, conceived as the domain of men.

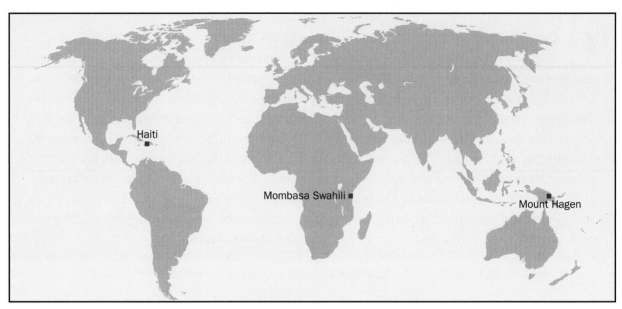

MAP 11.1 Location of societies whose EthnoProfiles appear in Chapter 11.

hostile public institutions that regularly discriminated against them. At the same time, women who stayed at home were not guaranteed protection because the public/private divide allowed men to evade legal accountability for physically abusing the women living in their private households. Indeed, feminist activism around the issue of spousal abuse spurred second-wave feminists to create a battered-women's movement, which has now become global (Merry 2003).

Feminist struggles in their own societies prompted some anthropologists to rethink many long-held assumptions about the contributions of women to human culture. Feminist anthropologists noted that most ethnographies, including those written by women, were based primarily on the views of male informants, even concerning matters pertaining to women. Thus, most discussions of "the culture" of a group in fact portrayed culture from the viewpoint of men (often high-status men). When women were discussed at all, it was usually in the context of marriage and the family, and the assumption seemed to be that women's cultural roles as wives and mothers followed "naturally" from the biological facts of pregnancy and lactation. However, Margaret Mead's demonstration in the 1930s of the lack of correlation between biological sex and culturally expected behaviours of males and females in society was

a well-known exception to this pattern (Figure 11.1). Building on Mead's work, it became commonplace for cultural anthropologists to use the term *sex* to refer to the physical characteristics that distinguish males from females (for example, body shape, distribution of body hair, reproductive organs, sex chromosomes).

By contrast, anthropologists used the term *gender* to refer to the culturally constructed roles assigned to males or females, which varied considerably from society to society. The distinction between sex and gender was an important theoretical breakthrough, and it became widely adopted by anthropologists and other social scientists. At the same time, the sex/gender distinction seemed to take for granted that even if there seemed to be a demonstrable lack of correlation between physical sex and the content of gender roles, all societies universally distinguished women from men. Such a dual categorization has been called a **gender binary**.

By the 1970s, some feminist anthropologists were concerned that both the gender binary and male domination of females might be universal. At that time, no persuasive evidence had been found to suggest that there had ever been societies organized as *matriarchies*—that is, societies where women as a group dominated men as a group. Today we know that this is not the case; there may have been matriarchies in the Mayan culture, which is discussed in the research by Kathryn Reese-Taylor et al. (2009) on the role of Mayan queens (see Chapter 12).

In 1974, Sherry Ortner published an article with the title "Is Female to Male as Nature Is to Culture?" Her

gender binary A dual gender categorization separating all women from all men.

FIGURE 11.1 Cross–cultural research repeatedly demonstrates that physical indicators of sex difference do not allow us to predict the roles that females or males may play in any particular society. In Otavalo, Ecuador, men were traditionally weavers (a), while traditional Tzotzil weavers were women (b).

answer at that time was yes. Her survey of a wide range of ethnographic and historical evidence suggested to her that male dominance was rooted in a universal form of binary thinking that opposed male to female, associated males with culture and females with nature, and valued culture over nature, regardless of the actual activities performed by men and women in a society. At best, women might be seen as *mediating* between culture and nature, but women were always seen as closer to nature than men, perhaps because women's bodies were so obviously bound up with the "natural" processes of pregnancy, childbirth, and lactation.

Ortner's rather pessimistic conclusion was challenged by other feminist anthropologists who adopted Marxian perspectives, looking beyond symbolic systems of culture to consider male domination in the context of wider social, political, and economic processes. Gayle Rubin (1975) argued that these wider processes shaped each society's particular "sex/gender system," and Eleanor Leacock (1983) argued that cases of male dominance in contemporary societies were less likely to reflect the original human condition than they were to show forms of institutionalized gender inequality influenced by the spread of capitalism. Leacock used ethnographic and historical evidence from North America and South America, Melanesia, and Africa to show how Western capitalist colonization had transformed egalitarian precolonial Indigenous gender relations into unequal, male-dominated gender relations.

British social anthropologist Marilyn Strathern encountered further complexities when, as a second-wave feminist, she first went to Mount Hagen, in New Guinea

(EthnoProfile 11.1). In the 1970s and 1980s, some ethnographers working in New Guinea were suggesting that in New Guinea, as elsewhere, males dominated females in order to control the reproductive powers of women. This interpretation was supported by the views of influential French anthropologist Claude Lévi-Strauss, who claimed that linguistic communication, marriage negotiations, and economic transactions were all forms of exchange controlled by men. Indeed, he argued, women were the most valuable exchange good of all (Figure 11.2).

In *The Gender of the Gift* (1988), Strathern challenged this interpretation, arguing that by imposing Western ideas of this kind on Melanesian cultural practices, Western anthropologists had misunderstood Melanesian

---

EthnoProfile 11.1

Mount Hagen

Region: Southeastern Asia

Nation: Papua New Guinea (western highlands)

Population: 75,000 (1960s)

Environment: Forested mountain slopes, grassy plains

Livelihood: Farming, pig raising

Political organization: Traditionally, some men of influence but no coercive power; today, part of a modern nation-state

For more information: Strathern, Marilyn. 1972. *Women in Between*. London: Academic Press.

FIGURE 11.2 Women working a field in Mount Hagen, Papua New Guinea.

gender relations. Western anthropologists had assumed that Western notions of *individuality* were universal; that is, that in all human societies, every human individual comes into the world as a self-contained, autonomous being with a unique identity. However, each Melanesian person is seen as being made up of parts contributed by relatives who were responsible for their coming into the world. These components persist and continue to connect them to their kin over the course of a lifetime. Importantly, these kin are both male and female, which means that every Melanesian has some male parts and some female parts, and Melanesians are best understood as **androgynous** rather than as either uniquely male or uniquely female.

What difference does it make to begin with an understanding of humans as androgynous individuals rather than as autonomous individuals divided into two "natural" kinds by a universal gender binary? In Melanesian societies, does it even make sense to talk about such phenomena as "male dominance" or "female submission"? Strathern concluded that even though Melanesians understood gender very differently than Euro-Americans, certain features of traditional Melanesian gender relations nevertheless produced forms of imbalance that tend to favour males over females.

androgyny A condition in which an individual person possesses both male and female characteristics.

men's studies/masculinities Research that focuses on the many different ways of being a man that can be identified in different places and times.

While neither men nor women were permanently subjugated to the will of the other gender, "men engaged with other men in the management of large-scale ceremonial exchanges from which women were excluded which may lead to men dominating women" (1988, 336). Melanesian women do not experience gender solidarity in ritual contexts and cannot count on other women to support them.

How Do Anthropologists Organize the Study of Sex, Gender, and Sexuality?

In the decades that followed the emergence of second-wave feminism, cross-disciplinary collaboration (and debate) about sex, gender, and sexuality diversified, both theoretically and substantively. One practical consequence has been ongoing discussion about what, in fact, the "field" should be called. Although terms such as *feminist anthropology* are still used by some (e.g., Lewin 2006), other scholars prefer to locate their work within the field of *women's studies*. In part, this reflects objections raised in connection with the association of "feminism" with the white, middle-class perspectives of many second-wave feminists; some women of colour have preferred to describe their analyses as *womanist* rather than *feminist* to emphasize the distinctiveness of the challenges faced by women who do not enjoy white, middle-class privileges. Many anthropologists and other social scientists have supported the move to combine the study of women, men, sex, gender, and sexuality in an inclusive field called *gender studies*. At the same time, not all women's studies scholars—anthropologists among them—have been convinced that folding women's studies into gender studies was a good move to make. They are concerned that sinking women's studies into gender studies cannot but dilute the attention paid to serious issues that women continue to face. This disagreement remains unresolved, its consequences visible in the many different names given to departments and programs in different universities that specialize in the study of women, men, sex, gender, and sexuality.

In any case, if one thinks of gender identities as parts of a larger "sex/gender system," studying women or men in isolation becomes immediately problematic. In fact, scholarship by anthropologists and other social scientists contributed to the growth of **men's studies** alongside women's studies; and just as women's studies scholars had found that there were many ways of being a woman, so too men's studies scholars identified a range of different ways of being a man, in different places and times; these were called different **masculinities**.

Early efforts to understand masculinities in Western societies stressed large-scale structures of domination and subordination, not only of women to men, but of some men to other men. The starkness of earlier approaches has been replaced by more nuanced understandings of how men in different societies engage with ideas and practices concerning masculinity, in our own and other parts of the world. Indeed, recent ethnography shows not only how men's ideas about masculinity vary cross-culturally, but how their views and practices change over time, both in the society itself and in the course of individual lifetimes. Ethnographic studies of issues affecting women far outnumber ethnographic studies of men and masculinities in different societies, but this is changing, leading to new empirical discoveries and theoretical innovations.

One example is the work of Marcia Inhorn, a medical anthropologist whose work in the Middle East began in the 1980s, with studies of how Egyptians coped with infertility. At that time, she found that many men were unwilling to accept publicly that they (and not their wives) were responsible for the couple's infertility, and their wives were willing to protect their husbands by not challenging this description. Inhorn (2012) also knew that a Muslim husband was traditionally considered justified should he choose to divorce an infertile wife. Nevertheless, she also found that Egyptian men of all social classes rarely exercised this option, remaining for many years in childless marriages with wives whom they loved, and who loved them. Inhorn called this phenomenon *conjugal connectivity*: "In the late 1980s, this was my first evidence that men were changing in the Middle East and . . . changing society with them" (58) (Figure 11.3).

In subsequent research, Inhorn has been able to challenge many stereotypes about Middle Eastern men that became further exaggerated following the 11 September 2001 terrorist attacks in New York City. She observes that these stereotypes are not only the product of Western media and ethnographies written (mostly) by men; they also draw on ideas expressed by Middle Eastern feminist scholars and on negative self-stereotypes that some Middle Eastern men themselves continue to hold. Key features of these stereotypes include the idea that Middle Eastern men all aspire to be family patriarchs who dominate their wives and children; that they are quick to defend family honour to the point of killing individuals, especially women, whom they believe have shamed their family; that they prefer to live together with other men who are related to them in the male line; and, finally, that their female kin *"buy into patriarchy."* This stereotype further insists that Middle Eastern women are estranged from their husbands because their marriages are arranged, because husbands are permitted to have multiple wives, and because wives are expected to produce many children, which in turn requires husbands to display extreme sexual potency. Large patriarchal families are supposed to contribute to "tribalism"—primary loyalty to the tribe over other political entities, such as the state. Tribal conflicts are said to promote violence and militarism, which is said to be reinforced by Islam, a religion that is regularly portrayed as promoting gender inequality and encouraging fanaticism to the point of waging *jihad*, or "holy war," against non-Muslims.

Inhorn forcefully rejects this composite stereotype of Middle Eastern men (2012). Even if some features of this caricature "may, at times and in certain places, be 'true' to the lives of some men," Inhorn points out that data she has gathered over the past 20 years demonstrate, on the contrary, that "masculinities in the Middle East, as elsewhere, are plural, diverse, locally situated, historically contingent and socially constructed" (2012, 50–1). Indeed, her research shows that Middle Eastern

Photo by Linda Davidson/The Washington Post via Getty Images

FIGURE 11.3 Contemporary practices of conjugal connectivity undermine patriarchal stereotypes about the ways Middle Eastern men relate to their wives and families. This political activist in Bahrain spends time with his wife and children every weekend.

men are coming to enact new kinds of masculinity, which she called *emergent masculinities,* that recognize the change in a male's life as men age: "change over the generations as male youth grow to adulthood; and changes in social history that involve men in transformative social processes (e.g., male labour migration, the rise of companionate marriage, the introduction of computers and the Internet into homes and workplaces)" (2012, 60). Practices of connectivity are part of emergent masculinities in the Middle East, as are the following:

> Men's desire to date their partners before marriage, men's acceptance of condoms and vasectomy as forms of male birth control, men's desires to live in nuclear family residences with their wives and children, and men's encouragement of daughters' education. All of these masculine practices are, in fact, emerging in the Middle East, but are rarely noticed by scholars or media pundits. (2012, 60)

It is precisely these kinds of emergent masculinities that Inhorn has encountered in her work on male infertility in Egypt, Lebanon, and the United Arab Emirates. Inhorn locates her research within the anthropology of science, technology, and medicine, a burgeoning field of anthropology we introduced in Chapter 1, which has taken the anthropological perspective and ethnographic methods into scientific laboratories, medical clinics, and hospitals in order to study the way that new technologies are being adopted by, and reshaping the lives of, people all over the world. Middle Eastern men are no exception, and the focus of anthropologists, including Inhorn, is on how assisted reproductive technology is becoming entangled with Middle Eastern cultural practices involving gender, religion, and family.

For further discussion about patrilineages, see Chapter 12, p. 267.

The concept of emergent masculinities is valuable because it has the potential to undermine toxic and inaccurate gender stereotypes about men, while providing more accurate understandings of how men remake their ways of being men under changing circumstances. Such efforts can also be seen in medical anthropologist Emily Wentzell's (2013) work with male patients in the urology ward of a hospital in Cuernavaca, Mexico, between 2007 and 2008.

Male sexual potency, and the ability of a man to engage in penetrative sex, has played a central role in traditional understandings of Mexican manhood, which is why the loss of this ability can be so threatening to a Mexican man. At the same time, Mexican masculinity has been negatively stereotyped in ways that compare with the toxic stereotypes of Middle Eastern men described by Inhorn. The Mexican stereotype, however, is rooted in a different culture and history. In Mexico, as elsewhere in Latin America, masculinity is traditionally defined in terms of practices associated with *machismo*—literally, "maleness." These practices include displays of aggression, an obsession with virility, and lack of emotional openness. In Mexico, the origin of this set of masculine traits is traditionally associated with the Spanish conquistadors, whose rape of Indigenous women is said to have produced *la raza* (the "race") of Mexicans who possess mixed European and Indigenous ancestry. Many of the men Wentzell spoke with agreed that traits associated with *machismo* have been passed on to subsequent generations of Mexican men. At the same time, they were often critical of these traits, either in themselves or in other men (such as their fathers), and were struggling to assert new ways of being Mexican men who were free of such traits. This was especially the case for younger married men, who were revising their ideas about family life and relations with their wives, in response to many of the same globalizing processes that Inhorn detected in the Middle East.

Older men—working-class men in particular—had grown up attempting to perform masculinity in ways that matched the traditional stereotype. This had meant, for many of them, expressing virility by pursuing many women, refusing to be faithful to their wives, drinking alcohol to excess, and working hard. Many believed that as long as they continued to be good providers—taking care of wives and children economically—they were fulfilling their duty as husbands and fathers. Their wives and children did not always agree. And when age and ill health began to undermine their ability to pursue sexual affairs or earn money, they were challenged to reconsider what it meant to be a man.

The older men Wentzell spoke with, however, were not faced with an either-or choice. Instead, they inventoried the various attributes they associated with an acceptable Mexican performance of manhood and deleted or replaced some attributes in response to the changing circumstances of their lives. For instance, a 68-year-old

In Their Own Words

The Consequences of Being a Woman

Bonnie L. Hewlett is an anthropologist who has spent many years working with women in the Central African Republic, women who told her they wanted to tell her their stories. One of these women she calls Blondine. Blondine tells of her marriage.

After Issa [her first husband] left, my second husband, Levi, saw me and wanted to marry me. He spoke so much he had no saliva in his mouth! I loved my second husband Levi. It was a good marriage, but over a long time I came to lose respect for my husband. The most important feeling in a marriage is respect. If you love your husband, you show him respect. But after some time of marriage, if he drank a lot of *embacko* [moonshine], he hit me. One time my friend heard the fighting and she came and said, "Why are you hitting your wife? Stop this!" After a few years in the marriage, Levi would drink and he'd talk and talk and yell and start fights. Sometimes I'd yell back, but most times I kept quiet until he fell asleep. Levi also neglected me, but not like the first husband, Issa. Levi searched for another wife. He did not ask me. I thought, "This can't be, not yet." If he had asked me before, if he had said, "My wife, can I search for another wife?" and explained to me, I would have said yes. But he married another woman and neglected me. He did not give me money or food and spent most of his nights with his other wife. I was so mad because he did not ask. I hit him. When Levi brought in the second wife, I hit her too. One time a man will look for another wife. Maybe because the other woman is beautiful and he says to himself, "I will marry her." If he tells the first wife, "Is it okay? She can help you with your work," then sometimes it is good to have two wives. The second wife becomes like a sister and respects the first wife. If they both have a good heart, they work together in the fields and help each other with the work in the house and it is good. But if the second wife is not obedient and respectful, then there is war.

After much hitting and fighting, we tried to reconcile and for a while we lived together, but when the second wife came, our husband said, "You two wives! Do not fight!!" When she'd come we worked together and prepared food for the family and we'd eat together. But then Levi began to neglect me. He slept too much with the second wife and bought her clothes and shoes and not me. I grabbed him by the neck and said, "My husband! Why do you not sleep with me? Tonight it is my turn!" When he came into the second wife's bedroom one night I grabbed his neck and said, "No! You sleep with me, not her!" If the husband organizes it good, it works so well! But if he does not, if he sleeps three nights with one and two nights with the other it does not work! Even so, when I heard them speak on the bed at night to each other, I listened and it made me so angry! I was jealous. I suffered and because of his neglect I divorced him. After Levi left, life was so difficult. I was alone with two children.

Source: Hewlett 2013, 163–4.

man whom Wentzell calls Johnny considered himself to have been both economically and sexually successful, working as a chef in the United States and engaging in penetrative sex with many women other than his wife. When Wentzell met him, however, he was in the hospital, facing the surgical removal of his cancerous penis. Prior to the surgery, Johnny was despondent, convinced that his manhood would disappear when his penis was removed. After the surgery, however, his mood was much more positive.

Johnny's loss of his penis was extreme. But many other older men Wentzell met, experiencing aging, illness, and increasing erectile difficulty, had similar worries about losing their manhood. In their cases, one possible solution might have been drugs like Viagra, Cialis, or Levitra, which, at the time of Wentzell's research, were being heavily marketed in Mexico as medication to treat what was coming to be called "erectile dysfunction," or ED. Wentzell initially thought that such drugs would have been seized upon by older men for whom sexual potency was central to their composite masculinities. However, many older men were not interested in taking the drugs. Their reasons varied but often included a revised composite masculinity in which the reckless virile behaviour of a young man was replaced by "responsible" forms of "mature masculinity," involving closer emotional relationships with wives, children, and grandchildren. In such composite masculinities, memories of past sexual conquests were adequate and did not play a central role in a future focused on mature domesticity.

Wentzell's study focused on composite masculinities, but she points out that the same approach can be taken to *composite femininities*, which she sometimes explored in relation to the wives of some of the men whom she had met in the hospital. Johnny's wife Mayra, for example, evaluated his past performance of manhood as a failure: he had been a poor provider, and he had left it to her to support their 12 children and survive a stillbirth on her own while he spent his earnings on other women, enjoying himself in the United States. Viewing Johnny's surgery as just reward for his past poor behaviour, she "asserted her own composite femininity, which foregrounded piety, responsibility, and the suffering often associated with 'good' womanhood in Roman Catholic contexts. . . . Mayra's mixture of physical caregiving and narrative critique seemed unconsciously strategic, reinforcing their couplehood through the embodied practice of care but putting her in control of the story" (2013, 30). In both these cases, Wentzell demonstrates that individuals' composite gender identity incorporates many features shaped by the historical, economic, political, and sociocultural settings in which they live their lives.

How Are Sex and Gender Affected by Other Forms of Identity?

As feminist scholars struggled to debunk supposedly universal "truths" about women, they came to realize that "women" itself is a problematic category. This became clear as comparative research revealed ways that other forms of identity, such as race and class, were deeply entangled with the ways women (and men) came to understand the meaning of gender. For instance, second-wave feminism had been energized by many white, middle-class women whose experiences of

women's oppression—being denied professional careers in the public sphere, being confined to roles as wives and mothers—were shaped by race and class privilege. But non-white feminists pointed out that non-white working-class women experienced oppression very differently—frequently as single mothers forced to work outside the home in dead-end jobs. These differences were the consequence not simply of male domination but also of structured racial and class oppression, a phenomenon now called **intersectionality**.

To recognize the reality of intersectionality is to recognize that every woman has multiple identities that intersect and complicate each other; taken together, they locate each woman differently (and, sometimes, surprisingly) with respect to other women (or men). Thus, in some settings, a middle-class African American woman might enjoy class-based privileges denied to a working-class white woman, whereas in other settings, the working-class white woman's race would allow her privileges that would override the class status of the middle-class African American woman.

Intersectionality can also be seen at work in the history of the Haitian state. Haiti began as a colony of France and achieved its independence following a successful revolt of black slaves against their white colonial masters (see EthnoProfile 11.2). As Nina Glick Schiller and Georges Fouron (2001) explain, however, "Haiti has its own particular and mixed messages about gender that give to women and men both rights and

EthnoProfile 11.2

Haiti

Region: Caribbean

Nation: Haiti

Population: 7,500,000

Environment: Rough, mountainous terrain, tropical to semi-arid climate.

Livelihood: About 80% of the population lives in extreme poverty

Political organization: Multiparty nation-state

For more information: Farmer, Paul. 1992. *AIDS and Accusation: Haiti and the Geography of Blame.* Berkeley: University of California Press.

FIGURE 11.4 The founders of the Haitian state borrowed from their former French masters an idea of gender that gave men control of family life. Women belonged to the Haitian nation, but until recently Haitian women who married foreigners lost their Haitian citizenship and their children were not legally recognized as Haitian.

responsibilities to family and nation" (133). Women appear in official stories about the Haitian Revolution, and some of them are even portrayed as heroines; most, however, are usually portrayed as silent wives and mothers. Moreover, the founders of the Haitian state borrow from their former French masters "a patriarchal idea of family as well as a civil code that gave men control of family life, wealth, and property" (Schiller and Fouron 2001, 134). Women belonged to the Haitian nation, but "state officials and the literate elite envisioned women as able to reproduce the nation only in conjunction with a Haitian man" (134). Until 1987, Haitian women who married foreigners lost their Haitian citizenship. High-status Haitian women are those who are supported economically by their Haitian husbands and who stay home with their children. Schiller and Fouron argue that many Haitians "still believe that to live by these values is to uphold not only family but also national honor" (135) (Figure 11.4).

By contrast, Haitian women who cannot live by these values are accorded low status. On the one hand, this means that they are not confined to the domestic sphere. On the other hand, for this very reason they are assumed to be always sexually available: "Men in Haiti see women alone or in the workplace as willing and able to trade their sexuality for other things they need. Men may ask rather than take, but often they are making an offer that women cannot afford to refuse" (Schiller and Fouron 2001, 139–40).

How Do Ethnographers Study Gender Performativity?

As we saw above, anthropologists (and others) who distinguish sex from gender long ago rejected the idea that a person's gendered beliefs or behaviour were somehow directly caused by that person's biological sex. Women—and men—regularly manage the contradictions that race, class, gender, and other identities create in the course of everyday life. It was misleading to think of culturally expected gender "roles" simply as obligations to which individuals learned to *conform*. Instead, these roles looked more like scripts that individuals learned to *perform*; and part of each performance involved deciding which features of which identities to highlight or downplay in any given social interaction. Understanding cultural identity as something people perform compels anthropologists to think of individuals as *agents* (or *actors*) who have mastered a range of skills that are appropriate for the public display of particular identities before particular audiences (Butler 1990) (Figure 11.5). Butler's work clearly outlines how displays of gender identity are examples of **gender performativity**; that is, gender is reconceived as something we "perform" or "enact," something we "do," not something we "are."

FIGURE 11.5 Feminist theorist Judith Butler receives an award in Frankfurt, Germany, in 2012.

gender performativity The concept that gender is something we "perform" or "enact," something we "learn to do," not something we "are born with."

Put another way, no single identity fully captures the inner life of any individual. From the perspective of performativity, culture can also be reconceived less as a set of imposed beliefs and behaviours and more as a set of *resources*—artifacts, actions, and interpretations—that can be deployed by individuals in order to enact before others the identities to which they lay claim. The notion of performativity has been widely applied by anthropologists and others to describe the way humans perform not only gender but also other forms of social identity, such as race or ethnicity (see Chapter 14).

Anthropologist Roger Lancaster (1994) explored the performativity of gender and sexual identity in the course of his fieldwork in Managua, Nicaragua, in the 1980s, as he studied the effects of the Sandinista Revolution on the lives of working people. While he was there, Lancaster learned about *cochones*. *Cochón* could be translated into English as "homosexual," but that would be highly misleading. As Lancaster discovered, working-class Nicaraguans interpret sexual relations between men differently from North Americans; we will explore these matters more fully later in the chapter. At this point, however, we want to discuss how Lancaster's discovery also prompted his recognition of the flexibility and ambiguity surrounding the *performance* of gender and sexuality in Nicaragua.

Lancaster was present one day when his *comadre* Aida bought a new blouse. After she showed it to everyone, her younger brother, Guto, picked it up and used it as a prop in an impromptu performance (1994, 559–60):

> With a broad yet pointed gesture, Guto wrapped himself in the white, frilly blouse, and began a coquettish routine that lasted for 15 or 20 minutes. . . . [He] added a purse and necklace to his ensemble. Brothers, sisters, even his mother, egged on this performance, shouting festive remarks . . . punctuated by whistles, kissing noises. Someone handed Guto a pair of clip-on earrings. With cheerful abandon, he applied a bit of blush and a touch of makeup. His performance intensified, to the pleasure of the audience. After disappearing for a moment into the bedroom, he returned wearing a blue denim

skirt. "Hombrote" (Big Guy), he shot in my direction, nuancing his usually raspy voice as if to flirt with me. I was astonished and no doubt my visible surprise was part of the clowning of the evening. "See, Roger," Aida kept remarking, "Look, Guto's a *cochón*, a queer."

What was going on here? When Lancaster later tried to interview those involved, he says, "no one would give me a *straight* answer" (1994, 560; emphasis in original). One participant laughingly suggested that perhaps Guto was a *cochón*. But Lancaster was puzzled because nothing in Guto's previous behaviour, nor in the behaviour of others who knew him, had suggested that he claimed or was accorded such an identity. Still, Guto's performance of "femininity" had been extremely skilful.

Lancaster entertained a series of possible, yet contradictory, interpretations of that performance. Was Guto mocking or embracing femininity? Was he engaging in homosexual flirtation with Lancaster, or was he masking same-sex desires by his over-the-top mimicry? Were he and his audience making fun of gender norms, or celebrating them, or simply blowing off steam? Lancaster recalled that he had been drawn into Guto's performance in the role of "straight man," and he speculated that perhaps Guto may have playfully "flirted" with him in an effort to reveal Lancaster's own sexual preferences. At that time, Lancaster had not yet explicitly disclosed his own identity as a gay man, and he wondered whether his friends used Guto's performance to test their suspicions. Still, this seemed an inadequate explanation: "As I was constantly reminded, my own conceptions of homosexuality did not exactly match up with those of my informants. It is not even quite clear to me what would have constituted a 'queer' response on my part . . . when plural others are playing, ambiguities multiply geometrically" (1994, 562).

Even though Lancaster could not provide a definitive explanation of what Guto's performance was all about, he insists that "play is not a trivial thing, and the simultaneously destructive and creative powers of laughter should never be underestimated" (1994, 561). This realization led him to reflect more deeply on what **transvestism**—the practice of dressing as and taking on mannerisms associated with a gender other than one's own—might mean, both in Nicaragua (where *cochones* traditionally perform during the festival of Carnival in

transvestism The practice of dressing as and taking on mannerisms associated with a gender other than one's own.

the manner Guto enacted) and perhaps elsewhere in the world (Figure 11.6).

Lancaster uses the term *transvestics* to encompass everything from these everyday forms of gender mimicry to fully fledged performances that cite not only gendered speech but also gendered forms of dress and bodily movement. All transvestic performers are not equally skilled, of course, but how their performances are judged varies, depending on context. Lancaster points out that in the context of North American drag balls, the performer may sometimes be evaluated positively by *convincingly* portraying another gender role, but in other contexts the drag performance fails unless it demonstrates an *ironic parody* of that other gender role.

Lancaster concluded that Guto's performance involved the portrayal of a stock Carnival figure in a manner that was both hostile and affectionate, and that this performance involved "play acting" (1994). Indeed, *cochones* are much admired for their transvestic performances, but not all the men who cross-dress in Carnival are *cochones*, and telling them apart is not easy. As a festival, Carnival involves turning the world upside down, and this involves upending a range of stereotypes about gender, sexuality, race, class, and ethnicity. As our previous discussion of intersectionality suggests, we agree with Lancaster that we humans "play our games freely, but we are not free to play them just any way we choose" (1994, 568). He suggests that play of this kind needs to be understood "as both a human universal and as a base condition of culture," which aligns with our discussion of play in Chapter 16.

How Do Anthropologists Study Connections among Sex, Gender, Sexuality, and the Body?

An important trend in sociocultural anthropology in recent decades has been attention to "the body," an object of study that is of obvious relevance to discussions of sex, gender, and sexuality. To understand the growth of interest in the body, remember that, for most of the twentieth century, sociocultural anthropology consistently downplayed human individuals (and their individual bodies) and instead highlighted patterns that characterized the social groups to which individual humans belonged. In recent years, anthropologists have turned to the work of Michel Foucault (Figure 11.7),

FIGURE 11.6 A Nicaraguan cowboy poses with a cross-dressing male during Carnival in Nicaragua.

Thornton Cohen / Alamy Stock Photo

whose writings highlight the way social power, particularly in modern Western societies, acts on individual bodies. Social institutions such as schools and armies regulate the actions of individual bodies in order to render them more efficient in the performance of particular skills or practices. At the same time, modern states depend on statistical information about their populations in order to devise ways of regulating those populations, engaging in what Foucault calls *biopolitics* (see Chapter 13). For example, campaigns to improve the well-being of citizens via medical interventions such as inoculations have allowed state institutions to increase the numbers of healthy individuals ready for the labour force, or the numbers of healthy recruits eligible to be drafted into the armed forces. Finally, Foucault argues, societies have devised ways of persuading individuals to bring their own bodily activities into conformity with social expectations, a phenomenon he calls "the care of the self." Foucault's theoretical framework has informed work in many areas of anthropological research but has mainly focused on documenting

FIGURE 11.7 French philosopher Michel Foucault.

the ways social intervention and regulation were mobilized to classify and produce particular forms of *sexual* embodiment over time (Foucault 1978).

Anthropologists have traditionally understood that human beings are plastic organisms who are open to the moulding processes of socialization and enculturation. This resonates with Foucault's understanding of the human body as a *docile* body; that is, a body that is easily taught, or, in Foucault's terms, a body "that may be subjected, used, transformed, and improved" through "disciplinary methods" that apply "an uninterrupted, constant coercion" of bodily activities, making possible "the meticulous control of the operations of the body" (1995, 136, 137). As we observed earlier, however, conceiving of human bodies as nothing more than passive, inert matter is problematic. As well, theorists in anthropology and elsewhere have drawn attention to the ways in which **affect** (visceral arousal, emotion, or feeling) is not opposed to rational thought but is in fact

affect Visceral arousal, emotion, or feeling.

entwined with thought in processes of making meaning in human lives.

Some of this research has focused on how individuals experience visceral feelings of desire that are at odds with cultural ideologies about gender and sexuality. One suggestion is that these forms of affect have the potential to disrupt ideologies concerning sexuality, making room for the development of alternative corporeal relations between individuals. Theoretical approaches of this kind offer ways of bringing material bodies back into discussions of sex, gender, sexuality, and human agency, without reducing bodily feelings to genetic or hormonal mechanisms.

Connections between Bodies and Technologies

Connections between humans and machines in contemporary societies can be found everywhere today, from computerized management of large informational databases in government and private industry, to online computer gaming, to your personal relationship with your smartphone. Science studies in anthropology are often located within the anthropology of science, technology, and medicine. As we saw earlier, this is the disciplinary location of medical anthropologists such as Marcia Inhorn and Emily Wentzell, whose research regularly involves the complex ways that human organisms are entangled with technologies. Furthermore the work of Marcia Inhorn demonstrates that the study of assisted reproduction also includes the study of sex, gender, and sexuality. In the past, medicine and technology were not viewed as having any intrinsic connection to the "natural" biological processes, such as human reproduction, and the failure of this natural process to produce living offspring was understood as equally "natural."

Today, however, in all parts of the world, individuals and couples (increasingly, same-sex couples) who want children of their own but are unable or unwilling to adopt may now use a variety of complex medical technologies and institutions. For example, sperm banks and egg banks at fertility clinics are used in procedures such as in vitro fertilization. These procedures are performed either on the individuals or couples seeking to become pregnant or on a female surrogate, who has agreed, for a fee, to gestate the embryo for the individual or couple. In addition, forms of prenatal testing, such as amniocentesis, are now standard technological interventions in pregnancies that may be otherwise uncomplicated.

How Do Anthropologists Study Relations between Sex, Gender, and Sexuality?

As we saw earlier, at one time, anthropologists agreed that "sex," while distinct from culturally shaped "gender," was a "natural" physical attribute clearly visible on the body, to be determined by inspection at birth (i.e., males have penises and females have vaginas) or at puberty (i.e., males grow beards and females grow breasts and start to menstruate). However, this way of classifying bodies, based on the presumption of a "natural" gender binary, turns out to be problematic. For one thing, the determination of the sex of newborns by visual inspection is by no means as straightforward as it may seem. Developmental biologist Anne Fausto-Sterling reports that "about one in a hundred infants is born without a consistent body sex" (2012, 313). That is, infants' patterns of sex chromosomes (XX for females, XY for males) may not correspond to the expected outward appearance of their genitals (an XX baby may have an enlarged clitoris and fused labia, an XY baby may have a tiny penis) or with their internal gonads (i.e., two ovaries for females, two testes for males).

Individuals who possess ambiguous genitalia have been called **intersex**, although many prefer to describe their condition as the result of a **disorder of sexual development**. Medical scientists are able to identify a number of developmental processes that can produce atypical genitalia in infants, some of which are associated with ongoing risks to the individual's health; however, many newborns with ambiguous genitalia face no such health risks. Still, infants with ambiguous genitalia may cause great anxiety for their parents, which has led to the elaboration of standard medical interventions in the United States soon after the birth of such infants. Decisions are made about the newborn's sex assignment (and the gender in which the child will be reared), and then surgery is performed to bring the external appearance of the infant's genitalia into line with this assignment; sometimes surgery is followed by additional hormonal treatments at puberty.

However, many adults who underwent these interventions in childhood have publicly declared that their own personal biographies have been far from "normal." Some have become activists who urge physicians and parents to delay or avoid such surgeries on infants altogether, in order to spare these children the surgical disfigurement and loss of sexual feeling that they experienced (Karkazis 2008). The issues are complex, but one thing is clear: the statistical frequency with which infants with ambiguous genitalia are born means that assigning newborns a sex is far from self-evident or unproblematic and is powerfully shaped by the cultural expectations and social practices of parents and physicians.

In this context, it is useful to reflect on a phenomenon Roger Lancaster described at the conclusion of his discussion of Guto's performance: namely, Guto's "breasts." Lancaster explained: "After adolescence, Guto, like some other boys in his extended family, had begun to grow small breasts. His older brother Charlie claimed that his own nipples sometimes produced *leche*, milk, as I discovered one day when I encountered him, concentratedly squeezing his nipples and asked him what he was doing" (1994, 572). What could have been responsible for this development? Lancaster could not know, but he speculated that perhaps the growth of breasts on Guto and Charlie might have been stimulated by exposure to pesticides in the countryside since some pesticides, when they decompose, can affect human bodies the way hormones do. This kind of fleshly malleability, which seems to carry meanings about our sex, gender, or sexuality, is what Lancaster calls "the transvestism of the body" (1994, 572). Guto and his brother managed these bodily changes by undergoing breast reduction surgery shortly before Guto's Carnival-esque performance with Aida's blouse.

Minimally, **sexuality** refers to the ways in which people experience and value physical desire and pleasure in the context of sexual intercourse. But contemporary anthropologists are more likely to refer to sexual*ities*, in the plural, to acknowledge the many ways in which sexual desires and pleasures have always been shaped historically by cultural, social, and political structures of the larger societies in which people live. Until recently, as we saw above, many Canadians took for granted that biological sex directly determined gendered behaviour.

intersex/disorder of sexual development Describes those individuals who possess ambiguous genitalia.

sexuality The ways in which people experience and value physical desire and pleasure in the context of sexual intercourse.

These assumptions underlie the view, long popular in Canada, that "normal" sexuality takes only one form—**heterosexuality**—which involves "natural" sexual attraction, leading to "natural" sexual intercourse, between males and females (i.e., individuals of different sexes).

To emphasize heterosexuality as the only correct form of human sexual expression is to subscribe to an ideology that anthropologists and others call **heteronormativity**: that is, the view that heterosexual intercourse is (and *should be*) the "normal" form that human sexual expression always takes. For example, heteronormative sexuality has been viewed in Euro-American societies as the appropriate form of sexuality within the nuclear family, formed around a heterosexual married couple who are expected to engage in exclusive sexual relations with one another in order to produce offspring. Claims that the nuclear family is the building block of Canadian society reflect what Foucault would call the biopolitical concern of the state to manage its population of citizens and regulate their reproduction. However, heteronormative thinking about sexuality has been undermined in recent decades, not only by scholarly work on varieties of human sexual expression but even more by activism by lesbians, gay men, and bisexual and transgender individuals, whose preferred ways of doing gender and enacting sexual expression challenge heteronormative standards.

From the perspective of these critics, people who continue to support heteronormativity are perceived to subscribe instead to **heterosexism**, a form of bias (like sexist bias) against all those who are not heterosexual.

Historians who study sexuality have demonstrated that heteronormative thinking and heteronormative sexual classifications are very recent phenomena that tend to be found mainly in Euro-American societies. Consider, for example, the concept of heterosexuality and its routine opposite, **homosexuality**—that is, sexual relations involving two males or two females (i.e., same-sex sexuality).

Many people assume that these terms identify stable forms of sexuality going back deep into the past, but this is not the case. David Halperin observes that the first appearance in print of the word *homosexuality* was in 1869, in German, in a pamphlet urging the German government not to criminalize "homosexual" relations between men; paradoxically, therefore, "'homosexuality' began life as a progay, politically activist coinage" (2014, 481). Before long, however, the term was appropriated by medical specialists called "sexologists," who turned it into a clinical term designating a particular variety of sexual deviance. By the end of the nineteenth century, however, individuals classified as homosexual by the medical authorities began to use the term **gay** to refer to themselves, an affirmative and empowering self-designation that became widespread over the course of the twentieth century.

Although the term *gay* may be applied to any person who is sexually attracted to someone of the same sex, it is more commonly used in reference to gay males and the cultures and practices associated with them. The term **lesbian** actually emerged in antiquity, but it originally referred to the Greek island of Lesbos, the home of the female poet Sappho, who was reputed to love females rather than males. The standard use of *lesbian* to describe female same-sex sexuality, however, only began around the turn of the twentieth century. In fact, the terms *homosexuality*, *heterosexuality*, and **bisexuality** (that is, sexual attraction to both males and females) were all invented by Euro-American medical researchers in the late nineteenth and early twentieth centuries, and *heterosexuality* did not assume its current meaning as the opposite of *homosexuality* until the 1930s (see Halperin 2014, 458–61). The terms **transgender** and **pansexuality** are even more recently established by medical researchers to clarify differences among individuals who, in one way or another, seem dissatisfied with the sex and gender assignments they received at birth and identify their

---

heterosexuality Sexual relations involving individuals of different sexualities (i.e., a man and a woman).

heteronormativity The view that heterosexual intercourse is (and *should be*) the "normal" form that human sexual expression always takes.

heterosexism A form of bias (like sexist bias) against all those who are not heterosexual.

homosexuality Sexual relations involving two males or two females (i.e., same-sex sexuality).

gay An affirmative and empowering self-designation for individuals medically classified as homosexual, which became widespread over the course of the twentieth century.

lesbian A term used to describe female same-sex sexuality around the turn of the twentieth century; based on the name of the Greek island of Lesbos, the home of the female poet Sappho, who was reputed to love women rather than men.

bisexuality Sexual attraction to both males and females.

transgender A term proposed in the 1960s by medical researchers to classify individuals who, in one way or another, seemed dissatisfied with the sex and gender assignments they had received at birth.

pansexuality Sexual attraction to males, females, and transgender males and females.

sexual expression with males, females, and transgender individuals.

Physicians now recognize *gender identity disorder* or *gender dysphoria* as a formal medical diagnosis, but many persons who claim a transgender identity deny the validity of this diagnosis, arguing that it is based on heteronormative bias. As with individuals diagnosed as "homosexual" in earlier decades, many individuals diagnosed with gender dysphoria insist that their sexuality is not a medical condition to be treated but a valid form of gender variation that requires recognition and support.

In the 1990s, some persons whose gender identities or sexual practices fell outside the range defined by "the heterosexual–homosexual continuum" began to refer to themselves as **queer**, taking back as a badge of pride a term once used to insult non-heterosexuals. The status of this term remains controversial, however: some view it as a convenient umbrella term for all those who reject heteronormativity; others use it to signify rejection of *all* categories of gender and sexual classification, including distinctions between lesbian, gay, bisexual, and transgender persons.

In the wake of sociopolitical breakthroughs such as the growing legal recognition of same-sex marriage, debates continue about how to distinguish between and label the many varieties of sexuality. For example, on 9 June 2015, following the highly publicized transition of former male Olympic athlete Bruce Jenner into a woman called Caitlyn, *The New York Times* published an article describing the difficulty of determining statistically the proportion of the US population who might be classified as "transgender" (Miller 2015). Being able to quantify more accurately the proportion of transgender individuals in the US population would have wide-ranging biopolitical effects, for good or for ill: as Miller notes, "knowing more about this population is important for policy-making in health, education, criminal justice, social services, sports, the military and more" (2015, A3). However, in Canada and the US the Census Bureau does not ask about gender identity, and many transgender persons hide their gender identity in order to avoid discrimination (Figure 11.8). At the same time, Miller also noted that "gender identity can be hard to define in a multiple-choice list. There are now more than 50 gender options on Facebook, for instance" (A3). Similarly, the "Transgender" page on Wikipedia provides several definitions of *transgender* and describes multiple and contradictory ways that people who call themselves transgender

FIGURE 11.8 Gender identity is complex and can become politicized, as illustrated by battles in the United States over access to public restrooms by transgender people.

might define what that label means (http://en.wikipedia.org/wiki/Transgender; accessed 21 October 2019). In part, the struggle over terminology reflects the desire of some transgender persons to gain public recognition of an identity label of their own choice as a claim to dignity; at the same time, the proliferation of labels reveals deep disagreements about what that identity might be.

Moreover, many millennials are choosing to now identify as **non-binary**, rejecting the need to identify as either male or female even though they do not consider themselves to be transgender. To be non-binary is to completely reject any continuation of the gender binary that used to be so pivotal to our Euro-Canadian understanding of what it means to be a person. Gender identity is a fluid construct that shifts as society grows and bends.

The conclusion seems inescapable that even in Euro-American societies, forms of sexual expression cannot be easily sorted into a handful of unambiguous categories in which sex, gender, and sexuality line up in predictable ways. On the contrary, the phenomena we call sex, gender, and sexuality would appear to be fluid and changing, not only over historical time but also in the biographies of many human individuals, even in Canada. Some scholars speak in terms of a *male-to-female continuum*, along

queer A self-identification claimed by some persons whose gender identities or sexual practices fall outside the range defined by "the heterosexual–homosexual continuum."

non-binary Self-identification that resists the gender binary, embodying the fluidity of gender as a social construct.

which individuals may plot the development of their own identifications in terms of sex, gender, and sexuality. Others may agree with David Halperin, whose history of the classification of sex, gender, and sexuality in Euro-American societies concludes that "Perhaps the final irony in all this is that the very word sex . . . has had the fine edge of its precise meaning so thoroughly blunted by historical shifts, conceptual muddles, and rearrangements in the forms of sexual life that it now represents that which is most resistant to clear classification, discrimination, and division" (2014, 484).

How Does Ethnography Document Variable Cultural Understandings Concerning Sex, Gender, and Sexuality?

In the wake of second-wave feminism and the rise of activism by lesbian, gay, bisexual, and transgender persons, anthropologists have in recent decades produced fresh ethnographic evidence concerning variations in beliefs and practices about sex, gender, and sexuality in the many communities where they carried out fieldwork, both within and outside the Western world. In many cases, the peoples and practices they write about have long histories that predate contact with Euro-American societies, which often came in the form of Western colonialism. Explorers and settlers often wrote about such practices, which scandalized them and which were officially forbidden by Christian missionaries. One example involves renewed attention to older writings about the cultural and sexual practices of the so-called *berdache*. Until the last decades of the twentieth century, the term *berdache* had been used by anthropologists to refer to Indigenous social roles in which men (and sometimes women) were allowed to take on the activities and sometimes the dress of members of the other sex. Today, many anthropologists refuse to use the term, as do many contemporary members of Indigenous societies. Rather, the more respectful term *two spirited* is used by individuals who view themselves as modern embodiments of these alternative-gender roles.

In the context of globalization in the twenty-first century, Euro-American ideas about sex, gender, and sexuality sometimes mix uneasily with local understandings, even when those local understandings themselves challenge traditional Western heteronormative assumptions. The following case studies further illustrate the range of ethnographic findings that continue to challenge taken-for-granted notions about sex, gender, and sexuality.

Female Sexual Practices in Mombasa

Anthropologist Gill Shepherd (1987) showed that traditional patterns of male–female interaction among Swahili Muslims in Mombasa, Kenya, make male and female same-sex relationships in this community intelligible (see EthnoProfile 11.3: Mombasa Swahilis; see also Figure 11.9). In the years when Shepherd did her research, she found that men and women in Muslim Mombasa lived in very different subcultures. For women, the most enduring relationship was between mothers and daughters, mirrored in the relationship between an older married sister and a younger unmarried sister. By contrast, relationships between mothers and sons and between brothers and sisters were more distant. Except in the case of young, modern, educated couples, the relationship between husband and wife was often emotionally distant as well. Because the worlds of men and women overlapped so little, relationships between the genders tended to be one-dimensional. Men and women joined a variety of sex-segregated groups for leisure-time activities, such as dancing or religious study. Within these same-sex groups, individuals competed for social rank.

EthnoProfile 11.3

Mombasa Swahilis

Region: Eastern Africa

Nation: Kenya

Population: 50,000 Swahilis among 350,000 total population of city (1970s)

Environment: Island and mainland port city

Livelihood: Various urban occupations

Political organization: Part of a modern nation–state

For more information: Shepherd, Gill. 1987. "Rank, Gender and Homosexuality: Mombasa as a Key to Understanding Sexual Options." In *The Cultural Construction of Sexuality*, ed. Pat Caplan, 240–70. London: Tavistock.

Of the some 50,000 Swahilis in Mombasa at the end of the 1980s, Shepherd reckoned that Western observers might classify perhaps 5000 as "homosexual." The number was misleading, however, because men and women shifted between what Euro-Americans call "homosexuality" and "heterosexuality" throughout their lives. Women were allowed to choose other women as sexual partners only after they had been married, widowed, or divorced. Both men and women were open about their same-sex relationships, and "nobody would dream of suggesting that their sexual choices had any effect on their work capabilities, reliability or religious piety" (Shepherd 1987, 241). Moreover, many women were quite clear about the practical reasons that had led them into sexual relationships with other women. Women with little money were unlikely to marry men who could offer them jewellery, shoes, new dresses, status, or financial security, but a wealthy female lover could offer them all these things. Also, a poor young woman in an unhappy marriage might have no way to support herself if she left her husband unless she had a lesbian lover to rely on.

According to Islamic law, Shepherd was told, a wealthy, high-ranking Muslim woman can only marry a man who is her equal or superior. A marriage of this kind would bring a great deal of seclusion, and her wealth would be administered by her husband. The wealthy partner in a female same-sex relationship, however, would be free of these constraints: "Thus, if she wishes to use her wealth as she likes, and has a taste for power, entry into a lesbian relationship, or living alone as a divorced or widowed woman, are virtually her only options" (Shepherd 1987, 257). Financial independence for a woman offered a chance to convert wealth to power. If she paid for the marriage of other people or provided financial support in exchange for loyalty, a woman could create a circle of dependants. Shepherd pointed out that a few women, some lesbians, had achieved real political power in Mombasa in this way (257).

Still, it was not necessary to be a lesbian to build a circle of dependants. Why did some women follow this route? The answer, Shepherd learned, is complicated. It was not entirely respectable for a woman under 45 or 50 to be unmarried. Some could maintain autonomy by making a marriage of convenience to a man who already lived with a wife and then living apart from him. Many women, however, found this arrangement both lonely and sexually unsatisfying. Living as a lesbian was less respectable than being a second, nonresident wife,

FIGURE 11.9 View of Mombasa.

but it was more respectable than not being married at all. The lesbian sexual relationship did not reduce the autonomy of the wealthy partner "and indeed takes place in the highly positive context of the fond and supportive relationships women establish among themselves anyway" (Shepherd 1987, 258).

Anthropologists working in Africa have described a range of relations between females (woman marriage, for example) that have been likened to European or American models of lesbian relationships, but disputes have arisen about whether such relationships always include an erotic involvement between the female partners. In a survey of this evidence, Wieringa and Blackwood noted that woman marriage could take many forms, some of which were more likely than others to include sexuality between the female partners. Among those where such sexual relations appear more likely are cases like that described by Shepherd "in which a woman of some means, either married (to a man) or unmarried, pays bride-wealth for a wife and establishes her own compound" (Wieringa and Blackwood 1999, 5).

Such evidence is not merely of academic interest. In the contemporary world of intensified global communication and exchange, Western and non-Western same-sex practices are becoming increasingly entangled with one another, leading to the emergence of local movements for "lesbian" and "gay" rights in African and elsewhere. In this context, in the late 1990s, the presidents of Zimbabwe, Kenya, and Namibia declared that homosexuality is "un-African." Based on the ethnographic evidence, however, Wieringa and Blackwood (1999) sided with those arguing that, on the contrary, it is homophobia that is un-African: "President Mandela from

South Africa is a striking exception to the homophobia of his colleagues. The South African constitution specifically condemns discrimination on the basis of sexual orientation" (27).

Transsexuality and Same-Sex Desire in Iran

Afsaneh Najmabadi is a scholar who has investigated the role of gender in the history of Iran. She left Iran as a young woman in the 1960s to study in the United States, where she became a feminist and political activist. She was deeply affected by the consequences of the Islamic Revolution in Iran in 1979, and, since that time, her research has explored how gender relations rooted in Iranian history were reworked in the course of the nineteenth century, as Iranian elites developed connections with the West and embarked on a self-conscious process of "modernization." Najmabadi also was interested in how, after the 1979 revolution, Iranians had responded to efforts by the religious authorities to expunge Western influences and to bring Iranian institutions and social practices into conformity with what they determined to be the requirements of Islamic law. She was particularly intrigued when, in 2003, there was a burst of attention in the Iranian and international press concerning what was being calling "the 'trans' phenomenon" (2013, 1). She knew that in the decade prior to the 1979 revolution, Iranian physicians had become involved in hormonal and surgical treatments for persons wishing to change their sex. By 2003, however, journalists seemed both surprised and puzzled that this sort of "progressive" treatment could be possible in an Islamic state; the same

state had ruled same-sex sexual relations to be illegal, often equating them with "sodomy," which was punished with the death penalty (2013, 1). After a 25-year absence, Najmabadi returned to Iran in 2005 to carry out ethnographic fieldwork that would explore all these matters more closely.

Najmabadi discovered that the distinctions between sex, gender, and sexuality developed by Western scholars did not easily map onto Iranian categories: most Iranians she spoke to did not recognize a distinction between sex and gender, and most also presumed a more or less direct causal link between an individual's sex/gender and the focus of his or her sexual desire: "the indistinction between gender/sex/sexuality . . . regularly disrupts attempts to separate the homosexual from the trans, even as that distinction is regularly invoked" (2013, 8). Iranians had also developed their own version of heteronormativity as a consequence of the "modernization" of Iranian family life: even Muslim theologians she spoke with seemed to take the existence of a heteronormative gender binary for granted (2013, 191). However, Iranian historical and cultural attitudes toward sex/gender/sexuality meant that the status of "trans" persons in contemporary Iranian society did not easily map onto "trans" identities recognized in the West. In Iran, she found that physicians linked "trans" identity with that of "intersex," which itself was associated historically with the category of "hermaphrodite" recognized in Islamic law. Just like infants born with ambiguous external genitalia, therefore, persons who believed that their inner soul or psyche was mismatched with their outer anatomy were considered to be entitled to hormonal and surgical interventions that would "clarify" their "true" sex/gender. This conclusion had been proclaimed lawful in a *fatwa* (or Islamic religious opinion) first issued in the 1960s by none other than Ayatollah Khomeini, leader of the Islamic Revolution in Iran and the highest-ranking Shi'a Muslim religious authority in recent Iranian history, whose authority remains unchallenged (2013) (Figure 11.10).

Najmabadi undertook participant observation in order to learn exactly how trans activists engaged psychological, medical, religious, and governmental authorities on an everyday basis; she also interviewed key figures in these different institutions. Although she expected to encounter rigid attitudes in officials, especially religious authorities, she describes herself as surprised and humbled by how many of them were not interested

Photo by Kaveh Kazemi/Getty Images

FIGURE 11.10 Iran's first religiously and legally recognized transsexual and her mother.

in denouncing sexual nonconformity, but who in their own ways were working to find humane solutions for affected individuals. The religious endorsement of treatment for what they termed "gender dysphoria" has made it possible for Muslim clerics, psychologists, physicians, and government bureaucrats to find some common ground, but it had taken the determined lobbying efforts of trans activists to persuade these officials to make needed changes.

At first, Najmabadi was surprised when trans activists told her that they did not want to "politicize" their cause. What they meant, she found, was that they did not want to turn their activism into a human rights issue that would involve the Iranian parliament passing legislation. Rather, they wanted to make sure that civil servants and others knew who they were and would continue to work with them, regardless of which political faction was in power. Their activism was intended to gain official awareness of the "needs" of trans people; to remove a series of medical, legal, and religious barriers; and to get support and protection from harassment, in order to make "livable lives" for themselves (2013, 12). By such methods, trans activists eventually gained official recognition as members of a "vulnerable" population deserving of state protection (2013, 214). Nevertheless, to become entitled to such protection, they had to pass a series of medical, psychological, and legal examinations designed to prove that they were indeed what they said they were. Once they obtained official certification as trans, they could have their name and sex/gender changed on their national identity papers, complete their sex-change treatments, and, if they wished, disappear into the Iranian population.

The high barrier to gaining formal trans certification in Iran points to another difference between Western and Iranian notions about sex, gender, and sexuality. The "filtering" process leading to trans certification was so intense because Iranian authorities wanted to make sure that the applicants they certified were *genuinely* "trans"; put another way, their goal was to *detect and exclude* candidates for trans status who did *not* experience "gender dysphoria" but who, in their view, were trying to mask their sexual attraction to members of their own sex/gender. Indeed, male-to-female trans persons in Iran were constantly suspected of trying to use sex change to hide what was interpreted as their shameful desire to be the passive male partner in sexual relations between males. Nevertheless, Najmabadi "never

saw the commission exercise the option of turning down an application altogether . . . there seemed to be a general attitude . . . that . . . it was their job to find a socially acceptable 'solution for the problem'" (2013, 18).

As noted earlier, relationships between couples whom Euro-Americans might classify as "gay" or "lesbian" are condemned as immoral and illegal in Iran; such "same-sex players" (as they are called in Persian) are forced to keep their relationships hidden from family and society, which causes them considerable hardship, especially when faced with what Najmabadi calls the Iranian *marriage imperative*: "The adulthood of everyone is bound to marriage. It is almost incomprehensible that someone would wish not to marry" (2013, 124). The pressure of the marriage imperative sometimes led non-heteronormative Iranians, who usually described themselves as "gay" or "lesbian," to wonder if they might be "trans" and ought to consider changing sex. Such thoughts were often prompted by their partners, who wanted to regularize their relationship and who might threaten to leave them if they did not agree to undergo sex change. Indeed, Najmabadi found attitudes amounting to homophobia among some non-heteronormative couples who insisted that they were not "same-sex players" and who strove to interpret their relationships with their partners in ways that did not violate hegemonic Iranian understandings of sex/gender/sexuality (2013, 248).

At the same time, some persons who obtained trans certification did not always go on to complete their transition. This might be because they could not afford to pay for the surgery right away. But it might also be because, even though they believed that they truly were trans, they also knew that their families and neighbours would never accept them as such. Najmabadi concluded that trans individuals—indeed, all non-heteronormative Iranians—were struggling to find a way to make a "livable" life by exploiting inconsistencies among the various restrictions and opportunities that governed their lives. One postoperative male-to-female trans person she knew "still lives as a man at home; it is very critical for her to remain a man with her family and in the neighborhood everyone knew her as a man. . . . When she is at her boyfriend's house, she explains, she goes into female clothes" (2013, 281). Najmabadi concluded,

What seemed to matter for trans subject-hood was articulated in terms of figuring out how to live livable lives—with families, with partners, in terms of employment, of getting medical and legal changes they wanted, and of what made them comfortable in different spaces of life . . . living livable lives, for some, called for flexibility and the ability to switch back and forth when necessary. (2013, 286)

As this study demonstrates, Western and non-Western LGBTQ issues have become increasingly entangled and complex in this globalized world. In fact, cross-cultural research repeatedly demonstrates that physical sex differences do not allow us to predict the roles that females or males will play in any particular society worldwide. In the next chapter, we continue to look at how roles are defined for members of a culture by considering who and how we are related to each other, whether that is as brothers and sisters or as wife (wives) and husband (husbands).

Chapter Summary

1. Cultural anthropologists have been interested in sex, gender, and sexuality since the beginnings of anthropology as a discipline and, since the 1930s, have insisted that biological sex needs to be distinguished from cultural rules for appropriate behaviour as a female or a male. Twentieth-century social movements for civil rights, women's rights, and the rights of gay, lesbian, bisexual, and transgender persons called into question the existence of a universal sex and gender binary in all human societies. Some anthropologists argued that sexist patterns in contemporary societies, in the West and elsewhere, were due primarily to the effects of capitalism and colonialism on Indigenous societies that had once supported more egalitarian relationships between men and women. Anthropologist Marilyn Strathern provided ethnographic evidence suggesting that Melanesian peoples tended to view males and females as androgynous. These efforts combined with work by scholars in other disciplines to produce an overall rethinking of how sex, gender, and sexuality ought to be understood.

2. The influence of feminism on anthropology initially led to a focus on the roles women played in different societies, but before long it became clear that women's roles could not be studied apart from the roles of men. Increasing attention to the ways sex, gender, and sexuality are differently enacted in different times and places led to a recognition that masculinities and femininities might be constructed in more than one way, even in a single society. Some anthropologists have used ethnographic data to demonstrate the processes by which new kinds of masculinity can develop over time, as new generations of men in particular societies confront challenges and opportunities that differ from earlier generations, as seen in Marcia Inhorn's discussion of emerging masculinities in the Middle East. Changes in masculinities also emerge over the life cycle, and Emily Wentzell's discussion of composite masculinities illuminates the process whereby Mexican men delete old elements and add new elements of their masculine identities as they come to terms with the challenges of aging and illness.

3. Women of colour developed approaches to sex, gender, and sexuality that went beyond the views of feminists who took the experiences of white middle-class Euro-American women as the norm, showing how experiences of gender oppression always intersected with other social statuses, such as race and social class. Ethnographers have identified patterns of intersectionality in their fieldwork and are able to provide comparative examples from different times and places.

4. Scholars and activists for gay, lesbian, bisexual, and transgender rights developed approaches that showed why gender roles were best understood as performances in which individuals attempted to enact forms of speech and behaviour that were considered appropriate in their societies. This made room for individual agency and for recognition that human affect could not be completely contained within any particular set of socially established definitions of sex, gender, or sexuality. The malleability of the human body, shaped by the skills we all learn that enable us to mimic others whose gender or sexuality differs from our own,

highlights a range of performance possibilities of gender and sexuality that, as Roger Lancaster argues, can deepen our understanding of what may count as "transvestism."

5. Work in the anthropology of science, technology, and medicine has drawn attention to the ways that humans are increasingly linked to, and dependent on, technologies. These arrangements can be seen in cases of cutting-edge medical technologies that allow infertile couples to produce biological offspring, as shown in Marcia Inhorn's research in the Middle East. But the connection between biology and technology in the production of human bodies that conform to a society's gender binary by means of surgery and hormones also demonstrates a similar kind of connection between biology and technology. Anthropologists and biologists have drawn attention to the high proportion of human infants who are born with ambiguous genitalia. In the United States, beginning in the 1960s, such infants were assigned a sex by physicians and parents, and surgery, hormone treatments, and other forms of therapy were used to bring such persons into alignment with the American gender binary. Such interventions have become controversial as adults who were subjected to these interventions as infants have grown up and protested what was done to them. Roger Lancaster persuasively argues that these surgically and hormonally mediated forms of anatomical reshaping may be usefully understood as a "transvestics of the body."

6. Scholars inside and outside anthropology have contributed to attempts to categorize the many categories of sex, gender, and sexuality that people have recognized in different times and places. Historians have provided useful information about the origins of the technical terms relating to sex, gender, and sexuality that are used today by Euro-American scholars and activists, which are briefly summarized in this chapter. The proliferation of distinct labels over time suggests to some observers that not only is there no gender binary but that it makes more sense to describe variation in sex, gender, and sexuality in terms of points on a continuum or in terms of gender fluidity.

7. In the context of globalization in the twenty-first century, Euro-American ideas about sex, gender, and sexuality have spread to many parts of the world that traditionally have thought about these phenomena in different ways. Sometimes Euro-American categories mix uneasily with local categories, even as those local understandings themselves challenge traditional Western heteronormative assumptions. Ethnographic studies of sex, gender, and sexuality from Kenya and Iran illustrate these kinds of variation and complication.

For Review

1. Explain the public/private divide with reference to gender issues.
2. Why do anthropologists and other scholars distinguish among sex, gender, and sexuality?
3. How does the concept of an "individual" self challenge universal assumptions about a heteronormative gender binary?
4. Distinguish between composite masculinities and composite femininities.
5. Explain intersectionality, particularly as it relates to issues of sex, gender, and sexuality.
6. What does it mean to say that gender is "performed"?
7. Explain how gender stereotypes have been used by colonial officials to model the relationship of colonizer to colonized.
8. Why do many contemporary anthropologists use the plural term *sexualities* rather than the singular term *sexuality*?
9. Discuss the history of the term *homosexuality* in western Europe and North America.
10. Using the case studies in the text, discuss how anthropologists analyze human sexual practices.

Key Terms

affect 246
androgyny 238
bisexuality 248
feminism 235
gay 248
gender binary 236
gender performativity 243
heteronormativity 248
heterosexism 248

heterosexuality 248
homosexuality 248
intersectionality 242
intersex/disorder of sexual
    development 247
lesbian 248
men's studies/masculinities 238
non-binary 249
pansexuality 248

patriarchy 235
public/private divide 235
queer 249
sexism 235
sexuality 247
transgender 248
transvestism 244

References

Butler, Judith. 1990. *Gender Trouble: Feminism and the Subversion of Identity.* New York: Routledge.

Farmer, Paul. 1992. *AIDS and Accusation: Haiti and the Geography of Blame.* Berkeley: University of California Press.

Fausto-Sterling, Anne. 2012. *Sex/Gender: Biology in a Social World.* New York: Routledge.

Foucault, Michel. 1978. *The History of Sexuality (La Volonté de Savoir).* New York: Pantheon Books.

———. 1995. *Discipline and Punish: The Birth of the Prison.* New York, Random House.

Halperin, David. 2014. *How to Be Gay.* New York: Belknap Press.

Hewlett, Bonnie L. 2013. *Listen, Here Is a Story.* New York: Oxford University Press.

Inhorn, Marcia. 2012. *The New Arab Man: Emergent Masculinities, Technologies and Islam in the Middle East.* Princeton: Princeton University Press.

Karkazis, Katrina. 2008. *Fixing Sex: Intersex, Medical Authority, and Lived Experience.* Durham, NC: Duke University Press.

Lancaster, Roger. 1994. *Life Is Hard: Machismo, Danger and the Intimacy of Power in Nicaragua.* Berkeley: University of California Press.

Leacock, Eleanor. 1983. "Interpreting the Origins of Gender Inequality: Conceptual and Historical Problems." *Dialectical Anthropology* 7 (4): 263–84.

Lewin, Ellen, ed. 2006. *Feminist Anthropology: A Reader.* Malden, MA: Wiley-Blackwell.

Merry, Sally. 2003. "Human-Rights Law and the Demonization of Culture." *Anthropology Newsletter* 44(2).

Miller, Claire C. 2015. "The Search for the Best Estimate of the Transgender Population." *The New York Times,* 8 June.

Najmabadi, Afsaneh. 2013. *Professing Selves: Transsexuality and Same-Sex Desire in Contemporary Iran.* Durham, NC: Duke University Press.

Ortner, Sherry. 1974. "Is Female to Male as Nature Is to Culture?" In *Woman, Culture, and Society,* edited by Michelle Zimbalist Rosaldo and Louise Lamphere, 68[en-dash]87. Stanford, CA: Stanford University Press.

Reese-Taylor, Kathryn, Peter Mathews, Julia Guernsey, and Marlene Fritzler. 2009. "Warrior Queens among the Classic Maya." In *Blood and Beauty: Organized Violence in the Art and Archaeology of Mesoamerica and Central America,* edited by Heather Orr and Rex Koontz, 39–72. Los Angeles: Cotsen Institute of Archaeology Press.

Rubin, Gayle. 1975. "The Traffic in Women. Notes on the 'Political Economy' of Sex." In *The Second Wave, A Reader in Feminist Theory,* edited by Linda Nicholson, 28–62. New York: Routledge.

Schiller, Nina Glick, and Georges Fouron. 2001. *Georges Woke Up Laughing: Long-Distance Nationalism and the Search for Home.* Durham, NC: Duke University Press.

Shepherd, Gill. 1987. "Rank, Gender, and Homosexuality: Mombasa as a Key to Understanding Sexual Options." In *The Cultural Construction of Sexuality,* edited by Pat Caplan, 240–70. London: Tavistock.

Strathern, Marilyn. 1972. *Women in Between.* London: Academic Press.

———. 1988. *The Gender of the Gift.* Berkeley: University of California Press.

Wentzell, Emily. 2013. *Maturing Masculinities: Aging, Chronic Illness, and Viagra in Mexico.* Durham: Duke University Press.

Wieringa, Saskia, and Evelyn Blackwood. 1999. "Introduction." In *Female Desires: Same Sex Relations and Transgender Practices across Cultures,* edited by Evelyn Blackwood and Saska Wieringa, 1–38. New York: Columbia University Press.

▲ An Inuit mother and daughter on Baffin Island, Nunavut, Canada, enjoy the sunshine. The young girl rides in her mother's *amauti*, the traditional parka worn by Inuit women in eastern Arctic Canada. Besides keeping both warm, the *amauti* encourages bonding between mother and child. Photo: RyersonClark/iStockphoto

12 Where Do Our Relatives Come From and Why Do They Matter?

Chapter Outline

This chapter will explore the ways anthropologists have investigated differences in human social organization in the key domain of kin and families. The variation these forms of human social organization display across space and over time is truly remarkable, but that does not mean that people are free to do or be whatever they like. Rather, the adaptive flexibility of long-lived, large-brained social animals such as humans develops over the life cycle in response to a range of sometimes unpredictable experiences. This kind of developmental response would be impossible if human behaviour were rigidly programmed by genes, firmly circumscribed by environments, or strictly limited by technologies.

Because human beings need one another to survive and reproduce, they have invented a variety of ways of creating, maintaining, and ending social ties with one another. This chapter focuses primarily on a range of forms of face-to-face relatedness, including kinship, marriage, and patterns of household composition, that different human groups have imagined and practised in different times and places. See Map 12.1 for locations of societies discussed in this chapter.

How Do Human Beings Organize Interdependence?

Human life is group life. How we choose to organize ourselves is open to creative variation, as we have seen.

But each of us was born into a society whose political, economic, and cultural practices were already well established when we arrived. These traditional practices make some kinds of social connections more likely than other kinds. As a result, much can be predicted about a child's probable path in life just by knowing the kind of social groups into which he or she is born. This chapter focuses on how such human experiences as sexuality, conception, birth, and nurturance are selectively interpreted and shaped into shared cultural practices that anthropologists call **relatedness**. Relatedness takes many forms: friendship, marriage, parenthood, shared links to a common ancestor, workplace associations, and so on. And these intimate everyday relationships are always embedded in, and shaped by, broader structures of power, wealth, and meaning.

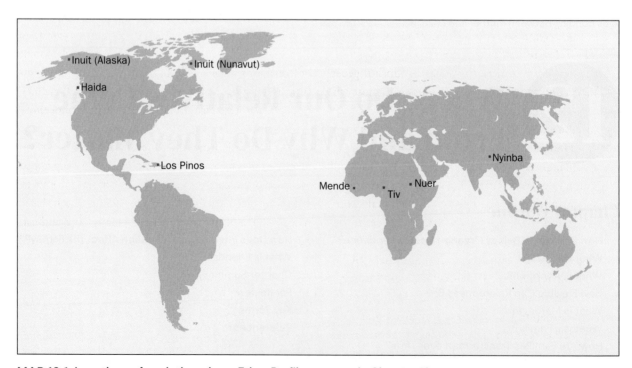

MAP 12.1 Locations of societies whose EthnoProfiles appear in Chapter 12.

For more than a century, anthropologists have studied those forms of relatedness believed to come from shared substance and its transmission (Holy 1996, 171). The substance believed to be shared may be a bodily one (blood, genes, or mother's milk, for example) or a spiritual one (soul, spirit, nurturance, or love, for example); sometimes more than one substance is thought to be shared. Systems of relatedness based on ideas of shared substance are called **kinship systems**. In the West as well as in many other parts of the world, people are thought to share a common substance because it was transmitted to them via the act of sexual intercourse between their parents that led to their conception and birth. Such ideas were close enough to Western beliefs for many anthropologists to conclude that all people everywhere based their kinship systems on the biology of reproduction. It was but a short step to conclude that Western beliefs about which people counted as one's "real" relatives were universally valid. In the early days, kinship studies in anthropology were based on the assumption that all societies recognized the same basic genealogical relationships between mothers and fathers, children and parents, sisters and brothers, and so on. But over the years, ethnographic evidence accumulated indicating that quite often people's understanding of kin ties was strikingly at odds with these genealogical relationships. In other cases, these genealogical relationships turned out to form but a small subset of the ways in which people created enduring connections with one another.

Is there some social glue that ensures social cooperation? In 1968, anthropologist David Schneider argued that North Americans' ideas of kinship generated the feeling of unending loyalty among all those who understood themselves to be related by ties of blood and sex. In many cases, however, human beings seek to establish (or find themselves belonging to) communities organized on regional, national, or global scales. As a result, they come to experience varying degrees of relatedness and solidarity with large numbers of individuals whom they will never meet face to face. As we will see in this chapter, human beings are perfectly capable of establishing and honouring ties of enduring diffuse solidarity that have nothing to do with blood or sex. Sociologist Zygmunt Bauman has argued, in fact, that "all supra-individual groupings are first and foremost processes of collectivization of friends and enemies. . . . More exactly, individuals sharing a common group or category of enemies treat each other as friends" (1989, 152).

Although a common enemy surely has the effect of drawing people together, it is rarely sufficient by itself to produce solidarity that endures. People in all societies have developed patterned social relationships that aim to bind them together for the long term, and some of these reach beyond, and even cut across, ties forged in terms of everyday relatedness. Consider, for example, the way members of Catholic monastic orders, who may neither marry nor bear children, nevertheless refer to one another as *brother*, *sister*, *father*, and *mother*. They also take as the prototype for these interpersonal relationships the formal role obligations of family members. But religious orders in many cases are large, international institutions fitting into the overall global hierarchy of the Catholic Church. Again, the kinds of connections established among members of such institutions reach far beyond the contexts of everyday, face-to-face relatedness.

As we already noted, anthropologists were the first social scientists to recognize that people in different societies classified their relatives into categories that did not correspond to those accepted in European societies. Coming to understand the complexities of different kinds of formal kin relations helped undermine the ethnocentric assumption that European ways of categorizing relatives were a transparent reflection of natural biological ties. Indeed, beginning anthropology students from many backgrounds regularly assume that the way they grew up classifying their kin reflects the universal truth about human relatedness. For this reason, we devote part of this chapter to introducing some findings from kinship studies in anthropology. Learning to distinguish between cross cousins and parallel cousins or considering some of the consequences that follow from tracing descent through women rather than men remain useful exercises that help overcome ethnocentric tendencies.

At the same time, the different classes of relatives identified in a formal kinship system may or may not be considered important in a particular society. Moreover, even when such kin categories remain important, ties of relatedness to people who are not formally kin may be as important as—or more important than—ties to formal

relatedness The socially recognized ties that connect people in a variety of different ways.

kinship systems Social relationships that are prototypically derived from the universal human experiences of mating, birth, and nurturance.

kin. Formal kin ties are supplemented by or replaced by other forms of relatedness in many societies, and these forms of relatedness take a variety of patterns and operate at different scales. This chapter pays particular attention to local, face-to-face forms of relatedness, including friendship, kinship, and adoption.

To recognize the varied forms that institutions of human relatedness can take is to acknowledge fundamental openness in the organization of human interdependence. This openness makes possible the elaboration and extension of ties of relatedness beyond face-to-face contexts. Structures of relatedness with increasingly vast scope tend to emerge when changed historical circumstances draw people's attention to shared aspects of their lives that more intimate forms of

relatedness ignore or cannot handle. New shared experiences offer raw material for the invention of new forms of common identity. Recognition of this process led political scientist Benedict Anderson to invent the term **imagined communities** to refer to "all communities larger than primordial villages of face-to-face contact (and perhaps even these)" (1983, 6). Anderson originally applied the concept of "imagined communities" to modern nation-states, but anthropologists were quick to note the range of communities included in his definition and have used the concept successfully to study different forms of human relatedness. The concept of imagined communities is important because it emphasizes that the ties that bind people into *all* supra-individual communities are *contingent*: they have not existed since the beginning of time, and they may disappear in the future. Put another way, imagined communities are social, cultural, and historical constructions. They are the joint outcome of shared habitual practices and of symbolic images of common identity promulgated by group members with an interest in making a particular imagined identity endure.

> **imagined communities** A term borrowed from political scientist Benedict Anderson to refer to groups whose members' knowledge of one another does not come from regular face-to-face interactions but is based on shared experiences with national institutions, such as schools and government bureaucracies.

In Their Own Words

Survival and a Surrogate Family

What is a family? How are families similar to, and different from, other forms of relatedness? In this excerpt from Gangsters without Borders: An Ethnography of a Salvadoran Street Gang, *anthropologist T.W. Ward addresses these questions from different points of view.*

Youth like José join gangs as a means of survival and self-defense, as a means of constructing an identity of self-worth, and as a way to create a surrogate family. The fact that the gang family can be as dysfunctional as the biological one it replaces—if not much more so—reflects the lack of positive role models and resources available to marginalized youth. As anyone who has studied gang members can attest, adolescents join street gangs in response to hostile neighborhoods, dysfunctional schools, aggressive (bullying) peers, lack of good-paying jobs, and absent, neglectful, or abusive parents or surrogate caretakers. Adolescents also join street gangs as a response to the poverty, racism, and discrimination they experience as the stigmatized and marginalized of society.

Street gangs are part of a deviant subculture, and therefore certain aspects of gang life tend to be shrouded in mystery, which leads to misinformation and misunderstanding. Because they live in a shadow of denial and deception, it is difficult to know what gang members do on a daily basis, much less what they really think and feel. Although partially based on reality, a distorted, stereotypical view of street gangs as highly organized, criminal organizations bent on murder and mayhem has been perpetuated by gang members and law enforcement officials tasked with the attempt to curb their criminal activities. Because it serves their different agendas, these actors have created a mythos about street gangs, which the media is all too eager to report. Despite the vast amount of academic research that has elucidated much of gang life and corrected this distorted view, there is still a large gap between the reality of street gangs and the public perception of what it means to be a gang member.

When I began the research for this book in 1993, like most people I had been conditioned by news, film, and television to believe this stereotype of gang members as tough "street thugs" who enjoy terrorizing others and spend most of their time selling drugs, robbing people, or doing drive-by shootings. Although this is partly true for a small minority of gang members, what I found over the course of eight and a half years of fieldwork was much more complex. Although the violence and criminality of gang life have been well documented and it is well known that some gang members are heavily involved with using and dealing drugs, what is missing from media descriptions of gang life is a holistic perspective that places this behavior in context. The media is not concerned with the fact that there is a great deal of variability of deviance between street gangs and that no two gangs are alike. Likewise, it ignores the enormous variability between individual members and the fact that most gang members are not involved in serious crimes of violence. Furthermore, the popular conception of a gang career does not consider the fact that the vast majority of members eventually retire from their gang and move on to a prosocial life.

For those who have had no direct contact with street gangs, what is least known about them is the flip side of their members' aggression and criminality: namely, the altruism or compassion expressed between homeboys and homegirls and the extent to which their gangs serve as adaptations to hostile environments. Street gangs thrive in the poorest neighborhoods in our urban communities. They are highly complex social organizations that serve multiple functions. Some gangs are like deviant social clubs providing camaraderie, excitement, and entertainment, which are an escape from boredom. Other gangs are like paramilitary organizations that provide protection and opportunity for economic gain

and positive "gangster" status. Regardless of the type of gang, most youth join street gangs in their search for a particular quality of life, a sense of self-worth, and a sense of belonging to a group that cares about their welfare and survival.

When gang members speak about their group as a (surrogate) family, they are referring to this aspect of love and concern for one another. For many, the gang temporarily fills a vacuum of love and respect. Although veterans of the gang life admit that their members usually fall far short of this ideology of sharing and caring for "fellow homies," the fact remains that, for many members, the gang replaces the dysfunctional families and communities that have neglected, abused, or abandoned them in one way or another. Most gang members call their gang a family because, at some level of functionality, it serves the essential purposes of caring and survival. As the gang members intuitively know, the core of any family is kinship, and love and compassion are expected by-products.

In order for the street gang to survive, much less thrive, it must provide some degree of safety and comfort to its members, some sense of status, and some sense of belonging. Otherwise, these disenfranchised youth would seek out some alternative to the gangster life. Generally speaking, the degree to which a gang serves this function of family is the degree to which an individual is committed to a hard-core version of the gangster life. He or she sees the gang as an acceptable substitute for his or her biological or fictive kin. For the most hard-core of gang members, the gang is the primary family they know or care about. For them, in addition to the questions of survival and status, the heart of the matter with street gangs is the matter of the heart, in terms of solidarity and bonding. The gang as surrogate family gives a person a sense of meaning and purpose in life, however distorted, destructive, or dysfunctional. It took me many years of conversation and observation to understand the complexity of how this played out between gang members over many places and many years.

What Is Kinship?

Our discussion of friendship, near the end of the chapter, contrasts the relationships people may develop with friends with other relationships based on kin ties. In this part of the chapter, we want to explore more fully how

traditional anthropological studies of kinship contribute to our understanding of the organization of human relatedness. People struggle to find ways to preserve certain ties of relatedness over time, reinforcing them with public affirmations and gift exchanges. These practices aim to provide scaffolding for enduring forms of social solidarity that strengthen the agency that group members can exercise jointly in their encounters with other groups. At the same time, such publicly acknowledged forms of relatedness can be experienced as a burden from which individuals try to escape.

Anthropologists who study formal systems of *kinship* pay primary attention to those publicly recognized sets of social relations that are prototypically derived from the universal human experiences of mating, birth, and nurturance. Anthropologists call relationships based on mating **marriage** (discussed below), which are referred to as **affinal relationships**; and those based on birth, **descent**—known as **consanguineal relationships**. Although nurturance is ordinarily seen to be closely connected with mating and birth, it need not be, and all societies have ways of acknowledging a relationship based on nurturance alone, which is called **adoption** in English. Although marriage is based on mating, descent on birth, and adoption on nurturance, marriage is not the same thing as mating, descent is not the same thing as birth, and adoption is not the same thing as nurturance. This is because the human experiences of mating, birth, and nurturance are ambiguous. Systems of relatedness in different societies highlight some features of these experiences while downplaying or even ignoring others. Europeans and North Americans know that in their societies mating is not the same as marriage, although a culturally valid marriage encourages mating between the married partners. Similarly, all births do not constitute valid links of descent: children whose parents have not been married according to accepted legal or religious specifications do not fit the cultural logic of descent, and many societies offer no positions that they can properly fill. Finally, not all acts of nurturance are recognized as adoption: consider, for example, foster parents

in Canada, whose custody of foster children is officially temporary. Put another way, through culturally created ties of kinship, a society emphasizes certain aspects of human experience, constructs its own theory of human nature, and specifies "the processes by which an individual comes into being and develops into a complete (i.e., mature) social person" (Kelly 1993, 521).

Marriage, descent, and adoption are thus selective. One society may emphasize women as the bearers of children and base its kinship system on this fact, paying little formal attention to the male's role in conception. Another society may trace connections through men, emphasizing the paternal role in conception and reducing the maternal role. A third society may encourage its members to adopt not only children but also adult siblings, blurring the link between biological reproduction and family creation. Even though they contradict one another, all three understandings can be justified with reference to the panhuman experiences of mating, birth, and nurturance.

Consider the Canadian kinship term *aunt*. This term seems to refer to a woman who occupies a unique biological position. In fact, an aunt may be related to a person in one of four different ways: as father's sister, mother's sister, father's brother's wife, or mother's brother's wife. From the perspective of Canadian kinship, all those women have something in common, and they are all placed into a single kinship category. Prototypically, a person's aunts are women one generation older than he or she is and are sisters or sisters-in-law of a person's parents. However, Canadians may also refer to their mother's best friend as *aunt*. By doing so, they recognize the strengths of this system of classification. By way of contrast, in Chile, *tía*, the Spanish term that translates as "aunt," is regularly used by children to refer to female friends of their parents. Indeed, people well into their early adulthood continue to use the term to refer to women who are taking on the role of "mother," but with whom they are not as intimate as they would be with their own mothers. US university students living with Chilean families frequently use the term *tía* to address the woman who, in English, would be called their "host mother."

Thus, kinship is an idiom. It is a selective interpretation of the common human experiences of mating, birth, and nurturance. The result is a set of coherent principles that allow people to assign one another group membership. These principles normally cover several significant

marriage An institution that transforms the status of the participants, carries implications about permitted sexual access, perpetuates social patterns through the production or adoption of offspring, creates relationships between the kin of partners, and is symbolically marked.

affinal relationships Kinship connections through marriage, or affinity.

descent The principle based on culturally recognized parent–child connections that define the social categories to which people belong.

consanguineal relationships Kinship connections based on descent.

adoption Kinship relationships based on nurturance, often in the absence of other connections based on mating or birth.

issues: how to carry out the reproduction of legitimate group members (marriage or adoption); where group members should live after marriage (residence rules); how to establish links between generations (descent); and how to pass on positions in society (succession) or material goods (inheritance). Taken together, kinship principles define social groups, locate people within those groups, and position the people and groups in relation to one another both in space and over time.

Kinship practices, rather than written statutes, clarify for people what rights and obligations they owe one another. But the first Westerners who encountered different kinship practices found some of them highly unusual. Western explorers discovered, for example, that some non-Western people distinguished among their relatives only on the basis of *age* and *sex*. To refer to people one generation older than the speaker required only two terms: one applying to men and one applying to women. The man who was married to their mother, or whom they believed to be their biological father, although known to them and personally important to them, was socially no more or less significant than that man's brothers or their mother's brothers. The explorers mistakenly concluded that these people were unable to tell the difference between their fathers and their uncles because they used the same kin term for both. They assumed that terms like *father* and *uncle* were universally recognized kinship categories. However, the people whom the explorers met were no more deluded than English speakers are when they assert that their father's sister and mother's brother's wife are equally their *aunts*.

The categories of feeling these people associated with different kin were as real as, but different from, the emotions Westerners associate with kin. Because the world of kin is a world of expectations and obligations, it is fundamentally a moral world charged with feeling. In some societies, a man's principal authority figure is his mother's brother, and his father is a figure of affection and unwavering support. A phrase like "God the Father" would not mean the same thing in those societies as it does in a society in which the father has life-and-death control over his children, and a mother's brothers are without significant authority.

The Role of Descent in Kinship

A central aspect of kinship is descent—the cultural principle that defines social categories through culturally recognized parent–child connections. Descent groups are defined by ancestry and consequently exist in time. They use parent–child links to transmit group identity and to incorporate new members. In some societies, descent group membership controls how people mobilize for social action.

Two major strategies are employed in establishing patterns of descent. In the first strategy, the descent group is formed by people who believe they are related to each other by connections made through their mothers and fathers *equally*. That is, they believe themselves to be just as related to their father's side of the family as to their mother's. Anthropologists call this **bilateral descent** (or *cognatic descent*). Two kinds of bilateral kinship groups have been identified by anthropologists. One is made up of people who claim to be related to one another through ties either from the mother's or the father's side to a common ancestor. This *bilateral descent group* is rare and is found among the Himba in southern Africa. The other kind, called a **bilateral kindred**, is much more common and consists of the relatives of one person or group of siblings.

The second major strategy, **unilineal descent**, is based on the assumption that the most significant kin relationships must be traced through *either* the mother *or* the father. Such descent groups are the most common kind of descent group in the world today, based on a count of the number of societies that continue to employ them. Unilineal descent groups that are made up of links traced through a father are called *patrilineal;* those traced through a mother are called *matrilineal*.

Bilateral Kindreds

The most common kind of bilateral descent group identified by anthropologists is called a *bilateral kindred*. This group includes all the people linked to an individual (or a group of siblings) through kin of both sexes on the mother's and the father's sides of the family—people conventionally called "relatives" in English (Figure 12.1). The bilateral

> **bilateral descent** The principle that a descent group is formed by people who believe they are related to each other by connections made through their mothers *and* their fathers equally (sometimes called *cognatic descent*).
>
> **bilateral kindred** A kinship group that consists of relatives of one person or a group of siblings.
>
> **unilineal descent** The principle that a descent group is formed by people who believe they are related to each other by connections made through *either* their mothers *or* their fathers.

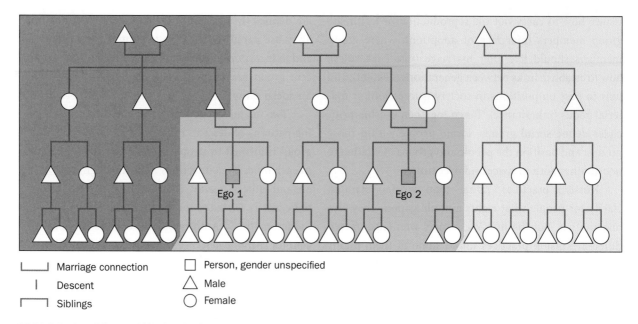

	Marriage connection		Person, gender unspecified
	Descent	△	Male
	Siblings	○	Female

FIGURE 12.1 Bilateral kindred; all people linked to an individual through kin of both sexes.

kindred are the kinship group that most Europeans and North Americans follow. In North American society, bilateral kindreds typically assemble when an individual undergoes a religious rite of passage (e.g., is baptized, is confirmed, or becomes a bar or bat mitzvah); when an individual graduates from high school, college, or university; or when an individual is married or buried. Bilateral kindreds centre on an individual (referred to as "Ego" in the terminology of kinship studies), and each member of that individual's bilateral kindred also has his or her own separate kindred. For example, Ego's father's sister's daughter has kindred that include people related to her through her father and his siblings—people to whom Ego is not related. This is simultaneously the major strength and major weakness of bilateral kindreds. That is, they have overlapping memberships and they do not endure beyond the lifetime of an individual Ego. But they are widely extended and can form broad networks of people who are somehow related to one another.

lineages The consanguineal members of descent groups who believe they can trace their descent from known ancestors.

patrilineage A social group formed by people connected by father–child links.

matrilineage A social group formed by people connected by mother–child links.

The Role of Lineages in Descent

Unilineal descent groups are found all over the world and are the most common type of descent group. Unilineal descent is based on the assumption that a person's most significant kin relationships are aligned through one's mother or through one's father. **Lineages** are unilineal descent groups whose members believe they can specify all the parent–child links that unite them. Lineages that are made up of links traced through a father are called *patrilineal*; those traced through a mother are called *matrilineal*. In a patrilineal society, women and men belong to a **patrilineage** formed by father–child links (Figure 12.2); similarly, in a matrilineal society, men and women belong to a **matrilineage** formed by mother–child connections (Figure 12.3). In other words, membership in the group is, on the face of it, unambiguous. An individual belongs to only one lineage. This is in contrast to a *bilateral kindred*, in which an individual belongs to overlapping groups. The *lineal* in patrilineal and matrilineal refers to the nature of the social group formed. These lineages are composed of people who believe they can specify the parent–child links that unite them. Although the abstract kinship diagrams that anthropologists draw include just a few people, lineages in the world vary in size, ranging from 20 or 30 members to several hundred. Interestingly,

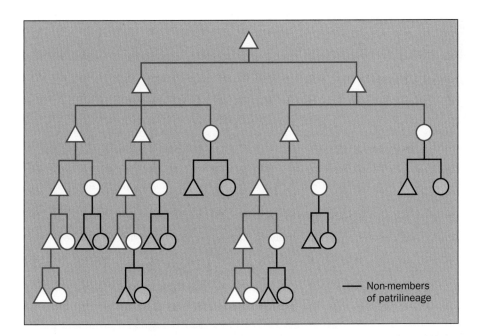

FIGURE 12.2 Patrilineal descent; all those who trace descent through males to a common male ancestor are indicated in white.

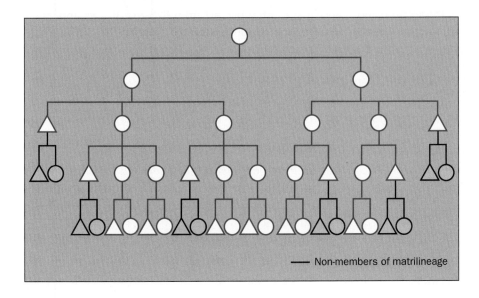

FIGURE 12.3 Matrilineal descent; all those who trace descent through females to a common female ancestor are indicated in white.

the types of lineages are not constant and may change through time. This is demonstrated in the work done by archaeologist Kathryn Reese-Taylor et al. (2009) on Mayan Queens during the Classic period. Their research outlines a shift in power from men to women that aligns with the Mayan civilization moving from a patrilineage to a matrilineage.

Lineage Membership

The most important feature of lineages is that they are *corporate* in organization—that is, a lineage has a single legal entity. The Ashanti, for example, think of a lineage as "one person," since (from the point of view of outsiders) all members of a lineage are equal *in law* to all others (Fortes 1953). For example, in the case of a blood feud, the death of any opposing lineage member avenges the death of the person whose death triggered the feud. Lineages also are important economically, in that they control private property and wealth, commonly areas of land, as a unit. Such groups are found only in societies where rights to use land are crucial and must be monitored over time. Lineages are also the main political associations in the societies that have them; people living in such societies recognize that their individual political or legal status comes mainly through the lineage to which they belong.

In Their Own Words

Mayan Queens: Rulers and Warriors

Canadian archaeologist Kathryn Reese-Taylor and her colleagues from the University of Calgary have begun to identify the powerful roles that wealthy Mayan women played during the Classic period of Maya civilization (c. 200–900 CE). Their interpretations of inscriptions and hieroglyphic representations are helping to recognize how important women were in battles fought in the homelands of the Maya and how possible changes from a patrilineal to a matrilineal kinship system occurred, demonstrating how political and kinship systems are intimately linked.

The importance of women in Maya society is no longer in question. Recent studies have highlighted the important roles played by women, particularly those in the royal courts. . . .

The results of our analysis have allowed us to greatly increase our understanding of Maya women's roles during the Classic period. Most significantly, we can now assert that during the later part of the seventh and early part of the eighth centuries, queens actually ruled independently, participated in battles, and captured enemies. In other words, for several women, the role of a Maya warrior queen was identical in all ways to that of warrior king.

Moreover, the visibility of women in the historic records grew after 623. The manner in which they were portrayed—conducting rituals, dedicating stelae [i.e., stone monuments], capturing prisoners—and, indeed, even the manner in which they were dressed, in the transgendered costume of the Maize God/Moon Goddess, all signify the power and authority royal women commanded in state politics. . . .

Our analysis has demonstrated that at the beginning of the seventh century, the roles of royal women in the central lowlands shifted dramatically. . . . [For example,] matrilineal descent appears to have become more important than patrilineal descent in the northern lowlands. We have also recognized an increased importance placed on matrilineal heritage in the texts and images of public art from 623 to 761. This implies a reformation in kinship systems during this period, at least among the elite of the central lowlands.

While additional research needs to be done to more fully understand Maya kinship systems, as well as gender identities, through this study we have detected a previously unrecognized link between the two. . . . Nonetheless, what is clear is that the shared representational systems—pictorial and textual—that existed in the corpus of Maya Lowland art are a rich source for continued investigation into gender roles, kinship systems, and expressions of political and military authority.

Source: Reese-Taylor et al. 2009, 39, 66–7.

In societies where lineages are found, the system of lineages can serve as a foundation for all social life. Lineage membership is transmitted in a direct line from father or mother to child. This means that in societies in which no other form of organization lasts, lineages can endure as long as people can remember from whom they are descended. Most lineages have a time depth of about five generations: grandparents, parents, Ego, children, and grandchildren. When members of a group believe that they can no longer accurately specify the genealogical links that connect them but believe that they are "in some way" connected, they form what anthropologists refer to as a "clan." A **clan** is usually made up of lineages that the society's members believe to be related to each other through links that go back into mythic times. Sometimes the common ancestor of each clan is said to be an animal that lived at the beginning of time. The distinguishing point is that lineage members can specify all the generational links back to their common ancestor, whereas clan members ordinarily cannot. Thus, a clan can be larger than any lineage and more diffuse in its membership.

clan A descent group formed by members who believe they have a common (sometimes mythical) ancestor, even if they cannot specify the genealogical links.

The Logic of Lineage Relationships

Lineages endure over time in societies in which no other form of organization lasts. Hence, they provide for the "perpetual exercise of defined rights, duties, office and social tasks vested in the lineage" (Fortes 1953, 29). In other words, in the societies where they are found, the system of lineages becomes the foundation of social life.

While lineages might look solid and unchanging, they are often more flexible than they appear. The memories people have of their ancestry are often transmitted in the form of myth or legend. Rather than accurate historical records, they are better understood in Malinowskian terms as mythical charters, justifications from the invisible world for the visible arrangements of the society.

For a discussion of the role of myths, see Chapter 16, pp. 386–9.

In showing how this relationship works, Fortes (1953, 29) quotes anthropologists Paul and Laura Bohannan, whose research was among the Tiv of Nigeria (see EthnoProfile 12.1: Tiv). The Bohannans observed that Tiv who had not previously viewed one another as kin sometimes renegotiated their lineage relationships, announcing publicly that they shared some of the same ancestors. Such changes were plausible to the Tiv because they assumed that traditional lineage relationships determined current social arrangements. If current social arrangements and tradition conflicted, therefore, the Tiv concluded that errors had crept into the tradition. Such renegotiation enabled the Tiv to keep their lineage relationships in line with changing legal and political relationships.

Patrilineages

By far the most common form of lineage organization is the patrilineage, which consists of all the people (male and female) who believe themselves to be related to each other because they are related to a common male ancestor by connections through men. The prototypical kernel of a patrilineage is the father–son pair. Although female members of patrilineages normally leave the lineages when they marry, they do not relinquish their interest in their own lineages. In a number of societies, they play an active role in the affairs of their own patrilineages for many years.

A classic patrilineal system was found among the Nuer of Ethiopia and what is now South Sudan (see

EthnoProfile 12.2: Nuer). At the time of his fieldwork in the 1930s, English anthropologist E.E. Evans-Pritchard (1940) noted that the Nuer were divided into at least 20 clans. Evans-Pritchard defined *clan* as the largest group of people who (1) trace their descent patrilineally from a common ancestor, (2) cannot marry each other, and (3) consider sexual relations within the group to be incestuous. The clan is subdivided, or segmented, into smaller lineages that are themselves linked to each other by presumed ties of patrilineal descent. The most basic level of lineage segmentation is the minimal lineage, which has a time depth of three to five generations (Figure 12.4).

EthnoProfile 12.1

Tiv

Region: Western Africa

Nation: Nigeria (northern)

Population: 800,000

Environment: Undulating plain—wooded foothills to sandbanks

Livelihood: Farming

Political organization: Traditionally, egalitarian; today, part of a modern nation-state

For more information: Bohannan, Laura, and Paul Bohannan. 1969. *The Tiv of Central Nigeria*. 2nd ed. London: International African Institute.

EthnoProfile 12.2

Nuer

Region: Eastern Africa

Nation: Ethiopia and South Sudan

Population: 300,000

Environment: Open grassland

Livelihood: Cattle herding and farming

Political organization: Traditionally, egalitarian tribes, no political offices; today, part of modern nation-states

For more information: Evans-Pritchard, E.E. 1940. *The Nuer*. Oxford: Oxford University Press. Also: Hutchinson, Sharon. 1996. *Nuer Dilemmas*. Berkeley: University of California Press.

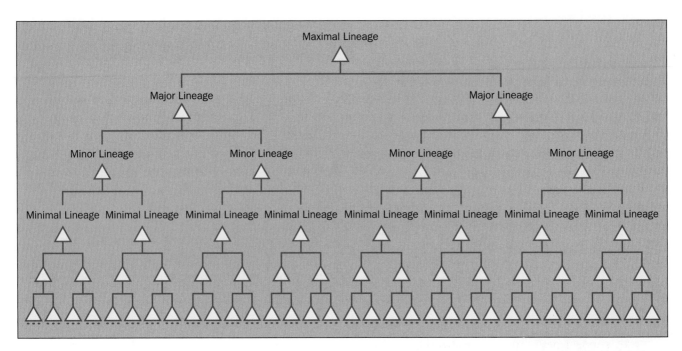

FIGURE 12.4 From a founder recognized by all descendants, lineages develop through *segmentation* across generations. The complexity of this segmentation is determined by the number and gender of the members of each generation.

Evans-Pritchard (1940) observed that the Nuer kinship system worked as a set of nested lineages: members of lineages A and B might consider themselves related because they believed that the founder of lineage A had been the older brother of the founder of lineage B. These two *minimal lineages*, as Evans-Pritchard called them, together formed a *minor lineage*—all those descended from a common father, believed to be the father of the two founders of A and B. Minor lineages connect to other minor lineages by yet another presumed common ancestor one more level back, forming *major lineages*. These major lineages are also believed to share a common ancestor and thus form a *maximal lineage*. The members of two maximal lineages believe their founders had been the sons of the clan ancestor; thus, all members of the clan are believed to be patrilineally related.

According to Evans-Pritchard (1940), disputes among the Nuer emerged along the lines created by lineages. Suppose a quarrel erupted between two men whose minimal lineages were in different minor lineages. Each man could recruit allies both from his own minimal lineage and from all the other minimal lineages that belonged in his major lineage. When members of the quarrelling minor lineages acknowledged (or were made to acknowledge by a mediator) that they were all part of the same major lineage, the dispute would be resolved. Similarly, the minor lineages belonging to one major lineage would ally if a dispute broke out that involved members of another, opposed major lineage. This process of nested groups moving apart or coming together in order to oppose one another at different levels of a hierarchy is called **segmentary opposition**, and it is a very common social process.

Evans-Pritchard (1940) noted that lineages were important to the Nuer for political purposes. Members of the same lineage in the same village were conscious of being in a social group with common ancestors and symbols, corporate rights in territory, and common interests in cattle. When a son in the lineage married, these lineage members helped provide the **bridewealth** cattle, the symbolically valuable goods paid to the bride's lineage in

segmentary opposition A mode of hierarchical social organization in which groups beyond the most basic emerge only in opposition to other groups on the same hierarchical level.

bridewealth The transfer of certain symbolically important goods from the family of the groom to the family of the bride on the occasion of their marriage. It represents compensation to the wife's lineage for the loss of her labour and child-bearing capacities. *Bridewealth* is sometimes referred to as *brideprice*.

compensation for the loss of her services. If the son were killed, they—indeed, all members of his patrilineage, regardless of where they lived—would avenge him and would hold the funeral ceremony for him. Nevertheless, relationships among the members of a patrilineage were not necessarily harmonious:

> A Nuer is bound through balanced reciprocal exchange to his paternal kin from whom he derives aid, security, and status, but in return for these benefits he has many obligations and commitments. Their often indefinite character may be both evidence of, and a reason for, their force, but it also gives ample scope for disagreement. Duties and rights easily conflict. Moreover, the privileges of [patrilineal] kinship cannot be divorced from authority, discipline, and a strong sense of moral obligation, all of which are irksome to Nuer. They do not deny them, but they kick against them when their personal interests run counter to them. (Evans-Pritchard 1951, 162)

Although the Nuer were patrilineal, they recognized as kin people who were not members of their lineage. In the Nuer language, the word *mar* referred to "kin": all the people to whom a person could trace a relationship of any kind, including people on the mother's side as well as on the father's side. In fact, at such important ceremonial occasions as a bridewealth distribution after a woman in the lineage had been married, special attention was paid to kin on the mother's side. Certain important relatives, such as the mother's brother and the mother's sister, were given cattle. A man's mother's brother was his great supporter when he was in trouble. The mother's brother was kind to him as a boy and even provided a second home after he reached manhood. If he liked his sister's son, a mother's brother would even be willing to help pay the bridewealth so that he could marry. "Nuer say of the maternal uncle that he is both father and mother, but most frequently that 'he is your mother'" (Evans-Pritchard 1951, 162).

Matrilineages

In matrilineages, descent is traced through women rather than through men. Recall that in a patrilineage, a woman's children are not in her lineage. In a matrilineage, a man's children are not in his.

Certain features of matrilineages make them more than just mirror images of patrilineages. First, the prototypical kernel of a matrilineage is the sister–brother pair; a matrilineage may be thought of as a group of brothers and sisters connected through links made by women. Brothers marry out and often live with the family of their wives, but they maintain an active interest in the affairs of their lineage. Second, the most important man in a boy's life is not his father (who is not in his lineage) but his mother's brother, from whom he will receive his lineage inheritance. Third, the amount of power women exercise in matrilineal societies is still hotly debated in anthropology. A matrilineage is not the same thing as a *matriarchy* (a society in which women rule); brothers often retain what appears to be a controlling interest in the lineage. Some anthropologists claim that the male members of a matrilineage run the lineage even though there is more autonomy for women in matrilineal societies than in patrilineal ones—that the day-to-day exercise of power tends to be carried out by the brothers or sometimes the husbands. A number of studies, however, have questioned the validity of these generalizations. Saying anything about matrilineal societies in general is difficult. The ethnographic evidence suggests that matrilineages must be examined on a case-by-case basis.

The Haida of Canada's northwest coast are a matrilineal people (see EthnoProfile 12.3: Haida), with each

EthnoProfile 12.3

Haida

Region: Northwest coast of North America

Nation: Canada

Population: 60,000

Environment: Maritime, cool

Livelihood: Fishing, whaling, collecting plants

Political organization: Traditionally, clans, public consensus; today, a tribal council within a modern nation-state

For more information: Boelscher, Marianne. 1988. *The Curtain Within: Haida Social and Political Discourse.* Vancouver: University of British Columbia Press.

matrilineage belonging to either the Raven or the Eagle *k'waalaa* (clan). Strong feelings of reciprocity and social responsibility exist between the Ravens and the Eagles, and membership in a particular matrilineage and its *k'waalaa* shapes individuals' identities as well as social relationships (Krmpotich 2010). The Haida use matrilineal identity to navigate such matters as their participation in potlatches, their use of property, whom they should marry, their social status, and whom they can ask for economic support.

A Haida matrilineage can be thought of as a broad network of families linked through ancestry, property, and common social responsibilities. The most closely related members of a matrilineage tend to share the strongest bonds, which are based on love, friendship, history, obligations, shared work, and commitment. Indeed, matrilineal kin form the basis of each person's sense of family, and they play integral roles in major life events—for example, by leading rites of passage; by preparing feasts, potlatches, weddings, and other celebrations; and by mourning the deceased (Krmpotich 2010, 162). At the same time, individuals are generally encouraged to marry outside of their *k'waalaa*, a practice that facilitates non-matrilineal kinship bonds (e.g., between children and fathers).

Haida often wear crests to represent the matrilineage to which they belong. The designs of these crests are owned and inherited by members of the *k'waalaa* to which they correspond, and they can be painted or embroidered onto garments and even tattooed onto a person (Figure 12.5). These material expressions

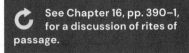

See Chapter 16, pp. 390–1, for a discussion of rites of passage.

perpetuate a sense of belonging and continuity of family and lineages. A significant factor in Haida kinship is the relationships between the living and the dead. Ancestors are often considered as guides for the living, providing opportunities and companionship. The recently deceased often accompany a relative for days or months after their death. Thus, kinship relationships are not only part of the living world; they transcend into the past, solidifying the matrilineal ties among the Haida (Krmpotich 2010, 163).

Kinship Terminologies

People everywhere use special terms to refer to people they recognize as related to them. Despite the variety of kinship systems in the world, anthropologists have identified six major patterns of kinship terminology based on how people categorize their cousins. The six patterns reflect common solutions to structural problems faced by societies organized in terms of kinship. Kinship terminologies suggest both the external boundaries and the internal divisions of kinship groups, and they outline the structure of rights and obligations assigned to different members of the society. They also provide clues about how the vast and undifferentiated world of potential relations may be divided.

What Criteria Are Used for Making Kinship Distinctions?

Anthropologists have identified several criteria that people use to indicate how people are related to one another. See Table 12.1 for a list of the most common to the least common criteria.

By the early 1950s, kinship specialists in anthropology had identified six major patterns of kinship terminology, based on how cousins were classified. In recent years, however, anthropologists have become quite skeptical of the value of these idealized models, in large measure because they are highly formalized, neglect all kin categories except cousins, and fail to consider the full range of people's actual kinship practices. Perhaps the main value to come from formal kinship studies is the fact that they took seriously the ways other people classified their relatives and were able to display the logic that informed such classifications.

Photo by Ann Johansson/Corbis via Getty Images

FIGURE 12.5 Haida use crests to physically represent the matrilineages to which they belong. Here, canoe paddles painted with family crests are stored in a longhouse on Graham Island, part of the Queen Charlotte Islands, in British Columbia.

TABLE 12.1 Most Common Criteria Used to Identify How People Are Related to One Another

Generation	Kin terms distinguish relatives according to the generation to which the relatives belong. In English, the term *cousin* conventionally refers to a non–sibling relative of the same generation as Ego.
Gender	The gender of an individual is used to differentiate kin. In Spanish, *primo* refers to a male cousin; and *prima,* to a female cousin. In English, cousins are not distinguished on the basis of gender, but *uncle* and *aunt* are distinguished on the basis of both generation and gender.
Affinity	A distinction is made on the basis of connection through marriage, or **affinity**. This criterion is used in Spanish when *suegra* (Ego's spouse's mother) is distinguished from *madre* (Ego's mother). In matrilineal societies, Ego's mother's sister and Ego's father's sister are distinguished from one another on the basis of affinity. The mother's sister is a direct, lineal relative; the father's sister is an affine; and they are called by different terms.
Collaterality	A distinction is made between kin who are believed to be in a direct line and those who are "off to one side," linked to Ego through a lineal relative. In English, the distinction of **collaterality** is exemplified by the distinction between *mother* and *aunt* or *father* and *uncle.*
Bifurcation	The distinction of **bifurcation** is employed when kinship terms referring to the mother's side of the family differ from those referring to the father's side.
Relative Age	Relatives of the same category may be distinguished on the basis of whether they are older or younger than Ego. Among the Ju/'hoansi, for example, speakers must separate "older brother" (*!ko*) from "younger brother" (*tsin*).
Gender of Linking Relative	This criterion is related to collaterality. It distinguishes *cross relatives* (usually cousins) from *parallel relatives* (also usually cousins). Parallel relatives are linked through two brothers or two sisters. **Parallel cousins,** for example, are Ego's father's brother's children or Ego's mother's sister's children. Cross relatives are linked through a brother–sister pair. Thus, **cross cousins** are Ego's mother's brother's children or Ego's father's sister's children. The gender of either Ego or the cousins does not matter; rather, the important factor is the gender of the linking relative (Figure 12.6).

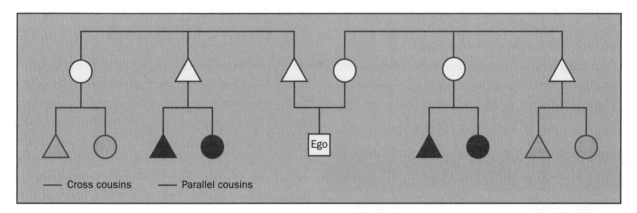

FIGURE 12.6 Cross cousins and parallel cousins. Ego's cross cousins are the children of Ego's father's sister and Ego's mother's brother. Ego's parallel cousins are the children of Ego's father's brother and Ego's mother's sister.

What Is Adoption?

Kinship systems sometimes appear to be fairly rigid sets of rules that use the accident of birth to thrust people into social positions laden with rights and obligations they cannot escape. Social positions that people are assigned at birth are sometimes called **ascribed statuses**, and positions within a kinship system have long been viewed as the prototypical ascribed statuses in any society. Ascribed statuses are often contrasted with

affinity Connection through marriage.

collaterality A criterion employed in the analysis of kinship terminologies in which a distinction is made between kin who are believed to be in a direct line and those who are "off to one side," linked to the speaker by a lineal relative.

bifurcation A criterion employed in the analysis of kinship terminologies in which kinship terms referring to the mother's side of the family are distinguished from those referring to the father's side.

parallel cousins The children of a person's parents' same-gender siblings (a father's brother's children or a mother's sister's children).

cross cousins The children of a person's parents' opposite-gender siblings (a father's sister's children or a mother's brother's children).

ascribed statuses Social positions people are assigned at birth.

achieved statuses Social positions people may attain later in life, often as the result of their own (or other people's) effort.

achieved statuses, those social positions that people may attain later in life, often as the result of their own (or other people's) effort, such as becoming a spouse or college graduate. All societies have ways of incorporating outsiders into their kinship groups, however, which they achieve by converting supposedly ascribed kinship statuses into achieved ones, thus undermining the distinction between them. We will use the term *adoption* to refer to these practices that allow people to transform relationships based on nurturance into relations of kinship.

Adoption and Naming among the Inuit of Nunavut

In some societies, such as that of ancient Rome, people distinguish between Ego's biological father (or *genitor*) and Ego's social father (or *pater*); they may also distinguish between Ego's biological mother (or *genetrix*) and Ego's social mother (or *mater*). Social parents are those who nurture a child, and they are often the child's biological parents as well. Among the Inuit of Nunavut, these distinguishing factors are not strongly acknowledged (see EthnoProfile 12.4). Rather, the Inuit view of extended

family encompasses the concept of "custom adoption"—a traditional form of adoption in which the adoptee maintains flexible relationships with her or his birth and adoptive families. As Valerie Alia (2007, 35) has observed, in Nunavut communities, "children move daily among the homes of birth and adoptive parents . . . receiving care, food, and companionship." Alia further notes that this form of adoption is generally considered to be "more welcoming and less stigmatized than adoption among *Qallunaat* [i.e., southerners]" (36). According to Alia's informants, "adoptions are a part of everyday life," and "giving a child for adoption is a way of making sure every *amauti* (or *amautik*) (the baby-carrying hood on a woman's parka, or *amautik*) carries a child" (36) (Figure 12.7). This practice of adoption encourages the formation of families, which contributes to a strong sense of community and provides families with many hands to help with hunting, fishing, preparing food, maintaining homes, and other sustenance tasks. Moreover, as Alia notes, "[w]hen communities are small and communication is open, adopted children grow up well nurtured and loved" (36).

To understand the cultural significance of custom adoption, it is important to understand the Inuit tradition of naming. According to the highly intricate *sauniq* naming system, Inuit parents and other relatives (usually women, sometimes men) assign the adoptee the name of a deceased relative. This act not only commemorates the deceased but also forms a vital, symbolic connection between the adoptee and her or his namesake, allowing the namesake to "live on" in the community. To the Inuit, the giving of a *sauniq* name is an act of extreme importance. As Alia (2007, 37) notes, "naming is a—perhaps *the*—central component of Inuit culture. It is

EthnoProfile 12.4

Inuit (Nunavut)

Region: North American Arctic

Nation: Canada

Population: 100,000

Environment: Arctic archipelago, tundra, shrub tundra

Livelihood: Hunting, fishing

Political organization: Traditionally, band societies; today, self-governing as part of a modern nation-state

For more information: McElroy, Ann. 2008. *Nunavut Generations: Change and Continuity in Canadian Inuit Communities.* Long Grove, IL: Waveland Press.

[Map labels: Ellesmere Island, GREENLAND, Banks Island, Baffin Bay, Victoria Island, Baffin Island, Inuit (Nunavut), Nunavut, Northwest Territories, 0 300 600 Kilometres]

FIGURE 12.7 An Inuit mother carries her daughter in her *amauti* on Baffin Island, Nunavut.

Lee Thomas/Alamy Stock Photo

often viewed literally as reincarnation—the embodiment of continuity from person to person and generation to generation." Guemple (1979, 51) offers additional insight into the connections between naming and relatedness:

> In Inuit society, children are not thought to be extensions of and therefore in some sense "owned" by their parents . . . [T]heir identity is . . . introduced into their bodies in the form of a name spirit . . . The bond between parents and child is the bond of "love" and the only persons whose personal sense of self-worth is affected by the actions of the child are his [or her] ritual relatives, most importantly his [or her] namesakes. (qtd in Alia 2007, 36)

How Flexible Can Relatedness Be?

Negotiation of Kin Ties among the Ju/'hoansi

Michael Peletz observes that many contemporary kinship studies in anthropology "tend to devote considerable analytic attention to themes of contradiction, paradox and ambivalence" (1995, 343). This is true of Richard Lee's analysis of kinship among the Ju/'hoansi. Lee learned that for the Ju/'hoansi "the principles of kinship constitute, not an invariant code of laws written in stone, but instead a whole series of codes, consistent enough to provide structure but open enough to be flexible." He adds, "I found the best way to look at [Ju/'hoansi] kinship is as a game, full of ambiguity and nuance" (2012, 67).

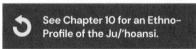
See Chapter 10 for an Ethno-Profile of the Ju/'hoansi.

The Ju/'hoansi have what seems to be a straightforward bilateral kindred with alternating generations. Outside the nuclear core of the system, the same terms are used by Ego for kin of his or her generation, his or her grandparents' generation, and his or her grandchildren's generation. Likewise, the same terms are used for Ego's parents' generation and children's generation. These terms have behavioural correlates, which Lee calls "joking" kin and "avoidance" kin. Anyone in Ego's own generation (except opposite-gender siblings) and in the grandparents' generation or the grandchildren's generation is joking kin. Anyone in Ego's parents' generation or

children's generation is avoidance kin, as are Ego's same-gender siblings. Relatives in a joking relationship can be relaxed and affectionate and can speak using familiar forms. In an avoidance relationship, however, respect and reserve are required, and formal language must be used. Many of these relationships may be warm and friendly if the proper respect is shown in public; however, people in an avoidance relationship may not marry one another.

The "game," as Lee puts it, in the Ju/'hoansi system begins when a child is named. The Ju/'hoansi have very few names: 36 for men and 32 for women. Every child must be named for someone: a first-born son should get his father's name; and a first-born daughter, her father's mother's name. Second-born children are supposed to be named after the mother's father and mother. Later children are named after the father's brothers and sisters and the mother's brothers and sisters. It is no wonder that the Ju/'hoansi invent a host of nicknames to distinguish among people who have the same name. Ju/'hoansi naming practices impinge upon the kinship system because all people with the same name will claim to be related. A man older than you with your name is called *!kun!a* ("old name"), which is the same term used for *grandfather*. A man younger than you with your name is called *!kuna* ("young name"), the same term used for *grandson*. It does not matter how people are "really" related to others with the same name or even if they are related at all according to formal kinship terminology; the name relationship takes precedence.

But the complications do not end there. By metaphorical extension, you call anyone with your father's name *father*; anyone with your wife's name, *wife*; and so on. Worse, "a woman may not marry a man with her father's or brother's name, and a man may not marry a woman with his mother's or sister's name" (Lee 2012, 79). Sometimes, a man can marry a woman but because his name is the same as her father's she can't marry him! Further, you may not marry anyone with the name of one of your avoidance kin. As a result, parents who do not want their children to marry can almost always find a kinship-related reason to block the marriage. Once again, it does not matter what the exact genealogical relationships are.

The name relationship ties Ju/'hoansi society closer together by making close relatives out of distant ones. At the same time, it makes nonsense of the formal kinship system. How is this dilemma resolved? The Ju/'hoansi have a third component to their kinship system, the principle of *wi*, which operates as follows: relative age is one of the few ways the Ju/'hoansi have of marking distinctions. Thus, in any relationship that can be described by more than one kin relationship, the older party chooses the kin term to be used. For example, a man may get married only to discover that his wife's aunt's husband has the same name he has. What will he and his wife's aunt call each other? According to the principle of *wi*, the aunt decides because she is older. If she calls him *nephew* (rather than *husband*), he knows to call her *aunt*.

The principle of *wi* means that a person's involvement with the kinship system is continually changing over the course of his or her lifetime. For the first half of people's lives, they must accept the kin terms their elders choose, whether they understand why or not. After midlife, however, they begin to impose *wi* on their juniors. For the Ju/'hoansi, kinship connections are open to manipulation and negotiation rather than being rigidly imposed from the outside.

Compadrazgo in Latin America

An important set of kinship practices in Roman Catholic Latin America is *compadrazgo*, or ritual co-parenthood. The baptism of a child requires the presence of a godmother and a godfather as sponsors. By participating in this ritual, the sponsors become the ritual co-parents of the child. In Latin America, godparents are expected to take an active interest in their godchildren and to help them wherever possible. However, the more important relationship is between the godparents and the parents. They become *compadres* ("co-parents"), and they are expected to behave toward each other in new ways.

Sometimes, the godparents are already kin; in recent years, for example, Nicaraguans have been choosing relatives living in the United States as *compadres* (Lancaster 1992, 66). A couple often chooses godparents whose social standing is higher than their own: the owners of the land they farm, for example, or owners of the factory where they work. Participating together in the baptism changes these unequal strangers into ritual kin whose relationship, although still unequal, is now personalized, friendlier, more open. The parents will support the godparents when that support is needed (politically, for

example), and the godparents will do favours for the parents. They even call each other *compadre* rather than, say, "Señor López" and "José."

Catherine Allen notes that the bonds of *compadrazgo*, in combination with marriage alliances and kinship,

> form constellations of mutual obligation and dependence that shift with time as new *compadrazgo* relationships are formed, young relatives come of age, and old bonds fall into disuse through death or quarreling. Like kin ties, bonds of *compadrazgo* can become as much a burden as an asset, and like kin ties they can be ignored or honored in the breach. (1988, 90)

What Is Marriage?

The forms of relatedness we have just described are intimately connected with another widespread social process: marriage. Marriages and households represent another form of relatedness that provides significant forms of social support that enable people to take part in wider patterns of social life. In many places, they also facilitate important economic and political exchanges between the kinship groups to which the marriage partners belong. Even when marriage is not connected with lineage or clan relations, marriage patterns provide frameworks for linking previously unrelated people to one another, embedding individuals within groups, and organizing individual emotional commitments and economic activities.

Toward a Definition of *Marriage*

Marriage and *family* are two terms anthropologists use to describe how mating and its consequences are understood and organized in different societies. Marriage involves more than living together and having sexual relations, and nowhere in the world is marriage synonymous with *mating*. In most societies, marriage also requires involvement and support from the wider social groups to which the spouses belong—first and foremost, from their families. A prototypical marriage (1) transforms the status of the participants; (2) stipulates the degree of sexual access the married partners are expected to have to each other, ranging from exclusive to preferential; (3) perpetuates social patterns through the production or adoption of offspring, who also have

---

compadrazgo Ritual co-parenthood in Latin America and Spain, established through the Roman Catholic practice of having godparents for children.

rights and obligations; (4) creates relationships between the kin of the partners; and (5) is symbolically marked in some way.

Many societies have long considered the prototypical marriage to involve a man and a woman. But as the following cases illustrate, marriage can take many forms.

Woman Marriage and Ghost Marriage among the Nuer

Among the Nuer, as E.E. Evans-Pritchard observed during his fieldwork in the 1930s, a woman could marry another woman and become the "father" of the children the wife bore (see EthnoProfile 12.2: Nuer). This practice, which also appears in some other parts of Africa, involves the distinction between pater and genitor. The female husband (the pater) had to have some cattle of her own to use for bridewealth payments to the wife's lineage. Once the bridewealth had been paid, the marriage was established. The female husband then got a male kinsman, friend, or neighbour (the genitor) to impregnate the wife and to help with certain tasks around the homestead that the Nuer believed could be done only by men.

Generally, Evans-Pritchard (1951) noted, a female husband was unable to have children herself "and for this reason counts in some respects as a man." Indeed, she played the social role of a man. She could marry several wives if she was wealthy. She could demand damage payment if those wives engaged in sexual activity without her consent. She was the pater of her wives' children. On the marriage of her daughters, she received the portion of the bridewealth that traditionally went to the father, and her brothers and sisters received the portions appropriate to the father's side. Her children were named after her, as though she were a man, and they addressed her as "Father." She administered her compound and her herds as a male head of household would, and she was treated by her wives and children with the same deference shown a male husband and father.

More common in Nuer social life was what Evans-Pritchard called the "ghost marriage." The Nuer believed that a man who died without male heirs left an unhappy and angry spirit who might trouble his living kin. The spirit was angry because a basic obligation of Nuer kinship was for a man to be remembered through and by his sons: his name had to be continued in his lineage. To appease the angry spirit, a kinsman of the dead man—a brother or a brother's son—would often marry a woman

"to his name." Bridewealth cattle were paid in the name of the dead man to the patrilineage of a woman. She was then married to the ghost of the dead man but lived with one of his surviving kinsmen. In the marriage ceremonies and afterward, this kinsman acted as though he were the true husband. The children of the union were referred to as though they were the kinsman's, but officially they were not. That is, the ghost husband was their pater and his kinsman, their genitor. As the children got older, the name of their ghost father became increasingly important to them. The ghost father's name, not his stand-in's name, would be remembered in the history of the lineage. The social union between the ghost and the woman took precedence over the sexual union between the ghost's surrogate and the woman.

Ghost marriage serves to perpetuate social patterns. Although it was common for a man to marry a wife "to his kinsman's name" before he himself married, it became difficult, if not impossible, for him to marry later in his own right. His relatives would tell him he was "already married" and that he should allow his younger brothers to use cattle from the family herd so they could marry. Even if he eventually accumulated enough cattle to afford to marry, he would feel that those cattle should provide the bridewealth for the sons he had raised for his dead kinsman. When he died, he died childless because the children he had raised were legally the children of the ghost. He was then an angry spirit, and someone else (in fact, one of the sons he had raised for the ghost) had to marry a wife to *his* name. Thus, the pattern continued, as, indeed, it does to the present day.

Why Is Marriage a Social Process?

Like all formal definitions, our definition of marriage is somewhat rigid, especially if we think of marriage as a ritual action that accomplishes everything at a single point in time. Thinking of marriage as a social process rather than a rigid form, however, is more inclusive of all forms of marriage, even those that may not perfectly fit the definition (Figure 12.8). For example, a marriage ritual may join spouses together, but their production of offspring who mature into recognized members of a particular social group takes time and cannot be assured in advance. Traditionally in some societies, a couple were not considered fully married until they had a child. A marriage sets up new relationships that bring together the kin of both spouses. These are called affinal relationships (based

Courtesy Robert H. Lavenda

FIGURE 12.8 Marriage is a social process that creates social ties and involves more than just the people getting married. Family and friends recognize the new couple after the formal ceremony in Venice.

Galen Rowell/Getty Images

FIGURE 12.9 This is an elaborate marriage in Rajasthan, India.

on *affinity*—relationships created via marriage) and contrast with consanguineal relationships (based on "blood" ties, i.e., on descent).

Marriage mediates relationships based on affinity and consanguinity and thus can play an important role in the formation of social groups. Marriage marks a major transformation of social position. It affects not only the newly married couple and their families but also the wider community, which is responsible for acknowledging the legitimacy of every new union (see Figure 12.9). Every society has its own forms of matchmaking. Sometimes marriages must be contracted within a particular social group, a pattern called **endogamy**. In other cases, marriage partners must be found outside a particular group, a pattern called **exogamy**. In Nuer society, for example, a person had to marry outside his or her lineage. In Canada, where the ideology of individualism leads many people to conclude that they can marry whomever they want, statistically people tend to marry within the bounds of certain

groups. For example, young people are often told to marry "your own kind," which usually means someone in their own ethnic, racial, or religious group or social class. Until recently, legal definitions of marriage in Canada also prohibited marriage between individuals of the same sex (see the "In Their Own Words" boxes).

Patterns of Residence after Marriage

Once married, spouses must live somewhere. There are four major patterns of post-marital residence. Most familiar to North Americans is **neolocal residence**, in which the new couple sets up an independent household at a place of their own choosing. Neolocal residence tends to be found in societies that are more or less individualistic in their organization.

When the married couple lives with (or near) the husband's father's family, the pattern is called **patrilocal residence**, which is observed by more societies in the contemporary world than any other residenc pattern.

---

endogamy Marriage within a defined social group.

exogamy Marriage outside a defined social group.

neolocal residence A post-marital residence pattern in which a married couple sets up an independent household at a place of their own choosing.

patrilocal residence A post-marital residence pattern in which a married couple lives with (or near) the husband's father.

In Their Own Words

Two Cheers for Gay Marriage

Roger Lancaster is a professor of anthropology and director of cultural studies at George Mason University. In this essay from the Anthropology News *of September 2004, he discusses some of the issues involved with gay marriage.*

Announcing his support for a proposed constitutional amendment to ban same-sex marriages, President Bush pronounced marriage, or more specifically the union of one man and one woman, to be "the most fundamental institution of civilization." Actually, it can hardly be said that monogamous heterosexual marriage is the sole form of union "honored and encouraged in all cultures and by every religious faith," as Bush claims. That's Anthropology 101. Nor can it be said that the idea of gay marriage runs counter to 5,000 years of moral teaching, as spokespersons for the Christian right insist.

What careful scholarship and "millennia of human experience" actually show is that marriage cannot be forever fixed into a one-size-fits-all formula. There's more than one way to live, to love, and to set up home and hearth.

Just What Is Marriage?

Marriage sometimes involves a formal union marked by a public announcement or a ritual—like a wedding. Or it might have the informal character of a union gradually acquired or consolidated over a period of time. What North Americans and Europeans call "common-law marriage" is the prevailing form of union in many parts of Latin America and elsewhere. For these (and other) reasons, anthropologists often avoid using baggage-laden terms like "marriage" when describing the broad sweep of institutions related to affinity, residency and kinship, opting instead for more portable (if off-putting) technical terms like "union" or "alliance."

Just how many forms of same-sex union one discerns across cultures and throughout human history will depend on what one counts as "same sex" and "union." Bonds of same-sex friendship, publicly announced and ritually marked by an officiating authority, amount to something very much like "marriage" in a great number of cultures. So do other forms of same-sex group affiliation, such as orders of nuns, certain priesthoods, the Band of Thebes, any number of warrior castes, and highly organized groups of women who

lived collectively on the Chinese Kwantung delta in the 19th century. Ironically, the very wedding vows that the president wants to "protect" derive from early Greek Christian same-sex commitment ceremonies, as historian John Boswell has shown in his final book, *Same-Sex Unions in Premodern Europe*.

Modern Love

What most Americans think of as "marriage" actually turns out not to be a universal institution, but a relatively recent invention. If you read St Paul or St Augustine, for instance, you'll see that the fathers of the early Christian Church were quite hostile to marriage. Far from celebrating the sexual union of one man and one woman, St Paul recommended celibacy for everyone and only grudgingly accepts marriage as a back-up plan: "Better to marry than to burn."

Although archaic texts sometimes refer to wedding feasts, marriage rituals involving the exchange of vows appear to develop fairly late in medieval Europe. The idea that an officiating authority—a priest—ought to be present during those vows comes later still. Later yet, the Church starts to keep records. And much later, the state becomes involved.

The revolutionary notion that one might marry, not in the political or economic interests of extended kin groups, but voluntarily and out of love, is an idea of distinctly modern vintage—one whose implications our culture continues to digest. And that's where we find ourselves today: in the throes of ongoing changes and contestations.

Social conservatives lament the decline of traditional families, the rise of divorce rates, the spread of cohabiting arrangements, the emergence of new family forms and, perhaps especially, the growing visibility of lesbian and gay relationships. They tap pervasive feelings of unease about the new arrangements. But logically, you can't have love without heartache. You probably can't have the idea that love is the sole legitimate basis for marriage without also having modern divorce rates. (Levelheaded people entered into the

Continued

spirit of this arrangement in the 1970s, when they began vowing "as long as we both shall *love*.") All said, these aspects of sexual modernity would seem to follow, more or less logically, from the idea that our relationships, like other contracts in a market economy, ought to be entered into freely. They would seem to follow from the idea that marriage ought to be based on love.

And once you have a modern culture of love, linked to that consummate American right, "the pursuit of happiness," it becomes difficult to justify arbitrarily excluding people from it.

Where Do We Go from Here?

Obviously, who's in and who's out of official kinship really matters. It counts in ways that are more than symbolic. There are real social, economic and health care implications. It's thus important to modernize the official definitions of marriage. But like most members of the gay left, I do worry about the fetishization of marriage and family in US political culture—a phenomenon not notably found in a single other industrial democracy. Claims about the supposed benefits of marriage, anguish over how to strengthen the family, and endless talk about "individual responsibility" have become panaceas in an era of declining wages, skyrocketing health care costs, vindictive welfare reform and social *in*security in general.

These collective fantasies distill a distinctly neoliberal picture of the world: the family, shored up by monogamous marriage (and sometimes enhanced by "covenant marriage"), is to act as a sort of state within the state, providing for individual members' welfare—precisely at a time when the state has renounced its historic responsibilities for social welfare (as I have shown in *The Trouble with Nature*).

In this skewed and surreal context, advocates of gay marriage sometimes sound more conservative than the conservatives. They sometimes present an astonishingly unrepresentative and unrealistic picture of gay and lesbian relationships. In a recent *Nation* article, Lisa Duggan pulls this quote from "The Roadmap to Equality," published by the Lambda Legal Defense and Education Fund and Marriage Equality in California: "Gay people are very much like everyone else. They grow up, fall in love, form families and have children. They mow their lawns, shop for groceries and worry about making ends meet. They want good schools for their children, and security for their families as a whole."

Frankly, I doubt that this suburban picture of children, school worries, lawnmowers, and domestic bliss really applies to more than a very small minority—perhaps as small as 3 or 4 percent—of the gay and lesbian community. I certainly want no part of America's deranged culture of lawn care. I also chafe at the idea, floated in the same guide, that denying marriage rights to lesbian and gay couples keeps them in a state of permanent adolescence. I don't *feel* like a permanent adolescent.

I've lived with my lover for over 15 years. I'd like some legal recognition of our relationship. I'd like the right to file joint taxes, if married couples are going to have that option, and the right to inherit each other's pensions and social security benefits. But I have no interest in quasi-religious rigmarole or moralizing platitudes. I don't feel that our relationship would benefit from the exchange of vows. And like most sound people of my generation, I'm skeptical of claims about the moral and existential benefits of being "shackled by forgotten words and bonds / And the ink stains that are dried upon some line" (as John Hartford once put it).

We need gay marriage, and we should fight for it. But we also need recognition of the true existent variety of ways people live and love. And everybody—whether they take the plunge or not—ought to have access to basic health care, affordable housing and a decent retirement. A one-size institution won't fit all. We need more options, not less. We need to be as radical as reality about these matters.

Source: Lancaster, Roger. 2004. "Two Cheers for Gay Marriage." *Anthropology News* 45 (6): 21–4.

It produces a characteristic social grouping of related men: a man, his brothers, and their sons (along with in-marrying wives) all live and work together. This pattern is common in both herding and farming societies; some anthropologists argue that survival in such societies depends on activities that are best carried out by groups of men who have worked together all their lives.

When the married couple lives with (or near) the family in which the wife was raised, the pattern is called **matrilocal residence**, which is usually found in

matrilocal residence A post-marital residence pattern in which a married couple lives with (or near) the wife's mother.

In Their Own Words

Marriage in Canada: The Evolution of a Fundamental Social Institution

Nicholas Bala, a professor in the Faculty of Law at Queen's University, reflects on the evolution of marriage laws in Canada generally, and on the shift to legal recognition of same-sex marriage in particular, as a consequence of changing social attitudes toward marriage and constitutional reform.

Marriage is one of the oldest social institutions, predating recorded history, law, and perhaps even religion. Marriage has not been a static social or legal institution, but rather has changed over the course of history in response to changing religious beliefs, social values and behaviours, technology, and even demographics. Similarly, there is great variation today in marital behaviours, attitudes, and laws about marriage in different countries.

Despite profound changes in the legal and social nature of marriage, marriage has remained a fundamental social institution, with primary responsibility for the nurturing and care of children. As society changes, the question which must be faced is whether the legal rules that were developed in the past to govern the definition of marriage and spousal relationships continue to best meet current social, economic, cultural, and spiritual needs and circumstances.

. . . [R]eligion historically established the legal basis of marriage throughout much of the world. In Canada and the United States, marriage law was largely based on Christian doctrine about marriage, in particular as reflected in English common law. . . . In both Canada and the United States, the laws and expectations for husbands and wives within marriage have changed dramatically over the past half century, setting the stage for the possible redefinition of marriage to include same-sex partners. . . . [M]arriage is now regarded as a "partnership of equals." Laws no longer refer to "husbands" and "wives," but are generally written in gender-neutral terms. Fathers and mothers are, in statutes, presumed to be equally capable of caring for their children. Spouses are viewed as legally equal. Gender roles in marriage are no longer *legally* prescribed.

Historically in Canada, there was great social [criticism] attached to adults who were "living in sin"—cohabiting without being married—and there was no legal recognition given to this type of relationship. Changing social mores in the 1960s and 1970s led to wider social acceptance of opposite-sex cohabitation outside of marriage and an increase in the incidence of what is often referred to in Canada as "common-law marriage." By 2001, 14 per cent of all Canadian opposite-sex couples residing together were unmarried, an increase from 6 per cent in 1981. Between 1972 and 1992, almost every province enacted legislation giving limited recognition to unmarried opposite-sex partners for a range of legal purposes such as spousal support.

At the same time, starting in 1977, provincial legislatures in Canada began to amend their human rights codes to add a prohibition of discrimination on the basis of sexual orientation. After the introduction of the Canadian Charter of Rights and Freedoms in 1982, most politicians and members of the Canadian public were prepared to accept that it was wrong to overtly discriminate against individuals on the basis of their sexual orientation in regard to such issues as employment. In a number of decisions starting in 2002, lower courts in most jurisdictions in Canada recognized that it is a violation of the Charter to deny same-sex partners the right to marry. By early 2005, courts in eight provinces and two territories had issued such rulings.

The government brought the Civil Marriage Act (Bill C-38) to Parliament in February 2005, to define a "civil marriage" as "the lawful union of two persons to the exclusions of all others." In the spring of 2005, there was intense lobbying of members of Parliament over same-sex marriage, with demonstrations, advertising, and letter-writing campaigns. Much of the anti–same-sex marriage advocacy was undertaken by conservative, faith-based groups. More liberal faith groups and civil liberties organizations supported changing the definition of marriage to allow same-sex partners to marry. There were Parliamentary Committee hearings and extensive media debates over same-sex marriage. Bill C-38 was passed by the House of Commons by a vote of 158 to 133 on 28 June 2005. The new marriage law came into force on 20 July 2005, after passage by the Senate.

Continued

The introduction of same-sex marriage in Canada has been motivated by a desire to respect the equality and human dignity of all Canadians, and in particular to recognize the social and emotional importance of the conjugal relationships of homosexuals (see Figure 12.10). This development also has considerable social value, as it promotes the interests of children who are being parented by same-sex partners, and it shifts some burdens which might otherwise fall on the state onto private shoulders (e.g., through allowances for spousal and child support). The recognition of same-sex marriage is of profound symbolic significance. The court decisions about same-sex marriage and the ultimate government response recognize the fundamental right of gays and lesbians to full equality under the law and provide important social validation of these relationships.

Source: Bala, Nicholas. 2005. "The Debates about Same-Sex Marriage in Canada and the United States: Controversy over the Evolution of a Fundamental Social Institution." *Brigham Young University Journal of Public Law* 20 (2): 195–220.

FIGURE 12.10 Definitions of marriage have evolved in Canada, with civil marriage of same-sex couples becoming legal in 2005 across the country. Here, Michael Leshner and Michael Stark, the first same-sex couple to marry in Canada, display their wedding bands.

association with matrilineal kinship systems. Here, the core of the social group consists of a woman, her sisters, and their daughters (along with in-marrying husbands). This pattern is most common among groups practising extensive agriculture.

Less common, but also found in matrilineal societies, is the pattern known as **avunculocal residence**. Here, the married couple lives with (or near) the husband's mother's brother. The most significant man in a boy's matrilineage is his mother's brother, from whom he will inherit. Avunculocal residence emphasizes this relationship.

Single and Plural Spouses

The number of spouses a person may have varies cross-culturally. Anthropologists distinguish forms of marriage in terms of how many spouses a person may have. **Monogamy** is a marriage form in which a person may have only one spouse at a time, whereas **polygamy** is a marriage system that allows a person to have more than one spouse at a time. Within the category of polygamy are two subcategories: **polygyny**, or multiple wives, and **polyandry**, or multiple husbands. Of the two, polygyny is far more common in societies around the world.

Monogamy

Monogamy is the most common spousal pattern in Canada and most industrialized nations. There are variations in the number of times a monogamous person can be married. Before the twentieth century, people in western European societies generally married only once

avunculocal residence A post-marital residence pattern in which a married couple lives with (or near) the husband's mother's brother (from *avuncular*, "of uncles").

monogamy A marriage pattern in which a person may be married to only one spouse at a time.

polygamy A marriage pattern in which a person may be married to more than one spouse at a time.

polygyny A marriage pattern in which a man may be married to more than one wife at a time.

polyandry A marriage pattern in which a woman may be married to more than one husband at a time.

unless death intervened. Today, some observers suggest that we practise *serial monogamy*—we may be married to several different people but only one at a time.

Polygyny

Polygynous societies vary in the number of wives a man may have. Islam permits a man to have as many as four wives but only on the condition that he can support them equally. Some Muslim authorities today argue, however, that equal support must be emotional and affective, not just financial. Convinced that no man can feel the same toward each of his wives, they have concluded that monogamy must be the rule. Other polygynous societies have no limit on the number of wives a man may have. Nevertheless, not every man can be polygynous. There is a clear demographic problem: for every man with two wives, there is one man without a wife. Men can wait until they are older to marry and women can marry very young, but this imbalance cannot be eliminated. Polygyny is also expensive, for a husband must support all his wives as well as their children (Figure 12.11).

Polyandry

Polyandry is the rarest of the three marriage forms. In some polyandrous societies, a woman may marry several brothers. In others, she may marry men who are related to each other and who all will live together in a single household. Sometimes a woman is allowed to marry several men who are not related, but she will live only with the one she most recently married. Studies of polyandry have shed new light on the dynamics of polygyny and monogamy, as well.

The traditional anthropological prototype of polyandry is based on marriage practices among some groups in Nepal and Tibet, where a group of brothers marry one woman. This is known as *fraternal polyandry*. During a wedding, one brother, usually the oldest, serves as the groom. All brothers (including those yet to be born to the husbands' parents) are married by this wedding, which establishes public recognition of the marriage. The wife and her husbands live together, usually patrilocally. All brothers have equal sexual access to the wife, and all act as fathers to the children. In some cases—notably among the Nyinba of Nepal (Levine 1980, 1988)—each child is recognized as having one particular genitor, who may be a different brother from the genitor of his or her siblings (see EthnoProfile 12.5: Nyinba). In other cases, all

FIGURE 12.11 The wives and children of a polygynous family.

the brothers are considered jointly as the father, without distinguishing the identity of the genitor.

There appears to be little sexual jealousy among the men, and the brothers have a strong sense of solidarity with one another. Levine (1988) emphasizes this point for the Nyinba. If the wife proves sterile, the brothers may marry another woman in hopes that she may be fertile. All brothers also have equal sexual access to the new wife and are treated as fathers by her children. Additional benefits of polyandry include the fact that land and wealth of a family of brothers will not be divided up between siblings, into smaller and smaller plots. Rather the land will be worked on jointly and wealth shared among the family.

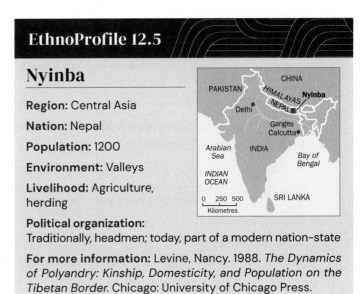

EthnoProfile 12.5

Nyinba

Region: Central Asia

Nation: Nepal

Population: 1200

Environment: Valleys

Livelihood: Agriculture, herding

Political organization: Traditionally, headmen; today, part of a modern nation–state

For more information: Levine, Nancy. 1988. *The Dynamics of Polyandry: Kinship, Domesticity, and Population on the Tibetan Border.* Chicago: University of Chicago Press.

According to Levine, Nyinba polyandry is reinforced by a variety of cultural beliefs and practices (1988, 158ff.). First, it has a special cultural value. Nyinba myth provides a social charter for the practice because the legendary ancestors are polyandrous, and they are praised for the harmony of their family life. Second, the solidarity of brothers is a central kinship ideal. Third, the corporate, landholding household, central to Nyinba life, presupposes the presence of a single wife with multiple husbands. Fourth, the closed corporate structure of Nyinba villages is based on a limited number of households, and polyandry is highly effective at checking the proliferation of households. Fifth, a household's political position and economic viability increase when its resources are concentrated.

The Distinction between Sexuality and Reproductive Capacity

Polyandry allows for a woman's sexuality to be distinguished from her reproductive capacity. This distinction is absent in monogamous or purely polygynous systems where a women's sexual and reproductive capacities are inseparable (except, perhaps, in prostitution), yet they usually accept such separation for men without question: "It may well be a fundamental feature of the [world view] of polyandrous peoples that they recognize such a distinction for both men and women" (Levine and Sangree 1980, 388). In the better-known polyandrous groups, a woman's sexuality can be shared among an unlimited number of men, but her child-bearing capacities cannot. Indeed, among the Nyinba, a woman's child-bearing capacities are carefully controlled and limited to one husband at a time. But she is free to engage in sexual activity outside her marriage to the brothers as long as she is not likely to get pregnant. As we saw in Chapter 11, Western assumptions about the relationship between sex, gender, and sexuality are not universal.

The Connection between Marriage and Economic Exchange

In many societies, marriage is accompanied by the transfer of certain symbolically important goods. Anthropologists have identified two major categories of marriage payments, called bridewealth or dowry.

Bridewealth, discussed earlier in this chapter, is most common in patrilineal societies that combine agriculture, pastoralism, and patrilocal marriage, although it is found in other types of societies as well (Figure 12.12).

Real photo postcard by J.W. Beattie

FIGURE 12.12 This photo from Santa Cruz Island (in the Solomon Islands) from 1906 shows bridewealth—in the foreground, reels of feather money on a rod, and in the background, other items of bridewealth carried on the women's heads.

When it occurs among matrilineal peoples, a post-marital residence rule (avunculocal, for example) usually takes the woman away from her matrilineage.

The goods exchanged as bridewealth have significant symbolic value to the people concerned. They may include shell ornaments, ivory tusks, brass gongs, bird feathers, cotton cloth, and animals. Cash may also be used. Bridewealth in animals is prevalent in eastern and southern Africa, where cattle have the most profound symbolic and economic value. In these societies, a man's father, and often his entire patrilineage, give a specified number of cattle (often in instalments) to the patrilineage of the man's bride. Anthropologists view bridewealth as a way of compensating the bride's relatives for the loss of her labour and child-bearing capacities. When the bride leaves her home, she goes to live with her husband and his lineage. She will be working and producing children for his people, not her own.

Bridewealth transactions create affinal relations between the relatives of the wife and those of the husband. The wife's relatives, in turn, may use the bridewealth they receive to find a bride for her brother in yet another kinship group. In many societies in eastern and southern Africa, a woman gains power and influence over her brother because her marriage brings the cattle that allow him to marry and continue their lineage. This is why Jack Goody and Stanley Tambiah (1973, 17) describe bridewealth as "a societal fund, a circulating pool of resources, the movement of which corresponds to the movement of rights over spouses, usually women." Or, as the Southern Bantu put it, "cattle beget children" (Kuper 1982, 3).

Dowry, by contrast, is typically a transfer of family wealth, usually from parents to their daughter, at the time of her marriage (Figure 12.13). It is found primarily in the agricultural societies of Europe and Asia but has been brought to some parts of Africa with the arrival of religions such as Islam that support the practice. In societies where both women and men are seen as heirs to family wealth, dowry is sometimes regarded as the way women receive their inheritance. Dowries are often considered the wife's contribution to the establishment of a new household, to which the husband may bring other forms of wealth. In stratified societies, the size of a woman's dowry often ensures that when she marries she will continue to enjoy her accustomed style of life. The goods included in dowries vary in different societies and may or may not include land (Goody and Tambiah 1973). There is perhaps a carryover from the European dowry in the Western practice of the bride's family paying for her wedding. However, dowry payments that may be

Dinodia Photos/Alamy Stock Photo

FIGURE 12.13 Dowries take many forms, depending on the cultural preferences of a given group of people. Here is a display of dowry items from Tamil Nadu, India.

dowry The wealth transferred, usually from parents to their daughter, at the time of a woman's marriage.

In Their Own Words

Law, Custom, and Crimes against Women

John van Willigen and V.C. Channa describe the social and cultural practices surrounding dowry payments that appear to be responsible for violence against women in some parts of India.

A 25-year-old woman was allegedly burnt to death by her husband and mother-in-law at their East Delhi home yesterday. The housewife, Mrs Sunita, stated before her death at the Jaya Prakash Narayana Hospital that members of her husband's family had been harassing her for bringing inadequate dowry.

The woman told the Shahdara subdivisional magistrate that during a quarrel over dowry at their Pratap Park house yesterday, her husband gripped her from behind while the mother-in-law poured kerosene over her clothes.

Her clothes were then set ablaze. The police have registered a case against the victim's husband, Suraj Prakash, and his mother.

—*Times of India*, 19 February 1988

This routinely reported news story describes what in India is termed a "bride-burning" or "dowry death." Such incidents are frequently reported in the newspapers of Delhi and other Indian cities. In addition, there are cases in which the evidence may be ambiguous, so that deaths of women by fire may be recorded as kitchen accidents, suicides, or murders. Dowry violence takes a characteristic form. Following marriage and the requisite giving of dowry, the family of the groom makes additional demands for the payment of more cash or the provision of more goods. These demands are expressed in unremitting harassment of the bride, who is living in the household of her husband's parents, culminating in the murder of the woman by members of her husband's family or by her suicide. The woman is typically burned to death with kerosene, a fuel used

Continued

in pressurized cook stoves, hence the use of the term "bride-burning" in public discourse.

Dowry death statistics appear frequently in the press and parliamentary debates. Parliamentary sources report the following figures for married women 16 to 30 years of age in Delhi: 452 deaths by burning for 1985; 478 for 1986, and 300 for the first six months of 1987. There were 1319 cases reported nationally in 1986 (*Times of India*, 10 January 1988). Police records do not match hospital records for third-degree burn cases among younger married women; far more violence occurs than the crime reports indicate.

There is other violence against women related both directly and indirectly to the institution of dowry. For example, there are unmarried women who commit suicide so as to relieve their families of the burden of providing a dowry. A recent case that received national attention in the Indian press involved the triple suicide of three sisters in the industrial city of Kanpur. A photograph was widely published showing the three young women hanging from ceiling fans by their scarves. Their father, who earned about 4000 Rs [rupees] per month, was not able to negotiate marriage for his oldest daughter. The grooms were requesting approximately 100,000 Rs. Also linked to the dowry problem is selective female abortion made possible by amniocentesis. This issue was brought to national attention with a startling statistic reported out of a seminar held in Delhi in 1985. Of 3000 abortions carried out after sex determination through amniocentesis, only one involved a male fetus. As a result of these developments, the government of the state of Maharashtra banned sex determination tests except those carried out in government hospitals.

Source: van Willigen, John, and V.C. Channa. 1991. "Law, Custom, and Crimes against Women." *Human Organization* 50 (4): 369–70.

perceived as inadequate can sometimes lead to tragic results, such as violence against women. For more on this, see "In Their Own Words" box.

What Is a Family?

Traditionally, Euro-Canadians have considered a family to be a mother, father, and their biological children. Early kinship studies were focused on finding units in other cultures that either compared to this model or could be contrasted by it. This is no longer the case, as new ideas of what *family* means in different cultural contexts, as well as in Western society, have evolved. As more and more research demonstrates, there is a variety of family structures around the world, and a new definition is needed. Essentially, a **family** is any group of individuals who provide for one another, regardless of their biological connection. While this new definition has its roots in Western LGBTQ community activism (see Chapter 11),

ethnographers such as Janet Carsten (2004) have found significant challenges to the idiom that "blood is thicker than water" in other societies. The Malays she interviewed and lived with considered children (and adults) who were fostered with them to progressively become a "blood" member of the family. As those being fostered or simply hosted partake of the host family's meals, their blood becomes more like that of the hosts, strengthening familial bonds. (Rice is a major source of nutrition and contributes to healthy blood.) Carsten observed that the ideal guest is one who decides to extend her stay indefinitely because she has been successfully incorporated into the host family. If she does decide to stay, she will no longer be considered a guest but a local and will perhaps even begin to take on the appearance and mannerism of her new family.

Anthropologists tend to distinguish the **conjugal family**, which is a family based on marriage—at its minimum, a husband and a wife (or a spousal pair) and their children—from the **non-conjugal family**, which consists of a woman or a man and her or his children. In a non-conjugal family, the spouse may be occasionally present or completely absent. Non-conjugal families are never the only form of family organization in a society and, in fact, cross-culturally are usually rather infrequent. In some large-scale industrial societies, including Canada, however, non-conjugal families have become increasingly common. In most societies, the conjugal family is co-resident—that is, spouses live in the same

family A group of individuals who can be considered as a single unit based on shared rights and responsibilities.

conjugal family A family based on marriage; at a minimum, a spousal pair and their children.

non-conjugal family A woman and her children; the husband/father may be occasionally present or completely absent.

dwelling, along with their children—but there are some matrilineal societies in which the husband lives with his matrilineage, the wife and children live with theirs, and the husband visits his wife and children. In Canada today, where many men as well as women are single parents, the view that a man and his children constitute a family is widely shared. This illustrates the ongoing reconfiguration of North American family relations, other features of which are described below.

Nuclear Families

The structure and dynamics of neolocal monogamous families are familiar to North Americans. These families are called *nuclear families*, and it is often assumed that most people in Canada live in them (although in 2010 only about one-quarter of the Canadian population did). For anthropologists, a **nuclear family** is made up of two generations: the parents and their unmarried children. Each member of a nuclear family has a series of evolving relationships with every other member: husband and wife, parents and children, and children with each other. These are the lines along which jealousy, competition, controversy, and affection develop in neolocal monogamous families; sibling rivalry, for example, is a form of competition characteristic of nuclear families that is shaped by the relationships between siblings and between siblings and their parents.

Polygynous Families

A polygynous family includes, at a minimum, the husband, all his wives, and their children. Polygynous families are significantly different from nuclear families in their internal dynamics. Each wife has a relationship with her co-wives as individuals and as a group (Figure 12.14). Co-wives, in turn, individually and collectively, interact with the husband. These relationships change over time, as the authors (Emily A. Schultz and Richard H. Lavenda) were once informed during their fieldwork in Guider, northern Cameroon (see EthnoProfile 14.2: Guider in Chapter 14). The nine-year-old daughter of the authors' landlord announced one day that she was going to become Lavenda's second wife. "Madame [Schultz]," she said, "will be angry at first, because that's how first wives are when their husbands take a second wife. But after a while, she will stop being angry and will get to know me and we will become friends. That's what always happens."

The differences in internal dynamics in polygynous families are not confined to the relationships of husband and wives. An important distinction is made between

Courtesy Robert H. Lavenda

FIGURE 12.14 Co-wives in polygynous households frequently co-operate in daily tasks, such as food preparation.

children with the same mother and children with a different mother. In Guider, people ordinarily refer to all their siblings (half and full) as brothers or sisters. When they want to emphasize the close connection with a particular brother or sister, however, they say that he or she is "same father, same mother." This terminology conveys a relationship of special intimacy and significance. Children, logically, also have different kinds of relationships with their own mothers and their fathers' other wives—and with their fathers as well.

Where there is a significant inheritance, these relationships serve as the channels for jealousy and conflict.

> **nuclear family** A family pattern made up of two generations: the parents and their unmarried children.

The children of the same mother, and especially the children of different mothers, compete with one another for their father's favour. Each mother tries to protect the interests of her own children, sometimes at the expense of her co-wives' children.

Competition in the Polygynous Family

Although the relationships among wives in a polygynous society may be very close, among the Mende of Sierra Leone, co-wives eventually compete with each other (see EthnoProfile 12.6: Mende). Caroline Bledsoe (1993) explains that this competition is often focused on children: how many each wife has and how likely it is that each child will obtain things of value, especially education. Husbands in polygynous Mende households are supposed to avoid overt signs of favouritism, but their wives do not all have equal status. To begin with, wives are ranked by order of marriage. The senior wife is the first wife in the household, and she has authority over junior wives. Marriage order structures the household but also lays the groundwork for rivalries. Wives are also ranked, however, in terms of the status of the families from which they came. Serious conflicts arise if the husband shows favouritism by paying for the education of the children of a wife from a high-status family before educating the older children of other wives or the children of wives higher in the marriage-order ranking.

The level of her children's education is important to a Mende woman because her principal claim to her husband's land or cash and her expectations of future support after he dies come through her children. She depends not only on the income that a child may earn to support her but also on the rights her children have to inherit property and positions of leadership from their father. Nevertheless, education requires a significant cash outlay in school fees, uniforms, books, and so on. A man may be able to send one child to a prestigious private school only if he sends another to a trade apprenticeship. These economic realities make sense to husbands but can lead to bitter feuds among co-wives and even divorce when wives blame their husband for disparities in the accomplishments of their children. In extreme cases, co-wives are said to use witchcraft to make their rivals' children fail their exams. To avoid these problems, children are frequently sent to live with relatives who will send them to school. Such competition is missing in monogamous households unless they include adopted children or spouses who already have children from a previous marriage.

Extended and Joint Families

Within any society, certain patterns of family organization are considered proper. In Canadian nuclear families, two generations live together. In some societies, three generations—parents, married children, and grandchildren—are expected to live together in a vertical **extended family**. In still other societies, the extension is horizontal: brothers and their wives (or sisters and their husbands) live together in a **joint family**. These are ideal patterns, and not all families are able or willing to emulate them. Note that extended families do not operate the way joint families operate, and neither can be understood as just several nuclear families that happen to overlap. Extended and joint families are fundamentally different from nuclear families with regard to the rights and obligations they engender among their members.

EthnoProfile 12.6

Mende

Region: Western Africa

Nation: Sierra Leone

Population: 12,000,000

Environment: Forest and savannah

Livelihood: Slash-and-burn rice cultivation, cash cropping, diamond mining

Political organization: Traditionally, a hierarchy of local chiefdoms; today, part of a modern nation-state

For more information: Little, Kenneth. 1967. *The Mende of Sierra Leone*. London: Routledge and Kegan Paul.

extended family A family pattern made up of three generations living together: parents, married children, and grandchildren.

joint family A family pattern made up of brothers and their wives or sisters and their husbands (along with their children) living together.

How Are Families Transformed over Time?

Families change over time: they have a life cycle and a lifespan. The same family takes on different forms and provides different opportunities for the interaction of members at different points in its development. New households are formed and old households change through divorce, remarriage, the departure of children, and the breakup of extended families.

Divorce and Remarriage

Most societies make it possible for married couples to separate. In some societies, the process is long, drawn out, and difficult, especially when bridewealth must be returned; a man who divorces a wife in such societies or whose wife leaves him expects some of the bridewealth back. But for the wife's family to give the bride-wealth back, a whole chain of marriages may have to be broken up. Brothers of the divorced wife may have to divorce to get back enough bridewealth from their in-laws. Sometimes a new husband will repay the bridewealth to the former husband's line, thus relieving the bride's relatives of this expense.

Grounds for Divorce

Depending on the society, nagging, quarrelling, cruelty, stinginess, or adultery may be cited as causes for divorce. In almost all societies, childlessness is grounds for divorce as well. For the Ju/'hoansi, most divorces are initiated by women, mainly because they do not like their husbands or do not want to be married (Lee 1992; Shostak 1981). After what is often considerable debate, a couple that decides to break up merely separates. There is no bridewealth to return, no legal contract to be renegotiated. Mutual consent is all that is necessary. The children stay with the mother. Ju/'hoansi divorces are cordial, Richard Lee (1992) tells us, at least compared with the Western norm. Ex-spouses may continue to joke with each other and even live next to each other with their new spouses.

Separation among the Inuit

Among the northwestern Inuit, the traditional view is that all kin relationships, including marital ones, are permanent (Burch 1970) (see EthnoProfile 12.7). Thus, although it is possible to deactivate a marriage by separating, a marriage can never be permanently dissolved. (Conversely, re-establishing the residence tie is all that is needed to reactivate the relationship.) A husband and wife who stop living together and having sexual relations with each other are considered to be separated and ready for another marriage. If each member of a separated couple remarried, the two husbands of the wife would become co-husbands, and the two wives of the husband would become co-wives; the children of the first and

second marriages would become co-siblings. In effect, a "divorce" among the Inuit results in more, not fewer, connections. Not all contemporary Inuit, especially those who are Christians, continue to follow this practice.

Blended Families

In recent years, anthropologists have observed the emergence of a new family type in Canada: the **blended family**. A blended family is created when previously divorced or widowed people marry, bringing with them children from their previous marriages. The internal dynamics of the new family—which can come to include his children, her children, and their children—may resemble the dynamics of polygynous families, as the relations among the children and their relations to each parent may be complex and negotiated over time.

The Flexibility of Marriage

It is easy to get the impression that marriage rules compel people to do things they really do not want to do. Younger people, for example, seem forced by elders to marry complete strangers of a certain kin category belonging to particular social groups; or women appear to

EthnoProfile 12.7

Inuit (Alaska)

Region: North American Arctic

Nation: United States (northwestern Alaska)

Population: 11,000 (1960s)

Environment: Arctic: mountains, foothills, coastal plain

Livelihood: Hunting, wage labour, welfare

Political organization: Traditionally, families; today, part of a modern nation–state

For more information: Burch, Ernest S., Jr. 1975. *Eskimo Kinsmen: Changing Family Relationships in Northwest Alaska.* American Ethnological Society Monograph, no. 59. St Paul: West

blended family A family created when previously divorced or widowed people marry, bringing with them children from their previous families.

be pawns in men's games of prestige and power. Marriage rules, however, are always subject to some negotiation, as illustrated by the marriage practices of the Ju/'hoansi of the Kalahari Desert (see EthnoProfile 10.1: Ju/'hoansi in Chapter 10). Richard Lee (2012) notes that all first marriages were set up by means of a long-term exchange of gifts between the parents of a bride and groom.

The Ju/'hoansi kinship system is as simple or as complex as people want to make it, and the game of kinship is extended to marriage. A girl may not marry a father, brother, son, uncle, or nephew or a first or second cousin. A girl may also not marry a boy with her father's or brother's name, and a boy may not marry a girl with his mother's or sister's name. In addition, neither a boy nor a girl should marry someone who stands in an avoidance relationship.

Consequently, for the Ju/'hoansi, about three-quarters of a person's potential spouses are off limits. In practice, parents of girls tend to be quite choosy about whom their daughter marries. As mentioned earlier, if they are opposed to a particular suitor, they will come up with a kin or name prohibition to block the match. Because the parents arrange the first marriage, it appears that the girl has very little to say about it. If she has an objection and protests long and hard, however, her parents may well call it off. This clear and insistent assertion of displeasure is not uncommon in the world. Even when a young woman follows the wishes of her parents for her first marriage, that first marriage may not be her last if dissatisfaction persists. Despite the parents' quest to find ideal spouses for their children, close to half of all first marriages among the Ju/'hoansi fail. However, as in many societies, only about 10 per cent of marriages that last five years or longer end in divorce (Lee 2012, 90).

Sometimes the contrast between the formal rules of marriage and the actual performance of marriage rituals can be revealing. Ivan Karp (1978) asks why Iteso women laugh at marriage ceremonies. During his fieldwork, Karp was struck by a paradox. The marriage ritual is taken very seriously by the patrilineal Iteso; it is the moment of creation for a new household, and it paves the way for the physical and social reproduction of Iteso patrilineages. But the ritual is carried out entirely by women who are not consanguineal members of the patrilineage! Despite the seriousness of the occasion and although they are carrying out the ritual for the benefit of a lineage to which they do not belong, Iteso women seem to find the ceremony enormously funny.

To explain this apparently anomalous behaviour, Karp suggests that the meaning of the marriage ritual needs to be analyzed from two different perspectives: that of the men and that of the women. The men's perspective constitutes the official (or hegemonic) ideology of Iteso marriage. It emphasizes how marriage brings the bride's sexuality under the control of her husband's lineage. It distinguishes between women of the mother-in-law's generation and women of the wife's own generation and stresses the woman's role as an agent of reproduction.

The women's perspective constitutes an unofficial (or counterhegemonic) ideology. For the men and women of a given lineage to succeed in perpetuating that lineage, they must control women's bodies. But the bodies they must control belong to female outsiders who marry lineage men. These same female outsiders direct the two ritual events crucial to lineage reproduction: marriage and birth. And men of the lineage are not allowed to attend either of these rituals. In sum, female outsiders control the continued existence of a patrilineage whose male members are supposed to control them!

Iteso women, Karp says, can see the irony in this: they are at once controlled and controlling. In the marriage ritual itself, they comment on this paradox through their laughter. In so doing, they reveal two things. First, they show that they know the men are dependent on them. Second, even as the men assert their control over women's bodies, the women's ritual actions escape the men's control. The official ideology of male control is subverted, at least momentarily, by the women's laughter. Even as they ensure that lineages will continue, they are able to comment on the paradoxical relation of women to men. It should be remembered, however, that all the women could do was comment on those relations; they did not have the power to change them.

How Does International Migration Affect the Family?

Migration to find work in another country has become increasingly common worldwide and has important effects on families. Anthropologist Eugenia Georges (1990) examined migration's effects on people who migrated to the United States from Los Pinos, a small town in the Dominican Republic (see EthnoProfile 12.8: Los Pinos). Migration divided these families, with some members moving to New York and some remaining in Los Pinos. Some parents stayed in the Dominican Republic while their children went to the United States. A more common pattern was for the husband to migrate and the wife to stay home. Consequently, many households in Los Pinos were headed by women. In most cases, however, the spouse in the United States worked to bring the spouse and children in Los Pinos to the United States.

This sometimes took several years because it involved completing paperwork for the visa and saving money beyond the amount regularly sent to Los Pinos. Children of the couple who were close to working age also came to the United States, frequently with their mother, and younger children were sent for as they approached working age. Finally, after several years in the United States, the couple who started the migration cycle would often take their savings and return home to the Dominican Republic. Their children stayed in the United States and continued to send money home. Households expanded across national borders, linked through nurturance, kinship, and obligation. Return migrants tended not to give up their residence visas and, therefore, had to return to the United States annually. Often, they stayed for a month or more to work. This also provided them with the opportunity to buy household goods at a more reasonable cost, as well as other items—clothing, cosmetics, and the like—to sell to neighbours, friends, and kin in the Dominican Republic (Figure 12.15).

Georges observes that the absent family member maintained an active role in family life despite the heavy psychological burden of separation. Although he might be working in a hotel in New York, for example, the husband was still the breadwinner and the main decision maker in the household. He communicated by visits, letters, and occasional telephone calls. Despite the strains of migration, moreover, the divorce rate was actually slightly lower in migrant families than in families whose members never migrated. This was in part because the exchange of information between Los Pinos and New York was both dense and frequent but also because strong ties of affection connected many couples. Finally, "the goal of the overwhelming majority of the migrants [from Los Pinos] I spoke with was permanent return to the Dominican Republic. Achievement of this goal was hastened by sponsoring the migration of dependents, both wives and children, so that they could work and save as part of the reconstituted household in the United States" (Georges 1990, 201). This pressure also helped keep families together.

EthnoProfile 12.8

Los Pinos

Region: Caribbean

Nation: Dominican Republic

Population: 1000

Environment: Rugged mountain region

Livelihood: Peasant agriculture (tobacco, coffee, cacao) and labour migration

Political organization: Part of a modern nation-state

For more information: Georges, Eugenia. 1990. *The Making of a Transnational Community: Migration, Development, and Cultural Change in the Dominican Republic.* New York: Columbia University Press.

In recent years, the Internet has come to play an increasingly important role in the lives of families that are separated by migration, education, work, and so on. Daniel Miller and Don Slater (2000) studied Internet use in Trinidad, finding that email and instant messaging have considerably strengthened both nuclear and extended families, allowing closer relations between distant parents and children, among siblings, and among other relatives. They remark on the experiences of a widow they knew who, depressed after her husband's death, was convinced by relatives to learn to use email to contact a beloved grandchild who had gone abroad.

FIGURE 12.15 As migration from the Dominican Republic to the United States has increased, more Dominicans are staying and bringing their families or creating families in the United States. Such celebrations of ethnic pride as the Dominican Day Parade in New York City have increased in recent years.

This experience was so valuable to her that she began to contact other relatives abroad and in Trinidad, and younger members of her family "swear it has given her 'a new lease of life'" (61). Overall, the use of the Internet offers anthropologists the opportunity to observe how family separation can be moderated and offers people around the world opportunities for relaxed, expansive, and everyday forms of communication that seem to have important effects on family life.

What Is Friendship?

Anthropologists have devoted surprisingly little attention to **friendship** and have found that it is no easier to define it than it is to define other such forms of relatedness as kinship or marriage. Nevertheless, a useful definition might be the relatively "unofficial" bonds that people construct with one another. These tend to be bonds that are personal, affective, and, to a varying degree from society to society, matters of choice (Bell and Coleman 1999). A recent work on friendship (Killick and Desai 2010) argues that friendship evades definition and that it can best be understood, at least from the perspective of the people who use the term in a particular society, as a relationship that contrasts with other ways of relating to people. One might go fishing with someone because he is your cousin, your friend, or the best fisherman in the area. For many anthropologists, particularly of an older generation, it would have been the kinship category to which attention was to be paid. Killick and Desai (2010) claim that it is essential to retain the analytic distinction between friendship and kinship, "since it is this aspect that appears to be of crucial importance in giving friendship its moral force in so many societies around the world" (2010). In other words, when someone from Canada says that her husband is her best friend, she is perfectly aware of the difference between the affinal relationship of husband and wife and that of the Canadian definition of best friend, and she uses the difference to highlight the kind of relationship she has with her husband.

In contemporary society, social networking programs such as Facebook are taking friendship in new

and unprecedented directions: what can it mean to have 900 friends? The line between friendship and kinship is often very fuzzy because there may be an affective quality to kinship relations (we can like our cousins and do the same things with them that we would do with friends), sometimes friends are seen after a long time as being related, and some societies have networks of relatedness that can be activated or not for reasons of sentiment, not just for pragmatic reasons. Friendship has been difficult for some anthropologists to study because in the past they have concentrated on trying to find regular long-term patterns of social organization in societies with non-centralized forms of political organization (Bell and Coleman 1999, 4). Bell and Coleman also note that the importance of friendship seems to be increasing: "In many shifting social contexts, ties of kinship tend to be transformed and often weakened by complex and often contradictory processes of globalization. At the same time new forms of friendship are emerging" (5). This is illustrated in Rio de Janeiro by Claudia Barcellos Rezende (1999), who observed the ways in which middle-class women and their maids could come to refer to each other as "friends." Within this hierarchical relationship, the distinctions that separated the women were not questioned in themselves, but the "friendship" consisted of affection, care, and consideration that both sets of women valued in their work relationship. It was a way of establishing trust: "What friendship invokes . . . is the affinity that brings these people together as parts of the same social world" (93) (see Figure 12.16).

Similarly, Magnus Course (2011) directs our attention to the way in which friendship and becoming a real person—*che*—are related among the Mapuche of Chile.

FIGURE 12.16 These two young men in Cameroon were the best of friends.

friendship The relatively "unofficial" bonds that people construct with one another that tend to be personal, affective, and often a matter of choice.

The Mapuche are one of the largest Indigenous groups in the Americas; there are about 1 million in Chile and another 40,000 in Argentina. For the Mapuche, Course asserts, conceptualization of the person is best characterized as "centrifugal"—that is to say that there is an open-ended movement through the lifespan outward from the kin relations that are "given" at birth to "chosen" friendship relations (Course 2011, 72). This is how personhood is constituted—one must go beyond relations with one's kin that one is born into to those relations that people create through their own volition that allows them to become *che*. This, Course tells us, is the central importance of friendship in the constitution of the Mapuche

person: "it is impossible to overestimate the importance of friends, as it is through the activation of the capacity to form relationships with un-related others that one becomes a true person" (2011, 73).

These examples demonstrate that human societies are able to organize human interdependency successfully across a broad range of variation in family forms and other relationships as noted in the friendship section. In the next chapter, we will look at another way that humans organize themselves via political relations, studying the ways we manage power, prestige, and/or wealth among different individuals and different groups.

Chapter Summary

1. Human life is group life; we depend upon one another to survive. All societies invent forms of relatedness to organize this interdependence. People in all societies recognize that they are connected to certain other people in a variety of ways and that they are not connected to some people at all. Anthropologists have traditionally paid closest attention to those formal systems of relatedness called kinship systems. But anthropologists also draw attention to other forms of relatedness, such as friendship, that may provide ways of counterbalancing relations with kin. Note that all forms of relatedness are always embedded in and shaped by politics, economics, and world views.

2. To recognize the varied forms that institutions of human relatedness can take is to acknowledge fundamental openness in the organization of human interdependence. New shared experiences offer raw material for the invention of new forms of common identity. Anthropologists now argue that all communities—even face-to-face communities—larger than a single individual are contingent, "imagined" communities. That is, all human communities are social, cultural, and historical constructions. They are the joint outcome of shared habitual practices and of symbolic images of common identity promulgated by group members with an interest in making a particular imagined identity endure.

3. The system of social relations that is based on prototypical procreative relationships is called

kinship. Kinship principles are based on, but not reducible to, the universal biological experiences of mating, birth, and nurturance. Kinship systems help societies maintain social order without central government. Although female–male duality is basic to kinship, many societies have developed supernumerary sexes or genders.

4. Patterns of descent in kinship systems are selective. Matrilineal societies emphasize that women bear children and trace descent through women. Patrilineal societies emphasize that men impregnate women and trace descent through men. Adoption pays attention to relationships based on nurturance, whether or not they are also based on mating and birth.

5. Descent links members of different generations with one another. Bilateral descent results in the formation of groups called *kindreds* that include all relatives from both parents' families. Unilineal descent results in the formation of groups called *lineages* that trace descent through either the mother or the father. Unlike kindreds, lineages are corporate groups. Lineages control important property, such as land, that collectively belongs to their members. In many societies, the language of lineage is the idiom of political discussion, and lineage relationships are of political significance.

6. Kinship terminologies pay selective attention to certain attributes of people that are then used to define different classes of kin. The attributes most often recognized include, from most to least

common, generation, gender, affinity, collaterality, bifurcation, relative age, and the gender of the linking relative.

7. Anthropologists recognize six basic terminological systems according to their patterns of classifying cousins. In recent years, however, anthropologists have become quite skeptical of the value of these idealized models because they are highly formalized and do not capture the full range of people's actual practices.

8. By prescribing certain kinds of marriage, lineages establish long-term alliances with one another. Two major types of prescriptive marriage patterns in unilineal societies are a father's sister's daughter marriage system and a mother's brother's daughter marriage system.

9. Achieved kinship statuses can be converted into ascribed ones by means of adoption.

10. From the complexities of Ju/'hoansi kinship negotiations to the unique features of *compadrazgo* in Latin America, anthropologists have shown clearly that kinship is a form of relatedness, a cultural construction that cannot be reduced to biology.

11. Marriage is a social process that transforms the status of the participants, stipulates the degree of sexual access the married partners are expected to have to each other, perpetuates social patterns through the production or adoption of offspring, and creates relationships between the kin of the partners.

12. Woman marriage and ghost marriage among the Nuer demonstrate that the social roles of husband and father or wife and mother may be independent of the gender of the persons who fill them.

13. There are four major patterns of post-marital residence: neolocal, patrilocal, matrilocal, and avunculocal.

14. A person may be married to only one person at a time (*monogamy*) or to several (*polygamy*). Polygamy can be further subdivided into *polygyny*, in which a man is married to two or more wives, and *polyandry*, in which a woman is married to two or more husbands.

15. The study of polyandry reveals how a society may distinguish a married woman's sexuality from her reproductive capacity, a distinction not found in monogamous or polygynous societies.

16. Bridewealth (or brideprice) is a payment of symbolically important goods by the husband's lineage to the wife's lineage. Anthropologists see this as compensation to the wife's family for the loss of her productive and reproductive capacities. A woman's bridewealth payment may enable her brother to pay bridewealth to get a wife.

17. Dowry is typically a transfer of family wealth from parents to their daughter at the time of her marriage. Dowries are often considered the wife's contribution to the establishment of a new household.

18. In some cultures, the most important relationships a man and a woman have are with their opposite-sex siblings. Adult brothers and sisters may see one another often and jointly control lineage affairs.

19. Different family structures produce different internal patterns and tensions. There are three basic family types: nuclear, extended, and joint. Families may change from one type to another over time and with the birth, growth, and marriage of children.

20. Most human societies permit marriages to end by divorce, although it is not always easy. In most societies, childlessness is grounds for divorce. Sometimes nagging, quarrelling, adultery, cruelty, and stinginess are causes. In some societies, only men may initiate a divorce. In very few societies is divorce impossible.

21. Families have developed ingenious ways of keeping together even when some members live abroad for extended periods. LGBTQ in North America have created families by choice, based on nurturance, which they believe are as enduring as families based on marriage and birth.

22. Friendships are relatively "unofficial" bonds of relatedness that are personal, affective, and, to a varying extent from society to society, a matter of choice. Nevertheless, in some societies, friendships may be so important that they are formalized like marriages. Depending on the society, friendships may be developed to strengthen kin ties or to subvert kin ties, because friendship is understood as the precise opposite of formal kin ties. This illustrates the ways in which people everywhere struggle to find ways to preserve certain ties of relatedness without being dominated by them.

For Review

1. What is relatedness? What form of relatedness does your family use for establishing family ties? How do concepts of relatedness reflect the idea that humans are biocultural organisms?
2. Define *kinship*, *marriage*, and *adoption*, and explain how each of these relationships is based on, but not reducible to, biology.
3. How have anthropologists traditionally distinguished between sex and gender? What factors might influence how a society defines and reinforces gender roles?
4. Compare bilateral kindreds and unilineal descent groups. What might be some advantages or disadvantages to membership in either type of group?
5. Prepare a chart of the key criteria used to distinguish different categories of kin, and provide a brief explanation and an example for each criterion.
6. Explain the differences between ascribed status and achieved status. In what situations might the distinctions between these categories be unclear?
7. What is the difference between *pater* and *genitor*, and between *mater* and *genetrix*? How do these concepts relate to most Westerners' understandings of adoption? How are they understood among the Nuer, in relation to woman marriage and ghost marriage?

8. Distinguish between endogamy and exogamy. In what ways might these practices simplify or complicate the task of finding a marriage partner?
9. Summarize the four main residence patterns that newly married couples may be expected to observe in different societies. What might be some advantages and disadvantages to each type of arrangement?
10. Discuss how different marriage patterns reflect variation in social understandings of male and female sexuality.
11. Explore the economic characteristics of marriage. Do you think that marriage is driven primarily by economic forces in Canadian society? Why or why not?
12. Summarize the major forms of a family discussed in this chapter. How would you describe your family structure?
13. Discuss the ways in which families and family structures change over time. How has the structure of your family changed over time?
14. Compare and contrast friendship and kinship. In what situations might these concepts overlap? What qualities do you consider necessary in a relationship to call someone a friend?
15. Using the EthnoProfiles in this chapter, discuss how anthropologists understand human sexual practices.

Key Terms

References

Alia, Valerie. 2007. *Names and Nunavut: Culture and Identity in Arctic Canada*. New York: Berghahn Books.

Allen, Catherine. 1988. *The Hold Life Has: Coca and Cultural Identity in an Andean Community*. Washington, Smithsonian Institution Press.

Anderson, Benedict. 2002. "The New World Disorder." In *The Anthropology of Politics*, edited by Joan Vincent, 261–70. Malden, MA: Blackwell Publishers.

——. 1983. *Imagined Communities*. New York, Verso Books.

Bala, Nicholas. 2005. "The Debates about Same-Sex Marriage in Canada and the United States: Controversy over the Evolution of a Fundamental Social Institution." *Brigham Young University Journal of Public Law* 20 (2): 195–231.

Bauman, Zygmunt. 1989. *Modernity and the Holocaust*. Cambridge: Polity Press.

Bell, Sandra, and Simon Coleman. 1999. "The Anthropology of Friendship: Enduring Themes and Future Possibilities." In *The Anthropology of Friendship*, edited by Sandra Bell and Simon Coleman, 1–19. Oxford: Berg.

Bledsoe, Caroline. 1993. "The Politics of Polygyny in Mende Education and Child Fosterage Transactions." In *Sex and Gender Hierarchies*, edited by Barbara Diane Miller, 170–92. Cambridge: Cambridge University Press.

Boelscher, Marianne. 1988. *The Curtain Within: Haida Social and Political Discourse*. Vancouver: University of British Columbia Press.

Bohannan, Laura, and Paul Bohannan. 1969. *The Tiv of Central Nigeria*. 2nd ed. London: International African Institute.

Burch, Ernest. 1970. "Marriage and Divorce among the North Alaska Eskimos." In *Divorce and After*, edited by Paul Bohannan, 152–81. Garden City, NY: Doubleday.

Burch, Ernest S., Jr. 1975. *Eskimo Kinsmen: Changing Family Relationships in Northwest Alaska*. American Ethnological Society Monograph, no. 59. St Paul, MN: West.

Carsten, Janet. 2004. *After Kinship*. New York: Cambridge University Press.

Course, Magnus. 2011. *Becoming Mapuche: Person and Ritual in Indigenous Chile*. Chicago: University of Illinois Press.

Evans-Pritchard, E.E. 1940. *The Nuer*. Oxford: Oxford University Press.

——. 1951. *Kinship and Marriage among the Nuer*. Oxford: Oxford University Press.

Fortes, Meyer. 1953. "The Structure of Unilineal Descent Groups." *American Anthropologist* 55: 25–39.

Georges, Eugenia. 1990. *The Making of a Transnational Community: Migration, Development, and Cultural Change in the Dominican Republic*. New York: Columbia University Press.

Goody, Jack, and Stanley Tambiah. 1973. *Bridewealth and Dowry*. Cambridge: Cambridge University Press.

Guemple, D. Lee. 1979. "Inuit Socialization: A Study of Children as Social Actors in an Eskimo Community." In *Childhood and Adolescence in Canada*, edited by Karigoudar Ishwaran, 39–53. Toronto: McGraw-Hill Ryerson.

Holy, Ladislav. 1996. *Anthropological Perspectives on Kinship*. London: Pluto Press.

Hutchinson, Sharon. 1996. *Nuer Dilemmas*. Berkeley: University of California Press.

Karp, Ivan. 1978. *Fields of Change among the Iteso of Kenya*. London: Routledge.

Kelly, Raymond. 1993. *Constructing Inequality: The Fabrication of a Hierarchy of Virtue among the Etoro*. Ann Arbor, MI: University of Michigan Press.

Killick, Evan, and Amit Desai. 2010. "Introduction: Valuing Friendship." In *The Ways of Friendship*, edited by Amit Desai and Evan Killick, 1–17. New York: Berghahn Books.

Krmpotich, Cara. 2010. "Remembering and Repatriation: The Production of Kinship, Memory and Respect." *Journal of Material Culture* 15 (2): 157–79.

Kuper, Adam. 1982. *Wives for Cattle: Bridewealth and Marriage in Southern Africa*. London: Routledge and Kegan Paul.

Lancaster, Roger. 1992. *Life Is Hard: Machismo, Danger, and the Intimacy of Power in Nicaragua*. Berkeley: University of California Press.

——. 2004. "Two Cheers for Gay Marriage." *Anthropology News* 45 (6): 21–24.

Lee, Richard B. 1992. *The Dobe Ju/'hoansi*. 2nd ed. New York: Holt, Rinehart, and Winston.

——. 2012. *The Dobe Ju/'Hoansi*. 4th ed. Belmont, CA: Wadsworth Publishing.

Levine, Nancy. 1980. "Nyinba Polyandry and the Allocation of Paternity." *Journal of Comparative Family Studies* 11 (3): 283–8.

——. 1988. *The Dynamics of Polyandry: Kinship, Domesticity, and Population on the Tibetan Border*. Chicago: University of Chicago Press.

——, and Walter Sangree. 1980. "Women with Many Husbands: Polyandrous Alliance and Marital Flexibility in Africa and Asia." *Journal of Comparative Family Studies* 11 (3): 325–34.

Little, Kenneth. 1967. *The Mende of Sierra Leone*. London: Routledge and Kegan Paul.

McElroy, Ann. 2008. *Nunavut Generations: Change and Continuity in Canadian Inuit Communities*. Long Grove, IL: Waveland Press.

Miller, Daniel, and Don Slater. 2000. *The Internet: An Ethnographic Approach*. Oxford: Berg.

Peletz, Michael G. 1995. "Kinship Studies in Late Twentieth-Century Anthropology." *Annual Review of Anthropology* 24 (1): 343–72.

——. 1995. "Neither Reasonable nor Responsible: Contrasting Representations of Masculinity in a Malays Society." In *Bewitching Women, Pious Men: Gender and Body Politics in Southeast Asia*, edited by Aihwa Ong and Michael Peletz, 76–123. Berkeley: University of California Press.

Reese-Taylor, Kathryn, Peter Mathews, Julia Guernsey, and Marlene Fritzler. 2009. "Warrior Queens among the Classic Maya." In *Blood and Beauty: Organized Violence in the Art and Archaeology of Mesoamerica and Central America*, edited by Heather Orr and Rex Koontz, 39–72. Los Angeles: Cotsen Institute of Archaeology Press.

Rezende, Claudia Barcellos. 1999. "Building Affinity through Friendship." In *The Anthropology of Friendship*, edited by Sandra Bell and Simon Coleman, 79–97. Oxford: Berg.

Schneider, David. 1968. *American Kinship: A Cultural Account*. Englewood Cliffs, NJ: Prentice Hall.

Shostak, Marjorie. 1981. *Nisa: The Life and Words of a !Kung Woman*. New York: Vintage.

van Willigen, John, and V.C. Channa. 1991. "Law, Custom, and Crimes against Women." *Human Organization* 50 (4): 369–77.

Ward, T.W. 2013. *Gangsters without Borders: An Ethnography of a Salvadoran Street Gang*. New York: Oxford University Press.

▲ Catalans protest Madrid's move to impose direct rule over Catalonia after the 2017 referendum, which resulted in the Catalan Parliament declaring independence from Spain. Photo: Concealed Resonances/Shutterstock

13 How Do Anthropologists Study Political Relations?

Chapter Outline

- How Are Culture and Politics Related?
- How Do Anthropologists Study Politics?
- How Do Anthropologists Study Politics of the Nation–State?
- What Happens to Citizenship in a Globalized World?

- Global Politics in the Twenty–First Century
- Chapter Summary
- For Review
- Key Terms
- References

Human societies are able to organize human interdependency successfully only if they find ways to manage relations of power among the different individuals and different groups. In this chapter, we survey approaches anthropologists take to the study of political relations in different societies, and we look at how intragroup relations tend to be controlled by those with power, prestige, and/or wealth.

Anthropologists have long been interested in the role of power in human societies. Why are members of some societies able to exercise power on roughly equal terms whereas other societies sharply divide the powerful from the powerless? In societies where access to power is unequal, how can those with little power gain more? What, in fact, is power?

Human societies are able to organize human interdependency successfully only if they find ways to manage relations of power among the different individuals and groups. When anthropologists study those that possess **power**, they consider how those who have power have the ability to transform a given situation. In this chapter, you will learn about the approaches anthropologists take to the study of political relations in different societies. Eric Wolf (1994) describes three different modes of social power:

1. *Interpersonal power or persuasion* involves the ability of one individual to impose his or her will on another individual.
2. *Organizational or authoritative power* highlights how individuals or social units can limit the actions of other individuals in particular social settings.
3. *Structural power* organizes social settings themselves and controls the allocation of social labour.

To lay bare the patterns of structural power requires paying attention to the large-scale and increasingly global division of labour among regions and social groups, the unequal relations between these regions and groups, and the way these relations are maintained or modified over time. The way in which clothing is manufactured now—in factories in Indonesia or El Salvador, Romania or China—for markets in Europe, North America, and Japan is an example of structural power. People are hired to work long hours for low wages in unpleasant conditions to make clothing that they cannot afford to buy, even if it were available for sale in the communities where they live. See Map 13.1 for examples of the diverse ways that humans create structures of social power mentioned in this chapter.

How Are Culture and Politics Related?

The study of social power in human society is the domain of **political anthropology**. In a recent overview, Joan Vincent argues that political anthropology continues to be vital because it involves a complex interplay among ethnographic fieldwork, political theory, and critical reflection on political theory (Vincent 2002, 1). Vincent divides the history of political anthropology into three phases. The first phase, from 1851 to 1939, she considers the "formative" era, in which basic orientations and some of the earliest anthropological commentaries on political matters were produced.

During this formative phase, four types of preindustrial political systems (see Table 13.1) were defined—bands, tribes, chiefdoms, and states—and anthropologists including Lewis Henry Morgan proposed that there was a singular, one-way progression of human political organization, from band to state, creating what was referred to as *unilineal cultural evolutionism*.

By the mid-twentieth century, the extravagant claims of some unilineal schemes of cultural evolutionism led most anthropologists to abandon such theorizing and evolutionary schemes. At this point, from 1942 to about 1971, the second phase of political anthropology developed, known as the classic era in the field. It is most closely associated with the flourishing of British

power **Transformative capacity; the ability to transform a given situation.**

political anthropology **The study of social power in human society.**

TABLE 13.1 Formal Categories Used by Anthropologists to Classify the Political Forms of Human Society

Category	Description	Example
Band/Egalitarian	A small, predominantly foraging society of 50 or fewer members that divides labour by age and sex only and provides relatively equal access for all adults to wealth, power, and prestige.	Ju/'hoansi of South Africa
Tribe/Ranked	A farming or herding society, usually larger than a band, that relies on kinship as the framework for social and political life; provides relatively egalitarian social relations but may have a leader who has more prestige (but not more power or wealth) than others. Sometimes called a *rank society*.	Hmong of Southeast Asia
Chiefdom/Stratified	A socially stratified society, generally larger than a tribe, in which a chief and close relatives enjoy privileged access to wealth, power, and prestige; has greater craft production but few full-time specialists.	Trobriand Islanders of the South Pacific
State	An economic, political, and ideological entity invented by stratified societies; possesses specialized government institutions to administer services and collect taxes and tribute; monopolizes use of force with armies and police; possesses high level and quality of craft production. Often has developed writing (particularly in early states).	Canada
Empire	Forms when one state conquers another.	Roman Empire

social anthropology rooted in functionalist theory, and it produced well-known works by such eminent figures as Elman Service and Morton Fried. This phase developed in the context of the post–World War II British Empire during the period of decolonization in the 1950s and 1960s. Topics of investigation during this period were considered the classic topics of political anthropology: the classification of preindustrial political systems and attempts to reconstruct their evolution; displaying the characteristic features of different kinds of preindustrial political systems and demonstrating how these functioned to produce political order; and studying local processes of political strategizing by individuals in non-Western societies (see, e.g., Lewellyn 1992).

By the 1960s, anthropologists had produced economic and political classifications of human social forms that mapped onto each other in interesting ways. As Matthew Johnson (1999, 141) summarizes,

> cultural anthropologists Elman Service and Morton Fried . . . have been particularly influential on archaeologists. Service gives us a fourfold typology ranging along the scale of simple to complex of band, tribe, chiefdom, and state. Fried offers an alternative [political] scheme of egalitarian, ranked, stratified, and state [societies]. . . .

Both start and stop at the same point (they start with "simple" gatherer–hunter societies, though their definitions of such societies differ, and end with the modern state). They both also share a similar methodology.

The **band** is the characteristic form of social organization found among foragers. Foraging groups are small, usually numbering no more than 50 people, and labour is divided ordinarily on the basis of age and sex. All adults in band societies have roughly equal access to whatever material or social valuables are locally available, which is why anthropologists call bands *egalitarian* forms of society.

A society identified as a **tribe** is generally larger than a band, and its members usually farm or herd for a living.

band The characteristic form of social organization found among foragers. Bands are small, usually no more than 50 people, and labour is divided ordinarily on the basis of age and sex. All adults in band societies have roughly equal access (egalitarian) to whatever material or social valuables are locally available.

tribe A society that is generally larger than a band, whose members usually farm or herd for a living. Social relations in a tribe are considered ranked, as there is often a leader who speaks for the group or who organizes certain group activities.

Social relations in a tribe are still relatively egalitarian, although there may be a leader who speaks for the group or organizes certain group activities. The leader often enjoys greater prestige than other individuals do, but this prestige does not ordinarily translate into greater power or wealth. Social organization and subsistence activities are usually carried out according to rules of kinship.

The *chiefdom* is the first human social form to show evidence of permanent inequalities of wealth and power, in addition to inequality of **status**. Ordinarily, only the chief and close relatives are set apart from the rest of society; other members continue to share roughly similar social status. Chiefdoms are generally larger than tribes and show a greater degree of craft production, although such production is not yet in the hands of full-time specialists. Chiefdoms also exhibit a greater degree of hierarchical political control, centred on the chief and relatives of the chief, based on their great deeds. Archaeologically, chiefdoms are interesting because some, such as the southern Natufians, who lived east of the Mediterranean Sea and were one of the first cultures in the world to domesticate plants and animals, apparently remained as they were and then disappeared, whereas others went on to develop into states. The **state** is a stratified society that possesses a territory that is defended from outside enemies with an army and from internal disorder with police. States, which have separate governmental institutions to enforce laws and to collect taxes and tribute, are run by an elite who possesses a monopoly on the use of force.

Note that these categories are not part of a unilineal evolution of culture, and a single social group may move back and forth between more than one of these forms over time. As well, most anthropologists who use these categories today do not think of them as sharply divided or mutually exclusive categories but, rather, as points on a continuum, with fuzzy boundaries between them.

By the 1970s and 1980s, a third phase had developed, in which the anthropology of politics posed broader questions about power and inequality (Vincent 2002, 3).

status A particular social position in a group.

state A stratified society that possesses a territory that is defended from outside enemies with an army and from internal disorder with police. A state, which has a separate set of governmental institutions designed to enforce laws and to collect taxes and tribute, is run by an elite that possesses a monopoly on the use of force.

Under conditions of globalization, anthropologists interested in studying power joined forces with scholars in other disciplines who shared their concerns, and they adopted ideas from influential political thinkers such as Antonio Gramsci and Michel Foucault to help them explain how power shapes the lives of those among whom they carry out ethnographic research. The cross-cultural study of political institutions reveals the paradox of the human condition. On the one hand, open cultural creativity allows humans to imagine worlds of pure possibility; on the other hand, all humans live in material circumstances that make many of those possibilities profoundly unrealistic. We can imagine many different ways to organize ourselves into groups, but, as Marx pointed out long ago, the past weighs like a nightmare on the brains of the living—and the opportunity to remake social organization is ordinarily quite limited.

Human beings actively work to reshape the environments in which they live to suit themselves. Because the resources available in any environment can be used to sustain more than one way of life, however, human beings must choose which aspects of the material world to depend on. This is why, inevitably, questions about human population growth and economic activity are intimately intertwined with questions about the distribution of power in society. Some archaeologists have suggested that population growth is a constant aspect of the human condition that determines forms of social organization. As Marshall Sahlins (1976, 13) points out, however, population pressure determines nothing more than the number of people that can be supported when the environment is used in a particular way. Members of a society can respond to that pressure in any of various ways: they can try to get along on less, intensify food production by inventing new technology, reduce their numbers by inventing new social practices (infanticide or forms of birth control), or migrate elsewhere. Indeed, the manner in

For a review of the connections between population growth and social inequalities in the human past, see Chapter 8.

which a group might choose to implement any of these options is not merely a result of too many people living in one place. Which members of the group will have to do with less? Which members will control technological innovation? Who will be expected to migrate? And will the ultimate decision be imposed by force or voluntarily adopted?

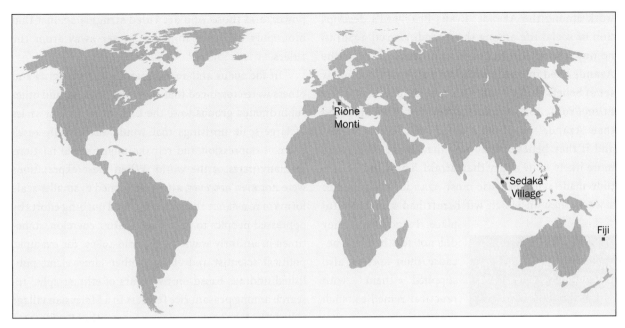

MAP 13.1 Location of societies whose EthnoProfiles appear in Chapter 13.

The answers offered to these questions by members of any particular society describe the niche these individuals have constructed for themselves. By building social and political alliances and mobilizing technology and material resources in order to make a living, ways of life are maintained and sustained over time.

How Do Anthropologists Study Politics?

Coercion

Political anthropologists in the early twentieth century were strongly influenced by Western philosophers who had assumed that the state was the prototype of "civilized" social power. For them, the absence of a state could mean only *anarchy*: disorderly struggles for power among individuals—what the English philosopher Thomas Hobbes (1588–1679) called the "war of all against all." This view assumes that power is best understood as physical force, or *coercion*. A fistfight might be seen as a typical, "natural" manifestation of attempts by individuals to exercise physical coercion. Although states that monopolize the use of force often perpetrated injustice or exploitation as a side effect, Hobbes and others viewed this as the necessary price for social order. Their assumption was that co-operative social living is not natural for human individuals because they are born with **free agency**—instincts that lead them

to pursue their own self-interest above everything else and to challenge one another for dominance.

Discussions of power as coercion tend to see political activity as competition between individual free agents over political control. When free agents make decisions, no larger groups, no historical obligations, no collective beliefs can or ought to stand in their way. Some believe that cultural evolution took a giant leap forward when our ancestors first realized that sticks and stones could be used as weapons not only against non-human predators but especially against human enemies. In this view, human history was driven by the production of better and better weapons, and civilizations were created and sustained by violence. But this is not the only way to understand human agency, as we will see.

Is Political Power Nothing More Than Coercion?

Early anthropologists such as Lewis Henry Morgan showed that kinship institutions could organize orderly social life in societies without states, and his observations were confirmed by later political anthropologists, such as E.E. Evans-Pritchard, based on his

free agency The freedom of self-contained individuals to pursue their own interests above everything else and to challenge one another for dominance.

work among the Azande. Evans-Pritchard's description of social life among the Azande ([1937] 1976) in no way resembled a war of all against all, although the Azande lived in a stateless society and held a complex set of beliefs about witchcraft, oracles, and magic (see EthnoProfile 16.6: Azande). Evans-Pritchard observed that Azande people discussed witchcraft openly, and if they believed they were bewitched, they were more likely to be angry than afraid. This kind of attitude made sense because most Azande subscribed to a world view in which witchcraft had a meaningful place. In addition, they did not feel helpless because their society also supplied them with practical remedies, such as vengeance magic, that

> ↻ For a more detailed exploration of Azande beliefs about witchcraft, oracles, and magic, see Chapter 16, pp. 397–9.

they could use to defend themselves if they thought they had been bewitched. Here, we see an example of what Wolf called organizational power that does not depend on state coercion. Instead, it depends on *persuasion*. Scaffolded by particular social institutions and practices, the belief system continues to appear natural and rational to members of the society; this is why ordinary, rational people support it.

How Do Anthropologists Study Resistance to Coercion?

What happens, however, if members of a society decide that the institutions and practices endorsed by their leaders are coercive, rather than legitimate? What if they decide to take action to overturn such coercion? History is full of examples of people rising up against their rulers, resisting coercion, and struggling to create new social relations that will provide greater freedom and justice. Indeed, stories about the founding of modern nation-states, such as France and the United States, often begin precisely with revolutionary accounts of successful resistance to oppression. The framework of analysis in which such accounts are located is dualistic: rulers monopolize

> **hidden transcripts** Private accounts by dominated groups of their oppression and alternatives to it developed outside the public political arena. These hidden accounts contrast with the views dominated peoples express in public political contexts that do not challenge the legitimacy of the dominant political order.

power, and those who are ruled struggle against that monopoly in order to wrest power away from the rulers.

In the 1960s and 1970s, many anthropologists and others were convinced that efforts by peasants and other subordinated groups were the first wave of a new series of large-scale uprisings that would successfully resist coercive oppression and remake unjust social relations in many parts of the world. When these expectations were not met, however, attention turned to smaller scale forms of resistance that demonstrated ongoing efforts by oppressed peoples to push back against coercion, sometimes in unlikely ways. In the mid-1980s, for example, political scientist and ethnographer James Scott published findings based on two years of ethnographic research among peasant rice farmers in a Malaysian village called "Sedaka" (a pseudonym; see EthnoProfile 13.1: "Sedaka" Village). He had learned that poor Malaysian peasants were at the bottom of a social hierarchy dominated locally by rich farmers and nationally by a powerful state apparatus. According to Scott, these peasants were not kept in line by some form of state-sponsored terrorism; rather, the context of their lives was shaped by what he called "routine repression": "occasional arrests, warnings, diligent police work, legal restrictions, and an Internal Security Act that allows for indefinite preventive detention and proscribes much political activity" (1987, 274).

He quickly realized that the poor peasants of "Sedaka" were not about to rise up against their oppressors. But this was not because they accepted their poverty and low status as natural and proper. For one thing, the peasants knew that overt political action in the context of routine repression would be foolhardy. As well, they had to feed their families. Their solution was to engage in what Scott called "everyday forms of peasant resistance": this included "foot dragging, dissimulation, desertion, false compliance, pilfering, feigned ignorance, slander, arson, sabotage, and so forth" (1987, xvi). These actions may have done little to alter the peasants' situation in the short run; however, Scott argued, in the long run they had the potential to be more effective than overt rebellion against state repression.

According to Scott, when peasants criticize rich landowners or rich landowners find fault with peasants, the parties involved are not just venting emotion. Instead, each side is simultaneously constructing a world view. Rich and poor alike are offering "a critique of things as they are as well as a vision of things as they should be . . . [they] are writing a kind of social text on the subject of human decency" (Scott 1987, 23). Scott (1990) refers to such peasant-formulated critiques and visions as **hidden transcripts**: private accounts of their oppression and alternatives to it, developed by dominated groups outside the public political arena. These hidden accounts contrast with the views that dominated peoples routinely express in public contexts that do not challenge the legitimacy of the dominant political order. The existence of hidden transcripts shows that even though these transcripts do not change their lived reality, the poor peasants are using them to recreate their lived experiences with meanings of their own choosing.

For Scott, the contrast between the world view of the state and the world view of peasants in "Sedaka" was revealed during the introduction of mechanized rice harvesting. Traditionally, rice harvesting had been manual labour. It regularly allowed poor peasants to earn cash and receive grain from their employers as a traditional form of charitable gift (Figure 13.1). In the late 1970s, however, the introduction of combine harvesters eliminated the rich farmers' need for hired labour, a loss that dealt poor families a severe economic blow. When the rich and poor talked about the harvesters, each side offered a different account of their effect on economic life in the village.

Scott tells us that both sides agreed that using the machines hurt the poor and helped the rich. When each side was asked whether the benefits of the machines outweighed their costs, however, consensus evaporated. The poor offered practical reasons against the use of combine harvesters: they claimed that the heavy machines were inefficient and that their operation destroyed rice paddies. They also offered moral reasons: they accused the rich of being "stingy," of ignoring the traditional obligation of rich people to help the poor by providing them with work and charity. The rich denied both the practical and the moral objections of the poor. They insisted that using harvesters increased their yield. They accused the poor people of bad faith. They claimed that the poor suffered because they were bad farmers and lazy, and they attributed their own success to hard work and prudent farm management.

Rich farmers, on the other hand, would never have been able to begin using combine harvesters without the outside assistance of both the national government and the business groups that rented the

EthnoProfile 13.1

"Sedaka" Village

Region: Southeastern Asia

Nation: Malaysia

Population: 300

Environment: Lush paddy land

Livelihood: Rice cultivation

Political organization: Village within a modern nation–state

For more information: Scott, James. 1987. *Weapons of the Weak*. New Haven, CT: Yale University Press.

machines to them at harvest time. Poor peasants were aware of this, yet they directed their critique at the local farmers and not at the government or outside business organizations. After all, the rich farmers "are a part of the community and therefore *ought* not to be indifferent to the consequences of their acts for their neighbors" (1987, 161). The stinginess of the rich did not just bring economic loss; it also attacked the social identity of the poor, who vigorously resisted being turned into nonpersons. The poor insisted on being accorded the "minimal cultural decencies in this small community" (Scott 1987, xvii). The only weapon they controlled in this struggle was their

FIGURE 13.1 Until recently, rice harvesting in rural Malaysia was manual labour that regularly allowed poor peasants to earn cash and receive grain from their employers as a traditional form of charitable gift.

ability, by word and deed, to undercut the prestige and the reputation of the rich. This strategy worked in "Sedaka" because rich local famers were not ready to abandon the traditional morality that had regulated relations between rich and poor; they still cared what other villagers thought of them. A shrewd campaign of character assassination might have caused at least some of the rich to hesitate before ignoring their traditional obligations to the poor, which would have helped the poor defend their claims to citizenship in the local community. Scott was convinced that if the wider political arena changed in the future, such that routine repression disappeared, many of the poor peasants he knew might well engage in open active rebellion.

Are There Limitations to Analyzing Power in Terms of Domination and Resistance?

Scott's studies of domination and the arts of resistance have become classics in anthropology because they move beyond crude understandings of political coercion as nothing but the exercise of brute force while they address the role of meaning and morality in political struggles and they reveal nuanced interpretations that members of oppressed groups are able to offer concerning their situation in the world. Scott himself had been influenced by the work of Antonio Gramsci (1971) who, among other things, offered a fresh view of how cultural understandings could play a role not only in consolidating power from above but also in resisting domination from below. Gramsci's perspective can be approached by considering two of his key concepts: domination and hegemony.

⟳ For an example of how humans actively engage with and revise their belief systems, see the discussion of culture change and cultural authenticity in Chapter 2, pp. 36–7.

What Are Domination and Hegemony?

Earlier in the chapter, we noted that anthropologists and others have offered different answers to the question of why people submit to institutionalized power. On one

ideology A world view that justifies the social arrangements under which people live.

domination Ruling with coercive force.

hand, they may have been coerced and fear punishment if they refuse to submit. On the other hand, they may submit because they believe that the power structures in their society are legitimate, given their understandings of the way the world works. What could lead people to accept coercion by others as legitimate (Figure 13.2)? A world view that justifies the social arrangements under which people live is sometimes called an **ideology**. Karl Marx argued that rulers consolidate their power by successfully persuading their subjects to accept an ideology that portrays domination by the ruling class as legitimate; dominated groups who accept the ruling class ideology were said to suffer from *false consciousness*. The concept of false consciousness is problematic, however, since it views people as passive beings incapable of withstanding ideological indoctrination. As we discussed in Chapter 2, this is not a plausible view of human nature.

More promising is the approach taken by Antonio Gramsci (1971). Writing in the 1930s, Gramsci pointed out that coercive rule—what he called **domination**—is expensive and unstable. Rulers do better if they can persuade the dominated to accept their rule as legitimate, both by providing some genuine material benefits to their subjects and by using schools and other cultural institutions to disseminate an ideology

FIGURE 13.2 Prior to colonial conquest by outsiders, Muslim emirs from northern Cameroon had coercive power.

Courtesy Robert H. Lavenda

justifying their rule. If they achieve all this—while also ensuring that none of these concessions seriously undermines their privileged position—they have established what Gramsci called **hegemony**. Hegemony is never absolute but always vulnerable to challenges: struggles may develop between rulers trying to justify their domination and subordinate groups who exercise agency by challenging "official" ideologies and practices that devalue or exclude them. Hegemony may be threatened if subordinate groups maintain or develop alternative, or *counterhegemonic*, cultural practices. Successful hegemony, by contrast, involves linking the understandings of dominant and subordinate groups into what appears to be mutual accommodation.

James Scott found the concepts of hegemony (and counterhegemony) to be helpful in his effort to explain key features of the struggle between peasants and landowners in "Sedaka" village. The hidden transcripts to which he refers are the raw materials out of which peasants are able to fashion a counterhegemonic critique of their situation, demonstrating that they are not suffering from false consciousness. Thus, if peasants refrain from engaging in public political critique, this is not because they have been brainwashed but because they are choosing to remain silent in the face of routine repression. The concept of hegemony is attractive to many anthropologists because it draws attention to the central role of cultural beliefs and symbols in struggles to consolidate social organization and political control.

Consider, for example, the Azande belief that people use witchcraft only against those they envy. The psychological insight embodied in this belief makes it highly plausible to people who experience daily friction with their neighbours. At the same time, however, this belief makes it impossible to accuse Azande chiefs of using witchcraft against commoners—because, as the Azande themselves say, why would chiefs envy their subjects? In this way, hegemonic ideology deflects challenges that might be made against those in power.

Research by anthropologists Jean and John Comaroff (1991) demonstrates how, from the beginning of the nineteenth century, the Tswana experienced a series of profound changes as they encountered European missionaries and merchants and settlers. Over this period, the Tswana were in some cases targets of explicit ideological power (i.e., for conversion to Christian religious practices and for participation in the growing market economy of South Africa). In other cases, however, they adopted new cultural forms seemingly without much notice. Changes in the clothing they wore, how they built their homes, how they farmed, how they learned to measure the time of day using clocks, how they learned to work for Europeans for wages and produce crops for the market, the consequences of learning to read and write—each of these might have seemed fairly insignificant at the time it occurred, but over time as these changes accumulated, they formed a new kind of silent, taken-for-granted background for everyday Tswana life. And yet the result of these changes was *not* the total absorption of the Tswana within a transplanted Western colonial culture. On the contrary, the encounter between the Tswana and Europeans also produced new cultural forms, creating a hybrid heritage that eventually contributed to the overthrow of apartheid in South Africa. Thus, the Comaroffs emphasize that hegemony may be powerful but it is never absolute, and there is always the potential for hegemony to be overturned (Comaroff and Comaroff 1991, 22–5).

Biopower and Governmentality

Foucault (1991) examined the way European thinkers from the Middle Ages onward had discussed what was necessary to sustain a peaceful, prosperous state. Together with colleagues, he identified the emergence of a new form of power in the nineteenth century. This form of power he called **biopower**, or *biopolitics*, which was preoccupied with bodies, both the bodies of citizens and the social body itself (Hacking 1991, 183). As Colin Gordon (1991, 4–5) summarizes, biopower refers to "forms of power exercised over . . . members of a *population*, in which issues of individual sexual and reproductive behaviours interconnect with issues of national policy and power."

---

hegemony The persuasion of subordinates to accept the ideology of the dominant group by mutual accommodations that nevertheless preserve the rulers' privileged position.

biopower Forms of power preoccupied with bodies, both the bodies of citizens and the social body of the state itself.

Anthropology in Everyday Life

Resistance in the Face of Assimilation

Historically, Canadian federal and provincial governments have pursued a policy of assimilation in their interactions with Indigenous groups. Assimilation strips individuals of their cultural differences with the ultimate goal of creating citizens who all share one culture's beliefs, values, and traditions. Canada's assimilation policy for Indigenous people was based on the ethnocentric notion that European culture, and by extension settler culture, was superior to that of Indigenous people. Treaties and the Indian Act allowed the government virtually absolute control over the lives of Indigenous peoples who all were, to varying degrees, wards of the state. This policy of assimilation resulted in the residential school throughout the nineteenth and twentieth centuries but also what is now referred to as the "Sixties Scoop." Lasting approximately from 1950 to 1990, this period of Canadian history saw individual provincial governments removing substantial numbers of Indigenous children from their families to be placed in government care. Children and youth considered to be neglected by their parents were placed in juvenile custody; adopted out to non-Indigenous families, sometimes across national borders; and/or moved from one foster home to another throughout their entire childhoods.

"Neglect" was open to interpretation, and accusations could be brought forward by any "interested member of the community." Even more alarming, neglect could be established if a child was not continually enrolled in school even though seasonal foraging practices did not allow for ongoing attendance. The mentality was, starting as early as the 1700s, that if settlers could remove Indigenous children from the "harmful" and "backwards" influence of their parents then they could destroy all cultural differences within a few generations. As we can clearly see today, however, Indigenous cultural traditions continue to live on as each generation has shown incredible resilience in the face of persistent oppression. Today, Indigenous young people are increasingly shaping Canada as they combine their knowledge of both Indigenous and settler culture to make a better present and future.

Critics of past policies have argued that governments need to encourage Indigenous self-determination, allowing Indigenous governments to establish and manage their own education and child-welfare agencies. An exciting step was taken in this direction recently with the creation of the Maskwacis Education Schools Commission in May 2018 in Alberta. Moreover, in a spirit of reconciliation and healing, the premiers of two provinces, Manitoba and Alberta, offered formal apologies in 2015 and 2018 to those affected by the Sixties Scoop. In addition, the federal government announced on 6 October 2017 that a settlement of $800 million would be paid to survivors. These are just a few small steps being taken toward better future relations between Indigenous and settler populations.

Source: The Truth and Reconciliation Commission of Canada. (2015). *Honouring the Truth, Reconciling for the Future: Summary of the Final Report of the Truth and Reconciliation Commission of Canada.* Kingston, Ontario: McGill-Queens University Press.

Before the 1600s, according to Foucault (1991), European states were ruled according to different political understandings. At that time, politics was focused on making sure that an absolute ruler maintained control of the state. Machiavelli's famous guide *The Prince* is the best known of a series of handbooks explaining what such an absolute ruler needed to do to maintain himself in power. But by the seventeenth century this approach to state rule was proving increasingly inadequate. Machiavelli's critics began to speak instead about *governing* a state, likening such government to the practices that preserved and perpetuated other social institutions.

The example of household management was a preferred model of government. But running a state as if it were a household meant that rulers would need more information about the people, goods, and wealth that needed to be managed. How many citizens were there? What kinds of goods did they produce, and in what quantities? How healthy were they? What could a state do to manage the consequences of misfortunes such as famines, epidemics, and death? In the 1700s, state bureaucrats began to count and measure types of people and things subject to state control, thereby inventing the discipline of statistics, what we would today refer to as *census taking*.

In this way, according to Foucault (1991), European states began to govern in terms of biopolitics, using statistics to inform their political policies. This, in turn, led to the birth of a new art of governing appropriate to biopolitics, which Foucault calls governmentality. **Governmentality** involves using the information encoded in statistics to govern in a way that promotes the welfare of populations within a state. To exercise governmentality, for example, state bureaucrats might use statistics to determine that a famine was likely and to calculate how much the suffering and death of citizens, and other losses, might cost the state. Bureaucrats would then come up with a plan of intervention—perhaps a form of insurance—designed to reduce the impact of famine on citizens, protect economic activity within the state, and thereby preserve the stability of the state and its institutions. Importantly, for Foucault, these interventions need to be understood not as directly coercive but, rather, as persuasive, even seductive, actions upon others' actions, sometimes described as the *conduct of conduct* (Foucault 1991).

In contemporary states, governmentality functions as a form of power that relies on accurate counting and measurements of individuals within a state's borders, for example through national censuses (Figure 13.3). However, as Ian Hacking (1991, 183) suggests, people must remain aware that the statistical information governments collect is not always used with their best interests at heart. After all, governments want to tax citizens, vaccinate and educate their children, restrict their activities to those that benefit the state, control their movements beyond (and sometimes within) state borders, and otherwise manage what they do. In the worst cases, detailed statistics can provide a government with the information it needs to act in stark opposition to the interests of a specific cultural, racial, or other group subject to its control. This was clearly the case in the late nineteenth century when the Canadian

> ↻ See Chapters 1 and 15 for more about the Truth and Reconciliation Commission's Calls to Action.

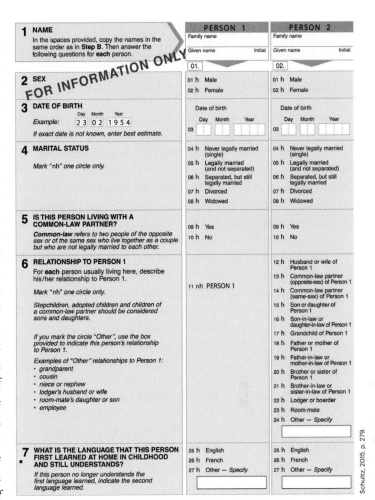

FIGURE 13.3 In order to govern, a state must know who it is governing. Censuses are one way that a state can gather the information it believes it needs.

government forced thousands of Indigenous people off their traditional lands and onto reserves and began sending their children to residential schools. The effects of these actions continue to be felt by Indigenous peoples across Canada today and are being addressed through the Truth and Reconciliation Commission (TRC) and its Calls to Action to reconcile the harm done by these residential schools. (See the "In Their Own Words" box on the Idle No More movement for an example of how some Indigenous people in Canada and elsewhere are standing up for themselves, in opposition to government forces that threaten their ways of life.)

governmentality The art of governing appropriately to promote the welfare of populations within a state.

In Their Own Words

Idle No More: Giving a Voice to the Voiceless

Researcher and writer Febna Caven outlines the strengths of the women leaders of the Idle No More movement as well as the strengths of the movement itself—a personal, global, and spiritual movement aimed at "empowering Indigenous communities to stand up for their lands, rights, cultures, and sovereignty" (Caven 2013, 6–7).

On 11 December 2012, on International Human Rights Day, northern Ontario Attawapiskat Chief Theresa Spence began a hunger strike, calling on Canadian Prime Minister Stephen Harper and Governor General David Johnston to "initiate immediate discussions and the development of action plans to address treaty issues with First Nations across Canada." Her peaceful resistance, emphasizing the importance of dialogue, catapulted the Idle No More movement to a new level of urgency. . . .

The Idle No More movement began as a thread of emails between four women from Saskatchewan: Jessica Gordon, Sylvia McAdam, Nina Wilson, and Sheelah McLean, who decided to make a "sincere effort to make some change." The context for their resolution was the Canadian Bill C-45, the government's omnibus budget implementation bill that includes changes to land management on the reservations. It attacks the land base reserved for Indigenous people, removes protection for hundreds of waterways, and weakens Canada's environmental laws. The women started a Facebook page to brainstorm ideas and [create] a plan for action. Gordon, who is from Pasqua Treaty 4 Territory, decided to name the page "Idle No More" as a reminder to "get off the couch and start working."

The movement's grassroots tactics were evident from the first major event, a mass teach-in at . . . an innovative community enterprise centre in Saskatoon, Saskatchewan, on 10 November 2012. Following the teach-in, . . . a series of rallies and protests spread across Saskatchewan to Manitoba and Alberta. Speaking to a reporter at one such rally, Wilson, a Nakota and Plains Cree from Treaty 4 White Bear territory said, "We are trying to help people get their voices back so that we can make more change and we are able to have more of a First Nations voice . . . not just a First Nations [voice] but an Indigenous voice, and not just an Indigenous voice but a grassroots voice, because it affects us all." And it does affect us all, as it does the environment.

Though it was the omnibus C-45 bill that led to the movement, Idle No More is not just about legislation. It is also a call for renewal of the Indigenous identities and lifeways. The leaders and spokespersons of the movement have no hesitation linking the political to the personal, as the personal is very much a part of the movement. From her teepee on the frozen Ottawa River, a stone's throw away from Parliament Hill, [Chief] Spence spent 44 days on hunger strike and recently said, "I am in this resistance because the pain became too heavy. I just could not take it anymore." She explained how the alienation and pain she feels stems from her years in the residential schools. "It was a closed chapter, until one day you realize this generation is facing the same pain we felt at resident school. We want a life of freedom and not a life of pain and fear for the [next] generation.". . .

As McLean, who is the only non-Indigenous member in the initial group of four women, says, "It is a very loving movement . . . and it's almost entirely female-led. Even though there are hundreds of men who support the movement, the vast majority of the movement's participants and organizers are women." The nature of the fluid, non-violent, and unifying movement is one that both reflects and engages women's agency. . . .

REUTERS/Chris Wattie

In December 2012, during the third week of her hunger strike, Attawapiskat Chief Theresa Spence meets with journalists in a teepee on Victoria Island in Ottawa, Ontario.

. . . Gordon, who has long served her community through non-profit organizations and by volunteering on committees and boards, has taken up the responsibility for monitoring the virtual space of the movement. She manages the movement's website, www .idlenomore.ca, and takes great care in ensuring that the events that get promoted and added to the Idle No More banner are all peaceful in nature. . . .

McAdam, who is from the Treaty 6 territory and a direct descendant of the treaty makers, is a scholar of Cree culture as well as law and human justice. . . . McAdam invokes Cree history and laws to unite the Indigenous people. She says ". . . when we say we are going to do something, the spirit world listens, your keepers listen, and our ancestors listen. When we say we are going to go 'support,' we mean *e we ni towh setohks ka ke yak*. This means we are doing more than supporting; our keepers [and our] spirits are going too. . . ."

Each of the four women leading Idle No More fills a valuable niche. But even as the movement has strong leadership . . ., the masses at the grassroots still retain their place at the core of the movement. As the movement leaders speak of disenfranchised communities left without potable drinking water, as the extended history of colonialism and violation of treaty rights are recalled, the focus still remains on dialogue so that solutions are sought together and not imposed. . . . Speaking up, dancing, and rallying together, co-creating, let's join too. Let us be Idle No More.

Source: Caven 2013, 6–7. Reprinted with permission from *Cultural Survival*.

How Do Anthropologists Study Politics of the Nation-State?

State societies are not new social forms. Nation-states, however, are a far more recent invention. Prior to the French Revolution, European states were ruled by kings and emperors whose access to the throne was officially deemed to have been ordained by God. After the French Revolution in 1789, which thoroughly discredited the divine right of kings, rulers needed to find a new basis on which to found legitimate state authority. The solution eventually adopted was rooted in political authority in **nations**: groups of people believed to share the same history, culture, language, and even the same physical substance. Nations were associated with territories, as were states, and a **nation-state** came to be viewed as an ideal political unit in which national identity and political territory coincided.

The building of the first nation-states is closely associated with the rise and spread of capitalism and its related cultural institutions during the nineteenth century. Following the demise of European colonial empires and the end of the Cold War, the final decades of the twentieth century witnessed a scramble in which former colonies or newly independent states struggled to turn themselves into nation-states capable of competing successfully in what anthropologist Liisa Malkki (1992) has called a "transnational culture of nationalism."

On the one hand, the ideology of the nation-state implies that every nation is entitled to its own state. On the other hand, it also suggests that a state containing heterogeneous populations *might be made into a nation* if all peoples within its borders could somehow be made to adopt a common **nationality**: a sense of identification with and loyalty to the nation-state. As political scientist Benedict Anderson pointed out long ago, nation-states should be understood as *imagined communities*: that is, as socially and historically constructed communities, associated with geographical territories whose residents have varying origins and backgrounds and lack regular face-to-face contact with one another. However, a shared identity could take shape over time as these heterogeneous residents came to participate in common, territory-wide, cultural practices, such as reading the same newspapers, travelling on shared infrastructure, or transacting business in the same territory-wide economic or bureaucratic institutions. Anderson was especially interested in how residents of a territorial unit such as a European colony, by virtue of their shared

nation A group of people believed to share the same history, culture, language, and even physical substance.

nation-state An ideal political unit in which national identity and political territory coincide.

nationality A sense of identification with and loyalty to a nation-state.

experiences, might come to imagine a shared territorial identity, which could become the foundation of national identity once the colony gained political independence. However, the willingness or ability for all residents of a nation-state to adopt national identity is far from guaranteed. Groups with other forms of identity that continue to persist within the boundaries of the nation-state are often viewed as obstacles to nationalism. If such groups successfully resist assimilation into the nationality that the state is supposed to represent, their very existence calls into question the state's legitimacy. Indeed, if their numbers are sufficient, they might well claim that they are a separate nation, entitled to a state of their own.

To head off this possibility, nationalist ideologies typically include some cultural features of subordinate cultural groups. Thus, although nationalist traditions are invented, they are not created out of thin air. That is, those who control the nation-state will try to define nationality in ways that allow for the acknowledgement of some aspects of the way of life of subordinate cultural groups so they will identify with and be loyal to the nation. Following Gramsci, Brackette Williams calls this process a **transformist hegemony**, which defines nationality in order to preserve the cultural domination of

transformist hegemony A nationalist program to define nationality in a way that preserves the cultural domination of the ruling group while including enough cultural features from subordinated groups to ensure their loyalty.

EthnoProfile 13.2

Fiji

Region: Oceania

Nation: Fiji

Population: 905,000

Environment: Tropical marine climate; volcanic mountains

Livelihood: Natural resource export, especially sugar; subsistence agriculture; tourism

Political organization: Multiparty nation–state

For more information: Kelly, John D., and Martha Kaplan. 2001. *Represented Communities: Fiji and World Decolonization.* Chicago: University of Chicago Press.

the ruling group while at the same time including cultural features from subordinate groups. Unfortunately, the practices of subordinated groups that are not incorporated into nationalist ideology are regularly marginalized and devalued. Continued adherence to such practices may be viewed as subversive, and practitioners may suffer persecution and even extermination. Other groups, by contrast, may be totally ignored. Ana María Alonso points out, for example, that Mexican nationalism is "mestizo nationalism" rooted in the official doctrine that the Mexican people are a hybrid of European whites and the Indigenous people they conquered. African slaves were also a part of early colonial Mexican society, but nationalist ideology erases their presence entirely (Alonso 1994, 396).

Nation Building in a Postcolonial World: The Example of Fiji

Nation building involves constructing a shared public identity, but it also involves establishing concrete legal mechanisms for taking group action to influence the state. That is, as John Kelly and Martha Kaplan (2001) argue, nation-states are more than imagined communities; they are also *represented* communities. For this reason, nation building involves more than constructing an image of national unity; it also requires institutions of political representation that channel the efforts of citizens into effective support for the state. But what happens when citizens of a nation-state do not agree about exactly what nation they are building or what kinds of legal and political structures are necessary to bring it about? One answer to these questions can be seen in the South Pacific island of Fiji, which became independent of Britain in 1970 and has experienced a series of political coups since 1987 (see EthnoProfile 13.2: Fiji).

At independence, the image of the Fijian nation was that of a "three-legged stool," each "leg" being a separate category of voters: "general electors" (a minority of the population including Europeans), "Fijians" (ethnic Fijians, descended from the original inhabitants of the island), and "Indians" (or Indo-Fijians, descendants of indentured labourers brought to Fiji by the British from Bombay and Calcutta in the nineteenth century). Kelly and Kaplan (2001) show that these three categories have deep roots in the colonial period, where they were said to correspond to separate "races." In the British Empire, race was an accepted way to categorize subordinated peoples, although in many cases—as in the case of the

Indo-Fijians—the people so labelled had shared no common identity prior to their arrival in Fiji.

These racial distinctions were concretized in colonial law, and the legal status of the ethnic Fijians was different from the legal status of Indo-Fijians. The status of ethnic Fijians was determined by a document signed by some Fijian chiefs with the British in 1874, which linked ethnic Fijians to the colonial government. The status of Indo-Fijians, by contrast, was determined by the contracts of indenture (*girmit*), which each individual labourer had signed to come to Fiji. Thus, ethnic Fijians were accorded a hierarchical, collective legal identity, whereas the Indo-Fijians had the status of legal individuals, with no legally recognized ties to any collectivity.

Thus, when Fiji's independence became real in 1970, the constitution insisted that races still existed in Fiji and that they had to vote separately. Since then, political parties have generally and increasingly followed racial lines, and the army has remained an enclave of Indigenous Fijians. When political parties backed mostly by Indo-Fijian voters won Fiji's 1987 election, the army staged a coup and took over the country after only a month. The constitution that was then installed in 1990 returned to even more naked discrimination against Indo-Fijians with regard to voting rights (Kelly and Kaplan 2001, 77).

The constitution was revised yet again, in a manner that favoured chiefly ethnic Fijian interests and seemed guaranteed to prevent parties backed by Indo-Fijian voters from winning control of the government in the 1999 election. To everyone's surprise, parties backing ethnic Fijians lost again. On 19 May 2000 came a second coup. Finally, after new elections in 2001, ethnic Fijians won control of the government. The new government lasted until a December 2006 military takeover. One of the military's demands was an end to the "race-based" voting system, to be replaced by a new "one citizen–one vote" system. However, in April 2009, the president suspended the constitution and appointed himself head of state. In September 2009, the British Commonwealth expelled Fiji for its failure to schedule democratic elections by 2010. An election was finally held in 2014, and Fiji was readmitted to the Commonwealth (Figure 13.4).

What lessons does this history suggest about nation building in postcolonial states? The issues are many and complex. But Kelly and Kaplan insist that the image of a united Fijian nation projected at independence was severely undermined by legal mechanisms of political representation carried over from the colonial period,

FIGURE 13.4 A Fijian citizen contemplates the list of candidates in anticipation of the 2014 national election.

particularly the race-based voting rolls. What became apparent in the years after independence was that Indo-Fijians and ethnic Fijians had imagined very different national communities. Indo-Fijians had supported the image of a nation in which all citizens, Indo-Fijian or ethnic Fijian or "general elector," would have equal status, voting on a single roll, working together to build a constitutional democracy. However, "few among the ethnic Fijians have yet come to see themselves as partners with immigrants" (Kelly and Kaplan 2001, 41). Ever since independence, and particularly after each coup, ethnic Fijians worked to construct an image of the Fijian nation based solely on traditions in which Indo-Fijians had no meaningful place. Thus, Kelly and Kaplan conclude, in Fiji (and in many other parts of the world), "'the nation' is a contested idea, not an experienced reality" (142).

Nation Building in a Postcolonial World: The Example of Nunavut

In Canada today, many Indigenous Canadians are struggling to achieve a nation-building goal very different from that of the Indo-Fijians. The First Nations, Inuit, and Métis peoples of Canada have long sought recognition of their nationhood and their inherent right to self-determination. They want to regain control of their affairs and to make their own decisions concerning the preservation and development of their distinct cultures. Many Indigenous groups seek an officially recognized form of self-government that would enable them to have more control over affairs within their communities and the power to deliver programs and services, such as education, child-welfare, and health care initiatives, that align with their values.

Anthropologists have devoted considerable attention in their research to traditional forms of leadership and government among Canadian Indigenous peoples. For example, there have been studies of the Iroquois Confederacy (a confederation of First Nations tribes that flourished in the seventeenth and early eighteenth centuries), chief-led governance among individual bands of the Northern Ojibwa and Cree, and the complexities of the Kwakiutl (Kwakwaka'wakw) and Haida sociopolitical groups of the northwest coast of North America. These studies demonstrate clearly that Indigenous people have always been quite capable of managing their own internal affairs without the interference of colonial administrators. Since the early days of Confederation, Indigenous people have expressed their desire to govern themselves once again in a way that they choose so that they can participate in a more equitable power-sharing arrangement with Ottawa and the provinces. This aim would require the creation of another level of government that recognizes Indigenous peoples as members of distinct groups that had an important and unique role in contributing to the formation of Canada.

Some of this power was finally granted in 1982, under section 35 of the Constitution Act, when the Canadian government recognized Indigenous peoples' right to determine matters related to their culture, identity, traditions, and language. However, because each nation is so unique, negotiations for more specific arrangements have been conducted on a nation-by-nation basis. For example, self-government arrangements have been settled with the Sechelt of British Columbia, the Cree-Naskapi

of Quebec, and various Yukon First Nations. At the same time, many non-Indigenous Canadians have been resistant to making such arrangements as they feel that the Canadian government has already made too many concessions to Indigenous peoples. Yet these concerns seem unwarranted as recent research demonstrates that those Indigenous communities whose members have been given greater autonomy in managing their own social programs and education have proven to be more efficient and less burdensome on the federal and provincial governments (Hedican 2008). Moreover, within these communities, resources have become more focused on the most important needs of First Nations groups, and Indigenous peoples have received more effective training for administrative positions.

Perhaps the most successful outcome of Canadian Indigenous peoples' fight for self-determination has been the creation of Nunavut, which became independent of the Northwest Territories on 1 April 1999 (Map 13.2). Inuit groups had been petitioning the federal government to create a separate territory for Inuit peoples since the mid-1970s. While formal negotiations began in the early 1980s, it wasn't until 1993

MAP 13.2 Nunavut became an independent Canadian territory on 1 April 1999. *Nunavut* means "our land" in Inuktitut, one of the major languages of the Inuit peoples. Approximately 85 per cent of those who occupy this area of the eastern Arctic are Inuit.

that the official documents—the Nunavut Act and the Nunavut Land Claims Agreement—were signed to create the new territory. (See EthnoProfile 12.4 in Chapter 12 for more information on the Inuit of Nunavut.) The latter of these documents, which was signed by representatives of the Inuit governmental organization known as the Tunngavik Federation of Nunavut as well as the Canadian government and the government of the Northwest Territories, granted Inuit peoples a variety of rights and powers, including the following: land title to 350,000 square kilometres of land, mineral rights to 35,000 square kilometres of land, equal representation of Inuit on environmental and wildlife boards, the right to harvest wildlife, a share of royalties from oil and gas and mineral development on Crown land, and the right to create their own self-governing body (PolarNet 2015). This land claim settlement represented the largest in Canadian history, and it marked the beginning of new relationships between Inuit peoples and the government of Canada. Many Indigenous peoples, both in Canada and around the world, also hope that it may provide a model for their own self-determination endeavours in the future.

Globalization and the Nation-State

The Fijian history described earlier points to the kinds of movements and mixing of people that were permitted and even encouraged in the age of European colonial empires, and how the consequences of these processes bequeathed a series of challenging problems to postcolonial territories that wanted to transform themselves into nation-states. Even as Fiji and other postcolonial states have been wrestling with these problems from the colonial past, however, ongoing changes in the world have begun to challenge the territorial boundaries that nation-states have struggled to erect around themselves. Since the end of the Cold War in 1989, processes of globalization, abetted by new forms of communication, transportation, and manufacturing, have unleashed flows of wealth, images, people, things, and ideologies across the world. The pressures of these global flows on the boundaries of nation-states have been profound. National governments have struggled, often in vain, to control what their citizens read or watch in the media: satellite services and telecommunications and the Internet elude state-ordered censorship. Nation-states allow migrants or students or tourists to cross their borders because they need their labour or tuition or vacation expenditures, but in so doing states must be content with the political values or religious commitments or families that these outsiders bring with them. Some have argued that weakening the boundaries between nation-states is a good thing, since border restrictions and censorship need to be overcome, but, almost 30 years after the end of the Cold War, the challenges posed by weakened borders have become more apparent. For example, the Schengen Agreement, adopted in 1999 by the European Union, eliminated passport controls between all member states except for Ireland and the United Kingdom, and it was hailed as a positive achievement. Twenty years later, however, enormous pressure has been put on the European Union by waves of refugees escaping economic and political pressures in their home nations: thousands of refugees have died attempting to cross the Mediterranean Sea from points in North Africa, and more recently, waves of refugees fleeing the Syrian civil war have passed through Turkey into Greece and then made their way northward by foot, seeking to settle in Germany and other European states that would accept them and offer them safety. Similar pressures have been felt in North America as refugees and migrants, seeking safety and a better life, have encountered increasing hostility on the southern border of the United States, including the erection of a border wall designed to keep them out. In many other parts of the world, political unrest has also pushed people across national borders in search of safety and continued means of survival, making many weakened states vulnerable to chaos and violence.

Migrants and refugees themselves often face a dilemma. On the one hand, they now form sizable and highly visible minorities in the countries of settlement, often in the poorer areas of cities. There they find opportunities for economic subsistence and political security, encouraging them to stay. On the other hand, hostility and sometimes violence are directed against them whenever there is a local economic downturn. Many migrants conclude that the possibility of permanent assimilation is unrealistic, which encourages them to maintain ties to their places of origin or to migrant communities elsewhere.

Migration, Trans-Border Identities, and Long-Distance Nationalism

The term *diaspora* is commonly used to refer to migrant populations with a shared identity who live in a variety of different locales around the world, but Nina Glick Schiller and Georges Fouron point out that not all such populations see themselves in the same way. Schiller and Fouron describe different types of "trans-border identities" that characterize different groups of migrants. They prefer to use the term **diaspora** to identify a form of trans-border identity that does not focus on nation building. Should members of a diaspora begin to organize in support of nationalist struggles in their homeland, or to agitate for a state of their own, they become **long-distance nationalists** (Schiller and Fouron 2002, 360–1). "Long-distance nationalism" was coined by political scientist Benedict Anderson to describe the efforts of émigrés to offer moral, economic, and political support to nationalist struggles in their countries of origin. In his original discussion, Anderson emphasized the dangerous

> **diaspora** Migrant populations with a shared identity who live in a variety of different locales around the world; a form of trans-border identity that does not focus on nation building.
>
> **long-distance nationalism** Members of a diaspora organized in support of nationalist struggles in their homeland or to agitate for a state of their own.
>
> **trans-border state** A form of state in which it is claimed that those people who left the country and their descendants remain part of their ancestral state, even if they are citizens of another state.
>
> **trans-border citizenry** A group made up of citizens of a country who continue to live in their homeland plus the people who have emigrated from the country and their descendants, regardless of their current citizenship.

FIGURE 13.5 The Dominican Republic permits emigrants who have become naturalized citizens of the United States to vote in Dominican elections. Here, a Dominican woman in New York campaigns in 2004 for a second term for President Hipólito Mejía.

irresponsibility of the "citizenshipless participation" of the long-distance nationalists: "while technically a citizen of the state in which he comfortably lives, but to which he may feel little attachment, he finds it tempting to play identity politics by participating (via propaganda, money, weapons, any way but voting) in the conflicts of his imagined *Heimat* [homeland]" (2002, 269–70).

Schiller and Fouron argue, however, that the conditions of globalization have led to new forms of long-distance nationalism that do not correspond to Anderson's original description. They point to the emergence of the **trans-border state**: a form of state "claiming that its emigrants and their descendants remain an integral and intimate part of their ancestral homeland, even if they are legal citizens of another state" (Schiller and Fouron 2002, 357). Trans-border states did not characterize periods of mass emigration in the nineteenth and twentieth centuries. At that time, nations sending emigrants abroad regarded permanent settlement elsewhere as national betrayal. They encouraged emigrants to think of migration as temporary, expecting them eventually to return home with new wealth and skills to build the nation. But in today's global world, political leaders of many states sending emigrants accept the likelihood that those emigrants will settle permanently elsewhere. Some may even insist that émigrés retain full membership in the nation-state from which they came, a form of long-distance nationalism that Schiller and Fouron call a **trans-border citizenry**: "Citizens residing within the territorial homeland and new emigrants and their descendants are part of the nation, whatever legal citizenship the emigres may have" (Schiller and Fouron 2002, 358).

Trans-border states and trans-border citizenries are more than symbolic identities: they have become concretized in law. For example, several Latin American countries, including Mexico, Colombia, the Dominican Republic, Ecuador, and Brazil, permit emigrants who have become naturalized citizens in countries such as the United States to retain dual nationality and even voting rights in their country of origin (Figure 13.5). Special government ministries are set up to address the needs of citizens living abroad. This is very different from Anderson's "citizenshipless participation." Schiller and Fouron stress that trans-border states and citizenries spring "from the life experiences of migrants of different classes" and are "rooted in the day to day efforts of people in the homeland to live lives of dignity and self-respect that compel them to include those who have migrated" (2002, 359).

But some trans-border citizenries face difficulties. First, their efforts at nation building are sometimes blocked by political forces in the homeland that do not welcome their contributions. This was the case for Haitians living abroad while Haiti was ruled by the Duvalier family dictatorship and for Cubans living abroad whose efforts have been blocked by the Castro revolutionary government. Second, the states in which immigrants have settled may regard as threatening the continued involvement of trans-border citizens in the affairs of another state. Such involvement has often been seen as even more threatening since terrorists destroyed the World Trade Center and attacked the Pentagon on 11 September 2001. Yet in an era of globalization, attempts to control migration threaten to block the flows of people that keep the global economy going. Moreover, the vulnerability of trans-border citizens in these circumstances often increases the appeal of long-distance nationalism (Schiller and Fouron 2002, 359–60).

The globalizing forces responsible for these changes have undermined previous understandings of what a world made up of nation-states should look like. Indeed, they reveal unacknowledged contradictions and weaknesses of actual nation-states. For example, the existence and strength of trans-border states and citizenries show that some nation-states—especially those sending migrants—are actually what Schiller and Fouron call *apparent states*: they have all the outward attributes of nation-states (government bureaucracies, armies, a seat in the United Nations), but in fact they are unable to meet the needs of their people (Schiller and Fouron 2002, 363). And the existence of apparent states also exposes inconsistencies and paradoxes in the meaning of citizenship in the nation-states where migrants settle.

Schiller and Fouron contrast legal citizenship with what they call substantive citizenship and point out that, for trans-border citizens, the two often do not coincide. **Legal citizenship** is accorded by state laws and can be difficult for migrants to obtain. But even those trans-border citizens who obtain legal citizenship often experience a gap between what legal citizenship promises and the way they are treated by the state. For example, people of colour and women who are United States citizens are not treated by the state the same way white male citizens are treated. By contrast, **substantive citizenship** is defined by the actions people take, regardless of their legal citizenship status, to assert their membership in a state and to bring about political changes that will improve their

lives. Some trans-border citizens call for the establishment of full-fledged **transnational nation-states**. That is, "they challenge the notion that relationships between citizens and their state are confined within that territory" and work for the recognition of a new political form that contradicts the understandings of political theory, but which reflects the realities of their experiences of national identity" (Schiller and Fouron 2002, 359).

Anthropology and Multicultural Politics in New Europe

One of the more interesting things about the early twenty-first century is that Europe—the continent that gave birth to the Enlightenment, to colonial empires, and (along with North America) to anthropology itself—has become a living laboratory for the study of some of the most complex social and cultural processes to be found anywhere in the world.

During the last half of the twentieth century, the countries of Europe, including Italy, were the target of large waves of migration from all over the world. One venerable working-class Roman neighbourhood, only a short walk from the Colosseum, is Rione Monti, which has a fascinating history of its own (EthnoProfile 13.3: Rione Monti; Figure 13.6). In 1999, anthropologist Michael Herzfeld (2003) moved into Rione Monti to explore social change in the uses of the past. Long-time residents of Monti share a common local culture, which includes use of the *romanesco* dialect rather than standard Italian and a strong sense of local identity that distinguishes them from "foreigners," including diplomats and non-Roman Italians. Their identity survived Mussolini's demolition of part of the neighbourhood in the early twentieth century. They successfully dealt with a local criminal underworld by mastering a refined urbane code of politeness. The underworld had faded away by the 1970s, but beginning in the 1990s, residents began to face two new challenges to their community.

legal citizenship The rights and obligations of citizenship accorded by the laws of a state.

substantive citizenship The actions people take, regardless of their legal citizenship status, to assert their membership in a state and to bring about political changes that will improve their lives.

transnational nation-state A nation-state in which the relationships between citizens and the state extend to wherever citizens reside.

EthnoProfile 13.3

Rione Monti (Rome)

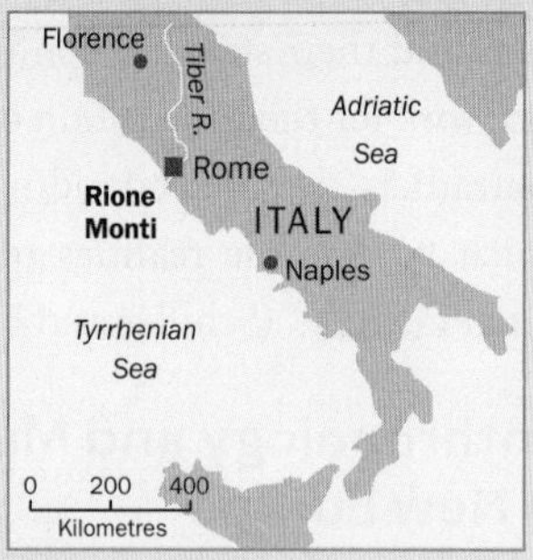

Region: Europe

Nation: Italy

Population: 15,300

Environment: Central neighbourhood in Rome

Livelihood: Urban occupations, ranging from tourism and factory work to restaurants, small businesses, bureaucratic, executive

Political organization: Neighbourhood in a modern nation-state

For more information: https://en.wikipedia.org/wiki/Monti_(rione_of_Rome)

First, historic Roman neighbourhoods became fashionable, and well-to-do Italians began to move into Rione Monti, pushing many workers into cheaper housing elsewhere. Second, in the 1990s, another group of newcomers arrived: immigrants from eastern Europe.

Italy is one of the more recent destinations of immigration into Europe, reversing the country's historical experience as a source, rather than a target, of immigration. However, after Germany, France, and Britain

FIGURE 13.6 Rione Monti is a neighbourhood in central Rome, Italy, where long-time residents and new immigrants are negotiating new forms of relationship.

passed laws curtailing immigration in the 1970s, Italy became an increasingly popular destination for immigrants from Africa, Asia, and Latin America; after the end of the Cold War came immigrants from outside the European Union (EU), including eastern Europe. Until recently, laws regulating immigration were few, and the country appeared welcoming. But this is changing: "Italy has not historically been a racist country, but intolerant attitudes towards immigrants have increased. To a large extent, this seems to be the result of a long-standing underestimation of the magnitude of the changes and thus poor policy implementation for a lengthy period, in spite of the best intentions officially proclaimed" (Melotti 1997, 91).

Umberto Melotti (1997) contrasts the distinctive ways in which immigration is understood by the governments of France, Britain, and Germany. According to Melotti, the French project is "ethnocentric assimilationism": since early in the nineteenth century, when French society experienced a falling birth rate, immigration was encouraged and immigrants were promised all the rights and privileges of native-born citizens as long as they adopted French culture completely, dropping other ethnic or cultural attachments and assimilating the French language and character (1997, 75). The British project, by contrast, is "uneven pluralism": that is, the pragmatic British expect immigrants to be loyal and law-abiding citizens, but they do not expect immigrants to "become British" and they tolerate private cultivation of cultural differences as long as these do not threaten the British way of life (79–80). (In many ways, Canadian immigration policy follows the British pattern, but multiculturalism is more firmly entrenched in our government policy and our national identity. At the same time, the practice of multiculturalism in Canada is somewhat uneven, as it privileges those who speak one of our two "official" languages [see Haque 2012], and it is not consistent in all regions [e.g., Quebec's policy of "interculturalism"; see Bouchard 2011].) Lastly, Melotti describes the German project as "the institutionalization of precariousness," by which he means that, despite the fact that Germany has within its borders more immigrants than any other European country and began receiving immigrants at the end of the nineteenth century, its government continues to insist that Germany is not a country of immigrants. Immigrants were always considered "guest workers," children born to guest workers were considered citizens of the country from which the worker came, and it remains very difficult for guest workers or their children born in Germany to obtain German citizenship. (This contrasts with France, for example, where children of immigrants born on French soil automatically become French citizens.)

Coming to terms with increasing numbers of Muslims living in countries where Christianity has historically been dominant is a central theme in political debates within Europe. Although almost all European states consider themselves secular in orientation (see Asad 2003), the relation between religion and state is far from uniform. France is unusual because of its strict legal separation between religion and state. In Britain, the combination of a secular outlook with state funding of the established Anglican Church has allowed citizens to support forms of religious inclusion that first involved state funding of Catholic schools for Irish immigrants and now involve state funding of Muslim schools for Muslim immigrants (Modood 1997; Lewis 1997). In Germany, where a secular outlook also combines with state-subsidized religious institutions, the state has devised curricula for elementary schools designed to teach all students about different religious traditions, including Islam, in ways that emphasize the possibility of harmonizing one's religious faith with one's obligations as a citizen. Although this approach may seem presumptuous or paternalistic, its supporters counter that its advantages outweigh its costs. Perhaps as a result of their own history, many contemporary Germans have less faith than the British that a civic culture of religious tolerance will automatically lead to harmony without state intervention and less faith than the French in the existence of a separate secular sphere of society from which religion can be safely excluded (Schiffauer 1997).

These are, of course, thumbnail sketches of more complex attitudes and practices. But they illustrate the fact that there is no single "European" approach to the challenges posed by immigration. In a way, each European state, with its own history and institutions, is experimenting with different ways of coping with the challenges immigration presents; and their failures and successes will influence the kinds of cultural institutions that develop in the twenty-first century. This is particularly significant in light of the fact that European nation-states have joined together in the EU, a continent-wide superstate with 28 members. Reconciling the diverse interests and needs of member states poses enormous challenges for EU members,

and issues surrounding immigration are among them. These challenges have increased even more sharply in recent years, as austerity policies within the EU have threatened the economic viability of states such as Greece, some of whose citizens have responded to the crisis by suggesting that Greece leave the European Union to find financial relief. Similarly, the free movement of EU citizens across state borders has generated anti-immigrant sentiments among some British citizens, which led to the so-called Brexit referendum in the United Kingdom, in which voters by a slim majority favoured cutting British ties with the EU, but, as of late 2019, this has still not been resolved. Finally, radical Islamic Middle Eastern terrorist groups such as ISIS (or the so-called "Islamic State") have managed to perpetrate violent terrorist incidents inside a number of European states, perhaps most notably the attacks in 2015 in Paris, first at the offices of the satirical newspaper *Charlie Hebdo* in January, and later coordinated attacks in November on several public venues in Paris, including the Bataclan concert hall. These events have further stimulated the growth of right-wing anti-immigrant and anti-Muslim political movements in many European countries.

Tariq Modood (1997) points out, for example, that European multiculturalism requires supporting conceptions of citizenship that allow the "right to assimilate" as well as the "right to have one's 'difference' . . . recognized and supported in the public and the private spheres"; multiculturalism must recognize that "participation in the public or national culture is necessary for the effective exercise of citizenship" while at the same time defending the "right to widen and adapt the national culture" (20). Modood further suggested that perhaps such tensions "can only be resolved in practice through finding and cultivating points of common ground between dominant and subordinate cultures, as well as new syntheses and hybridities. The important thing is that the burdens of change . . . are not all dependent on one party to this encounter" (1997, 20).

Anthropologist John Bowen's (2010) recent fieldwork in France documents the process Modood describes. Bowen has worked among the many French Muslims "who wish to live fulfilling *and* religious lives in France" (4). He has paid particular attention to the work of a number of French Muslim religious teachers and scholars, whom he calls "Islamic public actors." Other French Muslims come to them for religious instruction and for advice about how to cope with the difficulties of living in a non-Muslim country. In turn, the Islamic public actors Bowen knows are working to craft solutions that, in their view, are true both to the laws of the French republic and to the norms and traditions of Islam.

For example, many French Muslims are concerned about how to contract a valid marriage in France. Ever since the French Revolution, France has refused to accept the legality of religious marriages and recognizes only civil marriages contracted at city hall (Figure 13.7). Yet Muslims who want to marry are often confused about whether a "secular" marriage at city hall is appropriate or necessary. Indeed, some Muslims have argued that city hall marriages are un-Islamic because they did not exist at the time of the Prophet Muhammad. But other Muslims, including some of Bowen's consultants, disagree with this position. They argue that there was no need for civil marriages at the time of the Prophet because, in those days, tribal life made it impossible to avoid the obligations of the marriage contract. But things are different today for Muslims in urban France: Bowen's consultants have seen many tragic outcomes when young women who thought they had a valid Muslim marriage were left by their husbands, only to discover that the French state did not recognize their marriage and could offer them no legal redress.

Because this was not the outcome that Islamic marriage was intended to produce, the Muslim scholars Bowen knows looked beyond traditional

FIGURE 13.7 A Turkish bride and groom in Clichy–sous–Bois, a poor suburb of Paris. Islamic and French legal scholars are both working to harmonize French and Islamic marriage practices.

Islamic marriage practices in order to clarify the larger purposes that Islamic marriage was supposed to achieve. They then asked if these purposes could be achieved using the French institution of civil marriage. One scholar told Bowen, "I say that if you marry at the city hall, you have already made an Islamic marriage, because all the conditions for that marriage have been fulfilled" (2010, 167). Those conditions include that both Islamic marriages and French civil marriages are contracts; that both require the consent of the spouses; and that the legal requirements imposed on the spouses by French civil marriage further the Islamic goal of keeping the spouses together. Given that this kind of reasoning is further strengthened by appealing to opinions on marriage drawn from the four traditional Sunni schools of Islamic law, many Islamic public intellectuals believe that a way can be found to craft acceptable practices for French Muslims in many areas of daily life.

Because Bowen agrees with Modood that accommodation has to go in both directions, he also shows how some French legal scholars are working to craft solutions to the challenges Muslim marriage practices present to French law. Most French judges agree, for example, that Islamic marriages or divorces contracted outside France remain valid when the parties involved move to France. But French judges can refuse to accept international rules for resolving legal conflicts if they decide that the solution would violate French "public order." Bowen found that the concept of public order is basic to the French legal system, referring "both to the conditions of social order and to basic values, and it limits the range of laws that a legislator may pass and the decisions that a judge may make" (2010, 173).

Violations of public order may include customs from outside France that are judged to "offend the morality and values" of French law. Some French jurists argue that consequences following from Muslim practices of marriage and divorce should not be recognized in France if they violate French and European commitments to the equality of women and men. Other French jurists, however, point to the practical problems that this argument creates: not recognizing the validity of Islamic divorces in France, for example, would mean that a woman divorced according to Islamic law abroad could not remarry if she came to France. Similarly, refusing to recognize polygamous marriage in France would deprive the children of all but a man's first wife of their rights under French and European law. In recent years, Bowen reports, French judges have devised two ways of crafting a solution to these unwelcome consequences. One has been to modify the concept of public order by making so-called "practical exceptions" for Muslims who immigrate to France. The other is to be more flexible with Muslim marriage and family practices as long as these arrangements involve individuals who are not French citizens. These pragmatic solutions are an improvement over what Bowen calls the "more blunt-instrument approach" associated with the older understanding of public order. Bowen (2010) concludes that in France today, Muslim and French jurists alike are both struggling to craft "the legal conditions for common life that are capacious enough to 'reasonably accommodate' people living in differing conditions and with differing beliefs, yet unitary enough to retain the hope that such a common life is conceivable" (178).

As these examples suggest, the struggles and dilemmas facing residents of Rione Monti are widespread across the new Europe. But the specifics of these residents' situation and the cultural resources at their disposal have their own particularity. Thus, the traditionally left-wing Monti residents have resisted attempts by neo-fascist politicians to get them to turn against immigrant families in the neighbourhood. Long-time Monti residents were initially unhappy with the location of the Ukrainian church in a building that overlooks the neighbourhood's central square because the churchgoers gather there twice a week, invading "their" space. Herzfeld found that the residents of Monti, like other Romans, claimed not to be racist and that they seemed less hostile to immigrants of colour than to Ukrainians. But Ukrainians were more numerous in Monti, and more threatening, because they looked like local people but in fact were competing with locals for work and space in the neighbourhood (Herzfeld 2009, 230). Local and immigrant Monti residents eventually did find ways to get along with each other (231). Indeed, during the years when Herzfeld was doing his ethnography, the mix of residents in Monti was changing in other ways, as young professionals, including professors from the nearby university, began to rent apartments in local buildings. The low-income artisans who had traditionally lived in these buildings were finding, however, that rents were rising, even as entire apartment blocks remained empty. The owners of the apartment buildings in these blocks had concluded that it was worth their while to keep their buildings empty until real estate prices rose, even if this precipitated a housing shortage.

Prior to this period, struggles between renters, landlords, and the city government of Rome regarding building permits or over rental rates were common. Such disputes had usually been resolved by negotiations among all interested parties, and the negotiations had been carried out according to the mostly extralegal rules of a traditional neighbourhood "code." As a result, low-income renters had often managed to avoid eviction from their apartments. But in the early years of the twenty-first century, the rules changed, in large part because some of the key players changed. A lot of outside money was entering the Roman real estate market, deployed by businessmen who knew nothing and cared less about whether low-income renters ought to be allowed to stay in building in desirable locations.

Still, Monti residents were politically active, and they banded together when threatened with eviction. Herzfeld followed closely the back-and-forth negotiations that ensued when the renters in one particular building staged a rent strike after the building's new owner threatened to evict current residents. This was the sort of action that, in the old days, would likely have been quietly resolved according to the neighbourhood code; and at first, the strikers were able to get the building's new owner to agree not to evict them. What nobody had counted on, however, was the clout of the wealthy outside buyers who had entered the Roman real estate market. The building's new owner then sold the building to another company, who then sold it to a third company, whose owners refused to honour the agreement that the original owner had made with the renters. The current owners then tried to sell the building to the city, which refused to pay the price they were asking: "It became clear that nothing further could be done; this company soon thereafter sold the property to yet another firm, one that was developing extensive interests in the neighbourhood, and the struggle finally came to an end" (2009, 297).

A key component contributing to this outcome was a change in the law that reflected struggles over what kinds of rights residents had to their homes. One of Herzfeld's informants, who had been active in Roman city government, explained to him that the power of the city to intervene in struggles against eviction had changed. In the past, the city had respected the view that people had a social right to their homes; but these rights were no longer legally protected:

> [U]nder the national constitution, it was now the owner's rights that were protected. . . . A set of laws, promulgated at the national level by the co- alition to which he had belonged at the city level, and reinforced by already existing constitutional guarantees for the rights of property owners, had now effectively undercut any serious prospect of resolving the dispute as an issue of the social right to a home. (2009, 297)

At first the strikers refused to give up, but their legal position was weak; within a year, they had been evicted. There was much bitterness among those forced to leave, and even though all of them eventually did find other places to live, many had to leave Monti, which under- mined their sense of community and identity.

The experiences of these Monti residents raise inter- esting and troubling questions about the rights of long- time residents in any place who discover that under the current regime of global neo-liberalism they apparently possess no rights that international capital is obliged to respect. Herzfeld observes that "the intense attachment to place that aroused my sympathies can also be the source of no less intense forms of cultural fundamen- talism and racism" (2009, 301). These responses are not limited to Europe; they can be found in many countries around the world, including Thailand, where Herzfeld next carried out fieldwork, following what turned into a 24-year-long battle by residents of an inner-city neigh- bourhood to resist being evicted so that the government might modernize space they occupied (Herzfeld 2016). However, Herzfeld insists that "there is no necessary connection between localism and racism and other forms of intolerance, and in fact what has impressed me throughout both field projects—one in Italy, the other in Thailand—has been the firmness with which some reject the seductions of intolerance in the midst of their own sufferings, even as they recognize the bitterness that drives others in far less attractive directions" (2009, 302).

flexible citizenship **The strategies and effects employed by managers, technocrats, and professionals who move regularly across state boundaries and who seek both to circumvent and benefit from different nation-state regimes.**

He adds that "none of this will make much sense except in the further context of a consideration of the history of nationalism, both in Italy and elsewhere" (2009, 302).

What Happens to Citizenship in a Globalized World?

Our discussion of nationality, nation-states, and nation- alism has briefly traced developments from the French Revolution through the spread of European colonial empires through the transformation of colonies into nation-states, ending with the softening of national boundaries that has occurred following post–Cold War processes of globalization. Challenges to national sovereignty—that is, a nation's ability to defend its bor- ders and govern itself—have been accompanied by changes in the meaning of citizenship, the rights and privileges of those persons considered legitimate mem- bers of the national population. What might citizenship mean in a twenty-first-century globalized world?

How Can Citizenship Be Flexible?

Schiller and Fouron's contrast between legal and sub- stantive citizenship suggests that notions of citizenship that previously seemed straightforward break down in the context of globalization. Another way of address- ing these contradictions is suggested by anthropologist Aihwa Ong, who speaks of **flexible citizenship**: "the strategies and effects of mobile managers, technocrats, and professionals seeking both to circumvent *and* benefit from different nation-state regimes by selecting different sites for investment, work, and family relocation" (2002, 174). Ong studied diaspora communities of elite Chinese families who played key roles in the economic success of the Pacific Rim in recent years. Although their success is often attributed by outsiders to "Chinese culture," Ong's research questions this simplistic explanation; she docu- ments the ways in which Chinese families responded creatively to opportunities and challenges they encoun- tered since the end of the nineteenth century, as they found ways to evade or exploit the governmentality of three different kinds of institutions: (1) Chinese kinship and family, (2) the nation-state, and (3) the marketplace.

The break from mainland Chinese ideas of kin- ship and Confucian filial piety came when Chinese first moved into the capitalist commercial circuits of

European empires. Money could be made in these settings, but success required Chinese merchant families to cut themselves off from ties to mainland China and to reinforce bonds among family members and business partners in terms of *guanxi* ("relationships of social connections built primarily upon shared identities such as native place, kinship or attending the same school" [Smart 1999, 120]).

The family discipline of overseas Chinese enabled them to become wealthy and provided the resources to subvert the governmentality of the nation-state. The orientation of these wealthy families toward national identity and citizenship, Ong explains, is "market-driven." In Hong Kong, for example, in the years leading up to its return to mainland China in 1997, many wealthy Chinese thought of citizenship not as the right to demand full democratic representation, but as the right to promote familial interests apart from the well-being of society (Ong 2002, 178). None of the overseas Chinese she knew expressed any commitment to nationalism, either local or long distance—quite the contrary. Relying on family discipline and loyalty and buttressed by considerable wealth and strong interpersonal ties, they actively worked to evade the governmentality of nation-states. For example, Chinese from Hong Kong who wanted to migrate to Britain in the 1960s were able to evade racial barriers that blocked other "coloured" immigrants because of their experience with capitalism and their reputation for peaceful acquiescence to British rule. When the British decided to award citizenship to some Hong Kong residents in the 1990s, they used a point system that favoured applicants with education, fluency in English, and training in professions of value to the economy, such as accountancy and law. These attributes fitted well the criteria for citizenship valued under the government of Margaret Thatcher, while other applicants for citizenship who lacked such attributes were excluded. Citizenship, or at least a passport, could be purchased by those who had the money: "well-off families accumulated passports not only from Canada, Australia, Singapore, and the United States but also from revenue-poor Fiji, the Philippines, Panama, and Tonga which required in return for a passport a down payment of U.S. $200,000 and an equal amount in installments" (Ong 2002, 183) (Figure 13.8).

Although wealthy overseas Chinese families had thus managed to evade or subvert both the governmentality of Chinese kinship and that of nation-states, they remained vulnerable to the discipline of the capitalist

FIGURE 13.8 Overseas Chinese are to be found in many parts of the world, as here in Kuala Lumpur, Malaysia. They are not always millionaire businesspeople but are shopkeepers and small businesspeople as well.

market. To be sure, market discipline under globalization was very different from the market discipline typical in the 1950s and 1960s. Making money in the context of globalization required the flexibility to take advantage of economic opportunities wherever and whenever they appeared. Ong described one family in which the eldest son remained in Hong Kong to run part of the family hotel chain located in the Pacific region while his brother lived in San Francisco and managed the hotels located in North America and Europe. Children can be separated from their parents when they are, for example, installed in one country to be educated while their parents manage businesses in other countries on different continents.

These flexible family arrangements are not without costs: "Familial regimes of dispersal and localization . . . discipline family members to make do with very little emotional support; disrupted parental responsibility, strained marital relations, and abandoned children are such common circumstances that they have special terms" (Ong 2002, 190). At the same time, individual family members truly do seem to live comfortably as citizens of the world. A Chinese banker in San Francisco told Ong that he could live in Asia, Canada, or Europe: "I can live anywhere in the world, but it must be near an airport" (190).

Ong concludes that, for these elite Chinese, the concept of nationalism has lost its meaning. Instead, she says, they seem to subscribe to a **postnational ethos** in which they submit to the governmentality of the capitalist market while trying to evade the governmentality of nation-states, ultimately because their only true loyalty is to the family business (Ong 2002, 190). Such flexible citizenship, however, is not an option for non-elite migrants: "whereas for bankers, boundaries are always flexible, for migrant workers, boat people, persecuted intellectuals and artists, and other kinds of less well-heeled refugees, this . . . is a harder act to follow" (190). Ong concludes that neither the positives nor the negatives associated with the practices of these overseas Chinese merchants should be attributed to any "Chinese" essence; instead, she thinks these strategies are better understood as "the expressions of a habitus that is finely tuned to the turbulence of late capitalism" (191).

Global Politics in the Twenty-First Century

Although traditional research in political anthropology began among small-scale societies that might at one time have functioned independently of their neighbours, the fact remains that these ethnographic studies were

> **postnational ethos** An attitude toward the world in which people submit to the governmentality of the capitalist market while trying to evade the governmentality of nation-states.

regularly carried out when these societies had been incorporated into European colonial empires. With the breakup of these empires, most colonial territories were transformed into independent nation-states. But as we saw in the case of Fiji, this transformation has been full of tension and struggle because different segments of the Fijian citizenry had different ideas about what that modern nation-state would look like and about who would be in charge. Even as such struggles to affirm national sovereignty continue in many parts of the world, these struggles have been complicated by global flows of capital, people, images, ideas, and ideologies. National boundaries have softened. In some cases, nation-states have given up claims to sovereignty over some of their citizens, but some of these same citizens, now moving in the same globalized contexts, have found new ways of asserting their own territorial citizenship. Because power is productive, the results may be positive or negative, depending on the specific case. At the end of the second decade of the twenty-first century, however, the globalized world is in a dangerous and unstable condition. While some have been able to benefit enormously from the growth of global capitalism, many others have been left out. As inequalities widen, local leaders and their followers struggle to manage the consequences, with or in spite of the intervention of outside powers. One major consequence has been the increased flows of migrants and refugees seeking to escape the violence. Many long taken-for-granted notions about identity and belonging now seem up for grabs everywhere on earth.

Anthropology in Everyday Life

Human Terrain Teams and Anthropological Ethics

Recently, an ethical dispute has emerged among anthropologists about the Human Terrain System, a United States Army program that hires small teams of civilian anthropologists and other social scientists to become embedded with US combat brigades in Iraq and Afghanistan. These teams are intended to provide relevant sociocultural information about the particular neighbourhoods and village communities in which the US military is operating. Backed by an elaborate 24-hour research centre in the United States, the Human Terrain System attempts to improve relations between US military personnel and Iraqis and Afghans they might encounter, to gather information on development needs, and to generate culturally informed strategic advice. The hope is that providing US military forces with a greater understanding of social and cultural contexts will help reduce misunderstandings and unintentional insults and ultimately help prevent bloodshed. This program was instantly controversial, raising the question, "Is this an appropriate use of anthropological knowledge?"

A number of anthropologists have been concerned that the service of anthropologists in military units, almost like spies, could compromise the integrity of the discipline. Anthropologist Hugh Gusterson was quoted as saying, "The prime directive is you do no harm to informants . . . [but] data collected by [Human Terrain Team] members can also be accessed by military intelligence operatives who might use the same information for targeting Taliban operatives" (Caryl 2009). Indeed, it might be used to target *supposed* Taliban sympathizers. As Gusterson puts it, "The product generated by the Human Terrain Teams is inherently double-edged" (Caryl 2009). The interests of the military units may not be the same as the interests of the embedded anthropologists. How can these anthropologists prevent their research from being used for purposes to which they object? Could working for the military betray informants' trust?

Further, some have argued that the Human Terrain System may undermine anthropological research anywhere, all of which depends on the trust anthropologists

An American civilian anthropologist talks to Afghan national army soldiers, who were providing security both for the April 2009 elections and for Human Terrain Team interviews with local people.

develop with the people with whom they work. If some anthropologists are working for a foreign military, how can community members be sure that an anthropologist in their community is not also working for a foreign military?

Chapter Summary

1. Contemporary cultural anthropologists are interested in how cultures change, but they are suspicious of evolutionary schemes that give the impression that social arrangements could not have been—or could not be—other than the way they are. They also point out that no society anywhere is static. The power that human beings have to reproduce or to change their social organization is an important focus of political anthropology.

2. The ability to act implies power. The study of power in human society is the domain of political anthropology. In most societies at most times, power cannot be reduced to physical force, although this is the Western prototype of power. Power in society operates according to principles that are cultural creations. As such, those principles are affected by history and may differ from one society to another.

3. Western thinkers traditionally assumed that without a state, social life would be chaotic, if not impossible. They believed that people were free agents who would not co-operate unless forced to do so. Anthropologists have demonstrated that power is exercised both by coercive and by persuasive means. They have been influenced by the works of Antonio Gramsci and Michel Foucault. Gramsci argued that coercion alone is rarely sufficient for social control, distinguishing coercive domination from hegemony. Rulers always face the risk that those they dominate may create counterhegemonic accounts of their experience of being dominated, acquire a following, and unseat their rulers. Foucault's concept of governmentality addresses practices developed in Western nation-states in the nineteenth century that aimed to create and sustain peaceful and prosperous

social life by exercising biopower over persons who could be counted, whose physical attributes could be measured statistically, and whose sexual and reproductive behaviours could be shaped by the exercise of state power.

4. Nation-states were invented in nineteenth-century Europe, but they have spread throughout the world along with capitalism, colonialism, and eventual political decolonization. Nationalist thinking aims to create a political unit in which national identity and political territory coincide, and this has led to various practices designed to force subordinate social groups to adopt a national identity defined primarily in terms of the culture of the dominant group. When subordinate groups resist, they may become the victims of genocide or ethnic cleansing. Alternatively, the dominant group may try to recast its understanding of national identity in a way that acknowledges and incorporates cultural elements belonging to subordinate groups. If the creation of such an imagined hybrid identity is not accompanied by legal and political changes that support it, however, the end result may be political turmoil, as shown in the recent history of Fiji.

5. The flows unleashed by globalization have undermined the ability of nation-states to police their boundaries effectively. Contemporary migrants across national borders have developed a variety of trans-border identities. Some become involved in long-distance nationalism that leads to the emergence of trans-border states claiming emigrants as trans-border citizens of their ancestral homelands even if they are legal citizens of another state. Some trans-border citizenries call for the establishment of full-fledged transnational nation-states. Struggles of these kinds can be found all over the globe, including in the contemporary states of the European Union.

6. The contrasts between formal and substantive citizenship suggest that conventional notions of citizenship are breaking down in the context of globalization. Diaspora communities of elite Chinese families have developed a strategy of flexible citizenship that allows them to both circumvent and benefit from different nation-state regimes. They seem to subscribe to a postnational ethos in which their only true loyalty is to the family business.

For Review

1. Consider the traditional four different types of societies that nineteenth-century anthropologists developed. Outline the characteristics that define each of these types and describe the differences between egalitarian, ranked, stratified, and state. What are the types of leaders found in each type?

2. Define *power*, and describe the three different kinds of power identified by Eric Wolf. How has each of these kinds of power influenced your life and the society in which you live?

3. Explain how power may be understood as physical force, or coercion. Do you agree that this is the best way to understand power? Why or why not?

4. Compare hegemony and domination. Why is *hegemony* a particularly useful term for anthropologists?

5. What is biopower? Consider how this is linked to national laws governing abortion.

6. Following Foucault, how does *governing* a state differ from *ruling* a state?

7. Why is self-determination important for Canadian First Nations? Discuss the Canadian government's failures to promote the welfare of Indigenous Canadians.

8. Outline the key points concerning multicultural politics in contemporary Europe, with particular attention to the different ways in which the United Kingdom, France, and Germany deal with immigration. How can ethnographic research illuminate the challenges faced by immigrants in Europe and elsewhere?

9. What are hidden transcripts? Where do they come from and how do they function?

10. What are everyday forms of peasant resistance? How does James Scott connect them with the political relations of dominant and subordinate categories of people in "Sedaka," Malaysia? How effective do they seem to be in the context Scott describes? Do you think similar forms of resistance would have similar outcomes in other places?

11. Should anthropologists work for military organizations? Who "owns" anthropological knowledge? How might being aligned with one "side" affect the work that anthropologists do? What would you do if you were faced with the chance to do anthropological fieldwork in which you were required to collect information on locals and report back to a military organization?

Key Terms

band 297
biopower 303
diaspora 312
domination 302
flexible citizenship 318
free agency 299
governmentality 305
hegemony 303
hidden transcripts 300

ideology 302
legal citizenship 313
long-distance nationalism 312
nation 307
nationality 307
nation-state 307
political anthropology 296
postnational ethos 320
power 296

state 298
status 298
substantive citizenship 313
trans-border citizenry 312
trans-border state 312
transformist hegemony 308
transnational nation-state 313
tribe 297

References

Alonso, Ana María. 1994. "The Politics of Space, Time, and Substance: State Formation, Nationalism, and Ethnicity." *Annual Review of Anthropology* 23: 379–405.

Anderson, Benedict. 2002. "The New World Disorder." In *The Anthropology of Politics*, edited by Joan Vincent, 251–70. Malden, MA: Blackwell.

Asad, Talal. 2003. *Formations of the Secular: Christianity, Islam, Modernity*. Palo Alto, CA: Stanford University Press.

Bouchard, Gerard. 2011. "What Is Interculturalism?" *McGill Law Journal* 56 (2): 435–68.

Bowen, John R. 2010. *Can Islam be French? Pluralism and Pragmatism in a Secularist State*. Princeton, NJ: Princeton University Press.

Caryl, Christian. 2009. "Reality Check: Human Terrain Teams." *Foreign Policy*, 8 September. http://www.foreignpolicy.com/articles/2009/09/08/reality_check_human_terrain_teams

Caven, Febna. 2013. "Being Idle No More: The Women Behind the Movement." *Cultural Survival Quarterly* 37 (1): 6–7.

Comaroff, Jean, and John Comaroff. 1991. *Ethnography and the Historical Imagination*. Boulder, CO: Westview.

Evans-Pritchard, E.E. (1937) 1976. *Witchcraft, Oracles, and Magic among the Azande*. Abridged ed., prepared by Eva Gillies. Oxford: Oxford University Press.

Foucault, Michel. 1991. "Governmentality." In *The Foucault Effect: Studies in Governmentality*, edited by Graham Burchell, Colin Gordon, and Peter Miller, 87–104. Chicago: University of Chicago Press.

Gordon, Colin. 1991. "Governmental Rationality: An Introduction." In *The Foucault Effect: Studies in Governmentality*, edited by Graham Burchell, Colin Gordon, and Peter Miller, 1–52. Chicago: University of Chicago Press.

Gramsci, Antonio. 1971. *Selections from the Prison Notebooks*. Translated by Q. Hoare and G.N. Smith. New York: International Publishers.

Hacking, Ian. 1991. "How Should We Do the History of Statistics?" In *The Foucault Effect: Studies in Governmentality*, edited by Graham Burchell, Colin Gordon, and Peter Miller, 181–96. Chicago: University of Chicago Press.

Haque, Eve. 2012. *Multiculturalism within a Bilingual Framework: Language, Race, and Belonging in Canada*. Toronto: University of Toronto Press.

Hedican, Edward. 2008. *Applied Anthropology in Canada: Understanding Aboriginal Issues*. 2nd ed. Toronto: University of Toronto Press.

Herzfeld, Michael. 2003. "Competing Diversities: Ethnography in the Heart of Rome." *Plurimundi* 3 (5): 147–54.

——. 2009. *Evicted from Eternity: The Restructuring of Modern Rome*. Chicago: University of Chicago Press.

——. 2016. *Siege of the Spirits: Community and Polity in Bangkok*. Chicago: University of Chicago Press.

Johnson, Matthew. 1999. *Archaeological Theory: An Introduction*. Oxford: Blackwell Publishers.

Kelly, John D., and Martha Kaplan. 2001. *Represented Communities: Fiji and World Decolonization*. Chicago: University of Chicago Press.

Lewellyn, Ted C. 1992. *Political Anthropology*. 2nd ed. South Hadley, MA: Bergin & Garvey.

Lewis, Philip. 1997. "Arenas of Ethnic Negotiations: Cooperation and Conflict in Bradford." In *The Politics of Multiculturalism in the New Europe: Racism, Identity, and Community*, edited by Tariq Modood and Pnina Werbner, 126–46. London: Zed Books.

Malkki, Liisa. 1992. "National Geographic: The Rooting of Peoples and the Territorialization of National Identity among Scholars and Refugees." *Cultural Anthropology* 7 (1): 24–44.

Melotti, Umberto. 1997. "International Migration in Europe: Social Projects and Political Cultures." In *The Politics of Multiculturalism in the New Europe: Racism, Identity and Community*, edited by Tariq Modood and Pnina Werbner, 73–92. London: Zed Books.

Modood, Tariq. 1997. "Introduction: The Politics of Multiculturalism in the New Europe." In *The Politics of Multiculturalism in the New Europe: Racism, Identity, and Community*, edited by Tariq Modood and Pnina Werbner, 1–25. London: Zed Books.

Ong, Aihwa. 2002. "The Pacific Shuttle: Family, Citizenship, and Capital Circuits." In *The Anthropology of Globalization*, edited by Jonathan Xavier Inda and Renato Rosaldo, 172–97. Malden, MA: Blackwell.

PolarNet.2015."WelcometoNunavut."http://www.polarnet.ca/polarnet/nunavut.htm

Sahlins, Marshall. 1976. *Culture and Practical Reason*. Chicago: University of Chicago Press.

Schiffauer, Werner. 1997. "Islam as a Civil Religion: Political Culture and the Organisation of Diversity in Germany." In *The Politics of Multiculturalism in the New Europe: Racism, Identity, and Community*, edited by Tariq Modood and Pnina Werbner, 147–66. London: Zed Books.

Schiller, Nina Glick, and Georges Fouron. 2002. "Long-Distance Nationalism Defined." In *The Anthropology of Politics*, edited by Joan Vincent, 356–65. Malden, MA: Blackwell.

Scott, James. 1987. *Weapons of the Weak*. New Haven, CT: Yale University Press.

——. 1990. *Domination and the Arts of Resistance*. New Haven, CT: Yale University Press.

Schultz, Emily A., Robert H. Lavenda, and Roberta Robin Dods. 2015. *Cultural Anthropology: A Perspective on the Human Condition*. Toronto: Oxford University Press Canada.

Smart, Alan. 1999. "Expressions of Interest: Friendship and *Guanzi* in Chinese Societies." In *The Anthropology of Friendship*, edited by Sandra Bell and Simon Coleman, 119–36. Oxford: Berg.

The Truth and Reconciliation Commission of Canada. 2015. *Honouring the Truth, Reconciling for the Future: Summary of the Final Report of the Truth and Reconciliation Commission of Canada*. Kingston, Ontario: McGill-Queens University Press.

Vincent, Joan. 2002. "Introduction." In *The Anthropology of Politics*, edited by Joan Vincent, 1–13. Malden, MA: Blackwell.

Wolf, Eric. 1994. "Facing Power: Old Insights, New Questions." In *Assessing Cultural Anthropology*, edited by Robert Borofsky, 218–28. New York: McGraw-Hill.

▲ Social classes often live within easy sight of one another. Here, prosperous downtown Mumbai is easily visible from the sprawling squatter settlements. Photo: Catalin Lazar/Shutterstock

14 **What Can Anthropology Tell Us about Social Groups and Inequality?**

Chapter Outline

- What Are Naturalizing Discourses?
- How Do Anthropologists Study Human Rights?
- Chapter Summary

- For Review
- Key Terms
- References

The ethnographic and historical records show that societies in which people enjoy relatively equal relations with one another have flourished in different times and places. But cultural constructions of human differences and the use of such cultural constructions to build societies based on unequal social relations also have a long history. This chapter discusses some key forms of social and cultural inequality in the contemporary world to which anthropologists have devoted attention.

In Chapter 13, we observed that most people in the world today come under the authority of one or another nation-state and that all nation-states are socially stratified. Stratified societies, you will recall, are societies made up of permanently ranked subgroups, in which the higher ranking groups have disproportionately greater access to wealth, power, and prestige than do lower ranking groups. But inequality in the contemporary world may be constructed out of multiple categories arranged in different, and sometimes contradictory, hierarchies of stratification. In Chapter 11, we discussed how some of these categories—sex, gender, and sexuality—intersect with other categories in the production of such hierarchies. In this chapter, we will pay close attention to some additional important social categories involved in the construction of hierarchies of social inequality. See Map 14.1 for the societies we discuss in this chapter.

What Are Naturalizing Discourses?

Note that *all* of these categories are culturally and historically created. At the same time, many members of the societies that anthropologists study—whether their own or those of other people—often argue just the opposite: that these categories have always been part of human society. Claims that consider social categories as eternal and unchanging, rather than the result of history or culture, have been called **naturalizing discourses**.

Anthropologists are suspicious of naturalizing discourses for three related reasons. First, they ignore historical evidence showing how present-day arrangements contrast with earlier social arrangements in society. Second, they ignore variations in social arrangements in other present-day societies, which also show that social life may be organized differently. Finally, they direct attention away from current social inequalities, insisting that these inequalities are so deeply rooted that attempting to change them would be impossible.

Anthropologist Brackette Williams (1989) has argued that naturalizing discourses rely on the imaginary reduction, or *conflation*, of identities to achieve persuasive power. For example, forms of identity such as gender or race or caste—and sometimes even class and ethnicity, not to mention kinship and other forms of relatedness—have been described or justified by someone at some time in terms of *shared bodily substance* (for example, bloodline within a family). Thus, living within the same territory is conflated with having the same ancestors and inheriting the same culture, which is further conflated with eating the same food or sharing the same blood or the same genes. Culture is reduced to blood, and "the magic of forgetfulness and selectivity, both deliberate and inadvertent, allows the once recognizably arbitrary classifications of one generation to become the given inherent properties of reality several generations later" (Williams 1989, 431).

Some of these patterns of inequality, such as class and caste, reach back thousands of years into human history. Others (e.g., race, ethnicity, and nationality) are closely associated with European colonialism beginning some 500 years ago. The spread of capitalism and colonial powers around the world reshaped numerous Indigenous cultures that predated their arrival and introduced new types of stratification into formerly independent, egalitarian societies.

Class

In general, **classes** are hierarchically arranged social groups defined on economic grounds. That is, members of higher ranked social classes have disproportionately high access to sources of wealth in the society, whereas

naturalizing discourses Claims that consider social categories as eternal and unchanging, rather than the result of history or culture.

class A ranked group within a hierarchically stratified society whose membership is defined primarily in terms of wealth, occupation, or other economic criteria.

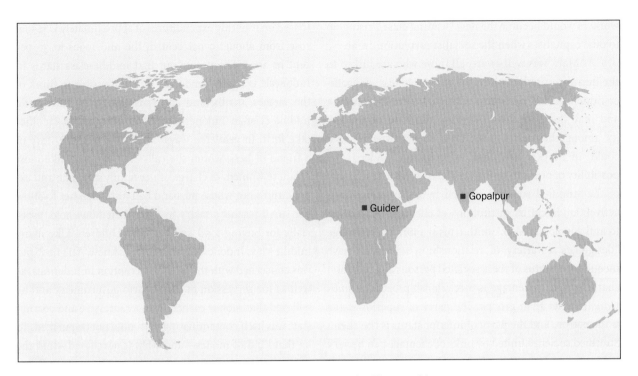

MAP 14.1 Location of societies whose EthnoProfiles appear in Chapter 14.

members of lower ranked classes have much more limited access to wealth (Figure 14.1).

The concept of class has a double heritage in modern anthropology, one stemming from Europe and the other from North America. European social scientists lived in states with a long history of social class divisions reaching back to the Middle Ages and, in some cases, to even earlier times. In their experience, social classes were well-entrenched and relatively closed groups. In the late 1700s, both the Industrial Revolution and the French Revolution promised to end the oppressive privileges of the ruling class and to equalize everyone's access to wealth. However, class divisions did not wither away in Europe during the nineteenth century; they just changed their contours. Followers of Karl Marx judged that, at best, an old ruling class had been displaced by a new one: feudal aristocrats had been replaced by bourgeois capitalists. The lowest level in European societies—rural peasants—were partially displaced as well, with the appearance of the urban working class. But the barriers separating those at the top of the class hierarchy from those at the bottom seemed just as rigid as ever.

As we described in Chapter 10, Marx defines classes in terms of their members' different relations to the means of production. This means that as long as a particular set of unequal productive relations flourishes in a society, the classes defined by these unequal roles in the division of labour will also persist. The French Revolution had triggered the displacement of aristocrats and peasants, who had played the key roles in European feudalism. They were replaced by new key classes—industrial entrepreneurs and the industrial working class—who were linked together within the capitalist mode of production. In time, Marx predicted, these industrial

FIGURE 14.1 Members of different social classes often live within easy sight of one another. Here, luxury apartments and squatter settlements rub shoulders in Rio de Janeiro, Brazil.

workers would become the new "leading class," rising up to oust capitalists when the socialist revolution came.

As Marx was well aware, all those who are linked to the means of production in the same way (e.g., as workers) often do not recognize what they have in common and may therefore fail to develop the kind of solidarity among themselves—the "class consciousness"—that could, in Marx's view, lead to revolution. Indeed, the possibility of peasant- or working-class solidarity in many of the stratified societies studied by anthropologists is actively undercut by institutions of clientage. According to anthropologist M.G. Smith ([1954] 1981, 31), **clientage** "designates a variety of relationships, which all have inequality of status of the associated persons as a common characteristic." Clientage is a relationship between *individuals* rather than groups. The party of superior status is the patron, and the party of inferior status is the client. Stratified societies united by links of clientage can be very stable. Low-status clients believe their security depends on finding a high-status individual who can protect them. For example, clientage is characteristic of *compadrazgo* (considered godparents in North American society) or of ritual co-parenthood relationships, found throughout Latin America. The Latin American societies in which *compadrazgo* flourishes are class societies, and parents who are peasants or workers often seek landowners or factory owners to serve as *compadres*, or godparents, at the baptism of their children. When the baptism ritual is completed, the parents and godparents of the child have a new, more relaxed relationship. They call each other "compadre" and can feel freer to seek one another out for support in times of need. While the lower status biological parents may seek out their higher status compadres for economic relief, the higher status individuals might seek out their lower status compadres for political support.

Class and Gender in Indonesia

In recent years, anthropologists have begun to pay attention to the concerns of the growing middle classes throughout the world. Carla Jones (2012, 151) studied the middle class in Indonesia, the world's fourth most populous country and the largest majority Muslim country in the world. Jones notes that market-research companies estimate that the middle-income segment of this population

(based on monthly expenditures of approximately US$300) rose from about 19 per cent in the mid-1990s to 30 per cent in 2009. She points out that middle-class status in Indonesia is highly gendered: "it is impossible to think of the virtues, thrills, and concerns associated with being middle class in Indonesia without seeing those qualities take form in gendered ways" (146). She tells the story of a friend of hers, whom she calls Ati, who was, like most Javanese women, in charge of her family's income and expenditures but whose husband had forbidden her to allow her small teacher's salary to enter their household, especially for buying food for their four children. Like many middle-class Indonesians whom Jones knew, Ati's husband was concerned with the level of corruption in Indonesia, as well as the repression of the Suharto government, and he believed that money earned from a repressive and corrupt state was itself contaminating and could not be purified. To let that kind of money—and what it purchased—into the private sphere of the household generated anxiety and also put the family at risk. Ati's solution was to use her salary to pay public school fees and to purchase school uniforms for her children. In this way, she returned the tainted money to the state and also complied with her husband's order.

This story suggests that members of the Indonesian middle class do not define themselves in terms of income or money. In fact, Jones notes that they do not even see themselves as members of a class, but rather "as people who are 'educated' or 'developed' and thereby have to pursue a commitment to 'truth, justice, ethics, or beauty' while needing 'to deny their privileged status'" (2012, 149). Some scholars argue that consumption is the key element uniting middle-class Indonesians because it is through their consumption patterns that they are able to distinguish themselves from both the lower class and the extremely wealthy.

Indonesian middle-class consumption patterns revolve around women. When the frugal, full-time housewife was seen as the model for middle-class distinction in the 1980s and 1990s, she was viewed as domesticating income used for family consumption. But the figure of the housewife also became associated with corruption because she was increasingly seen as a woman who pressured her income-earning husband through her feminine impulse to consume, corrupting her husband as he strove to satisfy his wife's consumption demands (Jones 2012, 155–6). More recently, the frugal housewife has been replaced by the woman who claims respectability through Muslim piety. But even this image has become tarnished: by consuming the latest elegant Islamic fashions, women are now

clientage The institution linking individuals from upper and lower levels in a stratified society.

criticized for pursuing piety as a fashion statement rather than as a religious statement (2012, 161).

Thus, consumption and femininity are closely linked components in the creation of selves shaped by class. Jones (2012) notes that these Indonesian examples overlap with experiences of middle classes elsewhere. Women, whether housewives, fashionably dressed pious women, or career women, have become symbols of a middle class with an ever-increasing desire for material things, which then increases their share of the burden of proving middle-class respectability.

Class and Caste in Canada

Marx's view of class is clearly different from the hegemonic view of class in Canada. For generations, Canadians have believed that they may pursue wealth, power, and prestige unhampered by the unyielding class barriers characteristic of traditional European societies. As a result, many social scientists trained in Canada (including cultural anthropologists) have tended to define social classes primarily in terms of income level and to argue that such social classes are open, porous, and permeable, rather than rigid and exclusionary. Upward class mobility is supposed to be, in principle, attainable by all people, regardless of how low their social origins are.

But the promise of equal opportunity for upward class mobility has not been realized by all those living in Canada. In the early twentieth century, social scientists concluded that an unyielding "colour bar" (for anyone who was not white) prevented upward class mobility. In Canada, this colour bar had a particularly limiting effect on individuals with Indigenous ancestry. In the United States, it had the greatest negative effect on those with African ancestry. In fact, the colour bar acts like a rigid barrier where one cannot move from a lower to upper class. This is similar to the caste system in India. Caste membership of an individual is given to one at birth and one cannot move from one caste into another. Membership in social classes is also ascribed at birth; but, unlike castes, classes are not supposed to be closed, and individual social mobility from one class into another should be possible (Sharma 1999). However, as we noted, the colour bar limits this social mobility in North American society.

Caste

The word **caste** was used by Portuguese colonizers who applied it to the stratification systems they encountered in South Asia in the fifteenth century. They understood that these societies were divided into a hierarchy of ranked subgroups, where sexual and marital links across group boundaries were forbidden.

Caste in India

The term *caste*, as most Western observers use it, combines two distinct South Asian concepts. The first concept, labelled as *varna*, is the widespread Hindu notion that Indian society is ideally divided into priests, warriors, farmers, and merchants—four functional subdivisions analogous to the estates of medieval and early modern Europe (Sharma 1999). The second concept is the existence of *jati*, which are localized groups; although *jati* names are frequently the names of occupations (e.g., farmer, saltmaker), there is no universally agreed-upon way to group the many local *jatis* within one or another of the four *varnas*. In any case, *varna* divisions are more theoretical in nature, whereas *jati* is the everyday term used in most of the local village settings.

Villagers in the southern Indian town of Gopalpur defined a *jati* for anthropologist Alan Beals (see EthnoProfile 14.1: Gopalpur). They said it was "a category of men thought to be related, to occupy a particular position within a hierarchy of *jatis*, to marry among themselves, and to follow particular practices and

EthnoProfile 14.1

Gopalpur

Region: Southern Asia

Nation: India

Population: 540 (1960)

Environment: Centre of a plain, some fertile farmland and pasture

Livelihood: Intensive millet farming, some cattle and sheep herding

Political organization: Caste system in a modern nation-state

For more information: Beals, Alan. 1962. *Gopalpur, a South Indian Village*. New York: Holt, Rinehart, and Winston.

caste A ranked group within a hierarchically stratified society that is closed, prohibiting individuals from moving from one caste to another.

occupations" (Beals 1962, 25). His informants compared the relationship between *jatis* of different rank to the relationship between older and younger brothers, where members of low-ranking *jatis* respect and obey members of high-ranking *jatis* in the same way that younger brothers respect and obey older brothers.

Villagers in Gopalpur were aware of at least 50 different *jatis*, although not all were represented in the village. *Jatis* are distinguished in terms of the foods they eat as well as their traditional occupations. In the Hindu belief system, certain foods and occupations are classed as pure, and others as polluting. In theory, all *jatis* are ranked on a scale from purest to most polluted. Ranked highest of all are the vegetarian Brahmins, who are pure enough to approach the gods. Carpenters and blacksmiths, who also eat a vegetarian diet, are also assigned a high rank. Below the vegetarians are those who eat "clean" or "pure" meat. In Gopalpur, this group of *jatis* included saltmakers, farmers, and shepherds, who eat sheep, goats, chicken, and fish but not pork or beef. The lowest ranking *jatis* are "unclean" meat eaters, who include stoneworkers and basketweavers (who eat pork) as well as leatherworkers (who eat pork and beef). Occupations that involve slaughtering animals or touching polluted things are themselves considered to be polluting. *Jatis* that traditionally carry out such activities as butchering and washing dirty clothing are ranked below *jatis* whose traditional work does not involve polluting activities (Figure 14.2).

FIGURE 14.2 Gautam Ganu Jadhao, a city worker, removes a cart full of sewage waste from a Bombay (Mumbai) neighbourhood in July 2005. People like him whose occupations are characterized as polluting are ranked at the bottom of the Hindu caste system.

Although the interdependence of *jatis* is explained in theory by their occupational specialties, the social reality is a bit different since it is primarily in the context of ritual that *jati* interdependence is given full play. For example, Gopalpur villagers require the services of a washerman when they need ritually clean garments or cloth; otherwise, most villagers wash their own clothing. To survive, one requires the co-operation of only a few *jatis;* "to enjoy life, participate in ritual, and do things in the proper manner requires the cooperation of many" (Beals 1962, 41).

Beals's study of Gopalpur documented three dimensions of caste relations in India that have become increasingly significant over time. First, Beals describes a rural village in which *jati* membership mattered most on ritual occasions. Second, Beals describes members of middle-ranking *jatis* in Gopalpur who treated one another as equals outside of ritual contexts. Third, Beals shows that middle-ranking *jatis* in Gopalpur in the 1960s were willing to use violence to block the upward economic mobility of members of a low-ranking *jati*.

In recent years, a number of low-caste groups in urban India have undertaken collective efforts to lift themselves off the bottom of society, either by imitating the ritual practices of higher castes or by converting to a non-Hindu religion (e.g., Buddhism or Christianity) in which caste plays no role. The national government has acted to improve the lot of the low castes by passing legislation designed to improve their economic and educational opportunities. In some cases, these measures seem to have succeeded, but violent reprisals have been common. In rural areas, many disputes continue to be over land, as in Gopalpur. However, even worse violence has been seen in urban India, as in 1990, when unrest was triggered by publication of a report recommending increases in the numbers of government jobs and reserved college places set aside for members of low castes. At the end of the twentieth century, relations between low-caste and high-caste Hindus were described as "conflictual rather than competitive in some localities," with "caste violence . . . recognized as a serious problem in contemporary India" (Sharma 1999, 67).

The principle of descent has also played a central role in the identification and persistence of race and ethnicity. As noted above, these categories are all closely bound up with historical developments over the past 500 years that built the modern world. Indeed, these categories are particularly significant in nation-states, and many

In Their Own Words

Caste and Class in Contemporary India

In the past half-century, class differentiation has become increasingly evident, especially in India's cities. Anthropologist Sara Dickey has worked in urban India for over 30 years, and she has studied how caste and class intertwine. Many Indians dream of moving into a higher social class; however, the hurdles poor people face are enormous and involve more than higher income alone.

Dickey points out that class status depends not only on economic capital but also on "cultural capital" (how you speak, how you dress, what kind of housing you live in, what kinds of consumer goods you possess) as well as on "social capital" (whom you know). Being able to amass sufficient amounts of all these kinds of capital is typically beyond the reach of most Indian citizens.

So what makes class mobility possible in India? Dickey contrasts two proposed answers to this question. One proposal, dating from the late twentieth century, argues that class status in India is an individual achievement. Scholars who take this position observe that within any Indian family, there are often stark differences between siblings, in terms of their access both to education and to jobs that provide high incomes. Dickey, however, proposes a second view, arguing that these differences should be understood as a consequence of the choices made by the families of the siblings in question. For example, it is families who decide whether or not they can afford to send one or more of their children to school because putting a child in school means not only additional expenses but also losing that child as a wage earner. As well, families must decide whether to send their children to government schools with inferior education or to private schools where English is the language of instruction. How many years children attend school is also a family decision, as are further decisions such as whether the family can help pay for university education, and if so, which subjects they are willing to allow their children to study. Note that education alone cannot ensure that students will be able to acquire all the additional forms of social and cultural capital that might permit their movement into a higher social class.

Against all odds, thanks to family support, luck, and timing, a woman Dickey calls Anjali seems to have successfully moved into a higher social class. Dickey first met Anjali in the city of Madurai in 1985, when Anjali was 7 years old. Her family's caste status was high, but her father worked driving a cycle rickshaw, and even though by Madurai standards they were not considered "poor," their financial situation was precarious. Unlike many girls, Anjali was allowed to attend school, and she did so well that her family allowed her to continue until she graduated from high school. She had hoped to go to university, but her family did not support this expensive ambition. However, when she suggested attending business school, her family did agree to help her. Anjali was also fortunate in being able to find a job that helped pay for her education, and she spent several years juggling work and her studies until she finally obtained her business degree. Shortly thereafter, she persuaded her family to help pay for a course in computer programming, which gave her desirable skills as the Indian tech industry began to grow. With these credentials, Anjali was able to get a job in a small business near home. When the firm Anjali worked for decided to move to another part of the city, she persuaded her family to take out a small business loan, which allowed her to set up her own firm in the offices of her former employer.

Anjali's family support had made these changes possible, and her parents and siblings benefited from her increased earning power. But this path to success was not entirely smooth as there was her dowry and her brother's marriage costs to consider.

Eventually, Anjali did get married to a man who was the son of a retired civil servant and who owned his own business. They fell in love and wanted to marry, but they did not do so until after their respective families had both approved of the match. Anjali's dowry included not just traditional wealth but the wealth represented by her business. After their marriage, Anjali moved into her husband's extended household. Her husband soon closed his own firm and joined Anjali's prosperous business, where they continued to work together successfully, bringing their young children to the office with them and bringing one of Anjali's younger brothers into the company. After a decade of marriage, Anjali appeared to have successfully moved into a higher social class, and that class status was likely to be perpetuated: both her children were enrolled in a prestigious English-language school in Madurai. But, as Dickey emphasizes, this class mobility depended on her family's support, even as her successes improved their own class standing in the eyes of others.

Source: Sara Dickey. 2016. *Living Class in Urban India.* New Jersey: Rutgers University Press.

contemporary nation-states, such as Canada, are of very recent, postcolonial origin. Clearly, to make sense of contemporary postcolonial forms of social stratification, we also need to look more closely at the categories of race and ethnicity.

Race

As we saw in Chapters 1 and 2, the concept of "race" developed in the context of European exploration, colonization, and conquest, beginning in the fifteenth century. Europeans conquered Indigenous peoples in the Americas, establishing colonial political economies.

> ↻ For an additional discussion of "race," please see Chapter 1.

By the end of the nineteenth century, light-skinned Europeans had established colonial rule over large territories inhabited by darker-skinned peoples, marking the beginnings of a global racial order (see Smedley 1995, 1998, among many others). Some European intellectuals argued at that time that the human species was subdivided into "natural kinds" of human beings called "races" that could be sharply distinguished from one another on the basis of outward phenotypic appearance. All individuals assigned to the same race were assumed to share many other common features, such as language or intelligence, of which phenotype was only the outward index. *Race* was used both to explain human diversity and to justify the domination of Indigenous peoples and the enslavement of Africans.

In Their Own Words

Racism, Colonialism, and Indigeneity in Canada

Professors Martin Cannon and Lina Sunseri have examined the continuing racism against Indigenous peoples in Canada. The following text is an excerpt from the conclusion to their edited volume Racism, Colonialism, and Indigeneity in Canada *(2011).*

On 27 September 2009, Prime Minister Stephen Harper announced to members of the G20 Summit—and the international community—that Canada is unique in being a country unmarked by histories of colonialism. "We . . . have no history of colonialism," he told world leaders, "so we have all of the things that many people admire about the great powers, but none of the things that threaten or bother them." Indigenous peoples and [non-Indigenous] Canadians alike listened in shock and disbelief. In saying these words, the prime minister seemed to contradict his own apology made to residential school survivors in Parliament about colonialism in June 2008. Moreover, his suggestion was that Indigenous efforts to challenge and rupture colonialism and dispossession are merely a "bother" and "threat" to the great powers of the world.

It is not uncommon to hear sentiments like these in Canadian society. Regrettably, they are not limited only to this country's leaders. In the classes we teach, we hear from educated Canadians that colonialism is a thing of the past, entirely disconnected from the present. These attitudes reflect a common sense or taken-for-granted

set of assumptions about the nature of colonial dominance, the nature of history, and the making of the nation. In some cases, these attitudes are shaped by hostility toward Indigenous peoples, anti-Indian organizing, and unwillingness to acknowledge histories of land dispossession, even institutionalized racism. On the other hand, these attitudes stem from misunderstanding, ignorance about contemporary colonialism, and a lack of clear vision informed by original nation-to-nation principles.

In writing this anthology, we have hoped to provide readers with a more thorough understanding of the racism that structures the colonial present. We have hoped to show that it is no longer possible to ignore Canada's origins as a colonial creation of both British and French settlers. . . . In summary, we also hope this book will spur readers to further contemplate and reflect on some of our major conclusions, including:

1. That neither racism nor Indigenous peoples are disappearing into the twenty-first century;

2. That the options available for repairing the mistrust and disavowal structuring modern colonial consciousness have already been set out in early historical and nation-to-nation-based agreements, such as the Guswentah or Two Row Wampum;

3. That poverty and economic marginalization continue as obstacles, requiring us to revisit colonial legacies and—in the first historical instance—the dispossession of lands before fully understanding, repairing, and eradicating them;

4. That Indigenous peoples continue to face serious disparities in educational attainments despite ameliorative efforts, the nature of which require us to consider histories of difference-making, anti-racist, and anti-colonial pedagogies, along with—and sometimes even before—strategies aimed at cultural awareness and revitalization . . .;

5. That institutionalized racism is not disappearing, especially as this has been directed toward Indigenous women, men, and nations through the Indian Act, Indian status distinctions, proposed amendments to the Indian Act . . ., and other interlocking systems of oppression based on sexism, colonialism, and patriarchy;

6. That racialized violence (e.g., Stonechild, Stolen Sisters, Ipperwash, Caledonia, Burnt Church, and Gustafsen Lake) continues to take place in Canada, embodying, in itself, the ongoing physical—and symbolic—removal of Indigenous peoples from their lands into the twenty-first century; and

7. That our resistance and resilience as peoples is not disappearing, as is evidenced by the contributions we continue to make in reformulating academia . . ., the arts, sports, and legal reform in Canada.

Dismantling colonial dominance requires breaking with cycles of oppression founded in the first instance upon histories of racism and sex discrimination. . . . Racialization, sexism, and heteronormativity have . . . intersected historically to place Indigenous men and women at a disadvantage relative to the state, the justice system, and each other. We therefore suggest that any meaningful discussions about racism and Indigeneity in Canada take these complex interrelationships into account, as they profoundly shape and structure the experiences of Indigenous peoples.

Colonial injustice racialized injustice. . . . [T]he Indian Act set into motion a way of thinking about identity, governance, and nationhood in racialized terms. . . . For better or worse, racism shapes the everyday experience of Indigenous peoples in Canada, but it does not prevent us from naming and then resisting its parameters.

Source: Cannon and Sunseri 2011, 263–5.

European thinkers, including many early anthropologists, devised schemes for ranking the "races of mankind" from lowest to highest. Not surprisingly, the "white" northern Europeans at the apex of imperial power were placed at the top of this global hierarchy. Darker-skinned peoples, such as the Indigenous inhabitants of the Americas or of Asia, were ranked somewhere in the middle. But Africans, whom Europeans bought and sold as slaves and whose homelands in Africa were later conquered and incorporated into European empires, ranked lowest of all. In this way, the identification of races was transformed into *racism*: the systematic oppression of members of one or more socially defined "race" by members of another socially defined "race" that is justified in terms of the supposed inherent biological superiority of the rulers and the supposed inherent biological inferiority of those they rule. It is important to emphasize once again that all the so-called races of human beings are *imagined communities*. As we emphasized in Chapter 7, there are no major biological discontinuities within the human species that correspond to the supposed racial boundaries created by nineteenth-century European scientists. In other words, the traditional concept of biological "race" in Western society is incoherent and biologically meaningless.

Nevertheless, racial thinking persists at the beginning of the twenty-first century, suggesting that racial categories have their origins not in biology but in society. Anthropologists have long argued that race is a culturally constructed social category whose members are identified on the basis of certain selected phenotypic features (e.g., skin colour) that all are said to share. The end result is a highly distorted but more or less coherent set of criteria that members of a society can use to assign people they see to one or another culturally defined racial category. Once these criteria exist, members of society can treat racial categories *as if* they reflect biological reality, using them to build institutions that include or exclude particular culturally defined races. In this way, race can become "real" in its consequences, even if it has no reality in biology.

The social category of "race" is a relatively recent invention. Audrey Smedley (1998, 693) reminds us that in the worlds of European classical antiquity and through the Middle Ages, "no structuring of equality . . . was associated with people *because of their skin colour*" (emphasis in original), and Faye Harrison (1995, 51) points out that "phenotype prejudice was not institutionalized before the sixteenth century." By the nineteenth century, most Europeans (including some early anthropologists) were attempting to classify all humans in the world into a few mutually exclusive racial categories. Significantly, from that time until today, as Harrison (1998, 612) emphasizes, "darker skin has come to symbolize the social bottom" (see also Smedley 1998, 694–5).

White domination of European and North American racial hierarchies has been a constant, but some anthropologists who study the cultural construction of whiteness point out that even in North America "whiteness" is not monolithic and that the cultural attributes supposedly shared by "white people" have varied in different times and places. In Canada during the late nineteenth century, white upper class Canadians considered themselves as distinct from the lower class immigrants from eastern Europe who settled large expanses of the western provinces. Today the meaning of *whiteness* in South Africa has been complicated by differences of class and culture separating British South Africans from Afrikaners (Hartigan 1997). For that matter, "blackness" is not monolithic, either. In Haiti, for example, white French colonists were expelled at independence in 1804, but an internal racial divide has persisted since then between the mass of black Haitians descended from freed slaves and a minority of wealthy, well-educated "mulattos" who originally comprised the offspring of white French fathers and black slave mothers. Throughout Haitian history, this mulatto elite has struggled to distinguish itself from the black majority, in the face of outsiders who have steadfastly refused to recognize any difference between the two groups. At times of unrest, however, the US government has regularly supported members of this elite, who have defended their interests by ruthlessly dominating other Haitians, especially the poor (Schiller and Fouron 2001). In the United States, the sharp "caste-like" racial divide between blacks and whites is currently being complicated by new immigrants identified with so-called brown/Hispanic and yellow/Asian racial categories. Harrison and others recognize that racial categorization and repression take different forms in different places.

A great example of how the lines between race, ethnicity, and nationality as sources of inequality may blur can be found in the history of Canada's immigration policy since the late nineteenth century. As Peter Li (2003, 15) notes, the Canadian government has used its immigration policy both "as a means to address the problems of labour shortages and economic development, and to regulate the social, cultural, and symbolic boundary of the nation." Around the end of the nineteenth century, most immigrants to Canada came from the United Kingdom and the United States (both of which had predominantly white populations at the time), and Canada's immigration policy remained fairly open. The first clear exception came in 1885 when the Canadian government passed an act imposing a "head tax" on Asian immigrants from China. When immigration from the United Kingdom and western Europe started to dry up, Canada began to actively recruit immigrants from the predominantly white nations of eastern and southern Europe (Figure 14.3). Around the same time, the Canadian government enacted legislation that restricted immigration from any non-European nation, especially the nations of Southeast Asia and Africa. During this period, Canadians with British or American ancestry were considered to be of higher social standing than immigrants from eastern or southern Europe, who in turn were considered to be of higher social standing than non-white immigrants. Even with various reforms between the end of World War II and today, many of which were ostensibly made to avoid excluding people based on race, our immigration policy remains highly selective, favouring immigrants from the United States and certain European nations (including the United Kingdom) over immigrants from less wealthy, typically non-white countries.

Colourism in Nicaragua

American anthropologist Roger Lancaster (1992, 215) argues that racism exists in Nicaragua but that it is "not as absolute and encompassing a racism as that which one encounters in the United States" even though it remains, in his opinion, "a significant social problem." One dimension of Nicaraguan racism contrasts the Spanish-speaking *mestizo* (or "mixed" European and Indigenous) majority of the highlands with the Indigenous Miskitos and African Caribbeans along the Atlantic coast. The highland *mestizos* Lancaster knew tended to regard these coastal groups as backward, inferior, and dangerous. These notions were overlaid with political suspicions deriving from the fact that Lancaster's informants were Sandinistas and that some Miskito factions had fought with the Contras against the Sandinistas after the Sandinistas deposed the dictator Anastasio Somoza in 1979.

But Lancaster came to see racism toward the coastal peoples as simply an extension of the pattern of race relations internal to highland *mestizo* culture that he calls **colourism**: a system of colour identities negotiated situationally along a continuum between white and black (Figure 14.4). In colourism, no fixed race boundaries exist. Instead, individuals negotiate their colour identity anew in every social situation they enter, with the result that the colour they might claim or be accorded changes from situation to situation.

Lancaster's informants used three different systems of colour classification. The first, or "phenotypic," system has three categories—*blanco* (white), *moreno* (brown), and *negro* (black)—that people use to describe the various skin tones that can be seen among Nicaraguan mestizos: "Nicaraguan national culture is mestizo; people's physical characteristics are primarily Indigenous; and in the terms of this phenotypic system, most people are moreno. In this system, *negro* can denote either persons of African ancestry or sometimes persons of purely Indigenous appearance, whether they are culturally classified as Indio or mestizo" (Lancaster 1992, 217).

Lancaster calls the second system that Nicaraguans use the "polite" system, in which all the colours in the phenotypic system are "inflated." That is, Europeans are called *chele* (a Mayan word meaning "blue," referring to the stereotypically blue eyes of people of European ancestry), white people are called *blanco*, and African people are called *moreno*. Polite terms are used in the presence of the person about whom one is speaking, and Lancaster was told that it was "a grave and violent offence to refer to a black-skinned person as *negro*" (1992, 217). In rural areas, for similar reasons, Indigenous people are called *mestizos* rather than *Indios*.

Lancaster calls the third system of colour terms the "pejorative and/or affectionate" system. This system has only two terms: *chele* (fairer skin and lighter hair) and *negro* (darker skin, darker hair). For example,

when the less powerful man in an interaction feels he is being imposed upon by the more powerful man, the former might express his displeasure by addressing the latter as *chele* or *negro*, both of which would be seen as

FIGURE 14.3 In the late nineteenth and early twentieth centuries, Canada's immigration policy began targeting farmers and other labourers from eastern Europe. The Ukrainian family pictured here arrived in Quebec City in 1911.

FIGURE 14.4 This photograph of Nicaraguan children shows a range of skin tones. In some parts of Latin America, such as Nicaragua and Brazil, such variation is used to create a system of classification based on lightness or darkness of skin tone that assigns people with relatively lighter skin to higher status, a phenomenon that anthropologist Roger Lancaster calls *colourism*.

colourism A system of social identities negotiated situationally along a continuum of skin colours between white and black.

In Their Own Words

Racialized Bodies, Disabling Worlds: Storied Lives of Immigrant Muslim Women

Parin Dossa reveals the lives of immigrant Muslim women living in Vancouver who are discriminated against not only because they are new to Canada but also because they have physical disabilities. Dossa describes how storytelling provides a way for these women to affirm their identities and their value as human beings.

My project . . . is to interrogate structures of exclusion and oppression by invoking the words and worlds of racialized women who have disabilities. I seek to demonstrate that people on the margins of society remake their world to affirm their agency and to avoid being perceived as helpless victims. . . . My goal is to bring to the fore issues of social justice and equality. . . .

In their everyday lives, persons with disabilities are given the societal message that they are lesser human beings. . . . My work aims to show that race and gender matter and that these social markers of difference cannot be dismissed under the seemingly neutral category of disability. . . . My data are derived from women in two communities in metropolitan Vancouver: South Asian Muslims from East Africa . . . and Iranian Muslims. Through their individual stories and testimonials I acquired an in-depth understanding of my key research question: What is it like to have a racialized body in a disabling world? . . . Exclusion and the social erasure of racialized individuals with disabilities have compromised their humanity. . . . Stories restore our humanity because they provide flesh to what may otherwise remain abstract (Jackson 2006). The participants in this study carry out this task of reconstituting personhood through speaking about their struggles, aspirations, and accomplishments. . . .

. . . For the women in this study, the starting point of their journeys is Canadian immigration policy, which has excluded them. . . . The premise at the root of this exclusion is that racialized persons who have disabilities cannot meet the labour skills criterion of the immigration policy; they are seen to be an anomaly. No value is attached to their desire to undertake waged work;

instead, they are cast as a population that consumes public services and therefore a drain on the system. . . .

. . . [T]he women in this study take it upon themselves to define their identities and claim the humanity denied them in their everyday lives. This is social justice at work. The women in this study speak in a testimonial voice, fully aware that their stories are links in a chain made up of many stories, each with its thread woven into the larger tapestry in the making. Furthermore, the women in this study do not refer to gender, race, and disability in exclusive terms. With varying emphasis, they interconnect these markers of difference in their lived realities. They are keen to ensure that their activist work, defined in their own terms, does not remain within the discrete spaces of their communities. They speak to advance the cause of a just society. . . .

The women bring forth their embodied, experiential knowledge of what it is like to be discriminated in a disabling world. They show how this world can be transformed into an enabling environment that is inclusive, where people can develop their potential as active citizens. . . . [Their] narratives reveal [their] desire to take their place in Canadian society in a way that positively acknowledges their differences of nationality, abilities, and gendered and race-based identities. The realization of this goal calls for the re-visioning of our social world: this is the mammoth task that the women pursue contextually and on the basis of their knowledge from the margins of society. From their special entry points into the dominant system, they see, hear, and question what others take as given reality.

Source: Dossa 2009, 4–8. © University of Toronto Press, 2009.

insulting. Paradoxically, members of families call one another *negro* or *negrito mio* as affectionate and intimate terms of address, perhaps precisely because these terms are "informal" and violate the rules of polite discourse (1992, 218).

Ethnicity

For anthropologists, **ethnic groups** are social groups whose members distinguish themselves (and/or are distinguished by others) in terms of **ethnicity**—that is, in terms of distinctive cultural features, such as language, religion, or dress. Ethnicity, like race, is a culturally constructed concept. Many anthropologists today would agree with John and Jean Comaroff (1992, 55–7) that ethnicity is created by historical processes that incorporate distinct social groups into a single political structure under conditions of inequality (see also Williams 1989). The Comaroffs recognize that ethnic consciousness existed in precolonial and precapitalist societies; however, they and most contemporary anthropologists have been more interested in forms of ethnic consciousness that were generated under capitalist colonial domination.

Ethnicity develops as members of different groups try to make sense of the material constraints they experience within the single political structure that confines them. This is sometimes described as a struggle between *self-ascription* (i.e., insiders' efforts to define their own identity) and *other-ascription* (i.e., outsiders' efforts to define the identities of other groups). In the Comaroffs' view, furthermore, the ruling group turns both itself and the subordinated groups into *classes* because all subordinated social groupings lose independent control "over the means of production and/or reproduction" (1992, 56).

One outcome of this struggle is the appearance of new ethnic groups and identities that are not part of any single earlier cultural group (Comaroff and Comaroff 1992, 56). In northern Cameroon, for example, successive German, French, and British colonial officials relied on local Muslim chiefs to identify for them significant local social divisions and adopted the Muslim practice of lumping together all the myriad non-Muslim peoples of the hills and plains. To the extent these groups were treated alike by colonial authorities and came to share a common situation and set of interests, members of

these groups developed a new, more inclusive level of ethnic identity. This new, postcolonial "Kirdi" identity, like many others, cannot be linked to any single precolonial cultural reality but has been constructed out of cultural materials borrowed from a variety of non-Muslim Indigenous groups who were incorporated within the colonial political order (see EthnoProfile 14.2: Guider and Figure 14.5). In a similar vein, francophone Québécois are an ethnic group that did not exist in

EthnoProfile 14.2

Guider

Region: Western Africa

Nation: Cameroon

Population: 18,000 (1976)

Environment: Savannah

Livelihood: Farming, commerce, civil service, cattle raising

Political organization: Traditionally, an emirate; today, part of a modern nation–state

For more information: Schultz, Emily. 1984. "From Pagan to Pullo: Ethnic Identity Change in Northern Cameroon." *Africa* 54 (1): 46–64.

ethnic group A group that shares similar values and norms defined by such things as language, geography, and religion.

ethnicity An ethnic group that a person identifies with or feels a part of to the exclusion of other groups, based on language, dress, religion, etc. Ethnicity emerges from historical processes that incorporate distinct social groups into a single political structure under conditions of inequality.

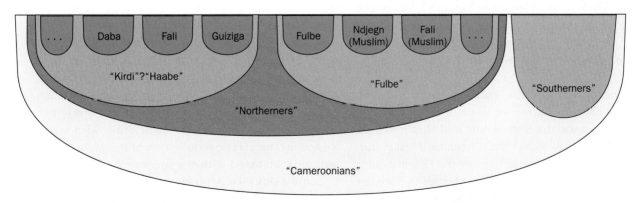

FIGURE 14.5 Nesting identities in northern Cameroon (1976).

precolonial times. This unique ethnicity represents a re-framed culture, based on a modified form of the French culture and a distinct Québécois language.

These ethnic groups joined together in a "patriotic front" to win a war of independence fought against white settlers. This confrontation took place at the highest level of the ethnic hierarchy, which the Comaroffs call "race." At this level, "Europeans" and "Africans" opposed one another, and each group developed its own encompassing ethnic identity. For example, Africans dealing regularly with Europeans began to conceive of such a thing as "African culture" (as opposed to European culture) and

"pan-African solidarity" (to counter the hegemony of the European colonizers). Conversely, in the British settler colonies of southern and eastern Africa, European immigrants defined themselves in opposition to Africans by developing their own "settler-colonial order" based on a caricature of aristocratic Victorian English society (Comaroff and Comaroff 1992, 58).

Guider began as a small settlement of non-Muslim Guidar. In 1830, it was brought into the Muslim Fulbe empire of Yola and remained a Fulbe stronghold under subsequent colonial rule. The Fulbe remained numerically dominant in town until after World War II; by

In Their Own Words

The Politics of Ethnicity

Stanley Tambiah reflects on the late twentieth-century upsurge in ethnic conflict that few people predicted because many assumed that ethnic particularisms would disappear within modern nation-states.

The late–twentieth–century has seen marginal subgroups emerge as major "political" elements and become major political collective actors in several societies. Moreover, today we are also faced with instances of majority ethnic groups within a polity or nation exercising preferential or "affirmative" policies on the basis of that majority status.

The first consideration that confirms ethnic conflict as a major reality of our time is not simply its ubiquity alone, but also its cumulative increase in frequency and intensity of occurrence. Consider these conflicts, by no means an exhaustive listing, that have occurred since the sixties (some of them have a longer history, of course): conflicts between anglophone and francophone in Canada; Catholic and Protestant in Northern Ireland; Walloon and Fleming in Belgium; Chinese and Malay in Malaysia; Greek and Turk in Cyprus; Jews and other minorities on the one hand and Great Russians on the other in the Soviet Union; and Ibo and Hausa and Yoruba in Nigeria; the East Indians and Creoles in Guyana. Add, to these instances, upheavals that became climactic in recent years: the Sinhala–Tamil war in Sri Lanka, the Sikh–Hindu, and Muslim–Hindu, confrontations in India, the Chackma–Muslim turmoil in Bangladesh, the actions of the Fijians against Indians in Fiji, the Pathan–Bihari clashes in Pakistan, and last, but not least, the inferno in Lebanon, and the serious erosion of human rights currently manifest in

Israeli actions in Gaza and the West Bank. That there is possibly no end to these eruptions, and that they are worldwide has been forcibly brought to our attention by a century-old difference that exploded in March 1988 between Christian Armenians and Muslim Azerbaijanis in the former U.S.S.R.

Most of these conflicts have involved force and violence, homicide, arson, and destruction of property. Civilian riots have evoked action by security forces: sometimes as counteraction to quell them, sometimes in collusion with the civilian aggressors, sometimes both kinds of action in sequence. Events of this nature have happened in Sri Lanka, Malaysia, India, Zaire, Guyana, and Nigeria. Mass killings of civilians by armed forces have occurred in Uganda and in Guatemala, and large losses of civilian lives have been recorded in Indonesia, Pakistan, India, and Sri Lanka.

The escalation of ethnic conflicts has been considerably aided by the amoral business of gunrunning and free trade in the technology of violence, which enable not only dissident groups to successfully resist the armed forces of the state, but also civilians to battle with each other with lethal weapons. The classical definition of the state as the authority invested with the monopoly of force has become a sick joke. After so many successful liberations and resistance movements in many parts of the globe, the techniques of guerrilla resistance now constitute a systematized and exportable knowledge. Furthermore, the easy access to the technology of warfare by groups in countries that are otherwise deemed low in literacy and in economic development—we have seen what Afghan resistance can do with American guns—is paralleled by another kind of international fraternization among resistance groups who have little in common save their resistance to the status quo in their own countries, and who exchange knowledge of guerrilla tactics and the art of resistance. Militant groups in Japan, Germany, Lebanon, Libya, Sri Lanka, and India have international networks of collaboration, not unlike—perhaps more solidary than—the diplomatic channels that exist between mutually wary sovereign countries and the great powers. The end result is that professionalized killing is no longer the monopoly of state armies and police forces. The internationalization of the technology of destruction, evidenced in the form of terrorism and counterterrorism, has shown a face of free-market capitalism in action unsuspected by Adam Smith and by Immanuel Wallerstein.

Source: Tambiah 1989, 431–32.

1958, however, individuals from over a dozen non-Fulbe groups had migrated to town, primarily from the surrounding countryside. By 1976, 83 per cent of household heads in town were recent migrants, and 74 per cent did not claim Fulbe origins.

In the Comaroffs' terms, all these groups, including the Fulbe, had lost political and economic independence with the coming of colonial rule and, under conditions of inequality, were incorporated by the colonizers as ethnic groups into the French colony of Cameroon. The Europeans uniformly admired the political, cultural, and religious accomplishments of the Muslim Fulbe. In their own version of indirect rule, they allowed Fulbe chiefs to administer territories they had controlled prior to colonization and, in some cases, handed over to them additional territories whose residents had successfully resisted Fulbe domination in precolonial times.

In 1976, the local ethnic hierarchy in Guider placed Fulbe at the top; and recent non-Muslim, non–Fulfulde-speaking migrants from rural areas, at the bottom. But in the middle were numerous individuals and families of Fulfulde-speaking Muslims who could claim, and in some cases be accorded, recognition as Fulbe by others in the town.

Fulbe identity had become an achieved status; it was the ethnicity claimed by the upwardly mobile in Guider. It was therefore possible for people born outside the dominant Fulbe ethnic group to achieve Fulbe status in their lifetimes (Schultz 1984). To do this, they had to be successful at three tasks: they had to adopt the Fulbe language (Fulfulde), they had to adopt the Fulbe religion (Islam), and they had to adopt the Fulbe "way of life," which was identified with urban customs and the traditional Muslim high culture of the western Sudan. Many Fulbe claimed that descent from one or another Fulbe lineage was needed in order to claim Fulbe identity. Nevertheless, they seemed willing to accept "Fulbeized Pagans" as Fulbe (e.g., by giving their daughters to them as brides) because those people were committed defenders of the urban Fulbe way of life. Those who were "Fulbeizing," however, came from societies in which descent had never been an important criterion of group membership. For these people, ethnic identity depended on the territorial affiliation of the group to which they were currently committed. From their perspective, in becoming Fulbe, they had simply chosen to commit themselves to Fulfulde, Islam, and life in "Fulbe territory," the town.

This example illustrates some of the key attributes often associated with ethnicity: it is fluid, malleable, something that can be voluntarily embraced or successfully ignored in different situations. Ambitious individuals and groups in an ethnically stratified society can manipulate ethnicity as a resource in order to pursue their interests. When nesting identities are present, people may regularly alternate between different identities in different contexts. Ethnic Fulbeization in northern Cameroon might be described as the formation of a "supertribe." Like the formation of caste alliances in India, it involves the expansion of group boundaries, allowing for the creation of stronger solidarity links among more people of different backgrounds. When such expanded alliances actually achieve increased success in political, economic, and social struggles, they may affect the very structures that gave rise to them (as the Shona–Ndebele alliance did in Zimbabwe) (Comaroff and Comaroff 1992, 61).

For dominant groups, however, defence of ethnic identity can be a way of defending privilege. Those who dominate may be threatened rather than flattered by subordinate groups who master elite cultural practices. Members of the dominant ethnic group may stress their cultural superiority and question the eligibility (and even the humanity) of subordinate groups who challenge them. It is at this point that anthropologists like Faye Harrison would argue that ethnicity becomes *racialized*. In her view, race differs from ethnicity precisely because it is used to "mark and stigmatize certain peoples as essentially and irreconcilably different, while treating the privileges of others as normative. This quality of difference, whether constructed through a biodeterminist or a culturalist idiom, is what constitutes the social category and material phenomenon of 'race'" (Harrison 1998, 613). Racialization in Western societies would thus bear a family resemblance to castification in South Asian societies.

Harrison (1995, 52) argues that by the middle of the nineteenth century, white northern Europeans, connecting their growing colonial power with their whiteness, began to racialize ethnic, religious, or class stereotypes associated with other Europeans (e.g., Irish, Jews, Italians, Poles, Slavs), viewing them as less human or, at any rate, differently human from themselves and attributing this difference to biologically inherited factors. Conversely, some racialized ethnic groups, such as the Irish, were able to reverse this process once they moved to North America, shedding their stigma and *ethnicizing* into just another "ordinary" Canadian or American ethnic group. Some social scientists might argue, or at any rate hope, that all racialized groups should be able to ethnicize sooner or later. But such a perspective risks ignoring the plight of racialized groups whose status never seems to change. Historians argue, for example, that the Irish were able to ethnicize precisely because they accepted the racialization of Indigenous peoples and individuals of African descent (see Allen 1997). Indeed, members of non-white races living in white-dominated countries are typically ranked below recent white immigrants on race- or ethnicity-based social hierarchies (see Harrison 1995, 49; see also Smedley 1998, 690).

For these reasons, Harrison argues that attempts to interpret race relations as ethnic relations in all contexts have "euphemized if not denied race" by failing to address the social, political, and economic factors responsible for keeping racialized groups excluded and stigmatized at the bottom of society (1995, 48). She agrees that certain racialized groups do engage in "ethnicizing practices emphasizing cultural heritage," but in her view such practices have never been able to overcome the "caste-like assumptions of the most systematically oppressive racial orders" (1998, 613; 1995, 54).

As we have seen, anthropologists have argued about which technical terms ought to be used to describe which forms of identity under which circumstances. We agree with Ursula Sharma (1999, 93) that social scientists should use a particular term only if it highlights a dimension of social relationships that would otherwise go unnoticed. Thus, ethnicity probably needs to be supplemented by the notion of race in order to distinguish the dehumanizing confinement of certain social groups to the bottom layers of society, and the use of castes with their hierarchical ranking highlights features of social organization that elude the usual scope of race, class, or ethnicity. Anthropologist Pnina Werbner (1997) further builds on these distinctions when she argues that in order to make progress in analyzing ethnic violence as a social force, practices of "everyday" ethnic identification need to be distinguished from racism.

Based on her research on multicultural social relations in Britain, Werbner distinguishes two different social processes: objectification and reification. *Objectification* simply refers to the intentional construction of a collective public identity; it is the process that produces "everyday" or "normal" ethnicity. Social relations between objectified ethnic groups are based on highly valued forms of collective identification, such as religion, dress, food, language, and politics. Interaction between groups that differentiate themselves along such lines ordinarily does not lead to violent confrontations (229). *Reification*, by contrast, is a form of negative racial or ethnic absolutism that encourages the violent elimination of targeted groups and is central to the practice of racism. It is violence that differentiates racism from everyday ethnicity; and if ethnic confrontation becomes violent, then it turns into a form of racism (234–5). For Werbner, making this distinction is crucial in multi-ethnic situations because when people fail to distinguish non-violent forms of everyday ethnicity from racism, they are, in effect, criminalizing valid ethnic sentiments and letting racists off the hook (233).

In many ways, the multicultural policy of Canada promotes what Werbner calls *objectification* while attempting to prevent what she calls *reification*. In practice, however, this policy is not always successful in preventing conflict. Ethnic tensions exist across Canada everywhere that diverse cultural systems

Anthropology in Everyday Life

Diverse Experiences with Intimate Relationships and Dating among South Asian Youth in the Greater Toronto Area

In a recent paper, Arshia Zaidi and colleagues (2014) asked the question, "How do ethnic identification, religion, religiousness, and gender intersect to shape second-generation South Asian youths' experiences of intimate relationships in Canada?" As background to their project, the researchers noted that, as recently as 2005, Canada was ranked seventh in the world in terms of the number of immigrants it receives; moreover, a significant number of these immigrants live in the Greater Toronto Area (GTA), making up just over 40 per cent of its population. Consequently, Toronto is often described as a "world in a city" (Siemiatycki 2011, quoted in Zaidi et al. 2014, 29). Many of these immigrants hail from South Asian countries such as India, Pakistan, Nepal, and Bangladesh, to name only a few.

The researchers also note that second-generation South Asian youth are often caught between the traditional value systems of their heritage countries and the contemporary value systems of their current homes, a difficulty that can sometimes lead to intergenerational conflict (28–9). In most "traditional" South Asian families, both those living in their original country and those living in Canada, young men and young women are strongly discouraged from forming intimate relationships with cross-gender peers before they are officially engaged or, in some cases, married (30). In addition, marriages are typically arranged by family members, and a heightened focus is placed on the preservation of premarital virginity to preserve

a family's honour (30). These cultural norms and expectations tend to be heavily gendered—women are expected to stay at home and be sexually conservative, while men are encouraged to venture out into the world and learn to support themselves and their families (31). In Canadian society, however, it is generally acceptable for youths to date cross-gender peers of their own choice, and there is a greater sense of gender equality in relation to dating.

In attempting to answer the central question of their paper, the researchers interviewed 56 unmarried second-generation South Asian youth between the ages of 18 and 25. The sample consisted of 30 females and 26 males, with equal numbers of Hindus and Muslims (20 each) and fewer Christians (only 16). The families of most of the youth originated in Sri Lanka, Pakistan, or India (36). The researchers' findings indicated that there was a gradual acceptance of and experience with intimate relationships, mainly among Hindus, followed in number by Christians and, lastly, Muslims. In addition, those youth whose ethnic identities most closely reflected the norms, values, and practices of their heritage countries and whose levels of religiosity were high, regardless of their faith, tended not to approve of premarital intimate relationships (48). Consequently, the researchers concluded that multiple factors relating to ethnicity, gender, and religious beliefs influence the degree to which second-generation immigrant youth accept their new country's values regarding dating and forming intimate cross-gender relationships.

---

coexist. While these tensions may not escalate into the sorts of large-scale ethnic conflicts we hear about in countries like Rwanda or Sudan, they do cause conflict, particularly when differing views on gender roles, religious beliefs, and sexuality are involved. And these tensions cause conflict not only between people of different ethnicities but also among members of the same ethnic group who interpret and express their ethnicity differently. Arshia Zaidi and her colleagues (2014) have examined these latter sorts of conflicts among South Asian youth in Canada. For a discussion of this work, see the "Anthropology in Everyday Life" box on the

experiences of South Asian youth living in Canada with forming intimate relationships and dating.

How Do Anthropologists Study Human Rights?

Concerns about and struggles against social inequality have only taken on more urgency in the context of globalization. In the midst of these struggles, concerns about human rights and their violation have been increasingly heard from all over the world. Anthropologists have been attentive to the spread of this discourse and the issues it raises, some of which we explore here.

Are Human Rights Universal?

Globalization has stimulated discussions about **human rights**: powers, privileges, or material resources to which people everywhere, by virtue of being human, are justly entitled. Rapidly circulating capital, images, people, things, and ideologies juxtapose different understandings about what it means to be human or what kinds of rights people may be entitled to. The context within which human rights discourse becomes relevant is often described as **multiculturalism**: living permanently in settings surrounded by people with cultural backgrounds different from your own and struggling to define with them the degree to which the wider society should accord respect and recognition to the cultural beliefs and practices of different groups. It is precisely in multicultural settings—found everywhere in today's globalized world—that questions of rights become salient and different cultural understandings of what it means to be human, and what rights humans are entitled to, become the focus of contention.

Human Rights Discourse as the Global Language of Social Justice

Discourses about human rights have proliferated in recent decades, stimulated by the original UN Universal Declaration on Human Rights in 1948 and followed by numerous subsequent declarations. For example, in 1992, the Committee for the Elimination of Discrimination against Women (CEDAW) declared that violence against women was a form of gender discrimination that violated the human rights of women. This declaration was adopted by the UN General Assembly in 1993 and became part of the rights platform at the Fourth World Conference on Women in Beijing, China, in 1995 (Figure 14.6). Anthropologist Sally Merry (2001) observes that this declaration "dramatically demonstrates the creation of new rights—rights which depend on the state's failure to

protect women rather than its active violation of rights" and that "the emergence of violence against women as a distinct human rights violation depends on redefining the family so that it is no longer shielded from legal scrutiny" (36–7).

Although CEDAW has proven particularly contentious, other human rights documents have been signed without controversy by many national governments. Signing a human rights declaration supposedly binds governments to take official action to implement changes in local practices that might be seen to violate the rights asserted in the declaration. Human rights discourses are common currency in all societies, at all levels.

Because of the wide adoption of human rights discourses throughout the world, some people have come to speak of an emerging "culture of human rights," which has now become "the preeminent global language of social justice" (Merry 2001, 38). Important to this dialogue is the inclusion of Indigenous peoples' rights in the UN declaration of 1989. As Jane Cowan, Marie-Bénédicte Dembour, and Richard Wilson (2001) write, it is "no use imagining a 'primitive' tribe which has not yet heard of human rights . . . what it means to be 'indigenous' is itself transformed through interaction with human-rights discourses and institutions" (5). These developments mean that anthropologists must take note of the important influence of this human rights discourse as it shapes the community-focused research that they do.

What counts as "human rights" has changed over time, not only because of the action of international bodies like the UN but also because of the efforts of an increasing number of NGOs that have become involved in various countries of the world, many of them deeply committed to projects designed to improve people's lives and protect their rights (Figure 14.7). As Merry (2001) says, these developments "have created a new legal order" (35) that has given birth to new possibilities throughout the world for the elaboration and discussion of what human rights are all about.

In addition, because the "culture of human rights" is increasingly regarded, in one way or another, as the "culture of globalization," it would seem to be a topic well-suited to anthropological analysis in itself. This is because, as we shall see, human rights discourse is not as straightforward as it seems. On the face of things, defending human rights for all people would seem unproblematic. Few people who are aware of the devastation wrought by colonial exploitation, for example, would

human rights Powers, privileges, or material resources to which people everywhere, by virtue of being human, are justly entitled.

multiculturalism Living permanently in settings surrounded by people with cultural backgrounds different from one's own and struggling to define with them the degree to which the cultural beliefs and practices of different groups should or should not be accorded respect and recognition by the wider society.

want to suggest that the victims of that exploitation did not have rights that needed to be protected at all costs. Yet when we look closely at particular disputes about human rights, the concept no longer seems so simple.

Cowan and her colleagues have noted that there are two major arguments that have developed for talking about the way human rights and culture are related. The first involves the idea that *human rights are opposed to culture* and that the two cannot be reconciled. The second involves the idea that a key universal human right is precisely one's *right to culture*. We will consider each in turn.

Rights versus Culture

Arguments that pit human rights against culture depend on the assumption that "cultures" are homogeneous, bounded, and unchanging sets of ideas and practices and that each society has only one culture, which its members are obligated to follow. As we saw in Chapter 8, this view of culture has been severely criticized by cultural anthropologists. But it is a view of culture that is very much alive in many human rights disputes because if people have no choice but to follow the rules of the culture into which they were born, international interference with customs said to violate human rights would seem itself to constitute a human rights violation. Outsiders would be disrupting a supposedly harmonious way of life and preventing those who are committed to such a way of life from observing their own culturally specific understandings about rights. Thus, it is concluded, cultures should be allowed to enjoy absolute, inviolable protection from interference by outsiders. This has been the position adopted, for example, by some national governments that have refused to sign the CEDAW declaration that violence against women violates women's human rights: "Many states have opposed this conception of human rights on cultural or religious grounds, and have refused to ratify treaties" (Merry 2001, 37). Nevertheless, by 2009, 186 countries had ratified CEDAW (https://treaties. un.org/Pages/ViewDetails.aspx?src=TREATY&mtdsg_ no=IV-8&chapter=4&lang=en).

Sometimes representatives of non-Western nation-states may feel free to dismiss rights talk as an unwelcome colonial imposition of ideas that, far from being universal, reflect ethnocentric European preoccupations. But such a dismissal of human rights discourse must be closely examined. In the case of the right of women to protection from violence, for example, Merry points out

FIGURE 14.6 Women protesting against violence at the Fourth World Conference on Women in Beijing, 1995.

that although some forms of violence against women may be culturally sanctioned in some societies, there are many forms that violence against women can take even in those societies, and not all of these are accorded the same amount of cultural support. As we saw in Chapter 2, practices such as female genital cutting could be justified in the past in some circumstances as an appropriate cultural action, but it is now being questioned and even outlawed in the societies where it was traditional. This suggests that "culture values" cannot be held responsible for everything that people do in any society

FIGURE 14.7 Women's shelters run by NGOs in Afghanistan provide a variety of services. Classmates applaud a fellow student after she stood up to read in a literacy class at one such shelter.

and that members of the same society can disagree about these matters and sometimes change their minds.

As talk about human rights has become incorporated into local cultural discussions in recent decades, anthropologists are not surprised to discover that the notion undergoes transformation as people try to make sense of what it means in their own local contexts (Cowan et al. 2001, 8). Being forced to choose between rights and culture, however, seems increasingly unviable in a globalizing, multicultural world. In their own anthropological work on these matters, Cowan and her colleagues (2001) are convinced that the rights-versus-culture debate exaggerates cultural differences. Like many cultural anthropologists today, they find that "it is more illuminating to think of culture as a field of creative interchange and contestation" (4). Such a view of culture makes it possible to find points of connection between the defence of certain human rights and the defence of particular cultural values.

Finally, it is worth asking if "culture" is sometimes used as a scapegoat to mask the unwillingness of a government to extend certain rights to its citizens for reasons that have nothing to do with culture. Cowan and colleagues observe that states like Indonesia and Singapore, which position themselves as stout defenders of "Asian values," have welcomed Western industrial capitalism. To reject human rights discourse because it contradicts "Asian values" would, at the very least, suggest "an inconsistent attitude toward westernization," which in turn feeds suspicions that the defence of "Asian values" may be a political tactic designed "to bolster state sovereignty and resist international denunciations of internal repression and political dissent" (Cowan et al. 2001, 6–7).

Rights to Culture

A second popular argument about the relationship between rights and culture begins from very different premises. This argument does not view universal "human rights" as alien and opposed to "cultures." Instead, it says that all peoples have a universal human right to maintain their own distinct cultures. The *right to culture* has already been explicit in a number of international rights documents.

This argument is interesting because it seems to concede that such things as universal human rights do exist after all. The list of universal rights is simply amended to include the right to one's culture. It draws strength from the idea that cultural diversity is intrinsically valuable and that people should be able to observe their own cultural practices free from outside interference. However, it calls into question the common understanding that people frequently cannot enjoy their full human rights until they are *freed* from the constraints of local cultures. A right to culture, therefore, shows how the very idea of rights and culture is transformed and contested by globalization.

One key issue in the struggle to protect the right to culture is shared by *any* claim to human rights. It concerns the kinds of legal mechanisms needed to ensure protection. The great promise of international documents like the UN Declaration on Human Rights seems to be that people are now free to bring allegations of human rights abuses to an international forum to seek redress. But in fact this is not the case. As human rights activists have discovered, human rights are legally interpreted as *individual* rights, not group rights. This means that people must demand that the *governments of the nation-states in which they are citizens* recognize and enforce the individual rights defended in international documents. International institutions like the UN have been unwilling to challenge the sovereignty of individual nation-states.

The defence of all human rights, including a right to culture, thus depends on the policies of national governments. Some activists see this as a serious contradiction in human rights discourse that undermines its effectiveness. Talal Asad recounts, for example, how Malcolm X argued in the 1960s that African Americans who wanted redress for abuses of their human rights should go directly to the UN and press their case against the government of the United States: "When you expand the civil-rights struggle to the level of human rights, you can then take the case of the black man in this country before the nations in the UN" (quoted in Asad 2003, 141). In fact, this is not the way the system was intended to work. Asad (2003) reminds us of the following:

> *The Universal Declaration of Human Rights* begins by asserting "the inherent dignity" and the "equal and inalienable rights of all members of *the human family*," and then turns immediately to the state. In doing so, it implicitly accepts the fact that the universal character of the rights-bearing person is made the responsibility of sovereign states. (137)

In this legal universe, African Americans (and similarly situated groups in other nation-states) occupied an anomalous position: "they were neither the bearers of national rights nor of human rights" (Asad 2003, 144). The recognition of the human rights of African Americans thus depended on persuading the *US government* to recognize those rights; the UN might use its persuasive power to urge such changes, but it had no coercive power to force the United States—or any other national government—to come into compliance.

Martin Luther King's strategy, Asad points out, took a very different tack, using arguments drawn from prophetic religious discourse and the discourse of American liberalism. His movement was aimed at "mobilizing American public opinion for change," and it was effective at pressing for progressive social change in a way that, among other things, was compatible with the division of labour set forth by the UN Declaration of Human Rights (Asad 2003, 146). In a globalizing world, however, this division of human rights labour—international bodies propose, but nation-states implement—is being challenged. For example, trans-border citizenries lack any forum in which their status and their demands are clearly accorded legitimacy. The right-to-culture movement has succeeded in recent years in highlighting such anomalies and eroding the traditionally recognized right of nation-states to determine the kinds of rights their citizens will be accorded (Cowan et al. 2001, 8–9). As in the case of the rights-versus-culture argument, however, the right-to-culture argument can be "called upon to legitimate reactionary projects as easily as progressive ones . . . the uses to which culture can be put in relation to rights are evidently multiple" (Cowan et al. 2001, 10).

Anthropological disciplinary commitments have allowed anthropologists to approach debates about rights and culture in ways that contribute something new to the discussion. These anthropological contributions can be seen in two ways. First, anthropologists have addressed the ways in which human rights discourse can itself be seen as culture. Second, their own struggles with the concept of "culture" allow them to mount a critique of some of the ways that this concept has been mobilized in discussions of human rights.

Rights as Part of Culture

Anthropological approaches are well suited for investigating the so-called culture of human rights that appears to have emerged in recent years. As in the cultures traditionally studied by anthropologists, the culture of human rights is based on certain ideas about human beings, their needs, and their ability to exercise agency, as well as the kinds of social connections between human beings that are considered legitimate and illegitimate. The entire question of "legitimacy" in human rights discourse points to the central role played by *law*, both as a way of articulating specific human rights and as a tool for defending those rights. Cowan and colleagues (2001) have drawn on earlier anthropological work in which systems of law were analyzed as cultural systems.

One important source has been the "law and culture" framework developed by anthropologists Clifford Geertz, Laura Nader, and Lawrence Rosen and non-anthropologists such as Boaventura de Sousa Santos. In this framework, "law is conceived as a worldview or structuring discourse. . . . 'Facts' . . . are socially constructed through rules of evidence, legal conventions, and the rhetoric of legal actors" (Cowan et al. 2001, 11). Analysts who talk about a "culture of human rights" as the new culture of a globalizing world point out that the key features of the human rights world view clearly indicate its origins in Western secular discourse. That is, it focuses on the rights of individuals, it proposes to relieve human suffering through technical rather than ethical solutions, and it emphasizes rights over duties or needs (Cowan et al. 2001, 11–12).

In the meantime, most anthropologists would probably agree that anthropology can clarify the idea of a "culture of human rights" (Cowan et al. 2001, 13). An understanding of culture as open, heterogeneous, and supple could be effective in helping us understand how human rights processes work.

How Culture Can Help in Thinking about Rights

To use the culture concept as a tool for analyzing human rights processes means looking for "patterns and relationships of meaning and practice between different domains of social life" that are characteristic of the culture of human rights (Cowan et al. 2001, 13). Since human rights are articulated in legal documents and litigated in courts, one of the most important patterns that become visible in the culture of human rights is the way they are shaped to accommodate the law. Groups and individuals who assert that their human rights have been violated regularly take their cases to courts of law. But this means that to get the courts to take them seriously, they must understand how the law operates. A key feature of this understanding involves a realistic awareness of the kinds of claims that the law pays attention to and the kinds of claims that it dismisses.

Looking at human rights law as culture reveals that only certain kinds of claims are admissible. As we saw above, the culture of human rights as currently constituted is best suited to redress the grievances of individuals, not groups. It also provides technical, not ethical, remedies, and it emphasizes rights over duties or needs. Plaintiffs are therefore likely to have a difficult time if they want to claim that their group rights have been violated, that they want the violator exposed and punished, or that the state itself has failed to fulfill its responsibilities toward them. Part of the human rights process therefore involves learning how to craft cases that will fit the laws. This can be tricky if the categories and identities recognized in human rights law do not correspond to categories and identities that are meaningful to the plaintiffs.

Anthropologists have worked with many social groups struggling with national governments to practise their culture freely. These political struggles regularly include claims about distinct and unchanging values and practices. As we saw earlier, these kinds of arguments for a right to culture are often cases of "strategic essentialism." That is, the unity and unchanging homogeneity of a particular "culture" is deliberately constructed to build group solidarity and to engage the state in a focused and disciplined way. But the "essentialism" that often comes to dominate discussions of group rights is not entirely a result of the strategies of activists. Once they choose to make their case in a court of law, they become subject to the "essentializing proclivities of the law" (Cowan et al. 2001, 11). Because human rights law recognizes only certain kinds of violations, groups with grievances must tailor those grievances to fit.

According to Merry, for example, groups like the Hawaiian Sovereignty Movement have successfully achieved some of their political goals by making claims based on the requirements of their "traditional culture." But this is because they live in a society that is "willing to recognize claims on the basis of cultural authenticity and tradition but not reparations based on acts of conquest and violation" (Merry 2001, 42–3). Outside the courtroom, many members of Indigenous groups think of their culture the way contemporary anthropologists think about culture: there are some common patterns but culture is basically unbounded, heterogeneous, and open to change. The conflict between these two understandings of culture has the potential to reshape their ideas about what their culture is. Groups that enter into the human rights process, thus, are entering into ethically ambiguous territory that is "both enabling and constraining" (Cowan et al. 2001, 11).

The Relationship between Human Rights and Humanitarianism

Over the course of the twentieth century, political conflicts in many parts of the world have engendered social upheaval and triggered population movements across political borders. However, French anthropologist Didier Fassin (2012) has detected a significant change in the way national governments and international organizations have come to respond to asylum-seekers in recent decades. Until the 1980s, the persecution and suffering of asylum-seekers had generally been interpreted as human rights violations. After that time, however, political asylum-seekers were increasingly lumped together with victims of earthquakes and tsunamis and addressed by a new form of governmentality, which Fassin calls humanitarianism: "a mode of governing that concerns the victims of poverty, homelessness, unemployment, and exile, as well as disasters, famines, epidemics and wars—in short, every situation characterized by precariousness" (x).

Humanitarian thinking includes the acknowledgement of a universal humanity, which is central to human rights discourse, but it also emphasizes "humaneness"; that is, "an affective movement drawing humans toward their fellows [which] creates the obligation to provide assistance and attention to others" (Fassin 2012, 2). When the discourse of humanitarianism replaces the discourse of human rights, outside observers are encouraged to regard all crises as equal and to experience empathy for the suffering of victims, rather than indignation at the violation of their human rights. The humanitarian response is to relieve suffering through charitable generosity. However, Fassin points out that this generosity is not as innocent as it may appear: "compassion is a moral sentiment with no possible reciprocity . . . those at the receiving end know quite well that they are expected to show the humility of the beholden rather than express demands for rights" (3–4). Thus, humanitarianism "always presupposes a relation of inequality" (4).

In Fassin's view, these changes are well illustrated by the history of the Sangatte transit centre in Calais, France, whose opening (and eventual closure) illustrates "the sidelining of asylum and the advent of humanitarianism . . . the process whereby the refugee issue became subordinate to migration control policy" (Fassin 2012, 141). Beginning in the 1980s, a succession of political crises in various parts of the globe propelled waves of refugees across Europe to Calais, the continental European terminus of the Channel Tunnel, the last barrier in their quest for political asylum in the United Kingdom. By the mid-1990s, however, the British began refusing requests for asylum and sending those who had been rejected back to France. By 1999, the population of suffering asylum-seekers in Calais was so large that the French government hired the Red Cross to manage a transit centre where they could stay. Many critics of Sangatte referred to it as a "camp," but it was an unusual camp because it was "not enclosed by barbed wire, and residents were free to come and go as they pleased" (Fassin 2012, 133). In Fassin's view, Sangatte was a paradoxical entity: "a place of indeterminate status, with a humanitarian mission but set up for reasons of security, though which foreigners were supposed to pass but where they were not supposed to stay. . . . Neither guests nor enemies, they enjoyed a furtive hospitality that conferred no rights—and in particular no right of asylum" (136). Residents were advised to return to their countries of origin, but were never informed that they might seek asylum in France, and less than 1 per cent ever did so (Fassin 2012, 140).

In 2002, the Sangatte transit centre closed, but asylum-seekers did not stop coming to France, and those who did directly experienced the consequences of the subordination of asylum to humanitarianism. Fassin (2012, 141–3) offers the example of a Haitian woman whom he calls Marie. Marie told Fassin that her father had been murdered as a political dissident, after which her mother had been abducted and presumed killed. After she was gang-raped by a group of young men who broke into her house, she and her boyfriend sought political asylum in France. Her first application for asylum was denied (probably, Fassin suggests, because she could not demonstrate that the gang rape had been politically motivated). An appeal was also denied and her case was closed. Marie became an illegal immigrant, hiding with a friend for two years until she was persuaded to see a doctor. The doctor who examined Marie wrote a report requesting that she be allowed to stay in France

on medical grounds because of her suicidal depression. However, when the results of Marie's blood tests came back, she was found to be HIV positive, probably as a consequence of the gang rape. Now diagnosed as suffering from advanced AIDS, she was quickly granted residence in France on humanitarian grounds.

The closure of Sangatte did not bring an end to the crisis posed by refugees living in Calais; with no protection or aid, they subsisted as best they could in public parks or on the beach, vulnerable to harassment by the police. Europe still remains a desirable destination for refugees fleeing violence and suffering in their home countries. But many Europeans continue to associate asylum-seekers with terrorism, or with undermining of the welfare state, or see them as a threat to Europe's identity as white and Christian. It is these anxieties, Fassin suggests, that have subordinated asylum to immigration policy. As circulation of individuals within the European Union has become freer, border control has become tighter. It is easier now to turn back asylum-seekers at airports, to deport undocumented immigrants, and even to hold them in camps outside Europe itself (2012, 156). Ironically, these policies have been promulgated because "the European space is also a space of the rule of law—and hence of rights, notably human rights" (2012, 155). Perhaps this explains why humanitarianism has become so popular in the contemporary world: it "bridges the contradictions of our world, and makes the intolerableness of its injustices somewhat bearable. Hence, it's consensual force" (2012, xi).

But anthropology is more than simply good to think with. Applying anthropological insights in an effort to cope with the challenges humans face in the contemporary world has a long history in our discipline. In recent years, perhaps the most successful and fastest growing field of applied anthropology has been medical anthropology. Drawing on many different schools of thought developed within our discipline, and sometimes borrowed from other disciplines as well, medical anthropology illustrates the range of significant practical interventions that an anthropological perspective can engender in our world.

Nationalism and Its Dangers

The most horrifying consequence of nation-building movements in the twentieth century has been the discovery of just how far the ruling groups of some nation-states are willing to go in order to enforce their version of national identity.

FIGURE 14.8 Relatives of the more than 8000 Muslim men and boys slaughtered in the 1995 Srebrenica massacre walk between rows of coffins next to freshly dug graves, looking for those belonging to their relatives, in a field in the town of Srebrenica, Bosnia and Herzegovina, on 31 March 2003.

After World War II, the world was shocked to learn about Nazi programs to "liquidate" Jews, "Gypsies" (Romani), and other groups that failed to conform to Nazi ideals of Aryan purity (Linke 1997). Many people hoped that the Nazi Holocaust was exceptional, but subsequent developments suggest that it may have been only the most dramatic example of an exterminationist temptation that accompanies all drives to nationalism. Sociologist Zygmunt Bauman argued in his book *Modernity and the Holocaust* (1989) that modern nation-states with rationalized bureaucracies and industrial technology were the first societies in history to make efficient mass extermination of deviants technically possible. In a transnational culture of nationalism, not to belong to a nation-state made up of loyal, ambitious, like-minded citizens is a severe, possibly fatal handicap. Using violence against all citizens who undermine claims of national homogeneity and common purpose may thus be a peculiarly modern way for insecure rulers of embattled nation-states to try to bring about solidarity and stability. In the late twentieth century, warring nationalities in the former Yugoslavia deployed selective assassinations and forced migration to rid their fledgling nation-states of unwanted "others," a policy known as *ethnic cleansing* (Figure 14.8). Thus, rather than relics of a barbarian past, ethnic cleansing, *ethnocide* (the destruction of a culture), and *genocide* (the extermination of an entire people) may constitute a series of related practices that are all signs of things to come. All are measures of the high stakes for which rulers of these nation-states see themselves competing.

Inevitably, such policies create populations of immigrants and refugees whose social status is anomalous and ambiguous in a world of nation-states and whose presence as new pockets of heterogeneity in a different nation-state sets the stage for new rounds of social struggle that may lead to violence.

Chapter Summary

1. Because membership in social categories such as gender, class, caste, race, ethnicity, and nation can determine enormous differences in people's life chances, much is at stake in defending these categories and all may be described as if they were rooted in biology or nature, rather than culture and history. Conceptualizing these forms of identity as essences can be a way of stereotyping and excluding, but it has also been used by many stigmatized groups to build a positive self-image and as a strategic concept in struggles with dominant groups. Although strategic essentialism may be successful in such struggles, it also risks repeating the same logic that justifies oppression.

2. The concept of *class* in anthropology has a double heritage: Europeans tended to view class boundaries as closed and rigid, whereas North Americans tended to view them as open and permeable. Class solidarity may be undercut by clientage relations that bind individuals to one another across class boundaries.

3. The stratification system of India has been taken as the prototype of caste stratification, although anthropologists also have applied the concept of *caste* to social hierarchies encountered elsewhere in the world. Local caste divisions (*jatis*) in rural India adhere to rules of purity and pollution that are defined in terms of the occupations their members

perform and the foods they eat and that govern whom they may marry. Members of *jatis* of similar rank do not observe most of these distinctions with one another, especially in urban settings. Caste associations in large cities of India use *jati* ties to promote their members' economic well-being. The use of violence by higher ranking *jatis* to block the advance of lower ranking *jatis* has increased in recent years. Contemporary anthropologists reject views of caste in India that portray it as internally harmonious and uncontested by those at the bottom of the hierarchy, pointing to the rise in caste violence in recent years.

4. The contemporary concept of "race" developed in the context of European exploration and conquest beginning in the fifteenth century as light-skinned Europeans came to rule over darker-skinned peoples in different parts of the world. The so-called races whose boundaries were forged during the nineteenth century are imagined communities; human biological variation does not naturally clump into separate populations with stable boundaries. Despite variations in opinions and practices regarding race over the centuries, a global hierarchy persists in which whiteness symbolizes high status and blackness symbolizes the social bottom.

5. Although ethnic consciousness existed in precolonial societies, contemporary anthropologists have been most interested in forms of ethnicity that were generated under colonial domination, when different groups were subordinated within a single political structure under conditions of inequality. This process can produce ethnic groups not continuous with any single earlier group and is often characterized by nesting, opposed identities that individuals often manipulate in order to achieve upward mobility. When dominant ethnic groups feel threatened, they may attempt to stigmatize subordinate groups by "racializing" them.

6. Discussions of human rights have intensified as global flows juxtapose and at least implicitly challenge different understandings of what it means to be human or what kinds of rights people may be entitled to under radically changed conditions of everyday life. But different participants in this discourse have different ideas about the relationship between human rights and culture. Some arguments about human rights include the right to one's culture. But most international human rights documents protect only individual human rights, not group rights. And even those who seek to protect their individual rights are supposed to appeal to the governments of their own nation-states to enforce rights defended in international documents.

7. Some anthropologists argue that a "culture of human rights" has emerged in recent years that is based on certain ideas about human beings, their needs, and their abilities that originated in the West. Some consider this culture of human rights the culture of a globalizing world that emphasizes individual rights over duties or needs and that proposes only technical rather than ethical solutions to human suffering. Anthropologists disagree about the value of such a culture of human rights in contemporary circumstances.

8. Because human rights law recognizes only certain kinds of rights violations, groups with grievances must tailor those grievances to fit the violations that human rights law recognizes. Groups that enter into the human rights process are entering into ethically ambiguous territory that is both enabling and constraining. Some anthropologists are concerned that a discourse of humanitarianism that responds to human suffering on compassionate grounds is pushing aside a discourse emphasizing human rights and social justice.

For Review

1. Class, gender, age, and ability intersect to shape individual and collective experiences on a daily basis. How do class and gender intersect in the life of an Indonesian housewife and her husband?

2. What are some stereotypes that people have about your ethnic group? Based on your experience, do you think these characteristics or behaviours can be scientifically backed up?

3. Does Canada have a class system? What would Marx say of Canadian society?

4. How does caste differ from class? Do you think that caste can be said to exist outside India? Why or why not?

5. Summarize the key arguments in the discussion of race in this chapter. Why does racism continue to be a problem even in societies where "race" is widely recognized to be a cultural construction?

6. In what ways is colourism in Nicaragua similar to and different from racism in Canada?

7. Summarize the main arguments in the discussion of ethnicity in this chapter. Describe how ethnicity is recognized in Canada.

8. Are ethnicity and race related? If so, how?

9. What are naturalizing discourses? Give an example.

10. Outline some of the issues with strategic essentialism. What are some of the potential drawbacks for marginalized groups who attempt to gain power and/or recognition through strategically essentializing their collective identities?

Key Terms

caste   329
class   326
clientage   328

colourism   335
ethnic group   337
ethnicity   337

human rights   342
multiculturalism   342
naturalizing discourses   326

References

Allen, Theodore. 1997. *The Invention of the White Race*. London: Verso.

Asad, Talal. 2003. *Formations of the Secular: Christianity, Islam, Modernity*. Palo Alto, CA: Stanford University Press.

Bauman, Zygmunt. 1989. *Modernity and the Holocaust*. Cambridge: Polity Press.

Beals, Alan. 1962. *Gopalpur: A South Indian Village*. New York: Holt, Rinehart, and Winston.

Cannon, Martin J., and Lina Sunseri, eds. 2011. *Racism, Colonialism, and Indigeneity in Canada: A Reader*. Toronto: Oxford University Press.

Comaroff, Jean, and John Comaroff. 1992. *Ethnography and the Historical Imagination*. Boulder, CO: Westview.

Cowan, Jane, Marie-Bénédicte Dembour, and Richard A. Wilson. 2001. "Introduction." IN *Culture and Rights: Anthropological Perspectives*, edited by Jane Cowan, Marie-Bénédicte Dembour, and Richard A. Wilson, 1–26. Cambridge: Cambridge University Press.

Dickey, Sara. 2016. *Living Class in Urban India*. New Jersey: Rutgers University Press.

Dossa, Parin. 2009. *Racialized Bodies, Disabling Worlds: Storied Lives of Immigrant Muslim Women*. Toronto: University of Toronto Press.

Fassin, Didier. 2012. *Humanitarian Reason: A Moral History of the Present*. Berkeley: University of California Press.

Harrison, Faye. 1995. "The Persistent Power of 'Race' in the Cultural and Political Economy of Racism." *Annual Review of Anthropology* 24: 47–74.

———. 1998. "Introduction: Expanding the Discourse on 'Race.' "*American Anthropologist* 100 (3): 609–31.

Hartigan, John, Jr. 1997. "Establishing the Fact of Whiteness." *American Anthropologist* 99 (3): 495–504.

Jackson, Michael. 2006. *The Politics of Storytelling: Violence, Transgression, and Intersubjectivity*. Copenhagen: Museum Tusculanum Press.

Jones, Carla. 2012. "Women in the Middle: Femininity, Virtue, and Excess in Indonesian Discourses of Middle Classness." In *The Global Middle Classes: Theorizing Through Ethnography*, edited by Rachel Heinman, Carla Freeman, et al., 145–68. Santa Fe, NM: School for Advanced Research Press.

Lancaster, Roger. 1992. *Life Is Hard: Machismo, Danger, and the Intimacy of Power in Nicaragua*. Berkeley: University of California Press.

Li, Peter. 2003. *Destination Canada*. Toronto: Oxford University Press.

Linke, Uli. 1997. "Gendered Difference, Violent Imagination: Blood, Race, Nation." *American Anthropologist* 99 (3): 559–73.

Merry, Sally Engle. 2001. "Changing Rights, Changing Culture." In *Culture and Rights: Anthropological Perspectives*, edited by Jane Cowan, Marie-Bénédicte Dembour, and Richard A. Wilson, 31–55. Cambridge: Cambridge University Press.

Schiller, Nina Glick, and Georges Fouron. 2001. *Georges Woke Up Laughing: Long-Distance Nationalism and the Search for Home*. Durham, NC: Duke University Press.

Schultz, Emily. 1984. "From Pagan to Pullo: Ethnic Identity Change in Northern Cameroon." *Africa* 54 (1): 46–64.

Sharma, Ursula. 1999. *Caste*. Buckingham, UK: Open University Press.

Smedley, Audrey. 1995. *Race in North America: Origin and Evolution of a Worldview*. Boulder, CO: Westview Press.

———. 1998. "'Race' and the Construction of Human Identity." *American Anthropologist* 100 (3): 690–702.

Smith, M.G. (1954) 1981. "Introduction." In *Baba of Karo*, edited by Mary Smith, 11–86. New Haven, CT: Yale University Press.

Tambiah, Stanley. 1989. "The Politics of Ethnicity." *American Ethnologist* 16 (2): 334–49.

Werbner, Pnina. 1997. "Introduction: The Dialectics of Cultural Hybridity." In *Debating Cultural Hybridity: Multi-Cultural Identities and the Politics of Anti-Racism*, edited by Pnina Werbner and Tariq Modood, 1–26. London: Zed Books.

Williams, Brackette F. 1989. "A Class Act: Anthropology and the Race to Nation across Ethnic Terrain." *Annual Review of Anthropology* 18: 401–44.

Zaidi, Arshia U., Amanda Couture-Carron, Eleanor Maticka-Tyndale, and Mehek Arif. 2014. "Ethnic Identity, Religion, and Gender: An Exploration of Intersecting Identities Creating Diverse Perceptions and Experiences with Intimate Cross-Gender Relationships amongst South Asian Youth in Canada." *Canadian Ethnic Studies* 46 (2): 27–54.

▲ A young girl practises writing in *fidel*, the script of the Amharic language of Ethiopia. Symbolic language both permits us to communicate with one another and sets up barriers to communication—there is no universally agreed–upon way of translating Amharic writing into the Latin alphabet. 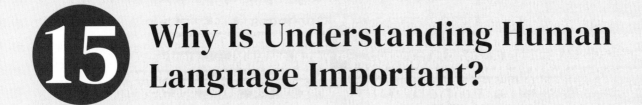 Photo: hadynyah/iStockphoto

15 Why Is Understanding Human Language Important?

Chapter Outline

Only human beings have symbolic language, and it is so deeply a part of our lives that we rarely even think about how unusual it is. In this chapter, you will learn about what makes human symbolic language different from other forms of animal communication. You will also explore its deep connections to other symbolic dimensions of social and cultural life, including the ways your patterns of thought, your sense of self, and even your personality are shaped by experiences in different kinds of symbolically shaped settings.

As we saw in Chapter 4, primates depend on learned behaviour to survive, and some primate species appear to have developed their own cultural traditions. Primates also communicate with one another in a variety of ways, most obviously by relying on vocal calls to alert one another about significant aspects of their environment—from the presence of food to the threat of a predator. In the past, some anthropologists hypothesized that human language was simply an elaboration of the call system of our ancestors, but this hypothesis proved to be incorrect, as we shall see below. In fact, the more anthropologists and other scientists studied human language, the more obvious it became that human languages are very different from primate call systems. Indeed, they came to realize that human language is a second learned system of communication that evolved in our lineage alongside the call system we inherited from our primate ancestors. Humans still possess a simple, species-specific system of calls, but because the languages we speak consist of complex symbols, our languages are distinct from call systems.

In Chapter 2, we defined a symbol as something that stands for something else. Human symbolic language is perhaps the clearest illustration of the central role played by symbols in all of human culture. Indeed, it is the dependence of human language on symbols that makes it such a flexible and creative system of communication—and far more powerful than any primate call system could ever be. So, when anthropologists talk about human language, they always mean human symbolic language. Therefore, as mentioned in an earlier chapter, we define language as the system of arbitrary vocal symbols human beings use to encode and communicate about their experience of the world and of one another. The role played by symbols in human language sets it apart from the apparently non-symbolic communication systems of other living species. Symbolic language has made possible many human achievements, but it is a double-edged sword: it allows people to communicate with one another, but it also creates barriers to communication, especially because not all humans speak the same language. There are approximately 7000 distinct languages spoken in the world today. This chapter explores the ambiguity, limitations, and power of human language and its connections to other forms of human symbolic activity.

What Makes Language Distinctively Human?

In 1966, the anthropological linguist Charles Hockett listed a number of different *design features* of human language that, in his estimation, set it apart from other forms of animal communication. Six of these design features are regularly used to define what makes human language a distinctive form of communication: *openness*, *displacement*, *arbitrariness*, *duality of patterning*, *semanticity*, and *prevarication*.

Openness

Openness indicates that human language is productive. Speakers of any given language not only can create new messages but also can understand new messages created by other speakers. Someone may have never said to you "Put this Babel fish in your ear," but, because you know English, you can understand the message. *Openness* might also be defined as "the ability to understand the same thing from different points of view" (Ortony 1979, 14). In language, this means being able to talk about the same experiences from different perspectives, to paraphrase using different words and various grammatical constructions. Indeed, it means that the experiences themselves can be differently conceived, labelled, and discussed. In this view, no single perspective would necessarily emerge as more correct in every respect than all others.

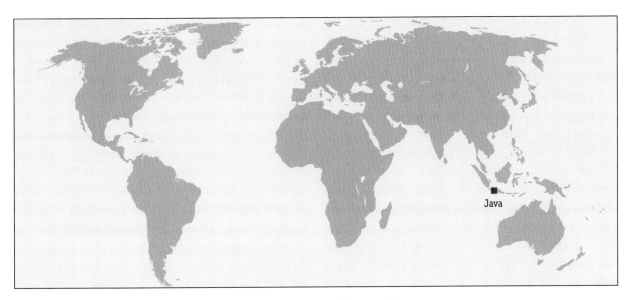

MAP 15.1 Location of Java whose EthnoProfile appears in Chapter 15.

The importance of openness for human verbal communication is striking when we compare, for example, spoken human language to the vocal communication systems (or *call systems*) of monkeys and apes. Biological anthropologist Terrence Deacon (1997) points out that, in addition to spoken symbolic language, modern human beings possess a set of six calls: laughing, sobbing, screaming with fright, crying with pain, groaning, and sighing, which coevolved alongside symbolic language. Linguistic anthropologist Robbins Burling (2005, 16) also emphasizes the difference between call systems and symbolic language:

> Language . . . is organized in such utterly different ways from primate or mammalian calls and it conveys such utterly different kinds of meanings, that I find it impossible to imagine a realistic sequence by which natural selection could have converted a call system into a language. . . . We will understand more about the origins of language by considering the ways in which language differs from the cries and gestures of human and non-human primates than by looking for ways in which they are alike.

Non-human primates can communicate in rather subtle ways using channels of transmission other than voice that we consider *paralanguage*. However, these channels are far less sophisticated than, say, American Sign Language. Burling points out that human sign languages share all the features of spoken human language, except for the channel of communication, which is visual instead of auditory. Ape call systems, by contrast, contain between 15 and 40 calls, depending on the species; and the calls are produced only when the animal finds itself in situations that include such features as the presence of food or danger, friendly interest, and the desire for company; or the desire to mark a location or to signal pain, sexual interest, or the need for maternal care. If the animal is not in the appropriate situation, it does not produce the call. At most, it may refrain from uttering a call in a situation that would normally trigger it. In addition, non-human primates cannot emit a signal that has some features of one call and some of another. For example, if an animal encounters food and danger at the same time, one of the calls takes precedence. For these reasons, the call systems of non-human primates are said to be *closed* when compared to open human languages.

Displacement, Arbitrariness, and Duality of Patterning

Closed call systems also lack *displacement*, our human ability to talk about absent or non-existent objects and past or future events as easily as we discuss our immediate situations. Although non-human primates clearly have good memories, and some species, such as chimpanzees, seem to be able to plan social action in advance (such as when hunting for meat), they cannot use their call systems to discuss such events.

Closed call systems also lack *arbitrariness*, the fact that there is no universal, necessary link between particular linguistic sounds and particular linguistic meanings. For example, the sound sequence /boi/ refers to a "young male human being" in English but means "more" or "many" in Fulfulde, a major language in northern Cameroon (see Figure 15.1). One aspect of linguistic creativity is the free, creative production of new links between sounds and meanings. Thus, arbitrariness and openness imply each other: if all links between sound and meaning are open, then any particular links between particular sounds and particular meanings in a particular language must be arbitrary. In non-human primate call systems, by contrast, links between the sounds of calls and their meanings appear fixed, and there is no easy slippage between sounds and what they stand for from one population to the next.

Arbitrariness is evident in the design feature of language known as *duality of patterning*. Human language, Hockett claimed, is patterned on two different levels: sound and meaning. On the first level, the arrangement of the small set of meaningless sounds (or *phonemes*) that characterize any particular language is not random but systematically patterned to create meaning-bearing units (or *morphemes*): in English, the final /ng/ sound in *song*, for example, is never found at the beginning of a sound sequence, although other languages in the world do allow that combination. The result is that from any language's set of phonemes (in English, there are some 36 phonemes) a very large number of correctly formed morphemes can be created. On the second level of patterning, however, the rules of **grammar** allow for the arrangement and rearrangement of these single morphemes into larger units—utterances or sentences—that can express an infinite number of meanings ("The boy bit the dog" uses the same morphemes as "The dog bit the boy," but the meaning is completely different). Since Hockett first wrote about the design features of human language, many linguists have suggested that there are more than just two levels of patterning in language—that there are levels of phonemes and morphemes as well as levels of sentence structure (*syntax*), meaning (*semantics*), and use (*pragmatics*). In each case, patterns that characterize one level cannot be reduced to the patterns of any other level but can serve as resources for the construction of more comprehensive levels. For example, units at the level of sound (or phonemes), patterned in one way, can be used to create units of meaning (or morphemes) at a different level, patterned in a different way. Morphemes, in turn, can be used to create units at a different level (sentences) by means of syntactic rules that are different from the rules that create morphemes, and syntactic rules are again different from the rules that combine sentences into discourse. Ape call systems, by contrast, appear to lack multilevel patterning of this kind (Wallmann 1992).

> **grammar** A set of rules that aim to fully describe the patterns of linguistic usage observed by speakers of a particular language.

FIGURE 15.1 *Him'be boi `don nder luumo* ("There are many people in the market").

Semanticity and Prevarication

Arbitrariness shows up again in the design feature of *semanticity*—the association of linguistic signals with aspects of the social, cultural, and physical world in which the speakers live. People use language to refer to, make sense of, and talk about objects and processes in their world (think about the way hockey fans discuss how the referees called [or missed calling] penalties during a hockey game). Nevertheless, any linguistic description of reality is always somewhat arbitrary because all linguistic descriptions are selective, highlighting some features of the world and downplaying others. (Semanticity is not the same thing as *semantics*, which refers to the formal study of meaning relations with a particular language.) Perhaps the most striking consequence of linguistic openness is the design feature *prevarication*. Hockett's (1966, 10) remarks about this design feature deserve particular attention: "Linguistic messages can be false, and they can be meaningless in the logician's sense." In other words, not only can people use language to lie, but also utterances that seem perfectly well formed grammatically may yield nonsense. An example is the following sentence invented by linguist Noam Chomsky (1957, 15): "Colourless green ideas sleep furiously." This is a grammatical sentence on one level—the right kinds of words are used in the right places—but on another level it contains multiple contradictions. The ability of language users to prevaricate—to make statements or ask questions that violate convention—is a major consequence of open symbolic systems. Apes using their closed call systems can neither lie nor formulate theories.

How Are Language and Culture Related?

Human language is perhaps the strongest example of a biocultural phenomenon. Within the past 100,000 years, changes to the human brain, our genetic structure, and the anatomy of the human mouth and throat combined to make language a biological possibility. At the same time, no human language can be restricted only to the sounds that come out of people's mouths. Languages are clearly cultural products with embedded meanings and behavioural patterns that stretch beyond individuals, across space, and over time. Anthropologists have long been particularly attentive to the multiple powerful dimensions of language, especially when ethnographic fieldwork in societies presented them with the challenge of learning unwritten languages without formal instruction. At the same time, anthropologists who transcribed or tape-recorded speech could lift it out of its cultural context to be analyzed on its own. Their analyses revealed grammatical intricacies and complexities suggesting that language was a good model for the rest of culture, including social relations, economic exchanges, and power interaction. It also became obvious that the way people use language provides important clues to their understanding of the world and of themselves. Indeed, some theories of culture are explicitly based on ideas taken from **linguistics**, the scientific study of language.

As with the culture concept, the concept of "language" has regularly involved a distinction between *Language* and *languages*. *Language* with a capital *L* (like *Culture* with a capital *C*) has often been viewed as an abstract property belonging to the human species as a whole, not to be confused with the specific *languages* of groups of people. This distinction initially enabled the recognition that all human groups possess fully developed *languages* rather than "primitive," "broken," or otherwise defective forms of vocal communication. Today, however, linguistic anthropologists realize that generalized views of "languages" can be as problematic as generalized views of "cultures." The difficulties associated with demarcating the boundaries between one language and another, or between dialects and languages, become particularly obvious in studies of pidgins, as we will see.

But drawing boundaries around particular languages is only one challenge. Attempting to define what a language can be used for—the functions it performs—can also be a point of debate. Many philosophers and linguists—indeed, many ordinary speakers—view language as primarily a vehicle for information transfer about some state of affairs in the world.

If we are to take a broad view of *human communication* as the transfer of information from one person to another, it immediately becomes clear that humans can communicate with one another nonverbally all the time, sending messages with the clothes they wear, the way they walk, or how long they keep other people waiting for them. Studies of this multidimensional communication are usually called *semiotics*, which refers to the study of meaningful signs and their use. In recent years, linguistic anthropologists have been attracted by the rich and suggestive approach to semiotics developed by American pragmatic philosopher Charles Sanders Peirce. Especially important has been Peirce's distinction between three types of signs:

1. *Iconicity.* The sign (or icon) *looks like* that which it represents (for example, the stylized image of a moving watch face or hourglass that appears on your computer screen indicates the passage of time while an operation is being performed).
2. *Indexicality.* The sign (or index) is *causally linked to* that which it signifies (for example, the verbal expression "y'all," which indexes, or points to, the speech that is characteristic of a particular region of the United States).

linguistics **The scientific study of language.**

3. *Symbolism*. The sign (or symbol) bears no intrinsic connection to that which it represents. Symbols exhibit the design feature of arbitrariness, that is, there is no necessary link between, say, the pattern of the red maple leaf on the flag of Canada and the territorial unit for which it stands. Thus, arbitrary links between symbols and what they signify must be learned.

One key strength of Peirce's types of signs is that they provide the theoretical apparatus needed to investigate the operations of semanticity, that is, for analyzing how language gets outside our heads and into the world. Peirce's three-part model of signs, moreover, is not limited to language but can also encompass meaningful relations conveyed by material objects and relations in the world. And because Peirce's model allows for the generation of new signs, it acts as a valuable way of tracing the meaningful connections between words *and* things that are at the core of human cultural relations.

The symbolic nature of human language makes it a flexible and creative system of communication. The role played by symbols in human language sets it apart from the apparently non-symbolic communication systems of other living species. Thus, when anthropologists talk about human language, they always mean human *symbolic* language.

> ↺ For a discussion regarding the use of the terms *Culture* and *cultures*, see Chapter 2, p. 30.

Many people often equate language with *spoken* language (speech), but it is important to distinguish *language* from *speech*. As well, remember that English can be communicated in writing, in Morse code, or in American Sign Language, to name just three unspoken media. Nevertheless, all human linguistic communication, regardless of the medium, depends on more than words alone. **Native speakers** of a language share not just vocabulary and grammar but also a number of assumptions about how to speak that may not be shared by speakers of a different language. Students learning a new language discover early on that word-for-word translation from one language to another does not work. Sometimes there are no equivalent words in the second language; but even when there are such words, a

native speaker A person who has spoken a particular language since early childhood.

word-for-word translation may not mean in language B what it meant in language A. For example, when English speakers have eaten enough, they say "I'm full." This may be translated directly into French as "*Je suis plein.*" To a native speaker of French, this sentence (especially when uttered at the end of a meal) has the nonsensical meaning "I am a pregnant [male] animal." Alternatively, if uttered by a man who has just consumed a lot of wine, it means "I'm drunk."

Learning a second language is often frustrating and even unsettling; someone who in his or her native language finds the world simple to talk about suddenly turns into a babbling fool. Studying a second language, then, is less a matter of learning new labels for old objects than it is of learning how to identify new objects that go with new labels. The student must also learn the appropriate contexts in which different linguistic forms may be used: a person can be "full" after eating in English but not in French. Knowledge about context is cultural knowledge.

How Do People Talk about Experience?

Each natural human language is adequate for its speakers' needs, given their particular way of life. Speakers of a particular language tend to develop larger vocabularies to discuss those aspects of life that are of importance to them. The Inuit of the Canadian Arctic Archipelago, for example, have long relied on ice and ice floes for subsistence hunting and winter travel. As a result, they have more than 100 words that describe ice and ice forms, including thick ice, thinning ice, old ice, and new ice. As another example, English speakers have created an elaborate vocabulary for discussing time, such as how we "waste time" or "save time." However, despite differences in vocabulary and grammar, all natural human languages ever studied by linguists have proven to be equally complex. Just as there is no such thing

> ↺ For more on the Canadian Inuit, see EthnoProfile 12.4 in Chapter 12, on p. 272.

as a "primitive" human culture, there is no such thing as a "primitive" human language.

Traditionally, languages are associated with concrete groups of people called *speech communities*. But, as Laura Ahearn points out, "complications set in . . . once we start trying to specify exactly what we mean by 'speech' and by 'community'" (2016, 120). As Ahearn observes, the definitions of these terms have varied over time; they have varied among formal linguists, sociolinguists, and linguistic anthropologists; and today there is still no overall agreement as to how narrowly or how widely these terms should be specified. In part, the answer depends on whether the research is primarily focused on a particular *language* or on the particular *group of people* who happen to speak that language (or languages). According to Ahearn, "Within linguistic anthropology, the most influential alternative to 'speech community' is the notion of 'community of practice'" (2016, 132). Especially influential has been a definition of *community of practice*, an integral aspect of sociolinguistics that was devised by linguistic anthropologists Penelope Eckert and Sally McConnell-Ginet:

> A community of practice is an aggregate of people who come together around mutual engagement in an endeavour. Ways of doing things, ways of talking, beliefs, values, power relations—in short, practices—emerge in the course of this mutual endeavour. As a social construct, a community of practice is different from the traditional community, primarily because it is defined simultaneously by its membership and by the practice in which that membership engages. (1992, 464)

Ahearn argues that the great advantage of thinking about a speech community as a community of practice is that it supports forms of research that "illustrate the emergent nature of communities and the inseparability of language from actual social contexts" (2016, 133). Such studies reveal the way different members of the community make use of linguistic resources in different ways. Nevertheless, because all languages possess alternative ways of speaking, members of particular speech communities do not all possess identical knowledge about the language (or languages) they share, nor do they all speak the same way. Individuals and subgroups within a speech community make use of linguistic resources in different ways. We use language in ways to express various aspects of our identities, such as our profession or our family relations. For example, many businesses will use specific acronyms as a form of everyday language that allow those working in that company to communicate but that are not necessarily apparent to those not working in that company. Consequently, there is a tension in language between diversity and commonality. Individuals and subgroups attempt to use the varied resources of a language to create unique, personal voices or ways of speaking. These efforts are countered by pressures to negotiate shared codes for communication within larger social groups. In this way, language patterns are produced, imitated, or modified through the activity of speakers. A particular language that we isolate at any given moment is but a snapshot of a continuing process.

How Do We Communicate without Language?

Before we begin to look more closely at humans' use of language, we must recognize that there are various ways in which we are able to send messages to one another without using language. For example, we can communicate through gestures, postures, facial expressions, and non-verbal vocalizations such as laughing or sobbing, and even through our use of the space around us. These sorts of **non-verbal communication** allow us to inform others about our feelings and even express our social and cultural identity. Indeed, we likely communicate well over 60 per cent of our messages non-verbally (Ottenheimer 2013, 131), and non-verbal communication can be as effective as language in transmitting simple messages between people. However, many of the non-verbal signals we use are culture specific, learned through living within a specific community; as such, accurate interpretation of these signals requires the receiver of the message to be aware of the non-verbal communication customs of the sender's culture.

When most people think about non-verbal communication, they usually think of **body language**: movements and postures that communicate attitudes and feelings non-verbally. The study of these sorts of cues is known as **kinesics**. In everyday interactions, we often use simple body movements—for example, a wave goodbye, a tap on the shoulder, a smile, a wink, or an impatient

non-verbal communication The process of sending and receiving messages without the use of words (e.g., through gestures, facial expressions, or non-verbal vocalizations). This is also referred to as *paralanguage*.

body language Movements and postures that communicate attitudes and feelings non-verbally.

kinesics The study of body movement, gestures, and facial expressions as a form of communication.

tapping of a foot—to enhance or even stand in for verbal messages. As with most forms of non-verbal communication, however, the meaning attached to these sorts of gestures tends to differ from culture to culture (Figure 15.2). Consider that Nicaraguans point at things with their lips and indicate questions by wrinkling their noses and that Comorans encourage others to come closer by moving a hand in what North Americans would interpret as a goodbye wave (Ottenheimer 2013, 132). Also consider that putting one's thumb and forefinger together in a circle with the other three fingers pointing upward means "okay" in Canada, while this same gesture conveys that something is worthless in France and may be considered an insult in some parts of Germany (142).

In addition to body language, smells, tastes, and non-verbal vocal sounds also communicate feelings and information. The smell of fresh baking can suggest home and comfort; the smell of cigars and perfumes can imply status; and pine or lemon scents can suggest cleanliness. Flavours tend to characterize certain cultures: for example, spicy foods such as salsas and curries are often associated with cultures from warmer climates, while less flavourful foods are typically linked with cultures from northern regions. Non-verbal vocalizations can convey a wide variety of messages, from a forceful declaration of anguish delivered through a sharp cry of pain to a subtle

comment of derision delivered through a soft laugh. (See the "In Their Own Words" box on the "Clinton cackle" for a great example of how complex messages can be conveyed through a well-timed laugh.)

Use of space is another way in which we send non-verbal messages. The study of how different societies perceive and use space is known as **proxemics**. A major focus of proxemics is the space we create around ourselves when interacting with others. Consider what you typically do when you meet someone new. Do you nod, bow, extend your hand, or give kisses on both cheeks? When you are having a conversation, how close do you stand to the other person? For most people, there is a point in space at which a conversation partner can be "too close"; how we define this point depends on both our culturally learned understanding of the space around us and our relationship with the other person. Edward T. Hall (1966), who was one of the first to look at proxemics, proposed the existence of four different kinds of interpersonal space that could be compared cross-culturally: intimate, personal, social, and public (Figure 15.3). The first two categories relate to the space we feel comfortable sharing with people with whom we have a close relationship (e.g., when talking to family or friends); the other two relate to the space we feel comfortable sharing with strangers (e.g., when standing in line at the grocery store or sitting in a waiting room). Generally, most Canadians

proxemics The study of how different societies perceive and use space.

FIGURE 15.2 The meaning attached to body language differs from culture to culture. A traditional Maori greeting in New Zealand is the *hongi*, in which two people welcome each other by pressing their noses and foreheads together.

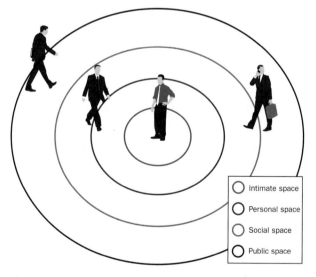

Intimate space
Personal space
Social space
Public space

FIGURE 15.3 People can be thought to have four spheres of interpersonal space: intimate, personal, social, and public. The amount of space we leave between ourselves and others depends on both our culturally learned understanding of the space around us and our relationship with the other person.

In Their Own Words

The "Clinton Cackle": Hillary Rodham Clinton's Laughter in News Interviews

Tanya Romaniuk of York University has recently investigated interviewees' use of laughter in response to an interviewer's questions in the context of broadcast news interviews (BNIs). In her investigation, she looks specifically at how United States politician Hillary Rodham Clinton (HRC) used laughter during interviews while she was campaigning for the Democratic nomination for president in 2007.

Through an examination of HRC's laughter in news interviews, I have attempted to describe some of the patterned ways in which laughter occurs, . . . and some issues that arise [in the context of BNIs]. Given that the turn-taking system for news interviews is designed for interviewees' answers to be responsive actions relevant only on the completion of a question (Clayman 2001), it is illuminating to consider how HRC negotiates this constraint through her use of laughter. Operating on the interviewer's talk while it is being produced allows HRC to provide implicit commentary on the talk without waiting until question completion, and prior to providing a substantive response. In this way, HRC demonstrates how laughter can be used as an interactional resource for interviewees in the context of news interviews. . . . In the context of BNIs, at least, the practice described [here] is one that other interviewees deploy in similar circumstances. . . .

. . . [I]t seems that there is no doubt that laughter is one interactional resource interviewees make use of in order to mitigate the force of an interviewer's adversarial questioning before providing a substantive response. While further research into this practice in the context of news interviews is certainly warranted, so too is work in other institutional contexts, in which interactional roles are also shaped and constrained by institutional identities. For example, [one researcher] found that in job interviews, applicants laughed more frequently than interviewers, just as [other researchers have] found that patients laughed more often than physicians in medical interviews. While I suspect that it is also more likely that interviewees laugh more often than interviewers in BNIs, this hypothesis, and others concerning the use of laughter in other institutional contexts, is worthy of exploration. Indeed, detailed analyses of laughter and its interplay with other verbal and non-verbal actions lead to a deeper understanding of the range of meanings it can convey in social interaction.

Source: Romaniuk 2009, 42.

---

feel uncomfortable standing within a metre of a stranger, while most Europeans feel comfortable standing half that distance from a stranger (Ottenheimer 2013, 136). It is important to be aware of how space is used among different communities and how it communicates important ideas non-verbally, especially when working with people from differing cultures.

How Do Languages Change over Time?

All languages change over time. The study of this evolution of language is known as **historical linguistics**, which investigates relationships between words and sounds within a language, as well as connections between different languages. For example, historical linguists may investigate the connections among the Nordic languages (in particular, Icelandic, Norwegian, Danish, and Swedish) by looking at the natural change of these languages over time and how contact with other cultures influenced their evolution. Iceland, for example, is an extremely isolated place in the North Atlantic region where, until relatively recently, the local language (Icelandic) was not heavily influenced by other cultures and changed primarily as a result of internal factors. As a result, Icelandic is most similar to the original Nordic language, Old Norse, which the Vikings would have spoken. The connections among modern Nordic languages indicate a genealogical relationship that historical linguists can use to reconstruct links between Nordic cultures across time. The further historical

historical linguistics The study of relationships between languages and how they change over time.

Languages continue to change in the present as well, and these changes tend to reflect cultural adaptations on a larger scale. Consider recent words associated with technology—for example, *smartphone*, *blog*, *Instagram*, *Snapchat* or even *Groupon*. These words did not exist a decade ago, but because they have been adopted by so many people, even on a global scale, we understand what they mean (Figure 15.4). Incorporating new words is not the only way that languages can change, however. Meanings of existing words and phrases can change as well. How would you define words like *spam* or *Twitter*? Until recently, *twitter* was a manner in which birds sing, while *spam* was the name of a luncheon meat (made of SPiced hAM) that was created in 1937. Often, these changes to language are generational and reflect *internal* changes to language and culture. As cultures change, new words must be invented and incorporated into the existing language to describe new technologies and experiences.

"Possessive pronouns? Um, iPod, yourPod, theirPod?"

FIGURE 15.4 As cultures change, new words must be invented and incorporated into the existing language to describe new technologies and experiences. Before the release of the first iPod in 2001, the word *iPod* would have meant little to most English speakers. Today, the term is widely recognized around the world, even by non-English speakers.

linguists trace modern languages back in time, the more connections they uncover. For example, tracing English back beyond 6000 years or so reveals its roots in the foundational Proto Indo-European (PIE) language, to which French, Spanish, Russian, and most other modern European languages also trace their roots. The analysis of when and how language groups diverged from one another is an important aspect of historical linguistics, one that is often used to supplement archaeological research. Similar words in discrete languages provide important evidence that archaeologists use to recreate migration patterns and invasions of different groups in the past. When speakers of different languages come into contact, they often borrow words from the unfamiliar language and incorporate them into their own language; this phenomenon is referred to as *external* language change.

> **linguistic competence** A term coined by linguist Noam Chomsky to refer to the mastery of adult grammar.
>
> **communicative competence** A term coined by anthropological linguist Dell Hymes to refer to the mastery of adult rules for socially and culturally appropriate speech.

What Does It Mean to "Learn" a Language?

Years ago studies of child language amounted to a list of errors that children make when attempting to gain what Chomsky calls **linguistic competence**, or mastery of adult grammar. For some time, however, linguists who study children's verbal interactions in social and cultural contexts have drawn attention to what children can do very well:

> From an early age they appear to communicate very fluently, producing utterances which are not just remarkably well-formed according to the linguist's standards but also appropriate to the social context in which the speakers find themselves. Children are thus learning far more about language than rules of grammar. [They are] acquiring communicative competence. (Elliot 1981, 13)

Communicative competence, or mastery of adult rules for socially and culturally appropriate speech, is a term introduced by American anthropological linguist Dell Hymes (1972). As an anthropologist, Hymes objected to Chomsky's notion that linguistic competence consisted only of being able to make correct judgments of sentence grammaticality (Chomsky 1965, 4). Hymes observed that competent adult speakers do more than follow grammatical rules when they speak. They are also able to choose words and topics of conversation appropriate to their social position, the social position of the person they are addressing, and the social context of interaction (Figure 15.5). The study of these socially appropriate rules forms a significant part of **sociolinguistics**, which is the study of language in relation to social factors, such as differences of regional, class, and occupational dialect, power and gender differences, and bilingualism.

How Does Context Affect Language?

Anthropologists are very much aware of the influence of context on how people use language. For example, consider the issue of using personal pronouns appropriately when talking to others. In English, the problem almost never arises because native speakers address all people as "you." But any English speaker who has ever tried to learn French has worried about when to address an individual using the second-person plural (*vous*) and when to use the second-person singular (*tu*). To be safe, most students of French use *vous* for all individuals, to avoid appearing too familiar with native speakers whom they do not know well. But certain difficulties remain. For example, if you are dating a French person, at what point in the relationship does the change from *vous* to *tu* occur, and who decides? Moreover, sometimes—for example, among university students—the normal term of address is *tu* (even among strangers); it is used to indicate social solidarity. English speakers who are learning French wrestle with these sorts of context-related linguistic dilemmas all the time. Rules for the appropriate use of *tu* and *vous* seem to have nothing to do with grammar, yet the choice between one form and the other indicates whether the speaker is someone who does or does not know how to speak French.

But French seems quite straightforward when compared with Javanese, in which all the words in a sentence must be carefully selected to reflect the social relationship between the speaker and the person addressed (see EthnoProfile 15.1: Java). In the 1950s, when Clifford Geertz (1960) first did fieldwork in Java, he discovered that it was impossible to say anything in Javanese without also communicating one's social position relative to the person to whom one is speaking. Even a simple request—such as "Are you going to eat rice and cassava now?"—requires that speakers know at least five different varieties of the language in order to communicate socially as well as to make the request. This example illustrates the range of diversity present in a single language and how different varieties of a language are related to different subgroups within the speech community.

FIGURE 15.5 Social and cultural contexts impact how children learn to communicate. For example, children in Canada often learn that it is appropriate to use formal grammar and polite terms in the context of a family dinner.

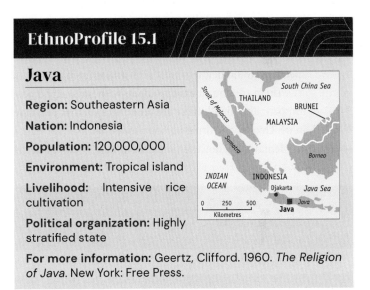

EthnoProfile 15.1

Java

Region: Southeastern Asia

Nation: Indonesia

Population: 120,000,000

Environment: Tropical island

Livelihood: Intensive rice cultivation

Political organization: Highly stratified state

For more information: Geertz, Clifford. 1960. *The Religion of Java*. New York: Free Press.

How Does Language Affect How We See the World?

During the first half of the twentieth century, two American anthropological linguists, Edward Sapir and Benjamin Whorf, observed that the grammar of different languages often described the same situation in different ways. They concluded that language has the power to shape the way people see the world. This claim

sociolinguistics The study of language in relation to social factors, such as differences of regional, class, and occupational dialect, power and gender differences, and bilingualism.

has been called the **linguistic relativity principle**, or the "Sapir–Whorf hypothesis." This principle has been highly controversial because it is a radical proposition that is difficult to test, and, when it has been tested, the results have been ambiguous.

The so-called strong version of the linguistic relativity principle is also known as *linguistic determinism*. It is a totalizing view of language that reduces patterns of thought and culture to the grammatical patterns of the language spoken. If a grammar classifies nouns in male and female gender categories, for example, linguistic determinists claim that speakers of that language are forced to think of males and females as radically different kinds of beings. By contrast, a language that makes no grammatical distinctions on the basis of gender supposedly trains its speakers to think of males and females as exactly the same. If linguistic determinism is correct, then a change in grammar should change thought patterns: if English speakers were to replace *he* and *she* with a new, gender-neutral third-person singular pronoun, such as *they*, linguistic determinists predict that English speakers would begin to treat men and women as equals.

There are a number of problems with linguistic determinism. First of all, there are languages such as Fulfulde in which only one third-person pronoun is used for males and females (*o*); however, male-dominant social patterns are quite evident among Fulfulde speakers. Second, if language determined thought in this way, it would be impossible to translate from one language to another or even to learn another language with a different grammatical structure. Because human beings *can* learn foreign languages and translate from one language to another, the strong version of the linguistic relativity principle cannot be correct. Third, even if it were possible to draw firm boundaries around speech communities (which it is not), every language provides its native speakers with alternative ways of describing the world. Finally, in many societies, people learn to speak more than one language fluently. Yet people who grow up bilingual do not also grow up unable to reconcile two contradictory views of reality. Indeed, bilingual children ordinarily benefit from knowing two languages, do not confuse them, can switch readily from one to another, and even appear to demonstrate greater cognitive flexibility on psychological tests than do monolinguals (Elliot 1981, 56). Consequently, bilingualism, or even multilingualism, is a highly valued skill, especially in our modern globalized world. In Canada, where students are given the opportunity to learn both of the country's official languages in school, approximately 17.5 per cent of the population is able to conduct a conversation in both French and English (Lepage and Corbeil 2013) (Figure 15.6).

In the face of these objections, other researchers offer a "weak" version of the linguistic relativity principle that rejects linguistic determinism but continues to claim that language shapes thought and culture. Thus, grammatical gender might not determine a male-dominant social order, but it might facilitate the acceptance of such a social order because the grammatical distinction between *he* and *she* might make separate and unequal gender roles seem "natural." Because many native speakers of English also are strong promoters of gender equality, however, the shaping power of grammar would seem far too weak to merit any scientific attention.

Neither Sapir nor Whorf favoured linguistic determinism. Sapir argued that language's importance lies in the way it directs attention to some aspects of experience rather than to others. He was impressed by the fact that "it is generally difficult to make a complete divorce between objective reality and our linguistic symbols of reference to it" (Sapir [1933] 1966, 9, 15).

In recent years, interest in the "Whorfian question" has been revived, and scholars have recognized that there are several different ways to ask about the

> **linguistic relativity principle** A position, associated with Edward Sapir and Benjamin Whorf, that asserts that language has the power to shape the way people see the world.

Janine Wiedel Photolibrary/Alamy Stock Photo

FIGURE 15.6 Canada is officially a bilingual country, and children across the country have the opportunity to learn both English and French in school.

relationship of language to thought. Especially exciting is the new perspective that comes from focusing on the influence of language in pragmatic contexts of use. Dan Slobin's "thinking for speaking" hypothesis, for example, suggests that the influence of linguistic forms on thought may be greatest when people prepare to speak to others on a specific topic in a specific setting: "One fits one's thoughts into available linguistic forms. . . . 'Thinking for speaking' involves picking those characteristics that (a) fit some conceptualization of the event, and (b) are readily encodable in the language" (Slobin 1987, 435). Slobin points out that related challenges are faced by speakers involved in "thinking for writing" or "thinking for translating." Thinking for translating is especially intriguing, particularly when translators must render features that are grammatically encoded in one language into a second language in which they are not encoded, or vice versa (Slobin 2003). For example, an English speaker who is trying to say "I like fast food" in Spanish will have to use a passive encoding—*me gusta la comida rápida* ("fast food please me"). This encoding is not easy for many English speakers to learn, precisely because it is not the standard English way to encode the thought.

Dedre Gentner and Susan Goldin-Meadow (2003) point out that some researchers still take a traditional Whorfian approach, viewing language as a lens through which people view the world. Others think of language as a tool kit, a set of resources that speakers make use of to build more elaborate conceptual structures. Still others think of language as a category maker, influencing the way people classify experiences and objects in the world. They note that the research that produces the most consistent evidence of the influence of language on thought comes from those who view language as a tool kit—that is, as a set of resources that speakers make use of for conceptual or communicative purposes. Nevertheless, they emphasize that defining the research question in such variable ways means that "we are unlikely to get a yes-or-no answer to the whole of Whorf's thesis. But if we have delineated a set of more specific questions for which the answer is no to some and yes to others, we will have achieved our goal" (Gentner and Goldin-Meadow 2003, 10–12).

Pragmatics: How Do We Study Language in Contexts of Use?

Pragmatics can be defined as the study of language in the context of its use. Each context offers limitations and opportunities concerning what we may say and how we

may say it. Everyday language use is thus often characterized by a struggle between speakers and listeners over definitions of context and appropriate word use. Linguistic anthropologist Michael Silverstein (1976, 1985) was one of the first to argue that the meaning of certain expressions in language cannot be determined unless we go beyond the boundaries of a sentence and place the expressions in a wider context of use. Two kinds of context must be considered: linguistic and non-linguistic. *Linguistic context* refers to the other words, expressions, and sentences that surround the expression whose meaning we are trying to determine. The meaning of *it* in the sentence "I really enjoyed it" cannot be determined if the sentence is considered on its own. However, if we know that the previous sentence was "My aunt gave me this book," we have a linguistic context that allows us to deduce that *it* refers to *this book*. *Non-linguistic context* consists of objects and activities that are present in the situation of speech at the same time we are speaking. Consider the sentence "Who is that standing by the door?" We need to look at the environment when the sentence is spoken to find the door and the person standing by the door. This is the non-linguistic context giving meaning to the words *who* and *that* (Figure 15.7).

By going beyond formal grammatical analysis, pragmatics directs our attention to **discourse**, or what we would consider a conversation, united by a common theme, among two or more speakers. Again, how the speakers interact and the social rules regarding how to conduct a proper discourse form an important component of sociolinguistics.

Ethnopragmatics

Linguistic anthropologists pay attention not only to the immediate context of speech, linguistic and non-linguistic, but also to broader contexts that are shaped by unequal social relationships and rooted in history (Hill and Irvine 1992). Alessandro Duranti (1994, 11) calls this **ethnopragmatics**, "a study of language use which relies on ethnography to illuminate the ways in

pragmatics The study of how language is used in conversation.

discourse A stretch of speech longer than a sentence united by a common theme.

ethnopragmatics The study of language use that relies on ethnography to illuminate the ways in which speech is both constituted by and constitutive of social interaction.

FIGURE 15.7 Being able to answer the question "What is that on the door?" requires that we examine the actual physical context at the moment we are asked the question to try to determine what *that* refers to: Is it the locks? Is it the door handles? Is it the studs on the door? Also, what part of the structure is the "door"?

which speech is both constituted by and constitutive of social interaction." These studies focus on how the rules of grammar, cultural values, and physical action are all conjoined (Hanks 1996, 11). This suggests that the source of meaning is in everyday routine social activity, or *habitus*, rather than in grammar and that phonemes, morphemes, syntax, and semantics are simply *linguistic resources* people can make use of, rather than rigid forms that determine what people can and cannot think or say.

If mutual understanding is shaped by shared routine activity and not by grammar, then communication is possible even if the people interacting with one another speak mutually unintelligible languages. All they need is a shared sense of "what is going on here" and the ability to negotiate successfully who will do what (Hanks 1996, 234). Such mutually co-engaged people shape *communicative practices* that involve spoken language but also include values and shared habitual knowledge that may never be put into words. Because most people in most societies regularly engage in a wide range of practical activities with different subgroups, each one will also end up knowledgeable about a variety of different communicative practices and the linguistic habits that go with them. For example, a college student might know the linguistic habits appropriate to dinner with her parents, to the classroom, to worship services, to conversations in the dorm with friends, and to her part-time job in a restaurant (Figure 15.8). Each set of linguistic habits she knows is called a *discourse genre*. Because our student simultaneously knows a multiplicity of different discourse genres she can choose among when she speaks, her linguistic knowledge is characterized by what Bakhtin called *heteroglossia* (Bakhtin 1981).

Heteroglossia is a set of coexisting linguistic norms and forms, each representing a different social subgroup. Because we all participate in more than one of these subgroups, we inevitably become fluent in many varieties of language, even if we speak only English. Our capacity for heteroglossia is an example of linguistic openness: it

FIGURE 15.8 When interacting with friends, young people tend to employ linguistic habits that are much less formal than those they might use when interacting with someone in a position of authority, such as a professor or an employer.

means that our thoughts and speech are not imprisoned in a single set of grammatical forms, as linguistic determinists argued. Indeed, if our college student reflects on the overlap as well as the contrasts between the language habits used in the dorm and those used in the restaurant, she might well find herself raising questions about what words really mean. To the extent that her habitual ways of speaking are deeply rooted in everyday routine activity, however, they may guide the way she typically thinks, perceives, and acts. And, so, the linguistic relativity hypothesis may be correct—not on the level of grammatical categories but on the level of discourse (Schultz 1990).

What Happens When Languages Come into Contact with One Another?

In local communities, speakers and listeners are, for the most part, able to use overlapping language habits to converse or argue about moral and political issues. This may also be the case when communities of speakers engage regularly with one another but do not all speak the same languages, or speak them equally fluently. Sometimes, however, communities find themselves sharing little more than physical proximity to one another and have radically different language traditions and no history of previous contact with one another. When these two differing groups come face to face and are forced to communicate, a new form of language—**pidgin**—may develop. There is no way to predict the outcome of such enforced contact on either speech community, but in many cases pidgin languages are created to communicate new shared experiences.

"When the chips are down, meaning is negotiated" (Lakoff and Johnson 1980, 231). The study of pidgin languages is the study of the negotiation of new meaning, the production of a new whole (the pidgin language) that is different from and not merely a different form of the languages that gave birth to it. The shape of a pidgin reflects the context in which it arises—generally one of colonial conquest or commercial domination. Vocabulary is usually taken from the language of the dominant group, making it easy for that group to learn. The system of pronunciation and sentence structure may be similar to the subordinate language (or languages), however, making it easier for subordinated speakers to learn.

What Is Linguistic Inequality?

Pidgins turn out to be far more complex and the result of far more active human input than we used to think, which is why they are attractive to linguists and linguistic anthropologists as objects of study. Where they co-exist, however, alongside the language of the dominant group (e.g., Hawaiian Pidgin English and English), they are ordinarily viewed as defective and inferior languages. Such views can be considered as a result of the situation that led to the formation of most of the pidgins we know about: European colonial domination. In a colonial or postcolonial setting, the language of the colonizer is often viewed as better than pidgin languages, which are frequently thought to be broken, imperfect versions of the colonizer's language. The situation only worsens when formal education, the key to participation in the European-dominated society, is carried out in the colonial language. Speakers of pidgin who remain illiterate may never be able to master the colonial tongue and may find themselves effectively barred from equal participation in the civic life of their societies.

To take one language variety as the standard against which all other varieties are measured might be described as "linguistic ethnocentrism," and such a standard may be applied to any language, not just pidgins. This is one kind of linguistic inequality: making value judgments about other people's speech in a context of dominance and subordination. A powerful example of the effects of linguistic inequality is found in the history of Indigenous children who were forced into the residential school system of Canada (Figure 15.9). Canada's residential school system provides a powerful and troubling example of how a dominant culture's linguistic ethnocentrism contributed to the loss of Indigenous languages. Indigenous children were taken away from their families, forced to attend residential schools, and prohibited from speaking Indigenous languages; and if they did speak them, they were punished for doing so.

> pidgin (1) A language with no native speakers that develops in a single generation between members of communities that possess distinct native languages. (2) A shared secondary language in a speech community in which speakers also use some other main language.

Bud Glunz/National Film Board of Canada. Phototheque/PA-134110

FIGURE 15.9 Canada's residential school system provides a powerful and troubling example of how a dominant culture's linguistic ethnocentrism contributed to the loss of Indigenous languages. Here, Cree students learn English in a classroom at an Anglican Church–run missionary school in Lac La Ronge, Saskatchewan, in 1945.

Beginning in the late 1880s, the government of Canada implemented an assimilation policy that required First Nations, Métis, and Inuit children to attend residential boarding schools. With the aim of "civilizing" the children (sometimes referred to as "taking the Indian out of the child"), the Canadian government provided funding for the schools, which were run by Christian churches of various denominations. By the 1930s to 1940s, approximately 50 per cent of all Indigenous children were living in these schools, separated from their families and cultures. More than 150,000 Indigenous children passed through the residential school system before the last federally funded schools closed in the late 1990s (Truth and Reconciliation Commission of Canada 2015, 3). Speaking Indigenous languages at school was strictly forbidden, and students who disobeyed the rules often faced severe physical and emotional punishments. For example, Celia Haig-Brown (1988, 11) recalls how her father, "who attended the Alberni Indian Residential school for four years in the twenties, was physically tortured by his teachers for speaking Tseshaht: they pushed sewing needles through his tongue, a routine punishment for language offenders." Isolated from their families for months on end, many students lost the ability to speak their own languages and, subsequently, were unable to pass on those languages to their children. Even as adults, many residential-school survivors were too

traumatized and ashamed to speak or relearn their original language. Others discouraged their children from learning their ancestral language, believing that fluency in English or French would make their lives easier. As a result, generations of Indigenous peoples in Canada are still experiencing the repercussions of language loss and cultural genocide. Marie Battiste (1986, xx) suggests that this type of forced assimilation and linguistic dominance can be considered the final stage of a "cognitive imperialism" that essentially "whitewash[ed] the tribal mind and soul."

On 11 June 2008, the Canadian government presented a formal apology to all who had been harmed in the residential school system, and numerous foundations were established to assist those who were in need of healing and reconciliation. Also established in 2008 was the Truth and Reconciliation Commission of Canada (TRC), which was given the task of investigating the full consequences of the Canadian residential school system. After years of conducting interviews and examining historical records, the TRC released its final report in early June 2015. On the topic of language loss, the report concluded that the residential school system had "contributed significantly to the fragile state of Aboriginal languages in Canada today":

Many of the almost ninety surviving Aboriginal languages in Canada are under serious threat of extinction. In the 2011 census, 14.5 per cent of the Aboriginal population reported that their first language learned was an Aboriginal language. In the previous 2006 census, 18 per cent of those who identified as Aboriginal had reported an Aboriginal language as their first language learned, and a decade earlier, in the 1996 census, the figure was 26 per cent. This indicates nearly a 50 per cent drop in the 15 years since the last residential schools closed.

Despite the establishment of cultural and language revitalization programs on reservations across the country, the statistics on Indigenous language use appear grim: across Canada, only 25 per cent of the Indigenous population is able to speak or understand an Indigenous language with full fluency (Norris 2007). Moreover, the majority of these speakers belong to older generations. Thus, as these speakers age and pass on, the Indigenous languages they speak will become increasingly endangered. Indigenous people living in urban areas face the greatest obstacles to learning and speaking their native languages because they are geographically isolated from their communities and may lack cultural support. At the same time, growing numbers of people—young and old, Indigenous and non-Indigenous—are recognizing the central importance of language to cultural identity and thus the urgent necessity to revitalize Indigenous languages. To help support these revitalization efforts and assist in learning these languages, Dr Bryan Gick (Bliss, Bird, Cooper, Burton, and Gick 2018), University of British Columbia, has worked with a group of colleagues and created a way of "seeing speech." Video recordings of ultrasound images were used to illustrate how a speaker's tongue moved in relation to specific sounds of western Canadian Indigenous languages, including *SENĆOŦEN* (Salish), *Secwe'pemc*, and *Halq'eméylem*. Learners were able to see how the speech was produced, rather than merely hear and mimic it. As a result, the acquisition rates for these learners was much faster, and learners felt much more confidence speaking in their new language (337). Also, see the "Anthropology in Everyday Life" box on Indigenous language revitalization.

What Is Language Ideology?

Building on early work on linguistic inequality, linguistic anthropologists have devoted much attention to the study of **language ideology**. Language ideology marks struggles between social groups with different interests, revealed in what people say and how they say it. Typically, a language ideology takes one language variety as the standard against which all other varieties are measured, positively or negatively. To employ a language ideology is to make value judgments about other people's speech in a context of domination and subordination, and such a standard may be applied to any language, not just to pidgins. An example of this occurs when French speakers from France consider their "form of French" the proper form; and the French spoken in Quebec, a lesser form. As linguistic anthropologist Kathryn Woolard puts it, language ideology represents the intersection "between social forms and forms of talk" (1998, 3)

Although the study of language ideology discloses a speaker's basic understandings of the world, it also reveals the ways in which our speech is always embedded in a social world of power differences. The way people monitor their speech to bring it into line with a particular language ideology illustrates that language ideologies "are active and effective . . . they transform the material

reality they comment on" (Woolard 1998, 11). In settings with a history of colonization, where groups with different power and different languages coexist in tension, the study of language ideologies has long been significant (Woolard 1998, 16). Linguistic anthropologists are well suited to study language ideologies because their linguistic training allows them to describe precisely the linguistic features (e.g., phonological, morphological, or syntactic) that become the focus of ideological attention while their training in cultural analysis allows them to explain how these linguistic features come to stand symbolically for a particular social group.

Language ideology in Canada is complex as the country was colonized by two predominately white nations to create a bilingual country, and internal struggles for power between these two groups continue today. The Official Languages Act (1969) recognized English and French as our two official languages, which has affected everything from labelling on food products to employment in federal agencies to funding for education. In essence, nation building and belonging in Canada are framed within the ideology of bilingualism and biculturalism. In doing so, Canada has created a positive image of itself as a tolerant and progressive society. However, even English and French are not treated equally in all communities across the country. French speakers living outside Quebec are often considered minorities and pressured to adopt English as their primary language. Likewise, English speakers living in Quebec are often considered minorities there and are pressured to adopt French as their primary language.

Canada's binary linguistic ideology has had even greater consequences for all those "others" who speak neither English nor French as their first language. This struggle for identity and belonging by linguistic "others" in Canada is discussed fully in Eve Haque's recent book *Multiculturalism within a Bilingual Framework* (2012). Haque argues that race, culture, and language are inextricably linked to notions of who we are as a nation. In many ways, "belonging" in Canada requires one to identify with one of the two official founding nations (England and France). Haque traces the numerous ways that the use and promotion of our two official languages

language ideology A marker of struggles between social groups with different interests, revealed in what people say and how they say it.

Anthropology in Everyday Life

Indigenous Language Revitalization

Without the language, we are warm bodies without a spirit.

—Mary Lou Fox, Ojibwe elder

Many linguists and linguistic anthropologists who specialize in the study of Indigenous languages in Canada are increasingly involved in collaborating with Indigenous peoples to preserve and revive Indigenous languages in the face of threatened decline or extinction. According to the 2011 Census of Population, over 60 distinct Indigenous languages, which are generally grouped into 12 language families (Statistics Canada 2012) (Map 15.2; Table 15.1). Each of these languages forms a crucial part of the history and cultural identity of the people who speak it, and of the people whose ancestors spoke it in the past. Thus, language revitalization is an essential component of cultural revitalization. Moreover, it is essential to the revival of Indigenous knowledge and to efforts toward self-governance and the promotion of Indigenous rights (Battiste 2012). For many Indigenous people, speaking their traditional language is not only an expression of identity, it is also an assertion of empowerment.

Despite a lengthy history of language loss, especially as a result of residential schooling, many Indigenous people today maintain hope for the success of their endeavours to revitalize their traditional languages.

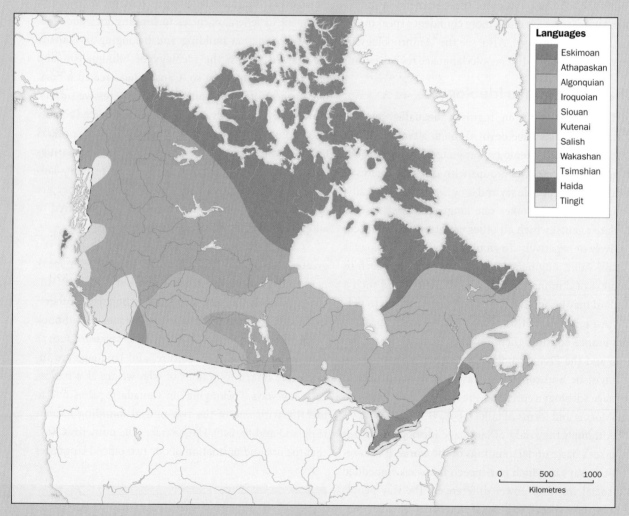

Languages
- Eskimoan
- Athapaskan
- Algonquian
- Iroquoian
- Siouan
- Kutenai
- Salish
- Wakashan
- Tsimshian
- Haida
- Tlingit

0   500   1000
Kilometres

MAP 15.2 Traditional distribution of Indigenous language groups, before contact with Europeans.

TABLE 15.1 Number and Location of Native Speakers of Indigenous Languages, Canada, 2011

Indigenous Language Families and Main Languages	Provincial and Territorial Main Concentrations	Number of Speakers[a]
Algonquian Languages	**Manitoba (24.7%), Quebec (23.0%)**	**144,015**
Cree languages	Saskatchewan (28.8%), Manitoba (24.0%), Alberta (21.9%), and Quebec (18.5%)	83,475
Ojibway	Ontario (46.3%) and Manitoba (44.3%)	19,275
Innu/Montagnais	Quebec (80.9%) and Newfoundland and Labrador (18.7%)	10,965
Oji-Cree	Manitoba (69.1%) and Ontario (30.7%)	10,180
Mi'kmaq	Nova Scotia (60.2%) and New Brunswick (27.5%)	8,030
Atikamekw	Quebec (99.9%)	5,915
Blackfoot	Alberta (97.5%)	3,250
Inuit (Eskimoan) Languages	**Nunavut (61.6%) and Quebec (31.3%)**	**35,500**
Inuktitut	Nunavut (63.1%) and Quebec (32.3%)	34,110
Athapaskan Languages	**Saskatchewan (40.5%) and Northwest Territories (22.7%)**	**20,700**
Dene	Saskatchewan (70.6%) and Alberta (15.2%)	11,860
Tlicho (Dogrib)	Northwest Territories (96.2%)	2,080
Slavey[b]	Northwest Territories (85.9%)	1,595
Carrier	British Columbia (98.0%)	1,525
Siouan Languages	**Alberta (76.9%) and Manitoba (16.6%)**	**4,425**
Stoney	Alberta (99.5%)	3,155
Dakota	Manitoba (62.5%) and Alberta (21.6%)	1,160
Salish Languages	British Columbia (98.0%)	2,950
Shuswap (Secwepemctsin)	British Columbia (97.0%)	675
Halkomelem	British Columbia (98.2%)	570
Tsimshian Languages	**British Columbia (98.1%)**	**1,815**
Gitksan	British Columbia (98.9%)	925
Nisga'a	British Columbia (96.7%)	615
Wakashan Languages	**British Columbia (95.3%)**	**1,075**
Kwakiutl (Kwak'wala)	British Columbia (98.0%)	495
Nootka (Nuu-chah-nulth)	British Columbia (90.6%)	320
Iroquoian Languages	**Ontario (82.7%) and Quebec (10.6%)**	**1,040**
Mohawk	Ontario (73.4%) and Quebec (18.3%)	545
Michif[c]	**Saskatchewan (40.6%), Manitoba (26.6%), and Alberta (11.7%)**	**640**
Tlingit	**Yukon (84.6%) and British Columbia (11.5%)**	**130**
Kutenai	**British Columbia (100%)**	**100**
Haida	**British Columbia (93.3%)**	**75**
Indigenous Languages[d]	**British Columbia (43.6%) and Ontario (30.2%)**	**1,010**
Total Indigenous Mother–Tongue Population	**Quebec (20.9%), Manitoba (17.7%), and Saskatchewan (16.0%)**	**213,490**

[a] Counts for languages within a family; do not add to the total of the language family because only the main languages are shown.
[b] Not otherwise specified.
[c] Michif is the traditional language of the Métis.
[d] Not included elsewhere.

Source: Statistics Canada. 2012. "Population with an Aboriginal Mother Tongue by Language Family, Main Languages within These Families, and Their Main Provincial and Territorial Concentrations, Canada, 2011." Table 1 in Aboriginal Languages in Canada. Catalogue no. 98-314-X2011003. Ottawa: Statistics Canada. http://www12.statcan.gc.ca/census-recensement/2011/as-sa/98-314-x/98-314-x2011003_3-eng.pdf

Continued

Many also refuse to consider those languages that have no fluent speakers as "extinct," instead referring to them as "sleeping languages" that can be "awakened" with effort (Huang 2009). In many communities, a major form this effort takes is the establishment of Indigenous-run language classes for young people. The hope among many Indigenous people is that by taking back responsibility for educating their children, they may one day be able to undo much of the cultural damage done by the legacy of the residential school system. And, in many communities, these efforts seem to be having a positive effect, as growing numbers of younger Indigenous Canadians are learning the language of their ancestors as a second language (Norris 2007). While learning these languages as second rather than first languages is not an ideal solution, it is an essential part of the process of language revitalization in situations where parents are no longer able to teach their children the language of their ancestors because they themselves are not fluent in that language (Norris 2007).

What role can anthropologists play in these sorts of community-based approaches to language revitalizations? A central goal for many linguistic anthropologists working in this realm is to record and document Indigenous languages as they are used by native speakers. These recordings can be very useful when working with elders who may have forgotten their native language, as listening to recordings of the language can reignite their memory and help them strengthen their language skills. Anthropological research can also help project leaders identify the most effective approaches, tools, and programs for working with any given group. For example, the Nunavut government has drawn on such research in creating television shows that teach Inuktitut to children and in planning language classes and speaking groups for adults. At the same time, input from anthropologists should never replace the voices of the people of the communities in which the programs are being run. To succeed, language revitalization initiatives must be collaborative, with community members playing a central role in their development and their implementation.

Source: http://indigenousfoundations.arts.ubc.ca/home/culture/languages.html

In Their Own Words

Borrowed Words, Mock Language, and Nationalism in Canada

Rachelle Vessey looks at how borrowed words are used as boundary markers by French- and English-speaking Canadians.

In Canada, where languages serve as symbols of the national divide, borrowed words used in discussions of the nation appear to have different meanings from their translation equivalents. They serve as a covert means of signalling group boundaries that are based not only on language, but also on the broader cultural elements that are indexed by languages. . . .

This study showed that *nationale* was used differently to *national* in English. . . . The term *nationale* seems to indirectly index French-speaking nationalism in Quebec, which appears to be marked as different from Canadian nationalism and predominantly negatively evaluated. As a result, the English use of the borrowed form *nationale* arguably constitutes mock language. In a similar way, in the French corpus the terms *Canadian* and *Canadians* were used differently to *Canadien/s* and *Canadienne/s*. . . . In the French data, *Canadian/s* appears to refer to "belonging to or association with Canada," but also indirectly indexes an English-speaking country, which is suggested to be separate from Quebec. Thus, the implicature of English-Canada French-Quebec group difference indicates that the French use of the borrowed form *Canadian/s* also constitutes mock language.

These words not only achieve meaning through their direct context . . . but also gain meaning from the wider context of the Canadian linguistic situation. . . . These examples have demonstrated that borrowed words have especially important meaning in multilingual and multicultural contexts, and they pose particularly interesting challenges to researchers. This case study of only two borrowed words in Canada suggests different understandings of language and nationalism in two

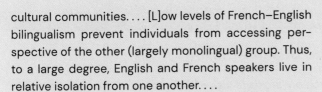

cultural communities. . . . [L]ow levels of French–English bilingualism prevent individuals from accessing perspective of the other (largely monolingual) group. Thus, to a large degree, English and French speakers live in relative isolation from one another. . . .

Perhaps ironically, many Canadians are not aware they live in isolation from the other group, because they see and hear speakers of the other official language (e.g., federal politicians and spokespeople) on a daily basis; however what they witness is often in translation. . . . [T]he other official language is rarely encountered in the original. . . . [R]ather than truly engaging the other language, Canadians sometimes use borrowed words to index belonging in specific linguistic and national communities.

Source: Vessey 2014, 186–7. Reprinted by permission of the publisher (Taylor & Francis Ltd, http://www.tandfonline.com).

creates a "convenient alibi for racial ordering" in a country that espouses multiculturalism. Bilingualism functions in a multiculturalist framework in Canada, creating unintended tensions and inequalities that are often contradictory in policy and in practice.

What Is Lost if a Language Dies?

At the beginning of the twenty-first century, many anthropologists and linguists have become involved in projects to maintain or revive languages with small numbers of native speakers. As touched on earlier in this chapter in relation to Indigenous languages in Canada, these languages are in danger of disappearing as younger people in the speech community stop using the language or never learn it in the first place. Communities concerned about language revitalization can range from Irish speakers in the United Kingdom to Mi'kmaq speakers in Nova Scotia to users of an Aboriginal sign language in Australia.

And the threats to these languages range widely as well. They include the spread of "world" languages, such as English, and the marginalization of one dialect in favour of a neighbouring dialect. They also include support for a "national" sign language (e.g., in Thailand) in place of local, "Indigenous" sign languages used by small communities, and the spread of technologies that can "save" people from being deaf (Walsh 2005). How seriously different "small languages" are endangered depends on what counts as small and how imminent the threat is perceived to be—and experts can differ in their evaluation of these matters.

Linguistic anthropologists have paid particular attention to Indigenous languages spoken by small communities who have experienced a history of colonization by outsiders and who are minorities within states where colonial languages dominate. At the same time, as Michael Walsh (2005) explains, Indigenous language situations are not all alike. In Guatemala, for example, "Mayan languages are spoken among a majority of the populations, and the languages are all closely related; so it is possible to have a more unified approach to Mayan language revitalization. Mayas in Guatemala are now using their languages in schools, and they are taking steps toward gaining official recognition of their languages" (296). Sometimes, however, colonial borders separate members of an Indigenous language community, meaning that speakers on one side of the border may be better supported in their language revitalization efforts than speakers on the other side of the border are. Examples include Ojibwe speakers (who are better supported in Canada than in the United States) and Quichua speakers (who receive different levels of support in Ecuador, Bolivia, and Peru) (Walsh 2005). And sometimes the ethnolinguistic practices of speakers can interfere with language retention: among Ilgar speakers in northern Australia, for example, conversation between opposite-sex siblings is forbidden. This means that a man finds himself "talking his mother tongue to people who don't speak it, and not talking it with the couple of people who do" (Evans 2001, 278; cited in Walsh 2005, 297).

Attempts to implement language revitalization have met with mixed success. Methods that work for literate groups (e.g., French speakers in Quebec) may be inappropriate for programs of language revival among speakers of languages that lack a long tradition of literacy, which is often the case with Indigenous languages in the Americas and Australia. In some cases, where prospects for revitalization are poor, it has been

In Their Own Words

Revitalizing Indigenous Languages in the Urban Amazon

Sarah Shulist of MacEwan University outlines her research on language loss and revitalization among the Kotiria, Indigenous peoples whose traditional homelands are in the northwest Amazon region of Brazil and Colombia. As Shulist notes, many Kotiria today face loss of their language as they move from rural areas to cities.

My work in the northwest Amazon of Brazil looks at the relationship between two of the most important social changes happening in the lives of Indigenous people, both in that region and in many others around the world—language shift and urbanization. Even though more and more of the world's Indigenous people are living in cities, language revitalization efforts are mainly being implemented in rural areas or recognized Indigenous territories/reserves. The presence of a larger and more diverse population, the disconnection from the territorial homeland, and the necessity of interaction with fundamentally different social structures and institutions make it very difficult to imagine ways of supporting Indigenous languages and cultures in these contexts.

The Kotiria (Wanano) people living in the city of São Gabriel da Cachoeira, Amazonas, are facing these challenges. In this small city of 13,000 people, 85 per cent of the population is Indigenous, and at least a dozen Indigenous languages are spoken by its inhabitants. The Kotiria's traditional territory is located in a remote part of the upper Uaupés (Vaupés) basin, in both Brazil and Colombia, and although there are only about 1000 speakers of the language left in total, the fact that it is still being learned as a first language by children in the rural areas means that it is in a stronger position than many other endangered languages of the world. The language has further been strengthened by the creation of a Kotiria-medium school within the Kotiria's traditional territory. This school is important both because it has led to an increase in materials available for learning and using the language, and because it has helped prevent the migration of families out of these communities in pursuit of educational opportunities for their children.

About 35 Kotiria families make their permanent homes in the city of São Gabriel, however, and the children born to those families do not formally learn the Kotiria language. In reflecting on their decision to live in an urban area, the parents of these children express less concern over the risk that the Kotiria language could disappear from use entirely—since they are confident that it remains strong in the rural communities—and more over the possibility that their children might become disconnected from their identities as Indigenous Kotiria people. Among the Kotiria, language is important not only to marking one's identity but also to coming to understand what it means to be Kotiria and what one's place in the world is. The Kotiria are one of many peoples in the northwest Amazon region who use language as a marker of kinship. This marker becomes particularly important when it comes to marriage, as individuals are required to marry someone from another language group (a practice known as "linguistic exogamy"). These social rules have meant that, among these groups, households were always made up of a mother who spoke one primary language and a father who spoke a different one. While children in the rural territories are usually raised speaking both languages of their parents (and often more), the fact that children use only one (the father's language) both to understand who they are and to determine who they can marry means that each person has a strong motivation to preserve his or her *own* language.

In the case of the Kotiria living in São Gabriel, the pressures created by urbanization include some that are common the world over and others that are unique to the Kotiria situation. Although small by North American standards, the size of São Gabriel means that speakers of Kotiria are dispersed throughout a relatively large population and do not encounter one another on a daily basis. Young people growing up in the city are influenced more by mainstream Brazilian (and global) entertainment than by Kotiria culture, and they prioritize romantic love matches over linguistic exogamy, reducing the importance they place on their linguistic choices. Kotiria adults—primarily the fathers, who are the ones expected to transmit their identities and cultural knowledge to their children—have to work in formal positions in order to earn money to support their family, which takes them away from their children during the bulk of the day. Their children, meanwhile, spend the majority of their days attending Portuguese-language schools. In the rural context, the patterns of subsistence agriculture and fishing incorporate children as they get older, and linguistic and cultural knowledge is transmitted as they accompany their parents in these routines.

The Kotiria demonstrate a central theme of language revitalization for urban Indigenous people—it is very difficult, if not impossible, to recreate the social and family structures that support the transmission of Indigenous languages in more traditional communities. For these people, who feel a very powerful sense of loss in seeing their children unable to speak their language, it is not enough to have documentary work that helps to ensure the continuity of their language in rural areas, when for various reasons they are unable to return to live in those communities. Despite the challenges they face, however, the urban Kotiria are beginning a process of recognizing that the effort needed to support their language is as much about the creation of new social

environments for using, transmitting, and discussing the language and cultural knowledge as it is about the development of pedagogical materials for teaching it. During my research visits to São Gabriel, I have helped to form an organization of Kotiria people, led by residents of the urban area, that will work to document and disseminate knowledge of their language and cultural practices in the city as well as in the rural communities. I have worked with members of this group in advocacy efforts to establish a Kotiria-medium school in the urban area, and to identify and understand the legal, ideological, and practical barriers that remain to be overcome in order to achieve this goal. We have also developed a set of strategies for the creation of new contexts in which the Kotiria language can be used, and for reaching young people who need to learn both the language and its importance for identity and cultural practice. Applying my anthropological training in order to better understand the social transformations taking place around language loss and the possibility of revitalization has led me to believe that linguistic anthropologists play a vital role in shaping effective programs and policy efforts.

Source: Courtesy of Sarah Shulist, 2015, MacEwan University.

suggested that the functions of the endangered language can be transferred to a different language. This is a well-known phenomenon in the case of colonial languages like Spanish and English, which have all experienced "indigenization" as the communities who adopt them tailor them to fit their own local communicative practices. Other scholars have pointed out that language loss is nothing new. In the ancient world, for example, the spread of Latin led to the extinction of perhaps 50 of the 60 or so languages spoken in the Mediterranean prior to 100 SCAP. However, the extension of Latin into ancient Europe also led to the birth of the Romance languages, some of whose native speakers (e.g., the French) express concern that the survival of their mother tongue is also threatened by the spread of global English (Sonntag 2003). New languages emerging from the processes of pidginization and creolization also continue to appear. For example, Copper Island Aleut is a hybrid of Russian and Aleut (Walsh 2005, 297).

Maintaining or reviving endangered languages faces many obstacles, not the least of which is the concern of many parents who care less about preserving their dying language than they do about making sure their children become literate in a world language that will offer them a chance at economic and social mobility. Some Indigenous groups are concerned that loss of language will mean loss of access to traditional sources of religious or spiritual power, which can only be addressed in the traditional tongue. Yet other Indigenous speakers would not like to see what was once a fully functioning mode of communication reduced to nothing but ceremonial use. Clearly, language endangerment is a very delicate topic of discussion. This is unfortunate, in Walsh's view, since practical solutions require "frank and forthright discussions of the issues . . . and good clear statements of advice" (2005, 308). But Walsh also believes that concerned people who want to save their languages ought to try to do what they can and not wait until scholarly experts arrive at consensus.

Anthropology in Everyday Life

Language Preservation in Baie Sainte-Marie: *Acadajonne ou Français?*

What is an endangered language? And why should such languages be saved? These questions framed the debates that occurred in the community of Baie Sainte-Marie, Nova Scotia, regarding *Acadajonne*, an endangered language thought by locals to represent an authentic form of French used in the late sixteenth and early seventeenth centuries. As Annette Boudreau and Lise Dubois (2007) discovered, the preservation of a language is often connected to political and symbolic values that are connected to social beliefs. Minority French-speaking communities outside of Quebec define themselves and their French language (sometimes referred to as *francité*) with respect to how they fit into the dominant anglophone society and the larger world of *la Francophonie* (worldwide speakers of French).

Baie Sainte-Marie is a small francophone community that exists within an anglophone-dominated region of Nova Scotia. The survival of the community is linked to its members' continued use of *Acadajonne*, which has significant historical meaning to them. Locals feel that their language connects them to their ancestors, French colonists who originally settled the Baie Sainte-Marie in 1604, were deported by the British in the late eighteenth century, and returned to reclaim the area by the mid-nineteenth century. This narrative of settlement, deportation, and resettlement creates a collective memory and sense of identity that ties the *Acadajonne* speakers of Baie Sainte-Marie together and to the region. Associated with residents' historical connection to place is the fact that *Acadajonne* is the oldest variety of French still spoken in North America. *Acadajonne* has numerous words that have survived since colonization. However, despite the importance of *Acadajonne* to those who speak it, there are both francophones who would suggest that this form of French is not worthy of being preserved and anglophones who would prefer English to be the only language used in the region.

While questions about the value of preserving *Acadajonne* as a distinct language have endured for generations, the debate intensified in the 1990s when a local community radio station began to use *Acadajonne* in its broadcasts. Today, those who support the use of what has long been a stigmatized form of French see the promotion of *Acadajonne* as a fight for legitimacy. Those who oppose its use suggest that it is not "proper" French and should therefore not be taught in schools or broadcast on airwaves; they suggest that widespread use of *Acadajonne* in the region may create a linguistic ghetto, or black hole, for *Acadajonne* speakers. In the course of their research, it became apparent to Boudreau and Dubois that the use of *Acadajonne* may be identified as a political resistance to the elite francophones in the area.

The power struggle between the two groups of francophones centres on the desire to gain social advantages through the use of language. And in this case, the promotion of tourism and commerce is an important consideration. Yet significant questions remain: Does the authenticity of Baie Sainte-Marie as an early French Acadian colony rest on whether or not *Acadajonne*, the language of the original settlers, continues to be used? Or is *Acadajonne* in fact a ghetto language that should be replaced with "proper" spoken French?

How Are Language and Truth Connected?

For the late Thomas Kuhn (1979), a philosopher of science, metaphor lay at the heart of science. Kuhn argued that changes in scientific theories were "accompanied by a change in some of the relevant metaphors and in corresponding parts of the network of similarities through which terms attach to nature" (416). Kuhn insisted that these changes in the way scientific terms link to nature are not reducible to logic or grammar: "They come about in response to pressures generated by observation or experiment"—that is, by experience and context. And there is no neutral language into which rival theories can be translated and subsequently evaluated as unambiguously right or wrong (416). Kuhn asks the question, "Is what we refer to as 'the world' perhaps a product of mutual accommodation between experience and language?" (416).

If our understanding of reality is the product of a dialectic between experience and language (or, more broadly, culture), then ambiguity will never be permanently removed from any of the symbolic systems that human beings invent. Reflexive consciousness makes humans aware of alternatives. The experience of doubt, of not being sure what to believe, is never far behind.

This is not merely the experience of people in Western societies. When E.E. Evans-Pritchard lived among the Azande of central Africa in the early twentieth century, he found that they experienced a similar form of disorientation (see EthnoProfile 16.6: Azande). The Azande people, he wrote, were well aware of the ambiguity inherent in language, and they exploited it by using metaphor (what they called *sanza*) to disguise speech that might be received badly if uttered directly. For example, "A man says in the presence of his wife to his friend,

'Friend, those swallows, how they flit about in there.' He is speaking about the flightiness of his wife and in case she should understand the allusion, he covers himself by looking up at the swallows as he makes his seemingly innocent remark" (Evans-Pritchard 1963, 211). Evans-Pritchard later observed that *sanza* "adds greatly to the difficulties of anthropological inquiry. Eventually the anthropologist's sense of security is undermined and his confidence shaken. He learns the language, can say what he wants to say in it, and can understand what he hears, but then he begins to wonder whether he has really understood. . . . [H]e cannot be sure, and even they [the Azande] cannot be sure, whether the words do have a nuance or someone imagines that they do" (228). However much we learn about language, we will never be able to exhaust its meanings or circumscribe its rules once and for all. Human language is an open system, and as long as human history continues, new forms will be created and old forms will continue to be put to new uses.

Chapter Summary

1. Symbolic language is a uniquely human faculty that both permits us to communicate with one another and sets up barriers to communication. The anthropological study of languages reveals the cultural factors that shape language use. Human symbolic language is also multifunctional, capable of performing many roles in speech events besides reference. In every language, there are many ways to communicate our experiences, and there is no absolute standard favouring one way over another. Individual efforts to create a unique voice are countered by pressures to negotiate a common code within a larger speech community.

2. Of Charles Hockett's design features of language, six are particularly important: openness, displacement, arbitrariness, duality of patterning, semanticity, and prevarication. Among other things, Charles Peirce's three-part theory of signs provides tools for explaining how human speakers link symbolic language to the wider world outside their heads.

3. Early linguistic anthropologists such as Edward Sapir and Benjamin Whorf suggested that language has the power to shape the way people see the world. This concept is called the "linguistic relativity principle." How this shaping process works is still investigated by some linguistic anthropologists, who argue that linguistic relativity should not be confused with linguistic determinism, which they reject.

4. Ethnopragmatics locates linguistic meaning in routine practical activities, which turn grammatical features of language into resources people can use in their interactions with others. It pays attention both to the immediate context of speech and to broader contexts that are shaped by unequal social relationships and rooted in history.

5. Because linguistic meaning is rooted in practical activity, which carries the burden of meaning, different social groups engaged in different activities generate different communicative practices. The linguistic habits that are part of each set of communicative practices constitute discourse genres. People normally command a range of discourse genres, which means that each person's linguistic knowledge is characterized by heteroglossia.

6. The study of pidgin languages is the study of the radical negotiation of new meaning. Pidgin languages exhibit many of the same linguistic features as non-pidgin languages. In colonial and postcolonial settings, the language of the colonizer is frequently viewed as superior to the language(s) of the colonized. The residential school system established in Canada in the 1880s for the forced assimilation of Indigenous children is an example of a dominant group's attempt to gain linguistic and cultural control over less powerful peoples in a postcolonial context.

7. Language ideologies are unwritten rules shared by members of a speech community concerning what kinds of language are valued. Language ideologies develop out of the cultural, social, and political histories of the groups to which they belong. Knowing the language ideology of a particular community can help listeners make sense of speech that otherwise would seem inappropriate or incomprehensible to them.

8. The design features of human language, particularly openness, seem to characterize human thought processes in general. The work of psychological anthropologists on human perception, cognition, and practical action overwhelmingly sustains the view that human psychological processes are open to a wide variety of influences.

online

For a thorough discussion of the descriptive aspects of language, see the Focus on Four Fields passage "Linguistic Anthropology: Components of Language" on the companion website.

For Review

1. What are the three reasons given in the text to explain why language is of interest to anthropologists? Explain why language is a key concept studied by anthropologists. How is it related to culture? How is it related to human biology?

2. Distinguish among language, speech, and communication. Explain the significance of these differences.

3. Summarize the key points for each of the six design features of language discussed in this chapter (openness, displacement, arbitrariness, duality of patterning, semanticity, and prevarication). How does each feature separate human language from the call systems used by monkeys and apes?

4. What is the difference between closed call systems and open symbolic languages?

5. Describe linguistic competence. How does it differ from communicative competence? Why do anthropologists draw a distinction between these two concepts?

6. Why do linguistic anthropologists emphasize the importance of context in language use?

7. What is the linguistic relativity principle? Summarize the problems with linguistic determinism, and describe the steps that contemporary linguists and linguistic anthropologists have taken to address these problems.

8. Explain the origins of pidgins and how this is an example of language inequality and colonization.

9. How was language used as a tool of power in residential schools in Canada? Include in your discussion the concept of language ideology.

10. What is language ideology? Summarize the case studies in this section of the text that analyze the language ideology of specific speech communities.

11. What is language revitalization? What are some of the difficulties in achieving language revitalization? What are some of the benefits? Use examples from this chapter in your answer.

Key Terms

body language 357
communicative competence 360
discourse 363
ethnopragmatics 363
grammar 354
historical linguistics 359

kinesics 357
language ideology 367
linguistic competence 360
linguistic relativity principle 362
linguistics 355
native speaker 356

non-verbal communication 357
pidgin 365
pragmatics 363
proxemics 358
sociolinguistics 361

References

Ahearn, Laura. 2016. *Living Language: An Introduction to Linguistic Anthropology*. 2nd ed. New York: Wiley-Blackwell.

Bakhtin, Mikhail M. 1981. *The Dialogic Imagination: Four Essays*. Edited by Michael Holquist. Translated by Michael Holquist and Caryl Emerson. Austin: University of Texas Press.

Battiste, Marie. 1986. "Micmac Literacy and Cognitive Assimilation." In *The Legacy*, edited by Jean Barman, Yvonne Hebert, and Don McCaskill, 23–44. Vol. 1 of Indian Education in Canada. Vancouver: UBC Press.

———. 2012. "Enabling the Autumn Seed: Toward a Decolonized Approach to Aboriginal Knowledge, Language, and Education." In *Schooling in Transition: Readings in Canadian History of Education*, edited by S.Z. Burke and P. MIlewski, 275–86. Toronto: University of Toronto Press.

Bliss, Heather, Sonya Bird, PEPAḴIYE Ashley Cooper, Strang Burton, and Bryan Gick. 2018. "Seeing Speech: Ultrasound-Based Multimedia Resources for Pronunciation Learning in Indigenous Languages" *Language Documentation & Conservation* 12: 315–38.

Boudreau, Annette, and Lise Dubois. 2007. "Francais, Acadien, Acadjonne: Competing Discourse on Language Preservation along the Shores of the Baie Sainte-Marie." In *Discourses of Endangerment*, edited by Alexandre Duchene and Monica Heller, 99–120. New York: Continuum Publishers.

Burling, Robbins. 2005. *The Talking Ape: How Language Evolved*. New York: Oxford University Press.

Chomsky, Noam. 1957. *Syntactic Structures*. Cambridge, MA: MIT Press.

———. 1965. *Aspects of the Theory of Syntax*. Cambridge, MA: MIT Press.

Clayman, Steven E. 2001. "Answers and Evasions." *Language in Society* 30 (3): 403–42.

Deacon, Terrence. 1997. *The Symbolic Species: The Co-evolution of Language and the Brain*. New York: W.W. Norton.

Duranti, Alessandro. 1994. *From Grammar to Politics: Linguistic Anthropology in a Western Samoan Village*. Berkeley: University of California Press.

Eckert, Penelope, and Sally McConnell-Ginet. 1992. "Think Practically and Look Locally: Language and Gender as Community-Based Practice" *Annual Review of Anthropology* 21: 461–90.

Elliot, Alison. 1981. *Child Language*. Cambridge: Cambridge University Press.

Evans-Pritchard, E.E. 1963. *Social Anthropology and Other Essays*. New York: Free Press.

Geertz, Clifford. 1960. *The Religion of Java*. New York: Free Press.

Gentner, Dedre, and Susan Goldin-Meadow. 2003. "Whither Whorf?" In *Language in Mind: Advances in the Study of Language and Thought*, edited by Dedre Gentner and Susan Goldin-Meadow, 3–14. Cambridge, MA: MIT Press.

Haig-Brown, Celia. 1988. *Resistance and Renewal: Surviving the Indian Residential School*. Vancouver: Tillacum Library.

Hall, Edward T. 1966. *The Hidden Dimension*. New York: Anchor Books.

Hanks, William. 1996. *Language and Communicative Practices*. Boulder, CO: Westview Press.

Haque, Eve. 2012. *Multiculturalism within a Bilingual Framework: Language, Race, and Belonging in Canada*. Toronto: University of Toronto Press.

Hill, Jane, and Judith Irvine, eds. 1992. *Responsibility and Evidence in Oral Discourse*. Cambridge: Cambridge University Press.

Hockett, Charles F. 1966. "The Problems of Universals in Language." In *Universals of Language*, edited by Joseph H. Greenberg, 1–29. Cambridge, MA: MIT Press.

Huang, Alice. 2009. "Languages: Aboriginal Languages in Canada." http://indigenousfoundations.arts.ubc.ca/home/culture/languages.html

Hymes, Dell. 1972. "On Communicative Competence." In *Sociolinguistics: Selected Readings*, edited by J.B. Pride and Janet Holmes, 269–93. Baltimore: Penguin.

Kuhn, Thomas. 1979. "Metaphor in Science." In *Metaphor and Thought*, edited by Andrew Ortony, 409–19. Cambridge: Cambridge University Press.

Lakoff, George, and Mark Johnson. 1980. *Metaphors We Live By*. Berkeley: University of California Press.

Lepage, Jean-François, and Jean-Pierre Corbeil. 2013. *The Evolution of English–French Bilingualism in Canada from 1961 to 2011*. Ottawa: Statistics Canada. http://www.statcan.gc.ca/pub/75-006-x/2013001/article/11795-eng.pdf

Norris, Mary Jane. 2007. "Aboriginal Languages in Canada: Emerging Trends and Perspectives on Second Language Acquisition." *Canadian Social Trends* 83 (Summer): 20.

Ortony, Andrew. 1979. "Metaphor: A Multidimensional Problem." In *Metaphor and Thought*, edited by Andrew Ortony, 1–18. Cambridge: Cambridge University Press.

Ottenheimer, Harriet Joseph. 2013. *The Anthropology of Language: An Introduction to Linguistic Anthropology*. 3rd ed. Belmont, CA: Wadsworth.

Romaniuk, Tanya. 2009. "The 'Clinton Cackle': Hillary Rodham Clinton's Laughter in News Interviews." *Crossroads of Language, Interaction, and Culture* 7: 17–49.

Sapir, Edward. (1933) 1966. *Culture, Language, and Personality*, edited by David Mandelbaum. Berkeley: University of California Press.

Schultz, Emily. 1990. *Dialogue at the Margins: Whorf, Bakhtin, and Linguistic Relativity*. Madison: University of Wisconsin Press.

Silverstein, Michael. 1976. "Shifters, Linguistic Categories, and Cultural Description." In *Meaning in Anthropology*, edited by Keith Basso and Henry Selby, 11–55. Albuquerque: University of New Mexico Press.

———. 1985. "The Functional Stratification of Language and Ontogenesis." In *Culture, Communication, and Cognition: Vygotskian Perspectives*, edited by James Wertsch, 205–35. Cambridge: Cambridge University Press.

Slobin, Dan. 1987. "Thinking for Speaking." *Proceedings of the Berkeley Linguistics Society* 13: 435–44.

———. 2003. "Language and Thought Online: Cognitive Consequences of Linguistic Relativity." In *Language in Mind: Advances in the Study of Language and Thought*, edited by Dedre Gentner and Susan Goldin-Meadow, 157–91. Cambridge, MA: MIT Press.

Sonntag, Selma K. 2003. *The Local Politics of Global English*. Lanham, MD: Lexington Books.

Statistics Canada. 2012. *Aboriginal Languages in Canada*. Catalogue no. 98-314-X2011003. Ottawa: Statistics Canada. http://www12.statcan.gc.ca/census-recensement/2011/as-sa/98-314-x/98-314-x2011003_3-eng.pdf

Truth and Reconciliation Commission of Canada. 2015. "Honouring the Truth, Reconciling for the Future: Summary of the Final Report of the Truth and Reconciliation Commission of Canada." http://www.trc.ca/assets/pdf/Honouring_the_Truth_Reconciling_for_the_Future_July_23_2015.pdf

Vessey, Rachelle. 2014. "Borrowed Words, Mock Language, and Nationalism in Canada." *Language and Intercultural Communication* 14 (2): 176–90.

Wallmann, Joel. 1992. *Aping Language*. Cambridge: Cambridge University Press.

Walsh, Michael. 2005. "Will Indigenous Languages Survive?" *Annual Review of Anthropology* 34: 293–315.

Woolard, Kathryn A. 1998. "Introduction: Language Ideology as a Field of Inquiry." In *Language Ideologies: Practice and Theory*, edited by Bambi Schieffelin, Kathryn Woolard, and Paul V. Kroskrity, 3–47. New York: Oxford University Press.

▲ *Mehndi* (temporary skin decoration drawn in dye derived from the henna plant) applied to the hands and feet is a wedding tradition in India and many other South Asian countries. Photo: gooddesign10/iStockphoto

16 How Do We Make Meaning?

Chapter Outline

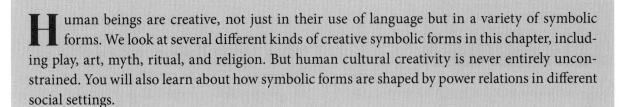

Human beings are creative, not just in their use of language but in a variety of symbolic forms. We look at several different kinds of creative symbolic forms in this chapter, including play, art, myth, ritual, and religion. But human cultural creativity is never entirely unconstrained. You will also learn about how symbolic forms are shaped by power relations in different social settings.

Building on the discussion of language and symbolism from the previous chapter, this chapter looks at human play, art, myth, ritual, and religion—dimensions of human experience in which the interplay of openness and creativity encounters rules and constraints, enabling people to produce powerful and moving symbolic practices that transform the character of human life. Map 16.1 illustrates the locations of the peoples referenced in this chapter.

What Is Play?

In Chapter 15, we explored the concept of "openness" in relation to language. *Openness* was defined as the ability to talk or think about the same thing in different ways and different things in the same way. If we expand openness to include all behaviour—that is, the ability not just to talk or think about but also to *do* the same thing in different ways or different things in the same way—we begin to define **play**. All mammals play, and humans play the most and throughout their lives.

Robert Fagen (1981, 1992, 2005) looks at play as a product of natural selection that may have significant fitness value for individuals in different species. Play gives young animals (including young human beings) the exercise they need to build up the skills necessary for physical survival as adults: fighting, hunting, or running away when pursued. Play may be important for the development of cognitive and motor skills and may be connected with the repair of developmental damage caused by either injury or trauma. It may also communicate the message "all's well," signalling "information about short-term and long-term health, general well-being, and biological fitness to parents, littermates, or other social companions" (Fagen 1992, 51). In species with more complex brains, playful exploration of the environment aids learning and allows for the development of behavioural versatility. Play also allows us to think symbolically and to imagine and

create systems of behaviour that lay at the heart of all cultures. Fagen (2005) suggests that play reflects natural selection for unpredictability. That is, to be able to produce unpredictable behaviours can be advantageous for an intelligent species faced with unanticipated adaptive challenges.

Evidence from archaeological sites suggests that play may have been an important aspect of childhood for our *Homo sapiens* ancestors and that it may in fact define our species' creative evolution and development of symbolic communication. Miniature artifacts that resemble full-size "adult" tools (e.g., bows and arrows, knives, scrapers, sewing needles) are interpreted as toys that children would have played with to learn essential skills necessary to become successful adults in their respective prehistoric cultures. These miniatures have been recovered from a variety of sites around the world, including Icelandic sites (Callow 2006), Mesoamerican sites (Joyce 2000), and Thule sites in the Canadian Arctic (Park 1998) (see the "Anthropology in Everyday Life" box on the archaeology of childhood). Evidence from various sites also suggests that children were apprentices, learning how to make their own artifacts using flint knapping (Högberg 2008) and potting techniques (Fewkes 1923; Smith 1998). In contrast, our closest hominin relatives, the Neanderthals, likely matured quickly, were less dependent on adults when they were young, and did not have time to play and be creative with toys, as their childhood was relatively short (Nowell 2013). Consequently, as April Nowell from the University of Victoria suggests, this lack of play time did not allow for Neanderthals to experience

play A framing (or orienting context) that is (1) consciously adopted by the players, (2) somehow pleasurable, and (3) systemically related to what is non-play by alluding to the non-play world and by transforming the objects, roles, actions, and relations of ends and means characteristic of the non-play world.

For a first-hand discussion of Nowell's research on Neanderthals and play, see the "In Their Own Words" box in Chapter 6, pp. 117–8.

"what if" fantasy games, test out artifacts, and experiment with different aspects of their world. It is highly likely that the "fantasy games" played by modern humans allowed for them to be more creative and to develop symbolic representations of their world (Nowell 2013, 29).

What Do We Think about Play?

Moving from everyday reality to the reality of play requires a radical transformation of perspective. To an outside observer, the switch from everyday reality to

Anthropology in Everyday Life

Archaeology of Childhood

Childhood can be a magical time—carefree days of toys and games. This is as true today as it was in prehistoric times. But, as every parent knows, child's play is serious business. It is how children learn to be grown-ups, to use the tools of adults, and to make their own place in society.

Although anthropologists have always been aware that children made up a significant proportion of prehistoric societies, the archaeological focus on children's activities is relatively new. Robert Park (1999), from the University of Waterloo, has done some novel work with "miniature" artifacts from Thule archaeological sites across Arctic Canada. His research provides a new perspective on the use of small artifacts and how children learned to become adults in prehistoric cultures. In his research, Park examines smaller versions of various utilitarian items, such as bows and arrows, and he suggests that these smaller artifacts were used by children to learn and practise how to be an adult in Thule culture. Ethnographic evidence from Inuit children collected by Diamond Jenness (1922) early in the twentieth century assists in the understanding of how children living in the Arctic played at being adults.

The Thule settled the Arctic Archipelago approximately 1000 years ago and adapted to their harsh surroundings by concocting an impressive array of highly specialized tools. The richness and diversity of their material culture is well represented in the archaeological record. The toys of the Thule children were almost as diverse as the tools and gadgets used by their parents. The remnants of these child-sized artifacts suggest nothing less than an extensive miniature material culture—one that can be plumbed by archaeologists just as surely as the full-sized culture it mimics.

Building on a rich body of ethnographic data drawn from oral traditions, records of casual visitors, and extensive studies by scholars, Park used data on more than 9700 artifacts (369 of which were miniatures) collected from 31 Thule sites in Canada and northern Greenland to explore childhood practices in the prehistoric Arctic. He divided the "miniature" artifacts into three broad categories that would be familiar to many children today: playing house, playing with dolls, and playing at hunting.

According to Jenness, playing house and playing at hunting were common practices among the Inuit children he observed. He noted that in summer the children liked to "set up house in an empty tent" (Jenness 1922, 170). In addition, "both boys and girls learn[ed] to stalk game by accompanying their elders on hunting excursions; their fathers [would] make bows and arrows for them suited to their strength" (170). One specific kind of play was restricted only to girls: that of making and playing with dolls. For boys, greater focus was placed on hunting activities where they learned how to use miniature harpoons to help pull ashore seals killed by the adults.

What is promising archaeologically about these kinds of findings is that they are clearly associated with a miniature material culture. The children at these sites engaged in a wide range of "play" that mimicked adult behaviour. This suggests that the Inuit practice of treating children as small adults was characteristic of their Thule ancestors as well. In a broader context, treating children as small adults is not unique to the Inuit of the early twentieth century or to the Thule of hundreds of years ago—the practice remains familiar to us today, although the degree to which it is expressed varies from culture to culture.

play reality may go undetected. However, sometimes the switch can have serious consequences for other people and their activities. In this case, play and non-play must be signalled clearly so that one is not mistaken for the other.

According to Gregory Bateson (1972), shifting into or out of play requires **metacommunication**, or communication about communication. Metacommunication provides information about the relationship between communicative partners. In play there are two kinds of metacommunication. The first, called **framing**, sends a message that marks certain behaviours either as play or as ordinary life. Dogs, for example, have a *play face*, a signal understood by other dogs (and recognizable by some human beings) indicating a willingness to play. If dogs agree to play, they bare their fangs and one animal attacks the other, but bites become nips. Both dogs have agreed to enter the *play frame*, an imaginative world in which bites do not mean bites. Within the play frame, a basic element of Western logic—that *A = A*—does not apply; the same thing is being treated in different ways. Human beings have many ways of marking the play frame: a smile, a particular tone of voice, a referee's whistle, or the words "Let's pretend." The marker says that "everything from now until we end this activity is set apart from everyday life." The second kind of metacommunication involves **reflexivity**. Play offers us the opportunity to think about the social and cultural dimensions of the world in which we live. By suggesting that ordinary life can be understood in more than one way, play can be a way of speculating about what can be rather than about what should be or what is (Handelman 1977, 186). When we say that jokes keep us from taking ourselves too seriously, for example, we are engaging in reflexive metacommunication. Joking allows us to consider alternative, even ridiculous, explanations for our experience.

What Are Some of the Effects of Play?

Helen Schwartzman (1978, 232–45) has demonstrated how play, through satire and clowning, may allow children to comment on and criticize the world of adults. A powerful example of this kind of commentary is described by anthropologist Elizabeth Chin (1999), who studied African American girls and their dolls in Newhallville, a working-class and poor neighbourhood

Courtesy Robert H. Lavenda

FIGURE 16.1 Play enables this girl in Guider, Cameroon, to incorporate her European doll into the world she knows.

in New Haven, Connecticut. Although "ethnically correct" dolls are on the market, very few of the girls had them because they cost too much. The poor children Chin knew in Newhallville had white dolls. But in their play these girls transformed their dolls in a powerful way by giving them hairstyles like their own. The original designers gave the dolls smooth, flowing hair to be brushed over and over again and put into a ponytail. But the girls' dolls had beads in their hair, braids held at the end with twists of aluminum foil or barrettes, and braids that were themselves braided together (315). Chin observes,

metacommunication Communication about the process of communication.

framing A cognitive boundary that marks certain behaviours as "play" or as "ordinary life."

reflexivity Critical thinking about the way one thinks; reflection on one's own experience.

In some sense, by doing this, the girls bring their dolls into their own worlds, and whiteness here is not absolutely defined by skin and hair, but by style and way of life. The complexities of racial references and racial politics have been much discussed in the case of black hair simulating the look of whiteness; what these girls are creating is quite the opposite: white hair that looks black. (315)

It is not that the girls did not realize that their dolls were white; it is that through their imaginative and material work they were able to integrate the dolls into their own world. The overt physical characteristics of the dolls—skin colour, facial features, hair—did not force the girls into treating the dolls in ways that obeyed the boundaries of racial difference. Their transformative play does not make the realities of poverty, discrimination, and racism disappear from the worlds in which they live; but Chin points out that "in making their white dolls live in black worlds, they . . . reconfigure the boundaries of race" and in so doing "challenge the social construction not only of their own blackness, but of race itself as well" (318) (Figure 16.1).

What Is Art?

In Western societies, art includes sculpture, drawing, painting, dance, theatre, music, and literature, as well as such similar processes and products as film, photography, mime, mass media production, oral narrative, festivals, and national celebrations. These are the kinds of objects and activities that first caught the attention of anthropologists who wanted to study art in non-Western societies. Whether non-Western peoples referred to such activities or products as "art," however, is a separate question. People everywhere engage in these kinds of playful creativity, yet activities defined as "art" differ from free play because they are circumscribed by rules. Artistic rules direct particular attention to, and provide standards for evaluating, the *form* of the activities or objects that artists produce.

Is There a Definition of Art?

Anthropologist Alexander Alland (1977, 39) defines **art** as "play with form producing some aesthetically

> **art** Play with form producing some aesthetically successful transformation-representation.

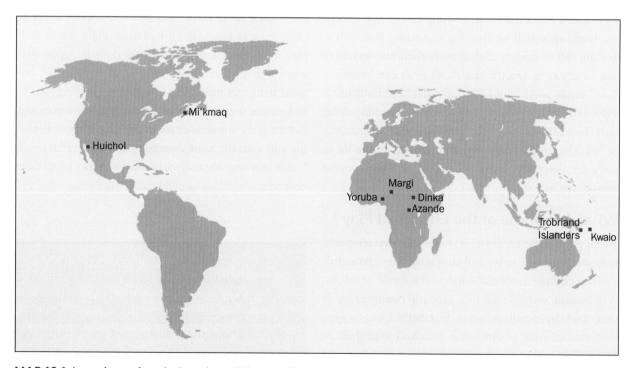

MAP 16.1 Locations of societies whose EthnoProfiles appear in Chapter 16.

successful transformation-representation." For Alland, *form* refers to the rules of the art game: the culturally appropriate restrictions on the way this kind of play may be organized in time and space. We can also think about form in terms of style and media. A *style* is a schema (a distinctive patterning of elements) that is recognized within a culture as appropriate to a given medium. The media themselves in which art is created and executed are culturally recognized and characterized (Anderson 1990, 272–5). A painting is a form: it is two-dimensional; it is done with paint; it is intentionally made; it represents or symbolizes something in the world outside the canvas, paper, or wood on which it is created. There are different kinds of paintings as well. There is the painting form called "portrait"—a portrait depicts a person, it resembles the person in some appropriate way, it is done with paint, it can be displayed, and more.

By "aesthetic," Alland (1977, xii) means appreciative of, or responsive to, form in art or nature. "Aesthetically successful" means that the creator of the piece of art (and possibly its audience) responds positively or negatively to it ("I like this," "I hate this"). Indifference is the sign of something that is aesthetically unsuccessful. It is probably the case that the aesthetic response is a universal feature in all human societies.

Aesthetic value judgments guide the artist's choice of form and material; they also guide the observers' evaluations. This implies that art involves more than just objects. V.N. Voloshinov ([1926] 1987) argues that art is a creative "event of living communication" (107), making it similar to ritual practices and involving the work, the artist, and the artist's audience. Artists create their works with an audience in mind, and audiences respond to these works as if the works were addressed to them. Sometimes their response is enthusiastic; sometimes it is highly critical. In addition, if aesthetic creation involves more than just the end product, such as a painting or a poem, attention needs to be paid to the process through which some product is made. James Vaughan (1973, 186) points out, for example, that the Margi of northeastern Nigeria do not appreciate a folktale as a story per se but, rather, enjoy the *performance* of it (see EthnoProfile 16.1: Margi).

To understand what Alland means by "transformation-representation," we can recall that the link between a symbol and what it represents is arbitrary. This means that symbols can be separated from the object or idea represented and appreciated for their own sake. They

EthnoProfile 16.1

Margi

Region: Western Africa

Nation: Nigeria

Population: 100,000 to 200,000 (1960s)

Environment: Mountains and plains

Livelihood: Farming, selling surplus in local markets

Political organization: Traditionally, kingdoms; today, part of a modern nation-state

For more information: Vaughan, James. 2006. *The Mandara Margi: A Society Living on the Verge.* www.indiana.edu/~margi

may also be used to represent a totally different meaning. Because transformation and representation depend on each other, Alland (1977, 35) suggests that they be referred to together (i.e., as transformation-representation). When a Javanese leather–puppet maker makes a puppet of the great mythic hero Arjuna, for example, he is representing the traditional form of the hero in his work, but he is also transforming a three-dimensional human form into a two-dimensional flat puppet made of buffalo hide, in which the colours, style, inclination of the head, and adornment stand for the internal state of the hero at a specific moment (Figure 16.2). At the same time, he is carrying out this work more or less skilfully and

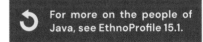
For more on the people of Java, see EthnoProfile 15.1.

is representing in his work the meanings that Arjuna carries for his Javanese audience.

Alland's definition of *art* attempts to capture something universal about human beings and cultural creativity. Similarly, anthropologist Shelly Errington (1998, 84) observes that all human cultures have "'symbolic forms': artifacts, activities, or even aspects of the landscape that humans view as densely meaningful." One dramatic example of this in Canada is the National War Memorial in Ottawa, which has a profound emotional impact on hundreds of thousands of people who visit it each year (see Figure 16.3). The memorial continues to draw offerings from visitors, not just wreaths and flowers but also messages of all kinds remembering those memorialized.

FIGURE 16.2 One of the great mythic heroes of Javanese *wajang* is represented here in a beautifully painted flat leather shadow puppet. The colour of the image; the angle of the head; the shape of the eye; the position of the fingers; and the style, colour, and quantity of the clothing all represent the inner state of the hero.

"But Is It *Art*?"

Many people—anthropologists included—have resisted the notion that art is only what a group of Western experts define as art. To highlight the ethnocentrism of Western art experts, they stressed that the division into categories of art and non-art is not universal. In many societies, there is no word that corresponds to *art*, nor is there a category of art distinct from other human activities. On the other hand, convinced that all people were endowed with the same aesthetic capacities, anthropologists felt justified in speaking of art and of artists in non-Western societies. Their goal was to recognize a fully human capacity for art in all societies and to redefine art until it became broad enough to include on an equal basis aesthetic products and activities that Western art

experts would qualify, at best, as "primitive," "ethnic," or "folk" art.

For example, some anthropologists focused on the evaluative standards that artists use for their own work and other work in the same form and how these may differ from the standards used by people who do not themselves perform such work. Anthony Forge (1967), for example, notes that Abelam carvers in New Guinea discuss carvings in a language that is more incisive than that of non-carvers. Forge and other anthropologists point out that artists in traditional non-Western societies created objects or engaged in activities that reinforced the central values of their culture. Thus, their work helped to maintain the social order, and the artists did not see themselves (nor were they understood to be) avant-garde critics of society as they often are in modern Western societies. Forge (1967) tells us that Abelam artworks are statements about male violence and warfare, male nurturance, and the combination of the two. These statements about the nature of men and their culture are not made by other means of communication, such as speech. Moreover, these statements are essential to Abelam social structure.

Recent work in the anthropology of art, however, has prompted many anthropologists to rethink this position. They have turned their attention to the way certain kinds of material objects made by tribal peoples flow into a global art market, where they are transformed into "primitive" or "ethnic" art. Some anthropologists, like Shelly Errington (1998), point out that even in the

FIGURE 16.3 The National War Memorial in Ottawa recognizes the importance of those who have given up their lives in times of conflict.

West many of the objects in fine arts museums today, no matter where they came from, were not intended by their makers to be "art." They were intended to be, for example, masks for ritual use, paintings for religious contemplation, reliquaries for holding the relics of saints, ancestor figures, furniture, jewellery boxes, architectural details, and so on. They are in fine arts museums today because at some point they were claimed to be art by someone with the authority to put them in the museum (Figure 16.4).

For these reasons, Errington distinguishes "art by intention" from "art by appropriation." Art by intention includes objects that were made to be art, such as Impressionist paintings. Art by appropriation, however, consists of all the other objects that "became art" because at a certain moment certain people decided that they belonged to the category of art. Because museums, art dealers, and art collectors are found everywhere in the world today, it is now the case that potentially any material object crafted by human hands can be appropriated by these institutions as "art."

To transform an object into art, Errington (1998) argues, it must have *exhibition value*—that is, someone must be willing to display it. Objects that somehow fit into the Western definition of art will be selected for the art market as "art." Looking at the objects that over the years have been defined as "art," Errington sees that the vast majority show certain elements to be embedded rather deeply in the Western definition of art: the objects are "portable (paintings, preferred to murals), durable (bronze preferred to basketry), useless for practical

purposes in the secular West (ancestral effigies and Byzantine icons preferred to hoes and grain grinders), representational (human and animal figures preferred to, say, heavily decorated ritual bowls)" (116–17). In other words, for Errington, art requires that someone *intend* that the objects be art, but that someone does not have to be the object's creator.

It can be fruitful to talk about art as a kind of play. Like play, art presents its creators and participants with alternative realities, a separation of means from ends, and the possibility of commenting on and transforming the everyday world. In today's global art market, however, restrictions of an entirely different order also apply. Errington (1998, 268) observes that the people who make "primitive art" are no longer "tribal" but have become

> modern-day peasants or a new type of proletariat. . . . They live in rain forests and deserts and other such formerly out-of-the-way places on the peripheries . . . within national and increasingly global systems of buying and selling, of using natural and human resources, and of marketing images and notions about products. Some lucky few of them make high ethnic art, and sell it for good prices, and obtain a good portion of the proceeds. Others make objects classed as tourist or folk art, usually for much less money, and often through a middleperson.

Others fulfill orders from elsewhere, "producing either masses of 'folk art' or expensive handmade items designed by people in touch with world taste and world markets" (269). Errington points out the bitter irony that international demand for "exotic" objects is growing at the very moment when the makers of these objects are severely threatened by international economic policies and resource-extraction projects that impoverish them and undermine the ways of life that give the objects they make their "exotic" allure. It should also be noted that what counts as fashionable decoration this year—"world taste"—may be out of fashion next year, leaving the producers with very little to fall back on.

"She's Fake": Art and Authenticity

Michelle Bigenho is an anthropologist and violinist whose multi-sited ethnography examines music performance in Bolivia, in part through her experiences performing with Música de Maestros (Figure 16.5).

FIGURE 16.4 Non-Western sculpture is transformed into art when it is displayed like Western art in a museum and viewed by members of the public who have the opportunity to look at it intensively (in this case, by Prince Charles).

Express Newspapers via AP Images

FIGURE 16.5 Música de Maestros in costume performing in a folklore festival in France.

This ensemble performs the works of master Bolivian composers of the past and attempts to recreate accurate performances of contemporary original music that they have studied in the countryside (Bigenho 2002, 4). During the time that Bigenho was part of the ensemble, there were both classically trained and traditionally trained musicians, of which three were foreigners: a Japanese musician who played the Andean flute; a Cuban musician who played violin; and Bigenho, an American, who also played violin. Along with a local dance ensemble, the musicians were invited to represent Bolivia in a folklore festival in France. As the bands were lining up, a member of the Belgian delegation walked over to Bigenho and announced, in French, "She's fake." The Belgian woman then "pointed to one of the Bolivian dancers dressed in her dancing costume with her long fake braids worked into her short brown hair. As she pointed, she said, 'She's real'" (88).

In this way, Bigenho (2002) raises the issue of the connection between "authenticity" and so-called folk art. How do the images that people in dominant nations have of "folk" or Indigenous peoples affect the production and circulation of Indigenous art? Can a Bolivian band include musicians from Japan, Cuba, and the United States and still be Bolivian? And who gets to decide what is authentic? Bigenho discusses a kind of authenticity that she calls "unique authenticity," which refers to the individual artist's new, innovative, and personal production, such as the original compositions of creative musicians. Unique authenticity is "the founding myth of modern concepts of authorship and copyright" (20). It concerns who owns cultural products and raises the issue of whether it is possible

to talk about collective creation and ownership of the music of a community, a people, or an ethnic group.

Bigenho came face to face with this issue when she compiled a cassette of music from one of the villages in which she worked. While the villagers recognized that the music they played was composed by individuals, they felt strongly that ownership of the music was collective. In doing so, they moved from uniquely authentic individual compositions—intellectual property—to collective ownership of a "culturally authentic representation"—cultural property (Bigenho 2002, 217). She discussed with the villagers how to register the copyright on the cassette. When Bigenho went to La Paz to register the copyright, however, she found that it was impossible to register the cassette under collective authorship or ownership. Ironically, *she* as the compiler could register the work but the people who created the work could not, unless they were willing to be recognized as individuals. According to Bolivian law, the music on the cassette was legally folklore,

> the set of literary and artistic works created in national territory by unknown authors or by authors who do not identify themselves and are presumed to be nationals of the country, or of its ethnic communities, and that are transmitted from generation to generation, constituting one of the fundamental elements of traditional cultural patrimony of the nation. (Bigenho 2002, 221)

As a result, the music was part of the "national patrimony" and belonged to the nation-state. Given the context of Bolivian cultural and ethnic politics, Bigenho reports that the villagers decided to try to gain visibility and connections as a collective Indigenous entity, which they believed would provide them with possible economic advantages; whether this belief was accurate remains to be seen. But similar struggles over the relationship between art and authenticity can be found all over the world.

What Is Myth?

We have suggested that play lies at the heart of human creativity. However, because the openness of play seems random, and thus just as likely to undermine the social order as to enhance it, societies tend to surround play with cultural rules, channelling it in directions that appear less destructive. Rules designed to discipline artistic expression

FIGURE 16.6 A vase painting illustrating part of the Popol Vuh, the Mayan creation story.

are one result of this channelling process. As we have seen, artists in various media are permitted a wide range of expression as long as they adhere to rules governing the form that expression takes. Societies differ in how loose or strict the rules of artistic form may be. Artists who challenge the rules, however, are often viewed negatively by those in power, who believe they have the right to restrict artistic expressions that question social, religious, or sexual precepts that ought not to be questioned.

In fact, all societies depend on the willingness of their members to not question certain assumptions about the way the world works. Because the regularity and predictability of social life might collapse altogether if people were free to imagine and act upon their own understandings of the world, most societies find ways to restrict the available options through the use of myth. Many people take the word *myth* to mean something that is false. But for anthropologists, **myths** are stories that recount how various aspects of the world came to be the way they are. The power of myths comes from their ability to make life meaningful for those who accept them. The truth of myths seems self-evident because they do such a good job of integrating personal experiences with a wider set of assumptions about how the world works. As stories that involve a teller and an audience, myths are products of high verbal art (and increasingly of cinematic art). Frequently, the official myth-tellers are the ruling groups in society: Indigenous elders, political leaders, religious specialists. They may also be considered master storytellers. The content of myths usually concerns past events (usually at the beginning of time) or future events (usually at the end of time). Myths are socially important because, if they are taken literally, they tell people where they have come from and where they are going and, thus, how they should live right now (Figure 16.6).

Societies differ in the degree to which they permit speculation about key myths. In complex Western societies, such as Canada, many different groups, each with its own mythic tradition, often live side by side. Multiculturalism is often toted as the dominant Canadian myth, which assumes that we are highly accepting of a wide variety of cultures and their beliefs. However, this is not always the case, and some groups appear to have higher status than others. For example, Canada's Official Languages Act gives English and French special status as the country's official languages and requires that government documents be prepared in both languages. In addition, our consumer packaging and labelling laws require that almost all items sold in Canada have labels that are written in both English and French. These laws uphold the power of the founding colonial powers, but they disregard the importance of Indigenous peoples and other groups in the country whose first language is neither English nor French.

Myths and related beliefs that are taken to be self-evident truths are sometimes codified in an explicit manner. When this codification is extreme and deviation from the code is treated harshly, we sometimes speak of **doctrine**. Societies differ in the degree to which they require members to adhere to orthodox interpretations of key myths. But even societies that place little emphasis on doctrine are likely to exert some control over the

> **myths** Stories that recount how various aspects of the world came to be the way they are. The power of myths comes from their ability to make life meaningful for those who accept them.
>
> **doctrine** Religious beliefs expressed through written and formal statements concerning the supernatural.

interpretation of key myths because myths have implications for action. They may justify past action, explain present action, or generate future action. To be persuasive, myths must offer plausible explanations for our experience of human nature, human society, and human history.

The success of Western science has led many members of Western societies to dismiss non-scientific myths as flawed attempts at science or history. Only recently have some scientists come to recognize the similarities between scientific and non-scientific storytelling about such events as the origin of life on earth. Scientific stories about origins, *origin myths*, must be compared and tested against material evidence in the natural world; the success of this match determines whether they are accepted or rejected. By contrast, non-scientific origin myths get their vitality from how well they match up with the social world.

How Does Myth Reflect—and Shape—Society?

Early in the twentieth century, anthropologist Bronislaw Malinowski introduced a new approach to myth. He believed that to understand myths we must understand the social context in which they are embedded. Malinowski argued that myths serve as "charters" or "justifications" for present-day social arrangements. In other words, a myth operates much like the Canadian Charter of Rights and Freedoms. That is, the myth contains some "self-evident" truth that explains why society is as it is and why it cannot be changed. If the social arrangements justified by the myth are challenged, the myth can be used as a weapon against the challengers.

Malinowski's ([1926] 1948) famous example is of the origin myths of the Trobriand Islanders (see EthnoProfile 16.2: Trobriand Islanders). Members of every significant kinship grouping knew, marked, and retold the history of the place from which their group's ancestress and her brother had emerged from the depths of the earth. These origin myths were set in the time before history began. Each ancestress-and-brother pair brought a distinct set of characteristics that included special objects and knowledge, as well as various skills, crafts, spells, and the like. On reaching the surface, the pair took possession of the land. That is why, Malinowski was told, the people on a given piece of land had rights to it. It is also why they possessed a particular set of spells, skills, and crafts. Because the original sacred beings were a woman and her brother,

EthnoProfile 16.2

Trobriand Islanders

Region: Oceania

Nation: Papua New Guinea

Population: 8500 (1970s)

Environment: Tropical island

Livelihood: Yam growing

Political organization:
Traditionally, chiefs and others of rank; today, part of a modern nation–state

For more information: Weiner, Annette. 1988. *The Trobrianders of Papua New Guinea*. New York: Holt, Rinehart, and Winston.

the origin myth could also be used to endorse present-day membership in a Trobriand clan, which depends on a person's ability to trace kinship links through women to that clan's original ancestress. A brother and a sister represent the prototypical members of a clan because they are both descended from the ancestress through female links. Should anyone question the wisdom of organizing society in this way, the myth could be cited as proof that this is indeed the correct way to live.

In Trobriand society, Malinowski found, clans were ranked relative to one another in terms of prestige. To account for this ranking, Trobrianders referred to another myth, or oral story, that helps to teach proper clan identity. In the Trobriand myth that explains rank, one clan's ancestor, the dog, emerged from the earth before another clan's ancestor, the pig, thus justifying ranking the dog clan highest in prestige. To believe in this myth, Malinowski asserted, is to accept a transcendent justification for the ranking of clans. Malinowski made it clear, however, that if social arrangements change, the myth changes, too—in order to justify the new arrangements. At some point, the dog clan was

↻ Detailed descriptions of various ways in which different cultures define kinship relationships can be found in Chapter 12, pp. 261–4.

replaced in prominence by the pig clan. This social change resulted in a change in the mythic narrative. The dog was said to have eaten food that was taboo. In so doing, the dog gave up its claim to higher rank. Thus, to understand a myth and its transformations, one must understand the social organization of the society that makes use of it.

Do Myths Help Us Think?

Beginning in the mid-1950s, a series of books and articles by the French anthropologist Claude Lévi-Strauss (1967) transformed the study of myth. Lévi-Strauss argues that myths have meaningful structures that are worth studying in their own right, quite apart from the uses to which the myths may be put. He suggests that myths should be interpreted the way we interpret musical scores. In a piece of music, the meaning emerges not just from the melody but also from the harmony. In other words, the structure of the piece of music, the way in which each line of the music contributes to the overall sound and is related to other lines, carries the meaning.

For Lévi-Strauss, myths are tools for overcoming logical contradictions that cannot otherwise be overcome. They are put together in an attempt to deal with the oppositions of particular concern to a particular society at a particular moment in time. Using a linguistic metaphor, Lévi-Strauss argues that myths are composed of smaller units—phrases, sentences, words, relationships—that are arranged in ways that give both a linear, narrative (or "melodic") coherence and a multilevel, structural (or "harmonic") coherence. These arrangements represent and comment on aspects of social life that are thought to oppose each other. Examples include the opposition of men to women; opposing rules of residence after marriage (e.g., living with the groom's father or the bride's mother); the opposition of the natural world to the cultural world, of life to death, of spirit to body, of high to low, and so on.

The complex syntax of myth works to relate those opposed pairs to one another in an attempt to overcome their contradictions. However, these contradictions can never be overcome; for example, the opposition of death to life is incapable of any earthly resolution. But myth can transform an insoluble problem into a more accessible, concrete form. Mythic narrative can then provide the concrete problem with a solution. For example, a culture hero may bridge the opposition between death and life by travelling from the land of the living to the land of the dead and back. Alternatively, a myth might propose that the beings who transcend death are so horrific that death is clearly preferable to eternal life. Perhaps a myth describes the journey of a bird that travels from the earth, the home of the living, to the sky, the home of the dead. This is similar to Christian thought, where the death and resurrection of Jesus may be understood to resolve the opposition between death and life by transcending death.

From this point of view, myths do not just talk about the world as it is but also describe the world as it might be. To paraphrase Lévi-Strauss, myths are good to think with; mythic thinking can propose other ways to live our lives. Lévi-Strauss insists, however, that the alternatives that myths propose are ordinarily rejected as impossible. Thus, even though myths allow for play with self-evident truths, this play remains under strict control.

Is Lévi-Strauss correct? There has been a great deal of debate on this issue since the publication in 1955 of his article "The Structural Study of Myth" (see Lévi-Strauss 1967). But even those who are most critical of his analyses of particular myths agree that mythic structures are meaningful because they display the ability of human beings to play with possibilities as they attempt to deal with basic contradictions at the heart of human experience.

For Malinowski, Lévi-Strauss, and their followers, those who believe in myths are not conscious of how their myths are structured or of the functions their myths perform for them. More recent anthropological thinking takes a more reflexive approach. This research recognizes that ordinary members of a society often *are* aware of how their myths structure meaning, allowing them to manipulate the way myths are told or interpreted in order to make an effect, to prove a point, or to buttress a particular perspective on human nature, society, or history.

What Is Ritual?

Play allows unlimited consideration of alternative perspectives on reality. Art permits consideration of alternative perspectives, but certain limitations restricting the form and content are imposed. Myth aims to narrow radically the possible perspectives and often promotes a single, orthodox perspective presumed to be valid for everyone. It thus offers a kind of intellectual indoctrination. But because societies aim to shape action as well as thought to orient all human faculties in the approved direction, art, myth, and ritual are often closely associated with one another. In this section, we will look at ritual as a form of action in a variety of societies.

How Can Ritual Be Defined?

For many people in Western societies, rituals are presumed to be religious—for example, weddings, Jewish bar mitzvahs, Hmong sacrifices to the ancestors, or the Catholic Mass. For anthropologists, however, rituals also include practices such as scientific experiments, college graduation ceremonies, procedures in a court of law, and children's birthday parties.

To capture this range of activities, our definition of **ritual** has four parts. First, ritual is a *repetitive social practice* composed of a sequence of symbolic activities in the form of dance, song, speech, gestures, the manipulation of certain objects, and so forth. Second, it is *set off from the social routines of everyday life*. Third, rituals in any culture *adhere to a characteristic, culturally defined schema*. This means that members of a culture can tell that a certain sequence of activities is a ritual even if they have never seen that particular ritual before. Fourth, ritual action is *closely connected to a specific set of ideas that are often encoded in myth*. These ideas might concern, for example, the relationship of human beings to the spirit world, how human beings ought to interact with one another, or the nature of evil. The purpose for which a ritual is performed guides how these ideas are selected and symbolically enacted. What gives rituals their power is that the people who perform them assert that the authorization for the ritual comes from outside themselves—from the state, from society, from a divine being, from a god, from ancestors, or from "tradition." They have not made up the ritual themselves; rather, the ritual connects them to a source of power that they do not control but that controls them.

How Is Ritual Expressed in Actions?

A ritual has a particular sequential ordering of acts, utterance, and events: that is, ritual has a *text*. Because ritual is action, however, we must pay attention to the way the ritual text is performed. The performance of a ritual cannot be separated from its text; text and performance shape each other. Through ritual

performance, the ideas of a culture become concrete, take on a form, and, as Bruce Kapferer (1983) puts it, give direction to the gaze of participants. At the same time, ritual performers are not robots but active individuals whose choices are guided by, but not rigidly dictated by, previous ritual texts; ritual performance can serve as a commentary on the text and even transform it. For example, Jewish synagogue ritual following the reading from the Torah (the five books of Moses, the Hebrew Bible) includes lifting the Torah scroll, showing it to the congregation, and then closing it and covering it. In some synagogues, a man and a woman, often a couple, are called from the congregation to lift and cover the Torah: the man lifts it and, after he seats himself, the woman rolls the scroll closed, places the tie around it, and covers it with the mantle that protects it. One of the authors of this text once observed a performance of this ritual in which the woman lifted the Torah and the man wrapped it; officially, the ritual text was carried out, but the performance became a commentary on the text—on the role of women in Judaism, on the Torah as an appropriate subject of attention for women as well as for men, on the roles of men and women overall, and so on. The performance was noteworthy—indeed, many of the regular members of the congregation seemed quite surprised—precisely because it violated people's expectations and in so doing directed people's attention toward the role of men and women in religious ritual at the end of the twentieth century as well as toward the Torah as the central symbol of the Jewish people.

What Are Rites of Passage?

Graduating from college, getting married, joining the military, and other "life cycle" rituals share certain important features, most notably that people begin the ritual as one kind of person (e.g., student, single, recruit), and by the time the ritual is over, they have been transformed into a different kind of person (e.g., graduate, spouse, soldier). These rituals are called **rites of passage** and are often linked to gender roles and behaviours. At the beginning of the twentieth century, the Belgian anthropologist Arnold Van Gennep (1960) noted that certain kinds of rituals around the world had similar structures. These were rituals associated with the movement (or passage) of people from one position in the social structure to another. They took place at births,

> **ritual** A repetitive social practice that is shared and scripted. It consists of sacred performances of symbolically meaningful cultural narratives.
>
> **rite of passage** A ritual that serves to mark the movement and transformation of an individual from one social position to another.

For a thorough discussion of gender roles and behaviours, see Chapter 11, pp. 243–5.

Anders Ryman/Alamy Stock Photo

FIGURE 16.7 Rites of passage are rituals that enable people to move from one position in the social structure to another. An Apache girl, accompanied by her godmother and a helper, moves into adulthood through the Sunrise Dance.

initiations, confirmations, weddings, funerals, and the like (Figure 16.7).

Van Gennep (1960) found that all these rituals began with a period of *separation* from the old position and from normal time. During this period, the ritual passenger leaves behind the symbols and practices of his or her previous position. For example, military recruits leave their families behind and are moved to a new place. They are forced to leave behind the clothing, activities, and even the hairstyle that marked who they were in civilian life.

The second stage in rites of passage involves a period of *transition*, in which the ritual passenger is neither in the old life nor yet in the new one. This period is marked by insecurity, ambiguity, and perceived danger. Often, the person involved is subjected to an ordeal or test given by those who have already passed through this rite. In the military service, this is the period of basic training, in which recruits (not yet soldiers but no longer civilians) are forced to dress and act alike. They are subjected to a grinding-down process, after which they are rebuilt into something new.

During the final stage—*reaggregation*—the ritual passenger is reintroduced into society in his or her new position. In the military, this involves graduation from basic training and a visit home, but this time as a member of the armed forces, in uniform and on leave—in other words, as a new person. Other rites of passage in youth culture in Canada include high school graduation and the informal yet significant ceremonies associated with

the eighteenth birthday, both of which are understood as movements from one kind of person to another.

The work of Victor Turner greatly increased our understanding of rites of passage. Turner concentrated on the period of transition, which he saw as important both for the rite of passage and for social life in general. Van Gennep (1960) referred to this part of a rite of passage as the "liminal period," from the Latin *limen* ("threshold"). During this period, the individual is on the threshold, neither here nor there, neither in nor out of a certain group. Turner notes that the symbolism accompanying the rite of passage often expresses this ambiguous state. **Liminality**, he tells us, "is frequently likened to death, to being in the womb, to invisibility, to darkness, to bisexuality, to the wilderness, and to an eclipse of the sun or moon" (Turner 1969, 95). People in the liminal state tend to develop an intense comradeship with each other in which their non-liminal distinctions disappear or become irrelevant. Turner calls this kind of social relationship **communitas**, which is best understood as an unstructured or minimally structured community of equal individuals.

Turner (1969) contends that all societies need some kind of communitas as much as they need structure. Communitas gives "recognition to an essential and generic human bond, without which there could be no society" (Turner 1969, 97). That bond is the common humanity that underlies all culture and society. However, periods of communitas (often in ritual context) are brief. Communitas is dangerous, not just because it threatens structure but also because it threatens survival itself. During the time of communitas, the things that structure ensures—production of food and physical and social reproduction of the society—cannot be provided. But someone always has to take out the garbage and clean up after the party. Thus, communitas gives way again to structure, which in turn generates a need for a new release of communitas. The feeling of communitas can also be attained by means of play and art. Indeed, it may well be that for people in contemporary nation-states the experience of communitas comes

liminality The ambiguous transitional state in a rite of passage in which the person or persons undergoing the ritual are outside their ordinary social positions.

communitas An unstructured or minimally structured community of equal individuals found frequently in rites of passage.

FIGURE 16.8 A crowd of hockey fans cheers on Team Canada during the 2010 Winter Olympic Games in Vancouver. These kinds of mass public events can create a feeling of communitas in today's nation-states.

through the climactic winning moments of a sports team (Figure 16.8), attendance at large-scale rock concerts, participation in mass public events like Carnival in Rio de Janeiro, Carnaval de Quebec in Quebec City, or the Calgary Stampede.

How Are Play and Ritual Complementary?

How does the logic of ritual differ from the logic of play? Play and ritual are complementary forms of metacommunication, although play is not real and not serious while ritual is considered important and very real. The movement from non-play to play is based on the premise of metaphor ("Let's make believe"); the movement to ritual is based on the premise of literalness ("Let's believe"). From the perspective of the everyday social order, the result of these contrasting premises is the "inauthenticity" of play and the "truth" of ritual.

Because of the connection of ritual with self-evident truth, the metacommunication of the ritual frame ("This is ritual") is associated with an additional metacommunication: "All messages within this frame are true." It is ritual that asserts *what should be* to play's *what can be*. The ritual frame is more rigid than the play frame. Consequently, ritual is the most stable liminal domain, whereas play is the most flexible. Players can move with

relative ease into and out of play, but such is not the case with ritual.

Finally, play usually has little effect on the social order of ordinary life; as a result, play can safely create a wide range of commentary on the social order. Ritual is different: its role is explicitly to maintain the status quo, including the prescribed ritual transformations. Societies differ in the extent to which ritual behaviour alternates with everyday, non-ritual behaviour. When nearly every act of everyday life is ritualized and other forms of behaviour are strongly discouraged, we sometimes speak of **orthopraxy** ("correct practice"). Traditionally observant Jews and Muslims, for example, lead a highly ritualized daily life, attempting from the moment they awaken until the moment they fall asleep to carry out even the humblest of activities in a manner that is ritually correct. In their view, ritual correctness is the result of God's law, and it is their duty and joy to conform their every action to God's will.

Margaret Drewal (1992) argues that, at least among the Yoruba, play and ritual overlap (see EthnoProfile 16.3: Yoruba). Yoruba rituals combine spectacle, festival, play, sacrifice, and so on and integrate diverse media—music, dance, poetry, theatre, sculpture (Drewal 1992, 198). They are events that require improvisatory, spontaneous individual moves; as a result, the mundane order is not only inverted and reversed but may also be subverted through power play and gender play. For example, gender roles are rigidly structured in Yoruba society. Yoruba rituals, however, allow some cross-dressing by both men

---

orthopraxy "Correct practice"; the prohibition of deviation from approved forms of behaviour.

EthnoProfile 16.3

Yoruba

Region: Western Africa

Nation: Nigeria

Population: 40,000,000

Environment: Coastal and forest

Livelihood: Farming, commerce, modern professions

Political organization: Traditionally, kingdoms; today, part of a modern nation-state

For more information: Bascom, William. 1969. *The Yoruba of Southwestern Nigeria*. New York: Holt, Rinehart, and Winston.

and women, providing institutionalized opportunities for men and women to cross gender boundaries and to express the traits that the Yoruba consider to be characteristic of the opposite sex, sometimes as parody but sometimes seriously and respectfully (Drewal 1992, 190).

How Are World View and Symbolic Practice Related?

Our previous discussions of language, play, art, myth, and ritual provided an overview of some of the ways human beings use culture to construct rich understandings of everyday experiences. In this section, we build on those insights and describe how human beings use cultural creativity to make sense of the wider world on a more comprehensive scale as they construct encompassing pictures of reality called **world views**.

What Are Symbols?

As they develop complex understandings of themselves and the wider world, people regularly devise symbols to organize this knowledge. As we saw earlier, a symbol—such as a word, an image, or an action—is something that stands for something else. Symbols signal the presence and importance of given domains of experience.

Some symbols, which anthropologist Sherry Ortner (1973, 1339) calls *summarizing symbols*, sum up, express, or represent for people "in an emotionally powerful . . . way what the system means to them." Examples include the cross representing the Christian faith or the Canadian flag representing our country and its citizens as a whole. These symbols represent a complex collection of ideas and feelings, which they draw our attention to all at once. Yet summarizing symbols often mean different things to different people. For example, while the Canadian flag might stand for patriotism, democracy, and freedom to many citizens, to others it may stand for limitations on civil rights or a history of colonization.

What Ortner calls *elaborating symbols* are essentially analytic. They allow people to sort out and label complex and undifferentiated feelings and ideas into comprehensible and communicable language and action. Elaborating symbols provide people with categories for thinking about how their world is ordered. For the Dinka—cattle herding people of eastern Africa—cattle are a key elaborating symbol. According to Godfrey Lienhardt (1961), cattle provide the Dinka (EthnoProfile 16.4) with most

of the metaphors they use for thinking about and responding to experience. For instance, Dinka perceptions of colour, light, and shade are connected to the colours they see in cattle. They even liken how their society is put together to how a bull is put together (Ortner 1973).

What Is Religion?

For many readers of this text, the most familiar form of world view is probably religion. The anthropological concept of religion, like many analytic terms, began as a description of a certain domain of Western culture. As a result, it has been very difficult for anthropologists to settle on a definition of religion that is applicable in all human societies. Scholars have often argued that a religion differs from other kinds of world views because it assumes the existence of a supernatural domain: an invisible world populated by one or more beings who are more powerful than human beings and able to influence events in the "natural" human world. The problem with this definition is that the distinction between "natural" and "supernatural" was originally made by non-religious Western observers in order to distinguish the real "natural" world from what they took to be the imaginary "supernatural" world. Many anthropologists who study different religious traditions believe that it is less distorting to begin with their informants' statements about what exists and what does not. In this

---

EthnoProfile 16.4

Dinka

Region: Eastern Africa

Nation: Sudan

Population: 2,000,000

Environment: Savannna

Livelihood: Principally cattle herding, but also agriculture

Political Organization: Traditionally, egalitarian with noble clans and chiefs; today, part of a modern nation–state

For more information: Deng, Francis Mading. 1972. *The Dinka of the Sudan.* New York: Holt, Rinehart, and Winston.

---

world views Encompassing pictures of reality that contain shared political, religious, and other moral beliefs that are created by the members of societies.

FIGURE 16.9 (a) The joint pilgrimage by Hindu worshipers to the Ganges River illustrates the social, active nature of religion. (b) This participant in the Hindu Thaipusam ritual pilgrimage in Singapore in 2004 has agreed to carry a kavadi for religious benefit. Kavadi can weigh 60 pounds (27 kilograms).

way, they are in a better position to understand the range of forces, visible and invisible, that religious devotees perceive as being active in their world.

For these reasons, John Bowen proposes that anthropologists approach religion in a way that begins broadly but that allows for increasing specificity as we learn more about the details of particular religious traditions. Bowen (2008, 4) defines **religion** as "ideas and practices that postulate reality beyond that which is immediately available to the senses." In individual societies, this may take the shape of beliefs in spirits and gods, in impersonal forces that affect the world, in the correct practice of ritual, or in the awareness that people's ancestors continue to be active in the world of the living. This definition encompasses both practices and ideas; religions involve actions as well as beliefs (Figure 16.9). Indeed, anthropologist A.F.C. Wallace (1966) proposes a set of "minimal categories of religious behaviour" that describe many of the practices usually associated with religions. Several of the most important are as follows:

1. *Prayer.* Where there are personified cosmic forces, there is a customary way of addressing them, usually by speaking or chanting out loud. Often,

people pray in public, at a sacred location, and with special apparatus: incense, smoke, objects (e.g., rosary beads or a prayer wheel), and so on.

2. *Physiological exercise.* Many religious systems have methods for physically manipulating psychological states to induce an ecstatic spiritual state. Wallace suggests four major kinds of manipulation: (1) drugs; (2) sensory deprivation; (3) mortification of the flesh by pain, sleeplessness, and fatigue; and (4) deprivation of food, water, or air. In many societies, the experience of ecstasy, euphoria, dissociation, or hallucination seems to be a goal of religious effort.

3. *Exhortation.* In all religious systems, certain people are believed to have closer relationships with the invisible powers than others have, and they are expected to use those relationships in the spiritual interests of others. They give orders, they heal, they threaten, they comfort, and they interpret.

4. *Mana. Mana* refers to an impersonal superhuman power that is sometimes believed to be transferable from an object that contains it to one that does not. The laying on of hands, in which the power of a healer enters the body of a sick person to remove or destroy an illness, is an example of the transmission of power. In Guider, Cameroon, some people believe that the ink used to copy passages from the Qur'an has power (see

religion "Ideas and practices that postulate reality beyond that which is immediately available to the senses" (Bowen 2008).

EthnoProfile 14.2: Guider). Washing the ink off the board on which the words are written and drinking the ink transfers the power of the words into the body of the drinker. All these examples illustrate the principle that sacred things are sometimes to be touched so that their power may be transferred to human beings.

5. *Taboo.* Objects or people that may not be touched are taboo. Some people believe that touching such objects or people may cause the cosmic power they contain to "drain away" or may injure the toucher. Many religious systems have taboo objects. Traditionally, Catholics were not to touch the Host (a form of sacred bread that they believe has been consecrated into the body of Christ) during Communion. Jews may not touch the handwritten text of the biblical scrolls. In ancient Polynesia, commoners could not touch the chief's body; even an accidental touch resulted in the death of the commoner. Food may also be taboo: many societies have elaborate rules concerning the foods that may or may not be eaten at different times or by different kinds of people.

6. *Feasts.* Eating and drinking in a religious context is very common. The Holy Communion of Catholics and Protestants is a meal set apart by its religious context. The Passover Seder for Jews is another religious feast. For the Huichol of Mexico (EthnoProfile 16.5), the consumption of peyote is set apart from other meals by its religious context. Even everyday meals may be seen to have a religious quality if they begin or end with prayer.

7. *Sacrifice.* Giving something of value to the invisible forces or their agents is a feature of many religious systems. This may be an offering of money, goods, or services. It may also be the immolation of animals or, rarely, human beings. Sacrifices may be made in thanks to the cosmic forces, in hopes of influencing them to act in a certain way, or simply to gain general religious merit.

How Do People Communicate in Religion?

Those who are committed to religious world views are convinced of the existence and active involvement in their lives of beings or forces that are ordinarily invisible. Some of the most highly valued religious practices, such as religious ecstasy or trance, produce outer symptoms that may

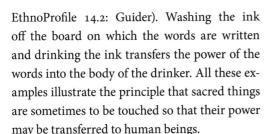

EthnoProfile 16.5

Huichol

Region: Latin America

Nation: Mexico

Population: 20,000

Environment: Mountainous terrain

Livelihood: Corn farming, deer hunting in recent past

Political organization: Traditionally, no formal organization, some men with influence; today, part of a modern nation-state

For more information: Myerhoff, Barbara. 1974. *Peyote Hunt.* Ithaca, NY: Cornell University Press.

be perceived by others; but their most powerful effects can be experienced only by the individual who undergoes them personally. What if you wanted to know what it felt like to experience religious ecstasy? What if you were someone who had had such an experience and wanted to tell others about it? What if you were convinced that the supreme power in the universe had revealed itself to you and you wanted to share this revelation with others? How would you proceed?

You might well begin by searching for metaphors based on experiences already well known to your audience. Thus, one Hindu Tamil worshiper in Kuala Lumpur who successfully went into trance during the festival of Thaipusam described his experience as "floating in the air, followed by the wind" (*Floating on the Air* 1973). And the Hebrew poet who wrote the twenty-third psalm of the Bible tried to express his experience of the power and love of his god by comparing his god to a shepherd and himself to a sheep. Many contemporary theologians argue that the language human beings use to talk about God is inevitably full of everyday metaphors (e.g., see Gillman 1992). Even those who claim to have had personal experience of the reality of God, of ancestral spirits, or of witchcraft will probably still find themselves forced to resort to poetic, metaphorical language if they want to explain that experience to other people—and perhaps even to themselves.

How Are Religion and Social Organization Related?

Anthropological research suggests that members of many religious traditions base their understanding of the structure of the universe on the structure of the society in which they live. One consequence of this mode of understanding is that forces in the universe are personalized. Thus, people seeking to influence those forces must handle them as they would handle powerful human beings. Communication is perhaps the central feature of how we deal with human beings: when we address each other, we expect a response. The same is true when we address personalized cosmic forces.

Maintaining contact with invisible cosmic powers is a tremendously complex undertaking. It is not surprising, therefore, that some societies develop complex social practices to ensure that it is done properly. In other words, religion becomes institutionalized. Social positions are created for specialists who supervise or embody correct religious practice.

Anthropologists have identified two broad categories of religious specialists: shamans and priests. A **shaman** is a spiritual specialist who is believed to have the power to contact invisible powers directly on behalf of individuals or groups. Shamans are often thought to be able to travel to the cosmic realm to communicate with the beings or forces that dwell there. They often plead with those beings or forces to act in favour of their people and may return with messages for them. The Ju/'hoansi, for example, recognize that some people are able to develop an internal power that enables them to travel to the world of the spirits—to enter "half death"—in order to cure those who are sick. Among the Inuit, shamans known as *angakkuit* have traditionally been relied on to cure the sick and provide spiritual guidance; in recent times, this form of shamanism has been integrated with Christianity, and *angakkuit* have become intermediaries teaching traditional beliefs and Christian ideology (Laugrand and Oosten 2010).

In many societies, the training that a shaman receives is long and demanding and may involve the use of powerful psychotropic substances. Repeatedly entering altered states of consciousness can produce long-lasting effects on shamans themselves, and shamans may be viewed with suspicion or fear by others in the

> ↻ For more on the Ju/'hoansi, see EthnoProfile 10.1. For more on shamanism and Christianity among Inuit societies in northern Canada, see Chapter 2, pp. 36–7.

> **shaman** A spiritual specialist who is believed to have the power to contact supernatural forces directly on behalf of individuals or groups.

society. This is because contacting cosmic beings to persuade them to heal embodies dangerous ambiguities: someone who can contact such beings for positive benefits may also be able to contact them to produce negative outcomes, such as disease or death.

The term *shaman* comes from the Tungus of eastern Siberia, where, at a minimum, it referred to a religious specialist who had the ability to enter a trance through which he or she was believed to be able to directly contact spiritual beings and guardian spirits for the purposes of healing, fertility, protection, and aggression in a ritual setting (Bowie 2006, 175; Hultkrantz 1992, 10). Siberian shamanism was associated with the idea that illness was caused by soul loss and that healing occurred through recovery of the soul (Figure 16.10). Thus, the shaman was responsible for dealing with spirits that were at best neutral and at worst actively hostile to human beings. The shaman could travel to the spirit world to heal someone by finding the missing soul that had been stolen by spirits. But a shaman

© A. Abbas/Magnum Photos

FIGURE 16.10 Using smoke from a juniper twig, Siberian shaman Vera heals a patient possessed by evil spirits.

who was jealous of a hunter, for example, was believed to be able to steal the souls of animals so that the hunter would fail, which could ultimately lead to starvation. In these societies, shamans are considered to be dangerous.

Shamanic activity takes place in the trance séance, which can be little more than a consultation between shaman and patient or a major public ritual, rich in drama. Becoming a shaman is not undertaken for personal development. In the societies in which shamanism is important, it is said that the shaman has no choice but to take on the role; the spirits demand it. It can take a decade or more to become fully recognized as a shaman, and it is assumed that the shaman will be in service to the society (for good or ill) for the rest of his or her life.

A **priest**, by contrast, is skilled in the practice of religious rituals, which are carried out for the benefit of the group or individual members of the group. Priests do not necessarily have direct contact with cosmic forces. Often, their main role is to mediate such contact by ensuring that the required ritual activity has been properly performed. Priests are found in hierarchical societies, and they owe their ability to act as priests to the hierarchy of the religious institution (Figure 16.11). Status differences separating rulers and subjects in such societies are reflected in the unequal relationship between priest and laity.

World Views in Operation

We have been discussing how world views are constructed, but most of us encounter them fully formed, both in our own society and in other societies. We face a rich tapestry of symbols, rituals, and everyday practices linked to one another in what often appears to be a seamless web. Where do we begin to sort things out? The following case study will offer some insight.

Coping with Misfortune: Witchcraft, Oracles, and Magic among the Azande

Anthropologist E.E. Evans-Pritchard, in his classic work *Witchcraft, Oracles, and Magic among the Azande* ([1937] 1976), shows how Azande beliefs and practices concerning **witchcraft**, **oracles**, and **magic** were related to one another (see EthnoProfile 16.6: Azande). He describes how Azande in the 1920s used witchcraft beliefs to explain unfortunate things that happened to them and how they employed oracles and magic to exert a measure of control over the actions of other people. Evans-Pritchard was impressed by the intelligence, sophistication, and

FIGURE 16.11 The complex organization of the Roman Catholic Church was illustrated at the funeral for Pope John Paul II in 2005.

EthnoProfile 16.6

Azande

Region: Central Africa

Nation: Democratic Republic of the Congo, South Sudan, Central African Republic

Population: 1,100,000

Environment: Sparsely wooded savannah

Livelihood: Farming, hunting, fishing, chicken raising

Political organization: Traditionally, highly organized, tribal kingdoms; today, part of modern nation-states

For more information: Evans-Pritchard, E.E. [1937] 1976. *Witchcraft, Oracles, and Magic among the Azande.* Abridged ed. Oxford: Oxford University Press.

---

priest A religious practitioner skilled in the practice of religious rituals, which he or she carries out for the benefit of the group.

witchcraft The performance of magic by human beings, often through innate supernatural powers, whether or not it is intentional or self-aware.

oracles Invisible forces to which people address questions and whose responses they believe to be truthful.

magic A set of beliefs and practices designed to control the visible or invisible world for specific purposes.

skepticism of his Azande informants. For this reason, he was all the more struck by their ability to hold a set of beliefs that many Europeans would regard as superstitious.

Azande Witchcraft Beliefs

The Azande Evans-Pritchard knew believed that *mangu* (translated by Evans-Pritchard as "witchcraft") was a substance in the body of witches, generally located under the sternum.[1] Being a part of the body, the witchcraft substance grew as the body grew; therefore, the older the witch, the more potent his or her witchcraft. The Azande believed that children inherited witchcraft from their parents. Men or women might be witches. Men practised witchcraft against other men; women, against other women. Witchcraft worked when its "soul" removed the soul of a certain organ in the victim's body, usually at night, causing a slow, wasting disease. Suffering such a disease was therefore an indication that an individual had been bewitched.

Witchcraft was a basic concept for the Azande, one that shaped their experience of adversity. All deaths were due to witchcraft and had to be avenged by magic. Other misfortunes were also commonly attributed to witchcraft unless the victim had broken a taboo, had failed to observe a moral rule, or was believed to be responsible for his or her own problems. For example, an incompetent potter whose pots break during the firing process may claim that witchcraft caused them to break, but everyone will laugh at the potter because they know he or she lacks skill. Witchcraft was believed to be so common that the Azande were neither surprised nor awestruck when they encountered it. Rather, their usual response was anger.

To the Azande, witchcraft was a completely natural explanation for events. Consider the classic case of the collapsing granary. Azande territory is hot, and people seeking shade often sit under traditional raised granaries, which rest on logs. Termites are common, and sometimes they destroy the supporting logs, making a granary collapse. Occasionally, when a granary collapses, people sitting under it are killed. Why

does this happen? The Azande are well aware that the termites chew up the wood until the supports give way, but to them that is not answer enough. Why, after all, should that particular granary have collapsed at that particular moment? To skeptical observers, the only connection is coincidence in time and space. Western science does not provide any explanation for why these two chains of causation intersect. But the Azande did: witchcraft caused the termites to finish chewing up the wood at just that moment; thus, that witchcraft had to be avenged by magic.

Dealing with Witches

To expose the witch, the Azande consulted oracles (see earlier definition). Pre-eminent among these was the poison oracle. The poison was a strychnine-like substance imported into Azande territory. The oracle "spoke" through the effect the poison had on chickens. When witchcraft was suspected, a relative of the afflicted person took some young chickens into the bush along with a specialist in administering the poison oracle. This person fed poison to one chicken, named a suspect, and asked the oracle to kill the chicken if that person were the witch. If the chicken died, a second chicken was fed poison, and the oracle was asked to spare the chicken if the suspect just named was indeed the witch. Thus, the Azande double-checked the oracle carefully; a witchcraft accusation was not made lightly.

People did not consult the oracle with a long list of names. They needed only to consider those who might wish them or their families ill: people who had quarrelled with them, who were unpleasant, who were antisocial, or whose behaviour was somehow out of line. Indeed, witches were always neighbours because neighbours were the only people who knew you well enough to wish you and your family ill.

Once the oracle identified the witch, the Azande removed the wing of the chicken and had it taken by messenger to the compound of the accused person. The messenger presented the accused witch with the chicken wing and said that he had been sent concerning the illness of so-and-so's relative: "Almost invariably the witch replies courteously that he is unconscious of injuring anyone, that if it is true that he has injured the man in question he is very sorry, and that if it is he alone who is troubling him then he will surely recover, because from the bottom of his heart he wishes him health and happiness" (Evans-Pritchard [1937] 1976, 42). The accused

---

[1]Beliefs and practices similar to those associated with Azande *mangu* have been found in many other societies, and it has become traditional in anthropology to refer to them as "witchcraft." This technical usage must not be confused with everyday uses of the word in contemporary Western societies, still less with the practices of followers of movements such as Wicca, which are very different.

then called for a gourd of water, took some in his mouth, and sprayed it out over the wing. He said aloud, so the messenger could hear and repeat what he said, that if he was a witch he was not aware of it and that he was not intentionally causing the sick man to be ill. He addressed the witchcraft in him, asking it to become cool, and concluded by saying that he made this appeal from his heart, not just from his lips (42).

People accused of witchcraft were usually astounded; no Azande thought of himself or herself as a witch. However, the Azande strongly believed in witchcraft and in the oracles; and if the oracle said someone was a witch, then it must be so. The accused witch was grateful to the family of the sick person for being informed. Otherwise, if the accused had been allowed to murder the victim, all the while unaware of it, the witch would surely be killed later by vengeance magic. The witchcraft accusation carried a further message: the behaviour of the accused was sufficiently outside the bounds of acceptable Azande behaviour to have marked him or her as a potential witch. Only the names of people who you suspected of wishing you ill were submitted to the oracle. The accused witch, then, was being told to change his or her behaviour.

Are There Patterns of Witchcraft Accusation?

Compared with the stereotypes of European American witchcraft—old hags dressed in black, riding on broomsticks, casting spells, causing milk to sour or people to sicken—Azande witchcraft seems quite tame. People whose impression of witchcraft comes from western European images may believe that witchcraft and witch-hunting tear at the very fabric of society. Yet anthropological accounts like Evans-Pritchard's suggest that practices such as witchcraft accusation can sometimes keep societies together. Anthropologist Mary Douglas (1970, xxvi–xxvii) looked at the range of witchcraft accusations worldwide and discovered that they fall into two basic types: in some cases, the witch is an evil outsider; in others, the witch is an internal enemy, either the member of a rival faction or a dangerous deviant. These different patterns of accusation perform different functions in a society. If the witch is an outsider, witchcraft accusations can strengthen in-group ties. If the witch is an internal enemy, accusations of witchcraft can weaken in-group ties; factions may have to regroup, communities may split, and the entire social hierarchy may be reordered. If the witch is a dangerous deviant, the

accusation of witchcraft can be seen as an attempt to control the deviant in defence of the wider values of the community. Douglas concluded that how people understand witchcraft is based on the social relations of their society.

Maintaining and Changing a World View

What makes a world view stable? Why is a world view rejected? Changes in world view are regularly connected to the practical, everyday experiences of people in a particular society. Stable, repetitive experiences reinforce the acceptability of any traditional world view that has successfully accounted for such experiences in the past. Connections to the land and traditional territories assist in keeping a world view strong. As Sarah King (2013) remarks, space and place are an important part of maintaining a stable world view for members of the Mi'kmaq First Nation in Atlantic Canada (EthnoProfile 16.7; see the "In Their Own Words" box on the importance of context in Mi'kmaq world views). When experiences become unpredictable, however, thinking people in any society may become painfully aware that past experiences can no longer be trusted as guides for the future, and traditional world views may be undermined (see Horton 1982, 252).

How Do People Cope with Change?

Drastic changes in experience lead people to create new interpretations that will help them cope with the changes.

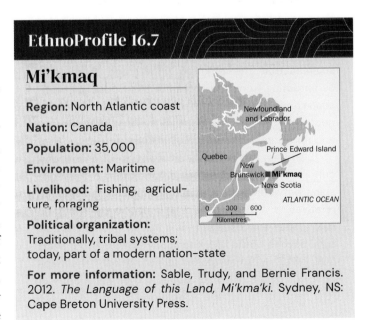

EthnoProfile 16.7

Mi'kmaq

Region: North Atlantic coast

Nation: Canada

Population: 35,000

Environment: Maritime

Livelihood: Fishing, agriculture, foraging

Political organization: Traditionally, tribal systems; today, part of a modern nation–state

For more information: Sable, Trudy, and Bernie Francis. 2012. *The Language of this Land, Mi'kma'ki.* Sydney, NS: Cape Breton University Press.

Sometimes the change is an outcome of local or regional struggles. The Protestant Reformation, for example, adapted the Christian tradition to changing social circumstances in northern Europe during the Renaissance by breaking ties to the pope, turning church lands over to secular authorities, allowing clergy to marry, and so forth. Protestants continued to identify themselves as Christians, although many of their religious practices had changed.

In Guider, Cameroon, lone rural migrants to town have frequently abandoned their former religious practices and taken on urban customs and a new identity through conversion to Islam. However, similar conflicts between new and old ways do not always lead to religious conversion. Sometimes, the result is a creative synthesis

> **syncretism** The synthesis of old religious practices (or an old way of life) with new religious practices (or a new way of life) introduced from outside, often by force.

of old religious practices and new ones, a process called **syncretism**. Under the pressure of Christian missionizing, for example, Indigenous people of Central America identified some of their own pre-Christian, personalized superhuman beings with particular Catholic saints. Similarly, Africans brought to Brazil identified Catholic saints with African gods, to produce the syncretistic religion Candomblé.

Anthropologists have debated the nature of syncretistic practices, noting that while some may be viewed as a way of resisting new ideas imposed from above, others may be introduced from above by powerful outsiders deliberately making room for local beliefs within their own more encompassing world view. The Romans, for example, made room for local deities within their imperial pantheon, and post–Vatican II Catholicism explicitly urged non-European Catholics to worship using local cultural forms (Stewart and Shaw 1994).

When groups defend or refashion their own way of life in the face of outside encroachments, anthropologists

In Their Own Words

The Importance of Context in Mi'kmaq World Views

Sarah King outlines the importance of context and place when studying Indigenous world views, drawing on examples from the Mi'kmaq First Nation living in Atlantic Canada.

Context is the hallmark of Indigenous philosophies and religions, as these are ways of being in which things are seen as interconnected, and the world is viewed in a holistic fashion. Traditional Indigenous knowledge is contextual. . . . [For example, Sable and Francis (2012)] suggest that the Mi'kmaq understand themselves as sprouting from and rooted in the landscape, *weji-sqalia'timk* (17). The knowledge of the people is connected to the place where they live and to human . . . and non-human relations. . . .

[L]and is the context of Indigenous philosophy, culture, and religion, as the embodiment of relationships between many (human and other-than-human) relatives. . . . "*Weji-sqalia'timk* is about an embodied landscape—a landscape that is still integral to the cultural psyche of the Mi'kmaq today" (Sable and Francis 2012, 25). . . . Mi'kmaw stories reflect not only "the mapping skill of the Mi'kmaq" but also their knowledge of "the sentient landscape" (Sable and Francis 2012, 42).

[For example, t]he Mi'kmaq serpent dance teaches respect for the powers of the land and the medicines, and it also "teaches of the seasons, the directions, the stars, the nature of reptiles, the bird that leads one to the medicine and values of respect and care in collecting plants" (90). . . .

Taking the land seriously as a fundamental organizing principle of Indigenous ways of knowing means recognizing how this principle leads to immense diversity. Nations, tribes, and communities all become who and what they are because of the *particular* place in which they are at home. . . . Context matters, not simply because it illuminates the importance of land as a fundamental principle to Indigenous peoples across North America, but because it leads us to the diversity of thinking and practices that is characteristic of lived Indigenous experience.

Source: King 2013, 499–507. Excerpts from pp. 499–500.

sometimes describe their activities as **revitalization**—a deliberate, organized attempt by some members of a society to create a more satisfying culture (Wallace 1972, 75). Revitalization arises in times of crisis, most often among groups who are facing oppression and radical transformation, usually at the hands of outsiders (e.g., colonizing powers). In Canada, cultural revitalization continues to take place in many Indigenous communities today. This process is perhaps most apparent in efforts to renew Indigenous languages, provide traditional education for Indigenous children, and revitalize aspects of Indigenous spirituality. In fact, evidence shows that efforts to revitalize Indigenous spirituality are actually increasing in many regions across Canada and the United States (Fonda 2011; Kosmin, Mayer, and Keysar 2001). In many cases, these efforts have been highly successful, especially among young people. The process of spiritual revitalization often leads to healthier communities, an increased sense of well-being in individuals, and a higher level of self-reliance in youth. Not surprisingly, then, it has also been linked to reduced suicide rates in a number of Indigenous communities in British Columbia and a more effective healing process among Indigenous individuals incarcerated in Canadian jails.

Revitalization movements engage in a "politics of religious synthesis" that produces a range of outcomes (Stewart and Shaw 1994). Sometimes syncretism is embraced. Other times it is rejected in favour of **nativism**, or a return to the old ways. Some nativistic movements expect a messiah or a prophet who will bring back a lost golden age of peace, prosperity, and harmony, a process often called *revivalism, millenarianism,* or *messianism.*

Nativistic movements often involve individuals in actively removing or avoiding any cultural practices associated with those who seek to dominate them. One such "anti-syncretistic" group is the Kwaio, who live on the island of Malaita in the Solomon Islands (see EthnoProfile 16.8: Kwaio). Almost all their neighbours have converted to Christianity, and the nation of which they are a part is militantly Christian. Members of other groups wear clothing, work on plantations or in tourist hotels, attend schools, and live in cities. The Kwaio have refused all this: "Young men carry bows and arrows; girls and women, nude except for customary ornaments, dig taro in forest gardens; valuables made of strung shell beads are exchanged at mortuary feasts; and priests sacrifice pigs to the ancestral spirits on whom prosperity and life itself depend" (Keesing 1982, 1).

EthnoProfile 16.8

Kwaio

Region: Oceania (Melanesia)

Nation: Solomon Islands (Malaita)

Population: 7000 (1970s)

Environment: Tropical island

Livelihood: Horticulture and pig raising

Political organization: Traditionally, some men with influence but no coercive power; today, part of a modern nation-state

For more information: Keesing, Roger. 1992. *Custom and Confrontation.* Chicago: University of Chicago Press.

Roger Keesing (1992) admits that he does not know exactly why the Kwaio responded in this way. He suspects that precolonial social and political differences between the Kwaio and their coastal neighbours influenced later developments. The colonial encounter itself was certainly relevant. In 1927, some Kwaio attacked a British patrol, killing the district officer and 13 Solomon Island troops. The subsequent massacre of many Kwaio by a police force made up of other Malaitans, followed by marginalization and persecution by the colonial government, also clearly contributed to Kwaio resistance.

The Kwaio maintain their old ways deliberately, in the face of alternatives; their traditional way of life is therefore lived in a modern context: "In the course of anticolonial struggle, *kastomu* (custom) and commitment to ancestral ways have become symbols of identity and autonomy" (Keesing 1992, 240). In the eyes of the Kwaio, the many Solomon Islanders who became Christianized and acculturated lost their cultural ties and thereby their ties to the land and to their past, becoming outsiders in their own homeland. Maintaining traditional ways is thus a form of political protest. From

revitalization A conscious, deliberate, and organized attempt by some members of a society to create a more satisfying culture in a time of crisis.

nativism A return to the old ways; a movement whose members expect a messiah or a prophet who will bring back a lost golden age of peace, prosperity, and harmony.

this perspective, many contemporary anti-syncretistic movements in the world, from fundamentalism of various religions to movements for national identity and cultural autonomy, can be understood as having aims very similar to those of the Kwaio, sparked by many of the same forces.

How Are World Views Used as Instruments of Power?

Within any particular cultural tradition, different world views often coexist. How, then, does a particular picture of reality become the "official" world view for a given society? And once that position is achieved, how is it maintained? To be in the running for the official picture of reality, a world view must be able, however minimally, to make sense of some people's personal and social experiences. Sometimes, however, it may seem to some members of society that barely credible views of reality have triumphed over alternatives that seem far more plausible. Thus, something more than persuasive ability alone must be involved, and that something is power. Powerless people may be unable to dislodge the official world view of their society. They can, however, refuse to accept the imposition of someone else's world view and develop an unofficial world view based on metaphors that reflect their own condition of powerlessness (Scott 1990).

How can world views be mobilized as instruments of power and control? First, a religious symbol can be invoked as a guarantee of self-evident truths when people in power seek to eliminate or impose certain forms of conduct. Holy books, like the Qur'an, may be used in this way. For example, a legal record from Guider, Cameroon, indicates that a son once brought suit against his father for refusing to repay him a certain amount of money. The father claimed that he had paid. Both father and son got into an increasingly heated argument in which neither would give ground. Finally, the judge in the case asked the father to take a copy of the Qur'an in his hand and swear that he was telling the truth. This he did. The son, however, refused to swear on the Qur'an and finally admitted that he had been lying. In this case, the status of the Qur'an as the unquestioned word of God, which implied the power of God to punish liars, controlled the son's behaviour.

Second, a symbol may be under the direct control of a person wishing to affect the behaviour of others. Consider the role of official interpreters of religious or political ideology, such as priests or kings. Their

In Their Own Words

Custom and Confrontation

In the following passage, the late Roger Keesing relays the words of one of his Kwaio informants, Dangeabe'u, who defends Kwaio custom.

The government has brought the ways of business, the ways of money. The people at the coast believe that's what's important, and tell us we should join in. Now the government is controlling the whole world. The side of the Bible is withering away. When that's finished, the government will rule unchallenged. It will hold all the land. All the money will go to the government to feed its power. Once everything—our lands, too—are in their hands, that will be it.

I've seen the people from other islands who have all become Christians. They knew nothing about their land. The white people have gotten their hands on their lands. The whites led them to forget all the knowledge of their land, separated them from it. And when the people knew nothing about their land, the whites bought it from them and made their enterprises. . . .

That's close upon us too. If we all follow the side of the Bible, the government will become powerful here too, and will take control of our land. We won't be attached to our land, as we are now, holding our connections to our past. If the government had control of our land, then if we wanted to do anything on it, we'd have to pay them. If we wanted to start a business—a store, say—we'd have to pay the government. We reject all that. We want to keep hold of our land, in the ways passed down to us.

Source: Keesing 1992, 184.

pronouncements define the bounds of permissible behaviour, as Roger Keesing (1982, 219) points out:

> Senior men, in Melanesia as elsewhere in the tribal world, have depended heavily on control of *sacred knowledge* to maintain their control of earthly politics. By keeping in their hands relations with ancestors and other spirits, by commanding magical knowledge, senior men could maintain a control mediated by the supernatural. Such religious ideologies served too, by defining rules in terms of ancient spirits and by defining the nature of men and women in supernatural terms, to reinforce and maintain the roles of the sexes—and again to hide their nature.

Keesing's observations remind us that knowledge, like power, is not evenly distributed throughout a society. Different kinds of people know different things. In some societies, what men know about their religious system is different from what women know and what older men know may be different from what younger men know. Keesing (1982, 14) suggests that men's control over women and older men's control over younger men are based on differential access to knowledge. It is not just that these different kinds of people know different things; rather, the different things they know (and do not know) enable them (or force them) to remain in the positions they hold in the society (Figure 16.12).

World views represent comprehensive ideas about the structure of the world and the place of one's own group, or one's own self, within that world. The ethnographic record offers a broad array of different world views, each testifying to the imaginative, meaning-making cultural capacity of humans. These models of the world, moreover, do not exist apart from everyday social practices; on the contrary, they are heavily implicated in our interactions with others. And when those interactions lead to crisis, humans respond by, among other things, seeking a way of making the crisis appear meaningful and therefore manageable. We are meaning-making, meaning-using, meaning-dependent organisms; and that is nowhere clearer than when a meaningful way of life is under assault.

Many of the cases in this chapter demonstrate the human ability to cope creatively with life, which reminds us that humans are not passive but active participants in the global world. Modes of livelihood that may benefit some human groups can overwhelm and destroy others. Western

© B&C Alexander/ArcticPhoto

FIGURE 16.12 Senior Dogon men carrying out fox trail divination. The knowledge and skills of elderly men, based on experience gained over a lifetime, provide their interpretations with an authority that those of people with less experience would not have.

colonialism and capitalism are clear examples of this. Today, modern technology is bringing respite to the global world, connecting us in new and ever-changing ways.

Why Study Anthropology?

All human beings, ourselves included, live in culturally shaped worlds, enmeshed in webs of interpretation and meaning that we have made. It is the task of anthropology and its practitioners to go out and record the vast creative diversity in the world that has been the history of our species. In our lifetimes, we will witness the end of many of those ways of life—and, if we are not careful, of all ways of life. This loss is tragic, for as these worlds disappear, so too does something special about humanity: variety, creativity, and awareness of alternatives.

Our survival as a species and our viability as individuals depend on the possibility of choice, of perceiving and being able to act on alternative situations we encounter in our daily lives. However, as alternatives are destroyed, or smashed, our own human possibilities are reduced. A small group of men and women have laboured in all corners of the earth, documenting human accomplishment in its variety and bringing it back and teaching it to others.

Certainly, our greatest human accomplishment is the creation of the beautiful worlds in which we live. Anthropologists have rarely given in to the idea that these worlds are pure and all good. They are not. There are no guarantees that human cultures will be compassionate rather than cruel or that people will agree with one another. There are not any guarantees that our species will survive. But there is a sense of knowing and hope that despite that fact we are a species bounded by our culture, we are also free to change it and the worlds we have created.

Studying anthropology, even at the introductory level, can have a powerful effect on students. It introduces students to new and different ways of life and demonstrates how similar yet unique the human species is. Knowing and experiencing cultural variety gives rise to reflection, and, with this, we experience the ultimate understanding of our own cultural tradition, which has been created by the generations who preceded us. We hope this book has enlarged your experience of humans and equipped you with the means to understand different cultures and the world around you in a less threatening, more tolerant manner.

Chapter Summary

1. Play is a generalized form of behavioural openness: the ability to think about, speak about, and do different things in the same way or the same things in different ways. Play can also be thought of as a way of organizing activities. We put a frame that consists of the message "This is play" around certain activities, thereby transforming them into play. Play also permits reflexive consideration of alternative realities by setting up a separate reality and suggesting that the perspective of ordinary life is only one way to make sense of experience. The functions of play include exercise, practice for the real world, increased creativity in children, and commentary on the real world. Play is likely linked to our evolution as modern humans capable of creativity and symbolic thought.

2. Art is a kind of play that is subject to certain culturally appropriate restrictions on form and content. It aims to evoke an aesthetic response from the artist and the observer. It succeeds when the form is culturally appropriate for the content and technically perfect in its realization. Aesthetic evaluations are culturally shaped value judgments. We recognize art in other cultures because of its family resemblance to what we call art in our own culture. Although people with other cultural understandings may not have produced art by intention, we can often successfully appreciate what they have created as art by appropriation. These issues are addressed in ethnographic studies that call into question received ideas about what counts as "authentic" art.

3. Myths are stories whose truth seems self-evident because they do such a good job of integrating personal experiences with a wider set of assumptions about the way the world works. The power of myths comes from their ability to make life meaningful for those who accept them. As stories, myths are the products of high verbal art. A full understanding of myth requires ethnographic background information.

4. Ritual is a repetitive social practice composed of sequences of symbolic activities, such as speech, singing, dancing, gestures, and the manipulation of certain objects. In studying ritual, we pay attention not just to the symbols but also to how the ritual is performed. Cultural ideas are made concrete through ritual action. Rites of passage are rituals in which members of a culture move from one position in the social structure to another. These rites are marked by periods of separation, transition, and reaggregation. During the period of transition, individuals occupy a liminal position. All those in this position frequently develop an intense comradeship and a feeling of oneness, or *communitas*.

5. Ritual and play are complementary. Play is based on the premise "Let us make believe," while ritual is based on the premise "Let us believe." As a result, the ritual frame is far more rigid than the play frame. Although ritual may seem overwhelming and all-powerful, individuals and groups can sometimes manipulate ritual forms to achieve non-traditional ends.

6. Anthropological studies of religion tend to focus on the social institutions and meaningful processes with which it is associated. Followers of religions can address personalized forces symbolically and expect them to respond. Maintaining contact with cosmic forces is complex, and societies have complex social practices designed to ensure that this is done properly. Two important kinds of religious specialists are shamans and priests.

7. Many anthropologists have attempted to display the rich, coherent tapestries of symbols, rituals, and everyday practices that make up particular world views and to demonstrate the high degree to which world views vary from one another. They have also studied the ways in which drastic changes in people's experiences lead them to create new meanings to explain the changes and to cope with them. This can be accomplished through elaboration of the old system to fit changing times, conversion to a new world view, syncretism, revitalization, or resistance.

8. Because religious knowledge is not distributed evenly among the members of societies, those who control such knowledge are often able to use it as an instrument of power to control other members of society.

For Review

1. Consider the definition of *play* in the running glossary, and explain the importance of each feature of this complex definition by examining Robert Park's research, as discussed on page 380.

2. What are the consequences of play for animals?

3. What is metacommunication? Can you provide an example of metacommunication? How do you use metacommunication in your own life?

4. How do Elizabeth Chin's observations about African American girls and their dolls in Newhallville, New Haven, Connecticut, illustrate the importance of play for understanding human symbolic practices?

5. What are the main components of the definition of *art* offered in this chapter, and why is each component important?

6. Distinguish "art by intention" from "art by appropriation."

7. What argument is made in this chapter concerning the role of "authenticity" in art? How does Michelle Bigenho's experience with Música de Maestros illustrate these points?

8. What are myths? List some myths that you believe in. What would be an example of a Canadian myth?

9. Compare Malinowski's view of myth with the view of Lévi-Strauss. How do the two relate to one another?

What are the advantages and potential drawbacks of each view?

10. Explain the significance of each of the major components of the definition of a ritual given in the text.

11. In what ways might a child's birthday party be understood as a ritual?

12. Describe each stage of a rite of passage. How do these stages apply to any rites of passage that you have undergone in your life?

13. How are play and ritual complementary? How do they differ?

14. List A.F.C. Wallace's minimal categories of religion and define and illustrate each of them.

15. Explain the differences anthropologists recognize between shamans and priests. Use the discussion of Inuit shamans to illustrate your answer.

16. What is syncretism? Christianity and Islam are religions followed by vast numbers of people from many different societies. Are these religions followed in precisely the same way by each and every follower? Explain why or why not using examples from this chapter.

17. Explain how world views can be used as instruments of power.

Key Terms

References

Alland, Alexander. 1977. *The Artistic Animal.* New York: Doubleday Anchor.

Anderson, Richard L. 1990. *Calliope's Sisters: A Comparative Study of Philosophies of Art.* Englewood Cliffs, NJ: Prentice Hall.

Bascom, William. 1969. *The Yoruba of Southwestern Nigeria.* New York: Holt, Rinehart, and Winston.

Bateson, Gregory. 1972. "A Theory of Play and Fantasy." In *Steps to an Ecology of Mind,* edited by Gregory Bateson, 177–93. New York: Ballantine Books.

Bigenho, Michelle. 2002. *Sounding Indigenous: Authenticity in Bolivian Music Performance.* New York: Palgrave.

Bowen, John R. 2008. *Religions in Practice: An Approach to the Anthropology of Religion.* 4th ed. Needham Heights, MA: Allyn and Bacon.

Bowie, Fiona. 2006. *The Anthropology of Religion: An Introduction.* 2nd ed. Malden, MA: Blackwell.

Callow, Chris. 2006. "Reconstructing the Past in Medieval Iceland." *Early Medieval Europe* 14 (3): 297–324.

Chin, Elizabeth. 1999. "Ethnically Correct Dolls: Toying with the Race Industry." *American Anthropologist* 101 (2): 305–21.

Deng, Francis Mading. 1972. *The Dinka of the Sudan.* New York: Holt, Rinehart, and Winston.

Douglas, Mary. 1970. "Introduction." In *Witchcraft Confessions and Accusations,* edited by Mary Douglas, vi–xxxviii. London: Tavistock.

Drewal, Margaret Thompson. 1992. *Yoruba Ritual: Performers, Play, Agency.* Bloomington: Indiana University Press.

Errington, Shelly. 1998. *The Death of Authentic Primitive Art and Other Tales of Progress.* Berkeley: University of California Press.

Evans-Pritchard, E.E. (1937) 1976. *Witchcraft, Oracles, and Magic among the Azande.* Abridged ed., prepared by Eva Gillies. Oxford: Oxford University Press.

Fagen, Robert. 1981. *Animal Play Behavior.* New York: Oxford University Press.

———. 1992. "Play, Fun, and the Communication of Well-Being." *Play and Culture* 5 (1): 40–58.

———. 2005. "Play, Five Gates of Evolution, and Paths to Art." In *Play: An Interdisciplinary Synthesis,* edited by F.F. McMahnon, Donald E. Lytle, and Brian Sutton-Smith, 9–42. Vol. 6 of *Play and Culture Studies.* Lanham, MD: University Press of America.

Fewkes, J.W. 1923. *Designs of Prehistoric Pottery from the Mimbres Valley, New Mexico.* Washington, DC: Smithsonian Institution Press.

Floating on the Air, Followed by the Wind. 1973. Film distributed by Indiana University Instructional Support Services, Gunter Pfaff (cinematographer) and Ronald A. Simons (psychiatric consultant). East Lansing: Michigan State University.

Fonda, Marc. 2011. "Canadian Census Figures on Aboriginal Spiritual Preferences: A Revitalization Movement?" *Religious Studies and Theology* 30 (2): 171–87.

Forge, Anthony. 1967. "The Abelam Artist." In *Social Organization: Essays Presented to Raymond Firth,* edited by Maurice Freedman, 65–84. London: Cass.

Gillman, Neil. 1992. *Sacred Fragments: Recovering Theology for the Modern Jew.* New York: Jewish Publication Society.

Handelman, Don. 1977. "Play and Ritual: Complementary Frames of Meta-Communication." In *It's a Funny Thing, Humour,* edited by Antony J. Chapman and Hugh C. Foot, 185–92. London: Pergamon.

Högberg, Anders. 2008. "Playing with Flint: Tracing a Child's Imitation of Adult Work in a Lithic Assemblage." *Journal of Archaeological Method and Theory* 15 (1): 112–31.

Horton, Robin. 1982. "Tradition and Modernity Revisited." In *Rationality and Relativism,* edited by M. Hollis and Steven Lukes, 201–60. Cambridge, MA: MIT Press.

Hultkrantz, Åke. 1992. *Shamanic Healing and Ritual Drama: Health and Medicine in Native North American Religious Traditions.* New York: Crossroads.

Jenness, Diamond. 1922. *The Life of the Copper Eskimos.* Ottawa: FA Ackland.

Joyce, Rosemary A. 2000. "Girling the Girl and Boying the Boy: The Production of Adulthood in Ancient Mesoamerica." *World Archaeology* 31 (3): 473–83.

Kapferer, Bruce. 1983. *A Celebration of Demons.* Bloomington: Indiana University Press.

Keesing, Roger. 1982. *Kwaio Religion: The Living and the Dead in a Solomon Island Society.* New York: Columbia University Press.

———. 1992. *Custom and Confrontation: The Kwaio Struggle for Cultural Autonomy.* Chicago: University of Chicago Press.

King, Sarah J. 2013. "Context Matters: Studying Indigenous Religions in North America." *Religion Compass* 7 (11): 498–507.

Kosmin, Barry A., Egon Mayer, and Ariela Keysar. 2001. *American Religious Identification Survey.* The Graduate Center of the City University of New York.

Laugrand, Frédéric B., and Jarich G. Oosten. 2010. *Inuit Shamanism and Christianity: Transitions and Transformations in the Twentieth Century.* Montreal: McGill-Queen's University Press.

Lévi-Strauss, Claude. 1967. *Structural Anthropology.* Translated by Claire Jacobson and Brooke Grundfest Schoepf. New York: Doubleday Anchor.

Lienhardt, Godfrey. 1961. *Divinity and Experience.* Oxford: Oxford University Press.

Malinowski, Bronislaw. (1926) 1948. *Magic, Science, and Religion, and Other Essays*. New York: Doubleday Anchor.

Myerhoff, Barbara. 1974. *Peyote Hunt*. Ithaca, NY: Cornell University Press.

Nowell, April. 2013. "All Work and No Play Left Little Time for Art." *New Scientist* 217 (2905): 28–9.

Ortner, Sherry. 1973. "On Key Symbols." *American Anthropologist* 75 (5): 1338–46.

Park, Robert W. 1998. "Size Counts: The Miniature Archaeology of Childhood in Inuit Societies." *Antiquity* 72 (276): 269–81.

_____. 1999. "The Archaeology of Childhood." *Discovering Archaeology* 1 (2): 81–93.

Sable, Trudy, and Bernie Francis. 2012. *The Language of this Land, Mi'kma'ki*. Sydney, NS: Cape Breton University Press.

Schwartzman, Helen. 1978. *Transformations: The Anthropology of Children's Play*. New York: Plenum Press.

Scott, James. 1990. *Domination and the Arts of Resistance*. New Haven, CT: Yale University Press.

Smith, Patricia Elaine. 1998. "When Small Pots Speak: The Stories They Tell." Master's thesis, McMaster University.

Stewart, Charles, and Rosalind Shaw. 1994. *Syncretism/Anti-Syncretism*. London: Routledge.

Turner, Victor. 1969. *The Ritual Process*. Chicago: Aldine.

Van Gennep, Arnold. 1960. *The Rites of Passage*. Chicago: University of Chicago Press.

Vaughan, James. 1973. "Engkyagu as Artists in Marghi Society." In *The Traditional Artist in African Societies*, edited by Warren d'Azevedo, 162–93. Bloomington: Indiana University Press.

_____. 2006. *The Mandara Margi: A Society Living on the Verge*. www.indiana.edu/~margi

Voloshinov, V.N. (1926) 1987. "Discourse in Life and Discourse in Art." In *Freudianism*, edited and translated by I.R. Titunik, in collaboration with Neil H. Bruss, 93–116. Bloomington: Indiana University Press.

Wallace, Anthony F.C. 1966. *Religion: An Anthropological View*. New York: Random House.

_____. 1972. *The Death and Rebirth of the Seneca*. New York: Vintage.

Weiner, Annette. 1988. *The Trobrianders of Papua New Guinea*. New York: Holt, Rinehart, and Winston.

Glossary

acclimatization A change in the way the body functions in response to physical stress.

Acheulean tradition A Lower Paleolithic stone-tool tradition associated with *Homo erectus* and characterized by stone bifaces, or "hand axes."

achieved statuses Social positions people may attain later in life, often as the result of their own (or other people's) effort.

adaptation The shaping of a useful feature of an organism by natural selection for the function it now performs.

adoption Kinship relationships based on nurturance, often in the absence of other connections based on mating or birth.

affect Visceral arousal, emotion, or feeling.

affinal relationships Kinship connections through marriage, or affinity.

affinity Connection through marriage.

affluence The condition of having more than enough of whatever is required to satisfy consumption needs.

African hybridization and replacement model The hypothesis that anatomically modern humans evolved in Africa between 300,000 and 100,000 years ago and then moved out into Europe, Asia, and Australasia, interbreeding to some extent with the hominin populations in those areas.

agriculture The systematic modification of the environments of plants and animals to increase their productivity and usefulness.

agroecology The systematically modified environment (or constructed niche) that becomes the only environment within which domesticated plants can flourish.

alleles All the different forms that a particular gene might take.

anagenesis The slow, gradual transformation of a single species over time.

anatomically modern human beings Hominins assigned to the species *Homo sapiens,* with anatomical features similar to those of living human populations: short and round skulls, small brow ridges and faces, prominent chins, and gracile skeletal build.

androgyny A condition in which an individual person possesses both male and female characteristics.

anthropoid The primate evolutionary grade that includes tarsiers, monkeys, apes, and humans.

anthropology The study of human nature, human society, human language, and the human past.

anthropomorphism The attribution of human characteristics to non-human animals.

applied anthropology The subfield of anthropology in which anthropologists use information gathered from the other anthropological specialties to solve practical cross-cultural problems.

aptation The shaping of any useful feature of an organism, regardless of that feature's origin.

archaeogaming The utilization and treatment of immaterial space to study created culture, specifically through video games.

archaeological record All material objects and structures created by humans and our hominin ancestors.

archaeology The specialty of anthropology that studies the human past by analyzing material remains left behind by earlier societies.

archaic *Homo sapiens* Hominins dating from 500,000 to 200,000 years ago that possessed morphological features found in both *Homo erectus* and *Homo sapiens.*

art Play with form producing some aesthetically successful transformation-representation.

artifacts Objects that have been deliberately and intelligently shaped by humans or our hominin ancestors.

ascribed statuses Social positions people are assigned at birth.

assemblages Artifacts and structures from a particular time and place in an archaeological site.

australopiths An informal term used to refer to all hominins that were the earliest bipedal hominins.

avunculocal residence A postmarital residence pattern in which a married couple lives with (or near) the husband's mother's brother (from *avuncular,* "of uncles").

band The characteristic form of social organization found among foragers. Bands are small, usually no more than 50 people, and labour is divided ordinarily on the basis of age and sex. All adults in band societies have roughly equal access to whatever material or social valuables are locally available.

bifurcation A criterion employed in the analysis of kinship terminologies in which kinship terms referring to the mother's side of the family are distinguished from those referring to the father's side.

bilateral descent The principle that a descent group is formed by people who believe they are related to each other by connections made through their mothers *and* their fathers equally (sometimes called *cognatic descent*).

bilateral kindred A kinship group that consists of relatives of one person or a group of siblings.

biocultural organisms Organisms (in this case, human beings) whose defining features are co-determined by biological and cultural factors.

biological anthropology (or physical anthropology) The specialty of anthropology that looks at human beings as biological organisms and tries to discover what characteristics make them different from other organisms and what characteristics they share.

biopower Forms of power preoccupied with bodies, both the bodies of citizens and the social body of the state itself.

bipedalism Walking on two feet.

bisexuality Sexual attraction to both males and females.

blades Sharp-edged stone tools that are at least twice as long as they are wide.

blended family A family created when previously divorced or widowed people marry, bringing with them children from their previous families.

bloodwealth Material goods paid by perpetrators to compensate their victims for their loss.

body language Movements and postures that communicate attitudes and feelings non-verbally.

bridewealth The transfer of certain symbolically important goods from the family of the groom to the family of the bride on the occasion of their marriage. It represents compensation to the wife's lineage for the loss of her labour and child-bearing capacities. *Bridewealth* is sometimes referred to as *brideprice*.

broad-spectrum foraging A subsistence strategy based on collecting a wide range of plants and animals by hunting, fishing, and gathering.

capitalism An economic system dominated by the supply–demand–price mechanism called the "market"; an entire way of life that grew in response to and in service of that market.

caste A ranked group within a hierarchically stratified society that is closed, prohibiting individuals from moving from one caste to another.

chiefdom A form of social organization in which a leader (the chief) and close relatives are set apart from the rest of the society and allowed privileged access to wealth, power, and prestige.

chromosomes Sets of paired bodies in the nucleus of cells that are made of DNA and contain the hereditary genetic information that organisms pass on to their offspring.

cladogenesis The birth of a variety of descendant species from a single ancestral species.

clan A descent group formed by members who believe they have a common (sometimes mythical) ancestor, even if they cannot specify the genealogical links.

class A ranked group within a hierarchically stratified society whose membership is defined primarily in terms of wealth, occupation, or other economic criteria.

clientage The institution linking individuals from upper and lower levels in a stratified society.

cline The gradual intergradation of genetic variation from population to population.

coevolution The interconnected relationship between biological processes and symbolic cultural processes, in which each makes up an important part of the environment and to which the other must adapt.

collaterality A criterion employed in the analysis of kinship terminologies in which a distinction is made between kin who are believed to be in a direct line and those who are "off to one side," linked to the speaker by a lineal relative.

colonization The act of settling a region, establishing control over the Indigenous peoples who live there, and appropriating local lands and resources for one's own use.

colourism A system of social identities negotiated situationally along a continuum of skin colours between white and black.

commodities Goods exchanged for cash.

commodity exchanges Impersonal economic exchanges typical of the capitalist market in which goods are exchanged for cash and exchange partners need have nothing further to do with one another.

common ancestry Darwin's claim that similar living species must all have had a common ancestor.

communicative competence A term coined by anthropological linguist Dell Hymes to refer to the mastery of adult rules for socially and culturally appropriate speech.

communitas An unstructured or minimally structured community of equal individuals found frequently in rites of passage.

compadrazgo Ritual co-parenthood in Latin America and Spain, established through the Roman Catholic practice of having godparents for children.

comparison A characteristic of the anthropological perspective that requires anthropologists to study similarities and differences across as many human societies as possible before generalizing about human beings and their activities.

complex societies Societies with large populations, an extensive division of labour, and occupational specialization.

composite tools Tools such as bows and arrows in which several different materials are combined (e.g., stone, wood, bone, ivory, antler) to produce the final working implement.

concentrations of particular artifacts Sets of artifacts indicating that particular social activities took place at a particular area in an archaeological site when that site was inhabited in the past.

conjugal family A family based on marriage; at a minimum, a spousal pair and their children.

consanguineal relationships Kinship connections based on descent.

consumption The using up of material goods necessary for human survival.

continuous variation A pattern of variation involving polygeny in which phenotypic traits grade imperceptibly from one member of the population to another without sharp breaks.

cranial capacity The size of the braincase.

cranium The bones of the head, excluding the jaw.

crosscousins The children of a person's parents' opposite-gender siblings (a father's sister's children or a mother's brother's children).

cultural anthropology The specialty of anthropology that shows how variation in the beliefs and behaviours of members of different human groups is shaped by sets of learned behaviours and ideas that human beings acquire as members of society—that is, by culture.

cultural imperialism The idea that some cultures dominate others and that domination by one culture leads inevitably to the destruction of subordinated cultures and their replacement by the culture of those in power.

cultural relativism Understanding another culture in its own terms sympathetically enough that the culture appears to be a coherent and meaningful design for living.

cultural resource management (CRM) Archaeological projects that are focused on mitigating the effects of development through identifying and interpreting significant cultural and heritage sites; sometimes referred to as "salvage archaeology."

culture Sets of learned behaviour, ideas, and material goods that human beings share as members of society.

Denisovans A population of Pleistocene hominins known only from ancient DNA recovered from two tiny, 41,000-year-old fossils deposited in Denisova Cave in Siberia.

dentition The sizes, shapes, and number of an animal's teeth.

descent The principle based on culturally recognized parent–child connections that define the social categories to which people belong.

design anthropology The use of anthropological methods to develop new product ideas.

diaspora Migrant populations with a shared identity who live in a variety of different locales around the world; a form of trans-border identity that does not focus on nation building.

digital heritage Digital information about the past available on the Internet. It can include a range of materials, from digitized documents and photographs, to images of artifacts, to video and sound recordings.

discontinuous variation A pattern of phenotypic variation in which the phenotype (e.g., flower colour) exhibits sharp breaks from one member of the population to the next.

discourse A stretch of speech longer than a sentence united by a common theme.

doctrine Religious beliefs expressed through written and formal statements concerning the supernatural.

DNA (deoxyribonucleic acid) The structure that carries the genetic heritage of an organism as a kind of blueprint for the organism's construction and development.

domestication Variety of ways that humans affected the reproduction of another species, with the result that specific plants and animals become more useful to and dependent on people.

domination Ruling with coercive force.

dowry The wealth transferred, usually from parents to their daughter, at the time of a woman's marriage.

Early Stone Age (ESA) The name given to the period of Oldowan and Acheulean stone-tool traditions in Africa.

ecofacts Biological remains that are likely associated with food consumption or other human activities.

ecological niche A species' unique position within the ecosystem in which it exists, which is shaped by its way of life (e.g., what it eats and how it finds mates, raises its young, relates to companions, and protects itself from predators).

economic anthropology "The part of the discipline [of anthropology] that debates issues of *human nature* that relate directly to the decisions of daily life and making a living" (Wilk 1996, xv).

egalitarian social relations Social relations in which no great differences in wealth, power, or prestige divide members from one another.

enculturation The process by which humans living with one another must learn to come to terms with the ways of thinking and feeling that are considered appropriate in their respective cultures.

endogamy Marriage within a defined social group.

ethnic group A group that shares similar values and norms, defined by such things as language, geography, and religion.

ethnicity An ethnic group that a person identifies with or feels a part of to the exclusion of other groups, based on language, dress, religion, etc. Ethnicity emerges from historical processes that incorporate distinct social groups into a single political structure under conditions of inequality.

ethnoarchaeology The study of the way present-day societies use artifacts and structures and how these objects become part of the archaeological record.

ethnocentrism The opinion that one's own way of life is natural or correct and, indeed, the only true way of being fully human.

ethnography A systematic study and description of a particular culture.

ethnology The comparative study of two or more cultures.

ethnopragmatics The study of language use that relies on ethnography to illuminate the ways in which speech is both constituted by and constitutive of social interaction.

evolution (1) The process of change over time. (2) A characteristic of the anthropological perspective that requires anthropologists to place their observations about human beings and their activities in a temporal framework that takes into consideration change over time.

evolutionary niche Sum of all the natural selection pressures to which a population is exposed.

evolutionary theory The set of testable hypotheses that assert that living organisms can change over time and give rise to new kinds of organisms, with the result that all organisms ultimately share a common ancestry.

exaptation The shaping of a useful feature of an organism by natural selection to perform one function and the later reshaping of that feature by different selection pressures to perform a new function.

excavation The systematic uncovering of archaeological remains through removal of the deposits of soil and other material covering them and accompanying them.

exogamy Marriage outside a defined social group.

extended family A family pattern made up of three generations living together: parents, married children, and grandchildren.

family A group of individuals who can be considered as a single unit based on shared rights and responsibilities.

features Non-portable items created by humans, such as house walls or ditches.

feminism The theory that women and men are equally human and therefore that women are entitled to enjoy the same rights and privileges as men.

feminist archaeology A research approach that explores why women's contributions have been systematically written out of the archaeological record and suggests new approaches to the human past that include such contributions.

fieldwork An extended period of close involvement with the people in whose way of life anthropologists are interested, during which anthropologists ordinarily collect most of their data.

flakes Chipped-off pieces of stone that may or may not have been used as small cutting tools.

flexible citizenship The strategies and effects employed by managers, technocrats, and professionals who move regularly across state boundaries and who seek both to circumvent and benefit from different nation-state regimes.

food collectors Societies that gather, fish, and hunt to subsist.

food producers Societies that depend on domesticated plants or animals or both to subsist.

framing A cognitive boundary that marks certain behaviours as "play" or as "ordinary life."

free agency The freedom of self-contained individuals to pursue their own interests above everything else and to challenge one another for dominance.

friction The awkward, unequal, unstable aspects of interconnection across difference.

friendship The relatively "unofficial" bonds that people construct with one another that tend to be personal, affective, and often a matter of choice.

gay An affirmative and empowering self-designation for individuals medically classified as homosexual, which became widespread over the course of the twentieth century.

gender The culturally constructed roles assigned to males or females, which vary considerably from society to society.

gender archaeology Archaeological research that draws on insights from contemporary gender studies to investigate how people come to recognize themselves as different from others, how people represent those differences, and how others react to such claims.

gender binary A dual gender categorization separating all women from all men.

gender performativity The concept that gender is something we "perform" or "enact," something we "learn to do," not something we "are born with."

gene The portion or portions of the DNA molecule that code for proteins that shape phenotypic traits.

gene flow The exchange of genes that occurs when a given population experiences a sudden expansion due to in-migration of outsiders from another population of the species.

gene frequency The frequency of occurrence of the variants of particular genes (i.e., of alleles) within the gene pool.

gene pool All the genes in the bodies of all members of a given species (or a population of a species).

genetic drift Random changes in gene frequencies from one generation to the next due to a sudden reduction in population size as a result of disaster, disease, or the out-migration of a small subgroup from a larger population.

genetics The scientific study of biological heredity.

genome The sum total of all the genetic information about an organism, carried on the chromosomes in the cell nucleus.

genotype The genetic information about particular biological traits encoded in an organism's DNA.

genus The level of the Linnaean taxonomy in which different species are grouped together on the basis of their similarities to one another. In modern taxonomies, genus is ranked between family (less specific) and species (more specific).

gift A good or service exchanged as part of social relations.

gift exchanges Non-capitalist forms of economic exchange that are deeply embedded in social relations and always require a return gift.

globalization Reshaping of local conditions by powerful global forces on an ever-intensifying scale.

governmentality The art of governing appropriately to promote the welfare of populations within a state.

grammar A set of rules that aim to fully describe the patterns of linguistic usage observed by speakers of a particular language.

grave goods Objects buried with a corpse.

haplorhines The suborder of primates that includes tarsiers, monkeys, apes, and humans.

hegemony The persuasion of subordinates to accept the ideology of the dominant group by mutual accommodations that nevertheless preserve the rulers' privileged position.

heteronormativity The view that heterosexual intercourse is (and *should be*) the "normal" form that human sexual expression always takes.

heterosexism A form of bias (like sexist bias) against all those who are not heterosexual.

heterosexuality Sexual relations involving individuals of different sexualities (i.e., a man and a woman).

heterozygous Describes a fertilized egg that receives a different particle (or allele) from each parent for the same trait.

hidden transcripts Private accounts by dominated groups of their oppression and alternatives to it developed outside the public political arena. These hidden accounts contrast with the views dominated peoples express in public political contexts that do not challenge the legitimacy of the dominant political order.

historical archaeology The study of archaeological sites associated with written records; frequently, the study of post-European contact sites.

historical linguistics The study of relationships between languages and how they change over time.

holism A perspective on the human condition that assumes that mind and body, individuals and society, and individuals and the environment interpenetrate and even define one another.

holistic A characteristic of the anthropological perspective that describes, at the highest and most inclusive level, how anthropology tries to integrate all that is known about human beings and their activities.

hominins All bipedal apes.

Homo The genus to which taxonomists assign large-brained hominins approximately 2 million years old and younger.

Homo erectus The species of large-brained, robust hominins that lived between 1.8 and 0.3 mya.

homology Genetic inheritance resulting from common ancestry.

homoplasy Convergent, or parallel, evolution, as when two species with very different evolutionary histories develop similar physical features as a result of adapting to a similar environment.

homosexuality Sexual relations involving two males or two females (i.e., same-sex sexuality).

homozygous Describes a fertilized egg that receives the same particle (or allele) from each parent for a particular trait.

human agency Human beings' ability to exercise at least some control over their lives.

human rights Powers, privileges, or material resources to which people everywhere, by virtue of being human, are justly entitled.

hybridization When members of two or more different species mate and produce viable offspring.

ideology A world view that justifies the social arrangements under which people live.

imagined communities A term borrowed from political scientist Benedict Anderson to refer to groups whose members' knowledge of one another does not come from regular face-to-face interactions but is based on shared experiences with national institutions, such as schools and government bureaucracies.

informants People in a particular culture who work with anthropologists and provide them with insights about the local way of life. Also called *respondents*, *collaborators*, *teachers*, or *friends*.

institutions Complex, variable, and enduring forms of cultural practices that organize social life.

intersectionality The notion that institutional forms of oppression organized in terms of race, class, and gender are interconnected and shape the opportunities and constraints available to individuals in any society.

intersex/disorder of sexual development Describes those individuals who possess ambiguous genitalia.

joint family A family pattern made up of brothers and their wives or sisters and their husbands (along with their children) living together.

kinesics The study of body movement, gestures, and facial expressions as a form of communication.

kinship systems Social relationships that are prototypically derived from the universal human experiences of mating, birth, and nurturance.

labour The activity linking human social groups to the material world around them; from the point of view of Karl Marx, labour is, therefore, always social labour.

language The system of arbitrary vocal symbols used to encode one's experience of the world and of others.

language ideology A marker of struggles between social groups with different interests, revealed in what people say and how they say it.

Late Stone Age (LSA) The name given to the period of highly elaborate stone-tool traditions in Africa, 40,000 to 10,000 years ago, in which blades were important.

legal citizenship The rights and obligations of citizenship accorded by the laws of a state.

lesbian A term used to describe female same-sex sexuality around the turn of the twentieth century; based on the name of the Greek island of Lesbos, the home of the female poet Sappho, who was reputed to love women rather than men.

liminality The ambiguous transitional state in a rite of passage in which the person or persons undergoing the ritual are outside their ordinary social positions.

lineages The consanguineal members of descent groups who believe they can trace their descent from known ancestors.

linguistic anthropology The specialty of anthropology concerned with the study of human languages.

linguistic competence A term coined by linguist Noam Chomsky to refer to the mastery of adult grammar.

linguistic relativity principle A position, associated with Edward Sapir and Benjamin Whorf, that asserts that language has the power to shape the way people see the world.

linguistics The scientific study of language.

long-distance nationalism Members of a diaspora organized in support of nationalist struggles in their homeland or to agitate for a state of their own.

macroevolution A subfield of evolutionary studies that focuses on long-term evolutionary changes, especially the origins of new species and their diversification across space and over millions of years of geological time.

magic A set of beliefs and practices designed to control the visible or invisible world for specific purposes.

mandible The lower jaw.

market exchange The exchange of goods (trade) calculated in terms of a multipurpose medium of exchange and standard of value (money) and carried out by means of a supply–demand–price mechanism (the market).

marriage An institution that transforms the status of the participants, carries implications about permitted sexual access, perpetuates social patterns through the birth of offspring, creates relationships between the kin of partners, and is symbolically marked.

material culture Objects created or shaped by humans and given meaning through cultural practices.

matrilineage A social group formed by people connected by mother–child links.

matrilocal residence A postmarital residence pattern in which a married couple lives with (or near) the wife's mother.

means of production The tools, skills, organization, and knowledge used to make a living.

medical anthropology The specialty of anthropology that concerns itself with human health—the factors that contribute to disease or illness and the ways that human populations deal with disease or illness.

meiosis The way sex cells make copies of themselves, which begins like mitosis, with chromosome duplication and the formation of two daughter cells. However, each daughter cell then divides again without chromosome duplication and, as a result, contains only a single set of chromosomes rather than the paired set typical of body cells.

men's studies/masculinities Research that focuses on the many different ways of being a man that can be identified in different places and times.

Mendelian inheritance The view that heredity is based on non-blending, single-particle genetic inheritance.

Mesopotamia The area made up of the Tigris–Euphrates river system, corresponding to modern-day Iraq, Kuwait, the northeastern section of Syria, and parts of Turkey and Iran. Often referred to as the "cradle of civilization" where early complex societies developed.

metacommunication Communication about the process of communication.

microevolution A subfield of evolutionary studies that devotes attention to short-term evolutionary changes that occur within a given species over relatively few generations of ecological time.

Middle Stone Age (MSA) The name given to the period of Mousterian stone-tool tradition in Africa, 200,000 to 40,000 years ago.

mitosis The way body cells make copies of themselves. The pairs of chromosomes in the nucleus of the cell duplicate and line up along the centre of the cell. The cell then divides, each daughter cell taking one full set of paired chromosomes.

mode of production The way that labour is organized within a society using specific tools, skills, organization, and knowledge.

modes of exchange Patterns according to which distribution takes place: *reciprocity*, *redistribution*, and *market exchange*.

monogamy A marriage pattern in which a person may be married to only one spouse at a time.

monumental architecture Architectural constructions of a greater-than-human scale, such as pyramids, temples, and tombs.

morphology The physical shape and size of an organism or its body parts.

mosaic evolution A process of change over time in which different phenotypic traits, responding to different selection pressures, may evolve at different rates.

Mousterian tradition A Middle Paleolithic stone-tool tradition associated with Neanderthals in Europe and southwestern Asia and with anatomically modern human beings in Africa.

multiculturalism Living permanently in settings surrounded by people with cultural backgrounds different from one's own and struggling to define with them the degree to which the cultural beliefs and practices of different groups should or should not be accorded respect and recognition by the wider society.

mutation The creation of a new allele for a gene when the portion of the DNA molecule to which it corresponds is suddenly altered.

myths Stories that recount how various aspects of the world came to be the way they are. The power of myths comes from their ability to make life meaningful for those who accept them.

nation A group of people believed to share the same history, culture, language, and even physical substance.

nationality A sense of identification with and loyalty to a nation-state.

nation–state An ideal political unit in which national identity and political territory coincide.

native speaker A person who has spoken a particular language since early childhood.

nativism A return to the old ways; a movement whose members expect a messiah or a prophet who will bring back a lost golden age of peace, prosperity, and harmony.

natural selection A two-step, mechanistic explanation of how descent with modification takes place: (1) every generation, variant individuals are generated within a species because of genetic mutation, and (2) those variant individuals best suited to the current environment survive and produce more offspring than other variants do.

naturalizing discourses Claims that consider social categories as eternal and unchanging, rather than the result of history or culture.

Neanderthals An archaic species of *Homo* that lived in Europe and western Asia 230,000 to 27,000 years ago.

neoclassical economics A formal attempt to explain the workings of capitalist enterprise, with particular attention to distribution.

Neolithic The "New Stone Age," which began with the domestication of plants 10,300 years ago.

neolocal residence A postmarital residence pattern in which a married couple sets up an independent household at a place of their own choosing.

niche construction When organisms actively perturb the environment in ways that modify the selection pressures experienced by subsequent generations of organisms.

nocturnal Active during the night.

non-binary Self-identification that resists the gender binary, embodying the fluidity of gender as a social construct.

non-conjugal family A woman and her children; the husband/father may be occasionally present or completely absent.

non-verbal communication The process of sending and receiving messages without the use of words (e.g., through gestures, facial expressions, or non-verbal vocalizations). This is also referred to as *paralanguage*.

norm of reaction A table or graph that displays the possible range of phenotypic outcomes for a given genotype in different environments.

nuclear family A family pattern made up of two generations: the parents and their unmarried children.

occupational specialization Specialization in various occupations (e.g., weaving or pot making) or in new social roles (e.g., king or priest) that is found in socially complex societies.

Oldowan tradition A stone-tool tradition named after the Olduvai Gorge (in Tanzania).

omnivorous Eating a wide range of plant and animal foods.

oracles Invisible forces to which people address questions and whose responses they believe to be truthful.

orthopraxy "Correct practice"; the prohibition of deviation from approved forms of behaviour.

paleoanthropology The study of human fossils and associated remains to understand our evolutionary history.

pangenesis A theory of heredity suggesting that an organism's physical traits are passed on from one generation to the next in the form of multiple distinct particles given off by all parts of the organism, different proportions of which get passed on to offspring via sperm or egg.

pansexuality Sexual attraction to males, females, and transgender males and females.

parallel cousins The children of a person's parents' same-gender siblings (a father's brother's children or a mother's sister's children).

patriarchy The domination of men over women and children.

patrilineage A social group formed by people connected by father–child links.

patrilocal residence A postmarital residence pattern in which a married couple lives with (or near) the husband's father.

phenotype The observable, measurable, overt characteristics of an organism.

phenotypic plasticity Physiological flexibility that allows organisms to respond to environmental stresses, such as temperature changes.

phyletic gradualism A theory arguing that one species gradually transforms itself into a new species over time, yet the actual boundary between species can never be detected but only drawn arbitrarily.

physical anthropology See *biological anthropology.*

pidgin (1) A language with no native speakers that develops in a single generation between members of communities that possess distinct native languages. (2) A shared secondary language in a speech community in which speakers also use some other main language.

play A framing (or orienting context) that is (1) consciously adopted by the players, (2) somehow pleasurable, and (3) systemically related to what is non-play by alluding to the non-play world and by transforming the objects, roles, actions, and relations of ends and means characteristic of the non-play world.

pleiotropy The phenomenon whereby a single gene may affect more than one phenotypic trait.

political anthropology The study of social power in human society.

polyandry A marriage pattern in which a woman may be married to more than one husband at a time.

polygamy A marriage pattern in which a person may be married to more than one spouse at a time.

polygeny The phenomenon whereby many genes are responsible for producing a phenotypic trait, such as skin colour.

polygyny A marriage pattern in which a man may be married to more than one wife at a time.

polymorphous Describes alleles that come in a range of different forms.

population genetics A field that uses statistical analysis to study short-term evolutionary change in large populations.

postcranial skeleton The bones of the body, excluding those of the head.

postnational ethos An attitude toward the world in which people submit to the governmentality of the capitalist market while trying to evade the governmentality of nation-states.

power Transformative capacity; the ability to transform a given situation.

pragmatics The study of how language is used in conversation.

prehensile The ability to grasp with fingers, toes, or tail.

priest A religious practitioner skilled in the practice of religious rituals, which he or she carries out for the benefit of the group.

primatology The study of non-human primates, the closest living relatives of human beings.

principle of independent assortment A principle of Mendelian inheritance in which each pair of particles (genes) separates independently of every other pair when germ cells (egg and sperm) are formed.

principle of segregation A principle of Mendelian inheritance in which an individual gets one particle (gene) for each trait (i.e., one-half of the required pair) from each parent.

prosimians The least complex evolutionary grade of the primates, which includes lemurs and lorises (now referred to as *strepsirrhines*).

provenance The three-dimensional position of an artifact within the matrix of an archaeological site.

proxemics The study of how different societies perceive and use space.

public/private divide A barrier that laws and customs erected between "private" domestic life in the family, conceived as "women's place," and public life, outside the family, conceived as the domain of men.

punctuated equilibrium A theory claiming that most of evolutionary history has been characterized by relatively stable species coexisting in an equilibrium that is occasionally punctuated by sudden bursts of speciation, when extinctions are widespread and many new species appear.

queer A self-identification claimed by some persons whose gender identities or sexual practices fall outside the range defined by "the heterosexual–homosexual continuum."

races Social groupings that allegedly reflect biological differences.

racism The systematic oppression of members of one or more socially defined "race" by members of another socially defined "race" that is justified in terms of the supposed inherent biological superiority of the rulers and the supposed inherent biological inferiority of those they rule.

reciprocity The exchange of goods and services of equal value. Anthropologists distinguish three forms of reciprocity: *generalized*, in which neither the time nor the value of the return is specified; *balanced*, in which a return of equal value is expected within a specified time limit; and *negative*, in which parties to the exchange hope to get something for nothing.

redistribution A mode of exchange that requires some form of centralized social organization to receive economic contributions from all members of the group and to redistribute them in such a way as to provide for every group member.

reflexivity Critical thinking about the way one thinks; reflection on one's own experience.

regional continuity model The hypothesis that evolution from *Homo erectus* to *Homo sapiens* occurred gradually throughout the traditional range of *H. erectus.*

relatedness The socially recognized ties that connect people in a variety of different ways.

relations of production The social relations linking the people who use a given means of production within a particular mode of production.

religion "Ideas and practices that postulate reality beyond that which is immediately available to the senses" (Bowen 2008).

replacement model The hypothesis that only one subpopulation of *Homo erectus*, probably located in Africa, underwent a rapid spurt of evolution to produce *Homo sapiens* 300,000 to 100,000 years ago. After that time, *H. sapiens* would itself have multiplied and dispersed, gradually populating the globe and eventually replacing any remaining populations of *H. erectus* or their descendants.

revitalization A conscious, deliberate, and organized attempt by some members of a society to create a more satisfying culture in a time of crisis.

rite of passage A ritual that serves to mark the movement and transformation of an individual from one social position to another.

ritual A repetitive social practice that is shared and scripted. It consists of sacred performances of symbolically meaningful cultural narratives.

sedentism The process of increasingly permanent human habitation in one place.

segmentary opposition A mode of hierarchical social organization in which groups beyond the most basic emerge only in opposition to other groups on the same hierarchical level.

sex The physical characteristics that traditionally distinguish two kinds of humans, females and males (for example, body shape, distribution of body hair, reproductive organs, sex chromosomes).

sexism The systematic sociocultural structures and practices of inequality, derived from patriarchal institutions, that continue to shape relations between women and men (based on an analogy with racism).

sexual dimorphism Observable phenotypic differences between males and females of the same species.

sexuality The ways in which people experience and value physical desire and pleasure in the context of sexual intercourse.

shaman A spiritual specialist who is believed to have the power to contact supernatural forces directly on behalf of individuals or groups.

site A precise geographical location of the remains of past human activity.

socialization The process by which humans as material organisms, living together with other similar organisms, cope with the behavioural rules established by their respective societies.

social organization The patterning of human interdependence in a given society through the actions and decisions of its members.

social stratification A form of social organization in which people have unequal access to wealth, power, and prestige.

sociolinguistics The study of language in relation to social factors, such as differences of regional, class, and occupational dialect, power and gender differences, and bilingualism.

species A distinct segment of an evolutionary lineage. Different biologists, working with living and fossil organisms, have devised different criteria to identify boundaries between species. For Linnaeus, a species is a Platonic "natural kind" defined in terms of its essence. For modern biologists, a species is a reproductive community of populations (reproductively isolated from others) that occupies a specific niche in nature.

state A stratified society that possesses a territory that is defended from outside enemies with an army and from internal disorder with police. A state, which has a separate set of governmental institutions designed to enforce laws and to collect taxes and tribute, is run by an elite that possesses a monopoly on the use of force.

status A particular social position in a group.

stereoscopic vision A form of vision in which the visual field of each eye of a two-eyed (binocular) animal overlaps with the other, producing depth perception.

strepsirrhines A suborder of primates that includes lemurs and lorises (formerly called *prosimians*).

subsistence strategies The ways that people in a particular society go about meeting their basic material survival needs.

substantive citizenship The actions people take, regardless of their legal citizenship status, to assert their membership in a state and to bring about political changes that will improve their lives.

surplus production The production of amounts of food that exceed the basic subsistence needs of the population.

survey The physical examination of a geographical region in which promising sites are most likely to be found.

symbol Something that stands for something else.

syncretism The synthesis of old religious practices (or an old way of life) with new religious practices (or a new way of life) introduced from outside, often by force.

taphonomy The study of the various processes that objects undergo in the course of becoming part of the fossil and archaeological records.

taxon Each species as well as each group of species related at any level in a taxonomic hierarchy.

taxonomy In biology, a classification system used to organize various kinds of organisms.

trans-border citizenry A group made up of citizens of a country who continue to live in their homeland plus the people who have emigrated from the country and their descendants, regardless of their current citizenship.

trans-border state A form of state in which it is claimed that those people who left the country and their descendants remain part of their ancestral state, even if they are citizens of another state.

transformist hegemony A nationalist program to define nationality in a way that preserves the cultural domination of the ruling group while including enough cultural features from subordinated groups to ensure their loyalty.

transgender A term proposed in the 1960s by medical researchers to classify individuals who, in one way or another, seemed dissatisfied with the sex and gender assignments they had received at birth.

transnational nation–state A nation-state in which the relationships between citizens and the state extend to wherever citizens reside.

transvestism The practice of dressing as and taking on mannerisms associated with a gender other than one's own.

tribe A society that is generally larger than a band, whose members usually farm or herd for a living. Social relations in a tribe are considered ranked, as there is often a leader who speaks for the group or who organizes certain group activities.

unilineal descent The principle that a descent group is formed by people who believe they are related to each other by connections made through *either* their mothers *or* their fathers.

variational evolution The Darwinian theory of evolution, which assumes that variant members of a species respond differently to environmental challenges. Those variants that are more successful ("fitter") survive and reproduce more offspring, who inherit the traits that made their parents fit.

witchcraft The performance of magic by human beings, often through innate supernatural powers, whether or not it is intentional or self-aware.

world views Encompassing pictures of reality that contain shared political, religious, and other moral beliefs that are created by the members of societies.

Index